Limited Classical Reprint Library

CLAVIS CANTICI:

OR,

AN EXPOSITION

OF

THE SONG OF SOLOMON.

BY THE
REV. MR. JAMES DURHAM,
LATE MINISTER OF THE GOSPEL IN GLASGOW.

WITH A PREFACE
BY
THE REV. GAVIN PARKER,
MINISTER OF BON-ACCORD PARISH, ABERDEEN.

Foreword by
Dr. Cyril J. Barber

Klock & Klock Christian Publishers, Inc.
2527 GIRARD AVE. N.
MINNEAPOLIS, MINNESOTA 55411

Originally published by
George and Robert King
Aberdeen
1840

0-86524-075-2

Printed by Klock & Klock in the U.S.A.
1981 Reprint

FOREWORD

Exposition's of Solomon's famous love-song abound. While some expositor's take the position of two primary characters, Solomon and the Shunamite, others prefer three, Solomon, the Shunamite and her faithful shepherd-lover in the hills near her home. By far the greatest number of commentators, however, apply the teaching of this portion of Scripture to the relationship which exists between Christ's Bride (i.e., the Church) and Himself as the Groom. James Durham (1622-1658) adheres to this form of application. Of his work Charles Haddon Spurgeon had this to say:

> Durham is always good, and he is at his best upon Canticles. He gives the essence of the good matter. For practical use this work is perhaps more valuable than any other Key to the Song.

We are all familiar with the stories of poor struggling lads aspiring to enter the ministry who, by God's grace and their own efforts obtained some form of education and became great preachers of the Word. In the case of James Durham, the opposite is true. Born into a wealthy home he could have enjoyed a life of ease and comfort. Instead, he studied at St. Andrews and Glasgow, and turning his back on the paternal estate, became a humble preacher of the Gospel.

Only eleven years of ministry were granted James Durham before he died. During that time he faithfully expounded God's Word and nurtured those souls committed to his care. He was a man of intense strength of conviction and discharged his duties with great diligence. The effort he put into his work undoubtedly shortened his life.

For one so young, Durham wrote voluminously. The only books to be published before his death at age thirty-six were *Heaven Upon Earth* (1657) and *A Commentary on the Book of Revelation* (1658). His other works, including *An Exposition of the Book of Job* (1659) were published posthumously.

Durham's *Exposition of the Song of Solomon* appeared ten years after his death when one might have expected that he would have been forgotten. To modern readers his writing may appear quaint, but it is full of love for the Lord and devotion to His cause. His style and application are also arresting and may bring conviction to the lukewarm of heart. Furthermore, the godly counsel and evident piety of the author are stimulating and revitalizing, even if one is not fully in accord with this able Scot's interpretation.

Viewed on its merits and the perspective of the writer, one is compelled to conclude with Gavin Parker, "it would be difficult to give [this work] too high a recommendation."

Cyril J. Barber, D.Lit.
Author, *The Minister's Library*

PREFACE.

The Theological works of Durham I have long considered among the very best productions of our Scottish Divines of the seventeenth century.

In his exposition of the sacred writings he excels in powerful, luminous, and faithful statements.

He exhibits also superior skill in discriminating the characters of men: and, as one taught by the Spirit of God, he clearly marks the distinctions between the precious and the vile.

Many of the more serious and spiritually minded in our land are well acquainted with his writings.

He possessed talents and learning—especially very extensive knowledge of sound Theology, by which he was well qualified to grapple with difficult portions of the lively oracles of God.

His Work on the Book of Revelation is a masterly production, and sufficient of itself to gain the author an honourable name among those who have been, and those who now are, mighty in the Scriptures.

His " Exposition of the Song of Solomon" is unquestionably very excellent. Those who have tasted that the Lord is gracious, esteem it highly, and receive from it many feasts upon Divine truth and upon the rich grace of the Lord Jesus Christ.

They may be pronounced blessed who understand and who relish the Song itself.

They do love, they do admire this wonderful production of the Holy Spirit: and to them, the Exposition by Mr. Durham will be welcome as a precious auxiliary to conduct them to the treasures of truth and of love which the inspired Song contains. The Key prefixed is also excellent, and must prove useful in making the words of the Holy Spirit more intelligible to many sanctified minds.

It is evident that the author had given deep attention to the inspired words of this Song, and that in answer to prayer the

Holy Spirit had guided him to correct knowledge of what is here written for the benefit of the church of God.

We have every reason to believe also, that it was the author's desire that many others should enjoy the light that shined from heaven into his own soul.

All who love God and truth, and salvation through Christ may now, and for ages to come, consult this Exposition, that they may with more advantage " Hear," and understand what the Spirit still speaks to the churches from this book of Divine inspiration.

As to the Song itself—the inspired subject of the Exposition— it would be difficult to give it too high a recomendation, it would be difficult to express in words one ten-thousandth part of its value. There is much cause for regret that even believers in Christ, enlightened in part by the Spirit of God, should be tempted to cherish prejudices against this precious portion of Divine revelation, or treat it with cold indifference.

The unrenewed, or those not taught by the Spirit of God, but still of the carnal mind—some of whom, even professing christianity—have in great numbers, and for long time, made light of it: yet, while the " natural man receiveth not the things of the Spirit of God," those who are spiritual know all the things, and relish and esteem all the things which are freely given them of God: to them this Book will be precious.

It is recommended by the Spirit of God in the opening words of the Book:—" The Song of Songs which is Solomon's."

Songs are lofty productions expressing elevation of thought, of imagination, feeling, desire, and enjoyment. A Song from heaven must be peculiarly sublime and animating. This is the Song of Songs, the most exalted of all the sublime productions of the Holy Spirit. In Scripture there are many Songs, even books of Songs besides this, but this Book contains the most ex- cellent of them all. As the house of God excels all other houses, or as the trees of God excel all other trees, so the one Song in this Book excels every other Song in the Book of God. Let no critic, let no man of talent, or literature, or science despise this Song,—IT IS SOLOMON's ! Solomon was the wisest of mere men : he was well taught : he studied much : he wrote much on many subjects : he was no novice in writing Songs :—

his Songs were one thousand and five—but this is the best of them all. Perhaps none of the rest had Divine inspiration to give any one of them authority among men. This Song written by Solomon is inspired by the Spirit of God. This Song therefore comes to the church with all the authority of Divine inspiration, and with all the weight of character possessed by Solomon, the man of wisdom, the anointed king of Israel, an eminent type of Messiah who is the light and joy of heaven and who announced himself as the light of the world.

The transcendant excellence of this Song appears in the varied and interesting subjects of which it treats. Although the name of God be not in it, his love to his people is described as powerful, tender, and immutable. In the person of the Redeemer— the beloved of God and of the church, Divine love enlivens a great proportion of the Song.

The kindness, the forbearance, the condescension, the intimacy, the faithfulness, the fervent zeal, the perfect wisdom, and the heavenly dignity and holiness of the Beloved Head of the Church, so frequently expressed and so clearly illustrated in this Song, do exhibit him as the Friend who loveth at all times.

The riches of Divine grace are here opened up as at the disposal of a king perfect in wisdom and righteousness; and who only waits for fit opportunities to satisfy the hungry soul with abundance of delights.

The nature of communion with God, by the mediation of Jesus Christ, is here explained as what is real, and practical, and useful, and conducive to peace and hope and joy.

The necessary influences and operations of the Holy Spirit are not only admitted, but also beautifully described: he gives life and vigour to the soul: he spreads loveliness over the garden and the fields: he gives progress to the flowers: and he prepares pleasant fruits for the people beloved of Jehovah.

The whole Song illustrates a life of faith on the Son of God. There are troubles and enemies: there are sorrows, and fears, and hopes, and pleasures to which others are strangers. Even "daughters of Jerusalem,"—persons very near in outward circumstances—do not intermeddle with the joys of believers although they may profess themselves expectants of the same salvation, and of the same heaven.

The song is excellent on account of the views which it opens up into the heaven of heavens. Believers now wonder at themselves as the objects of the sovereign love of God while here below, and though they do not know what they shall be, yet this Song affords assurance that they shall be near unto Jehovah,—not to be treated with indifference or coldness, but to be the objects of his peculiar love and the happy recipients of his bounty to eternal ages. The Song is pastoral; it places before us many a scene of loveliness: and all these scenes will be exhibited and enjoyed in the paradise of God. The fruits of grace on earth are excellent, but they point to far higher excellence in the heavenly paradise where the tree of life continually blossoms, and affords all varieties of pleasant fruits, to feast, to cheer, and to delight the redeemed of the Lord.

Yet let it be observed, that to enjoy the friendship described in this Book, it is necessary to have Christ revealed in the soul: it is necessary to approve of his character, to love him, to esteem him, to desire him above all created things: it is also necessary to be united to him by a true and living faith. Sinners for all that they may pretend, are cold hearted toward the holy Saviour, until they see his glory, and taste that the Lord is gracious, and enjoy communion with him as their beloved and esteemed friend. A believer cannot have delight in Jesus himself, nor yet in the Songs which celebrate his peculiar excellence until with decision and with experience he can say, "My Beloved is mine and his desire is towards me."

This inspired Song has been but little esteemed and enjoyed in the visible church. Many who profess to love Christ see little in it to admire. But in this apathy, or blindness, or dislike, is exhibited the very same spirit of the daughters of Jerusalem who said, "what is thy Beloved more than another beloved?"

We have reason however to believe that this neglected part of Divine revelation shall be brought from obscurity and shall shine as a brighter light in the world during the millenial ages. We are encouraged to expect more abundant effusions of the Holy Spirit than have ever been received on the earth, and more numerous conversions to God. Every convert illumined by the Holy Spirit will love the Lord Jesus Christ in sincerity. The portions of Scripture by which the Holy Spirit takes of the things of Christ to show to believers will be more studied and the rich treasures of grace and of truth contained in them will be the more eagerly welcomed and the more abundantly enjoyed. Then this Song—" The Song of the Lamb"—the Song that describes the glory and the grace of the Lamb's person and the righteousness and the faithfulness of his ways shall be much read and studied and sung by living Christians in the church of God.

After the shaking of nations and of churches; and when the sincere followers of Jesus shall have got liberty to break away from the abominations of corrupted christianity, when the God of salvation shall have given them fortitude to keep by themselves as a people distinct from the other religious people of the world, they shall be seen by the inhabitants of heaven as so many conquering heroes, who through grace had obtained " the victory over the beast, and over his image, and over his mark, and over the number of his name." They shall stand in the view of all heaven, and near many of the inhabitants of the earth, having the harps of God. In that place of splendour, light, and purity, as represented by the Holy Spirit, " they sing the song of Moses the servant of God, and the song of the Lamb, saying, Great and marvellous are thy works Lord God Almighty; just and true are thy ways, thou King of Saints." The song of Moses has long been esteemed in the visible church. The triumph of Divine Almighty power over the enemies of the church has been frequently sung. But the time is coming when the bold and triumphant notes of praise in the song of war shall be accompanied or followed and sweetened with more gentle and peaceful sounds, by celebrating, as in this Song of the Lamb, the glory and grace, the righteousness and truth of Immanuel the King of saints, whom Jehovah hath appointed HEAD over all things to the church.

In writing and preparing for publication, this Exposition of the Song, it may be said that the esteemed author did sow the good seed. Yet in our land there are many who make light of salvation. The seed was sown as by the way side: birds of the air devoured it. While many men cared little about it, Satan, as the leader of all who hate spirituality and holiness in religion, had got it almost out of sight. It was cast into the shade; it was little known; and but few enquired after it. There was difficulty in procuring a copy; and perhaps greater difficulty in getting many people to bestow on it a careful perusal. Some

thought it heavy and fanciful, and many saw no need for con-
sulting any exposition of the Song of Solomon. Some people
however do esteem this work, and among these are some of the
excellent of the earth.

Those who love God will feel obliged to Mr. King for ven-
turing, at his own expense, to send forth a new and beautiful
Edition. It is to be hoped, and prayed for, that, by the sovereign grace of God granted to many who peruse this work,
it may be made highly useful in the church of Christ, as a means
of awakening many who have sat down at ease under a super-
ficial profession of Christianity, and of encouraging those who
have no evidence of vital interest in the Lord Jesus Christ to
flee to him as the only sure refuge of the guilty and to accept
him with humility and gratitude as a compassionate and bene-
volent and all-sufficient Saviour.

But I deem it altogether uncalled for, to add another word
in recommendation of this Work. The truth in it will speak
for itself.

May the Great Teacher, promised to the church—the Spirit
of Truth—take of the things of Christ contained in this inspired
Song, and so exhibit them to the understanding and to the
heart, as to guide every inquirer to the saving knowledge of all
the truths revealed from heaven!

GAVIN PARKER.

ABERDEEN,
14th March, 1840.

To the Right Honourable, truly Noble, and Religious Lady, my Lady Viscountess of KENMURE.

Madam,

Many have been the helps and furtherances that the people of God, in these latter times, and more especially in these lands, have had in their Christian course and way to heaven: in which respect, our blessings have not a little prevailed above the blessings of our progenitors, who, as they enjoyed not such plentiful preaching of the gospel, so were they not privileged with so many of the printed, and published labours of his servants, succinctly and clearly opening up the meaning; and by brief, plain, familiar, and edifying observations, making application of the holy scriptures in our own vulgar language, and that even to the lowest capacities: a rich treasure highly valuable above all the gold of both Indies, and the greatest external blessings of the most potent and flourishing nations; and the more to be valued, if we call to remembrance, how that not very many years ago, the Christians in this same island, would have travelled far to have heard a portion of the scriptures only read to them, and would very liberally and cheerfully have contributed of their substance for that end; and would withal carefully have sought out, and at high rates made purchase of a Bible, a New Testament, or any small treatise (then very rare and hard to come by) affording but the least measure of light on the scriptures (which in those dark times were to them much as a sealed book in comparison of what they have been in the late bright and glorious sun-shine of the gospel to us) though to the manifest hazard of being burnt quick for so doing. O how highly would these precious souls have prized, and how mightily would they have improved the frequent, pure, plain, and powerful preachings, and many excellent writings, wherewith Britain and Ireland, have to admiration been privileged of late years! Sure their laborious, painful, costly, and hazardous diligence, in seeking after the knowledge of God, according to his word, will rise in the judgment against this care-

less, lazy, negligent, and slothful generation, who, in the
use of so many various and choice helps, have so patent
and easy access to know, and serve him, with that which
almost costs them nothing.

We have now—besides the large English Annotations,
and the Dutch lately Englished on the whole scriptures,
and some notable pieces of English divines upon several
parts of them—the book of Psalms, all the small Prophets,
the gospels according to Matthew, and John, the epistles
to the Galatians, Ephesians, Philippians, Colossians, and
Hebrews, the two epistles of Peter, the Revelation, and
this Song of Solomon, solidly explained, and in short
notes, sweetly improved by the ministers and divines of
our own church, for the benefit, not only of scholars (who
have many large helps in other languages ;) but also, yea,
principally, of such as cannot, on several accounts conveniently make use of the other ; and yet it may be, (which
is for a lamentation) there are many particular persons,
and not a few whole families, that can read, and might
easily come at such books, mainly designed for their edification, who concern themselves so little in these impor-
tant things, that they look not after them, though in their
secret and family reading of the scriptures, they might be
thereby singularly profited. Oh ! do we thus despise the
goodness of God, and vilify the riches of his bounty ? Is
this to run to and fro, that scripture-knowledge may be
increased; to cry after knowledge, and to lift up our
voice for understanding ; to seek her as silver, and to
search for her as for hid treasure ? or, is this to look on
scripture wisdom, making wise to salvation, as the principal thing, and with all our getting to get understanding?
How much, alas ! have we set light by, and loathed this
manna, that hath from heaven for many years fallen frequently and abundantly, as it were, about our camps ?
No doubt, as we begin sadly to feel already (but, ah !
our stroke is above our groaning) so we have further
ground to fear, that our holy and jealous God, may for
this and other such provocations (whereby we have evidently manifested our detestable indifferency and great
unconcernedness in things of greatest concernment) send
us a famine not of bread, nor a thirst of water, (these
comparatively were light afflictions;) but of hearing the
words of the Lord, so that we shall wander from sea to
sea, and from the north even to the east, and shall run to

and fro to seek the word of the Lord, and shall not find it; and in his wrathful, yet spotless and just providence, order some such revolution, as it shall be accounted a crime punishable by bonds, torture, and death, to read, or have such books, yea, even the book of God itself. O for opened eyes to see what helps and privileges we have enjoyed, and do in part yet enjoy, and grace suitable to improve them.

Amongst these many helps, what my blest husband, the Author of this piece, hath, according to the grace given unto him, contributed, shall not, I hope, be the least acceptable and useful to the church, he having by the good hand of his God upon him, been led to open up two books of the holy scriptures, wherein belike the Lord's people did very much desire to know the mind of the Spirit, they being somewhat darker, and less easily understood, than many, if not than any of all the rest,—the book of the Revelation, and this book of Solomon, the Song of Songs, or the most excellent Song; containing the largest and liveliest discoveries of the love of Jesus Christ, the King, Bridegroom, and Husband of his church, to her his Queen, Bride, and Spouse; and of hers to him, with those spiritually glorious interviews, holy courtings, most superlative, but most sincere, commending and cordial entertainings of each other, those mutual praisings and valuings of fellowship;—those missings, lamentings, and bemoanings of the want thereof;—those holy impatiencies to be without it, swelling to positive and peremptory determinations, not to be satisfied, nor comforted in any thing else, those diligent, painful and restless seekings after it, till it be found and enjoyed, on the one hand;—and those sweet, and easy yieldings to importunity, and gracious grantings of it, on the other; with those high delightings, solacings, complacencies, and acquiescings in, and heartsome embracings of one another's fellowship:—Those failings, faultings, lyings a-bed, and lazinesses, and thereupon, when observed, those love-faintings, swarfings, swoonings, seekings, and sorrowings on the one side; and those love-followings, findings, pityings, pardonings, passings by, rousings, revivings, supportings, strengthenings, courings, confirmings, and comfortings, with most warm and kindly compellations, on the other: (O let men and angels, wonder at the kingly condescending, the majestic meekness, the stately stooping, the high humility, and the lofty lowliness that conspicuously shines forth here on the Bridegroom's part!) —Those love-languishings, feverings, sickenings, holy violentions, apprehendings, and resolute refusings to let go on the one part, and those love-unheartings, heart-ravishings, captivatings, and being overcome: those love-arrests, and detainments in the galleries, as if nailed (to speak so with reverence) to the place, and sweetly charm-ed into a kind of holy impotency, to remove the eye from looking on so lovely an object, on the other :)—Those bashful, but beautiful blushings, humble hidings, and mo-dest thinking shame to be seen or heard speak, on the Bride's part, and those urgent callings, and in a manner compellings, to compear, with those serious professings of singular satisfaction, to hear her sweet voice, and to see her comely countenance on the Bridegroom's part:— Those frequently claimed, avouched, boasted of, and glo-ried in, mutual interests :—Those love-restings, and re-posings on the arm, and on the bosom of one another, with these serious and solemn chargings and adjurings not unseasonably to disturb and interrupt this rest and re-pose :—Those mutual kind invitings, and hearty accept-ing of invitations ; those comings and welcomings ; those feastings, feedings, and banquetings on all manner of pleasant fruits, chief spices, and best wines, even the rar-est and chiefest spiritual dainties and delicates :—Those pleasant, refreshful airings and walkings together in the fragrant fields, villages, woods, orchards, gardens, ar-bours, umbrages, and as it were, labyrinths of love:— Those stately magnificent and majestic describings of one another, as to stature, favour, beauty, comely proportion of parts, curious deckings and adornings, sweet-smelling odoriferous anointings, powderings, and perfumings, hold-ing forth their respective qualifications, endowments, ac-complishments, perfections, and excellencies, whereof all things in the world, bearing such names, are but dark, dull, and empty resemblances :—[In which commending descriptions the Bridegroom seems holily to hyperbolize, and the Bride, though doing her best, doth yet fall hugely below his matchless and incomparable worth, which is exalted far above all the praise of men and angels ; his also of her are many more and more brightly illuminated and garnished with delectable variety of admirably op-posite similitudes, than hers are of him, because his love is infinitely more strong, and his skill in commending infinitely greater and more exquisite, and because withal her jealousies, and suspicions of his love, are not easily removed, nor the persuasions of his so egregious esteem of her easily admitted, though doubtless, he who is the chief of ten thousands, and altogether lovely, hath infinitely the preference and pre-eminence, whereof, if there were not another, that is a demonstrative, and undeniable evidence, that all the splendour and glory, wherewith she thus shineth, is derived and borrowed by her, as but a little twinkling state from him, that great light, the Sun of righteousness. O what will he make of his church when sinless and in heaven, when he makes so much of her, when sinful and on earth! and how incomprehensibly glorious must he be in himself, that puts such passing glory on her!]—These transports of admiration at one another, held forth in the several Behold's, O's, Who's, and How's, prefixed to their respective compellations and commendations :—and finally these vehement joint-longings, to have the marriage consummated and the fellowship immediate, full, and never any more to be interrupted.

From this little hint, may it not be said, that the ravishing passions and passionate ravishings of most purely spiritual, chaste, and ardent love, burning like coals of juniper, and flaming forth in the excellentest expressions imaginable, do quite surpass, transcend, and out-vie those of the most strongly affectionate lovers in the world, whether wooers, or married persons? nay, these scarcely serve darkly to shadow forth those; for, indeed, this marriage, and marriage-love, betwixt Christ and his church is a great mystery, and deservedly so called, by the apostle : the incarnation of the Son of God, with what he was made, died and suffered out of mere free love to the elect, that he might bring about and accomplish this blest match betwixt him and them, and so bestow all his purchase, nay, himself on them ; this, this I say, is without all controversy the great mystery of godliness : O the height and the depth, the breadth and length of the love of Christ, whereof, when all that can be said of it, were it by the tongues of men and angels is said, that must needs be said, that it is a love which passeth knowledge : who can speak suitably, and as he ought of this noble, notable and non-such subject, the love of Christ to his church, that breathes so sweetly and strongly

throughout this Song, and that doth by its sovereign influence so powerfully draw forth the church's love after
him : a heart be-drenched with, and a tongue and pen
dipped in the sense of this love, would do well ; sure the
reading, writing, speaking, hearing, and meditating of this
Song, treating of so transcendently excellent a theme, and
in so spiritually sublime and lofty a strain, calls for a most
spiritual and divine frame of heart ; to the attaining
whereof, that the author might help himself and others, he
did, as from one principal motive, pitch on this book, and
preach on it at great length to the people of his charge in
Glasgow : (in which sermons, he went through pleasant
variety of much choice and rich matter, wonderfully
suited to the several cases of his hearers, especially of the
most seriously and deeply exercised Christians ;) and
thereafter, lecture on it more shortly, only opening up the
meaning of the text, and giving some succinct, but very
sweet notes from it, designing, (at the urgent importunity of several friends, who had been much refreshed by his
larger sermons) these lectures for the more public edification of the church ; by which also he speaketh now the
third time more particularly to the people of Glasgow, on
this precious subject. I suppose I may without vanity
say, that the frame of his spirit did in a good measure
suit such a spiritual purpose, and was more and more
spiritualized by his conversing in, and handling of it : he
was a disciple whom Jesus much loved ; and who by very
intimate and familiar acquaintance with him, was privileged to lean, as it were, on his bosom ; most dearly also
did he love his master ; and from a principle of sincere
love to him, watchfully and tenderly fed his sheep and
lambs. He did withal, as a special friend of the Bridegroom, stand by to hear his voice, having therein his joy
fulfilled, and was effectually taught the excellent art of
of commending the Bridegroom, and of wooing a Bride
for him ; so that this much beloved and very loving disciple, was fitted beyond many of his fellows to treat of
the love betwixt Christ and his church. O that the reading of this savoury comment on this sweetest and most
spiritual text, may, according to the author's desire and
design, through God's blessing, contribute to make those
that are after the flesh to be after the Spirit, and those
that are after the Spirit, as to their state, to mind more
the things of the Spirit, as to their frame ! Sure there was

never more need; for, alas! we are generally undone, through a great remainder of the carnal mind, which is death, and are lamentably little spiritually minded, though to be so be life and peace. It may verily be doubted, if there hath been any generation of Christians before this, that have so little minded the things of the Spirit, and have so strongly favoured the things of the flesh, that have set their affections so little on things above, and so much on things on the earth, notwithstanding of so many and mighty pullings of providence at them.

I hope, noble Madam, with whomsoever this piece shall fall short of the author's aim, it shall not with you, to whom he designed the dedication of it, as he shewed to an intimate friend on his death-bed: it is true, he did not very much please dedicatory epistles, as savouring often, in his opinion, somewhat of adulation; yet such was the true sense of his singular obligations to your Ladyship, and the deep conviction of the sincerity and eminency of the grace of God in you, (whom looking on as indeed a mother in our Israel, he thought it a privilege to have his only daughter, after her mother's death, a while under your educating inspection, of whom you had no reason to be ashamed, she having more especially betwixt that time and her death, though but very young, in modesty, sobriety, gravity, humility, self-deniedness, and in the serious and profound exercise of godliness resembling her blest father to the life, whom through grief for his death she did not long out-live) that he resolved to dedicate this piece to you: which part of his latter will, I durst not but fulfil; and had I been with any such predetermination left to my own choice, your Ladyship would have been the very person pitched upon, not only on the account of my husband's and my own esteem of you, but also of your constantly continued kindness to his family since his death.

Let me, Madam, say it, for provoking you to be yet more for God, and to exercise yourself yet further unto godliness, that your praise is much in the churches of Christ, as otherwise, so through several dedications of books, and missive letters now printed and published from some of the most faithful and famous men in this church, whereby all readers of them are some way alarmed to enquire what this Lady of honour may be, that hath been in so high esteem with so holy, grave, and discerning men.   Since your religion is thus talked of, and spread abroad in several places, (so that I need say nothing) I hope you will endeavour, through grace, in the frame of your spirit, and in your whole deportment to suit this savoury report that hath gone of you ; and that not in order to the getting or keeping such a name for yourself, but as the native, necessary, and unconstrained result of the power of the life of the grace of God within, and in order to the glorifying of him, by whom you were called, and that betimes, even in the morning of your days, to the fellowship of Jesus Christ our Lord by the gospel ; wherein he hath graciously helped you now these forty years and upward, as I suppose, under all the times, changes, and revolutions, that have gone over you (which have not been few, nor inconsiderable) to continue stedfast, without any back-drawing, wavering, shrinking or staggering, reflecting upon, or blemishing your holy profession, and to follow the Lord fully ; a rare and singular mercy, which but few professors of such old standing, especially in these days, have obtained.

Let all the favour and grace you have found in his sight, and all the respect you have had from his choice servants make you constantly speak yourself thus in the ear,—Should such a person as I, do that which would displease him, and make any that seek him, sad or ashamed for my sake.   And, what manner of person ought I to be, in all holy conversation and godliness.

Now, Madam, that it may be thus with your Ladyship, and that you may be fat and flourishing, bringing forth fruit in old age, that you may in waiting on God, renew your strength, run and not be weary, walk and not faint, yea, mount up with wings, as the eagle, putting forth fresh strength in this last stage of your race, and that it may be the one thing done by you, and all the Lord's people, to forget the things that are behind, to reach forth unto the things that are before, and to press hard toward the mark for the prize of the high calling of God in Christ Jesus, is the desire of,

Right honourable, your Ladyship's singularly obliged
Debtor, for all duties of love and service,
MARGARET DURHAM.

TO THE

CHRISTIAN READER.

I HAVE been desired by some interested in the publishing of the ensuing Exposition of the Canticles to peruse it, and to communicate unto thee my thoughts concerning it; upon the first request, I judged this labour altogether needless, on the account of that reputation, which the known piety and abilities of its author, have in the church of God. And this he hath deservedly, not only from his personal holiness and useful labours in the work of the ministry, but also from those other eminent fruits of his study, which being formerly published, have recommended him to the thoughts of unprejudiced persons, as one of good learning, sound judgment, and every way " a workman that needeth not to be ashamed." The perusal of this Exposition hath much confirmed me in the same thoughts and apprehensions. The book of the Canticles is not in any part of it, much less in the whole, a meet subject for every ordinary undertaker to exercise upon. The matter of it is totally sublime, spiritual, and mystical; and the manner of its handling universally allegorical. So did God think meet in his manifold wisdom to instruct his church of old, whilst it tabernacled under those clouds and shadows, whose departure and flying away it so earnestly breathes after in this very book. God committed unto it then, in his oracles, the same treasure of wisdom and grace, as he doth now unto us under the gospel, only he so folded them up under types and allegories, that they could not clearly and distinctly look into them, he having provided " some better things for us, that they without us should not be made perfect." The nature of those types and allegories, with the distinction between them, is briefly, but excellently discoursed by our author in his preface, as a necessary prœludium unto his whole Exposition. There was always then a virtual, spiritual light and heat, a mystery of wisdom in this book: but so wrapt up, so encircled and enclosed in its manner

B 5

of expression, and universal respect unto Christ, not then
actually exhibited, as that it shines not forth, it gives not
out its beauty and glory, until touched and affected by a
beam of immediate gospel light, and its covering be taken
off by him who removes the vail of Moses, and of all
the prophets, both from their writings and the minds of
them that do believe. I shall not here enquire particularly
what express understanding in and of the things divinely
revealed in this book, the church had under the Old Testament, whilst they "searched diligently into the grace of
Christ here declared," and "which his Spirit herein testi-
fied unto them." Nor shall I stay to manifest how great
a darkness as to the true and useful apprehension of the
mind of God in this holy allegory, seems to have been
upon some whole ages of the Christian church. This is
certain, that ever since this heavenly treasure was committed to the sons of men, such a beauty, glory, and excellency have beamed from the matter contained in it,
with the manner of its declaration, and the impress of the
wisdom of God in both, that all who have had a due reverence unto divine revelation, have been filled with an
holy admiration of it, and a desire to look into the mystery contained in it. But whereas, as was intimated;
the things contained in it, are, "the deep things of God,"
which none can search out to perfection, but the Spirit of
God; and the manner of its delivery is not only absolutely
allegorical, the reducing of the just and due intendment
of which kind of expression unto that which is proper, requires great heedfulness, skill, and diligence, both in
things spiritual, when their subject is such, and in the
nature of those schemes or figures of speech, but also
suited unto a measure of light, and understanding which
we are not thoroughly acquainted withal; these things
falling in conjunction with the imperfection and weakness
of all, with the curiosities of some who have undertaken
this exposition, many mistakes have ensued thereon; yea,
some attempts of this kind have seemed to be designed to
divert the minds of men from the direct scope and intendment of the Holy Ghost throughout this whole book. The
Jews in their Targum, a work of great and public esteem
amongst them, are larger on this book, than any other in
the whole Bible. It seems indeed to have been a later
endeavour than most of their other Paraphrases, seeing
express mention is made in it, not only of their Talmud, but

also of sundry Talmudical fables, as of their two Messiahs, Ben-David, and Ben-Joseph, of their anti-messiah, Armillus, of their eating and drinking Leviathan with the wine of paradise in their vainly expected kingdom. But it may be these are later corruptions, and not the conceptions of the first author of that work. However, they plainly acknowledge the mystery and allegory of the whole, ascribing the things mentioned to the transactors between God and the church, partly historically, partly prophetically, with such a respect unto the Messiah, as in sundry places is not to be despised. From them, have some learned persons of late taken occasion to wrest the whole allegory into an history, and a prophecy: but with more sobriety than they, and with more respect to the analogy of faith, with the lights and times of the New Testament. It is, in my judgment, no hard matter to evert that supposition, and cast it out of further consideration; but this is not a place to engage in that undertaking: but I do suppose, that he who will seriously consider the uncertainty and arbitrariness of their conjectures in the application of things here spoken unto, the distinct times and seasons which they would have intended, will find himself somewhat unable to give a firm assent unto their assertions, though he should be desirous so to do. The more general persuasion of learned men is, that the whole is one holy declaration of that mystically spiritual communion, that is between the great Bridegroom and his Spouse, the Lord Christ and his church, and every believing soul that belongs thereunto. This being the nearest, surest, and most firm relation that is between them, the ground of all that he did for the church, and continues yet to do, and of all the duty that he requires from it, that intercourse in faith, love, delight, rest, and complacency that is between them, is here expressed, in words suggested by and from the wisdom of God: and as the whole Song carries this design and intention evidently in the face of it; so the safe rules of attending to the true meaning of the original words, the context of the discourse, the nature of the allegorical expressions, the just period of the Dialogists, or Interlocutors, the analogy of faith, by collation with other scriptures, and the experience of believers in common, will through the supply and assistance of the Spirit upon their fervent supplications, lead humble and believing enquirers, into such acquaintance with the mind of God, in the several particulars of it, as may tend to their own, and others' edification. This course our author steered, and that, if I greatly mistake not, with eminent success. He was no doubt liable to mistakes, as we are all; nor is his Exposition proposed, as that which should prescribe to the judgments, or give bounds to the enquiries of others, whom God hath endued with the like gifts and grace. But this, I suppose, I may say without offence, that it will be hard for any to discover, either defect in judgment, or untruth in affection, or the ommission or neglect of any rule, means, or advantages that might, or ought to be used in enquiry after the mind of God, in this work, or a want of perspicuity, and plainness in the discovery, or expression of his conceptions upon it. I am persuaded every reader, whose mind is exercised about, and conversant in these things, whose heart hath an experience of their power and reality, will find that light and strength added to what he hath attained, and that assistance and direction towards what he is yet reaching out after, as that he will not forbear to give that testimony to the author in this matter, as is due to a faithful and skilful labourer, in this excellent part of the harvest of the Lord; and to the judgment of such alone I do appeal: and this consideration refers me to these thoughts which I before expressed, viz. the uselessness of any recommendation of this treatise unto those who are willing conscientiously to enquire into the sacred truths treasured up in this excellent portion of scripture, and to improve them unto their own advantage in faith and obedience. The whole of what I can contribute unto the furtherance of the usefulness of this treatise, is to recommend it in. my poor supplications, unto the grace of him, who supplied this seed to the sower, that he would bless it in the hearts and minds of them that read it, with an increase unto holiness and eternal life:

So prays, thy friend and servant in the work of the gospel,

JOHN OWEN.

May 20, 1669.

CLAVIS CANTICI.

A KEY, USEFUL

FOR

OPENING UP THE SONG.

THIS is a place of scripture, the exposition whereof many in all ages have shunned to adventure upon; and truly I have looked upon it of a long time, as not convenient to be treated upon before all auditories, nor easy by many to be understood; especially because of the height of spiritual expressions, and mysterious raps of Divine Love, and the sublime and excellent expressions of the Bridegroom therein contained, which would require much liveliness of frame, and acquaintance in experience with the things here spoken of, and nearness in walking with God, as being necessary for finding out the mind and meaning of the Spirit of God therein: yet we are now brought by help of his grace, to essay the interpretation of it, upon these following considerations.

I. Because it is acknowledged by all, not only to be authentic scripture, but an excellent piece thereof; and therefore is to be made use of by the church, and not to lie hid, nor to be laid aside, as if the meaning thereof were not to be searched into, because it seems dark and obscure.

II. Because the subject and matter of it is so divine, carrying along with it many various cases, both of particular souls, as also, of the church, both visible and invisible, with many excellent commendations of Christ the Bridegroom, which ought to be the subject of his friends' meditations, and cannot but be profitable, if he bless them; there being here maps, almost for all conditions.

III. Because the style and composition is so divine and excellent, carrying the affections along with it, and captivating them in the very reading; so that few can read this Song, but they must fall in love with it; we would therefore see what is within it, if, at least, we may get a taste of that which doth so sweetly relish.

IV. It seems the Holy Ghost, by putting it into such a mould intended to commend it: and if it be true that all the poetical pieces of scripture, ought especially to be learned and taken notice of; so should this, it being so commended to us in that frame.

V. The strain and subject of it is so very spiritual, that it necessitates the students thereof, to aim at some nearness with God; and ordinarily it leaves some stamp upon their affections, which is not the least cause, nor the smallest encouragement to me in this undertaking.

We shall not stand to prove the authority of it; it carries a Divine style in its bosom, nor is there need to enquire who was the penman of it, it being clear that Solomon who was furnished with wisdom and understanding, as never a king before or since was, is honoured to be the Amanuensis of the Holy Ghost, in putting this Song upon record. Whether after, or before his backsliding, it is not much to us; though it be most probable that it was after, in the warmness of a spirit sensible of this so great deliverance: for here we may, as it were, see him making use of that experience of the vanity of all things he had found, coming to the fear of God as the conclusion of the whole matter; whereof this Song of Love is not a little evidence, and which looks like his own saying, Eccl. xii. 13.

The means which are necessary for our more perspicuous handling, and your more profitable hearing of this profound scripture will be,

I. Some acquaintance with the whole word of God, but mainly the book of the Psalms, and other Songs recorded in the Word; as also, with the gospel, and such places as have most likeness to it.

II. Acquaintance with the cases of others, either by reading, or mutual fellowship; but most of all, it is requisite, that one have some experimental knowledge of the way of God towards his own heart: he who is so wise as to observe these things, even he shall understand this loving kindness of the Lord: such kind of experience is one of the best commentaries upon this text.

III. Watchfulness over ourselves, keeping our heart with all keeping, and studying a tender frame of spirit, that we may have a conscience always void of offence towards God: looseness all the week will not be a frame for the Canticles. It is not the simple being of grace, but the lively operation and exercise thereof, which prompts and disposes either to speak to purpose, or to hear of this with profit: he would grow in grace who would grow in knowledge here: neither have others ground to expect that this secret of the Lord shall be with them, or that they shall be of a quick understanding, who fear him not: one may have grace, and not a lively frame for this, except grace be acting and in exercise.

IV. Much conversing with the Bridegroom, especially by prayer, that he who causes the dull to understand doctrine, may manifest himself, and open our eyes to behold wondrous things, that he may bless us in the knowledge of his will in this we undertake, which so especially concerns him and us; for, this scripture may be dark to these who speak on it, if this be not, and a sealed book to you who hear it, if these things be wanting: whereas, "if these be in us and abound, we shall neither be barren nor unfruitful" in the knowledge of this piece of sacred scripture.

Now, that we may have the more clear access to speak profitably of the matter of this Song, and that our way of opening and applying of it (which may possibly in some things be different from others) may be the better cleared. We shall, 1. Permit some propositions concerning it. 2. Draw come conclusions from these; both which we shall endeavour shortly to clear and confirm, as useful to be taken along in our proceeding.

The first proposition then in this: This Song is a piece of divine Scripture, and a most excellent part thereof (which we shall speak to more fully on the title) and so of equal authority with other scriptures (wherein holy men spoke, as they were inspired by the Holy Ghost) and tendeth to the edifying of the church, and making of the man of God perfect, even as they do: for,

I. This Song hath ever been received into the Canon, and accounted (as they speak) for canonic, as the rest of the scriptures were. It was never questioned by the Jews (as *Mercer. præfat. ad Cant.* cleareth) but was still received by them, and transmitted to the Gentile churches who received the scriptures of the Old Testament from them, who had the oracles of God in keeping : and that the same hath been universally received by Christians, may appear by the records of the councils, and writings of the fathers, where the catalogue of the books of the holy scripture is set down.

II. It carrieth the authority of the Holy Ghost engraven upon it, as evidently as any piece of scripture, not only as to its matter, manner of expression, divine style ; but mostly in that divine power and efficacy it hath on hearts and spirits (especially of the more discerning, who best know Christ's voice as his sheep) whereby it relishes so sweetly, and elevates them to such an holy ravishment, that it obtaineth the testimony from all, that there is something divine in it, and more than can be in human writings, even though they cannot particularly tell the meaning of it ; that holding true here, which one said of a book which was something obscure, " That which I understand," said he " is excellent : therefore I judge that which I understand not, to be so also, though it exceed my reach."   And that it is Christ who speaketh, and that it is the language of the Holy Ghost, and can be applied to no other, is by a divine conviction extorted from the reader, and hearer of it ; so that confessedly and deservedly, it beareth this title, a " Song of Songs."

This Song must either be attributed to the Spirit, as the chief author of it, (though Solomon was the penman) or we must say, it was not only penned, but indited merely by some man, (Solomon, or whoever he be) led by his own spirit, or some other spirit, without the Spirit of God : but none of these last can be said.   What other spirit can so speak of Christ and the church ?   What other song, even of the most holy men, can be compared to this ?   Was it ever equalled ?   Or can it be equalled ? And if it cannot be the fruit of the spirit of a mere man, though in the most holy frame, then it must be inspired by the Spirit, in wonderful wisdom, and a most divine style, compacting the mysteries of communion with God in Christ, in this short Song ; wherefore we say, it is justly called a " Song of Songs," whereby its is preferred not only to all human songs, but even to other scriptural songs, which were blasphemous to do, were it not of a divine rise and authority.

There are two objections which sometimes have been started by some ; but they will not be of weight to infringe this truth. The first is, that there is no passage of this Song cited in the New Testament. But citation of scriptures in the New Testament doth not give authority to them. They are cited as having authority, and not to get it; and therefore there are many scriptures in the Old Testament which were never cited in the New: although it may be said, there are many near resemblances, at least, in the New Testament, to divers passages in this Song; as the often styling the church a Vineyard, Matt. xx. and comparing the church's union with Christ to Marriage, Matt. xxii. &c. That " Christ standeth at the door and knocketh," Rev. iii. 20. taken as it were, from Song v. 2. The virgins falling on sleep, Matt xxv. The efficacy of grace, called drawing, John vi. 44. taken from chap. i. 4, &c. Christ in the parables called a King, or, the King (which by way of eminency is applied to HIM, Psal. xlv. 1, 2.) Neither is the second objection of greater weight, viz. That no proper name of God is to be found in this Song: for, 1. It is so also in other scriptures, as in the book of Esther: the scripture's authority doth not depend on naming the name of God, but on having his warrant and authority. 2, This Song being Allegorical and Figurative, it is not so meet nor consistent with its style, to have God named under proper names, as in other scriptures. Yet, 3. There are titles and descriptions here given to an excellent person, which can agree to none other, but Christ the eternal Son of God : as " the King," " O thou whom my soul loveth," "the chief of ten thousand," " the Rose of Sharon," and the like, whereby HIS eminency is singularly set out above all others in the world.

In sum, there are none of the characters usually condescended on as necessary for evidencing the authority of holy scripture, wanting here; this Song being a divine subject, received into the canon, bearing a divine stamp, having much majesty in its style, agreeing with itself and other scriptures fully; impartially speaking out the blots and adversities of the bride, as well as her beauty and prosperity, and written by a prophet and penman of holy writ, viz. Solomon.

The second proposition is, That this Song is not to be taken properly, (and κατα το ρητον) or literally, that is, as the words do at first sound; but it is to be taken and understood spiritually, figuratively and allegorically, as having some spiritual meaning contained under these figurative expressions, made use of throughout this Song: my meaning is, that when it speaketh of a Marriage, Spouse, Sister, Beloved, Daughters of Jerusalem, &c. these expressions are not to be understood properly of such, but as holding forth something of a spiritual nature under these.

I grant it hath a literal meaning; but I say, that literal meaning is not immediate, and that which first looketh out, as in historical scriptures, or others which are not figurative; but that which is spiritually, and especially meant by these allegorical and figurative speeches, is the literal meaning of this Song: so that its literal sense is mediate, representing the meaning, not immediately from the words, but mediately from the scope, that is, the intention of the Spirit, which is couched under the figures and allegories, here made use of: for, a literal sense (as it is defined by Rivet out of the school-men) is that which floweth from such a place of scripture, as intended by the Spirit in the words, whether properly or figuratively used, and is to be gathered from the whole complex expressions together, applied thereunto, as in the exposition of parables, allegories and figurative scriptures is clear: and it were as improper and absurd to deny a figurative sense (though literal) to these, as it were to fix figurative expositions upon plain scriptures, which are properly to be taken.

For there is a two-fold literal sense of scripture, 1. Proper and immediate, as where it is said, " Solomon married Pharaoh's daughter." The second is figurative and meditate, as when it is said, Matth. xxii. 2. " A certain king made a marriage to his son," &c. Both have a literal meaning. The first immediate, fulfilled in Solomon: the second is mediate, setting out God's calling Jews and Gentiles unto fellowship with his Son: and so that parable is to be understood in a spiritual sense. Now we say, this Song (if we would take up its true sense and meaning) is not to be understood the first way, properly and immediately, but the second way, figuratively and mediately, as holding forth some spiritual thing under borrowed expressions, which will further appear from these things:

I. There can be no edification in setting out human love (amongst parties properly understood) so largely and lively; and yet edification must be the end of this Song, being a part of scripture; it must therefore have a higher meaning than the words at first will seem to bear.

II. There can be no parties mentioned, besides Christ

and his Bride, to whom this Song can agree ; nor can any proper meaning thereof be assigned, which can make it applicable to these parties : and therefore it cannot be understood properly, but figuratively, and that not of any other, but of Christ and believers : to Solomon it cannot agree in its application, nor to his queen, yea, to no man, if it be taken in a proper sense : for, 1. These commendations given to the Bridegroom, chap. v. to the Bride, chap. iv. 6, 7. if properly understood, would be monstrous, blasphemous, and ridiculous; such as to have " teeth like a flock of sheep," and a " head like Carmel," &c. and so in many other things.   2. Some things are attributed to this Solomon, who is the subject of this Song, that were not within Solomon's reach ; as that, his presence at the table, chap. i. 12. " Maketh her spikenard to smell," which influence cannot proceed from one man more than another, and chap. iii. 10. where it is said, " He made a chariot, and paved it with love," which is no material thing, and so could be no pavement in Solomon's chariot.   3. That Solomon being the penman of this Song, yet speaketh of Solomon in the second person, " Thou, O Solomon," chap. viii. 12. makes it appear that some other was designed than himself ; and many such like expressions that fill up the matter of this Song (such as spices, gardens, &c.) cannot be understood properly of these very things themselves, but of some other thing vailed under them : and so also, when she is called, " Terrible as an army with banners," it cannot be understood of Solomon's queen : and applying it to the church, we cannot understand it of any carnal terror, which the external aspect of the church doth beget in beholders.

III. The style and expressions will bear out more than any human love, or any human object, upon which men set their love : we are sure, no such love would be proponed to believers as a warranted pattern for their imitation, as if it would be commendable in them to be so much ravished and taken up even with the most lovely creature.

IV. Many things here are inconsistent with human love and that modesty that is required in it (as the Hebrews themselves, *apud Mercer*, observe) as to propone him to others, to excite them to love him, others undertaking to follow after him, her speaking to him in her sleep, chap. v. 2.   Running in the night through the streets, and slighting him at the door ; which by no means can admit a proper, literal, and immediate sense, but must needs aim at something figurative. Besides, what reason can there be to plead a proper sense here, more than in other figurative scriptures of the same sort, as of these that speak of the soul's union with Christ, under the similitude of a marriage, and particularly that of Psalm xlv. which is, as it were, a compend of this Song, and is looked upon by all as figurative?

If it be enquired in what sense we call this Song figurative, whether as typical or allegorical? The answering and clearing of this question will further us in the interpretation of this excellent scripture. We shall therefore shew, 1, How allegorical properly so called, differeth from typical. And, 2. Why we call this Song allegorical, and not typical.

Allegorical scriptures, or allegories (we take allegory here as divines do, who take it not as grammarians, or rhetoricians, for a continued discourse of many figures together) properly and strictly taken (for sometimes allegory may be taken largely, and so may comprehend whatever is figurative, whether typical, tropological, analogical, &c. as the apostle taketh it, Gal. iv. speaking of Abraham's two sons, which is properly a type) differeth from types, or typical scriptures, thus,

Firstly, Types suppose still the verity of some history, as Jonah's casting in the sea, and being in the fish's belly three days and three nights, when it is applied to Christ in the New Testament, it supposeth such a thing once to have been: allegories again, have no such necessary supposition, but are as parables, proponed for some mystical end. Thus, while it is said, Matt. xxii. 2. " A certain king made a marriage," "planted a vineyard," &c. That place supposeth it not necessary as to the being of the allegory, that ever such a thing was, it may be an allegory without that; but a type cannot be without reality in the thing, or fact, which is made a type.

II. Types look only to matters of fact; and compare one fact with another (as Christ lying in the grave for such a time, to that of Jonah, who did lie so long in the whale's belly) but allegories take in words, sentences, doctrines, both of faith and manners, as in the former examples is clear.

III. Types compare persons, and facts under the Old Testament, with persons and facts under the New, and are made up of something that is present, prefiguring another

to come : allegories look especially to matters in hand,
and intend the putting of some hid spiritual sense upon
words, which at first they seem not to bear, whether the
allegory be only in the Old Testament, or only in the
New, or in both, it looks to the sense and meaning, being
so considered in itself, as the words may best serve the
scope, and teach, or manifest the thing-the Spirit intends,
without any comparison betwixt this, and that of the Old
Testament and New : yea, an allegory may be in precepts, as " Muzzle not the mouth of the ox," and " cut off
the right hand," &c. which have an allegoric sense in them.

IV. Types are only historical, as such, and the truth of
fact agreeing in the antitype, make them up, it being clear
in scripture that such things are types : for we must not
forge types without scripture warrant : but allegories are
principally doctrinal, and in their scope intend not to clear,
or compare facts, but to hold forth and explain doctrines,
or by such similitudes to made them the better understood,
and to move and affect the more, or the more forcibly to
convince, as Nathan made use of a parable, when he was
about to convince David, 2 Sam. xii. 1, 2, &c.

V. Types in the Old Testament respect only some
things, persons, and events. as Christ, the gospel, and its
spreadings, &c. and cannot be extended beyond these : but
allegories take in every thing that belongs either to doctrine, or instruction in faith, or to practice for ordering
one's life.

Hence we may see, that allegories are much more extensive in their meaning and application, than types,
(which cannot be extended further than some one thing)
and so are much more doctrinal, and concern both the faith
and manners of God's people much more, and may for
that, more warrantably be applied and made use of for
these ends.

Secondly, We say, that this Song is not typical, as
being made up of two histories, viz. Solomon's marriage,
and Christ's : nor doth it any way intend the comparing
of these two together in the events, as to their facts, or
deeds : but it is allegoric, not respecting Solomon, or his
marriage, but aiming to set out spiritual mysteries in
figurative expressions, in such a manner as may most
effectuate that end, for enlightening the judgment and
moving of the affections, without any respect to that story
or fact of Solomon's : for,

1. The strain and series of it, is clearly allegoric, as the reading and considering of it will clear. 2. There can be no history to which it can relate, unto which the things spoken in this Song can be properly applied, as is said. 3. Solomon's marriage was at least twenty years before this Song was written : see on Song vii. 4. concerning the tower of Lebanon, and compare it with 1 Kings vii. 1, 2. and chap. vi. ult. Therefore it cannot be thought so much as to be penned on that occasion, as an Epithalamium which was to be sung that night on which he was married, and although occasion of penning of it were taken from that, yet would it not prove it typical, and to respect that as its type. 4. What more is this allegory of a marriage to be accounted typical, than other places of scripture, where this same manner of expression is used ? 5, If it be partly typical, how is this type to be made up ? For Christ's love unto, and marriage with his church, is not set out here as peculiar to the New Testament, but is applicable to believers under the Old : there can therefore be here no comparing of facts of the Old Testament, with any thing answering to them in the New.

If it be said, Solomon's marriage typified Christ's marrying of the Gentiles. I answer, beside that there is no scripture for this conjecture (and it is hard to coin types without scripture authority, otherwise we might make Solomon a type in his many wives, possibly, and in many other such things ; also that of his marrying Pharaoh's daughter was against the law, as well as this) it cannot be said that this Song setteth out only Christ's love to the Gentiles ; or the believing Gentiles, their carriage and love to him : for, was it not fulfilled (in that which they could make its antitype) before Christ came in the flesh, in the believing Jews ? yea, before ever that marriage was : and therefore, there can be no typical respect had to that marriage here. Besides, it would much darken the spiritualness and divineness of this Song, to make it in such a way typical, as having any proper fulfilling, or meaning, that were possibly verified in the deed of any man. We conclude then, that this Song is simply allegoric.

We come now to a third proposition, which is this : The divine mystery intended, and set forth here, is the mutual love and spiritual union, and communion that is betwixt Christ and his church, and their mutual carriage towards one another, in several conditions and dispensations. The comprehensive sum of this, is contained in this Song, and compended by the Spirit, for the comfort and edification of the church, under these figurative expressions: this we say, is the scope and subject-matter of this Song: for,

I. If the intent of this Song be to set out the spiritual carriage, amongst spiritual parties, and the spiritual love which each hath to other, then it must set out Christ's love to his church, and hers to him: the reason is, because there are no other spiritual marriage parties known, but Christ and his church; there is no other spiritual marriage, or spiritual marriage love, but this: but this Song in its scope is to set out a spiritual marriage, of spiritual parties, and their spiritual love, therefore it must set out this.

II. The scope of this Song must be agreeable to the matter contained in it. Now the matter contained in it, can agree to no other parties, and be approved in no other love: therefore these descriptions given to the Bridegroom, can be given to no other but Christ; and these given to the Bride by him, can be given to no other but the church, and must speak out no less love than that love of Christ's, the expressions being far beyond the love of all others: this will more fully appear in the opening up of the Song.

III. What is the scope of these allegories, in other scriptures, as that of Psalm xlv. that of planting a vineyard, Mat. xxi. that of marriage, chap. xxii. (which none can deny) is meant of espousing spiritually. (See this same allegory of marriage, Jer. iii.; Hos. ii. 3; Ezek. xvi.; Matt. xxii.; Luke xiv.; 2 Cor. xi. 1; Rev. xix. 8;) that must be the scope of this also. For, 1, There cannot be two spiritual marriages, to which these scriptures and this can be applied. 2, Scripture must agree with scripture, and one more obscure place, must be expounded by others more clear; and therefore seeing this scope is clear in other scriptures of this nature, we may conclude it is the scope here also; that Psalm xlv. doth agree with the expressions and strain of this Song, is clear by comparing them; and that it speaketh of that spiritual marriage betwixt Christ and his church, is clear by the citations drawn from it, and applied to that end by the Apostle, Heb. i. 8, 9.

IV. Either this must be its scope, or it must have some

other scope, or none at all. To say none at all, is blasphemous : if it be said another scope than this, then it must
either be such a scope as agreeth with these other scriptures, or which differeth from them ; but not such as differeth from them, that cannot be said; therefore it must be
the same : and so it setteth out Christ's way with his
church, and hers with him, drawing them, as it were, in
a map together.

Object. If any would argue, that it might better be prophetically applied, as foretelling events in the church, as
some do : for answer, I. We suppose, it would be hard to
make that out to be the scope and intention of the Spirit.

II. It would be more hard to get help from other scriptures, in the application of it to such events, and such
times ; and so this would leave it wholly to uncertainty,
or men's pleasure, as their invention and groundless conjectures, would lead them to apply it : (as we fear some
good men have taken too much liberty, without any ground
but mere conjectures, to wrest the scope of this Song) and
besides, such an interpretation would exceedingly spoil believers of that instruction and consolation, which the true
scope giveth them ; for then they were not to apply it to
themselves, or to the church, but at such a time, and in
such an age; because, if it shall be once fulfilled in others,
or, if it be not applicable to them, because they live not
in such a time, it will certainly mar their confidence in
making any comfortable application of it to themselves.

Besides, these considerations may clear, that in its
scope, it cannot be properly prophetical of such and such
times and events, but dogmatical and practical, for believers' use, in all times and events.

1. If the scope and matter of this Song will agree
to any one time, or if all of it will agree to believers at
any time, then it cannot be prophetical ; for, prophecy
supposeth a diversity of time for divers events, and cannot be said at any one time alike to be fulfilled ; but all the
subject of this Song may be fulfilled in one believer or
other, at any one time ; there are still some enjoying
Christ, some deserted, some praying, some suffering, &c.
and so of whatever part of it we can think upon, it may
be said of one time, as well as of another, that it hath its
accomplishment in one believer or other ; and therefore
it is not properly prophetical.

2. If all of it may now be applied to believers, yea, and

at any time before the end of the world, may be as well applied as being then fulfilled, as well as when it was written, then it is not prophetical, seeing prophecies have their particular accomplishments; but all parts of this Song, even the first parts, may now be applied, and will still agree to believers, as properly as it did in Solomon's time. Therefore, &c.

3. If all the parts of it were in the same way applicable to, and true, in the cases of believers, than when it was written, even as now, or will be before the end, then it was not intended to be prophetical, but doctrinal, narrative, and consolatory: but the first is true; were there any believers in Solomon's days, but these commendations, properties, promises, practices, &c. did agree to them, as they do to us? and was not Christ's way such to them also as it is to us?

4. Consider further, if the scope of it be to set out Christ's way to his church, and hers to him, as it is said; and if according to this scope, it should be made use of by a believer in any time, then it is not prophetical, but doctrinal, as hath been said: but the former is true, as is cleared. Therefore, &c.

5. If it be applicable to believers, according to their several cases, and if it be the case agreeing with any part of this Song, which grounds the application of it to any party, and not the time when that case is not; then it is not prophetical, deducing cases by times, but doctrinal, &c. applying directions, warnings, and comforts to believers' cases, in whatsoever time.

6. The matter of it is the ordinary cases which are incident to believers in all times, and what may make it look prophetical-like, may be considered in the Exposition.

7. If its scope be one and the same with other allegories of this kind, then it is not prophetical, but doctrinal: but the former is true: therefore, &c. The truth of both which, may appear by what is said, and will further appear in that which followeth.

We leave this then, and come again to the proposition, viz. that the great scope of this Song is to set out that mutual love and carriage that is between Christ and his church: that this proposition, which is a main one, may be the more clear, we shall take it in five distinct branches.

I. It holdeth out, we say, the church's case, and Christ's care of her, in all her several conditions, and under all

dispensations ; such as, 1. Her sinful infirmities, and failings in duties, chap. i. 6, and v. 2, 3.   And also, under
liveliness in duties, chap. i. 2, 3, 4, and v. 5, almost
throughout.   2. Under crosses, chap. i. 6, as being a "lily
among thorns," and hated of the world, chap. ii. 2, and also
in prosperity, wherein she is commended as terrible, chap.
vi. 10.   3. as deserted and sick of love, chap. iii. 1, 2, and
v. 4, 5.   And again, as enjoying her beloved, chap. i. 4,
and iii. 4, 5.   4. As under faithful shepherds, and lively
ordinances, chap. i. 4, and iii. 4, 5, and also, as under carnal watchmen, chap. v. 7.   And in all these, her various
conditions, in all ages, are painted forth, before Christ's
incarnation as well as now, without respect to any particular time or age : for, ceremonial things are not here
meddled with, but what was spiritual : besides, the church
then, and now is one, as in the next consideration will be
cleared.   5. As in private dealing with Christ, and
longing after him, and praying for him, chap. iv. 6, and
viii. 1, &c. almost throughout ; and also, what she was in
public duties, going to the watchmen, chap. v. 7, and iii.
3, and what she was in fellowship with others, chap. v. 8,
9, and chap. vi. 1, 2.   6. It sets out believers as more
strong, and furnished with a greater measure of grace
and knowledge, and also, as more weak in gifts and
graces.   7. And lastly, it holds forth the same believers,
as more and less lively in their conditions.

This book in its matter, is a comprehensive sum of all
these particulars formed in a Song, put together, and
drawn as on a board, for the believer's edification ; to
shew, 1. What should be, and will be their carriage when
it is right with them, as to their frame.   2. What are
their infirmities, and what they use often to fall into, even
they who are belivers, that they may be the more watchful.   3. To shew what they may meet with, that they
may make for sufferings, and not stumble at them when
they come.   4. That the care and love of Christ to them,
in reference to all these, may appear, that they may know
upon what grounds to comfort themselves in every condition, and may have this Song, as a little magazine, for
direction, and consolation in every condition.

Therefore this Song is not to be restricted to any particular case or time, and is (even by Bernard, serm. I.)
therefore observed to differ from other spiritual Songs, in
three things : 1. That it is penned upon no particular oc-

casion, as others are ; such as that of Moses, Exod. xv.
and Judg. v. &c. 2. That it is composed by way of conference between several parties. 3. That there are in
this conference more parties than two ; Christ, the Bride,
Watchmen, Daughters of Jerusalem, &c. all which do shew
its extensiveness, and comprehensiveness in respect of its
subjects and use.

II. This Song holdeth forth the church's, or Bride's
conditions, under all her several considerations : we may
consider the Bride, or church four ways, all of which we
will find here : 1. As visible, and visibly professing Christ,
and worshipping him in ordinances : in this respect there
are Watchmen spoken of ; a mother's house ; gardens of
many believers together, and a vineyard let out to keepers,
and a mother having children, (called also Daughters of
Jerusalem) who are professing believers, and such like,
which agree only to the church, as visible.

2. Consider her as invisible, having true faith in Christ,
spiritual union with him, love to him and real exercise of
graces, &c. Thus Christ is hers, and she is his ; she is
drawn by him, and brought into the chambers of lively
sense and communion : thus she is near him, or absent
from him, and such like, which only agree to the church,
or saints, as members of the invisible church, having real
(and not only professed) union with Christ ; and thus she
is distinguished from the mother's children, which are
outward professors of the visible church ; and thus the
most of the commendations she gets throughout this Song,
agree unto her as invisible : neither can it be thought
strange that both these considerations take place in one
and the same Song : For, 1. That distinction of the
church visible and invisible, is not a distribution of a
whole into distinct parts ; as, suppose one would divide a
heap of chaff and corn, into corn and chaff ; but this is a
distinct uptaking of the same whole, (viz. the church)
under two distinct considerations ; as, suppose one would
consider the foresaid heap, as it is a heap, comprehending
both corn and chaff, or as it is only comprehensive of corn ;
so the church thus distinguished, is but one, considered in
whole, as having both renewed and unrenewed in it, and
as having renewed only ; yet so as the renewed are a part
of the whole, under one consideration, viz. as they are
visible professors ; and also, are the invisible church, being
distinctly considered, as they have more than a visible pro-

fession : therefore the likeness being so great and near, it
is no marvel they be frequently conjoined in this Song,
so as they must be distinguished in respect of these distinct considerations, seeing the visible church in its consideration as such, comprehends the visible militant church
under it, but not contrarily. 2. It is ordinary upon this
ground, thus to conjoin them in other scriptures, as when
an epistle is written to a church, some things are said of it,
and to it, as visible, some things again are peculiarly applicable to believers, who are members of the invisible
church in it ; as by looking to these epistles, Rev. ii. 3 ;
it is clear, all are comprehended in every epistle, yet is
the matter diversely to be applied, and these who have
ears to hear, (that is, are real members of the invisible
church also) are particularly spoken unto, although indefinitely : and why then may not the church in both these
considerations, be spoken of here in this Song.

3. If we consider either the visible, or invisible, church,
as whole or catholic, something is spoken to her under that
consideration, namely, as catholic ; so she is said to be
one, chap. vi. 9, made up of many, the mother having
many daughters, a vineyard instrusted to all the keepers,
having some children beloved, others hated, &c. which
must be applicable to her, as so considered.

4. If we look to particular members, either, 1. As professors of the visible church, such as the daughters of Jerusalem, seeking the Beloved with the Bride, and one of
them are distinct from another, and from the watchmen ;
such are the threescore queens, and fourscore concubines,
as distinct from the church, considered as one. Or, 2.
As members in particular of the invisible church ; so the
Bride is distinguished from other professors, and believers ; she speaks to them, and they to her ; chap. ii. So
is one queen and concubine distinguished from another :
thus also is the church considered in general, and in indi-
viduals in their carriage ; yea, it serveth much to the scope
of edifying believers that the church in these respects, be
thus distinctly considered and looked upon : neither will
this be thought strange, if we consider, that the church,
however understood, and the particular and individual
members thereof (especially of this invisible church) are of
an homogeneous nature ; so that what may be said of the
whole may be said of all its parts, and what may be predicated concerning the whole essentially, may be predi-

cated of every part, &c. As when we consider the whole element of water, it is water; so when we consider a drop, it is also water: and what essential properties do agree to the whole, as such, agrees to every drop of the whole; so it is in the church, all saints, members of the invisible church, have the same spirit, faith, and privileges: the same covenant, husband, &c. and what thus essentially agrees to one, agrees to all, and what may be said of all, may be said of one: I say in essentials, because, though there be many circumstantial, and gradual differences, as one believer may be stronger than another, &c. yet that will not mar this oneness, and agreement in essentials. Yet,

III. We say, every thing in this Song, is not to be applied to all within the church, or to the church, under every consideration in the same manner; what agreeth to the church as visible, will not, at least, in the same manner agree to her, considered as invisible, *& contra;* nor will every thing which agrees to a believer in one case, agree to all; nay, not to that same believer always. Therefore, there is great need of wariness in application, that the word may be rightly divided, and the divers cases of the church and particular believers would be rightly taken up for that end: every place is not to be applied to all (though sometimes a place may be taken up under divers considerations, as from other scriptures, and the formerly cited epistles is clear) but what agrees to every one would be so applied, and solely upon that consideration, and under that notion, as it agrees unto such a person, or such a case.

For helping us in this distinct application, it is necessary that we lay down these following rules:

Firstly, We must weigh the particular scope of such a place of scripture, if it speak something concerning a believer in particular, or the church in general; if it set out some outward, or some inward thing concerning them.

Secondly, We would consider the matter spoken to, and see how it agreeth, whether to the church under one consideration, or under another; and if the matter predicated of her, or attributed to her, will agree to her as visible, or as invisible only, for so it is to be applied; if to the whole church, or if to all its members, and every particular believer; for so it is to be understood.

Thirdly, We would see, how the same matter is applied in other Songs and scriptures, and it will be safe for us to follow the same way of application here.

Fourthly, We would consider what the particular circumstances that may be observed in such a particular scripture, will help in finding out the sense ; as who speaketh, to whom, in what frame, on what occasion, &c. Yet,

IV. We say, that this Song doth most generally agree, and is especially applicable to the cases of particular believers : because,

1. The scope is not so much to speak to all collectively, as distributively to hold forth the several cases, that all of them at all times are subject unto ; for although every place do not point out the case of the church in general, or her duty, yet we conceive it is still in every part, pertinent to some one believer or other : such places must therefore be understood distributively.

2. The nature and strain of the most of those things mentioned in this Song, generally will agree best, if not only to particular believers ; as to love Christ, to seek him, to be commended so by him, to be out of one case into another, pursuing after him from one duty to another; which indeed shews the way of the church in general, but so as considered in the exercises of her individual members, and in the intercourse of communion, which useth to be betwixt Christ and them, and so agreeth to the church, only in respect of particular believers.

3. There is a plurality of parties speaking, differenced not only from carnal professors, but from one another, who are commending the Bride, and so loving her and Christ also ; which says, that the several parts of this Song must especially be distributively considered of believers severally.

4. There is no time, we can conceive all believers to be in the like case, so that one case or word will not suit them all ; as to be " sick of love," to have his right hand under her head, &c. Something then must agree to one, something to another, and both also at different times to the same persons : and therefore we must consider this Song, as speaking distributively the church's condition, to be applied according to the several cases of the saints, and and according to their several conditions ; some things as spoken to one, and some things to another.

5. The putting of these exercises in a Song, as it were to be learned and sung by particular believers (as a little compend, both of what concerns their faith and manners)

was certainly for helping their memories, and furthering their consolation ; which would be much impaired, if in singing of it, particular believers might not suck their own consolation in particular from Christ's words unto them : and what can hinder but a believer may say, " I am, HIS, and HE is mine," and that these and other places applicable to them, may not be so applied, seeing their comfort and edification is the scope of this Song ?

V. The last branch of the proposition is, that this Song holdeth forth the same love, and care in Christ to his church and the same exercises and duties of believers, under figurative terms, which are plainly and properly holden forth in other scriptures, which are not figurative, such as are in the gospel, in the Psalms, &c. There are no new, strange, or uncouth cases here : but believers' ordinary cases, there is no uncouth way of Christ's here, but what he useth to his church : it is often the folly and vanity of men's minds, that when expressions of scripture look somewhat strange like, they suppose still some uncouth and strange thing to be there, and therefore loathe that which is plain. It is true, the cases mentioned here, are most spiritual, having love often drawn in its most bright and lively colours, yet for substance, the exercises are the same, which in other plain scriptures are otherwise expressed ; for, it must express the same cases, or, we must say, it expresseth something different from them, not incident ordinarily to believers, and not mentioned any where in scripture which to affirm, were both dangerous and absurd : besides, Christ being still the same in his way with believers, and they having still the same spirit, and being still under the same covenant, &c. we can conceive no other thing here, but what he hath expressed concerning himself and them, other-where in scripture. And certainly the scope of this Song, is rather in a sweet way, to compact together the ordinary cases of believers, and their consolations, for their edification, than to pitch on strange things, or make new cases, which would not be so profitable unto them, and would wrong, and enervate the great intent of this Song.

We proceed now, and shall draw some conclusions from these propositions.

First Conclusion. We may then warrantably read and expound this Song; it being scripture, it must be edifying, and ought to be made use of. It is true, this, and some other scriptures, were of old restrained by the Jews, from the younger sort, that none should read them, but those who were at thirty years of age : Origin marks for pieces of holy scripture thus restrained by them : the history of the creation, Gen. i.   The description of God's appearance, Ezek. i. and of his temple, chap. xl. &c. And especially this Song, because the matters in them were so sublime, that there needed more than ordinary humility and experience in those who should meddle with them ; this indeed, saith men ought to be sober, and with holy fear search these scriptures : but that restraint (if peremptory) was unwarrantable, seeing the Lord hath put none such on his people, as to any portion of sacred scripture. And though this Song be obscurer than many other scriptures ; yet, generally the reading of it, and hearing of it, will affect, and as to the composing of the Spirit, edify as much, as other more plain scriptures : which saith, it is to be enquired into, that the meaning being found out, the profit reaped thereby may be the more distinct and apparent.

Second Conclusion. We gather from what hath been said, that seeing this Song may be expounded, then doctrines for grounding our faith, and directing our practice, may warrantably be drawn from it, for the edification of God's people, seeing it is scripture ; and although it be allegoric, it is in a special way useful for edification, and may as bread be broken to the children : it is not only consistant with the nature of plain scriptures, but also of allegories, that they be thus extended in their use. We shall clear this conclusion in these three,

I. There may be doctrines drawn from this Song, in reference to all cases that are incident to a believer.   As 1. In reference to the case of the church, in all its considerations, visible or invisible, catholic, or particular.   And, 2. In reference to the more private and personal cases of believers ; doctrines instructing them both in faith and manners, &c.   For the doctrines must rise as extensively as their scope and matter ; and these are of a great reach and extent, as formerly hath been said ; such doctrines then, when handled in this Song, would not be thought strange, nor unsuitable to it ; but the broader they arise, the Spirit's wisdom and contrivance in this Song, will be the more wonderful and evident.

II. These doctrines must not be taken from the words

properly, but allegorically understood, according to the
intention of the Spirit in them, even as from parables,
and other clearer allegories and figures in scripture, it
useth to be done.

III. These doctrines so drawn, when rightly concluded
from the text and scope, are solid and sure, useful for
faith and manners, as doctrines drawn from other places
of scripture are : for, 1. It is certain, that many scriptures
are allegorically set down, and is their authority therefore any way less than that of other scriptures ? And if
their authority be such in themselves, as is the authority
of other scriptures; then their exposition and doctrines
drawn from them, must be solid and useful, as these that
are drawn from other scriptures : or, 2. We must say,
there is no use of such scriptures, which were blasphemous ; and if they be useful, there may be solid uses drawn
from them, as from other scriptures. 3. Our Lord useth
parables and allegories often in the gospel, and that in
things relating both to faith and manners : which saith,
the use of them is solid and safe, when they are rightly
understood and applied.

All the difficulty is in the right understanding of them,
and because allegories are frequent in scripture, and this
Song is wholly made up of allegories : therefore, both for
removing prejudices and facilitating our way, I shall speak
something to these three, 1. We shall shew what an allegoric exposition, or rather the exposition of an allegory
is. 2. When it is necessary to understand a scripture
allegorically. 3. How to walk in attaining the solid
meaning, or how to know if such a thing be the meaning
of an allegoric scripture.

I. There is a great difference betwixt an allegoric
exposition of scripture, and an exposition of allegoric
scripture : the first is that which many fathers and school-
men fail in, that is, when they allegorize plain scriptures
and histories, seeking to draw out some secret meaning,
other than appeareth in the words ; and so will fasten many
senses upon one scripture. This is indeed unsafe, and is
justly reprovable ; for, this maketh clear scripture dark,
and obtrudeth meanings on the words, never intended by
the Spirit : as, suppose one speaking of Goliah's combat
and David's, should pass by the latter, and expound
Goliah to be the flesh or the devil, and David to be the
Spirit, or Christ : such expositions may have some plea-

santness, but often little solidity; and such who most
commonly thus interpret scripture, often fall into errors.
As guilty of this fault, Origen is generally complained of,
though more also be guilty, as might be cleared by many
instances.

II. An exposition of an allegoric scripture, is, the opening and expounding of some dark scripture (wherein the
mind of the Spirit is couched and hid under figures and
allegories) making it plain and edifying, by bringing out
the sense according to the meaning of the Spirit in the
place, though at first, it seemed to bear out no such thing:
so Mat. xiii. Christ expoundeth that parable, or allegory,
(for though retoricians make a difference between similitudes, or parables and allegories; yet, in divinity there is
none, but that allegories are more large and continued)
calling the seed the word; the sower, the Son of Man, &c.
This way of expounding such dark scriptures, is both useful and necessary, and was often used as edifying by our
Lord to his disciples: now, it is this we speak of, which
teacheth how to draw plain doctrines out of allegories,
and not to draw allegories out of plain histories, or doctrines.

It may be asked then, where are we to account a place
of scripture allegoric, and are we to seek out some other
meaning, than what at first appeareth?

Answ. 1. When the literal proper meaning looketh
absurd-like, or is empty, and nothing to edification: as when
it is said, we must eat Christ's flesh, whereby believing is
expressed; and so, these scriptures that do command to
"pluck out the right eye," "cut off the right hand," "take
up our cross," &c. All which, if literally understood, were
absurd and ridiculous; and therefore, the mistaking such
scriptures, hath occasioned many errors, as that of Anthro-
pomorphit's attributing members, viz: head, hands, feet,
&c. to God; and passions, yea, infirmities, as anger, repenting, &c. because the scripture speaking of God after
the manner of men, doth allegorically attribute to him,
eyes, hands, wrath, &c.

2. These places of scripture are to be accounted allegoric, which reach not the scope of edification, intended by
them if literally understood; as when Christ hath spoken
of sowing, the disciples thought, that something more was
intended than at first appeared; for his aim could not be
to discourse of husbandry to them; so gathers the apostle

an allegory from these words, " Thou shalt not muzzle the mouth of the ox, that treadeth out the corn." And so also, that and the like precepts, discharging the Jews, the sowing their fields with divers grains, &c. Which though they be not wholly allegoric, but have in the letter their own truth, yet, somewhat in these beyond what appears, was aimed at by the Spirit: for saith the apostle, " Doth God care for oxen ?" that is, that precept hath a further scope, 1 Cor. ix. 9, 10.

3. When a literal sense obtrudes some falsity on the scripture, then such a scripture is to be understood allegorically; as when Christ said, " destroy this temple, and I will build it up in three days;" it is not to be understood of the material house, or Jewish temple, because then Christ's word would not have had its accomplishment; but allegorically of his body; so, when Christ saith, except a man eat his flesh, he shall not live, John vi. 53. It cannot be understood literally, seeing all who have obtained life, did never eat his flesh in a carnal bodily way.

4. Any scripture is to be accounted allegorical, when the literal sense agreeth not with other scriptures, and is repugnant to the analogy of faith, or rules of right manners: as, when we are commanded to heap coals of fire upon the head of our enemy. Now, it were against the command of not avenging ourselves, if literally and properly understood: it must therefore signify some other thing.

5. When a literal sense answereth not the present scope of the speaker, and the speaker would be thought impertinent, if his words were properly taken, then it would seem necessary to expound it as an allegory; so, Matt. iii. 10. when John is pressing repentance, he saith, " The axe is laid to the root of the tree." &c. And that parable of Christ's Luke xiii. 7, speaking of the husbandman that spared his tree three years. If these places were only properly understood, they would not enforce repentance, which is aimed at; they must therefore be expounded, as having something more in them, of a deeper reach, which may conduce to that scope.

And seeing according to these rules all the absurdities mentioned would follow, if this Song were literally and properly expounded, it must therefore be taken allegorically, and the doctrines must be drawn from its inside, or scope, when the vail of the allegory is laid by.

But, III. Because it is dangerous, to leave men to coin what exposition they please of such scriptures, therefore as upon the one hand, it is absurd to cast all doctrines from them, as unsolid ; so, upon the other hand, we would see what may fix us in a solid exposition, and so what may be esteemed a well-grounded doctrine, drawn from such an allegory.

I shall, in order to our help in this, name five rules, whereof the last is safest.

1. Some allegories at the first view seem plain, and imprint their meaning on those that have the least capacity, that it may be known, at least, what in general they aim at ; and therefore, such are left frequently in scripture unexpounded, and are used to press most obvious truths, such as that of John, Matt. iii. 10, " The axe is laid to the root of the tree ;" and " he hath his fan in his hand," &c. The meaning whereof, is at first obvious to be a peremptory certification, pressing present repentance : so is the parable of the marriage, Matt. xxii. 1, which at first view, appears to be understood of espousing believers to Christ as their husband : and so Christ's command to " take up the cross," &c. These, as to their meaning, are obvious ; and we think such is this Song in its general series ; the very reading of it seems to imprint, that Christ and his people must be taken up as the parties, and the love here spoken of, must be such as is betwixt them ; and though particular expressions be dark, thus far it is obvious.

2. The meaning of an allegory, may be gathered from the common use of such phrases and expressions, in our common use, so kissing and embracing, &c. signify love, and are expressions of mutual affection. In an allegory then, these, and such like, are to express analogically some spiritual thing, answerable in our spiritual life to such things in our bodily life : thus they express spiritual love and the sense of it. Thus eyes, hands, feet, &c. applied to God, denote some singular property in him : if allegorically applied to believers, they denote some qualification of the new man, that hath some analogy, and resemblance to these, as knowledge, activity, patience, &c. because, by our eyes we see, by our hands we work, and by our feet we walk and travel, &c. Thus are they transferred, to hold out some other thing than appeareth at first from the words, and the work of the interpreter is to bring out the scope and matter in plain expressions, that it may look

like the thing it is, and which is aimed at as the scope.

3. It is helpful in expounding of allegories, to know how such phrases are expounded in other places; as when some things are spoken of David that cannot literally agree to David, then see who is meant in other places of scripture by him. If it cannot be known what is meant by a marriage tie here, seeing it can be no human thing, see what other spiritual marriage is spoken of in any other place of scripture, and who are the parties, and this is to be expounded by that.

4. Being to interpret any allegorical place of scripture, we would see, not only to the scope of all scripture, and the analogy of faith in general; but to the scope of the Spirit in that place: as for example, if we would understand what is intended by the parable of the prodigal, we would first consider the scope, which is to show God's ready welcome of a sinner, and then level the exposition, as serving to illustrate that scope. So we would consider what is the Bride's scope, chap. v. 10, and it is to describe Christ: and chap. vii. 1, we would consider what is the Bridegroom's scope; and it is to describe her. So then it agrees with the scope, to open these places, and apply them to what is commendable in him, and her: and thus the exposition and doctrines from it, do not only suit with the analogy of faith, and are not contrary to sound doctrine; but also suit with the intention of the Spirit there, and are agreeable to it: for the Holy Ghost under general commendations, may include all particulars, which may serve to make out the general; and so when the scope is to hold Christ out, as all desires, then whatever makes him appear desirable, and standeth with the analogy of the expression, may well stand with that scope: this is sure, especially when negatively it is inferred; that is, when such a scope necessarily inferreth such a doctrine, and when that scope could not be attained, if such a doctrine were not supposed: as when in general, Christ and his church are holden out to stand in a near relation together, and so to carry on towards each other, as being under such a relation; this will necessarily infer a covenant, and an union by faith upon the grounds of it, and some evidencing of the proofs of Christ's love, &c. because without these, that relation could never have been, nor can it without them be, understood by us.

5. The last rule, which we call most sure, is this: then

we may safely conclude, that we have reached the true meaning of an allegorical scripture, when from the scripture in the same, or other places, agreeing with the scope of the present allegory, we gather in plain expressions what is meant thereby, or what was intended by the Spirit in such an allegorical expression; as when Christ clears the parable of the Sower, he calleth the seed the Word, &c. which makes the meaning clear, and above question; or, when a plain expression is mixed in with the allegory. So that expression, chap. i. 2; " Let him kiss me," &c. in the words following is expounded by a more plain expression, viz. "thy love is better," &c. Hence we solidly gather that by kisses are meant love: and this doctrine is sure, Christ's love is vehemently desired by the Bride. These ways for finding out what is the sense of such scriptures, are safe; and therefore, that saying, symbolic scriptures are not argumentative, is to be understood with a limitation, viz. except in so far as the scope and meaning of the Spirit is known, and in so far as the allegory, or the several parts thereof agreeth with, and conduce to the clearing and making up of the known scope.

All these ways going together, and taken along with us, we may, through God's blessing, undertake the opening of this Song, and draw doctrines from it so expounded; not only agreeable to other scriptures and the analogy of faith, but also as agreeable to the scope of this Song; yea, even the scope of such a portion of it, though possibly every expression in its meaning, be not so fully reached; which is not the thing we dare promise, but humbly to essay the making of it in some measure clear, relishing, amiable, and comfortable to God's people. And so we leave this conclusion.

The *Third Conclusion* and last is, that the doctrines which this Song yieldeth for all conditions, and which for believers' use are to be drawn from it, are the same plain, solid spiritual truths which are drawn from other scriptures, wherein Christ's love to his church and people, and their exercises are set down: and if in its exposition, it resolve in the same meaning with other scriptures, then must also the doctrines be the same; and therefore such doctrines concerning faith and manners, for believers' direction in all cases, as ariseth from the gospel, and other plain scriptures, psalms, and histories, may be solidly drawn from this Song: and such when they are drawn, are solid (being according to the foresaid general rules) and weight is to be laid on them, in a christian walk. We shall therefore endeavour to make this out, that when the doctrine of faith, repentance, diligence, &c. and such other doctrines as are in the gospel, concerning the covenant, or Christ, are spoken of, ye may not think it strange, or unsuitable to this Song. And therefore we say,

1. If the doctrines be suitable to the scope and matter contained in this Song, then they are sure and solid, and weight is to be laid upon them : but the doctrines concerning Christ's love to, and care of his church, and concerning her exercise of faith, repentance, &c. are suitable to the scope, and agreeable to the matter of it, or thus, if the scope and matter of this Song do agree with the gospel (I call the gospel what in the New Testament is more fully holden forth, and more clearly) in the scope and matter of it ; then must the doctrines which arise from it, be the same with these that rise from the gospel : but the first is true, as is formerly cleared, therefore must this last be so also. And what is the scope of the gospel, but to set forth Christ's love to his church, to show her duty &c.? and is not that same scope here also? only what is preceptively, or doctrinally delivered there, is here (as it were) acted in a sort of comedy, and compiled in a Song, but still for the same end.

2. If the same allegories in other places of scripture, will bear solid doctrines concerning Christ, his covenant, faith, &c. even such as are in plain scriptures ; then must this Song do the like, seeing it is the word of God, tending to the same scope with these. But it is clear, Isa. v. 2 ; Jer. iii.; Mat. xxii.; Rev. xix. 7, that the same allegories of vineyards, fruits, and marriage, &c. are used, and to the same scope with this, and are made use of to yield solid doctrines concerning faith, fruitfulness, and other doctrines belonging to a believer's faith and practice : therefore it must be so here ; for though this Song be larger, and is made up of more allegories together, that will not alter the nature of it, or of the doctrines which must be drawn from it.

3. If we compare this Song with the xlv. Psalm, it cannot be denied, 1. But that Psalm and this Song are to one scope, and of one style or strain, in prosecuting that scope ; it is a Song of love for the King, and a spiritual marriage is the subject thereof, as is clear from the very

reading of it. 2. It cannot be denied, that solid proofs and doctrines, concerning many points of faith and practice, which are in other plain scriptures, are, and may be warrantably drawn from it, even as if it were plain gospel: therefore must the doctrines be such which arise from this Song also, for that Psalm is used even by the apostle, Heb. i. 8, 9, to confirm the great truths of the gospel.

4. If this whole Song be one piece, and of one nature, driving all along the same general scope, then such doctrines, as the places in it which are clear, do yield; such I say, must be contained (if we would discern them) in these places of it which are most obscure: but what is most plain in this Song, speaks out such plain doctrines, experience, &c. therefore what is more obscure, may be resolved in such also: for we may best know what kind of doctrines floweth from what is obscure, by the places that are more clear, seeing God in the most dark scriptures ordinarily hath inserted some plain passages, or given some hints of his mind, to be as a key for opening all the rest. Now, if we will for instance, consider some such places as these, "My Beloved is mine," &c. "I called but he gave me no answer," they yield plain doctrines, as other plain scriptures do: and therefore, seeing it is one continued Song, and each of these dark and plain places answer one another, to continue the series of the discourse upon the same subject, we may know by what is plain, how to understand what is couched within that which is more dark.

5. As one piece of the allegory is to be resolved, so by proportion must all the rest, there being one thread and scope: now, that some pieces of the allegory may be expounded in clear doctrines concerning Christ and his church, may be gathered from paralleling some parts of it with other scriptures: as if we compare that excellent description of Christ, chap. v. 10, with that which John sets down, Rev. i. 13; we will see a great resemblance betwixt the two (if this last have not respect unto the former) especially in that which is spoken anent his feet and legs, and his countenance; but it is certain, that description, Rev. i. 13, is given him with a purpose to describe him, and to set out the several attributes and excellent qualities he is furnished with, as omniscience by his eyes, justice by his legs walking surely; omnipotence by his arms, &c. which are particularly so applied in the epistles to the seven churches, chap. ii. and iii. and after-

ward : if then there, by the Spirit's warrant, we may draw
from Christ's being said to have eyes, that he is omniscient
(and so in other properties) may we not also think, that
seeing it is the same Spirit that speaks here in the particular description which is given of Christ and the Bride
in their several parts, that these same particular properties may be aimed at ; and may we not make use of such
interpretations elsewhere given, for our help in the like
particulars, and so also in other things ?

6. Thus we argue, either this Song is so to be resolved,
as hath been said, and such doctrines are to be drawn from
it as arise from the gospel, for expressing the way of
believers with Christ, and his with them ; or then, 1.
There are no doctrines to be drawn from it, but this Song
is a mere complement, and but ignorantly, with holy blind
affection to be sung, which is absurd : or, 2. The doctrines
are but to be guessed at, and so the truth of them is only
conjectural, which will come near the former absurdity,
and spoil the believer of any solid edification he could have
from it; or, 3. It must contain such a kind of love, such
cases and doctrines concerning Christ and believers, which
are different from the gospel, and the cases of saints plainly recorded elsewhere : now this would necessitate an
uncertainty of its meaning, and hazard the coining of two
ways of Christ's dealing with his people, as also of theirs
with him, two unions, two marriages, &c. or, 4. It must
contain the same doctrines concerning faith, Christ, the
covenant, the church, &c. which are contained in other
scriptures, and in the gospel, which was the thing to be
proved.

We have been the larger on this, to obviate two extremes, that men are given to follow, in reference to this
Song. 1. Some loathing plain truths, which are plainly
delivered in scriptures, properly to be taken ; and because
this in expression and strain differeth, they conclude there
must be some uncouth, strange, and odd thing here. It is
true, if we look to the degree of warm affections that
breathe forth here, we may conceive that there is something odd and singular in this Song : but, as to the kind
of doctrine here delivered, there is nothing new ; and to
imagine the contrary, were as if a man supposed, there
behoved to be some strange liquor or meat, in curious-like
glasses, and dishes, because the master of an house might
use variety of vessels, for the delectation of the feasters,

yet still giving the same solid food and drink, though diversely prepared; or, as if a man would suppose, Paul and Barnabas, Christ our Lord, and John, did preach different gospels, because they were of different gifts, and had a different manner of expression. 2. On the other hand, some are ready to cast at this book as useless, because they see not plain truths at the first in it, and possibly think all endeavours to expound it, or draw doctrines from it, but a guessing, and are ready to offend, when they meet with nothing but some such truths as are obvious in some other scriptures. This wrongs the worth, and divine authority of this scripture also, and though many (and we among others) may misapply some things in this Song, yet to say they cannot be rightly applied, or that such doctrines as we have before mentioned, are not native to it, is too precipitant, to say no more.

For further declaring and confirming of these propositions and conclusions, we shall answer some objections, or questions which may be proposed concerning what is said.

1. It may be objected, if allegoric scriptures be so to be expounded, and such doctrines to be drawn from them; then why are such scriptures set down under such figurative expressions; might they not be better in plain words? or might not such plain scriptures be rather expounded, which bear such doctrine with less difficulty.

Answ. If this were urged, it would not only reflect on this Song, but on many places of scripture, and also, on the expounding of such scriptures; yea, it would reflect on the wisdom of the Spirit, and his sovereignty, who may choose what way he pleases, to express his mind to his people, and whatever way he take to do this, sure it is still the best, and it may warrant us to acquiesce in the way he hath taken to speak his mind, that it is he that speaks: yet, there may be good ends given of this his way, or weighty reasons (even for our behoof) why he speaks to his people in such terms, and language: as 1. Here he putteth all the conditions of a believer together, as in one map, which are more sparsely, and (as it were) here and there, to be found elsewhere through the scriptures; we have them here compended together, in a sort of spiritual dependence one upon another, and in a connexion one with another, and they are put in a song to make them the more sweet and lovely; and under such poetical and figurative expressions, as best agreeth with the nature of Songs, and poetical writings; that so believers may have them together, and may sing them together, for the help of their memory, and up-stirring of their affections.

2. Their figures and similitudes, have their own use, to make us the better take up, and understand the spiritual things which are represented by them; when in a manner, he condescends to illustrate them by similitudes, and so to teach (as it were) to our senses, things which are not otherwise so obvious: for which cause, Christ often taught by parables the great mysteries of the gospel.

3. Thus not only the judgment is informed, but it serveth the more to work on our affections, both to convince us of, and to deter us from what is ill, when it is proposed indifferently in an allegory, as Nathan in his parable to David did: and also, it conduceth the more to gain our affections to love such things as are here set out, wherefore even heaven itself is so described from similitude of such things as are in account with men, Rev. xxi. 22. And Christ's love becomes thus more comfortable, and our relation to him the more kindly-like, when it is illustrated by marriage, and the kindly expressions of a husband and wife; for this also, God is compared to a Father, and his pity to a Father's pity to children, to make it the more sensible and comfortable.

4. Thus also any knowledge that is attained, or any impression that is made, is the better fixed and kept; similitudes are often retained, when plain truths are forgotten, as we may see in experience: yea, the retaining of the similitude in the memory, doth not only keep the words in mind, but helps to some acquaintance with the things which are signified, and furthereth us in understanding the manner, how such and such things the Lord doth to his people are brought about.

5. Thus both the wisdom and care of God, and his Spirit appeareth, who taketh divers ways to commend his truth unto men, and to gain them to the love of it, that they who will not be affected with plain truth, he may by more taking expressions, commend unto them the same thing; which is the reason why he hath given divers gifts and ways of holding forth his truth unto ministers; some have one way, like sons of thunder; some another, like sons of consolation; and yet all to carry on the same end that one may be helpful unto the other. Indeed if God

had delivered his truth only in obscure terms, the objection might seem to have some weight; but when he doth it in both plain and obscure ways, this is his condescendency and wisdom, by all means seeking to gain some.

6. Thus also the Lord removeth occasion of loathing from his word, by putting it in some lovely artifice, in the manner of its delivery; and also, he doth hereby provoke his people to more diligence, in searching after the meaning of it; it being often our way to esteem least of what is most obvious, and most of that which is by some pains attained.

7. Thus also the Lord maketh the study of his word delectable, when both the judgment and affections are jointly wrought upon; and to shew that all the believer's conditions may be matter of a sweet song to him; whereas some things, if plainly laid down would not be so cheerfully digested. Thus he maketh the saddest matter sweet, by his manner of proposing it.

8. Also the Lord useth to keep the songs, and spiritual allowance of his own, somewhat veiled from the rest of the world; for " they have meat to eat which the world knoweth not of," that believers may see, and feed sweetly where they discern nothing, and that they having this commented on by experience betwixt him and them, may sing that song, which none other in the world can learn, as the hundred and forty and four thousand do, Rev. xiv. 1, for thus it is said, Matt. xiii. 9, 10, 11, &c. that Christ spake in parables, that not only he might condescend to the weakness of his own, so as they might bear it, Mark. iv. 33, 34, but also that others, " seeing might see, and not perceive." Often that same way which his own gets good of, proveth a stumbling to others, through their own corruption.

9. There may be also something of God's design here, to try the humility and sincerity of his people if they will stoop to every way he useth, because it is his, and such humbly receive it, as being that which (though it seem to others foolishness, yet) makes them wise unto salvation. The mockers taunted Ezekiel's message under this notion, that he spake parables, Ezek. xx. 49, but Zech. xi. 10, 11, when the prophet broke the two staves (which was a dark and mysterious-like action) the poor of the flock waited on him, when (as it is like) others stumbled also. By all which, we may see, why the Lord hath so compacted together, plain useful doctrines, under such expressions in

this Song; and also, why our undertaking to open it, may be well constructed, even though the same truths may elsewhere as clearly arise; yet these truths are here in such a way connected together, and so not only proposed, but also commended unto us, as will not any where else be found.

Object. 2. If any say, the raising of such gospel doctrines, makes this Song look more like the gospel of the New Testament, than a song of the old:

Answ. 1. Is it the worse, that it looks like the gospel? Or, are not such doctrines (if they follow from it) the better and more comfortable? Certainly there is no doctrine more edifying and comfortable to believers, and more like, or more becoming Christ's way with believers, or theirs with him (which is the scope and subject of this Song) than gospel-doctrines are. High soaring words of vanity, and mysteries having nothing but an empty sound, are much more unlike this spiritual Song than these. 2. If it set out Christ's way to believers, even under the Old Testament, and believers' way of keeping communion with God even then; is not that the same gospel way which we have now? Their faith and communion with God, stood not in the outward ceremonies, which were typical; but in the exercise of inward graces, faith, love, &c. which are the same now as then. Was not Christ the same to them as to us? had they not the same spirit, covenant, &c. and so the cases and experiences of, or incident to believers then, are also applicable to us now? That Christ was then to come, and hath now suffered, and that the way of revealing him then, was some way different from that we have now, will not make another gospel, covenant, faith, yea, nor church; we being grafted in that same stock which they once grew upon, and being by faith heirs of the same promises, which some time they possessed.

Object. 3. If any should yet doubt, if Solomon knew or intended such doctrines as these, and that therefore they cannot be well digested, if drawn from this Song, beyond his mind and meaning. I Answer, 1. Our great purpose is to know what the Spirit intended, and not what Solomon understood; and if this be the Spirit's intention to set out Christ's way with his church; then such doctrines as agree therewith, must be agreeable to his meaning. 2. Yea, suppose Solomon and other prophets should be ignorant, in a great measure of the meaning of such things, as the Spirit foretold by them, as it is not impossible in some extraordinary things, especially when their knowledge in these was not essential to the truth of their prophecy, (for they might have a kind of nescience in the particulars, though they were sure the things they delivered were in the complex prophecy God's word) yet, will any say, that we should limit the words spoken by them, to their understanding of them? If so, by what rule would we know, or how they did understand them?

3. Therefore we say, it was with Solomon here as with other prophets (as Isaiah and others) who spake many of the gospel-truths, which in particular they might not so fully know, as we do now, when these prophecies are fulfilled; yet was it never doubted, but the most deep mysteries of the gospel, were contained in their prophecies.

Yet, 4. We say there is no ground to think, but Solomon knew much of the mind of the Spirit in the Song, yea, more than any learned man now a-days. For, 1. He was not only a believer, but one eminent for gifts and knowledge; and none will say but he was so for divine knowledge as well as human: as his books particularly Prov. iv. viii. ix. chapters, in his description of Christ, the substantial wisdom of the Father, &c. do shew: and can it be thought, he wrote this book, without any sense of what he wrote? 2. Can it be thought, but that he levelled what he wrote here at a scope; and that afterwards himself made use of it, for his edification and comfort? which could not be done, if he had not understood the most of these gospel-mysteries, upon which all this sweet conference betwixt Christ and believers is founded. 3. His writing in such terms shews, the words were not ignorantly fallen upon; but he, having knowledge of all herbs, spices, &c. and how to apply them to spiritual things, pitched upon these as the most pertinent similitudes, which are therefore by the special wisdom of the Spirit, made use of in this Song, as in other of his writings; yea, certainly his knowledge, how spiritual mysteries are couched up in these similitudes, and represented by them, was beyond what we can reach unto now: and therefore we dare not insist, or be peremptory in the particular application of these similitudes. 4. The subject of this Song not being prophetical, but narrative and doctrinal, containing such exercises, as might be, and certainly were found in believers, even then, and such dispensations as they used to meet with, will any say he was a stranger unto them, see-ing there was access to know these much better, than pro-phecies of things which were to come? Yea, 5. Is there any thing here but what in other scriptures of the Old Testament (and especially Songs and Psalms) is to be found where the cases and exercises of God's people are set down? And it needs not be thought strange, if we equal him in knowledge with others of his time, or before him; and that he sets down in a more artificial manner, according to his measure of gifts, that which others set down in more plain terms, yet both by the same Spirit.

We may then confidently hazard, to draw the same doctrines concerning Christ, the gospel church, &c. from it, that are to be found in other more clear and plain scriptures. One of the Fathers (Athanas. in Synops.) comparing this Song with other scriptures of the Old Testament, says, " It is as John Baptist among the pro-phets, other scriptures speak of Christ as coming," (saith he) " and afar off; this speaks of him, and to him, as already come, and near hand ;" and indeed it is so ; for so even then, he was sometimes very familiar and present both to the faith and sense of his people as well as now. Thus also even Origen (though in plain scriptures too luxuriant, yet in this he) seems to own this same scope. Thus also Zanch. in Eph. v. makes it a compend and copy of the spiritual marriage with Christ. And Bodius in Eph. page 114, says, It is " *ipsius fidei, et Religionis Christi-anæ, medulla.*"

If it be said, if we interpret this Song after this manner, then all the observations will run upon believers' cases only; which would seem to say, that no doctrines may be drawn from it, for the edification of those who are yet unrenewed ; and what use can it then be of to them, who yet are the greater part in the church?

Answ. 1. The gospel hath doctrines suitable to all with-in the church : and this Song being in substance, Christ's way with his church must also contain doctrines useful for all within the same.

2. In this Song the church is not only considered as invisible, and united by true faith to Christ ; but also as visible, and as under external ordinances, as hath been said ; and in that respect, it furnishes doctrines fit for all.

3. This Song will furnish doctrines useful for these, as other parables or allegories of that kind do, which Christ used often even for the edification of such.

4. Doctrines from all places of scripture, may be raised
by analogy; as from such places, where God holdeth
forth the way he useth with his own, when they have
wronged him by sin, which is to humble them, and bring
them to repentance, ere they see his face again, sin becomes bitter even to them: from such places, I say, we
may gather by proportion, that God's way with unrenewed sinners, whom he minds to bring to peace and friendship with himself, is to humble them and make sin bitter
to them, seeing the recovery of peace and the first found-
ing of peace, as to this is brought about after the same
manner.

5. From such places as speak directly Christ's special
love to believers, there may be drawn good uses and applications to others; partly, to engage them to him who so
loves his own: partly, to terrify these who are not his,
by their being debarred from any right to such excellent
privileges.

6. Where the Bride's carriage is commendable, it is a
copy and pattern to all, even as examples and precepts
are ordinarily given in common to all, and serve to direct
every one in what they should aim at: and also to convince for what they are short of: the duties she is taken
up with, being moral, her example in these, must lay an
universal obligation upon all, and in such things wherein
she faileth through infirmity, her carriage serveth well to
deter all from these evils.

In the last place: for better understanding of the subject of this Song, we would take along with us, 1. Some
observations. 2. Some rules.

1. The subject thereof is to hold forth the mutual and
interchangeable exercise, and out-lettings of love as well
betwixt Christ and particular believers, as betwixt him
and the church: as also, his various dispensations to the
Bride, her divers conditions and tempers and both his and
her carriage under them, and her outgates.

2. The manner how this sweet subject is set down, is
by way of dialogue, in several conferences, after a drama-
tic way, (as it is called) because thus the mutual love of
these parties, is best expressed: in which there are, 1.
The principal parties in the discourse. 2. Others, as
friends or attendants, waiting on: in the gospel, John iii.
28, 29, there are mentioned the bridegroom, and his
friends, and the bride: and children of the marriage

chamber are spoken of, Matt. ix. 15, by which are understood virgins and companions, that attend her, and also go forth to wait on him ; which are of two sorts, some wise, being really so, some foolish being wise in profession only, Matt. xxv. 1, 2. There is also mention made of a mother, Gal. iv. 26, who hath two sorts of children, some born after the flesh, and but children (as it were) of the bondwoman ; others born after the spirit, and true members of the church invisible : the former persecute the latter : and of both kinds of children, are some of all ranks, amongst priests, apostles, ministers, &c.

We will find all these parties in this Song, acting their several parts.

1. The Bridegroom is Christ, John iii. 34, called the one husband, 2 Cor. xi. 2, for there is not another spiritual husband, to whom believers can be matched ; he is the king's son, for whom the marriage is made Matt. xxii. 1. 2, &c. He is the Lamb, unto whose marriage the hearers of the gospel are invited, Rev. xix. 9, and Psalm xlv. He is the king unto whom the queen is to be brought after she is adorned ; by this name he is also styled in this Song, " The King," chap. i. 4, 12, &c. and the " Beloved ;" those, and such titles are given to him which cannot be understood to be attributed to any but to Christ only, by believers.

2. The Bride is the church and every believer in divers considerations (as is said before) who are married to Christ, and are to be made ready and adorned for the solemnizing of the marriage. Of the nature of this marriage see more, chap. viii. 8.

3. The Bridegroom's Friends are honest ministers, who rejoice to see him great ; such as John was, John iii. 29, and such were the apostles, John xv. 15. Such are here the watchmen, trusted with the over-sight and edification of others, spoken unto, chap. ii. 15, and spoken of, chap. iii. 3.

4. The Virgins, or Children of the marriage-chamber, are here called " Daughters of Zion," chap. iii. 11, and " of Jerusalem" (many whereof are weak, ready to stumble, chap. i. 6, and of little knowledge, chap. v. 9, and ready to stir up the Bridegroom, chap. iii. v.) and the virgins that love Christ, chap. i. 3, and the upright, chap. i. 4.

5. The Mother is the universal visible church, wherein are many true believers, who are converted to Christ by the word and ordinances dispensed therein, and to which also many hypocrites belong as members.

6. The Children of the promise, and true Virgins that love Christ; the Children of the bond-woman, and the flesh, are unrenewed professors in the church, as also, false teachers, who act their part here likewise, chap. i. 6. and ii. 15. and v. 7.

3. This conference, as it is betwixt Christ and the believer, is followed as betwixt married parties. 1. In the titles, they attribute to each other. 2. In their claiming of this relation one in another, as that he is hers, and she is his. 3. In their expressions, which are such as use to be betwixt most loving parties, who live exercising conjugal love, most kindly and intimately together. The reason whereof is, 1. To shew the near union that is betwixt Christ and his church ; there is a relation, and a most near relation, betwixt them, that is not betwixt him and any others. 2. To shew the kindly effects of that relation in both the parties, especially the faithfulness and tenderness of the husband, in walking according to it in every thing. 3. It is to sweeten every piece of exercise the believer meets with ; yea, to make all dispensations digest the better, seeing they are dispensed and ordered by such a loving husband. 4. It is for warming the believer's heart the more to Christ, and to make this Song heartsome and delightsome, that so believers may have always a marriage Song, and every night may be to them as a marriage night.

4. The purpose or subject of this Song, is Christ, and divine things of all sorts : but mainly the experiences of grown christians, held forth in most noble and lively expressions, as was before a little cleared.

5. The scope of all is, to express the desirableness of fellowship with the Bridegroom, and how the Bride thirsteth and longeth for it, and how careful she is to entertain it, and by laying out his matchless excellencies to commend him to others ; which also seems to be the scope and design for which this scripture is given to the church ; and so her breathing after communion with him, doth here begin the conference, verse 2, " Let him kiss me," &c.

6. The manner of their expression is, 1. Sweet and loving : and therefore, this conference is carried on, under the terms of marriage, and the titles of beloved, my ove, spouse, &c. (as being the most lively that can express that relation, and most apposite for entertaining of mutual love) are here made use of. 2 The manner of expression is something obscure, though sweet, that so the Lord's people may be stirred up to painfulness, and diligence in

searching out his mind ; and also, because the mysteries
here contained are great, and cannot as they are in themselves, be conceived: therefore that they may be illustrated,
parables are used as Matt. xiii. 34, compared with Mark
iv. 33, where it is clear, that the intent and effect of the
Lord's speaking by parables, is to help some to take up
these mysteries, and to leave some ignorant. 3. The
Spirit of God doth here make use of borrowed expressions,
the more lively to set out the spiritual matter contained
under them ; and by things most taking, and best known
to our senses, to hold out divine mysteries, unto which
these expressions are to be applied. 4. Often these same
expressions, are made use of in one place, in speaking to
the Bridegroom, and in another, speaking to the Bride,
he calling her " chief amongst the daughters," and she
him, " chief amongst the sons," but in a different sense:
for, he styles her from his acceptation of her, and from
his imputation, and communication of his graces to her :
but she styles him from his own excellency and worth,
he having all in himself, and nothing borrowed from any
other, but imparting that which is his, to her.

The rules we would take along with us in our proceeding, are these :

1. We would find out who speaks in every passage of
this Song ; for this serves much to clear what is spoken.

2. We would carefully ponder what is the purpose of
the Spirit in every part thereof.

3. We must apply, and conform expressions to the scope,
and expound them by it, and not stick too much in following of every thing, which these allegories seem to bear ;
but draw the doctrines from them, being compared with
the scope, and other places of scripture, not insisting too
far upon the similitudes.

4. We are to take special notice of the Bride's frame, in
her manner of speaking ; for we may observe that often
in the vehemency of her passionate love, she breaks out
without any seen connexion, or order, as chap. i. 2, and
by cut, broken, and vehement expressions, in her divers
frames, and tender fits, as her case is up, or down, (abruptly, as it were) she useth to express herself.

5. We must not apply all sorts to the church, as to
shut out believers, nor contrarily ; but take in both where
both may come in ; and more especially apply to the one,
where the purpose makes most for it, as hath been said.

AN EXPOSITION,

&c.

CHAPTER I.

Ver. 1. The Song of Songs, which is Solomon's.

Before we enter upon the purpose of this chapter, or give the division of it, we would first speak to the title contained, verse 1.

We account this title scripture, it being in the original, even as other titles prefixed to divers psalms, as to Psal. li., cii., &c. In it three things are set down. 1. The nature of this scripture. 2. Its excellency. 3. Its instrumental author, who was made use of by the Spirit in penning of it.

1. For the nature of this scripture, it is a Song. Songs in scripture, are such portions or books thereof, as were specially intended to be made use of, for the praising of God, and the edifying and comforting of his people in singing of them. Three sorts of them were in use amongst the Hebrews (as the titles of our Psalms do clear, and as they are mentioned by the apostle, Eph. v. 19.) 1. Psalms: such were used both with voice and instruments. 2. There were hymns (so the cxlv. Psalm is intituled) such in the matter of them, were wholly made up of praise, and what immediately led to that. 3. There were spiritual songs, which were more extensive in the matter, taking in histories, cases, and exercises of all sorts; and might be sung with the voice, without instruments, either publicly, or privately, of this last sort is this Song, intended to be made use of in the praises of God; and so composed, both for the matter and manner, as it might best attain that end, and prove edifying and comfortable also to believers, in their singing of it.

2. The excellency of this Song is expressed in this, that it is a "Song of Songs," a most excellent song, this being the manner how the Hebrews express their superlatives.

While it is called a " Song of Songs," it is compared with, and preferred to all other songs: and we conceive the comparison is not only betwixt this and human songs; But 1. It is compared with, and preferred to all those which Solomon wrote, and it is preferrable to all these thousand and five mentioned, 1 Kings iv. 32.   2. It is compared with all other scriptural songs, such as are recorded, Exod. xv. and Judges v. &c. of all which, this is the most excellent, as being, 1. Purposely intended to treat of the most choice and excellent subject, to wit, Christ and his church, which is not done upon particular occasions, as in other songs, but is the great purpose that is only designed, and pursued.   2. It treats of Christ and his church in their most glorious, lively, and lovely actions, to wit, his care of and his love unto his church, and that in its most eminent degree; and also, of her love to him in its various measures and workings.   3. It is in a most excellent manner composed, by way of conferences and sweet colloquies betwixt these two parties, having in it many excellent expressions, and variety of them, well interwoven with sundry cases of several sorts, to make the whole draught the more taking and excellent.   4. It is set forth in a most lovely, excellent, majestic style and strain, which exceedingly ravishes and captivates affections, making the love contained in it, sweetly savour and relish through the beautiful garment of borrowed expressions, which is put upon it.   5. It is a most excellent song, in respect of its comprehensiveness; here is an armory and store-house of songs, in this one, where there is something treasured up for every case, that may be edifying and comfortable, which will not be so found in any other song; there being something here suiting all sorts of believers, under all the variety of cases and dispensations, wherewith they are exercised; and also all the relations under which the church standeth; all which, should commend this Song unto us.

It is recorded of the Hebrews, that whatever scripture was delivered in a poetical frame, they accounted themselves specially bound to take notice of that, and to get it by heart; and indeed it is not for nought, that some scriptures, and not others, are cast in that mould; and something of this, as the intent of the Holy Ghost, may be gathered from Moses his putting his last words into a Song, Deut. xxxii. that they might be the better remembered.

The third thing in the title is the penman made use of by the Spirit, in the writing and recording this Song: it is Solomon, a great man, rich, wise, yea, an elect saint; yet one, who had also fallen into many foul faults, whom the Lord hath suffered to die, without recording expressly any thing of his recovery, though we make no doubt of it; which (because Bellarmine, *lib.* 3 *de Justif.* chap. 14. page 368, Tannovius and others, are at pains in contradicting this, yea, Augustine doubts of it, because nothing is directly recorded of his recovery) we shall endeavour to make clear from these considerations,

1. From the Lord's promises to him, 2 Sam. vii. 14, 15, where these three things are observable, which the Lord undertakes concerning him, 1. That he will be to him a Father. 2. That he will correct him with the rods of men, if he shall sin: which saith he would not eternally punish him. 3. That he would not do with him as he did with Saul, whom he rejected; he would not take away his mercy from Solomon, as he had done from him: and if no more were in these promises, but what is temporal, there would be no great consolation in them to David (whose consolation is one chief part of the scope at that place.) Besides, these promises, Psalm lxxxix. 31, 32, 33, (which are the same with these, 2 Sam. vii.) are looked upon as specially evidences of God's love, and peculiar promises of his saving covenant.

2. When he is born, the Lord gives him his name, yea, sends Nathan, 2 Sam. xii. with this warrant, to name him Jedidiah, because the Lord loved him; which cannot be a love flowing from any thing in him, as if he had been well pleased with his carriage, (Solomon had not yet done any thing good or evil) but it must be a love prior to his works, and so not arising from his good deeds, and therefore not cut off by his sins: which being like the love God had to Jacob, before he had done good or evil, Rom. ix, 11, must speak out electing love, as it doth in that place.

3. He is made use of by the Spirit, to be a penman of holy writ, and a prophet of the Lord; all which are by our Lord, Luke xiii, 28, said, to "sit down with Abraham, Isaac, and Jacob, in the kingdom of heaven;" and there is no reason to exclude him, seeing that universal (all the prophets &c.) would not be a truth unless he were there; and though some wicked men have prophesied, as Balaam did, yet are they never accounted as prophets of the Lord

as Solomon was, but false prophets and enchanters; neither were they penmen of the holy writ; who were as Peter calleth them, 2 Pet. i. 21, " Holy men of God, speaking as they were inspired by the Holy Ghost."

4. Neither are the peculiar privileges he was admitted unto, to be forgotten; by him the Lord built the temple, by him the covenant was explicitly renewed with God, 1 Kings viii. 9, and his prayers are often particularly mentioned, to be heard; yea, after his death, some testimonies are recorded of him, which cannot consist with his rejection: see 2 Chron. xi. 17, where the ways of Solomon are put in, as commendable with David's, though there were defects in both; and this being immediately after Solomon's death, it would seem he left the worship of God pure, and so had turned from his idolatry, though all the monuments of it were not abolished. And especially in this, he was singularly privileged, that, in a most lively way, he was the type of our blessed Lord Jesus, in his intercession, reign, and peaceable government: besides, that by particular covenant, the kingdom of Christ, and his descent from him, was established to him.

5. It is of weight also, that it seems more than probable, that Solomon wrote Ecclesiastes after his recovery; it being neither among the Proverbs, nor Songs which are mentioned, 1 Kings iv. 32. And in it, he speaks out the experience he had both of folly and madness, and the vanity he had found in all created things, even when he had perfected his essay of all the possible ways of attaining either the knowledge of their perfections, or satisfaction in the enjoyment of them.

The scriptures therefore hath not left his recovery altogether dark; yet as to any historical narration thereof, the Lord hath so ordered, that he passeth away under a cloud, for these good ends:

1. Thereby, Solomon is chastised with the rods of men (even after death) upon his name; for, his miscarriages are set down expressly, but his recovery (as to any direct testimony thereof) is passed over.

2. By this, the Lord maketh his displeasure with Solomon's ways known; though he had favour to his person, and gave him his soul for a prey.

3. Thus the Lord would affright others from declining, and hereby teacheth his people, to be afraid to rest upon gifts; yea, or upon graces, seeing he hath left this matter

so far in the dark, as might yield an occasion (as it were) to question the eternal condition of Solomon.

4. It may be also, that Solomon after his recovery, did never recover his former lustre, nor attain to such a profitable way of appearing in God's public matters for which formerly he had been so observable : for so it is taken notice even of David, after his fall, that his following life is stained, as different from what went before : therefore it is the commendation of Jehoshaphat, 1 Chron. xvii. 3, that he walked in the first ways of his father David, which certainly is not done to condemn David's state after that time, but to leave that mark (as a chastisement) on his failings : and seeing Solomon's were greater, therefore may this silence of his recovery be more universal as to him.

Before we draw any thing from this, by way of use, I shall answer a doubt, and it is this, how can all these thousand and five songs mentioned, I Kings iv. 32, be lost, without wronging the perfection of canonic scripture ? Or, what is come of them ? Or, what is to be accounted of the loss of them ?

Answ. We say, 1. The scriptures may be full in the articles of faith, even though some portions thereof, which were once extant, were now amissing ; except it could be made out, that some points of faith were in these books, which are not to be found in other scriptures. 2. Yet, seeing it is not safe and it wants not many inconveniences, to assert that any book once designed of God to his church, as a canon, or rule of faith and manners, should be lost—and seeing it is not consistent with that wise providence of his, whereby he hath still carefully preserved the treasure of his oracles in his church ; we rather incline to say, that though these songs were possibly useful, and might be written by the Spirit's direction ; yet, that they were not intended for the universal edification of the church nor enrolled as a part of his word, appointed for that end. Neither can it be thought strange, that it should so be ; for that a thing be scripture, it is not only needful, that it be inspired, but also that it be appointed of God for public use. It is not improbable, but Isaiah, Moses, David, Paul, and others, might have written many more writings, upon particular occasions, or to particular persons, which were useful in themselves for edification ; and yet were never appointed of God to be looked upon or received as scriptures for public use in his church; so do we account of these Songs mentioned in the objection, and other writings of Solomon, now not extant: and it may be, the Spirit hath pitched on this Song to be recorded as the sum and chief of all the rest; as he did pitch upon some particular prayers of David and Moses &c. passing by others.

And lastly, We are rather to be thankful, for the great advantage we have by this, than anxiously to inquire what hath become of the rest.

There are four things we would propose for use, from the title of this Song.

First, That singing of believers' cases, even their several cases is allowable: or, that singing of divers and different cases, yea, even their saddest cases, is not inconsistent with, but very agreeable unto the work of praise: ye see, this is a Song for the nature of it; which Song is to be sung, yet for matter exceeding comprehensive of all sorts of cases, and these various.

There are (amongst others) five cases, in which to sing doth sometimes stumble, at least, stick much with those who are weak and tender; all which, we will find cleared in the Bride's practice of singing this Song.

I. It is doubted, if sad cases should be sung, seeing, James v. 13, It is said, "Is any man merry, let him sing Psalms." *Answ.* It is true, those who are merry should sing, but not only they, no more than only they who are afflicted should, pray: it is not our case, nor our cheerful disposition, but the duty that should be respected in this work of praise; yea, we should sing for cheering our disposition, and mitigating and sweetening our crosses: so doth the Bride here sing her sufferings, chap. i. 6; chap. v. 7, when she was smitten; yea, her desertions, she putteth these also in a song.

II. It is stumbled at sometimes, to sing complaints of our own sinfulness, and to turn our failings into songs; what matter of cheerfulness is there in these may one think; but we say, here she doth so, "mine own vineyard have I not kept" (saith she) chap. i. 6; "I sleep," &c. chap. v. 2. It is a ground of cheerfulness that we may sing over these unto God, with expectation to be pardoned and delivered from them, as Psalm lxv. 3.

III. When the matter is different from our case, some think it is hard to sing such Psalms. *Answ.* Certainly in this Song, there are different, yea, contrary cases; yet none can think, but a believer may sing it all at one time. Yea, 2. There had never then been a Psalm sung in public; for in no congregation, can all the members ever be in one case. 3. The same might be objected against public prayers also, seeing there may be many petitions that are not suitable to all joiners; yet hath the Lord commanded both public praying and praising.

IV. When the matter, which is sung, is above us, being a thing we have not yet reached, and so cannot assert it in our particular condition as truth, as these words, Psalm xviii. 20, 21, " I have kept his ways," &c. *Answ.* By this Song, all, at least most part of believers, are made to sing many things, beyond their own attainments possibly; yea, chap. viii. 12, that phrase, " My vineyard which is mine, is before me," is of the same extent with that, Psalm xvii. 20.   Yet will not any think, that the Spirit propounding this Song and that Psalm, as a subject for public praise, did ever intend that none should sing it, but such as were as holy as David; yea, it would seem, that if either David, or Solomon, had stuck to the absolute perfection which these words seem to hold forth (if they be expounded according to the strict rule of the law, and be not taken in an evangelic sense) that neither of them would, or could have sung them: yea, it is observable, that in this Song, there are spots mentioned; and not keeping of the vineyard, chap. i. 6. is one part of the Song, as well as keeping of it, chap. viii. is another.

How then may we join in these? *Answ.* 1. We sing not our own sense, and experience only, but what may attain the end of praise; which is attained, in our acknowledging what others have reached, though we ourselves come short. 2. Not only our own case, as particular members, is to be sung; but in public we take in the praises of the whole body. 3. That expression, chap. i 6, " Mine own vineyard," &c. holds forth the sense she had of her negligence, not as if she had in no way done her duty, but she confesseth her failings in it; which she sings to the praise of that free grace, that had pardoned her. Again, the other expression, chap. viii. 12, " My vineyard which is mine, is before me," expresseth her sense of her sincerity, blessing God for it, and refreshing herself in the acknowledging of it: and both these may agree, as to some measure, in the believer's experience, at one and the same time: though when the believer sinneth more grossly, they do not so well agree to him, except in respect of different times and cases.

In praising then, we would neither simply look to our frame, nor to the matter in itself, which is to be sung, nor to the cases we are in, as if these were the warrant of our singing, or the rule to regulate us in it: but unto these three things. 1. The end wherefore singing is appointed. 2. The command. 3. The notion, or consideration, in respect of which the believer joineth in the duty of praise.

Firstly, The ends are principally three. 1. Glorifying God, and making his praise glorious: thus histories of the Lord's dealing with his people of old, and thus the cases of others, in our singing of them, serve to that end, that he did such works, that such a case was once sung to him, and such a saint was so dealt with: otherwise, we might scruple to sing Psalm xliv. 1, " We have heard with our ears, our fathers have told us," and other scriptures, as well as cases: and so the most part of the subject of praise and the book of the Psalms, would be laid aside as useless, and not so much as to be read; for we ought not to read, or say an untruth, more than to sing it.

A second end is, edifying of others with whom we join, as well as studying edification ourselves: so, Col. iii. 16, the end to be proposed in singing, is, " Teaching and admonishing one another, in psalms, and hymns, and spiritual songs." And suppose, some found themselves unsuitable in their own case, to the purpose that is to be sung, yet will it not teach them what they should be, and admonish them, because they are not such?

A third end we are to aim at in singing, is our own cheering and refreshing, " Making melody in our hearts to the Lord," Eph. v. 19. Which ariseth not always from the matter simply considered, as it holds true in our own experience: but. 1. From our conscientious going about it, as a piece of worship to God, and so doing, we are accepted in that. 2. From the heartsomeness of that soul-refreshing exercise of praise; and so that scripture which might be more saddening in meditation to us, yet should be cheering in praise, because it is then used in that ordinance. 3. From the possibility that is herein discovered, of attaining such a blessing, frame, or experience, because once a saint did attain it: and since they were men of the like passions, and infirmities with us, why may not we aim at, and hope to be made saints of the like graces with them, since they were what they were, by the grace of God? 4. From this, that it was once made good in another, which mercy should be a ground to us, to mention it to the Lord's praise. 5. From its being a part of scripture, appointed for his praise, whether it agree with our case, or not: that being the end wherefore it was designed to be sung, is a sufficient warrant for our joining in the singing thereof.

Secondly, We would consider the command we have, not only to praise, but to praise in these words of David, and other penmen of holy Psalms; for which cause, God hath furnished his church with songs (but not so with forms of prayers, to which he would have us astricted) and that for preventing doubts concerning the matter: For, 1. If God did propone these songs to be sung, then they are fit to praise him. 2. If he did allow none to sing them but such as had no hesitation or scruple to assert them, with application to themselves; then, either never should they be sung, or never in public: but, 3. Did he not appoint them to be used in David's time? and joiners then were not all of one size; sure, they had never been committed to public use, if none might have joined in singing them, but these who could sing them from their own experience: or, will a believer be challenged for praising God, in the rule and words laid down by him? certainly not: however he may be challenged, if he be not suitably affected in the singing of them.

Thirdly, We would consider the notion, or capacity under which believers join in this duty; for they join either as parts of the whole church, and so they go about their part of the duty of praise (as the matter holdeth true in any member indefinitely, even as they join in prayers) so being that which is sung, be allowed matter for that end: or they join as true believers, and then what points out infirmity, they look on as agreeing to their flesh; what points out sincerity, they as spiritual, though not perfect, join on that account in the thankful acknowledging of it; what confesseth a sin, if guilty, they acknowledge it; if not, they bless God they are preserved by grace; yet they are made to see their corruption, which hath the seed of that sin in it, and take warning; as in singing the li. Psalm is requisite, when all are not under that guilt which David there confesseth.

V. A fifth case in singing, which hath been matter of doubting to some, is when they are put to sing with others, who possibly are strangers to God. *Answ.* Such may be cleared from this, that the Bride joineth with "the Daughters of Jerusalem;" often they have a share in holding up this Song: so doth she go to the watchman, being willing to join with them who smote her: and certainly this and other songs, being to be sung in public in the congregation, and such a congregation, as none will plead that it ought to have been separate from, it is clear they joined, and that upon the account of the former grounds.

Second. The second thing we are to observe for use, is from the commendation of this Song, being for its excellency, " a Song of Songs :" and it is this, that, the believer hath the choicest Song, and most excellent mirth in the world, not such songs, or joy as the world hath, or giveth, John xiv. 27. Yea, their songs, are such songs, as none can learn, but themselves, Rev. xiv. 3. O how happy and cheerful a life might a believer have, if he did not sometimes mar his own comfort! All is most excellent which he hath, his songs are so, for they have the most excellent subject, to wit, Christ, Psalm. xlv. and the most excellent grounds of rejoicing, and most solid ; the largest, sweetest, and most comfortable allowance in the world. Considering all this Song together, though it hath sundry sad and perplexing cases, yet it is most excellent: for, right thoughts of Christ, will make every condition sweet, and a song ; nothing will come wrong to a believer; Christ, Christ maketh up all, and maketh all excellent: every condition with him is excellent; whoso covets him, coveteth what is best ; whoso neglects him, neglects what is only worth the seeking, and what can only afford a song to the owner, and it is clearness in Christ's worth, and an interest in him, that turns all conditions into a song.

Third. From the author (I mean the penman) consider, that piety and tenderness is not unbecoming, but is rather an ornament to the most noble, most rich, and most wise men in the world : it is a greater glory to Solomon, and a greater evidence of his eternal good condition, that he was acquainted with, and taken up in holy exercises, than that he was a king ; yea, places, parts, riches, &c. are beautiful, when made subservient to piety ; piety maketh these to shine on Solomon : and the Spirit also maketh use of natural and moral wisdom, which the Lord had bestowed upon him, to set out deep mysteries in these writings; which shews, that the Lord would have any measure of these gifts he hath bestowed on us, adorned with the exercise of grace, and made subvervient to his glory. Also, we may see here, that much business in men's common affairs, and a tender walk, are not inconsistent; if men would prudently manage their time, they might have access to their employments, and keep a spiritual frame also, as Solomon, David, and others did. It is our corruption, and not the multitude of lawful employments, that distracts us; David went home to bless his own family, in the midst of public affairs, 2 Sam. vi. 20.

Fourth. From the consideration of the penman (stained with such faults) made use of by God in the composition of this Song; we may observe, 1. That neither place, parts, nay, nor graces, will exempt any man from falling: O believers, what need is there to be watchful and humble! may not these examples of David, Solomon, Peter, &c. lay your pride, and put you to your arms, and necessitate you to be upon your watch? who of you will lay claim to Solomon's knowledge, experience, or privileges? yet even he, the penman of this sweet scripture, had his affections to God cooled, and became an offence even to this day; what is spoken of his fearful backsliding and fall, being still a rock of offence, upon which many still break their necks. 2. There may be much corruption dwelling beside much light and grace, and yet, the one not fully put out, or extinguish the other. 3. Grace hath fitted and made use of many a knotty tree for the Lord's work: for what Solomon naturally hath been, may appear in his carriage (seeing men's sinful carriage and way, is but the product of the natural corruption that is in their hearts) notwithstanding he is thus made use of. 4. Corruption may lie long under grace's feet, and grace may attain to a great height, and yet corruption may again strangely break out, and grace be brought very low. What knowledge had Solomon! what prescience and clearness had he gotten by the Lord's appearing to him! what hearing of prayer! how useful was he in God's work, in building the temple, ordering all the Levites; &c. and continued thus eminent for many years, even till he was well stricken in years; and then fell so foully! how may this strike us with fear! It is much to win fair off the stage, without a spot. Be humble, and he that standeth, let him " take heed lest he fall." 5. Grace can wash foul spots out of believers' garments, seeing, no question Solomon's was washed : and as he was recovered, so grace is able to recover the saints from their most dangerous and fearful backslidings. 6. Sometimes the Spirit will honour the penmen of holy writ, by mentioning and recording their names, other times not, as is clear from some books, unknown by whom they were written. The Lord doth in this according to his pleasure, and as he seeth it may tend to edification.

Verse 2. Let him kiss me with the kisses of his mouth : for thy love is better than wine.

HAVING spoken to the title we come now to the Song itself : which being by way of conference, or dialogue, we shall divide the several chapters, according to the number of the speakers, and their several intercourses in speaking ; and so in this chapter, we have five parts. In the 1st. the Bride speaks, to verse 8. In the 2d. the Bridegroom, to verse 12. In the 3d. the Bride again, to verse 15. And 4th. the Bridegroom speaks, to verse 15. And lastly, the Bride, in the two last verses.

The Bride begins this sweet conference, verse 2. and continues to verse 8. 1. She speaks to Christ, verse 2, 3, 4. Then 2. to the daughters of Jerusalem, verse 5, 6. Lastly, She turns herself again to the Bridegroom, verse 7.

In the first of these, there is, 1. Her aim and desire, by way of an earnest wish laid down, verse 2. 2. The motives that stir up this desire in her and whereby she presseth it on him, verses 2, 3. 3. There is a formal prayer set down, verse 4, which is amplified in these three, 1. In the motive proposed. 2. In the answer obtained, and felt. 3. In the effects that followed on it.

Her great wish is, " Let him kiss me with the kisses of his mouth." That it is the Bride that speaks, is clear ; she begins, not because love ariseth first on her side (for here she begins, as having already closed with him, and therefore she speaks to him, as one who knows his worth, and longs for the out-lettings of his love) but because such expressions of Christ's love, as are to be found in this Song, whereby his complacency is vented and manifested towards us, doth first presuppose the working of love in us, and our exercising of it on him, and then his delighting (that is his expressing his delight) in us : for although the man first suit the wife (and so Christ first sueth for his Bride) yet when persons are married, it is most suitable, that the wife should very pressingly long for, and express desire after the husband, even as the Bride doth here after Christ's kisses, and the expressions of love.   Of this order of Christ's love, see chap. viii. verse 10.

In the words consider, 1. What she desires; and that is, "the kisses of his mouth." 2. How she points Christ forth, by this significant demonstrative, HIM. 3. Her abrupt manner of breaking out with this her desire, as one that hath been dwelling on the thoughts of Christ, and feeding on his exellency; and therefore now she breaks out, "Let him kiss me," &c. as if her heart were at her mouth, or would leap out of her mouth, to meet with his.

1. By kisses, we understand most lovely, friendly, familiar, and sensible manifestations of his love; kisses of the mouth are so amongst friends, so it was betwixt Jonathan and David, and so it is especially betwixt husband and wife.

Next, there are several delightsome circumstances, that heighten the Bride's esteem of this, the so much desired expression of his love.   The first is implied, in the person who is to kiss, it is HIM, "Let HIM kiss,", he who is the most excellent and singular person in the world.   The second is hinted in the party whom he is to kiss, it is ME, "Let him kiss ME," a contemptible despicable creature; for so she was in herself, as appears from verses 5, 6, yet this is the person, this love is to be vented on. 3. Wherewith is he to kiss?   It is with the "kisses of his mouth;" which we conceive is not only added as an Hebraism, like that expression, "The words of his mouth," and such like phrases, but also to affect herself, by expressing fully what she breathed after, viz. kisses, or love, which are the more lovely to her, that they come from his mouth, as having a sweetness in it, (chap. v. 16.) above any thing in the world.   That Christ's love hath such a sweetness in it, the reason subjoined will make clear, "for thy love is," &c. That which is here kisses, is immediately denominated loves; it is his love that she prizeth, and whereof kisses were but evidences.

They are kisses, in the plural number, partly to shew how many ways Christ hath to manifest his love, partly to show the continuance and frequency of these manifestations, which she would be at: the thing which she here desires, is not love simply, but the sense of love; for she questions not his love, but desires to have sensible expressions of it, and therefore compares it not only to looks, that she might see him, but to kisses; which is also clear from the reason annexed, while she compares his love to wine.

Again, her manner of designing Christ, is observable—HIM. It is a relative, where no antecedent goes before, yet certainly it looks to Christ alone, as the reasons shew: here no rules of art are kept, for love stands not on these: this manner of speaking is to be found also in moral authors, when one eminent is set forth, who is singularly known beside others, as having in the estimation of the speakers no match: so Pythagoras' scholars used to say of their master, αυτος εφη,—"He said it": and in scripture, when the saints speak of the Lord, they thus design him, because they are not afraid to be mistaken, Psalm lxxxvii. 1, "His foundation," &c. and Isa. liii. 2, "He shall grow up like to a tender plant." This is neither for want of titles due to him, or rhetoric in her, but because in this manner of expression the saints set forth, 1. Christ's singular excellency, which is such, that he hath no match, or equal, there is but one Him. 2. Their singular esteem of him, whatever others think, 1 Cor. viii. 6, "To us there is but one Lord, Jesus:" only Christ is esteemed of by them. 3. A constant and habitual thinking, and meditating on him; for though there be no connexion in the words expressed, yet what is expressed, may have, and hath connexion with the thoughts of her heart; and if all were seen that were within, it would be easily known what HIM she meant: and so we are to gather its dependence on the affection, and meditation it flows from, rather than from any preceding words; for here there are none. 4. It is to shew, her thoughts of Christ were not limited, or stinted to her words, or her speaking of HIM: for though there be no words preceding, to make known who this HIM is, spoken of; yet we may well conceive her heart taken up with desire after HIM, and meditation on HIM: and so there is a good coherence,—" let Him," that is, HIM I have been thinking on, HIM whom my soul desires, he only whom I esteem of, and who hath no equal, &c. This sort of abruptness of speech, hath no incongruity in spiritual rhetoric.

Whence we may observe, 1. That Christ hath a way of communicating his love, and the sense of it to a believer, which is not common to others. 2. That this is the great scope and desire of believers, if they had their choice, it is to have sensible communion with Christ : this is their one thing, Psalm xxvii. 4. It is the first and last suit of this Song, and the voice of the Spirit and Bride, and the last prayer that is in the scripture, Rev. xxii. 17. 3. That belivers can discern this fellowship (it is so sweet and sensible) which is to be had with Jesus Christ. 4. That they have an high esteem of it, as being a special signification of his love. 5. That much inward heart fellowship with Christ, hath suitable outward expressions flowing from it. 6. That believers in an habitual walk with Christ will be abrupt in their suits to him, sometimes meditating on him, sometimes praying to him. 7. That where Christ is known, and rightly thought of, there will be no equal to him in the heart.

2. In the next place, she lays down the motives that made her so desire this ; which are rather to set forth Christ's excellency, to strengthen her own faith, and warm her own love in pursuing after so concerning a suit, than from any fear she had of being mistaken by him, in being as it were, so bold and homely with him in her desires. 1. The reason is generally proposed, verse 2, and enlarged and confirmed, verse 3. The sum of it is, thy love is exceeding excellent, and I have more need, and greater esteem of it, than of any thing in the world, therefore I seek after it, and hope to attain it.

There are four words here to be cleared, 1. " Thy loves" (so it is in the original, in the plural number) Christ's love is sometimes (as the love of God) taken essentially, as an attribute in him, which is himself, "God is love," 1 John iv. 8. Thus the Lord, in his love, is the same in all times. 2. For some effect of that love, when he doth manifest it to his people, by conferring good on them, and by the sensible intimations thereof to them : so it is, John xiv. 21, 23. We take it in the last sense here ; for she was in Christ's love, but desired the manifestations of it ; and it is by these that his love becomes sensible and refreshful to believers. It is loves in the plural number, although it be one infinite fountain in God, to show how many ways it vented, or how many effects that one love produced, or what esteem she had of it, and of the continuance and frequency of the manifestations thereof to her ; this one love of his was as many loves.

The second word to be cleared, is " wine." Wine is cheering to men, Psalm civ. 15, and makes their heart glad : under it here is understood, what is most cheering and comfortable in its use to men.

3. Christ's love is better, 1. Simply in itself, it is most excellent. 2. In its effects, more exhilarating, cheering, and refreshing, And, 3. In her esteem; to me (saith she) " It is better ;" I love it, prize it, and esteem it more, as Psalm iv. 7, 8. " Thereby thou hast made my heart more glad," &c. This his love is every way preferable to all the most cheering and refreshing things in the world.

4. The inference, " for," is to be considered : it shew-eth that these words are a reason of her suit, and so the sense runs thus, because thy love is of great value, and hath more comfortable effects on me, than the most de-lightsome of creatures, therefore let me have it. Out of which reasoning we may see what motive will have weight with Christ, and will sway with sincere souls in dealing with him, for the intimation of his love ; for the love of Christ, and the sweetness and satisfaction that is to be found in it, is the great prevailing motive that hath weight with them : and sense of the need of Christ's love, and esteem of it, and delight in it alone, when no creature-comfort can afford refreshing, may, and will warrant poor hungry and thirsty souls, to be pressing for the love of Christ, when they may not be without it ; which shews,

1. That a heart that knows Jesus Christ, will love to dwell on the thoughts of his worth, and to present him often to itself, as the most ravishing object, and will make use of pressing motives and arguments, to stir up itself to seek after the intimations of his love. 2. That the more a soul diveth in the love of Christ, it is the more ravish-ed with it, and presseth, yea, panteth the more after it : it was HIM before, " Let him kiss me," as being some-thing afraid to speak to him ; it is now, THOU, " THY love," &c. as being more inflamed with love, since she began to speak, and therefore more familiarly bold, in pressing her suit upon him. 3. The exercise of love strengthens faith: and contrarily, when love wears out of exercise, faith dieth : these graces stand and fall together, they are lively and languish together. 4. Where Christ's love is seriously thought of and felt, created consolations will grow bare, and lose all relish; wine, and the best of

creature-comforts, will lose their savour and sweetness with such a soul, when once it is seen how good he is. 5. An high esteem of Christ, is no ill argument in pressing for, and pursuing after his presence ; for to those that thus love and esteem him, he will manifest himself, John xiv. 21, 23. 6. Where there hath been any taste of Christ's love, the soul cannot endure to want it, it cannot enjoy itself, if it do not enjoy him ; this is the cordial that cheereth it in any condition, and maketh every bitter thing sweet.

Verse 3. Because of the savour of thy good ointments, thy name is as ointment poured forth ; therefore do the virgins love thee.

THE second reason (which is also a confirmation and enlargement of the former) is verse 3, and it runs upon these supposed and implied grounds. 1. That there are many precious excellencies in Christ. So that, 2. The speaking of his name, is as if a man would open a sweet savouring box of ointment, as that woman did, John xii. 3. There is no title, or office, or qualification in Christ, but all are savoury; his very garments smell of myrrh, and aloes, and cassia, &c. Psalm xlv. 8. 3. It suppones that this worth and loveliness of Christ, ravishes all that ever knew him (here called virgins) with love to HIM : and therefore (which is the strength of the reason) it is no marvel, would she say, I love him so fervently, and desire so earnestly the manifestations of his love, which I have found so sweet.

So the verse may be taken up in these four things, 1. Christ's furniture ; he hath many savoury ointments, and good. 2. The further explication, and amplification of this his commendation, expressing both what she meant by ointments, and also the abundance and freshness of these ointments which were in Christ, in these words, "thy name is as ointment poured forth." 3. The effect that followed on these, or the attractive virtue of them, which is such, that the most chaste, who kept their affections from other objects, are yet without prejudice to their chaste nature, taken up and ravished with that loveliness of Christ : " Therefore" (saith she) "do the virgins love thee. 4. There is the scope, which is partly to shew the reality of Christ's worth, which not only she, but all

believers were in love with; partly to show, that it was
no strange thing, to see her so taken up with him, it
would be rather strange if it were otherwise; seeing it is
not possible for any to see and taste what Christ is, and
not be ravished with his love.

Ointments are both of an adorning and refreshing nature, especially to the sense of smelling, Psalm civ. 15.
" Ointment makes men's faces to shine," and the house
where it is, to savour, when it is precious and good, John
xii. 3. Men in vanity use sweet powders, and such things
as these, which can but little commend them; but Christ's
ointments are his graces, Psalm xlv. 2, wherewith he is
anointed, for opening the blind eyes, for preaching glad
tidings to the poor, to bind up the broken-hearted, to
give the oil of joy for mourning, &c. as it is, Isa. lxi. 1,
2, 3. Which qualifications, are both more delightsome
and savoury, in themselves, and to the soul that is sensible of its need of them, than any ointments the high priest
of old used, which were but typical of the graces and
qualifications wherewith Christ is furnished: hence is in
the gospel, 2 Cor. ii. 14, 15, (whereby these graces are
manifested) called " a sweet savour."

Again, these ointments are said to be good: so are
they in their nature, and in their effects on sinners, as is
clear from Isa. lxi. 1, 2, &c. And 2. They are said to
savour; the scent and smell of them is sweet and refreshful to the spiritual senses. And 3. They are called his
(thy good ointment:) they are his, not only as he is God,
having all-sufficiency essentially in him, but as Mediator,
having purchased eternal redemption, and having " the
Spirit without measure" communicated to him, John iii.
34, and in that respect, " anointed with the oil of gladness
above his fellows," Psalm xlv. 7, that out of his fulness
we might all receive, grace for grace, John i. 14. Our
graces being of that same nature, that his are of. It is
comfortable, that Christ hath many good ointments; that
they are his own, and that he hath the right of disposing
of them, and that as Mediator they are given unto him
for that very purpose.

Observ. 1. Grace is a cordial and savoury thing, no
ointment is like it. 2. Christ abounds in grace, he is
" full of grace and truth," John i. 14. Hence our wants
are said to be made up, " according to his riches in lory
by Jesus Christ," Phil. iv. 19. 3. They are goodg and

execellent graces and qualifications, wherewith the Mediator is furnished; such as do exactly answer all the necessities and wants of empty and needy sinners.

2. The commendation is explicated, or illustrated by a similitude : the thing she explains, and which she understood by ointments, is his name : the similitude whereby it is illustrated, is, " ointment poured forth," Christ's name is Himself or the knowledge of Himself, or every thing whereby Himself is made known, his attributes, word, works, especially those of redemption, his ordinances, covenant, promises, &c. which are all his name (for so the preaching of the gospel is called the bearing of his name, Acts ix. 15, and making known, or declaring his name, Psalm xxii. 22. Heb. ii. 12, &c.) This is the thing illustrated. Now this name is compared, not to ointment simply, as sealed up in a box, but to ointment as poured forth and diffused. Whereby, 1. The abundance of these graces is holden forth; there is no scarcity of them in him. 2. His liberality in communicating of them, he pours them out, as one opening a box of ointment, should so diffuse and distribute it. 3. By this is set out the lively savouriness of his graces ; they savour not only as ointment closed up, but as ointment diffused. In a word, there is nothing in Christ (for whatever is in him, is comprehended under his name) but the unfolding of it will be more refreshful, and abundant in spiritual delights, than if men would break and open many boxes of costly ointments, and pour them all out on others.

Observ. 1. Believers are not soon satisfied in taking up, or expressing of Christ's worth. 2. Christ and all that is in him, is as full of spiritual life and refreshing, as a box that is full of the most precious ointment : Christ is well stored with grace, it is " poured into his lips," Psalm xlv. 2. 3. This savour of Christ's graces is not felt by every one, the box of his ointments is not open to all, but only to some, and that is to them that believe ; for to them he is precious, and every thing that is in him, is most cordial and savoury to the believer. 4. The more Christ and his worth be enquired into, it will savour the better, and be the more refreshful (for it is his name which is this ointment) Christ in his excellent worth, through men's strangeness to him, is unknown in the world ; they do not enquire into this savoury name, but if he were once known, they would find that in him, that would make them give over their other unprofitable pursuits, and pant after him.

The effect of these his ointments (which is a proof of the reality of this truth, and the third thing in the verse) is in these words, "therefore do the virgins love thee." By virgins here, are not understood bare professors, but sincere believers, who are not counterfeit in their affection, nor so common in their love, as to bestow it on any creature whorishly, but who reserve it for Christ only : so the church is called, 2 Cor. xi. 2, "a chaste virgin ;" and so these who were kept unspotted, and sealed for the Lord, Rev. xiv. 4, 5, are called virgins. They are here called virgins in the plural number, because this denomination belongs to all believers, distributively, and in particular. They are said to love Christ, that is, whatever others do, who have no spiritual senses, and whose example is not to be regarded ; yet these (saith she) desire thee only, and delight in thee only : and this differenceth true virgins from others.

If it be asked, whether that be single love, which loves Christ for his ointments ; we answer Christ's ointments may be two ways considered, 1. As they make himself lovely and desirable ; so we may, and should love him, because he is a most lovely object, as being so well qualified and furnished. 2. As by these, many benefits are communicated to us ; thus we ought to love him for his goodness to us, although not principally, because no effect of that love is fully adequate, and comparable to that love in him, which is the fountain from which these benefits flow ; yet, this love is both gratitude and duty, taught by nature, and no mercenary thing, when it is superadded to the former. Hence observe,

1. All have not a true esteem of Christ, though he be most excellently lovely : for, it is the virgins only that love him. 2. There be some that have an high esteem of him, and are much taken with the savoury ointments, and excellent qualifications wherewith he is furnished. 3. None can love him and other things excessively also ; they who truly love HIM, their love is reserved for HIM, therefore they are called virgins : it is but common love, and scarce worth the naming, that doth not single out its object from all other things. 4. They who truly love HIM, are the choice and wale of all the world beside ; their example is to be followed and weight laid on their practice (in the essentials of spiritual communion, more than

on the example of kings, scholars, or wise men : so doth she reason here from the virgins, and passeth what others do.   5. True chaste love to Christ, is the character of a virgin-believer, and agrees to them all, and to none other.   6. The love that every believer hath to Christ, is a proof of his worth ; and will be either a motive to make us love HIM, or an aggravation of our neglect.

Verse 4. Draw me, we will run after thee. The king hath brought me into his chambers : we will be glad and rejoice in thee, we will remember thy love more than wine : the upright love thee.

BEING now more confirmed in her desire, from the reasons she hath laid down, she comes in the 4th verse more directly to propound and press her suit : for rationally insisting upon the grounds of grace, in pressing a petition, both sharpens desire, and strengthens the soul with more vigour and boldness, to pursue its desires by prayer.   In the words we may consider, 1. The petition.   2. The motive made use of to press it.   3. The answer, or grant of what was sought.   4. The effects of the answer following on her part, suitable someway to her engagement.
The petition is " draw me," a word used in the gospel, to set forth the efficacious work of the Spirit of God upon the heart, engaging the soul in a most sweet, powerful, and effectual way to Jesus Christ; " None can come to me" (saith Christ) " except the Father draw him," John vi. 44.   It is used here, to set forth the Bride's desire to be brought into fellowship with Christ by the power of this same Spirit, that as she desires a visit from Christ, so she desires his Spirit, that he may by his powerful operations draw her near to him.   And although a believer be not at a total distance from Christ, and so needs not renovation as one in nature doth ; yet considering that a believer may fall into a deadness of frame, as to the lively exercise of grace, and a great distance, as to any sensible sweet communion with Jesus Christ, and that it must be by the power of that same Spirit (without which even these that are in Christ can do nothing) that they must be recovered, and again brought to taste of the joy of his salvation (as is clear from David's prayer, Psalm li. 10. to have " a clean heart created in him," see ver. 12, of that Psalm.)   And that there are degrees of communion with

him, and nearness to him, none of which can be got at without the Spirit's drawing, more than being made near at the first in respect of state : I say all these things being considered, it is clear, that this petition is very pertinent, even to the Bride, and doth import these particulars : 1. A distance, or ceasing of correspondence for a time, and in part, betwixt Christ and her. 2. Her sense and resentment of it, so that she cannot quietly rest in it, being much unsatisfied with her present case. 3. An esteem of Christ and union with him, and a desire to be near, even very near him ; which is the scope of her petition, to be drawn unto him, that she may have (as it were) her head in his bosom. 4. A sense of self-insufficiency, and that she had nothing of her own to help her to this nearness, and so a denying of all ability for that in herself. 5. A general faith, that Christ can do what she cannot do, and that there is help to be gotten from him (upon whom the help of his people is laid) for acting spiritual life, and recovering her to a condition of nearness with himself. 6. An actual putting at him (so to speak) and making use of him by faith, for obtaining from him, and by him, quickening, efficacious and soul-recovering influences, which she could not otherwise win at. 7. Diligence in prayer ; she prays much, and cries for help when she can do no more.

II. The motive whereby she presseth this petition, is, " We will run after thee:" wherein we are to consider these three things, 1. What this is to run : which is, in short, to make progress Christ-ward, and advance in the way of holiness, with cheerfulness and alacrity (having her heart lifted up in the ways of the Lord) for the believer's life is a race, heaven is the prize, I Cor. ix. 24. and Phil. iii. 13, 14, &c. and the graces and influences of the Spirit give legs, strength, and vigour to the inner-man to run, as wind doth to a ship, to cause her make way ; as it is, Psalm cxix. 23, " Then I shall run in the way of thy commandments, when thou shalt enlarge my heart," which is, on the matter, the same with drawing here. And this running is opposed to deadness, or slowness in her progress before : now (saith she) I make no way, but draw me, and we shall go swiftly, speedily, willingly, and cheerfully. Hence we may gather.

1. That often when there is desertion as to Christ's presence, that there is an up-sitting in duty and the exercise of grace. 2. That bonds in duty are as observable and

heavy to believers, as want of comfort. 3. That there is in them an high estimation, and a serious desire of enlargement in duty, or of liberty to run in the way of God's commandments. 4. This desire is very acceptable with Jesus Christ, and therefore is made use of as a motive in pressing her petition before him : he takes it well, when a believer is like to lie by and sit up, that he look up to him, and pray and pant for help, to set him to his feet again.

2. Consider why the person is changed, " draw me," (saith she) and "we" shall run : if we take the church collectively under "me," then " we," will set out the particular members ; and it is this much, do me good, or pour thy Spirit on the church, and we shall run in our stations who are members : it is the better with all the members, when it is well with the church in general. But it would seem to look to particular believers, the effect of drawing being most proper and peculiar on them : and so it is to be understood thus, if thou wilt draw me, and by the power of thy grace work effectually upon me, then many more shall get advantage by it : which holds true, partly, by reason of the sympathy that is amongst the members of that one body ; partly, because a work of grace fits and engages one the more to be forth-coming for the good of others : partly, because of the influence which liveliness in one, may have upon the quickening and stirring up of others : even as often, when deadness begins in one, it leaveneth and infecteth more ; so by God's blessing may liveliness do. This same argument is made use of by David, Psalm, xci, when he is dealing for the establishment and liberty of God's Spirit, then (saith he) ver. 12, 13, " I will teach sinners thy way, and they shall be converted unto thee." He was not only purposed to stir up himself, and walk tenderly in the strength he should receive, but that he would lay out himself for the good of others, and he promiseth himself success therein through the grace of God. And so Joshua, xxiv. 15, " I and my house will serve the Lord :" which speaks, that his serving the Lord, would have influence upon his house. Experience doth often make out, that a lively soul in a congregation or family, will readily occasion and provoke others, to stir and seek with them.

3. The force of the reason, in the connexion it hath with the petition, imports, 1. That she was much in love

with holiness, and had an ardent desire after more of it.
2. That she resolved to improve her receipts, for the edification of others. 3. That these designs were very acceptable to Christ. 4. That except she were drawn, she
would come short of both. 5. A cheerful engaging to be
forth-coming to his honour and the good of others, and to
undertake what he shall call to, and fit for: these go well
together, that when we see and are sensible, that we of
ourselves, as of ourselves, can do nothing. 2. Cor. iii. 3.
yet we may humbly engage, " To do all things through
Christ strengthening us :" in a word, I have need (would
she say) to be drawn, if holiness be needful : and I hope
thou who respectest holiness in me and others of thy people, will grant what I seek. Her engaging to run, if he
would draw, is no vain undertaking ; but a humble pressing motive, holding forth some sincerity given from him,
but no ability in herself, but as he who hath given her to
will, must also work in her to do.

III. The third thing in the verse, is the return, or grant
of this suit ; the King (saith she) "hath brought me into his
chambers, he hath indeed brought me where I was desirous
to be. The words, " he hath brought me," being compared with the petition, " draw me," and the effects following, whereby she changeth from praying to praising, and
and that with expressions holding forth a kind of surprisal,
do evidence this to be a real return to her prayer, and a
comfortable alteration upon, and change in her condition.

In this answer, consider, 1. What she receives—a noble
privilege ; she is admitted into the king's chamber to nearness with HIM, which she longed for, and now she hath it.
Chambers are the most intimate places of familiar fellowship, especially with kings, where none but courtiers indeed come. They were the places where the Bridegroom
and the Bride rejoiced together ; and it hath a tacit opposition to a salutation by the way, or admission to outer
rooms, this to which she is admitted is more, yet is it
something here attainable ; which we conceive, is the
enjoying of that love she formerly sought for, and which
afterward she engaged to remember, as having now obtained it. In a word, she is where she would be, as the
effects shew.

2. Consider who brought her into these chambers ; it is
the King, even HIM she prayed unto, to draw her, he hath
heard her : this King (as being the chief of all that ever

bare that name) is called the King by way of eminency; and so, Psalm xlv. 1, 2, and Zech. iv. 9. He is not only King, and supreme as God, having the same essential dominion with the Father, over all the creatures; but also, (which is here especially meant) as Mediator, he is a King by donation, Psal. ii. 6, 7, and also by conquest, having purchased his kingdom with his blood, and by the power of his spiritual arms that are effectual upon the hearts of sinners, brings them subject to him, Psalm xlv. 5. So he confesseth himself to be a King before Pontius Pilate, John xviii. 36, 37, although his kingdom be not of this world. It is he, who by his blood hath made access for believers to nearness with God, as it is, Eph. ii. 18: through that new and living way, Heb. x. 19, 20: so that she may well say, he brought her in. She attributes this to him expressly, 1. For his commendation, and to give him the acknowledgment due to him in this work, which would never have been wrought without him: all nearness and access to God, all progress in holiness, and comfort in duties, should not only be sought by, and from Christ; but he acknowledged for these, and the praise of them returned to him.

2. She observes the return of her prayer, and his readiness to be entreated, I prayed to him to draw (saith she) and he did it effectually; he drew me, and brought me into his chambers. Here we may say, 1. Christ is easily entreated, Isa. lxv. 24, " Before they call, I will answer." 2. Believers should observe returns of prayer, and bless Christ for them. 3. She acknowledgeth he had brought her into the chambers, to magnify and to commend the mercy the more: it is the greater honour, that not only she is there, but that the King himself (like the prodigal's father) met her, and took her in: Christ's convoy is much worth, and sinners may hazard forward with it, and not despair of access. 4. She attributes it to him, that she may keep mind of his grace, whereby she stands and enjoys these privileges; and that she may be still humble under them, as having none of these from herself: it is much, under sense and a fair gale of flowing love, to carry even, and to be humble: and it is rare to be full of this new wine, and bear it well.

3. Consider the importance of the word in the original, it is here translated, " he brought me in," as it is, chap. ii. 4; but the word in that conjugation, in which it is

used in the first language, signifieth, he made me come, or go in ; implying, 1. A sort of averseness, and inability in herself. 2. Many difficulties in the way. 3. An efficacious work overcoming all these, and effectually bringing her over all, as the same word is used, Psalm lxxviii. 71, where God's bringing David from the fold to be king, over so many difficulties, is spoken of.

IV. The last thing in the verse is, the effect following on this her admission, which is both exceeding great, spiritual cheerfulness in herself, and gladness of heart also in others, whereby both her own, and their hearts were much enlarged in duty, as she undertook (and therefore the person from " me" to " we" is changed again) for before (she saith) " he brought me," &c. but now, " we will be glad," &c. The effects by way of gratitude, are in two expressions, 1. " We will rejoice and be glad in thee." And 2. " We will remember thy love more than wine :" and as she took her motive, while she desired Christ's love, from that esteem which all believers (under the title of virgins) had of it, so now, having obtained what she sought, she confirms her estimation of that enjoyment, from the experience of the same believers, under the name of " upright ;" that by such an universal testimony in both assertions, she might the more confirm her faith anent the reality of Christ's worth, seeing her esteem of him did flow from no deluded sense in her, but was built on such solid reasons, as she durst appeal to the experience of all believers, who thought Christ well worthy the loving : and so this is not only brought in here to shew the nature of believers, whose disposition inclines them natively to love Christ ; but also to shew the excellent loveliness of Christ, as an object worthy to be loved, in the conviction of all that ever knew him. The first expression holds forth a warm change upon her affections ; no sooner is she admitted into the chambers, but she crieth out, " O we will rejoice and be glad in thee." Where, 1. Ye have her exercise and frame ; it is to rejoice and be glad : cheerfulness and joy, disposing the heart to praise, are sometimes called for as well as prayer. If we look on this joy as it stands here, it says, 1. There are degrees and steps in communion with Christ ; and the saints are sometimes admitted to higher degrees thereof, than at other times : sure it is a heartsome life to be near Christ, and in his chambers. 2. This joy, and that nearness with Christ, which is the ground of it, are both often the effect of prayer, and follow upon it, when faith is in a lively way exercised in that duty. 3. That faith exercised on Christ, can make a sudden change to the better in a believer's case, Psalm xxx. 6, 7, &c. 4. That a believer should observe the changes of Christ's dispensations, the returns of their own prayer, and be suitably affected with them, whether he delay the answer, or give them a present return.

The second thing in the expression, is the subject of this joy, it is "in thee," not in corn, or wine; not in their present sense, but in him as the Author of their present comfortable condition, and as being himself their happiness, even in their greatest enjoyments, according to that word, 1. Cor. i, 31, " Let him that rejoiceth, rejoice in the Lord :" and this qualifies joy, and keeps it from degenerating into carnal delight, when he "that rejoiceth, rejoiceth in the Lord ;" and it is a good character to try such joy with, as may warrantably pass under that name of the joy of the Lord, and as will have that effect with it, to strengthen us in his way, Neh. viii. 10.

3. We may consider a twofold change of the number in the Bride's speaking, it is " we," which was " me ;" " the King brought me," (said she) but now " we" will rejoice. The reasons were given on the petition ; and further, we may add here, that it is to show her being conformed in her practice to her undertaking ; and to show that that admission of hers redounded to the good of more, and ought to take them up in praise with her. The other change of the person is, from the third to the second, from " he," the " King," to " thee," in the second person (we will rejoice in thee) which shews a holy complacency and delight, sometimes making her to speak of him, sometimes to him, yet so, as she loves to have Christ both the object and subject of her discourse, and the more he is to her, she is the more satisfied : this being another character of spiritual joy and exulting in Christ, it still makes him to be the more to them, and they are still pressing under it, to be the nearer to him.

The second effect is, " we will remember thy love more than wine." What is understood by "love" and " wine," as also, why the number is changed from the singular to the plural, hath been formerly cleared. The word " remember," doth import these three things, I. A thankful ac-

knowledgment of the favour received, and a making of it
to be remembered to his praise; this remembering is opposite to forgetting, Psalm ciii. 2, from which we may
observe two things, 1. The acknowledgment of the mercies we have received, is a necessary piece of the duty
of praise; they will never praise for a mercy, who will
not acknowledge they have received it: forgetfulness and
unbelief do much mar praise. 2. They that pray most
for any mercy, will most really praise when it is received;
and this last is a duty as well as the former, but is not
made conscience of, nor suitably performed, but by hearts
that acknowledge God's goodness to themselves. II. It
imports, a recording of this experience of God's goodness,
for her own profit for the time to come: thus every manifestation of his grace is to be kept as an experience for
afterwards, when that frame may be away, and he may
hide his face, whereupon there will follow a change in the
believer's frame: it is good keeping the impression of his
kind manifestations still upon the heart; so the Psalmist
endeavoured, Psalm cxix. 93, "I will never forget thy
precepts: for with them thou hast quickened me." III. It
imports, the doing of both these with delight, "we will
remember thy love" (saith she) "more than wine," that is,
the thoughts of Christ's love doth and shall relish more
sweetly than wine, or any comforts amongst creatures;
the very thoughts of it are, and will be so cordial and refreshful.

The last expression, "the upright love thee," is added
for comfirmation, as was said on verse 3, and may be
looked upon as brought in by way of obviating an objection. Who (might it be said to the Bride) will so rejoice
in Christ with thee? She answers, whatever the most
part of the world do, yet those who have spiritual senses,
love Christ as I do. The difference betwixt this and the
former expression, in the end of the third verse, is in two,
1. Though the persons be the same, yet she gives them
different styles; there she calls them "virgins," as being
chaste in their love, not joining themselves to idols, nor
going a whoring after creatures: here she calls them
"upright," as being sincere, neither dissemblers, nor hypocrites, but such as were really that which they appeared
to be, having a practice suitable to their profession; such
was Job, Job. i. 1. "An upright man;" such was Natha-
nael, John i. 47, "An Israelite indeed:" these have not

double ends, nor double hearts, but are straight, and may abide the touch-stone, their practice being their very heart turned outward. The other difference is in the scope: formerly they were brought in, as being desirous of Christ, as she was; here as delighted with Christ when he is enjoyed, both go together: and whoever are desirous after him, will be delighted in him, while present; and afflicted for, and affected with his absence: in both she evidenceth a suitableness in her frame to the generation of God's people, and cares not from whom she may differ, if she be conformed to them.

Observ. 1. Where there is love to Christ, there is sincerity in practice; neither is there true love to be found in any hypocrite; for, sincerity and love to Christ go together. 2. Sincerity is a characteristic of a virgin, and true believer: if we would know who are the "virgins" spoken of, verse 3; she tells us here, they are the "upright." 3. All who are sincere, or upright, come in in one category and reckoning; they are all of the same spiritual nature, or disposition, and what may be said of one of them (as to that) may be said of them all. 4. God reckons believers, not by the degree of their progress, but by the kind and nature of their walk, if it be sincere, or not; that is, if they be straight as to their ends, motives, and manner in duties, or not. 5. These characters which agree in common to believers as such, and these cases which agree with the ordinary way of all the saints in scripture, are solid, and weight may be laid upon them in concluding our sincerity, or the goodness of our state; but peculiar evidences, or singular experience, should not be leaned unto in that, as if our uprightness, or the goodness of our state, could not be made out without these, wherein possibly an hypocrite can go nearer to resemble a child of God, than in that which is more ordinary to saints as such.

Verse 5. I am black, but comely (O ye daughters of Jerusalem) as the tents of Kedar, as the curtains of Solomon.

6. Look not upon me, because I am black, because the sun hath looked upon me: my mother's children were angry with me, they made me the keeper of the vineyards; but mine own vineyard have I not kept.

In the fifth and sixth verses, we have the second piece of the Bride's first discourse, and it is the speech she hath to the "daughters of Jerusalem:" wherein, verse 5, she gives a description of herself: then verse 6, applies and clears it for some edifying use unto these beginners.

For clearing of this place, let us, 1. See, who these "daughters of Jerusalem" are. 2. What is the scope of these words. 3. What is their dependence upon, and connexion with, the former. 4. What is more particularly the meaning of them.

By "daughters of Jerusalem" in common, are certainly understood professors, members of the church; and so born in and belonging unto Jerusalem; but because there are members of several sorts, some strong, some weak, some sound, some unsound, some tender, some profane; we must inquire a little further who are meant by these "daughters of Jerusalem," they being often mentioned in this Song.

First, We look on them as distinct from "mother's children," mentioned in the following verse as a party different from the "daughters" here spoken to; and so they are not to be accounted amongst the profane, bitter heart-enemies of godliness, who yet live in the church: they are not the worst then of them that are in the visible church. 2. We take them also as distinguished from the "virgins" and "upright," who loved and delighted in Christ in the former verse. For, chap. v. 8, 9, and vi. 1, we will find them very ignorant of Christ, although they have some affection. In a word, we take them to include two sorts of professors, 1. Such as are weak and scarcely formed, yet are docile, and have respect to outward ordinances and godliness, in the practice of it: so their respect to the Bride, and the question propounded by them, chap. v. 9 doth clear. 3. They comprehend such as are formed believers, really honest, and who have some sound beginnings, yet mixed with much weakness, ignorance and infirmity, and so not come up the length of grown Christians; such who need milk, and cannot endure strong meat; so their question and undertaking, chap. vi. 1, doth evidence: they were daughters, while yet they were really very ignorant of Christ, and were ready to provoke him before he pleased, (as the often repeated charge the Bride gives them throughout this Song imports) and they were daughters still, even after they were something better taught and engaged. We find, 1 John ii. 13, the apostle speaks of three sorts, 1. "Fathers," that are grown

believers, rich in experience, such we esteem to be understood by the Bride in this Song. 2. " Young men," who
are strong well advanced believers, such were the virgins
and upright here made mention of. A third sort are styled
" little children," that is, some who (as it were) are yet on
the breasts, and that in knowledge, practice, or experience,
had not come to a consistence, or to have their senses exercised to know good or evil, as it is, Heb. v. 14, such we
account these " daughters of Jerusalem," and so may comprehend under them professors, who stand not in the way
of their own edification, though they be weak.

2. The scope of her discourse to them, is to prevent
their stumbling at the cross, or being deterred from godliness, because of any blackness, or spots that were to be
seen in her ; it being a great stumbling to weak professors, to see sufferings accompanying tenderness (especially when it is persecuted, and pursued by professors of the
same truth) as also to see infirmities and sinful blemishes
in persons eminently godly ; now her scope is, for their
edification, to condescend to satisfy them in both.

3. The reason why she breaks in with this discourse
upon the back of the former (which shows the connexion)
may be twofold, 1. To remove an objection that might
be made, if any should say, what needs all this rejoicing ?
are ye not both stained with sin, and blackened with sufferings ? she answers by a distinction, granting that in
part she was black, and that was truth, yet that blackness
was not inconsistent with comeliness, which she clears,
and that therefore she might in part rejoice also. The
other way that this depends on the former, is, that she
may further her project of engaging others to rejoice
with her, she endeavours to remove these two occasions
of stumbling (taken from the failings and sufferings of
the godly) out of the way of weak professors, that she
may get them along with her : and so it agrees well
with the scope.

More particularly consider the. words, wherein she
endeavours to satisfy these doubts, and ye will find
these things in them, 1. She concedes what is truth. 2.
Qualifies it by a distinction. 3. Illustrates it. And
these three in the 5th verse. 4. In verse 6, she applies it. And 5, more particularly explicates it. 1. then
(saith she) I answer, by conceding what is truth, " I am
black," both with crosses and corruptions ; that cannot be

denied. 2. She qualifies her concession, though I be
black yet I am comely, that is, I am not universally, or
altogether unlovely, mine estate is mixed, being made up
of crosses and comforts, corruptions and graces, beauty
and blackness. 3. She illustrates this description of herself, or her mixed condition, by two similitudes, both
tending to one thing, or one of them tending to set forth
her blackness, the other her beauty, I am (saith she) like
" the tents of Kedar" which were blackish and of no great
value, being, by those who lived in them, so frequently
transported in such hot countries ; this sets forth her
blackness. The second similitude is, that she was like
the " curtains of Solomon :" he built glorious dwellings,
and being a rich king, no question had rich hangings ;
this sets forth her beauty ; as if she would say, Ye must
not judge of my worth from one side, especially my out-
side, or upon one consideration, for I have in me both to
humble and comfort me. It may be also, though these
tents of Kedar were not outwardly beautiful, yet they
were within well furnished ; and that the curtains of Solomon which were most rich, had outer-coverings of smaller
value, as the tabernacle had of badgers' skins ; and so
the similitudes illustrate her condition, and set out the
thing more to the life. As Kedar's tents (saith she) look
poor and base like, yet if ye look within, they are glorious ; so think not strange, if I appear without beauty to
the eye, there may be, yea, there is comeliness within, if
ye could discern it, for " within the king's daughter is all
glorious," Psalm xlv. 13, which way of distinguishing, is
a notable piece of spiritual wisdom and learning, and a
great means of peace in ourselves ; when what is true of
infirmities is acknowledged, and yet the conclusion that
tentation would infer is denied. Here observe, 1. The
conditions of believers, even the best of them are mixed
of good and ill, sin and grace, comfortable privileges and
sad sufferings. 2. There is a mixture of blackness in believers' beauty even in their best frame and condition, for
she is now in the king's chamber, and yet we find her
saying, " I am black." 3. Believers, if they would consider what they are rightly, would look on themselves
as having contraries in them. 4. Where challenges
are just and well grounded, they should be acknowledged and taken with. 5. It is wisdom so to acknowledge our sin, as we may difference it from any work of

God's grace in us.   6. Believers, their observing of their sinfulness, should not make them deny their grace ; and their observing their grace, should not make them forget their sinfulness.   7. The cross that follows godliness, or the stain and spot that is on a godly person, is sooner taken notice of by onlookers, than either the advantages that follow holiness, or the graces and spiritual beauty of holy persons; this makes it needful to remove this offence. 8. When it may be edifying, believers should assert the worth and beauty of holiness, and their own comeliness thereby, as well as confess their own infirmities ; and Christian communion will require both.

Having illustrated her answer, in the fourth place she applies it, verse 6, " Look not upon me" (saith she) " because I am black," seeing I am comely as well as black : look not on me only as such, and think it not strange that I am so : looking here, implieth indignation and disdain. And so, " look not," is here to be taken, 1. As being a caveat against indignation or disdain : "look not," &c. that is, disdain me not as if nothing desirable were in me; for sin often waiting on the affliction of God's people, obscures the beauty of grace, and makes them to be disdained and undervalued in the world.   2. This " look not," is a caution to dissuade them from gazing, or curious wondering at any cross that was on her, or sin that was in her : it should not be the object of their curiosity, much less of their delight or contentment to see it so, Obadiah 12.   It is condemned in Edom, " thou shouldst not have looked upon the day of thy brother." Next, while she saith, " look not upon me, because I am black," she doth not dissuade them from looking on her blackness simply, but from looking only on it ; that should not be the alone ground of their search into their condition, but they should take notice of what good was in her as well as what was wrong : so then her blackness should not be the only cause of their looking on her, it should not be their work to ask after her crosses and infirmities, and no more ; this she supposes may affright and terrify them : and so it is implied here, that on-lookers often pore more on believers' infirmities, than on their graces ; and this is the fruit which follows, they procure a stumbling and a fall to themselves.

4. In the rest of the 6th verse, she doth more fully explicate her answer, in so far as concerned her blackness,

(for so the words run in this 6th verse) two ways, 1. In setting out her sufferings in general. 2. In a more particular distribution of the kind and occasions of her seeming unloveliness. Generally her sad condition is expressed in these words, " the sun hath looked upon me." The sun in those countries had great heat, as we see in Jonah iv. 8, where the beating of the sun upon him did sore vex him ; Jacob also says, it burnt him in the day-time, Gen. xxxi. 40, Therefore, Matt. xiii. 6, 21, the Lord expresseth persecution under the similitude of the scorching heat of the sun. Here the meaning is (as if she had said) it is no marvel I be black, I have been made obnoxious to all sorts of persecution, and therefore can have no outward beauty, but must be in the eyes of the world contemptible, even as one cannot endure the hot sun-beams and not be blackened. So there are in this expression these things imported, 1. Persecution. 2. Vehement persecution. 3. Visible effects following it, she is thereby made black. 4. A continuance under it. So the sun's looking on her, till she be made black imports. 5 There is her patient enduring of it. 6. There is her sense of it. Yet, 7. She is not ashamed of it, while she shews this her suffering to be no cause, why others should stumble at her.

Afterward, she proceeds more particularly, to describe, first her sufferings, then her infirmities. She describes her sufferings, 1. In the instruments of them. 2. The cause of them. 3. The nature of them. The actors are not heathens, but " mother's children ;" the visible church is the common mother, who hath children born after the flesh, as well as after the Spirit ; these children are professors of the same truth, but really not only strangers, but heart-enemies to godliness, and true tenderness ; such was Ishmael, and such are all unrenewed persons, who are children of the flesh, and such there will be (Gal. iv. 29) so long as there is a church visible : such instruments the apostle complains of, 2 Cor. xi. 26, that he had perils from false brethren within, as well as from strangers without. This is not only mentioned to shew there are such enemies, but to set out more fully the church's strait ; she is often more bitterly, and more subtilly persecuted by those who are called Christians or professors of the gospel, than by heathens themselves.

2. The cause of her sufferings, as from men, is " they were angry with me," (saith she ;) she had not done them

any personal wrong (as David often asserts of himself, in the like case) though she was not free of sin against God; but it proceeded from a malicious, malignant disposition of the natural men of the world, who, as they hate Christ, so do they hate all that are his, John xv. 18, 19, accounting them as the off-scourings of all men, and troublers of the world continually, upon no other ground, but because they are not such themselves, and because God hath chosen them out of the world. This shews both the causelessness of their persecution, as also the degree of bitterness that it did proceed from. From which, *Observ.* 1. There are no such bitter enemies unto a godly person, as a graceless malignant professor : see Isa. lxvi. 5. 2. No sort of persecution doth blacken, or obscure the beauty of an honest believer so much, as the foul, bitter reproaches of malignant professors. Yet, 3. Believers are often even under that cross. And 4. The best beloved believer, even Christ's Bride, will not in the world eschew it; innocency will be no guard, but to the conscience within. And if the Bridegroom himself, while he was in the world, did not escape it, the Bride cannot think to go free.

3. The nature of her sufferings is expressed thus, "they made me the keeper of the vineyards." That this implies suffering, and no trust put on her, the scope and her complaint make it clear : besides that it is given as the evidence of the hatred and malice of these persecutors. This general expression then, being compared with other scriptures, will import these ingredients in her suffering, which occasioned her blackness. 1. That her suffering was heavy and painful; for it was a great drudgery, to be put to keep the vineyards; to be made keeper, was to watch both night and day, and so no wonder she was scorched. Matt. xx. 11. The bearing burdens in the vineyard, in "the heat of the day," is spoken of as the greatest weight, and heaviest piece of their work. 2. That her suffering was reproachful; for, the keeping of the vineyards was a base and contemptible service, therefore it is said. Jer. lii. 16, that the poor, who were not taken notice of, were left to dress the vines; and it is a promise, Isa. lxi. 5, that his people should have freedom from that drudgery, and strangers should be employed in it for them. 3. That her sufferings occasioned sad distractions to her in the worship and service of God; for, in scripture sometimes, vine-dressing is opposed to the

worshipping of God, as a distracting, diverting exercise,
which is very afflicting to God's people : therefore when
they have a promise of more immediate access to God's
worship, it is said, they shall be liberated from such diverting employments, Isa. lxi. 5, 6, and instead of these,
they shall get another task, to wit, to " be priests to the
Lord, and ministers of our God," as if these exercises
were somewhat inconsistent together, and so she opposeth
her own proper duty to this, in the next words ; in a
word, these malignant brethren procured her pain, shame,
and distraction from the service of God, as much as they
could, and in a great part prevailed.

Observ. 1. Malice in rotten professors against godliness, will sometimes come to a great height. 2. Malice
in wicked men thinks nothing of true tenderness, or of
those who truly are so ; but esteems them, and useth them
as if they were base and vile. 3. Often in outward things,
the profanest members of the church have the pre-
eminence ; and the most godly, as to these things, are in
the meanest and basest condition ; so as sometimes, they
appoint the godly as their slaves, to their work. 4. Often
while wicked professors are in power, the truly godly are
under affliction.

Though this suffering was sharp, yet she resents her
sinful infirmities much more sadly, in the words following,
" But" (saith she heavily) " mine own vineyard have I
not kept :" and this her slothfulness and unwatchfulness
made her black, and also procured the blackness that was
on her by her sufferings. This part of the verse implies,
1. The Bride's privilege. 2. Her duty. 3. Her sin.
4. Her sense of it. 1. Her privilege is, she hath a
vineyard of her own, besides these she was put to keep.
The similitude of a vineyard here, is to be taken in another sense than in the former expression : neither are we
to think strange of this, seeing similitudes are to be in-
terpreted according to the different scope of expressions,
and places in which they are used. By " vineyard" then
here, is to be understood the particular privileges, graces
and talents of any sort, which are given of God to a believer : these are the things she should have watched
over ; the neglecting thereof, brings blackness on her,
and procures heavy challenges, called a " vineyard" here ;
and also, chap. viii. 13, partly, because there are many
several graces to be found in believers, as plants planted

in them ; partly, because these will furnish them matter
of continual exercise and labour ; and partly, because
what they have, they are to improve, that there may
be fruit on them, and rent brought in to the master that
intrusted them, chap. viii. 12, 13. This vineyard is
called hers, because the special oversight and charge
of it was committed to her. 2. Her duty is to keep and
watch over this vineyard, that is, to improve the talents
she hath gotten, to see that no plants be unfruitful, and
that no hurt from any cause inward, or outward annoy
them : Christianity or godliness, is no idle talk, every
privilege hath a duty waiting on it. 3. Her sin is, that
what with other diversions, and what from her own unwatchfulness, she had neglected the keeping of this vineyard ; so that this one task which was put in her hand,
she had not discharged ; but laziness came on, and the
vineyard was not dressed, thorns and nettles grew, and
tentations brake in, and this marred her fruitfulnes : in a
word, she was no way answerable to the trust that was
put on her by Christ. 4. She resents this : where these
things may be taken notice of, 1. She sees it, and observes
it. 2. She acknowledges it. 3. She is sensible of it, and
weighted with it as the greatest piece of her affliction.
It is ill to be unwatchful, for that may draw on both
fruitlessness and heaviness on a believer ; but it is good to
observe and be affected with it, and to be walking under
the sense of it, even in our most joyful frame, such as hers
was here.

Here then, *Observe*, 1. Believers have a painful laborious task of duty committed to them. 2. They may much
neglect this work and task wherewith they are intrusted.
3. Neglect and sloth make the weeds to grow in their
vineyard, and the building which they ought to keep up,
to drop thorough. 4. It is not unsuitable, or unprofitable
for believers, in their most refreshing conditions and
frames, sadly to remember their former unwatchfulness,
and to be suitably affected therewith. 5. Believers should
be well acquainted at home, how it stands with them as to
their own condition and state. 6. They who are best
versed in their own condition, will find most clearly the
cause of all their hurt to be in themselves ; whatever is
wrong in their case, themselves have the only guilty hand
in it.

If any should ask, how makes this last part of the verse

for her scope, in removing the offence before these weak
beginners? I answer, it doth it well: for, saith she,
there is no reason ye should stumble, or be troubled because of my afflictions, they were without cause, as to men,
though I am under much sin and guilt before God: neither scare at godliness or joy in Christ, because of my infirmities; for, these spots came from mine own unwatchfulness, and not from godliness in itself (which is the soul's
special beauty) therefore take warning from my slips, and
study to prevent the bringing on of such a stain and blot
upon your profession, by security and negligence; but
esteem not the less, but the more of Christ, his people and
ways, and the beauty of holiness, which is to be seen in
them, because by my unwatchfulness and untenderness,
I have marred this beauty in myself, and that is the reason
I look so deformed-like.

Verse 7. Tell me (O thou whom my soul loveth) where thou
feedest, where thou makest thy flock to rest at noon: for
why should I be as one that turneth aside by the flocks of
thy companions?

In the seventh verse, we have the third part of the
Bride's first speech; in which she turneth herself from
the daughters to the Bridegroom; and the scope of what
she speaks here, is, that by applying herself by prayer
and faith to Christ Jesus (who is, and whom she for comfort acknowledges to be, the great and good Shepherd of
his sheep, John x. 11,) she may be guarded against the
hurtful effects of those two evils which she acknowledged
in the former verse, viz. afflictions and sinful infirmities; in respect of the one, she desires Christ's guiding;
and in respect of the other, his consolation; that so
she being under his charge, may be upheld by him, and
kept from miscarrying: that this is the scope, and so depends upon the former verse, especially the last part of
it, will be clear by comparing the last part of this verse,
and the last part of the former together. There are these
three in it, 1. The title given to Christ. 2. The petition, or thing sought. 3. The argument whereby it is
enforced.

1. The title is a sweet and affectionate one, " O thou
whom my soul loveth." In this title these things are implied, 1. A loveliness in Christ, and such a soul-affecting

and ravishing loveliness, as no creature-beauty hath, or can have. 2. An ardent and vehement love in her towards him, so that she might say, her soul loved, honoured, desired, and esteemed him. 3. A disrelishing of all things besides Christ, as nothing; he is the only object her soul loves, he alone hath her heart, and is in the throne as chief in her affections, and hath no allowed co-partner there, to whom this title may be applied. 4. It is implied, what title Christ will best accept of, even that which bears out most affection to him; there can be no greater honour, or more acceptable piece of respect put on him by a believer, than this, to own him, and avow him as the only object of his soul's love; as the Bride doth here, "O thou whom my soul loveth!"

2. The thing that is here sought by the Bride, is set down in two petitions, meeting with the two-fold strait she was in, viz. of crosses and infirmities; and because fear of sin weighted her most, she begins with the suit that might guard against that, and in the reason presseth it most. The first petition then is, "tell me where thou feedest," (thy flock,) for "feeding" here, is to be understood actively, that is, where he feeds others: and not passively (as in other places) where he feeds and delights himself. The second petition is, "Tell me where thou makest thy flock to rest at noon:" that is, make me know where and how thou comfortest and refreshest thy people, under scorching persecutions and trials: so these petitions go upon the relation that is between Christ and his people, of shepherd and flock, which is frequent in scripture. In sum, that which she seeks, is this, thou who guidest all thine, as a shepherd doth a flock, let me know how thou orderest thy people, and carriest them through in times of snares, and where thou refreshest them in times of trouble: these being the two great duties of a shepherd, are well performed by Christ. 1. It is his work to feed them, and lead them in wholesome and safe pastures, Psalm xxiii. And, 2. To give them quiet and cool resting places in the time of heat, when the sun becomes scorching; and therefore prayeth she to him, seeing thou dost both these to thine, let me know the right way of partaking of the benefit of thy care. Which two petitions imply, 1. That there is a near relation betwixt Christ and all believers; he is the Shepherd, and they the flock, Isa. xl. 11; Ezek. xxxiv. 11, 12;

Psalm xxiii. 1, 2. 2. That Christ's flock may be, yea, usually are in hazard both of sin or straying, and also of affliction. 3. That Christ Jesus is tender of his people, in reference to any hazard they are in of sin or suffering; he is "the good Shepherd," John x. 11, " He carries the lambs in his bosom," Isa. xl. 11. " He stands and feeds his flock," Mic. v. 4. 4. That he hath resting places, and shadows for refreshing and hiding his people, in all the storms and heats they may meet with. 5. That believers sometimes under straits, may not know well how either to rid themselves out of temptations, or to quiet themselves under crosses, till he help them with light and strength : they cannot know the well whence their supply and consolation cometh, till it be discovered, as it was to Hagar. 6. That even then, when they know not how to be guarded against sin, and shadowed under suffering, Christ knows both, and hath help in both these cases provided for them. 7. That as it is he who must guide them in snares, and support them in sufferings ; so believers, when they are at their own wit's end in respect of both, ought even then to look for help and direction in these from him.

3. The reason presseth for his guiding, with a great weight ; "for why" (saith she) "should I be as one that turneth aside, by the flocks of thy companions ?" in which these things are implied, 1. That Christ may have companions, (not who are indeed so, but) such who set themselves up equally beside him, and make it their design to have others to follow them, but do not follow Christ themselves ; thus heretics, false Christs, Matt. xxiv. 23, 24, lusts, idols, or whatever is equalled or preferred to Christ, and not subjected to him, is made, as it were, his companion : sure, the scope shews, they were not friendly companions ; but it speaks the nature of corrupt men, who are seducers, and the sin of seduced people, that the one seek to themselves, and the other attributes to them, too much. 2. That these companions may have flocks, and many followers, even as our Lord Jesus hath, so Matt. xxiv. 23 ; 2. Peter ii. 1, &c. 3. That believers, if not by Christ's care prevented, may go astray after some of these companions, and throng on in a way of error and defection with them. 4. That believers will be afraid of this ill, and also sensible of their own proneness to it. 5. It imports an abhorrence and indigna-

tion at that evil, of being carried away a whoring from Christ, " why" (saith she) " should I be," &c. ?   6. She accounts it a great mercy to be kept in Christ's way, and makes it a main piece of her prayer, that this may be granted to her as her mercy.   7. She exercises faith on Christ, and vents her requests by prayer to him, concerning every thing she wants ; be wanting what will, she betakes herself to him, for the obtaining of it.   8. Where there is a loathness to go astray, or fall into snares, it will stir up to serious wrestling with Christ to prevent it.   9. Hazard of sin to believers, (who are sensible of their inclination to go astray) and weakness to hold on in God's way, is a great motive, that being made use of in prayer, hath much weight for obtaining direction, and an hearing from Christ ; as it is a notable spur to stir up to pray seriously, " for" (saith she) "why should I be," &c. which speaketh forth her indignation against every wrong way, and her expectation, that if any thing prevailed with him, that would ; and so we will find her success in this suit, to follow in the next words.

PART II.—CHRIST'S WORDS.

Verse 8.   If thou know not (O thou fairest among women) go thy way forth by the footsteps of the flock, and feed thy kids beside the shepherds' tents.

From the 8th verse to the 12th, follows Christ's express return to her former suit ; and because it is he that speaks, we take it up as the second part of the chapter. In the **Bride's** condition there was, 1. Crosses and afflictions. **2. Sins** and infirmities. 3. Snares and hazard of new failings. Now Christ so frames his answer, as he may meet with all her necessities most comfortably and lovingly ; and because she was most affected with the fear of sin, he answers that first : and so he doth, 1. In order to her being guided against snares, give a direction for her duty, verse 8. 2. In order to her consolation under her suffering, and the sense of her failings, he commends her, verse 9, 10. 3. He gives her a promise, in order to her further consolation, verse 11.   The scope of all is, to comfort her ; and every part of the answer being from Christ's mouth, may be effectual for that end.

In the direction, verse 8. there is, 1. The title he gives her. 2. The directions themselves, which are two. 3. A supposition, or ground upon which he gives them.

1. The title he gives her is, " O thou fairest among women", which is much from Christ to the Bride, who immediately before styled herself black: believers who are humble under the sense of their own infirmities, are nevertheless highly esteemed by Christ; nor are always his thoughts of believers as theirs are of themselves; nay, by the contrary, blushing at their own deformity, is a chief part of their beauty. The giving her this title, implies these three things, 1. A real worth in a believer, beyond the most noble person in the world. 2. A real respect unto, and esteem that Christ hath of them, which he hath of none other. 3. Wonderful tenderness, condescending for her consolation, to intimate these his thoughts of her to herself, now when she was otherwise sadly afflicted, and under a double distress.

If it be asked, how these excellent titles and commendations may be applied to a sinful believer. *Answ.* These four ways, 1. By communication and participation of the divine nature, they have a stamp of the Spirit of holiness imparted to them, whereby they resemble God, 2 Peter i. 4, and none other in the world can compare with them in this. 2. In respect of the imputation of Christ's righteousness, wherewith they are adorned, and which they have put on, which makes them very glorious and lovely, so that they are beautiful beyond all others, through his comeliness put upon them. 3. In respect of Christ's gracious acceptation, whereby he doth esteem otherwise of them than of the most royal and beautiful in the world, they find such favour in his eyes. 4. In respect of his design, project and purchase ; she is so, and to be made so in end ; he will have his people made completely beautiful and spotless, before he have done with them, Eph. v. 26. " Without spot and wrinkle :" all which are peculiar to a believer, of whom glorious things are spoken and written, which are applicable to none other.

2. The directions are two. Wouldst thou know, saith he, how to be kept out of snares? then 1. Look how the old worthies walked, and follow their way. 2. Have respect to the public ordinances, and hold near them, that you may have direction from the word, by these to whom I have committed the trust of dispensing the same : I have (saith

he) no new light to give you, nor any new way to heaven
to shew you, nor any new means, ordinances, or officers to
send amongst you, nor yet must ye expect immediate re-
velations ; but walk in the light that shines to you, by the
preaching of the word by my ministers, who are the under shepherds, which I have set over you : for thus I
guide all by my counsel, whom I afterward receive to glory.

The first direction (" go thy way forth by the footsteps
of the flock") holds forth, 1. That all believers, of old and
late, are of one flock, of one common concernment, and
under the care of one chief Shepherd : this is the flock
spoken of, verse 7, whereof Christ is Shepherd. 2. That
there is but one way to heaven, for the substantials of
faith and godliness, in which they that went before have
walked, and these that follow after must walk in the same
way, if ever they think to come there. 3. That there are
many in all ages, whom God hath helped in trying times
to keep in his way, and have been carried well through all
difficulties to heaven. 4. That believers should observe
these beyond others, as being especially worthy of imitation. 5. That they should, and may follow the commendable practices of believers in former times, and not affect
singularity. 6. That it is commendable, and often safe
in times when new opinions and doctrines bear sway, to
follow their way, who we are sure went before us to
heaven, Heb. xiii. 7 ; 1 Thess. ii. 14 ; Heb. vi. 14. This
imitation of others, is to be limited with that necessary
caution, in so far as the practice of others agrees with the
first pattern, Christ, 1 Cor. xi. 1. In a word, this direction shews there is no way, but the good old way to be
asked for, and followed in the most declining times, Jer.
vi. 16, and that we should keep the very print of their
steps, studying to be followers of their faith, who have
been honourably carried through before us.

The second direction puts them to the right use and
improvement of the ministry of the word, which he will
have them to respect ; "feed thy kids beside the shepherds' tents." Shepherds here in the plural number, are
the servants of that one Shepherd, whose own the sheep
are : so ministers are called often shepherds, or pastors,
both in the Old and New Testament, 1. Because of their
relation to Christ, by whom they are intrusted to feed his
sheep ; he is the owner, they are but shepherds, Ezek.
xxxiv. 2. Because of their relation to the flock, which

is committed to their care, and for which they must give an account, Heb. xiii. 17. 3. Because of the nature of their charge, as being assiduous, difficult, and tenderly to be gone about; for, such is the work and care of a shepherd, as we may see by what Jacob speaks of himself, when he had the charge of Laban's flock, Gen. xxxi. 40. 4. To shew the necessity of that ordinance. And 5. The respect people ought to have to them who are over them in the Lord: no flock needs a shepherd more than a congregation needs a minister ; people without labourers, being like sheep without a shepherd, Matt. ix. 36, under a sad necessity of wandering and being lost.   Next, " shepherds' tents" are mentioned, with allusion to these parts where shepherds in the wilderness carried tents about with them ; and so to be near the tent, was to be near the shepherd : it is like they kept lambs and kids nearest unto their tents, because they needed more oversight than the rest of the flock ; for a lamb to be at its liberty in a large place, was dangerous, Hosea iv. 16.   By "kids," we understand young, unexperienced believers or professors, whereby it is clear, 1. That there are kids and young ones in Christ's flock.   Yea, 2. That the strongest believers, even the Bride, have their own infirmities ; and there are some particulars wherein they are weak : for this direction is given to the Bride, as a particular and experienced believer ; and seeing ordinarily weak believers are called lambs, and unrenewed men goats, it may be kids here are mentioned to point at the relics of sinful nature, even in believers, which is the reason why they need still oversight. 3. It is clear, that the office of the ministry, is a standing, perpetual, and necessary office in the church, otherwise this direction would not always satisfy the believer's question here proposed.   4. The strongest believers, have need and use of a ministry.   5. It is a great part of a minister's charge, to keep believers right in snaring and seducing times, Eph. iv. 12, 13, &c.   6. Believers should make use of public ordinances, and Christ's ministers, especially in reference to snares and errors ; and they should take their directions from them, and in their difficulties consult with them, and their counsel should be laid weight upon.   7. Allowed dependence on a ministry, is a great means to keep souls from error ; whereas on the contrary, when no weight is laid on a ministry, unstable souls are hurried away.   8. Christ hath given no immediate, or extraordinary way to be sought unto and made use of, even by his Bride, in her difficulties; but the great means he will have her to make use of, is a sent ministry, and therefore no other is to be expected: it is no wonder therefore the devil (when his design is to cry down truth and spread error) seeks to draw the Lord's people from the shepherds' tents; and no wonder souls, who once do cast off respect to their overseers, be hurried away with the temptations of the times, as in experience hath often been found a truth. 9. Ministers should have a special eye on the weakest of the flock, their care should be that the kids may be next them; our blessed Lord doth so, when the lambs are carried in his own bosom, Isa. xl. 11. And therefore, seeing weak believers have most need of Christ's oversight, if they begin to slight the ministry and ordinances, they cannot but be a ready prey; and the devil hath gained much of his intent when he hath once gained that. O that men would try whose voice that is, that saith, come back from the shepherds' tents (when Christ says, abide near them.) It is as if a wolf would desire the lambs to come out from under the shepherd's eye: and lastly, when Christ gives this direction to his own Bride, we may see he allows none to be above ordinances in the militant church; it will be soon enough then, when they are brought to heaven, and put above the reach of seducers.

3. The supposition is in these words, " If thou know not," &c. which is not any upbraiding answer, but tendeth to insinuate the direction the more; I have given you means (saith he) and so he puts her back to the serious use of these, as he sent Paul, Acts ix. to Ananias, to have his mind made known by him: which implies, 1. That a believer may be in many things ignorant. 2. That Christ pities the ignorant, and hath compassion on them who are out of the way, or in hazard to go out of the way, Heb. v. 3. That believers should not in praying to Christ, neglect the ordinary means in seeking knowledge: nor in using them, neglect him: she prays to him, and he directs her in them. 4. Directions for a believer's walk, given by Christ's ministers from his word, are his own, and are accounted by him as if he did immediately speak them himself. 5. Christ would have his ministry and ordinances kept up in esteem and request amongst his people: therefore, he will not be particular in giving

answer to his Bride, but sends her to them, that she might know the usefulness of them, and learn to know his mind from them. 6. They cannot expect to make great progress in religion that neglect the ministry, seeing it is to them that Christ recommends his own Bride ; if people were enquiring at Christ, what should they do now in a time, when temptations to error and defection abound ? no other answer were to be expected, than what he gives to his Bride here : yea, if Abraham were entreated to send some from the dead, to advise people to abhor profanity and error : his answer would be, they have Moses and the prophets, they shall have no other, and no other would prevail, if these ordinances do not : people should conscientiously, and thriftily use the means and light they have ; for, it is by such the Lord trains his own Bride : and though he will admit her as a courtier to his chamber, yet this familiarity he admits her to, is in the use of ordinances, and he will have no believer above ordinances and need of ministers, while he keeps them within the compass of snares.

Verse 9.   I have compared thee, O my love, to a company of horses in Pharaoh's chariots.

10.   Thy cheeks are comely with rows of jewels, thy neck with chains of gold.

The commendation follows, verses 9, 10, in which the Bridegroom hath respect to two things, which afflicted her most in her condition, 1.   That she was in hazard to be a prey to every sin, and to every enemy. 2. That she lay under many blots, and was made black by her own miscarriages ; therefore the Lord, that he might comfort her against those, is brought in speaking thus ; thou art neither so weak, nor so black and unbeautiful as the world thinks thee, and as thou esteems of thyself; my testimony of thee is better to be believed, than either the world's, or thy own ; and I assert thee to be stately and strong, beautiful and comely.

1. verse 9.   He sets out her stateliness, strength and courage, by a similitude taken from horses, are (saith he) horses stately and strong? for so in Job is the horse described, chap. xxxix. 19, 20, &c.   And is not a company of them much more stately, especially a company of Egyptian horses, which were the best in the world? 2

Chron. i. 17; Isa. xxxi. 1. And if any in Egypt were beyond others, certainly Pharaoh the king had such in his own chariots. Now (saith he) if these be lovely, strong and stately, then thou art so; for, "I have compared thee" to such: this expression, "I have compared thee," bears out the confirmation of the assertion; for, it is not men that thinks thee so, but I who know where true worth is, and who can be surety for my own assertion, I have said thou art as strong as these. I have likened thee to them, and made thee like them. This holds forth these things, 1. That there is an excellent courage and boldness, wherewith the believer is furnished beyond others, he is bold as a lion, Prov. xxviii. 1, both in duties and sufferings. 2. That there is in believers an undauntedness of spirit, and an unconquerableness, that overcome they cannot be; better fight with all Pharaoh's chariots, than with them, Zech. xii.; Rev. xii. 3. The words hold out, that there is an infallible certainty in this truth; we have here Christ's verdict of it, he in his reckoning counts believers so, and he cannot be mistaken. 4. There is the cause, why the Bride is so strong and stately, he makes her so: and so these words "I have compared thee," may be taken efficiently, I have made thee comparable, or made thee to be like them; and there is an article in the original, which may confirm this, and the words may be turned, like my company of horses, or of my horses; which shews that, as believers themselves are Christ's, so also, whatever stock of spiritual strength and courage they have, it is his, and from him: and that they are Christ's and made use of by him, shews the use of their strength, Micah iv. 13, and so, Zech. x. 3, they are called my "goodly horse." 5. It implies this, that it becomes not believers to droop, faint, or be discouraged under difficulties, seeing he hath past such a sentence, or given such a verdict of them; it is a reflecting on him, as if it were not so with them as he affirms, or as if he did bear false testimony concerning them. Now this courage, strength, and boldness which is here attributed to believers, is to be understood of that which is competent to them peculiarly as believers; and their success in all their spiritual conflicts, is still to be looked upon with respect to the event, which is ever to be more than conquerors, in the issue at least, whatever appears for the present.

The second part of the commendation is, verse 10.

Wherein her comeliness and beautiful adorning is set out: though thou think thyself black (saith he) yet, " thy cheeks are comely with rows of jewels," and " thy neck with chains of gold :" what is meant by neck, or cheeks, or chains, or rows of jewels, we think not necessary to be particularly inquired into ; the allusion is to women, who in those places, by such ornaments used to be adorned; and possibly there is here also an allusion to the horses of great ones, who are said to have chains of gold about their necks, Judges viii. 26.

The scope and sum of the verse may be taken up in these things, 1. That though the Bride have some infir- mities, yet there is exceeding great comeliness and love- liness to be seen in her, she is said to be comely, and that out of Christ's own mouth : certainly grace puts much real beauty upon the person that hath it. 2. That she hath more ornaments than one, there are here jewels in the plural number, and chains of gold also; one grace goes never alone, neither is imputed righteousness and sanctification ever separate ; who ever hath one grace, hath all. 3. That this beauty which is to be seen on be- lievers, is universal, as to the subject ; for, here one part of the body is adorned, as well as another, both neck and cheeks ; the whole man is renewed, and the person is justified. 4. This comeliness grows not of any stock within the believer, nor is it natural to him, but it is com- municated, or imparted beauty, such as is put on ; a come- liness proceeding from the beneficence of another, and is the work of a cunning workman. See Ezek. xvi. 10, 11, where similitudes, like these in this text are made use of.

Verse 11. We will make thee borders of gold, with studs of silver.

In the 11th verse for confirming of the former consola- tion, he gives her a promise ; the scope whereof is to ob- viate an objection which jealous sense might make against what he hath said : how shall beauty be obtained, or con- tinued, might she say ? whence shall it come, seeing I am so black and loathsome ? to this he answers, as it were, by a sweet promise, " we will make," &c. Wherein we may consider, 1. The thing promised, it is "borders of gold" and " studs of silver." 2. The party promising, and undertaking the performance of it : " we will make" them to thee, saith he.

Borders of gold and studs of silver, (it is like) have been some special ornaments in these days, and that which is here pointed at by them, in general seems to be an addition to what formerly the Bride possessed, he would add to her beauty, and gloriously complete it : and certainly it must be an excellent work ; which needs such workers as are here spoken of. We take the thing promised, to comprehend the increase, continuance and perfecting of her comeliness and beauty ; in which work the blessed Trinity are engaged : and so, the second thing is, who undertakes it. "We will make thee" saith the Bridegroom ; this word make, in the original is used for making of man at first, Gen. i. 26. As also, for renewing of him, and begetting holiness in him, Psalm c. because it is no less work to renew, than to create man. The number here is changed from the singular, I have compared, &c. verse 9, to the plural, we will, &c. As it is also in the first making of man, from the singular, " He made" heaven and earth, to the plural, "let us make man according to our image ;" as if the Holy Ghost, purposely in mentioning this renewing-work of grace, did allude to the first work of man's creation. And this, 1. To show the excellency of it, not that God was put to any deliberation, but that the work was and is, exceeding excellent, and therefore deliberately as it were gone about. 2. To show, that man hath no more hand in his renovation than in his first creation, that is, he is no more of himself able to bring about the one than the other. By this "we," we do not understand God speaking of himself in the plural number, as in some languages, for honour's cause, kings do of themselves : for, 1. If that were more honourable, then it would have always been used for God's honour, especially at solemn times, such as when the law was given ; but we find the contrary true from the scripture. 2. Although that manner of speaking be used in some other languages, yet it is never so used in the Hebrew tongue (as by those who understand it, is asserted, and by some of the most learned Jews is acknowledged) and therefore we understand the Trinity of persons in one God-head to be here understood ; for, this one is also three, the Father, Son and Spirit, having a joint design in promoving the salvation of the elect, Isa. lxi. 1, 2. And grace being a work, and gift prayed for, from them all, Rev. i. 4, 5, it must be understood of these three blessed persons of the Holy Trinity, this work being common to the three persons of the Godhead, and communicable to no other. This then makes the consolation strong: for, saith Christ, although the perfecting of your grace be a great task, and far above your reach, yet fear not, we the Father, Son, and Spirit have undertaken it, and shall make it out to you.

Hence we may learn, 1. That grown believers, even the Bride, hath need of more grace and spiritual comeliness; there is a necessity of looking after a further growth in those, even to be transchanged from glory to glory, 2 Cor. iii. *ult.* 2. That growing in grace, and perseverance therein, is a great consolation and comfort to a true believer; and therefore the promise of it is given to the Bride for that end here. 3. That neither growth in grace, nor perseverance therein, is a work of the believer's own working, but the omnipotency of grace is exercised here. 4. There is plurality of persons in the one Godhead; the Godhead, that is, " I," is also " we." 5, All the persons of the blessed Trinity concur, and are engaged in promoving the holiness, and in perfecting the beauty of a believer. 6. All the graces of a believer are pieces of the workmanship of the Holy Trinity: grace then must be an excellent thing. 7. The perfecting and perseverance of a believer is infallibly sure and certain, seeing all the persons of the Godhead are engaged in this work; and they who this day are believers, may promise this to themselves. 8. Much of believers' beauty is yet in the promise, and in the perfecting, so that it hath its defects and imperfections while they are here. 9. What is promised is so sure, that it ought to be no less comfortable, than if it were enjoyed; for the promise ought to have no less weight for that end, than the former commendation. 10. Christ allows his people freedom from anxiety, because of things that are to come, and to be comforted in him against the fears of those as well as to draw consolation from him against any evil that is present; therefore is this intimated unto them. 11. Believers ought still to hold all their enjoyments and privileges as from him, and the expectation of what is coming, as well as the performance of what is past. 12. Faith in the promise, hath a large comprehensive object to rest upon, and to draw consolation from, even the power of the Godhead, and what may be by the Father, Son, and Spirit created, and brought about for a believer's good, even though it have not at present a being; "we will make thee" what is wanting, and what is needful, says the promise; creating power is engaged to through his work concerning them, "I create the fruit of the lips," Isa. lvii. 19; And "I will create Jerusalem a joy," &c. More cannot be desired, and less the Lord allows not.

PART III.—BRIDE'S WORDS.

Verse 12.   While the King sitteth at his table my spikenard sendeth forth the smell thereof.

13.   A bundle of myrrh is my well-beloved unto me; he shall lie all night betwixt my breasts.

14.   My beloved is unto me as a cluster of camphire in the vineyards of En-gedi.

THE third part of the chapter follows in these three verses, 12, 13, 14. In it the Bride expresseth how refreshful Christ was to her, and how she did solace herself in him; this she holds forth, not only in the sweet and warm title she gives him; but further in these three things, 1. She declares the comfortableness of the fellowship she had with him, verse 12. 2. By two comparisons she illustrates it, in the beginning of the 13th and 14th verses. 4. She sets forth the warmness of her own affections to him in the end of verse 13.

The titles she gives him are two, 1. "The King," whereby his sovereignty and majesty is set forth. The second is, "beloved" or "well-beloved," a title importing much love and affection: it differs from that title, "my love," which he gave her, verse 9, for that is a compellation given to her by him, as from a superior to an inferior, or as from an husband to a wife; this title which she here gives him, is as from an inferior, as a wife to her husband. The first holds forth condescending tenderness; the second respective love; but both agree in this, that they are most loving and affectionate titles.

She sets forth the comfortableness of Christ's fellowship, verse 12. Where, we are to consider these three things, 1. The privilege of his sweet company which she enjoyed, in these words, "the King sitteth at his table." 2. The effect thereof, held forth in this similitude, "my

spikenard," &c. 3. The connexion of these two, in this
expression, " while the King sitteth," &c.

1. The King here spoken of, is Christ, as was cleared.
verse 4. " His table," or feasting-house is the gospel,
Prov. ix. 1, &c. where the " feast of fat things" is prepared, Isa. xxv. 6. His sitting at his table, or her sitting
with him at it, imports familiar fellowship with him by
the gospel : so the " table of the Lord" is taken, 1 Cor. x.
21, and Matt. xxii. 4. The comfortable fellowship that
is to be had with him by the gospel, is held forth under
the similitude of a great feast ; as fellowship in glory and
enjoying of him there, is set out by eating and drinking
with him at his table, Luke xxii. 29, 30. Now this is
most friendly, when Christ not only furnishes a table,
Psalm xxiii. 5, but he comes and sits down, and sups with
them, and admits them to sup with him, Rev. iii. 21. It
is called his table, because he both furnishes it, and is
master and maker of the feast, yea, the matter of it also.

2. The effect of this fellowship is " my spikenard
sendeth forth the smell thereof." Spikenard here, signifies the graces of the Spirit wherewith the believer is
furnished out of the treasure of the sweet spices that are
in Christ: which are compared to spikenard, because
grace is precious in itself, and savoury and pleasant to
God, Psalm cxli. 2, and to others also, who have spiritual
senses. To send forth the smell, is to be in lively
exercise, and to be fresh and vigorous ; grace without
smell, or lively exercise, being like flowers somewhat
withered, that savour not, or like unbeaten spice, that
sends not forth its savour.

3. There is the connexion of this effect (which is so
comfortable to her) with Christ's presence, as the cause ;
it is while she sits, that her spikenard sendeth forth its
smell, it is then, and not else, that her graces flow ; such
influence hath his presence on her, as a cool wind hath on
a garden, for making the smell thereof to flow out, as it
is, chap. iv. 16.

Here *Observ.* 1. Christ the Bridegroom is a king. 2.
It makes all his condescending to sinners the more lovely,
admirable and comfortable, that he is so excellent ; that
he being such a King, sitteth at the table with poor believers, is much ; love in Christ, brings his majesty, as it
were, below itself, to feed and feast his poor people.
3. There is a way of most sweet and comfortable com-

munion to be had even with the King in his own ordinances. 4. There is a great **difference** betwixt an ordinance, or duty, and Christ's presence in it; these are separable. 5. It is Christ's presence that makes a feast to a believer, and makes all gospel ordinances, and duties so refreshful. 6. Believers may. and will observe when Christ is at the table, and when not: and it will be empty to them when he is absent. 7. All the provision wherewith believers' table is furnished, and they are feasted is Christ. 8. Christ should have a continued dwelling in the believer, and they a continual conversing with him, as those who diet ordinarily at one table.

The effect (namely the flowing of her graces) and its connexion with his presence, as the cause, shews, 1. There is a stock of grace, and spikenard in them, with whom Christ useth to sup, and there is no other but such admitted to his table. 2. The graces of the Spirit in believers, may be in a great part without savour, void of lively exercise, almost dead as to their effects. 3. It is exceedingly refreshful to believers, to have their graces flowing and acting. 4. Christ's presence hath much influence to make all things lively and savoury; where he sits, all things that are beside him (as it were) blossom and savour: the graces of his people are then very fresh and lively. And, 5. Though grace be savoury in itself, yet in Christ's absence, that savour will be restrained, and not sent forth; for it is implied, that when the King sat not at his table, her spikenard did not send forth its smell. 6. Christ's company, or fellowship with him, will not only be prized by believers, as it brings sensible comfort to them; but also as it revives their graces, and makes them lively.

2. Her satisfaction in Christ's fellowship, verses 13, and 14, is illustrated in two similitudes, whereby her holy fondness (to speak so) on him appears. The first similitude is, "a bundle of myrrh." Myrrh was a precious and savoury spice, made use of in the "anointing oil," Exod. xxx. 23. and in embalming Christ's body. A bundle of it, signifies abundance of it; not a stalk, or a grain, but a bundle that must be of more worth, and virtue than a lesser quantity. The second similitude, to the same scope is a "cluster of camphire," or cypress; a sweet odoriferous and precious wood in these parts; and a cluster of it, implies a congeries of it, having much of its excellency

bound up together : and under these two similitudes (because one is not enough to set forth the thing) is understood
a most precious, refreshful excellency which is to be found
in Christ, and wherewith the most desirable excellency
amongst the creatures being compared, he is much more
excellent than they all ; he is more sweet and precious
than a cluster, even of that camphire which grows in the
vineyards of En-gedi, where, it is like, the most precious
of that kind grew. Now these expressions hold forth, 1.
Christ's preciousness. 2. His efficacy and virtue. 3. His
abounding in both ; the worth and virtue that is in him
cannot be comprehended, nor told. 4. The Bride's wisdom
in making use of such things to describe Christ ; and her
affection in preferring him to all other things, and in satisfying herself in him, which is the last thing in these verses.

This respect of hers, or the warmness of her affection
to him, is set forth two ways, 1. In that expression, " he
is unto me," (which is both in the beginning of the 13th
and in the be ginning of the 14th verse) whereby is signified, not only Christ's worth in general, but, 1. His
savouriness, and loveliness to her in particular : she
speaks of him, as she herself had found him. 2. To express what room she gives him in her affection, he was
lovely in himself, and he was so to her, and in her esteem;
he is (saith she) a bundle of myrrh unto me, a cluster of
camphire to me : this is further clear from that other expression, namely, " he shall lie all night" (saith she) " betwixt my breasts," even as one hugs and embraces whom
they love, or what they love ; and keeps it in their arms,
and thrusts it into their bosom ; so (saith she) my beloved
shall have my heart to rest in, and if one room be further
in than another, there he will be admitted. Which imports,
1. Great love. 2. A satisfying her spiritual senses on him.
3. Tenaciousness in keeping and retaining him, when he is
gotten, and great lothness to quit, or part with him. 4. It
shews his right seat and place of residence ; the bosom and
heart is Christ's room and bed. 5. It shews a continuance
in retaining him, and entertaining him, she would do it not
for a start, but for all night. 6. A watchfulness in not in-
terrupting his rest, or disquieting of him, he shall not be
troubled (saith she) but "he shall lie all night," unprovoked
to depart. These are good evidences of affection to Christ,
and offer ground for good directions how to walk under
sensible manifestations, when he doth communicate himself.

PART IV.—CHRIST'S WORDS.

Verse 15.   Behold, thou art fair, my love : behold, thou art fair, thou hast doves eyes.

THESE words contain a part of that excellent and comfortable conference between Christ and the Spouse : there is here a mutual commendation one of another, as if they were in a holy contest of love, who should have the last word in expressing of the other's commendation.   In the verse before, the Bride hath been expressing her love to Christ, and he again comes in upon the back of this, expressing his esteem of her, and that with a behold, —"behold," &c.

If ye look upon this verse in itself, and with its dependance on the former words, it will hold out these things.   1. That love-fellowship with Christ must be a very heartsome life, O the sweet, mutual satisfaction that is there : 2. That Christ must be a very loving and kindly husband ; so have all they found him, that have been married to him : and therefore, Eph. v. 27.   He is proposed as a pattern to all husbands, and may well be so. That our Lord Jesus thinks good sometimes to intimate his love to believers, and to let them know what he thinks of them : and this he doth, that the believer may be confirmed in the faith of his love : for this is both profitable, and also comfortable, and refreshful.   Lastly, from the connexion observe, that there is no time wherein Christ more readily manifests and intimates his love to believers, than when their love is most warm to him.   In the former verse, she hath a room provided between her breasts for him, and in these words our Lord comes in with a very refreshful salutation to her : for though his love go before ours in the rise of it ; yet he hath ordered it so, that the intimation of his love to us, should be after the stirring of ours towards him, John xiv. 21.

In the commendation that he here gives her, consider these five particulars, 1. The title he gives her, "my love." 2. The commendation itself, "thou art fair." 3. The note of attention prefixed, "behold." 4. The repetition of both. 5. A particular instance of a piece of that beauty he commends in her.

1. The title is a very kindly and sweet one : and this

makes it lovely, that therein he not only intimates, but appropriates his love to her, allowing her to lay claim thereto as her own ; " my love," saith he ; and it says, that there can be nothing more cordial and refreshful to believers, than Christ's intimating of his love to them ; and therefore, he chooseth this very title for that end : the men of the world exceedingly prejudge themselves, that they think not more of this, and study not to be acquaint with it.

The commendation that he gives her is, " thou art fair." If it be asked, what this imports ? we may look upon it these three ways, 1. As it imports an inherent beauty in the Bride. 2. As it looks to the clearness and beauty of her state, as being justified before God ; and this she hath, as being clothed with the righteousness of Christ. 3. As it holds forth Christ's loving estimation of her, that though there were many spots in her ; yet he pronounces her fair (and lovely, because of his delight in her, and his purpose to make her fair) and without spot, or wrinkle, or any such thing : from all which, these three truths may be gathered, 1. That such as are Christ's, or have a title to him, are very lovely creatures, and cannot but have in them exceeding great loveliness, because there is to be found with them a work of his grace, a new creature, and a conversation some way levelled to the adorning of the gospel. 2. Christ Jesus hath a very great esteem of his Bride, and though we cannot conceive of love in him, as it is in us ; yet the expressions used here, give us ground to believe, that Christ hath a great esteem of believers, how worthless soever they be in themselves. *Lastly,* comparing this with verse 5, we may see, that believers are never more beautiful in Christ's eyes, than when their own spots are most discernible to themselves ; and oft times when they are sharpest in censuring themselves, he is most ready to absolve and commend them.

The third thing is, the rousing note of attention which is prefixed ; and this is here added to the commendation of the Bride, for these reasons, which may be as observations, 1. That he may shew the reality of that beauty that is in believers, that it is a very real thing. 2. That he may shew the reality of the estimation, which he hath of his Bride. 3. It imports a desire he had to make her believe, and a difficulty that was in bringing her to believe, either the beauty that was in her, or his estimation of her ; and therefore is this note of attention doubled. She hath

her eyes so fixed on her own blackness, that she hath
need to be roused up, to take notice both of the grace of
God in her, and also of the esteem that Christ had of her.

The particular that he commends in her, in the last part
of the words is, " thou hast dove's eyes." He insists not
only in the general, but is particular in this commendation
he gives her. And this shews, 1. Christ's particular observation not only of the believer's state, frame and carriage in general, but of their graces in particular. 2. That
there may be some particular grace, wherein believers
may be especially eminent; even as it is in corrupt, natural men, that are still under the pollution and dominion
of the body of death ; yet there is some one or other predominant lust that is strongest : in some sort it is so with
the believer, there is some one thing or other, wherein
grace especially vents, and puts forth itself in exercise.
Abraham is eminent for faith, Moses for meekness, Job
for patience : and hence the believer is considered sometimes under the notion of one grace, and sometimes of another, as we may see, Matt. v. 3. That our blessed Lord
Jesus hath a particular delight in the holy simplicity and
sincerity of a believer : or, holy simplicity and sincerity,
puts a great loveliness upon believers ; for, by this, " thou
hast dove's eyes," we conceive to be understood a holy
simplicity, separating her in her way, from the way of
the men of the world : for, while their eyes, or affections
run after other objects, hers are taken up with Christ ;
for by eyes are set out men's affections in scripture ; so,
Matt. vi. 22, and often in this song, the eyes signify the
affections, as in that expession, " thou hast ravished me
with one of thine eyes," &c. The eyes being some ways
the seat, and also the doors of the affections. Now " dove's
eyes" set out not only the Bride's affection, and love to
Christ, but also the nature of her love, which is the thing
here mainly commended, as simplicity, chastity, and
singleness, for which that creature is commended, Matt.
x. " Be simple as doves." And this is the commendation
of the love that true believers have to Christ, that it is
chaste, single and sincere love : singleness is the special
thing Christ commends in his people. It is that for which
believers are so much commended, Acts ii. 46.

PART V.—BRIDE'S WORDS.

Verse 16. Behold thou art fair, my beloved, yea, pleasant:
also our bed is green.
17.   The beams of our house are cedar, and our rafters of fir.

WE come to the last part of the chapter, in the two
last verses, in which the Bride commends Christ's beauty,
and the sweetness of fellowship with him : he had been
commending her, and now she hastens to get the commendation turned over on him, " behold thou art fair," &c.
And there are two things which she here commends, 1.
She commends the Bridegroom himself, " behold thou,"
&c. 2. She commends fellowship with him under the similitude of bed, house, and galleries, verse 16, 17. From
the connexion of this with the former purpose, ye may
see how restless believers are, when they meet with any
commendation from Christ, till they get it turned over to
his commendation and praise ; and this is the property of
believers, to be improving every good word they get
from Christ, to his own commendation that speaks it ; this
is the end and design why grace is bestowed upon believers, that it may turn in the upshot and issue to the
commendation of his grace. 2. That there is nothing
more readily warms the hearts of believers with love and
looses their tongues in expressions of commending Christ
than the intimation of his love to them ; this makes their
tongue as the " pen of a ready writer," Psal. xlv. 1.
More particularly in this commendation the Bride gives
him, ye will find these four things, 1. There is the style
she gives him, " my beloved." 2. There is the commendation given, and it is the same with the commendation
which in the former verse he gave her. 3. The note of
attention prefixed, " behold." *Lastly*, an addition to the
commendation Christ gave her, while she turns it over
upon him, and which is as a qualification of Christ's
beauty ; because one expression will not do it, she makes
use of two, " thou art fair" (saith she) " yea, pleasant :"
he had said she was fair ; nay, (saith she) " thou art fair,"
&c. She turns it over to him, because the same things
that are commendable in her, are infinitely and much
more commendable in him ; that which is in a believer,
being the extract of the principal which is in him, Christ

being the principal, and the graces that are in the believer but the transcript, or copy: all these things are in Christ like the light in the sun, and in the believer but like the light in the moon, communicated to it by the sun; and they are in Christ as in their own element and ocean, and in the believer but like some little stream communicated from that infinite fountain; and it is upon this ground, that the same commendation given by Christ to her, is turned over by her to him: and it is even as much as if she had said to him, my beloved, what is my fairness? it is thou who art fair, I am not worthy to be reckoned fair, the commendation belongs to thee, thou art worthy of it: and this is the nature of love in believers, to blush (in a manner) when Christ commends them, and to cast all such commendations back again upon him, that they may rest upon Christ, as the party who deserves them best.

From the title ye may see here, 1. Much humility in the Bride, and also much reverence and respect to Christ, which is the reason why she will not let the commendation lie upon her, but puts it back upon him: love to Christ, and estimation of him, aims always at this, that whatever is commendable in the believer, should ultimately resolve upon him. 2. Here is much familiarity, notwithstanding of her humility, in that she calls him "my beloved" as he called her "my love." Humility and reverence, an high estimation of Christ, and confidence in him, and familiarity with him go all well together in the believer; and the believer should labour to have all these in exercise together, and should never let one of them part from another. In a word, it is a humble familiar way in believing, which we should aim at. 3. One special thing that makes Christ lovely to believers, and natively stirreth them up to commend him is, when they are clear anent his love to them.

If it be asked, why she turns over this commendation to him in the second person, "thou art," &c? *Answ.* She doth it, 1. To testify her sincerity, that she was not flattering, nor complimenting, but she durst make him witness of what she said. 2. To show that there are many spiritual conferences, and sweet colloquies between the souls of believers and Christ, wherein they are familiar with him, which none knows, nor can know, but Christ and they; for, she is speaking to him when no body knows, and he to her. 3. Because there are many divine experiences of believers, that are scarcely communicable to any other, but Christ: and therefore she will tell them over to him.

The commendation she puts upon him, is even the same which he before gave her, " thou art fair" (saith she) and that which she aims at in this, is, 1. To set forth the exceeding great beauty that is in our Lord Jesus; which beauty is spiritually to be understood, namely of the qualifications wherewith he is furnished, having grace " poured into his lips," Psalm xlv. 2; John i. 14. 2. The great esteem that the believer hath of Christ, and that both for what he is in himself, and for what he is to him: "thou art fair" in thyself (saith she) and "fair" to me; and it says, a little glimpse of Christ's beauty, has an attractive efficacy upon the heart of a believer: when Christ Jesus is seen, it puts a wonderful stamp of love upon the hearts of his people; he hath a very amiable aspect, that cannot but get love in the beholders: as they said that heard him, never man spake as he speaks; so they that have seen him, will say, never man's countenance looked like his; amongst all the sons of men he bears the standard, and hath a loveliness wherein he is beyond them all: no wonder, he being " the brightness of his Father's glory, and the express image of his person." 3. It is to shew, wherefrom all her beauty was derived (as was hinted before) it was from his; if I be fair (saith she) it is because thou art fair, it is thy beauty that puts beauty upon me.

The third thing, is, the " behold" prefixed, and it holds out these three, 1. The excellency and admirableness of the matter: Christ's beauty, is a subject of a most transcendent and admirable excellency. 2. Her seriousness in the expressions of his commendation, as having her heart at her mouth, while she speaks of it, being so affected and taken up with it. 3. Though he needed not, yet she needed up-stirring herself: and there was need she should stir up others, and therefore this word, for her own, and others' cause, is prefixed.

The last part of this commendation, is (as we said) an addition to what he spoke in her commendation: " yea, pleasant," saith she; this pleasantness and loveliness doth relate to the communicativeness of Christ's worth, his communicating of what is lovely in him to others; it had not been enough for us, that he had been lovely in himself as God, if he were not also lovely by that relation that is between him and a believer in the covenant of grace, whereby there is not only a communicableness, but also an actual communication of these things to a believer, which may make him lovely and beautiful before God. And this makes Christ pleasant, that of "his fulness we receive, and grace for grace," John i. 16. When the believer shares of Christ's fulness, he cannot but be beautiful, and Christ cannot but be pleasant; and indeed if we could express any thing of the importance of the word, it is a most material and massy expression of that inexpressible worth that is in him, and likewise of a believer's estimation of it; and, 1. In the general it imports this, a difficulty in commending Christ rightly; there cannot be words gotten for it; the thing that is commendable in him, is so large, that words, yea, the most superlative of them, come far short in setting him forth. 2. It sets forth, how unsatisfied believers are with their own expressions of that worth, which they see to be in him; they think the first word unsuitable, and therefore they pass on to another, and in the close, they are forced as it were to give it over, and to say, thou art altogether lovely. 3. It imports, that there is no kind of thing that may commend Christ, wherein he is defective; he hath not only the materials of beauty (so to say) but he hath the form: all things that are in Christ, are wonderfully delightsome and pleasant to look on. *Lastly*, this expression implies, an exceeding great refreshfulness and contentedness, which Christ Jesus doth yield to a believer; and that exceeding great satisfaction and delight, that a believer may have in looking on Christ: this word "pleasant," speaks their actual feeding upon the beautiful sight they have gotten of him, so that they cannot be withdrawn from it: must not Christ be lovely, when his people get eyes to see him? and must it not be a heartsome life to be in heaven, where they behold him, who is fair and lovely, as he is, and have their eyes fixed on him for ever, when he is so beautiful even here-away, where we see him but darkly, through a glass, and much of his beauty is vailed from our eyes?

That which follows, is the enlargement of the Bride's commendation of Jesus Christ, as he is called a beloved, or husband, for she follows that allegory in commending his bed, house, and galleries; and this is the scope, to show how excellent and stately a husband he was. And,

2. How happy and comfortable a life his Bride had in communion and fellowship with him.   In the words, these three are to be cleared, 1. What is commended, as "bed," "house," &c. 2. The several commendations given to these. 3. The title of claim or relation under which they are commended, "our bed," &c.

That which is commended, is expressed by three words, 1. "Bed." 2. "The beams of our house," 3. "Rafters." In sum, it is this, that as husbands (who are in good condition) have beds to solace in with their Brides; houses to dwell in, and galleries to walk in, for their refreshing, and have these excellently adorned according to their rank; so our blessed Husband excels in these. By bed, is understoood the special means of nearest fellowship with, and enjoying of Christ; the bed being the place of rest, and of the nearest fellowship between the Bridegroom and the Bride.

Its commendation is, that it is green: that is, 1. Refreshful, like the spring. 2. Fruitful, and so the similitude of greeness is opposed to a disconsolate, barren, unfruitful condition, Psalm. xcii, 12, 13, and Jer. xvii. 8. So then, that which is here pointed at, is, that nearness with Christ, is both exceeding heartsome and refreshful, and also hath much influence on believers to keep them fresh, and make them fruitful.

The second thing commended, is "the beams of the house;" the house is of a larger extent than the bed: it signifies the church, wherein Christ dwells with his Bride; the beams of it, are the ordinances, word, sacraments, promises of the covenant, &c. whereby the house is both compacted together, and sustained; there being no living with Christ, nor fellowship with him, without these. The commendation is, that it is of cedar, 1. Cedar was a durable wood. 2. Excellent and precious, chap. iii. 10. 3. It was typical of Christ, and therefore used in the ceremonial services: so this commendation holds forth the excellent nature of the ordinances, and promises, being of great worth, precious and perpetual in their use to the church, while upon earth: but it doth especially hold forth the eternal excellency and worth, and the durable power and strength of Christ, the main corner-stone of this building, Eph. ii. 20, 22.

The third word is, "rafters": it is on the margin, galleries, and so we take it, being rendered so, chap. vii 5.

The word signifies, to run alongst: and the scope here is to show what pleasant walks there are with Christ; or, how pleasant a thing it is to walk with him. As to dwell with him, and lie, or bed with him, so to walk with him, must needs be pleasant: and this metaphor (with the rest) is here made use of, it being ordinary in this Song, under such expressions, to hold forth the love-fellowship, that is betwixt Christ and his church. Now these galleries are said to be of " fir," or cypress, a durable wood. This word is not elsewhere in scripture, but the scope shews it is some fine thing, and points out the unspeakable satisfaction and pleasure which is to be had in a life of walking with him.

She claims title to all these, bed, house, galleries; she saith not, thy bed, nor my bed (whereby. chap. iii. she signifies her own carnal ease and rest) but, our bed, our house, &c. whereby she points at somewhat which both of them had joint interest in, and did together converse into; although her interest be communicated from him; yet she keeps the manner of speech suitable to husband and wife.

These words show, 1. That there be several degrees of fellowship with Christ, and several ways and means, for entertaining of it: some more near, as when he lay betwixt her breasts: some more mediate (when, as it were) he and she only live together in the house, which may point at her trading with Christ in the ordinances, but without sensible manifestations: and also believers walking with him in their ordinary callings, even when they are not in duties of immediate worship which is signified by galleries. 2. Any of these degrees and means of fellowship, are excellent in themselves, and to be pressed and sought after by the believer. 3. The nearest means of fellowship with Christ, is most refreshful to spiritual sense; the bed more than the house. 4. Yet though it be so, believers should not divide them; but should think much of all the means and ordinances, even as long as they abide here. 5. There is a mutual relation betwixt Christ and his Bride, which gives a mutual interest in, and relation to all that is his; whatever is his, it is ours, his bed is ours, his house ours, &c. 6. Believers that can lay claim to Christ, may and should claim interest in all that is his. 7. This makes every dispensation lovely, and ever step of our walk heartsome, when under every dispensation, and in every step of our walk, we are living a life of fellowship with Christ: to be spending all our time in lying, dwelling and walking with Christ, O how sweet a life were that! 8. The means of fellowship with Christ in all places and times, are so well contrived, and so large and refreshful, as they contribute exceedingly to make a believer cheerful in all duties of worship, and in all his conversation; for we here see, there are bed, house, and galleries provided in order to her keeping company with Christ.

CHAPTER II.

PART I.—CHRIST'S WORDS.

Verse 1. I am the rose of Sharon, and the lily of the valleys. 2. As the lily among thorns so is my love among the daughters.

THIS second chapter contains the same scope, and runs in the same strain with the former. It hath two principal parts: in the first, Christ speaks in the first two verses. In the second, the Bride continues, to the end.

Again, in these two verses, Christ doth first commend himself, verse, 1. 2. He describes his Bride, verse 2.

That it is he who speaks, appears thus; 1. It is clear, at first looking upon the words, that he speaks in the second verse, and who else can be thought to speak in the first? he is the " I" in the first verse, who claims the Bride by this possessive particle "my" in the second. 2. The words, " I am the rose of Sharon," &c. are stately, becoming him alone to speak them: like these, " I am the true vine," " I am the bread of life," &c. And so majestic is the commendation, that it can agree to none other, but to him. 3. The Bride's work is to commend him, and not herself, especially with a commendation, beyond what he giveth her, verse 2, and therefore the first verse must be Christ's words, not hers.

The scope is, (for her instruction and comfort now in affliction,) that he may make her know himself: the very knowing of Christ is comfortable, and it is one of the most excellent, rare, and ravishing things he can show his Bride, to show her himself, or to make her know him: neither can he choose a subject more profitable in itself, or more welcome to her, to insist on, than to display his own beauty, whereby she may see her blessedness in such a match.

In the first verse then, Christ comes in commending himself, " I am the rose of Sharon, and the lily of the valleys." The rose is a sweet savouring flower, and so is the lily : Sharon and the valleys are added, because the roses and lilies that grew there, were the best that were to be found. He is said to be that "rose," or "the rose" and "the lily," as if there were no other, to distinguish him, as excellent and singular from all others. He thus sets forth himself to show, 1. That Christ Jesus hath a most lovely savour, and a most delightful and refreshful smell, to them that have spiritual senses to discern what is in him. 2. That there is nothing refreshful in creatures, but is more eminently and infinitely in him ; therefore he is called the rose and the lily. 3. That whatever excellency is in Christ, is singularly and incomparably in him ; there is no other rose, or lily but he ; and what excellency is to be found in others, doth not deserve the name, being compared with him. 4. That he is never suitably commended, till he be lifted up above all. 5. That none can commend Christ to purpose but himself ; he takes it therefore on him, " I am," &c. He can indeed commend himself effectually and none but he can do it. 6. That he manifests more of his loveliness to those who have gotten a begun sight and esteem of it : for, she had been commending it formerly, and now he discovers more of it to her. 7. That it is one of Christ's greatest favours to his Bride, and one of the special effects of his love, to set out himself as lovely to her, and to bear in his loveliness upon her heart ; and this is the scope here.

In the second verse, he describes his Bride. Here we have these things to consider, 1. What she is ; a "lily." 2. What others of the world beside are called here ; the " daughters" (so men without the church are to the church, and corrupt men in the church are to believers) that is, daughters of their mother the world ; no kindly daughters to her, they are thorns. 3. The posture of Christ's Spouse, she is " as a lily among thorns," a strange posture and soil, for our Lord's love and lily to grow in.

The lily is pleasant, savoury, and harmless ; thorns are worthless, unpleasant and hurtful. The lily's being compared with them, and placed amongst them, sets out both

her excellency above them, and her sufferings from them.
In general, *Observ.* 1. Christ draws his own beauty
and the Bride's together, thereby to show their kindred
and sibness (so to speak) she is not rightly taken up, but
when she is looked upon as standing by him ; and he not
fully set forth, nor known without her. 2. He took two
titles to himself, and he gives one of them to the Bride,
the "lily ;" but with this difference, that he is "the lily,"
she "as" or like "the lily :" setting forth, 1. Wherein
her beauty consists, it is in likeness to him. 2. From
whom it comes, it is from him, her being his love, makes her
like the lily. 3. The nearness of the mystical union, that
is between Christ and his Bride ; it is such, that thereby
they some way share names, Jer. xxiii. 6, and chap.
xxxiii. 16. 4. He intermixes her beauty and crosses together, drawing them on one table, to give her a view of
both ; and that for her humbling, and also for her comfort ;
it is not good for believers, to look only to the one without the other.

More particularly, *Observ.* 1. Christ's Bride is very
lovely and beautiful. 2. The children of the world are
natively hurtful to her. 3. In Christ's account the believer is exceedingly preferable to all others, of whatsoever place, or qualifications in the world. 4. Christ's
relation and affection, doth not always keep off outward
afflictions from his own Bride. 5. It is native to believers
to have a crossed life in the world, their plantation here
among thorns speaks it. 6. That the crosses are of more
kinds than one, which believers are environed with, thorns
grow on all hands beside Christ's lily. 7. Holiness and
innocency will not always prevent wrongs and injuries
from others, thorns will wrong even the lily. 8. Christ
observes here, how she looks in her sufferings, and so he
takes special notice, how his people carry in a suffering
lot. 9. It is commendable to keep clean under sufferings,
and to be lily-like, even amongst thorns.

PART II.—BRIDE'S WORDS.

Verse 3.   As the apple-tree among the trees of the wood, so is
my beloved among the sons: I sat down under his shadow
with great delight, and his fruit was sweet to my taste.

THE second part of the chapter may be subdivided in
two ; first, from the third verse, the Bride comes in, speak-

ing as in a lively frame, to verse 8. 2. From that to the end, she speaks as being at some distance with the Bridegroom.

In the first part, 1. She commends Christ, and lays down this commendation, as the ground of her consolation, verse 3. 2. She proves it by her experience, *ibid.* 3. Explains the way of her coming to that experience, verse 4. 4. She cries out under the sense of it, verse 5. 5. She shews his tender care of her in that condition, verse 6. And lastly, expresseth her fear, lest there should be any change to the worse in her condition, and her care to prevent it, verse 7.

The dependence of the third verse upon the second, is clear: she takes the commendation out of Christ's mouth, which he gave her, and after that same manner almost turns it over on him, as she had done, chap. i. 16, and then comforts herself in him: hath she crosses? then he hath a shadow to hide her, and with this she settles herself, and doth not complain of her sufferings, Hence, *Observ.* 1. There is no staying of the heart against afflictions, but in Christ, 2. It is better for believers to insist in commending him, than describing their crosses.

Here there is, 1. The Bride's esteem of the children of the world, called here the "sons," they are like wild barren trees, that give no fruit, or comfort: the world is exceeding little worth, especially to those who know Christ. 2. Her esteem of Christ, he is like the "apple-tree;" there is great odds betwixt Christ and all the world; there is ever fruit to be found on him, and a shadow in him. This is proven by her experience (for they who have felt and tasted how sweet he is, can speak somewhat of this) I encountered with many difficulties (says she) like scorchings of the sun: (see on chap. i. verse 5.) and could find no shelter, nor refreshment amongst the creatures: but I resolved to make use of Christ by faith, in reference to them (even as men do, by interposing a tree betwixt them and the heat, that they may have a shadow) and I found refreshing and ease, by the benefits and privileges that flow from Christ, and are purchased by him, and are enjoyed by virtue of an interest in him; which were very comfortable, even as sweet apples from an apple-tree, are refreshful to one sitting under its shadow in a great heat.

Observ. 1. Believers may be scorched with outward

and inward heat; they may be exercised not only with sharp outward afflictions, but also with the sense of God's wrath, and with the fiery darts of Satan's temptations. 2. Christ is a complete shadow, and a cure for all. 3. They that would find Christ a shadow from the heat, must make use of him, and employ him for that end; they must "sit down," &c. 4. Believers never flee to his shadow till some heat scorch them; for, her being scorched with heat, is supposed here as that which made the shadow refreshful. 5. Faith in Christ, will compose believers in the midst of the greatest difficulties; it will set them down, &c. yea, and delight them also. 6 Much of the nature and exercise of faith, in its use-making of Christ, appears in its interposing of Christ betwixt us and wrath, or whatever may be troublesome to us, and in the quieting of ourselves upon that ground; for, this is it that is meant by sitting down under his shadow. 7. There are many choice and excellent fruits in Christ, that flow from him to believers. 8. All the spiritual benefits and privileges that believers enjoy, are Christ's fruits; they are his fruits by purchase and right, and by him communicated to believers. 9. Believers eat and feed, and may with his blessed allowance do so upon what is his. 10. Christ's fruits are exceeding sweet, when they are eaten; they are satisfying, and, as it were, sensibly sweet. 11. These sweet fruits are neither eaten, nor the sweetness of them felt by believers, till they go to Christ's shadow, and sit down delightsomely under his righteousness; then they become refreshful.

Verse. 4.   He brought me to the banqueting house: and his banner over me was love.

SHE proceeds in expressing her cheerful condition, by shewing the way of her access to it, verse 4, " He brought me," &c.   Wherein, 1. She sets out the sweetness of the enjoyment of Christ's sensible love, by comparing it to a feast, or house of wine. 2. She tells who it was that brought her to it, "he brought me." 3. The manner how she was brought to it; it was by the out-letting of his love, " his banner" (saith she) " over me was love." The first expression sets forth three things, 1. The great abundance of satisfying and refreshing blessings, that are to be found in Christ; such abundance of provision as useth to be laid up at a feast, or in a banqueting-house, 2. His liberal allowance thereof to his own, who for that end hath laid up this provision for them. 3. The nature of the entertainment; it is a feast of the best and most cordial things, a house of wine: the second is, "he," that is Christ, "brought me in." It shews, 1. Believers' impotency to enter in there of themselves, and their want of right, that may give them access to the blessings that are laid up in Christ. 2. That it is Christ who makes their access; he purchased an entry by his death, he applies his purchase by his Spirit, and dispenseth it by his office, and so brings them in. 3. It suppones a freedom of grace in the bringing them in: they are brought in by his mere favour. 4. It contains a thankful remembrance, or acknowledgment of this deed of Christ's and an holding of this favour of him. The third holds forth the manner how she is brought in; it is under a "banner of love:" a stately manner; it was love that brought her in: the expression implieth, that not only it was love that moved him to bring her in, but that he did it in a loving manner which amplifieth and heightens his love; She comes in marching, as it were in triumph, having love like a banner, or colours, adorning this march, and making way for her entry; so that even in the manner of her being brought in, the general predominant, visible thing (as it were) that appeared, was love. *Observ.* 1. Christ will sometimes bring his people into the sense of his love, exceeding lovingly and kindly, even as to the manner of engaging them. 2. Believers should observe this way with them. 3. This loving manner, in the way of his dealing with his people, doth exceedingly commend his love, and is an heightening consideration of it. 4. Christ's love is in itself a most stately and triumphant thing. 5. It is only the love of Christ that secures believers in their battles and march against their spiritual adversaries; and indeed they may fight, who have love for their colours and banners.

Verse 5. Stay me with flagons, comfort me with apples; for I am sick of love.

SHE is almost overcome with this banquet, and therefore cries out for help, verse 5. Here consider, 1. The case she is in, 2. The cure she calls for. 3. From whom she seeks it.

Her case is, that she is "sick of love." This is not to be taken for the fainting of a soul under absence, and the want of sense ; all the context before and after, and the scope, will show it otherwise with her ; but it is a sickness from the weight and pressure of felt inconceivable love, damishing her (as it were) and weakening her, she cannot abide that sight and fulness which she enjoys.

2. The cure she desires confirms this, "stay me," (saith she) or support me, for I am like to fall under it ; and "comfort me," the word is strengthen me, or bed me, straw me with, or in apples, let me lie down amongst them. The first expression looks to the house of wine where she was, which suppones no want, and may be rendered, "stay me in flagons," as seeking support in this holy fill of the Spirit, whereby she was staggering. The second looks to the apple-tree, verse 3. And she would ever roll herself among the apples that come from this tree ; and like the disciples, Matt. xvii. 4. saith (as it were) "It is good to be here ;" she would even be fixed and lie down in that posture, never to part with this happy condition again.

3. Those she speaks to, and from whom she seeks help, are expressed in the plural number (as is clear in the original) which shews a ravishment and kind of rapture in this exclamation ; not observing to whom she speaks, but expressing her delight in that which she enjoyed, yet mainly intending Christ (as the disciples did, Matt. xvii. not knowing what they said) for it is he who applies the cure in the next verse.

Observ. 1. Love will have a great out-letting at sometimes beyond others, as if a dam were gathered, and then letten out. 2. Sense of love in a high degree will straiten and weight a believer, as over-burdening and overpowering him, so as he is put to say Hold, and wo's me ; as it is, Isa. vi. 5 : the nature of God's presence is such, and our infirmity so unsuitable thereto. 3. Love is lovely when the believer is almost dotting with it, and staggering under the weight and power of it. 4. It can cure even the same sickness it makes. These flagons and apples are the only remedy, though our bottles be now weak, and can hold but little of this new wine.

Verse 6.   His left hand is under my head, and his right hand doth embrace me.

SHE expresseth Christ's care of her in this condition, ver. 6th as a most loving husband, he sustains her in his arms, in this swoon and swarf, which from joy she falls into, as the words do plainly bear.   *Observ.* 1. Christ's love is a sensible sustaining thing, and is able to support the heart under its greatest weakness.   2. As Christ is tender of all his people, and at all times, so especially when they are in their fits of love-sickness.   3. As believers would observe Christ's love at all times, so especially when they are weakest; for then they will find it both seasonable and profitable so to do.

Verse 7.   I charge you, O ye daughters of Jerusalem, by the roes, and by the hinds of the field, that ye stir not up, nor awake my love till he please.

THIS verse contains her care to entertain this condition, and the way she takes for that end.   They are the Bride's words, is, 1. Clear from the scope and matter.   2. From the expressions she useth, speaking of him, " my love," and " till he please ;" for, it becomes to give Christ his own liberty in staying, or going, and it were not for our good that our pleasure were the rule in our fellowship with him.   Now in order to the securing of this comfortable condition to herself, first she adjures and charges, which is, 1. To show the concernment of the thing.   2. Her seriousness in it ; for, she is in very great earnest.   3. A fear of misguiding this condition.   4. A difficulty so to prevent the hazard, as to keep all quiet.
    2. The parties she speaks to, while she thus adjures, are the " daughters of Jerusalem :" giving them the lesson she would take to herself, because they had need to be thus guarded.   *Observ.* 1. That professors are in hazard to mar their own enjoyments, and to interrupt an intimate fellowship with Christ.   2. Beginners are readiest to fall into this sin.   3. Seriousness will stir up believers to be watchful over themselves, and will make them press others to be so also.
    The expression, " by the roes and hinds of the field," is but added, for keeping the strain of this song (which is composed in an allegoric way, and every similitude is not

to be narrowly searched into) and to show how tenderly
they ought to watch, to prevent this hazard, as men having to do with "roes and hinds of the field," is but added,
for keeping the strain of this song (which is composed in
an allegoric way, and every similitude is not to be narrowly searched into) and to shew how tenderly they ought
to watch, to prevent this hazard, as men having to do
with roes, who are soon stirred ; shewing that a little
thing may stir up Christ, and mar the comfortable fellowship that is between him and his people.

3. The charge itself is, that " they stir not up nor awake
the beloved ;" as a wife would say (when her husband is
come home and resting in her arm) be quiet all, and let no
din be in the house to awake him : and this charge reaches
herself, as well as others ; when she as the mother, commands all the little ones, or children (as it were) to be
quiet, that Christ may not be stirred up, and made to remove ; she ought to be much more careful in this herself.
Hence, *Observ.* 1. If a sensible presence be not tenderly
entertained, it will not last. 2. Believers should be most
careful then, when they are admitted to near and sensible fellowship with Christ, that nothing may fall out which
may provoke him to depart. 3. The least sinful motions
and stirrings of corruption should be suppressed, as having
a great tendency to provoke and stir up the beloved to be
gone.

Lastly, This charge is qualified in these words, " till he
please." Which does not imply, that she gives them leave
at any time to stir him up ; but the meaning is, see that
by your fault he be not awaked, till his own time come.
Observe then, 1. Christ guides his visits and love-manifes-
tations, by his sovereignty and pleasure. 2. He may
withdraw from his people without respect to any particular provocation, as having sinful influence thereupon. 3.
Christ's pleasure is believers' rule, in the things that are
most precious to them : here she acquiesces, even to his
withdrawing, when he shall please. 4. Believers may
have peace, and be quiet under absence, if they have not
sinfully provoked Christ to withdraw : for this is the thing
the Bride aims at, as to herself, in this her care. 5. Often
believers are guilty in marring Christ's fellowship with
them before he please, and they might enjoy Christ's company much longer oftentimes, if they did not sin him out
of house and doors.

Verse 8.   The voice of my beloved! behold he cometh leaping
  upon the mountains, skipping upon the hills.
9. My beloved is like a roe, or a young hart: behold he
  standeth behind our wall, he looketh forth at the windows,
  shewing himself through the lattice.

THESE words contain a case of the Bride's, different
from her case in the former words; there she was in
Christ's arms; here she sees him afar off; there she was
endeavouring to keep him still; here she is sensible that
he is away, and verse *ult.* is praying for his return.   Observe then from the connexion, the most satisfying and
comfortable conditions of a believer, while upon earth, are
not abiding; even the Bride must experience distance,
as well as presence.   2. Sometimes sensible presence will
not continue, even when believers are most careful to retain it, as we find she was in the words before.

Her distance hath two steps, 1. There are some views
of Christ, and some intercourse with him, though afar off,
in this chapter: then 2. She is deprived even of that, in
the first part of the chapter following: and readily distance once begun, doth proceed from a lesser to a greater
degree before it be removed.

More particularly, we would observe here, I. What is
Christ's carriage, when the Bride doth not enjoy sensible
presence in so lively a way: and that in two things, 1.
What he is doing: he is coming, leaping, standing behind the wall, looking through the lattice, &c.   2. What
he is saying; he is speaking to her, and, as it were, writing
kind love-letters to her at that same time: Christ is both
doing and speaking kindly to a believer, even when he is
away to sense, if it be well discerned.   II. We may see
what is the Bride's carriage suitable to his, in four
steps (worthy to be imitated by believers, for their own
peace, in their disconsolate condition.)   1. She observes
what he doth, though it be but a twilight discovery she
hath of him.   2. She records what he saith, and reads
his epistle often over.   3. She comforts herself in keeping
the faith of her interest, and the hope of future enjoying
of him, clear.   And, 4. Prays in the mean time, for some
manifestations of his love, till that come.   The first is,
verses 8, and 9.   The second, verses 10. to 16.   The third
verses 16, and 17.   The fourth in the close of the 17th
verse.

In her observation of Christ's way with her, verse 8.
Consider, 1. His practice, which she observes. 2. Her
observation of it. 3. How she is affected with it. And
lastly, her expression of it.

The first of these is contained in these words, " He
cometh leaping upon the mountains, skipping upon the
hills." There are four things here to be taken notice of,
1. A supposed distance, for when he is said to be coming,
he is not present : this distance is not in reality, as to
the union that is betwixt Christ and a believer, that is
always the same, but it is to be understood as the sense
of his presence which may be interrupted. 2. It is said
" he cometh ;" coming imports his drawing near to remove
the distance, as being already on his way. *Observ.* 1. It
is his coming that removes the distance between him and
his people : the first motion of love is still on his side.
And, 2. even when Christ is absent, if he were well seen,
he is making way for our nearer union with him, and is
upon his way coming again, John xiv. 3. Even when he
is away he is still coming, though it may be afterward the
distance seem to grow greater, and the night of absence
darker. The third thing is, that there are mountains
which he comes over, that is something standing between
him and us, marring our access to him, and his familiarity
with us, till he remove it, as mountains obstruct men's
way in travel ; and so difficulties in the way of God's work
are compared to mountains, Zech. iv. 7. " Who art thou, O
great mountain ?" &c. So here, as there are difficulties
to be removed, before the union betwixt Christ and us be
made up ; so also there are particular sins, as perjury,
breach of covenant, and other clouds of guiltiness, which
must be removed, ere his presence can be restored, after
he goeth away. Again, coming over mountains, maketh
one conspicuous and glorious afar off ; so Christ's march
and return to a believer is ever in triumph, over some
great ground of distance, which makes him discernibly
glorious. 4. Christ is said to be leaping and skipping :
which imports, 1. An agility in him, and a facility to
overcome whatever is in the way. 2. A cheerfulness and
heartiness in doing of it ; he comes with delight over the
highest hill that is in his way, when he returns to his
people. 3. It holds forth speediness : Christ comes quickly,
and he is never behind his time, he cannot mistryst a believer ; his term-day is their necessity, and be sure he will

meet with them then. 4. It imports a beauty, majesty
and stateliness in his coming, as one in triumph; and so
he comes triumphantly and in great state; and what is
more stately than Christ's triumphing over principalities
and powers, and making a shew of them openly, by overcoming the difficulties in his way to his Bride.

The second thing in the verse, is her observation of
this; Christ in his way is very discernible to any that is
watchful, and believers should observe his way when
absent, as well as present. If it be asked how she discerned it? there is no question, faith is here taking up
Christ according to his promise, John xiv. 3, " If I go
away, I will come again;" and faith lays hold on this:
faith is a good friend in desertion, for as we may here see,
it speaks good of Christ even behind his back: when sense
would say, he will return no more, faith says he is coming,
and prophesies good of Christ, as there is good reason.

The third thing is, how she is affected with it; this observation proves very comfortable to her, as her abrupt
and cut expression imports, " the voice of my beloved:"
as also the " behold," she puts to it, which shews, 1. That
her heart was much affected with it. 2. That she thought
much of it. 3. That it was someway wonderful that
Christ was coming, even over all these difficulties to her;
there is no such ravishing wonder to a sensible believing
sinner, as this, that Christ will pass by all his sins, yea
take them all on himself, and come over all difficulties
unto him, therefore is this, behold, added here.

The fourth thing is her expression of this, which confirms the former, and it is such as sets out a heart, as it
were, surprised, and overcome with the sight of a coming
friend. Hence, *Observ.* 1. A sinner's thoughts of a coming
Christ, will be deeply affecting; and these thoughts of
him are mis-shapen and of no worth, that do not in some
measure cast fire into, and inflame the affections. And,
1. A heart suitably affected with the power of Christ's
wonderful grace and love will be expressing somewhat of
it to others, as the Bride is doing here.

In the 9th verse the observation of his carriage is continued : where, 1. He is commended. 2. His carriage is
described, with her observation of it. The commendation
she gives him is, " He is like a roe, or a young hart:" these
creatures are famous, for loving and kindly carriage to
their mates, as also for loveliness and pleasantness in them-

selves, Pro. v. 19. Thus he is kindly and loving: O so
kind as Christ is to his church and chosen! Jonathan's
love to David passed the love of women, but this surpasseth
that, beyond all degrees of comparison. 2. He is timeous
and seasonable, in fulfilling his purposes of love to his
Bride; no roe or hart for swiftness is like him in this:
and this may be the ground, from which she concludeth
that he was coming and leaping in the former words, because Christ's affections, and way of manifesting them,
is such as this.

2. His carriage is set forth in three steps, held forth in
allegoric expressions. The 1. is, " he stands behind our
wall," that is as a loving husband may withdraw from
the sight of his spouse for a time, and yet not be far away,
but behind a wall, and there standing to see what will be
her carriage, and to be ready to return; or as nurses will
do with their little children, to make them seek after
them; so says she, though Christ now be out of sight, yet
he is not far off, but, as it were, behind the wall; and it is
called " our wall," in reference to some other she speaks
with, of him; and a wall, because often we build up these
separations ourselves, betwixt him and us (Isa. lvi. 1.)
that hides Christ, as a wall hides one man from another;
yet even then Christ goes not away, but waits to be gracious, as weary with forbearing: there is much love on
Christ's side, in saddest desertions, and our hand is often
deep in his withdrawings: it is sad when the wall that
hides him, is of our building: there is often nothing betwixt him and us, but our own sin.

The second step is, " he looketh forth at the window,"
which is to the same purpose. The meaning is, though I
get not a full sight of him, yet he opens, as it were a window, and looks out, and I get some little glance of his
face: sometimes Christ will neither (as it were) let the
believer in to him, nor will he come out to them; yet he
will make windows, as it were, in the wall and give blinks
of himself unto them.

The third step is, " he shows himself through the
lattice :" that is, as there are some windows that have
tirlesses, or lattices on them, by which men will see
clearly, and yet be but in a little measure seen; so, says
she, Christ is beholding us, though we cannot take him up
fully: yet the smallest bore whereby Christ manifests himself, is much and to be acknowledged. All this she ob-

serves with a "behold," as discerning something wonderful in all these steps: Christ hath several ways of communicating his love to his people (and that also even under desertions and withdrawings) and there are several degrees of these, yet the least of them is wonderful, and should be welcomed by believers, if it were to see him but through the lattice.

Verse 10.   My beloved spake, and said unto me, rise up my love, my fair one, and come away.

11.   For lo, the winter is past, the rain is over and gone ;

12.   The flowers appear on the earth, the time of the singing of birds is come, and the voice of the turtle is heard in our land ;

13.   The fig tree putteth forth her green figs, and the vines with the tender grape give a good smell. Arise my love, my fair one, and come away.

HAVING put by her observation of his carriage, she comes to speak to the second part, namely, what was her carriage : and it was to read over, or think over with herself, or to tell over to others, what Christ had said unto her : this is a main piece of spiritual wisdom, to fill Christ's room in his absence with his word and call, and to read his mind only from these, the best interpreters of it. These words prefaced to Christ's epistle, or sermon, "my beloved spake, and said unto me," are not idly set down, before she tell, what the words which he spake were, But, 1. It shews she delights in repeating his name, for she had made mention of it before, verse 8. 2. It shows what commended Christ's epistle, or words to her, it was not only the matter therein contained (though that was warm and sweet) but it is come (saith she) from my beloved, it was he that said this, it was he that sent me this word. 3. It shews her discerning of his voice ; and her assurance, that the word, call, and promise, (she was refreshing herself with) was his word, and no devised fable. It is a notable ground of consolation in Christ's absence to believers, when they are clear, that such and such gracious words come out of Christ's own mouth to them. 4. It says, that fellowship with Christ, is no dumb exercise ; those that are admitted to fellowship with him, he will be speaking with, otherwise than with the world. And, 5. That a believer hath an ear to hear, not

only what the minister saith, but also what Christ saith.
6. It is the word as from Christ's own mouth, that hath
an effectual impression ; and a believer will receive it as
such, that it may leave such an impression upon his heart.
7. When Christ quickens a word, it will be sweet ; and
such a word will be retained, so that those who have been
quickened by it, will be able long afterwards to repeat it :
it is our getting little good of the word of the Lord, that
makes us retain it so ill.   8. It affords much satisfaction
to a believer, when he can say, Christ said this or that to
me, and that it is no delusion.   9. What Christ says unto
the spirits of his own, in communion with them, may
bide the light, and is, on the matter, that same which he
says in the word and gospel, as we will see in the following discourse, which for this end, and for the edification
of others, and honour of the beloved, she tells over.

We may take these words or epistles of Christ's, as directed to three sorts (as the duty here pressed, " rise and
come away," will bear,) 1. To those that are dead in sins,
whom Christ by his voice quickens, and makes to rise,
John v. 28.   Although this be not the immediate intent
of it, as it is spoken to a believer ; yet considering the
scope of recording this, and the matter contained in it, it
may well be thought useful to engage those who are yet
strangers to Christ, there being still but the same way of
making at the first, and afterward recovering nearness
with him, viz. by faith in him ; and so it will press receiving of, and closing with Christ.   2. We may consider it as spoken to believers, but to such as sleep, or are
sitten up ; so it presseth quickening.   And, 3. As spoken
to believers in a disconsolate, discouraged condition ; so
its scope is to stir, quicken, rouse and comfort Christ's
Bride, in any of these two last cases, that he may bring
her into more nearness of fellowship with himself and to
more boldness in the use-making of him ; which is the
great scope he aims at.

There are three parts of this sermon, or epistle, 1.
There is a kindly invitation, that mainly respects the
pressing of faith, from verse 10, to 14.   2. There is a
loving direction, or two, verse 14, looking especially to
the practice of duties.   3. Lest any thing should be wanting, he gives a direction concerning the troublers of her
peace, verse 15.

In all these parts, there are four things common to be

found in each of them. 1. Some sadness in her condition supposed. 2. Some directions given to cure it. 3. Some motives used, to press the practice of these directions. 4. Some repetitions, to show his seriousness in all, and the concernment of the thing spoken.

The case wherein those who are here spoken to, are supposed to be, in this first part of Christ's sermon, verse 10, &c. is, 1. Deadness, total, or partial: believers may be under a decay, and be in part dead. 2. It is supposed that they are secure, and not vigorous; but insensible, in a great part, of that ill. 3. That they are disconsolate, and heartless under distance and deadness: which ills often meet together.

The direction he gives in order to the helping of this, is in two words, 1. " Rise." 2. " Come away." Which says, that as she was now in a case of strangeness to Christ, so there was a necessity of rousing herself, and coming out of it; such a necessity as there is for a straying wife to return to her husband. Now these words are a sweet call of a kind husband, inviting to this return, and showing the remedy of straying, and estrangement from him. Rising imports, 1. One that is settled some way, in a condition opposite to walking and running. 2. A stirring up of themselves as unsatified therewith, and desirous to be out of it, with some endeavour to be up again : declining from Christ puts souls still down, and holds them at under. 1. " Come away," holds forth a term from which she is to come, from that condition she was in, whatever it was, it was not good : men are in no desirable condition, when Christ calls them. 2. A term to which she is to come, and that is Christ; it is to follow the Bridegroom ; to get her brought to a nearer union and communion with him, is the great thing he aims at. 3. An act whereby she passeth from what she was, and turning her back on that, moves towards him, that she may thereby attain nearer union and fellowship with him. By both which, we conceive the exercise of faith in him, is mainly holden forth, 1. Because faith is ordinarily in scripture set forth by coming, Isa. lv. 1 ; John v. 40 ; John vi. 35, and this expression suits well the act of faith. 2. Because it is the only means of making up the distance betwixt him and us: decay in the exercise of faith, and distance from Christ, go together ; and the exercise of faith, and nearness with him, are also inseparable companions. This is the meaning then,—why liest thou in this discouraged, decayed and comfortless condition? there is another, and a far better, to wit, a lively and comfortable condition allowed upon thee; Christ calls thee to exercise faith in him, for recovering of thy case. And this now is set down imperatively by way of command, that we may know that believing in Christ, or keeping communion with him by faith, are not left to our option, but are laid on by a peremptory command, for necessitating us to the exercise of it, 1 John iii. 23, as a thing most acceptable to him, with which he cannot be angry, nor will he call obedience thereunto presumption.

3. When he hath given the invitation; he presseth it most seriously and weightily; for though it be our concernment, we are not easily induced even to believe: O but the world is much mistaken in this, that think it an easy matter to believe! And also he would have us knowing; he allows us the comfortable exercise of faith in him, with all his heart (if we may speak so) when he thus presseth and persuadeth us to it; likewise we may gather, that it is no common thing which he exhorts unto, when he doth so seriously press it, but it is of most weighty concernment to us.

There are three ways he maketh use of, to press it: 1. By excellent, loving titles, "my love," and "fair one;" which are given here, especially to let her know he loved her, and thereby to encourage her to follow the call. The faith of his love, hath no little influence upon our acting faith in particulars on him. 2. To show that he is no rigid, nor severe censurer of a discouraged believer, no, "my fair one" (saith he) even when she hath many spots; Christ will raise no ill report on his own, whatever be their failings. 3. He presseth it from the special relation he hath to her, "my love," and "my fair one," which makes all his words very kindly, and shows an obligation on her, by the covenant-relation that stood between them to be his, and to subject herself to his directions, according to that word, Psal. xlv. 10, "Hearken O Daughter," &c. "Forget thy father's house," &c. And therefore she ought to leave all and cleave to him: Christ requires nothing from us, but according to the covenant, that ties us to communion or cohabitation (to speak so) with Christ, and it is a most binding obligation; if this prevail not in pressing us to duty, that we are Christ's, nothing will pre-

vail: it is no little practick in believers, to be like the
relation they stand in to Christ; what, my love (saith he)
becomes it you to be so strange? " Rise and come," &c.
Some other thing is allowed to you than to others, and
some other thing is called for from you, than is to be
found in the way of others.

The third way he insisteth to urge this (for the call,
and kindness come still on his side, even when we are in
the fault) is by most pressing arguments of three sorts.
The first is verse 11. " Rise" (saith he) " and come away,"
for there is no hazard now to travel this journey, because
what may scare you is done away. The winter cold and
storm is past, and the rain that makes rivers unpassable
and journeys dangerous and wearisome (therefore, it is
said Matt. xxiv. 20, "pray that your flight be not in the
winter") these are over. This suppones, 1. There was a
sharp winter, and a bitter rain (as it were) whereby the
way of fellowship with God, was unpassable, till these
were removed; the sword (as it were) standing to keep
sinners from paradise, that is, the sentence and curse of
the broken law, and the wrath of God pursuing therefor;
which was indeed a fearful winter, and storm that made
the sun dark, and the day gloomy, therefore is God's
wrath in scripture compared to " terrible blasts and tem-
pests," and " who can stand before his cold?" Psalm
cxlvii. 17. 2. It says, that now these are done away by
Christ; and by his call in the gospel, he assures his people, they shall find them fully removed, so that there is
no wrath nor curse, that any who yields to it needs to
fear. 3. It implies that the gospel brings good news,
and there is none better than this, that God's justice is
satisfied, and his wrath removed. 4. It imports, that
Christ can bear sure testimony to this, that wrath is over,
because he paid a price to remove it, and therefore sinners
may take his word, and follow his call. And, 5. That
believers are sometimes ready to suspect, more than they
have ground, that there is some storm yet before them;
but Christ hath made all fair weather, ere he call: O great
argument! he calls not to fight, but to gather the spoil:
he puts not believers to the sea, till he himself hath made
all calm: believers meet with blasts and storms sometimes, but readily that is when their back is on Christ,
and not when their faces are to him-ward: the wind of
wrath is not in a sinner's face that seeketh Jesus, but the
word saith to such "fear not," Mark xvi. 6, "ye seek him."

2. He presseth her to rise and come, from some heart-some encouragement he propones, verse 12. There is a great change (saith he) now, when the angry winter is over, all things are pleasant and lovely. 1. " The flowers appear," that shows there is heat and warmness in the earth, and it is an effect of the spring, and a proof that winter is past. Hereby the fruits of grace, appearing in the change that is wrought upon sinners, may be signified, as is frequently hinted in this Song, where the church is called a garden, and believers are the flowers: come, (saith he) grace hath made others to come through the ground, who once were like flowers in the winter, under ground, but now they appear and flourish. 2. " The time of the singing of birds is come." As in the spring, birds sing, which in the winter drooped: so (saith he) now many poor sinners have changed their sad note, and begin to sing, who once were sinking under fears ; and the good news of the gospel, like " the voice of the turtle, is heard in our land ;" these good tidings have been sent even to us, which is no little evidence of love, and no small confirmation to faith. That the news of the gospel, and the consolation of sinners thereby, is here understood, is very agreeable to the scope : and these prove the removing of wrath, and are encouraging for stirring sinners up to the exercise of faith. And O how heartsome, and re-freshful is the spiritual spring, when the " day-spring from on high" visits us ! (as these things mentioned in the text, are in the natural spring very pleasant, and tend to pro-voke men to go and recreate themselves in the fields.) And this is the particular scope of this place : there is never a sinner hath gotten good of Christ, but it proves him to be very kind ; and the blessed change Christ hath wrought on them, should encourage others to believe, especially when it is the day of their visitation, and the Sun of righteousness hath become warm by the gospel unto them, or unto the place and society in which they live. 3. He presseth his direction and call, by the very presentness and now, of the season of grace, verse 13, " The fig-tree putteth forth," &c. Which shews not only, that summer is near, but that " it is even at the door," Matt. xxiv. 32, 33. And (saith he) the vines bud and give a smell ; whereby is holden forth, the thriving of the plants of God's vineyard, under the dispensation of grace, as we may see verse 15. All these prove that " now is

the acceptable time, and now is the day of salvation ;" and there are large allowances of consolation to them that now will accept of Christ's offers, and be subject to his call : therefore, saith he, even to us, sit not the time when all is ready, but up, and come away : and that "the voice of the turtle is heard in our land," (that is even the church wherein we live) proves it to be the season of grace also ; for, it is long since the time of the turtles' singing hath come to us, and their voice is yet still heard : and this says the season of grace is amongst our hands, now when Christ's call comes to our door, and therefore it should not be neglected.

And so he doth in the fourth place, repeat the call in the end of verse 13, " Arise my love," &c. And this repetition is to shew, 1. His willingness to have it effectual, if sinners were as willing, it would soon be a bargain. 2. Our sluggishness in not answering at once, therefore must word be upon word, call upon call, line upon line, precept upon precept. 3. To bear out the riches of his grace and love in this call, wherein nothing is wanting that can be alleged to persuade a sinner to close with Christ, and to press one that hath closed with him to be cheerful in him : what a heartsome life might sinners have with Christ, if they would embrace him, and dwell with him in the exercise of faith ! they should have always a spring-time, and possess (to say so) the sunny side of the brae of all the world beside, walking in gardens and orchards, where the trees of the promises are ever fruitful, pleasant, and savoury to sight, smell, taste ; and every word of Christ, as the singing of birds, heartsome and delightful to the ear ; and all of them healthful to the believer. Who will have a heart to sit Christ's call? or if they do, who will be able to answer it, when he shall reckon with them? It will leave all the hearers of the gospel utterly inexcusable. *Lastly,* this repetition shews the importunateness, and the peremptoriness of his call ; he will have no refusal, neither will he leave it arbitrary, if we will come, when we will come, or what way : but he straitly enjoineth it, and that just now : it is always time to believe, when Christ calls, and it is never time to shift, when he persuades. All this says, Christ must be a kind and loving Husband ; how greatly play they the fool, that reject him ! and how happy are they who are effectually called to the marriage of the Lamb !

Verse 14. O my dove, that art in the clefts of the rock, in
the secret places of the stairs : let me see thy countenance,
let me hear thy voice ; for sweet is thy voice, and thy countenance is comely.

THIS 14th verse, contains the second part of Christ's
sweet and comfortable sermon ; wherein, besides the title
which he gives his Bride, there are three things, 1. Her
case. 2. The directions which he propones, as the cure of
her case. 3. The motive pressing it.

The title is, " my dove :" this hath a sweet insinuation
and motive in it. Believers are styled so, 1. For their
innocent nature, Matt. x. 16. 2. For their tenderness,
and trembling at the word of the Lord, Hos. xi. 11 ; Isa.
xxxviii. 14. Hezekiah mourned as a dove. 3. For their
beauty and purity, Psalm lxviii. 13. 4. For their chaste
adhering to their own mate, in which respect, that of
Isa. xxxviii. 14, is thought to allude to the mourning of
the one, after the other's death : This shews what a believer should be, and who deserves this name.

The condition of this dove is, that she is " in the clefts
of the rock, and in the secret places of the stairs :" it is
ordinary for doves to hide themselves in the rocks, or
holes in walls of houses ; and this similitude is used sometimes in a good sense, as Isa. lx. 8, sometimes in an ill
sense, as pointing out infirmity, and too much fear and
silliness, Hos. vii. 11, Ephraim is a silly dove without
heart, that goes to Egypt, &c. The Bride is here compared to a dove hiding itself, in the last sense, out of unbelief and anxiety, taking her to poor shifts for ease, and
slighting Christ, as frightened doves that mistake their
own windows, and fly to other hiding-places ; the scope
being to comfort and encourage her, and the directions
calling her to holy boldness, and prayer to him (implying that these had been neglected formerly) doth confirm
this. Then says the Lord, my poor heartless dove, why
art thou discouraged, taking thee to holes (as it were) to
hide thee, fostering misbelief and fainting ? that is not
the right way.

What then should she do (might it be said) seeing she
is so unmeet to converse with him, or look out to the view
of any that looks on ? He gives two directions, holding
forth what was more proper, and fit for her case, 1. Let
me see thy countenance (saith he). Like one that is asham-

ed, thou hidest thyself as if thou durst not appear before me, but come (saith he) let me see thy countenance. This expression imports friendliness, familiarity, and boldness in her coming before him: so this phrase of seeing one's face is taken, Gen. xliii. 3, 5, and 2 Sam. xiv. 32, as the not shewing of the countenance, supposeth discontent or fear; so then the Lord calls by this to holy familiarity with him, and confidence in it, in opposition to her former fainting and misbelief. The second direction is, let me hear thy voice. To make him hear the voice, is to pray, Psalm v. 3, and under it generally all the duties of religion are ofter comprehended: it is like, discouragement scared the heartless Bride from prayer, and she durst not come before him; do not (saith he) but call confidently upon me in the day of trouble, and time of need. *Observ.* 1. Prayer never angers Christ (be the believer's case what it will) but forbearing of it will. 2. Discouragement when it seizes on the child of God, is not soon shaken off; and therefore he not only gives one direction upon another, but also adds encouragements and motives suitable to these directions.

And so we come to the third thing in the verse, the motives he makes use of to press his directions, which are two, 1. "Sweet is thy voice." 2. "Thy countenance is comely." What is my voice and countenance, might she say (for proud unbelief is exceeding humble, and subtile, when it is opposing, and quarreling with Christ's call) yea, (saith he) thy voice is sweet; there is no music in the world so pleasant to me, as the prayer of a poor believer. Now this doth not so much commend our prayers, as it shews his acceptation of them, and the excellency of his golden censer, that makes them with his odours so savoury before God, Rev. viii. 3. And, 2, (saith he) thy countenance though there be spots on it, yet to me it is comely, therefore let me hear thy voice, let me see thy countenance. Christ had rather converse with a poor believer, than with the most gallant, stately person in all the world. Besides, *Observ.* 1. Fainting may overmaster even a poor believer, and misbelief may mire him. 2. There are often foolish feckless shifts made use of by believers, for defending misbelief and discouragement, when they are under temptation. 3. Faithless fears, and discouragement may come to that height, as to scare believers from Christ's company, and mar them in prayer to him. 4. Misbelief bears out still this to a tempted soul that Christ cares not for it; yea, that he disdains such a person and his company. 5. Christ is tender of fainting believers, and of their consolation, even when they suspect him most, and when their suspicions are most unreasonable and uncharitable to him, Isa. xlix. 14, 15. 6. Christ allows poor believers a familiar and confident walk with him ; they might all be courtiers, for the access that is allowed them, if they did not refuse their allowance, and sinfully obstruct their own access thereto. 7. Christ loves to be much employed by his people, and there is nothing more pleasing to him, than frequently to hear their voice. 8. He is a sweet and gentle constructer of them, and their service ; and is not rigid, even when often they have many misconstructions of him. 9. The more discouragement seizeth upon the soul, there should be the more prayer, and thronging in upon Christ ; for there is no outgate to be expected, but in that way. 10. None needs to fear to put Christ on their secrets ; or they need not so to fear (if they be sincere) that they spill their prayers, as thereby to be kept from prayer, or made heartless in it ; for it is Christ that hears them, whose censer, Rev. viii. 6, makes them savoury before God : "let me hear thy voice," is no little encouragement in that duty : and the right consideration of it, would help to much boldness in prayer ; and especially considering, that the God who is the hearer of prayer, is our Beloved.

Verse 15.   Take us the foxes, the little foxes that spoil the vines : for our vines have tender grapes.

THIS 15th verse contains the last part of Christ's sermon ; wherein, as he had formerly given directions in reference to her particular walk, so here he evidenceth his care of her external peace : that Christ speaks these words, the continuation and series of them with the former, the scope (which is to make full proof of his care) and the manner how the duty here mentioned is laid on, to wit, by way of authority, makes it clear. There are three things in them, 1. An external evil incident to the church, and that is, to be spoiled by foxes. 2. A cure given in a direction ; take them, &c. 3. He gives reasons to deter all from cruel pity in sparing of them, "for," &c. In clearing the case here supposed, as incident to the church, we are to consider, 1. What these vines are. 2. What be these foxes. 3. How they spoil the vines. For clearing the first, consider, that the visible church is often compared in scripture to a vineyard, Matt. xxi. 33. And the particular professors, especially believers, are as the vine trees that grow in it; so, Isa. v. 7, "the vineyard of the Lord is the house of Israel," collectively, "and the men of Judah are his pleasant plants." They are called so, 1. For their fecklessness in themselves, Ezek. xv. 2, 3, &c. yet excelling in fruit beyond others. 2. Because of God's separating them from others, and taking pains on them above all others, Isa. xxvii. 2, 3, for these and other reasons, they are called vines. Next, by foxes are understood false teachers Ezek. xiii. 4. " O Israel, thy prophets" (that is, thy flattering teachers, as the context clears) "are as foxes in the deserts." And, (Matt. vii. 15,) they are called wolves in sheep's clothing: hereby are meant, not all those who in something differ in their own judgment from the received rule, if they vent it not for corrupting of others, or the disturbing of the church's peace; but those who are, in respect of others, seducers, teaching men to do as they do, in that which tends to the church's hurt; and such also, as by flattery and unfaithfulness, destroy souls, proportionally come in to share of the name, as they do of the thing signified thereby, as that place of Ezekiel, before cited, and chap. xxxiv. 2, 3, doth confirm. Now they get this name for their resembling foxes, in three things, 1. In their abominable nature; wherefore they are called, foxes, wolves, dogs, &c. and such like, which are abhorred and hated of all men; and so are these most hateful to God, and so ought they to be with all others. 2. For their destroying, hurtful nature, in their destroying of the church; therefore called "ravening wolves," Matt. vii. 15; and "grievous wolves," Acts xx. 29; "who subvert whole houses," Tit. i. 11; "and whose word eateth as doth a grangrene," 2 Tim. ii. 17. 3. They are compared to these for their subtilty, a fox being famous for that, for which cause Herod is called a fox, Luke xiii. 32. So false teachers speak lies in hypocrisy, 1 Tim. iv. 2 ; creep into houses, their doctrines eat as a canker insensibly: and they are, 2 Cor. xi. 13, 14, called " deceitful workers :" and as their master Satan can transform himself into an angel of light, so do they themselves into the ministers of Christ: all such beasts whatever their shape be, are hateful to Christ and his church. 3. These false teachers or foxes, are said to "spoil the vines," for foxes hurt not a vineyard, or a flock of lambs more than false teachers do the church. 1. Corrupting the purity of doctrine. 2. Obscuring the simplicity of worship. 3. Overturning the beauty of order and bringing in confusion. 4. Spoiling her bond of unity, and rending the affections, and dividing the ways of her members, thereby dissipating the flock. 5. Extinguishing the vigour and life of christian practice; diverting from what is more necessary, to hurtful and vain janglings, which do still increase to more ungodliness, and have never profited them who are occupied therein, Heb. xiii. 7. 6. By ruining souls, carrying them headlong to the pit, 2 Pet. ii. 1, and iii. 16. There is no hurt nor hazard the church of Christ meets with, or ever met with, more grievous and dangerous, than what she meets with from such, although this be an exercise and trial, ordinarily incident to her.

2. The cure the Lord provides, is, the furnishing of his church with discipline, and the giving of directions for managing of it in these words, "Take us," &c. wherein consider these four, 1. To whom it is directed. 2. What is required. 3. A motive insinuated in the expression, "take us." 4. The extent of the direction, for the obviating of a question. It may be supposed to be directed to one of four. 1. Either to the Bride; or, 2. To angels; or, 3. To magistrates; or, 4. To church guides. Now it is to none of the first three, therefore it must be to the last and fourth: first, It is not to the Bride: for, 1. The word "take" in the original, is in the plural number, and signifieth take ye: now the Lord useth not to speak to the church, but as to one. 2. He says, "take us," and so taking the Bride in with himself, as a party for whom this service is to be performed, the speech must be directed to some third. 2. It is not directed to angels, these are not spoken to in all this Song, and this being a duty to be performed while the church is militant, they come not in to gather the tares from the wheat, till the end of the world, nor to separate the bad fish from the good, till the net be fairly on the shore. 3. This direction cannot be given to the magistrate; for, besides that he is not mentioned in this Song, nor as such, hath he any part in the ministry of the gospel, or is capable to be thus spoken unto

(although the duty from the force of its argument will also reach him in his station, because he should, so far as he can, prevent the spoiling of Christ's vineyard in his place) besides this, I say, this direction must take place in all times, whenever the church hath such a trial to wrestle with, otherwise it were not suitable to Christ's scope, nor commensurable with her need : now for many hundreds of years the church wanted magistrates to put this direction in practice, yet wanted she not foxes, nor was she without a suitable capacity of guarding herself against them, by that power wherewith Christ hath furnished her. It remains therefore, 4. That it must be spoken to Christ's ministers, and officers in the church, called rulers in the scripture, and in this Song, watchmen and keepers of this vineyard, as by office, contradistinguished from professors, chap. iii. 3, and v. 7, and viii. 11, 12. Such the church never wanted, such are required to watch, (Acts xx. 24.) against wolves, and such in the church of Ephesus are commended, (Rev. ii. 3, 4,) for putting this direction in execution. 2. The duty here required is to take them, as men use to hunt foxes till they be taken : and this implies all that is needful for preventing their hurting of Christ's vines : Christ's ministers are to lay out themselves in discovering, confuting and convincing, censuring and rejecting them, Tit. iii. 11. That is, not to endure them that are evil, but to try them judicially, as it is, Rev. ii. 2.

Observ. 1. Christ's church is furnished with sufficient authority in herself, for her own edification, and for censuring of such as would obstruct the same. 2. This church authority is not given to professors in common, or to the Bride as the first subject, but to their guides, Christ's ministers and servants. 3. It is no less a duty, nor is it less necessary to put forth this power against false teachers, than against other gross offenders : so did Paul, 2 Tim. i. *ult.* and so commands he others to do, Tit. iii. 10, heresy and corrupt doctrine being also a fruit of the flesh ; Gal. v. 20, as well as other scandalous sins.

3. There is a motive to press this, implied, while he saith, "take us ;" which words insinuate, that it is service both to him and her, and that ministers are his servants, and the church's for Christ's sake. It shows also his sympathy, in putting himself (as it were) in hazard with her (at least mystically considered) and his love in com-

forting her, that he thinks himself concerned in the restraint of these foxes, as well as she is.

4. The direction is amplified to remove an objection.
Say some, all heresies, or all heretics are not equal, some
comparatively are little to be regarded, and it is cruelty
to meddle with these, that seem to profess fair.   No (saith
he) take them all, even the " the little foxes ;" for, though
they be but little, yet they are foxes, though they be not
of the grossest kind (as all scandals in fact are not alike,
yet none is to be dispensed with) so they are (saith he)
foxes, and corrupt others ; for, a little leaven will leaven
the whole lump (often small-like schisms, or heresies,
such as the Novatians and Donatists, &c. have been exceedingly defacing to the beauty of the church) therefore,
(saith he) hunt and take them all.   How small a friend
is our Lord to toleration ? and how displeased is he with
many errors, that the world thinks little of ? Magistrates,
ministers and people may learn here, what distance ought
to be kept with the spreaders of the least errors, and how
every one ought to concur in their stations, for preventing
the hurt that comes by them.

The last thing in the verse, is the reasons wherewith
this direction is backed and pressed : The first is, all of
them " spoil the vines :" error never runs loose, and heretics never get liberty, but the spoiling of the vines one
way or other follows ; and can beasts be suffered in a
garden, or orchard, and the plants not be hurt ?

2. If any say, they are but little foxes, and unable to
hurt.   He answers this, and adds a second reason, in saying " the grapes are tender ;" or, " the vines are in the
first grapes" that is as they (while scarce budding or
sprouting) are easily blasted by a small wind, so the work
of grace in a believer, or Christ's ordinances in his church,
are most precious and tender wares, and cannot abide
rough hands ; even the least of seducers, or corrupt
teachers, may easily wrong them ; they are of such a nature, as they may soon be spoiled, if they be not tenderly
and carefully looked to.   *Observ.* 1. They that have
grace should be tender of it ; it may easily be hurt.   2.
Gracious persons, should not think themselves without
the reach of hazard from corrupt teachers ; for, this is
spoken of the Bride, " the foxes spoil the vines." 3. Our
Lord Jesus is exceedingly tender of the work of grace,
in and amongst his people, and where it is weakest, he is

some way most tender of it. 4. This argument here made use of, says also, that those who are most tender of his church, and the graces of his people, will be most zealous against false teachers even the least of them ; for these two are joined together in him, and are in themselves necessary to preserve the one, and restrain the other ; and the suffering of these to ramble and run without a check, cannot be the way of building, but of spoiling Christ's church.

The third motive, or reason pressing the watchmen to have a care of the vines, is hinted in the possessive particle, " our," " for our vines," &c. which is relative to the watch-men, whom he takes in with himself, as having a common interest in the church ; the church is his, and theirs, as the flock is the owner's, and the shepherd's, who are particularly set to have the over-sight of it ; for, the shepherd may say, this is my flock, which no other servant can say : and this is a great piece of dignity put upon ministers, to be " fellow workers with Christ," 2 Cor. vi. 1, &c. and binds on their duty strongly ; for, saith Christ here to them, ye will have loss also, if ye see not to it, because ye must account for the vineyard, wherewith ye are intrusted ; It is yours, and yet ye are not absolute lords, for it is also mine, I am the owner of it ; and so the vines are both theirs and Christ's, their interest speaks how naturally they should care for them ; his interest shews the dependency both ministers and people ought to have on him.

Verse 16.   My beloved is mine, and I am his ; he feedeth among the lilies.
17.   Until the day break, and the shadows flee away, turn my beloved, and be thou like a roe or a young hart upon the mountains of Bether.

Now follows the two last parts of her carriage in the Beloved's absence ; first after she hath (as it were) read over this epistle, she comforts herself in his love, and her interest in him though he be absent. (It is a good use of his word, when it is made use of, for strengthening our faith in him, when sense is away). There are two parts of this consolation, 1. Her faith is clear for the present, verse 16.   2. Her hope is solid in the expectation of an excellent day coming, verse 17.   Next, verse 17. she puts up a prayer for a gracious visit, which she knows he will allow upon her until that day come ; and this is the last thing here recorded of the Bride's carriage in the Bridegroom's absence.

In the 16th verse, the faith of her interest in him, is, 1. asserted, " My beloved is mine, and I am his." 2. It is vindicated, or established against an objection in the following words, " he feeds," &c. The assertion holds out an union betwixt him and her, " I am his," &c. or, as it is in the original, " I am to him, and he is to me :" such as is the union betwixt married persons, Hos. iii. 3, which the tie of marriage brings on : even such is this which follows covenanting with God ; for, this union presupposeth it, and is founded on it, Ezek. xvi. 8, " I entered into a covenant with thee, and thou becamest mine," or "to me ;" although (saith she) he be not here, yet he is my husband, and that tie stands betwixt me and him, which is no little privilege ; and in this she comforts herself under absence.

Observ. 1. There is an excellent union, and peculiar tie betwixt Christ and believers, which none other can lay claim to but they : It is excellent, as will easily appear, if we consider these properties of it. 1. It is a near union, they are "one flesh," Eph. v. 27, as man and wife ; " they are flesh of his flesh, and bone of his bone." 2. It is a real and not imaginary union (though it be spiritual and by faith) it makes and transfers a mutual right of the one to the other, and hath real effects. 3. It is mutual on both sides, Christ is wholly hers, and she is wholly dedicated to him. 4. It is a kindly union, such as is betwixt husband and wife, and followed with the fruits of a most sweet relation. 5. It is a union which is some way full ; whole Christ is hers, and she by consent and title is wholly his. 6. It is an indissolvable union, there is no dissolving of it by any thing that can fall out, otherwise the consolation were not solid. Again, *Observ.* 2. That this relation which the believer hath to Christ, is the great ground of his happiness and consolation, and not any sensible presence, or any dispensation, or gift communicated by Christ to him. 3. That believers may attain assurance, and clearness anent their interest in him, and may come to know really that Christ is theirs, and believers should aim to be through in this, that their " calling and election may be made sure" to themselves, 2 Pet. i. 10. 4. Believers when they have attained clearness, should acknowledge it, and comfort themselves in it, and not raise new disputes about it. 5. This clearness may consist with absence and want of sensible presence, and there is no case, wherein a believer should stick faster to his confidence, than in such a case, when under desertion and absence, as the Spouse doth here.

2. She vindicates her faith in these words, " He feedeth among the lilies." The words may be looked upon as the preventing of an objection, for it might be said, If Christ be yours, where is he? Is it likely that he is yours, when he is so far away? For, the faith of clearness will be assaulted and set upon, and it is not easily maintained, and unbelief takes the advantage of Christ's absence from sense, to brangle it; so that unbelief and temptation especially sets on then: therefore, she answers it thus, " He feedeth among the lilies," that is, he is kind to his people, and present with them, though now I see him not; faith may, and will argue from Christ's love to his people in general, and from the promises that speak to all, when there seems to be nothing singular in the believer's own condition, from which he can take comfort. By lilies are understood all believers: the church was called a lily, verse 2. Here all believers are so called, as partaking of that same beauty and savour, and because planted in the same true garden. Christ was called a lily, verse 1. and here all believers are called lilies, shewing, 1. That all believers have a conformity to Christ, and partake of the divine nature and Spirit that is in him. 2. That all believers in things that are essential to grace and holiness, have conformity one to another, they have the same faith, Spirit, covenant, Husband, &c. although in circumstantials and degrees, there be differences. Next, this " feeding" amongst them, shews, 1. A special gracious presence in his church, and among believers; there he "walketh among the seven golden candlesticks, Rev. ii. 1. 2. A special delight he hath in them, and satisfaction to be amongst them, as a man delighteth to walk in his garden: it is " his meat" (John iv. 32, 34.) " and drink" to do them good; so then (saith she) he is kind to all his people, and is so to me, though for the time I see him not: and thus also she answers the question, chap. vi. 1, 2, even when Christ is a-seeking, and she was enquiring after him. *Observ.* 1. Christ's care of his church, and love to his Bride, is no less under absence, than when his presence

is sensibly enjoyed. The consideration of this, tends much to further the consolation of believers, and it becomes them well to believe this, when under desertion and absence, and so to ward off temptations.

The solid exercise of faith never wants hope waiting on it, therefore, 2dly, Verse 17, that follows, for completing the Bride's consolation in these words, "until the day break, and the shadows," &c. Though there be shadows (saith she) and vails betwixt him and me, in this night of desertion ; yet there is a day coming when these, by his presence, shall be made to flee away, and I shall see him as he is. There is a twofold day spoken of in scripture, 1. A day of Christ's presence here upon earth, Luke i. 78. " The day-spring from on high hath visited us." 2. The day of his glorious appearing, commonly called the great day ; and in a singular way called here " the day," because it hath no night of interruption following thereupon, and because it goes as far beyond what believers possess now, as day exceeds the night ; therefore it is called " the morning," Psalm xlix. 14, in which the just shall have the dominion ; and, the dawning of the day, and, the rising of the day-star in our hearts, 2 Pet. i. 19, which is there opposed to the clearest prophecies and ordinances, which are but as a candle in a dark place in respect of that day. Now we conceive the last and great day is signified here, I. Because that is her scope, to comfort herself in the hope of what is coming. II. Because she opposeth it to the present means, as to shadows, even to faith itself, for that she enjoyed for the time ; and also to sensible presence, which in the next words she prays for, till the day dawn. By " shadows" is meant, whatever mars the immediate, full, and satisfying enjoying of Christ, which as shadows, hides him from us, or darkens him that we do not see him as he is, or gives but small and dark representations of him, (like shadows of the body) which are very unproportioned unto his own excellent worth. They are said to " flee away," because a glimpse of Christ then, when he who is the Sun of righteousness, shall shine at the break of that day, shall dispel and dissipate them more fully and quickly, than this natural sun when rising, doth scatter darkness and shadows that go before it. And by " until," we understand the setting of a fixed term, which distinguisheth one time from another, as Gen. xxxii. " I will not let thee go until thou

bless me ;" so saith she, until that day of immediate presence come, let me have love-visits, as is expressed in the
following words. *Observ.* 1. There is an excellent day
coming to believers, wherein Christ shall be immediately
enjoyed and seen, and wherein the soul shall be comforted
with no mediate object, or created excellency, but shall
see his face, and be filled with the fulness of God. 2.
While here there are many shadows even betwixt Christ
and the strongest believers ; " we see but darkly as in a
glass," 1 Cor. xiii. 12. There is, 1. A shadow of desertion, and his hiding of himself. 2. A shadow of ordinances,
where he is seen, yet but darkly, like a face in a looking-
glass. 3. A shadow of sinful infirmities, drawing vails
betwixt Christ and us, and hiding his face from us, Isa.
lix. 2. 4. A shadow of natural infirmity ; for, not only
are we ready through unbelief to slander him, but by
reason of weakness (like narrow or old bottles) we are
not capable of him, and unable to contain him. III. At
that day of his appearing, all these shadows will instantly
be done away : there will not one tear be left on any believer's cheeks, there will be no affliction or desertion to
hide him from them, but they shall be for ever with him :
there will then be no ordinances, nor temple, Rev. xxi.
22, " but the Lord God, and the Lamb himself, shall be
the temple" and light of his people : nor will there be
any sinful infirmities then to interpose betwixt him and
them ; death, the curse and corruption, will be cast into
the lake : no unclean thing accompanies the believer into
the New Jerusalem ; nay, no imperfect thing is there,
for whatever is imperfect, and whatever was in part, is
then done away, 1 Cor. xiii. 10, and what is perfect will
then come ; the soul in its faculties will then be perfected,
capacitated and dilated, to conceive, take up, and delight
in God ; and the body perfected, made glorious and spiritual, like the glorious body of our Lord Jesus, Philip, iii.
ult. 4. The hope of that day, and of the fleeing away of
all shadows then, is (and no marvel it be) very refreshful
to the Lord's people : and believers in all their darknesses
should comfort themselves and others from the hope of it,
1 Thess. iv. *ult.* 5. And all that are Christ's, or whoever
have faith in Christ, and fellowship with him by virtue of
his covenant, may expect at that day to enjoy Christ immediately and fully, and to see him as he is : O that men
believed this ! and that many were thronging into his cove-

nant now, as they would not desire to be cast from his presence in that day! yet, 6. All shadows are never removed till then ; the believer must, and some way will submit to Christ's way of ordering it so, and not seek it should be otherwise till then.

In the last place, the Bride falls about the exercise of prayer, in the rest of this verse ; faith and hope in exercise always stir up to prayer : for, these graces do not foster laziness and security, but incite and provoke to duty (it is a good token when faith and hope are so accompanied) therefore she turns her to prayer, in which she speaks to him as to her beloved : clearness of interest, as it helps notably to many things, so to confidence in prayer especially. The petition (importing still absence) hath these two in it, 1. The suit itself, " turn." 2. The enforcing and enlarging of it, " be like a roe," &c. Turning here, implies, 1. Sense and feeling of his absence. 2. Her serious desire to have Christ again. 3. That his absence may be removed by his own returning, and so the change of her case to the better must flow from him. And, 4. That she may ask this from him, and expect by prayer in faith to obtain it, believing prayer being the best means to effectuate this. Next, she enforceth and enlargeth her petition, " be thou like a roe," &c. that is, seeing (saith she) all shadows will not be removed till that time, what is my suit for the time ? it is even this, that thou wilt give me visits of thy presence, and be like " a roe or a young hart on the mountains of Bether." The word " Bether," signifies division, and so it may be made use of here : so long (saith she) as these mountains divide betwixt me and thee, Lord, be not a stranger, but swiftly, easily, and kindly (as the roes come over mountains to their mates, Prov. v. 19.) come thou to me, and comfort me with frequent love-visits, until that time come, that thou take me to thee, to enjoy thee fully and immediately. *Observ.* 1. It is lawful for believers to desire sensible presence, even here-away : yea, it is suitable, they should often long and pray for it. 2. Where the hope of heaven is solid, sensible manifestations of Christ's love will be most ardently sought for : it will never prejudge one of their satisfaction and full payment, then, that they have gotten a large earnest-penny here, she knows that will never be reckoned up to her. 3. Much prayer, flowing from, and waiting upon the exercise of faith and hope, is a notable way to bring the soul to the enjoyment of sense. 4. The believer hath a heartsome life, and a rich inheritance, Christ here, and Christ hereafter; "the lines are fallen unto him in pleasant places." 5. She grounds her suit on the marriage-relation and tie betwixt him and her, "my Beloved" (saith she). A covenant-claim to Christ, is the most solid ground upon which believers can walk in their approaches before him, and in their pleadings with him. 6. He allows believers to plead for his company, from this ground, that he is theirs by covenant, as he pleads for their company, on that same ground, verse 10, &c.

CHAPTER III.

BRIDE.

Verse 1. By night on my bed I sought him whom my soul loveth : I sought him, but I found him not.
2. I will rise now, and go about the city in the streets, and in the broad ways I will seek him whom my soul loveth: I sought him, but I found him not.

THIS chapter hath three parts, 1. The Bride's sad exercise under the want of Christ, and in seeking after him till she find him, to verse 6. 2. The daughters of Jerusalem come in, commending the Bride, verse 6. 3. The Bride, from verse 7, to the end, returns to discourse of, and commend the excellency and amiableness of Christ.

In her exercise consider, 1. Her case. 2. Her carriage in several steps. 3. Her success in every step. 4. Her practice when she hath obtained her desire : or, we may take them up in these two, 1. Her sad condition, and her carriage under it. 2. Her outgate and her carriage suitable thereto. Her case is implied in two words, in the beginning of verse 1. 1. It was night with her. 2. She was on "her bed." By "night," is ordinarily understood darkness and affliction, opposite to light of day and joy ; and here her exercise being spiritual, it must imply some spiritual affliction, or soul-sad spiritual exercise. So "night" is taken, Psalm xlii. 8. "He will command his lovingkindness in the day, and in the night" (while the day comes, that his loving kindness be intimated) "his song shall be with me," &c. The scope shews, that it is

a night of desertion she is under, through the want of
Christ's presence whom she loves : his presence, who is
the Sun of righteousness with healing under his wings,
makes the believer's day ; and his absence is their night,
and makes them droop, as being under a sad night of soul
affliction ; therefore is it, that she seeks so carefully after
his presence. 2. Her being " on her bed," is not taken
here, as implying nearness with him, for the scope shows
he is absent ; but a laziness of frame on her spirit, opposite to activeness and diligence, as it is taken, chap. v.
verse 3, and so it is opposed to her after-rising and diligence, and therefore it is also called " my bed," implying
that she was here alone in a secure comfortless frame, and
therefore for this, it is distinguished from " our bed," chap.
i. 16, and " his bed" afterward, verse 7, where she is allowed rest, and spiritual ease, and solace in his company ;
but here on her bed she hath no such allowance, whatever
carnal ease and rest she takes to herself: believers have
their own fits of carnal security, when they give their
corruptions rest, that is, their own bed : and it is a heartless lair (to speak so) to lie alone and want the Beloved :
this is her case, wanting Christ, yet lying too still, as contented some way in that condition ; though it cannot continue so with believers, it will turn heavy and perplexing
at last to them, as it doth here to the Bride : and sure,
the easiest time under security is not so comfortable and
profitable to believers, as is an exercise that takes them
more up ; therefore afterward she prefers rising and
seeking, to this woful rest.   It shows, 1. That believers'
distance and darkness may grow ; for, in the former
chapter, Christ was absent, yet, as through a window or
lattice, there were some glimpses of him ; but here it is
" night," and there is not so much as a twilight discovery
of him. 2. Often, distance with Christ, and security and
deadness (as to our spiritual life) go together: when
Christ is absent, believers then usually fall from activity
in their duty, Isa. lxiv. 7. " No man stirreth up himself
to lay hold on thee," and the reason is, " thou hast hid
thy face," &c. Matt. xxv. 5, " While the Bridegroom
tarried," even the wise virgins " slumbered and slept."
   Her carriage, or way that she takes in this case, is set
out in four steps : The 1. Is in these words, " I sought
him, whom my soul loveth." Consider here, I. The title
Christ gets, " him, whom." &c. Christ got this name be-

fore, and now several times she repeats it, And it holds
forth, 1. The sincerity of her love, it was her soul and
heart that loved him.   2. The degree and singularity of
it, no other thing was admitted in her heart to compare
with him, he bears the alone sway there in respect of the
affection she had to him, it is he and none other, upon
whom her soul's love is set, otherwise, this title would not
suitably designate him ; Christ loves well to have such
titles given to him, as may import the heart's special
esteem of him.   3. It shews, that even in believers' lowest
conditions, there remains some secret soul-esteem of Christ,
and that in their judgment he is still their choice and
wale above all the world.   Yet, 4. That their practice
while security prevails, is most unsuitable to their convictions and judgment,   II. Consider her practice and
carriage.   While Christ is absent her practice is not altogether a lying by, without the form of religion ; for, (saith
she) on my bed " I sought him," that is, I prayed and
used some means, but in a lazy way, not stirring up myself vigorously in it.   *Observ.* 1. Believers in a secure
frame, may keep some form of duty, yet their duties are
like the frame of their heart, lifeless and hypocritical.   2.
There is much of believers' practice, such as themselves
will find fault with, when they come to look rightly upon
it ; yea, even much of their way, while they keep up the
form of duty, is but like the sluggard, Prov. xxvi. 14,
turning themselves upon their beds, as the door upon the
hinges ; not lying still nor altogether daring to give
over the form, yet little better on the matter, because
they make no effectual progress, nor can they say their
soul is in and with their service, which they perform.   3.
Her success, as to this step, is, " but I have found him
not," that is, I was nothing the better, these sluggish endeavours did not my business : every form of seeking will
not obtain, and one may seek Christ long in their ordinary
formal way, ere they find him ; yet it is good not to give
over, but to observe the form : life and love is not altogether gone, when one discerns absence and their own
laziness, with discontent.

When this doth not reach her design, she proceeds to
a more lively step, verse 2, and that is, to get up, and
seek him in a more active and stirring way : which says,
1. She observed the continuance of her distance, and
what came of her prayers and seeking : which is a goo

beginning of one's recovery, and winning to their feet after a fit of security and decay. 2. It says, it is often good for a believer, as to his rousing, and his recovering of spiritual life, that sense is not always easily obtained ; this activity had not followed (readily) had not Christ constrained her to it, by cross dispensations and disappointments. In this step we have, 1. Her resolving to fall about a more active way in seeking him. 2. Her performance. 3. Her success. *First*, Her resolution is, " I will rise now" (saith she) "and go about the streets," &c. In which there are these three, 1. What she resolves to do ;—not to give over (for that should never be given way to) but to bestir herself more actively in duty, " I will rise and go" from the bed to the streets of the city and seek him there. By "city" is understood the church, whereof all members are "fellow-citizens," Eph. ii. 19. It is called so, 1. For its order and government ; so the church is as a city, that hath watchmen and laws. 2. For its unity ; it is one commonwealth and incorporation, Eph. ii. 12. This Jerusalem is a city compacted together, Psalm cxxii. 3. 3. For its privileges, whereof all believers (who are the burgesses and fellow-citizens) are partakers, Eph, ii. 19, and unto which all others who are without, are strangers. Her "going into the city," suppones a communicating of her case to others for help, and her using of more public means, opposite to her private dealing with herself on her bed, verse 1. even as rising imports a stirring of herself to more activity in the manner of performing these duties, opposite to her seeking him formerly while she lay still on her bed : the thing then resolved upon is to this sense, what am I doing? are there not more means, in the use of which I may seek Christ? Is there not another way of enquiring after him, than this lazy formal way? I will up and essay it. There are many means given for a believer's help, and when one fails, another may be blessed, and therefore, believers are still to follow from one to another ; and where true love to Christ is, it will make them do so, and spare no pains till they meet with him. Again, verse 2. Ere she gets to her feet, and goes to the streets, &c. she deliberately resolves it, " I will rise," &c. which shows, 1. That her former disappointment did put her to a consultation what to do, and made her more serious ; and this is the use that ought to be made of disappointments in the duties of religion. 2. That there will be heart-deliberations in a christian walk, when it is serious; and they are the best performances and duties, that are the results of those. 3. Serious resolutions are often very useful, and helpful in duty; for, they are engagements, and spurs to stir up to duty, when we are indisposed for it. 4. It is good cordially to resolve upon duty, when the practice of it is somewhat difficult or obstructed; for, this both speaks sincerity, and also helps to lessen the difficulty which is in the way of duty. 5. Resolutions to set about duty are sometimes the greatest length believers can win at, while under indisposition; and this much is better than nothing, because it draws on more.

This resolution is qualified, " I will rise now" (saith she); that is, seeing these sluggish endeavours doth not avail me, I will delay no longer, but will now presently fall about it in more earnest. It is the sign of a sincere resolution, when it doth not put off or shift duty, but engageth the soul in a present undertaking of it, Psalm cxix. 59, 60.

Next, her performance, or her putting this resolution in practice, doth accordingly follow instantly, " I sought him" (said she) that is, in the streets, &c. *Observ.* 1. It is not a resolution worth the mentioning, that hath not practice following ; for every honest resolution is followed with practice, whatever shortcoming wait upon it. 2. Honest resolutions are often to duty, like a needle that draws the thread after it; and believers should not fear to resolve on duty from fear of coming short in performance, if their resolutions be undertaken in the strength of Christ, as this was, as is clear by considering her former frame, which was such as would give no great encouragement to self undertakings in duties.

Lastly. Her success, or rather her disappointment follows in these words, " but I found him not," even then when I was most serious in seeking him, I missed him still; which is not only spoken to show the event, but also by way of regret, she is deeply affected with it. *Observ.* 1. When the Lord's people have been formerly lazy, Christ may keep up himself, even when they become more active, rather hereby chastening their former negligence, than being offended at their present diligence in duty. 2. It is sad when Christ is missed even in duty, and that once and again. 3. She continues to be a dis-

tinct observer of the fruits both of public and private duties
which is a commendable practice, and to be made conscience of by all the seekers of his face.

Verse 3.   The watchmen that go about the city, found me ; to
whom I said, saw ye him whom my soul loveth?

THIS verse contains the third step of the Bride's carriage ; being now abroad, the watchmen found her, and
she enquires for her beloved at them : and her success in
this may be gathered from what follows, she doth not
upon recourse to them immediately find him, but is put
to go a little further.   In the words, there is, 1. An opportunity or means for finding Christ, met with.   2. Her
improving of it.   3. Her success which is implied, as is
said.
   I. The means holds forth these three things, 1. What the
church is ; it is a city, wherein there is order, and a common fellowship, as hath been said, verse 2.   2. The minister's office is here implied : this city hath " watchmen ;"
so are ministers called Ezek. iii. 17 ; Isa. lxii 6 ; Heb.
xiii. 17.   Which words imports, 1. That the church is a
city in danger, having outward and inward enemies, and
therefore needing watchmen.   2. That there is the office
of a ministry appointed in the church for guarding against
and preventing her danger ; and that some are peculiarly
designed, and separated from others for that purpose ;
some who may be called " watchmen," which others cannot be said to be ; and so they are here distinguished from
believers or private persons.   3. This office is most necessary, burdensome, and of great concernment to the
safety of the church, as watchmen are to the city ; for so
watch they over the souls of the people committed to their
trust.
   Again these watchmen, are in the exercise of their
duty, They went about the city : which shows their diligence according to their trust ; at least, it holds forth the
end wherefore they are appointed.   *Observ.* There is but
one city or church, and all ministers are watchmen of that
one church, given for the edification of that body ; and
they should watch, not only for this or that post (to say
so) but for the safety of the whole, as watchmen that
stand at their post, for the good of the whole city.
   These watchmen found her, that is, (as we conceive)

by their doctrine they spoke to her condition, and by their searching and particular application, made the two-edged sword of the word reach her; as if they had discernably pointed her out, beyond all the rest of the congregation: which shews, 1. The efficacy of the word when rightly managed, Heb. iv. 12, It "is a discerner of the thoughts and intents of the heart. 2. That God can make it find out one in the midst of many others, when the minister knows not; and can make it speak to a believer's case, or any other particular person's condition, as if he did know and aim at them particularly. 3. That ministers should be searching, and differencing in their doctrine, as their several conditions, and various exercises of hearers require: that is, they ought to put differences betwixt the precious and the vile, and rightly to divide the word of truth, or to lay every one's portion to them so as it be not given in gross, or heaped together to all, but to every one their own allowance. In sum then, that which she says, is this, when I had gone abroad, (saith she) in heaviness to hear (if so I might meet with Christ in public) God made some watchmen speak to my condition particularly, as if one had acquainted them with it.

II. Her improving of this opportunity (coming as it were, beyond her expectation) follows in the next words: she cries out in an abrupt manner, "Saw ye him;" she thinks they can help her, being acquainted with such cases, and therefore she will consult them; that is, she follows in, upon the little experience she had felt of their skill, to seek for help from them, and for that end to communicate her case to them, as it were after sermon is done, or when some convenient time offers. *Observ.* 1. That believers that are serious, will let no fit opportunity for meeting with Christ pass; they are accurate observers, and frugal managers of them all. 2. She observes and is glad when a word speaks home to her case, and finds her; and this is indeed the disposition of a sound and serious believer. 3. Ministers should be well acquainted themselves with soul-sickness, and expert in the various exercises and cases incident to the people of God, both in order to the finding out their disease, and the cause of it (who often can scarce make language of their own condition themselves) and also in order to the making suitable applications for the cure of it; for, this is to have the tongue of the learned, to speak a word in season. 4. Believers often can say little of their cases but in a broken and confused way; which says, ministers had need to be the better acquainted with the spiritual cases and exercises of souls, that they may understand by half a word what they would say. 5. Believers should advert well to whom they communicate their case, this should not be done to all.   6. Ministers are suitable physicians (though not the sole, or only physician) to whom believers should make known their soul-exercises and cases, and therefore, there should be much spiritual sympathy betwixt their people and them.   7. It is a great encouragement to a distressed soul, to impart its case to a minister, when in his public doctrine he useth to speak pertinently unto it.   8. It is not unsuitable for exercised souls (besides the public hearing of their minister) to have their particular queries to him in private. 9. How Christ shall be obtained, is a suitable subject for ministers and people, in their converse together, to be mainly taken up with ; and holy anxiety concerning this, is a frame fit for making addresses to ministers ; they may indeed come to ministers with such questions, who are much in longing after him.   10. There may be much tenderness in affection and love, where there is much weakness in knowledge.   He is the " him" whom her soul loveth, even now when she knows not where he is ; and the most grown believers may be sometimes brought to this low ebb in their condition, for good ends, and for demonstrating the usefulness and necessity of public ordinances, even to them.   11. An exercised soul prizeth most a ministry ; and such spiritual exercises (as are here mentioned) do cherish their esteem of that ordinance, when other debates among a people often do derogate from its due esteem.   12. Ministers should not cast affection, nor reject zeal in weak christians, even though these be joined with some infirmities, and may occasion some more trouble to themselves : but where sincerity is, there should be an overcoming condescendance as to both these, and the questions of a tender soul should be by them entertained, as having learned at their Master, not to break a bruised reed.   13. Tender exercised souls usually confine their questions to their own soul's case ; there is no abstract curious query here, nor for the fashion proposed, nor any needless debate about extrinsic things, or the faults or practice of others : but, " Saw ye him whom my soul loveth ?"   This is the sore upon which she keeps her finger, and this is the wound which she keeps bleeding, till he bind it up.

III. The success of her meeting with the watchmen, and of this query she puts to them, though it be not expressed, yet it is implied in the first words of the next verse, which being compared with this, holds out two things, 1. That she did not presently find an outgate from under her sad case, for she behoved to go further. 2. It was but a little further that she is put to go, till she find him ; which says, that her endeavours were not altogether fruitless. *Observ.* 1. Christ will sometimes let believers know, that all means without him are empty, and that he is restricted to none of them ; yea, nor to any fellowship, no not of the most powerful minister. 2. Public means do not always bring present ease unto believers under disquieting cases, yet, (to say so) they dispose and make way for it in private ; and one may get the good of an ordinance, and of fellowship with ministers or christians, though not in the mean time, yet afterward even when they are retired at home ; and it is as good a time thereafter, yea, and better for their behoof.

If it be asked here, what we should judge of these watchmen, if they were tender or not? The ground of the doubt is, because chap. v. 7, watchmen that are not tender are spoken of, which yet are there said to find the Bride. *Answ.* There is a twofold finding, 1. When one searches an exercised condition for this end, that he may contribute something for the exercised person's ease and help. 2. When one follows or searches after tenderness in others, that we may find some advantage against them, thereby to make the heart of the righteous sad : the one finds, as a friend finds another : the other as an enemy or mocker finds another : the first sort of finding is to be understood here in this chapter, for the watchmen here carry as friends ; the second sort of finding, chap. v. 7, for there they carry as mockers : which will appear by these differences, 1. Here she propones her case to them for their help, it is like being encouraged thereto, by their finding out her case before in the preaching of the word, but chap. v. 7. she doth no such thing. 2. When they find her, chap. v. 7, they smite her and put her to shame, which makes her silent : but their finding her here, doth encourage her. 3. Though here she find not Christ instantly, yet she says not as in the for-

mer steps, " I found him not," she could not altogether
say so, and immediately after she finds him ; but chap. v.
she goes long seeking him, after she meets with the
watchmen ; yea, goes from them heavier, and more
wounded than when she came : and this Song being to
hold forth the various conditions of a believer, and it being incident to them sometimes to fall in tender hands,
and sometimes, yea, often in the hands of those which are
rough and untender, we judge it safest to understand this
place of the first, and chap. v. of the last, and especially
because this makes most for the believer's instruction and
consolation, which is here aimed at, and this is more suitable to the scope of the Song, than that both should be
understood one way.

Verse 4.   It was but a little that I passed from them, but I
found him whom my soul loveth : I held him, and would not
let him go, until I had brought him into my mother's house,
and into the chamber of her that conceived me.

THE beginning of this verse, contains the last step of
the Bride's carriage, and also her desired success, She
went "a little" further, and " but a little," and she finds
him whom her soul loveth : public ordinances and fellowship with godly men, are very useful and necessary, but
not to be rested on ; and they who find not the desired
outgate by these, should not immediately give over the
business as desperate and hopeless ; for, there is something even beyond these to be aimed at, " a little further"
must be gone, which is the first thing in the verse : and
we conceive it doth import these two, 1.   A more immediate going to Christ himself, (as if the ministers had
said) ye must go over and beyond means, to Christ
himself, and denying these, lean and rest, and that wholly
on him : they go beyond means, that rest not on them,
and are denied to them in the use of them, as that man,
Matt. xvii. 14, that brought his son to the disciples, to
get the Devil cast out, and when they did it not, he
went not away, but stayed for Christ himself, and told
the case to him : Christ can do when means fail, and
we should trust him, when they seem to disappoint us :
how feckless are the best of ministers, when himself
is not present ?   2. This going " a little further," doth
not import the doing of any duties she had not done,

but a more vigorous and lively manner of going about these. There had some heartlessness, unbelief, and indisposition stuck to her, in all the former steps and strugglings ; now she steps further in, and goes further in the use of these same means ; and not speaking to the minister, when she finds that the moving of his lips cannot assuage her grief, she looks through to the Master, and vigorously addresses herself to the exercise of faith in him, and of prayer to him, &c. in a more serious way than she had done before. *Observ.* 1. Sometimes believers may lay too much weight on outward and public means ; they may rest too much there, and go on further than these. 2. It is God's goodness, by disappointment in means, to train his people on to a further length of power and life in their practice. 3. It may be when a believer hath satisfied himself in going about all external means, and that in the due order, hath neglected none of them, that there is still somewhat more to do, as to the bettering of his inward frame. 4. It is not a desperate business, nor are believers forthwith to conclude that their hope is perished, because they have not attained their desire in the use of means for a time. 5. It is not a less practique in the soul-exercises, to go over and beyond means and ordinances in suing for Christ, than to go about them ; and the last is no less necessary than the first. 6. Believers in the use of means, should join these three together, 1. Making conscience of means ; and yet, 2. For the success, looking higher than they ; and, 3. Not standing when they find not instantly ease, or satisfaction by them.

The second thing here, is her success, which is according to her desire, " I found him" (saith she) ; when I had pressed but a little further, he sensibly and surprisingly made himself known to me. *Observ.* 1. Christ is not far off from his people when they are seeking him, whatever they may think when he hides himself. 2. They who love Christ, and conscionably follow all means for obtaining him are not far from finding, nor he far from manifesting himself to them. 3. They who sincerely press forward to the life of ordinances beyond the form, and by faith take themselves to Christ himself for the blessing, not resting on their performances will not long miss Christ, yea, it may be, he will give them a sensible manifestation of himself sooner than they are aware ; for, " the

Spirit is obtained, not by the works of the law, but by the hearing of faith," Gal. iii. 2. 4. A soul that sincerely loves Christ, should not, and when in a right frame will not give over seeking Christ till it find him, whatever disappointment it meets with ; and sure such will find him at last. 5. Christ found after much search, will be very welcome, and his presence then will be most discernible. 6. Believers should no less observe, and acknowledge their good success in the means, than their disappointments ; there are many who often make regrets of their bonds, that are deficient in acknowledging God's goodness when they get liberty.

Next, In this verse we have her carriage set down, when she hath found him ; she doth not then lay by diligence, as if all were done, but is of new taken up, with as great care to retain and improve this mercy, as before she was solicitous to attain it : whether a believer want or have ; whether he be seeking, or enjoying, there is still matter of exercise for him in his condition. This her care to retain Christ (which is the fourth thing in the first part of this chapter) is laid down in three steps. 1. She endeavours to hold him that she again lose not the ground she had gained. 2 She seeks to have other members of that same church getting good of Christ also : and these two are in this verse. 3. When his presence is brought back to the church and ordinances, her care is to admonish, yea, charge that he be entertained well with them, lest they should provoke him to be gone, verse 5.

The first step then of her care is, " I held him and would not let him go :" as a wife having found her husband, whom she much longed for, hangs on him lest he depart again, so doth she ; which is an expression both of her fear, love, care, and faith. This holding of Christ, and not letting him go, imports, 1. A holy kind of violence, more than an ordinary, wherewith the Bride strives and wrestles to retain him. 2. That Christ (as it were) waits for the believer's consent in this wrestling, as he saith to Jacob, Gen. xxxii. 26, " I pray thee, let me go :" which upon the matter seems to say, I will not go, if thou wilt hold me, and have me stay. 3. It imports an importunate adhering to him, and not consenting upon any terms to quit him. And lastly it imports the singular and inexpressible satisfaction she had in him ; her very life lay in the keeping him still with her, and therefore she holds him, and cannot think of parting with him.   Now this presence of Christ (being spiritual) cannot be understood in a carnal way, nor can they be carnal grips that retain him ; and his power being omnipotent, it cannot be the force of a frail creature that prevails, but it is here as in Hos. xii. 2, 3, In Jacob's prevailing, "he wept and made supplication," that is, an humble, ardent suing to him by prayer, with a lively exercise of faith on his promises (whereby he allows his people to be pressing) engageth him to stay ; he is tied by his own love that is in his heart, and his faithfulness in his promises, that he will not withdraw, and deny them that, for which they made supplication to him, more than if he were by their strength prevailed over, and overcome ; as a little weeping child will hold its mother or nurse, not because it is stronger than she, but because the mother's bowels so constrain her, as she cannot almost, though she would, leave that child ; so Christ's bowels yearning over a believer, are that which here hold him, that he cannot go ; he cannot go, because he will not.   Here we have ground to observe the importunateness of sincere love, which is such, as with an holy wilfulness it holds to Christ and will not quit him, as Jacob said, " I will not let thee go."   2. We may observe here the power of lively faith (to which nothing is impossible) love and faith will stick to Christ against his own seeming entreaties, till they gain their point, and will prevail, Gen. xxxii. 28.   3. See here the condescending, the wonderful condescending of the Almighty, to be held by his own creature, to be, as it were, at their disposal, " I pray thee, let me go," Gen. xxxii. 26, and Exod. xxxii. 10, " Let me alone, Moses ;" so long as a believer will not consent to quit Christ, so long keeps their faith grip of him, and he will not offend at this importunity ; yea, he is exceedingly well pleased with it : it cannot be told how effectual prayer and faith would be, if fervent and vigorous.

The second step of her carriage, which is the scope of the former ; namely of her holding him, is in these words, "till I had brought him to my mother's house to the chambers of her that conceived me."   By "mother" in scripture is understood the visible church, which is even the believer's mother, Hos. ii. 1, " Say to Ammi (my people) "plead with your mother."   So chap. i. 6, this mother hath children, both after the flesh and after the spirit, the former hating the latter ; and chap. viii. 5. It is the mother that hath ordinances, for the Bride's instruction. The church visible is called the mother, because, 1. By the immortal seed of the word, the Lord begets believers in his church, to which he is Husband, and the Father of these children ; she is the Wife and Mother that conceives them, and brings them up. 2. Because of the covenant tie that stands betwixt God and the visible church, whereby she may claim right to him as her husband (the covenant being the marriage contract betwixt God and the church) which is therefore the ground of the former relation of mother. Again, Christ is said to be brought into the church not only when his ordinances are pure in her, (which is supposed to be here already; for verse 3, there were watchmen doing their duty, and dispensing pure ordinances) but when there is life in them, the presence and countenance of his Spirit going along with them, that they may be powerful for the end appointed: as it was one thing to have the temple, the type of his church, and another, to have God's presence singularly in it ; so it is one thing to have pure ordinances set up in the church, and another, to have Christ's presence filling them with power: now (saith she) when I got Christ, I knew there were many fellow-members of that same church, that had need of him, and I was importunate that he might manifest himself in his ordinances there, for their and my good. Church ordinances, are the allowed and ordinary means of keeping fellowship with Christ, and they are all empty when he is not there. *Observ*. 1. That even true believers have the visible church for their mother, and it is written of them as their privilege, that they were born there, Psal. lxxxvii. 4, 5. 2. Believers should not disclaim the church in which they are spiritually begotten and born, nor their fellow-members therein; but reverence her as the mother that gave them life, and carry respecfully toward her as such ; " honour thy father and mother" being a moral command, and the first with promise. See Psalm cxxii. 3, 6. 3. When believers get nearest Christ for themselves, it is then the fit time to deal with him for others, especially for the church whereof they are members ; it is Moses' only express suit, Exod. xxxiv. 9, when God admits him to his company (in presenting whereof it is said, verse 8, he made haste) " I pray thee, O Lord, go amongst us." 4. It is true tenderness, when one is admitted to more nearness with God than others, not to separate from the church whereof they are members, and as it were to carry Christ to their own chamber ; but to endeavour to have Christ brought also to the church, that what is wanting of life amongst her members, or the rest of the children, may be made up by his presence. 5. They who are tender of their own comfort, and of retaining Christ's presence with themselves, will be careful to have others, not yet sensible of their need of it, nor acquaint with it, made partakers thereof also. 6. Believers in their serious applications to Christ for the church whereof they are members may prevail much, and have much influence for obtaining his presence there, and for the putting of every thing in a better frame for the good of others. 7. A kindly member of the church, is brought up ordinarily in that church, and by that mother, where she was conceived, therefore she goes back to her mother's house, for they have breasts to nourish, who have a womb to bring forth in this respect, and yet here were both children that hated her, chap. i. 6, and watchmen that smote her, chap. v. 7, yet to this mother's house she goes. In a word, this is, as a kind spouse living in her mother's house, having after long seeking found her husband, will be desirous to have him home with her, not only for their mutual solace, but for the comfort of all the family ; so do believers, living yet in the church, desire to improve their credit and court with Christ, for the good of the whole church, that where she was conceived, others may be conceived also : where Christ's ordinances are, there ordinarily are children begotten of God ; and where a church conceives seed, and brings forth to him, it is a token he hath not given her a bill of divorce, nor will disclaim her to be his wife ; so much less, the children ought not to disclaim her as their mother : it is a shame that many who profess to be children, either are not yet conceived, or the mother that conceived them, is despised by them ; it is strange if the father will own such as children, who not only cry out against, but curse their mother, and place a piece of religion in this.

Verse 5. I charge you, O ye daughters of Jerusalem, by the roes and by the hinds of the field, that ye stir not up, nor awake my Love till he please.

THE third part of her care is in this verse, when she hath prevailed with him, to give his presence and countenance to her mother's house, then she turns to the daughters of Jerusalem, the visible professors and members of the church, charging them, that now seeing Christ is returned, they would be careful to entertain him well, and not to provoke him to withdraw. These words were spoken to the former chapter, verse 7, where they have the same general scope, which is to shew her care of having Christ retained; but in this they differ, there they look to her particular enjoyment of Christ; here they look (as the scope and connexion with the former words shew) to his presence in the church, or her mother's house, lest that should, by the daughter's fault, be interrupted: the first shews a believer's care, conjuring all (as it were) that nothing in her might provoke him: this shews what should be the church's care in reference to his visible presence, and blessing (to say so) in his church: now (saith she) Christ is amongst you, O ye who are of my mother's house, beware of putting him away; and in this she deals with them, as considered in their visible church state and relation, and not as real believers; the charge being to all: and therefore in the following verse, and chap. viii. 5, the daughters return an answer, which they do not, chap. ii. 7, because here she directs her words to the visible professors; whereas, chap. ii. 7, her scope was only to compose herself, seeing the presence she enjoyed was only to her particular sense. Here, *Observ.* 1. As there is more of Christ's sensible presence, and also of distance from him, in his way with particular believers at one time than another; so is there, in respect of his way to his church: sometimes he is not in the mother's house, sometimes he is. 2. As every believer should endeavour to retain Christ in his presence with their own souls, so all the members of a visible church should be careful to prevent his departure from his ordinances. 3. Often it is with Christ's presence in his church, as it is with the condition of particular believers in it; if they be secure, and he away from them, then often he is from the " mother's house" also ; if they be lively, and he with them, then he is brought back again to the church with them. 4. As Christ may withdraw, if provoked and not entertained, from a private believer, so he will do from a church, if they hold not fast what they have received, and walk not answerably thereto. 5. Church members, by their sins, have much influence on Christ's removal from amongst them ; yea, sometimes it may come to pass, when the body of a church turn despisers of the gospel, that no intercession of the godly, for preventing his departure, will prevail, even though Noah, Daniel, and Job were amongst them, Jer. xv. 1, and Ezek. xiv. 14. 6. Believers, that know the hazard of provoking Christ, and what a loss the loss of his presence is, should interpose seriously with new unexperienced beginners, and give them warning faithfully concerning this their hazard. 7. As a believer, in respect of the visible church, stands under the relation of a child to a mother ; so, in respect of visible professors, they stand under the relation of brethren and sisters, and should keep religious communion with them, even as such, that being an external duty that lieth upon them. 8. True love to Christ will be affected even with the wrongs that others do to him who is their beloved, and will endeavour to prevent his being wronged and provoked, as she doth here. 9. True love to others, will not only put to pray and intercede for them, and employ all the court the believer hath with Christ for their good (as the Bride did in the former verse) but will also manifest itself in giving faithful admonitions, advertisements, &c. and in doing what else may prevent sin in them.

DAUGHTERS OF JERUSALEM.

Verse 6. Who is this that cometh out of the wilderness like pillars of smoke, perfumed with myrrh and frankincense, with all powders of the merchant?

THE visible professors having now gotten a serious charge (because they are not easily engaged ; and it mars the good of our fellowship one with another in admonitions and warnings, when we are not serious even in the manner of our dealing with others) they are some way put into a little piece of warmness and admiration more than ordinary (as ordinarily Christ's return to a church and his ordinances in it, after a palpable decay, hath some stir and affectionate like motions accompanying it, such as were to be found in John's hearers, John v. 35.)   And in this affected and stirred condition they answer the Bride's charge, " O who is this ?" say they, importing they have more respect to the godly, and shew forth more evidences of it in their expressions, than ever they used formerly to do.

That these are the words of the daughters of Jerusalem, may be cleared from these things, 1. That they are placed on the back of her charge to them ; and when she charges, they used to answer (as chap. v. 9, and viii. 5,) and then she proceeds to speak to them ; even so it is here ; for, the words hold forth a mutual conference betwixt her and them, and therefore the words of this verse will be most pertinently understood as spoken by them.   2. They are the same words on the matter, and spoken on the same occasion with these, chap. viii. 5. which we will find to be spoken by them.   3. They can agree to none other. To say, they are the words of angels, is not warrantable, they not being a speaking party in this song : to say, they are the Bride's own words, will not suit with the commendation that is given to her, and of her in them, as by a distinct party : neither can they be Christ's words spoken immediately by him : for chap. viii. 5. where these words upon the matter are repeated, she is said to ascend, " leaning on her beloved ;" and he is spoken of, and looked on as a third, both from the Bride and the speaker.   It remains then, that they must be the words of the daughters of Jerusalem, wondering at the change that was to be seen on the church, her case being now compared with what it was before ; and wondering at believers in her, upon the same account also, as almost mistaking them, and so they speak as having other affections to them than they had before.   It is like that wondering expression, Isa. xlix. 21.   Thou shalt say (to wit, when the sudden change comes) " Who hath begotten me these ?" or, as it is, Rev. iii. 9, where it is promised to the church of Philadelphia, that others should " fall down, and worship at her feet," as being convinced now, that Christ loves his church.   And that this verse is spoken of the Bride, the words in the original, being in the feminine gender, puts it out of question ; for, they are in the original, as if it were said, " Who is she that cometh up," &c.

The words contain a commendation of the church, expressed both in the matter, and also in the manner of the
expression (being by way of question) and it is given by
visible professors, some whereof may be more tender than
others, yet both contradistinguished from the Bride. The
commendation hath three part or steps. 1. She " cometh,"
or (as it is chap. viii. 5.) " ascends from the wilderness :"
it is like before this manifestation of Christ, the Church
was dry and withered-like, in a wilderness condition,
without any beauty or lustre; but now that condition is
changed, when Christ is present, she ascends and comes
out of it : and this wilderness (considering her ascent from
it) signifies the world, wherein believers sojourn in the
way of heaven (as Israel did in the wilderness to Canaan)
and wherein there is no true content, nor satisfying rest
sought by them, nor to be found by any, therefore is their
back on it, though formerly they seemed to be settled in it
with the rest of the worldly ; thus the heavenliness of believers in their conversation is set out.

2. She comes like " pillars of smoke ;" this looks not in
all things to ordinary smoke but (as the after-words do
clear) to the "smoke of incense," &c.   Now she ascends
like smoke in a calm day, and like pillars of it together,
making heavenward, as the smoke of incense, which being
commanded in God's worship, was acceptable to him : and
as smoke fleeing from kindled fire cannot but ascend,
(especially new kindled) cannot but have smoke, and that
in abundance ; so now the church being warmed, and of
fresh inflamed and made lively with Christ's presence,
cannot but send out a sweet savour, which discernibly
ascends upward from the world (which is but a wilderness)
as smoke doth from the earth.

3. She is "perfumed with myrrh and frankincense, and
all the powders of the merchant :" that is, as precious
powders are used to make one savoury, so the believer
being replenished with the graces of Christ's Spirit, (often
in this song compared to sweet spices, chap. i. 12. and iv.
6, 13, 14, 16, &c.) and these graces being now quickened
by his presence, they cast a delightful savour to them
with whom such believers converse : so it was, Acts ii.
ult. and the ordinances, being powerful and lively, will
have such a powerful influence, as to be a " sweet savour in
in every place," 2 Cor. ii. 14, 15, and to leave some conviction of their amiableness and excellency, even upon the

consciences of those who will never get good of them, so
that there is no costly ointment or powder, that will so
perfume a person or place, as the gospel will do a church:
especially when immediately on the back of Christ's return,
he doth in an extraordinary manner countenance the dispensing of his own ordinances, so that even the temporary
believer is made in a manner, to receive the gospel with joy.

Next, the manner of the expression is by way of question, and admiration, " who is this ?" say they, we never
saw the like of her, she hath no match ; and so the question expresseth a wonderful beauty and loveliness in her,
and a great conviction and astonishment in them. In reference to which two, these things are to be learned, 1.
That there is nothing more lovely and savoury in itself,
than grace exercised in a believer's walk, and Christ's
ordinances beautified with his own presence in his church.
2. That where Christ's ordinances in his church, and the
graces of his Spirit in the hearts of his people are made
lively with his presence, they will be in their beauty very
discernible to others, and will be much admired, spoken
of, and commended by them. 3. That this beauty is
usually most fresh, when Christ returns to his people and
church, after he hath been a while away; for, then tenderness is in life amongst them. 4. The world in itself,
and being compared with Christ's church (especially in
their estimation, whose eyes God hath opened) is but a
miserable wilderness, and cannot give a heartsome being
or place of abode to a believer. 5. Believers have a more
noble design to compass, than to sit down and take up
their rest in this world, their faces bend upwards, and
their backs are upon it. 6. Christ's presence gives life
to a believer's motions, and ravisheth them upward, as fire
put to fuel necessitates smoke to ascend. 7. A heavenly-
minded believer is a comely sight, and a world-denied
professor will extort a commendation, even from ordinary
on-lookers. 8. As there is more of the exercise of true
grace amongst believers, by Christ's more than ordinary
presence with them, and in his church; so there is often
a more than ordinary warmness and motion in the generality of church-members at such a time, whereof yet many
may be unsound, as no question all the daughters of Jerusalem were not sound. 9. The church of Christ and believers in it, will look much more beautiful to professors
at one time than at another, and they will be much more

taken with this beauty sometimes than at other times; for, chap. i. 5, 6. The daughters of Jerusalem were in hazard to stumble at her spots; here they are ravished with her beauty as thinking her another thing than she was before. 10. Christ's presence will indeed put another face, both on a church and person, and make them every way different (but still to the better) from what they were. 11. The more active, believers be in exercising their graces, they will have the more fresh relish and savour; for, her ascending here, makes all her perfumes to flow.

BRIDE.

Verse 7.   Behold his bed, which is Solomon's: threescore valiant men are about it, of the valiant of Israel.
8.   They all hold swords, being expert in war: every man hath his sword upon his thigh, because of fear in the night.

THE Bride, being commended in the former verse by the daughters of Jerusalem, as being jealous that they gazed upon her, to the prejudice of the Bridegroom, and being ever restless till every commendable thing that is in her, redound to his praise, to whom she owes, and from whom she derives all her beauty; she steps in hastily with a " behold," as having a far more wonderful and excellent object to propose to them, to wit, Christ Jesus, the true Solomon himself, whose loveliness and glory should take them all up, rather than any poor perfections they saw in her.

That this is the scope, the matter will clear, especially, verse 11, where, what she would be at, is propounded in plain terms; and her sudden coming in with a " behold," as in chap. i. 6, doth confirm it.   That they are the Bride's words also, the scope and connexion bear out; this being her disposition, that she can suffer no commendation from Christ, nor from any other to stay or rest upon her, but is restless till it be turned over to his praise, as, chap. i. 16, ii. 3, &c.   There is none so tender of him, or jealous of his honour, as Christ's Bride is: again, the daughters being spoken unto, and Christ spoken of as a third person, it can be no other that speaks here, but the Bride; what! (saith she) are ye taken with any loveliness ye see in me? I will propose to you a far more excellent object.

And this short but very sweet discourse, holds forth
Christ, lovely and glorious in three most excellent steps,
wherein by a notable gradation, Solomon is ever mentioned ; his name (who was a special type of Christ) being
borrowed to design him, while his glory is set forth.   He
is described, 1. From his bed, verses 7, 8.   Whereby is
set forth, the excellent happiness and quietness that believers have in enjoying him.   2.   From his chariot, a
most stately piece of work by which is signified that excellent means (to wit, the covenant of redemption revealed
and preached) whereby our Lord Jesus brings his people
to his rest, verse 9, 10.   3.   She propounds his own most
excellent self, and that crowned with the stately majesty
and glory of his love, beyond which there is no step to
proceed, but here she sits, and willeth all others to be
taken up, in " beholding him," as the only desirable and
heart ravishing object, verse 11.

For opening of the first, in the 7th and 8th verses, we
have these five things to consider.   1.   Who this Solomon
is.   2.   What this bed is.   3.   What this guard, that is
about it, doth signify.   4.   For what end that guard is
appointed.   5.   The use of the note of attention, behold,
which is prefixed.

1.   By Solomon, David's son properly, is not understood, this scope will not agree to him (he was indeed a
great king, " but a greater than Solomon is here") therefore seeing in scripture, Solomon was typical of Christ,
as from Psalm lxxii, and other places may be gathered ;
through all these verses, by Solomon, is understood Christ,
the beloved, and Bridegroom, who especially was typified
by Solomon in these things : 1.   Solomon had a great
kingdom from the river to the sea, and so will our Lord
have many subjects.   2.   As Solomon was, so Christ is, a
powerful, rich king ; our Lord Jesus hath all power in
heaven and in earth committed unto him.   3.   Solomon
was a royal, magnificent king, sought unto from all parts
of the earth ; and so the name and glory, wherewith the
Mediator is furnished, is above every name in heaven and
in earth.   4.   Solomon was a wise judicious king ; and
singular for that : and so in our Lord Jesus " dwells all
the treasures of wisdom and knowledge ;" there is no need
to fear that any thing that concerns his people will miscarry in his hand.   5.   Solomon had a peaceable reign
(for which cause he had that name) and his government

was blessed and happy to his people and servants ; and so
our Lord Jesus is the " Prince of peace," Isa. ix. 6, and of
his government there is no change : and happy are his
subjects, and blessed are his servants, for the one half of
his glory, magnificence, wisdom, &c. and of their happiness
can neither be told nor believed.   This is an excellent
person, and a most stately king, who yet is the believer's
Bridegroom ; Christ's Bride is nobly and honourably
matched.

2. By bed here, is understood the same thing that is
signified by it, chap. i. 16, to wit, that access, nearness
and familiarity that the believer hath with Christ, and
whereunto he admits them that are his ; and the rest, solace and refreshment that they enjoy in fellowship with
him : beds being especially appointed for these two, 1.
For refreshing and rest, Isa. lvii. 2, and Psalm cxxxii. 3.
2. For the mutual fellowship of husband and wife.   So
then, by this is holden forth the excellent, refreshing and
soul-ease, that a believer may have in the enjoying of
Christ ; there is no bed that can give quietness, rest and
solace, like this.   Again it is called " his bed" 1. To distinguish it from hers, chap. iii. 1.   There is great odds
betwixt the two, as was hinted upon that verse.   2. To
shew, that although she be admitted to it (and therefore
it is called " ours," chap. 1. 16,) yet it is wholly procured
and framed by him alone.   3. It is called " his," to show
the communion that a believer hath with Christ in his refreshings.   O sweet ! It is Christ's own bed, if he lie well,
they lie well who are married to him ; It is his peace
which they enjoy here, " my peace I leave with you, my
peace I give unto you," &c. John xiv 27.   And it is his
glory and throne, that they are made partakers of hereafter, when they are set down on the same throne with
him.   Again, it is called " his bed, which is Solomon's :"
which expression, is added to show where the weight of
this wonderful refreshing lies, to wit, in this, that the rest
(which he invites them to behold) is no mean man's, it is
Solomon's ; yea, a greater than Solomon's, whose curtains
and hangings are much above his, chap. i. 6.   If Solomon's servants were happy that were admitted to his presence, how wonderfully happy are believers, Christ's
Bride, who are admitted to his own bed : the dignity of
believing and union with him, should be read out of the

dignity and glorious majesty of the person with whom we are united.

3. There is a guard mentioned here, which in relation to Christ, shews his stateliness, and in relation to us, shews our safety and security, that as kings (and it is like, Solomon) used to be attended by guards, for stateliness and security, that quietly they may rest (their guards watching about them) so this rest that a believer hath in Christ, O it is sure! there is an excellent guard compassing them about. It is particularly described, 1. In its number, they are "sixty" that is a competent and sufficient number. 2. They are "valiant," gallant, courageous men, that will not fail to execute orders : they are the choice men of Israel, that Solomon had to watch his bed, they are choice ones our Lord makes use of for the security of believers. 3. They are orderly disposed for their security, they are "about it," on all hands, there can be no approach made upon believers, to the prejudice of the repose they have in Christ. 4. They are well armed ; yea, always at their arms, in a posture of defence, "they all hold swords," none of them want arms, and they have them still in readiness. 5. They are not only stout, but skilful, "expert" men, who have been tried and well proved : none of his people needs to suspect Christ's watch over them, dexterous is he in preserving poor souls. 6. "Every one hath his sword girt on his thigh," and is standing at his post. All the expressions tend to shew that here, and here only, in Christ's bed may a soul rest secure ; there is no access for wrath to seize upon them that are in Christ, nor to devils to pull them from Christ ; for, He and his Father are stronger than all, and none is able to pluck them out of his hand. Believers have a notable security and defence, Christ's bed and his guard, if he be sure, they are sure, one watch watcheth both him and her. The same power of God, Isa. xxvii. 2, the twenty thousand of angels, which are his chariots, Psalm lxviii. 17, are for the believers' protection in Christ's company, "pitching their tents about them," Psalm xxxiv. 8. In a word, they are not only guarded with angels, but with divine attributes, the wisdom and power of God, and this makes them dwell in safety.

The end of all this ; is, for "fear in the night ;" there are no nights to Christ himself, and so no fear ; yea, Solomon the type, having such a peaceable kingdom, it is not like he had much fear; but the fear is in respect of believers, who are admitted to Christ's company and fellowship : for preventing their fears, he hath settled all firmly, as if guards were set for their security. Hence we gather, that the believer is supposed to be in the bed with him, otherwise there is no use of this guard; and his bed here is a piece of work that is framed not only for himself, but also for the daughters of Jerusalem, as the following chariot is. By night here is understood believers' darkness and lightless conditions (to speak so) wherein fears, doubts, challenges, &c. are most ready to assault, as affrightments use to befal men in the night. These words, "because of fear in the night," hold forth the use that our Solomon hath of that guard, to wit, for quieting his poor people, against the doubtings, difficulties, discouragements, and such like, whereto believers are so subject in their drooping, night-conditions; though when light shines, they are little troubled. These words shew, I. That Christ's Bride admitted to fellowship with him, may have her black and dark nights. 2. That believers, who have thought themselves above doubtings and fears, when things went well with them, yet in nights of temptation, darkness, and trial may be overtaken with many sad fears; it is not always day with them, and when it is night with them, they are apt to fear. 3. That believers in their nights, and under their fears have good security and an excellent guard ; yea, their safety and defence is as good then, as when there is no night nor fear ; how dark soever their night be, Christ's guard will sufficiently preserve them. 4. Christ is tender even of believers' fears, and hath provided so well for their peace, as he hath appointed means, not only to prevent their hurt, but also to prevent their fears : for, "because of fear" hath he appointed this guard. 5. There is no king or monarch so well attended and guarded, or who may sleep so secure and sound as a believer: his guard is still at their post, and they are valiant men, that cannot fail; for, 1. He is at peace with God ; and he that is within the peace of God, hath the warrant, right, and advantage of it to "guard the heart and mind," Phil. iv. 7. 2. The believer hath all the promises, and confirmations of oath and seals, in which it is impossible for God to lie, to secure and quiet him. 3. He hath the watch of angels, Psalm xxxiv. 7, pitching their tents about him, and chariots of angels waiting on him.   4. He hath God himself, and his almighty power for his defence, who alone may make him dwell in safety, wherefore he may lie down with confidence, and also sleep with quietness, Psalm iv. 8.   It is good sleeping in Christ's bed, there is not so good rest to be found any where in the world : so then, by the guard is understood, whatever contributes for confirming believers' faith, and strengthening them against their fears of being interrupted in their rest, which (being in Christ) is allowed upon them.

5. A " behold" is prefixed to all this, and that deservedly, 1. To shew the wonderfulness of what she was to say, O how wonderful is it, if believed !   2. To provoke, and stir up to observe and take notice of it ; few are acquainted with believers' privileges, and if they had not been recorded in the word, we durst never have likened or evened ourselves to them.   3. It is to shew an holy impatiency in her affection, in breaking in so with this discourse, as more fervently desirous to fill their mouths and hearts with the commending of Christ, than what they were about in commending of her ; a notable diversion, and sign of love in a friend of the Bridegroom, who with John the Baptist is content to decrease, so he may increase : true believers should and will endeavour more the commendation of Christ, in their fellowship together, than to commend any grace, gift, or what else they have gotten from him ; they will not conceit, or cry up their graces and gifts as they are theirs, for that were base ingratitude, but withal they mention what they have received, partly to endear him to themselves, and partly to commend him to others ; and thus they design to return him his own with advantage, wherein nevertheless they are the gainers, even while they seem to give what they have received.

Verse 9.   King Solomon made himself a chariot of the wood of Lebanon.

10.   He made the pillars thereof of silver, the bottom thereof of gold, the covering of it of purple ; the midst thereof being paved with love, for the daughters of Jerusalem.

THE second piece of work, mentioned for the commendation of the worker, is a chariot, described at large, verses 9, 10.   For clearing of the words, we are to enquire concerning these three things. 1. Its worker or former. 2. The end for which it is framed. 3. Concerning this chariot itself.

The author or maker thereof, is Solomon, and that King Solomon, that is Christ, as was cleared before, he is mentioned thrice under this name; but there is a gradation here that is observable, 1. He is called Solomon, verse 7. 2 King Solomon, verse 9. 3. King Solomon crowned, or, crowned King Solomon, verse 11. The longer she speaks of Christ, and insists in mentioning his excellency, her thoughts draw the deeper, she sets him up the higher, and becomes warmer in her apprehensions, affections, and expressions concerning him: acquaintance with him, would make one speak eloquently of him, he that is the worker and former of this chariot, is a most excellent king, it must needs then be a stately, royal piece of work.

2. There are two ends mentioned wherefore he makes it, 1. It is to himself, that is, for his own glory, and that thereby he may in a special way hold forth himself to be glorious, and that particularly in his grace; for, though he made all things for himself, yet is he said especially to manifest his glory in doing good to his people; and what serves for the manifestation of his grace, is in a peculiar manner made for himslf: so Isa. xliii. 7, 21. "This people have I formed for myself" (in a far other way than he formed nations) "they shall" (in a singular way) "shew forth my praise;" that is, the praise of his goodness, wherein his way was peculiar to them: and the paving of this chariot with love, and appointing of it for the daughters of Jerusalem, doth confirm this also, that it is the praise of grace that especially shines in this piece of work. And the second end, subordinate to the former is in the end of verse 10, in these words "for the daughters of Jerusalem," that is, for their good that are weak and far short of perfection; it is not only fitted for his glory, but also, it is fitted and confirmed to them, so as it may procure and bring about their good. *Observ.* 1. In the greatest pieces of Christ's workmanship, he had mind of poor sinners yet unglorified, his delight was with them before the world was, Prov. viii. 31. 2. The glorifying of grace is the great thing Christ aims at in all his contrivance and way toward his church and people. 3. He hath knit his own glory and the good of his people together; that same work which is for himself, is also for them, that if he

obtain his end, they cannot but be well; his glory and their good, ride (to say so) in one chariot. 4. For as stately a person as our Lord Jesus is, he disdains not to be occupied in making works, and as it were framing chariots, for the behoof of his people : rather than they should want what may further them in their way, he will make and furnish them himself.

3. The third is the work itself, which indeed is very admirable, as the worker and ends are : it is a chariot, several ways described, both in its matter, form, and furniture. The word translated chariot is no where else in scripture, it is translated bed on the margin, it is by the Septuagints expressed by such a word as signifieth, to be carried, and to carry, as chariots and litters (wherein men are carried) used to be carried by horses : we think it fitly expressed by chariot, not only because the word is different from that which is translated bed, verse 7, but, 1. The immediate end and use seems to be different also ; for, as stately kings use their beds for repose and rest in their chambers, and their chariots to ride in when they go abroad, and wherein their queens may ride with them ; so is it here. As Christ hath a bed for believers' quieting, he hath also a chariot for safe conveying and carrying them through their journey, till they come to their complete rest, this being no less necessary for believers (such as the daughters of Jerusalem are) than the former.

In short, by this chariot we understand the way of redemption in general, as it is contrived in the eternal council of God, and so called the covenant of redemption, and also as it is preached and manifestated to us in the gospel. The reasons why we thus apply it, are, not only because there is no other thing that it will agree unto ; for, 1. It is a work of Christ and so not Christ himself. 2. It is a work of special grace for his own, and that while they are in the way (for the elect in heaven are not daughters of Jerusalem) therefore it is no common work of creation, or providence, or of glory in heaven. 3. It is for the church's good, and therefore cannot be understood of her; for, besides that the several parts of its description will not suit her, not only Christ, but the daughters of Jerusalem are to be borne in this chariot; and we know not a fourth thing imaginable, that can be understood by it but the covenant of redemption revealed in the gospel. But, 2. The covenant of redemption is that work of Christ's wherein most eminently the glory of his grace and love to sinners doth appear, which makes him wonderfully lovely and admirable ; (to set forth which is the present scope) it therefore must be here understood. 3. That work is signified by this chariot, whereby Christ communicates his love to poor sinners, and carries them through, therefore it is said to be "paved with love" for that end ; now there is no partaking of special love from Christ, but by this covenant, nor was there ever another means made, or appointed for conveying love to them, or for bringing them through to the partaking of it, but this same covenant; therefore it must be understood. 4. All that is spoken of this chariot, as it will be applicable to no other thing, so will it well agree to the covenant of redemption manifested and preached in the gospel. 1. It may well be compared to a chariot, because by it poor believers are carried through as in a chariot, borne up and sustained by it, even in the way: yea, in it and by it they triumph and ride in triumph, (as he in his gospel rides prosperously) and if it be that wherein he rides, it must be that wherein they ride also, and therefore well compared to a chariot, because both he and they triumph by it. 2. It is eminently and peculiarly Christ's workmanship, he made this covenant for their behoof, and entered himself surety, undertaking for them, when there was none upon their side of the covenant to undertake but he the Mediator; and therefore is he styled Jesus and Redeemer, and it is by his purchase (having procured this unto them) that they are admitted to it, and carried through in it. 3. It is in a peculiar way contrived and framed for the glory of his grace, and the good of his people, as hath been said ; by it is manifested in the church the manifold wisdom of God, and the riches of the grace of Christ ; if ever a piece of work was made for the good of sinners, and the glory of grace, this is it, without which all the creatures had been uncomfortable ; yea, hurtful to them. 4. It may be said to be of the "wood of Lebanon," that is excellent and durable, for so the wood of Lebanon was, for which cause it was made use of in building of the temple ; and so all the materials of this covenant, and its properties are excellent and durable, it is an everlasting covenant, that fails not, and vanishes not away, but endures for ever. 5. The form is suitable also, "he made the pillars thereof" (saith she) "of silver :" pillars in a piece of work signify, 1. De-

coration. 2. Orderliness. 3. Stateliness, for which cause
when "wisdom builds her house," Prov. ix. 1, 2, "she
heweth out seven pillars ;" and Solomon made pillars for
the temple, the inscriptions whereof signified their end
and use, Jachin and Boaz, stability and strength, 2
Chron. iii. 17. And they are as silver pillars to shew
their excellency, and so this covenant hath precious promises, as the pillars thereof, able to support believers, and
hath all these so well ordered and contrived that every
thing is excellently in its own place ; this covenant is
therefore said to be "well ordered in all things, and sure,"
the pillars will not shrink, shake, nor bow, 2 Sam. xxiii. 5.
6. It hath a "bottom" and that of "gold :" a bottom is to
shew its stability and firmness to sustain and keep up
those who ride in it, and gold shews its solidity and preciousness, it is a rich bottom, therefore the New Jerusalem
is said to have streets of pure gold. Rev. xxi. 22. So
this covenant hath a sure foundation, elect and precious ;
this covenant cannot be unbottomed, and sinners cannot
fall through, if once in it. 7. It hath "a covering," and
that "of purple :" a cover is to preserve and save from any
thing that may fall from above ; and purple or scarlet
(for in scripture both are one, as may be seen, Matt. xxvii.
28, compared with Mark xv. 17.) sets out the excellency
and efficacy of that cover, it is not of every thing, it is of
purple ; and this in scripture way made use of to be dipt
in the blood of the sacrifices, Heb. ix. 14, which was
called, verse 20, "the blood of the covenant," typifying
the application of Christ's blood : this is the cover of the
covenant, the worth and efficacy of Christ's satisfaction,
whereby all in covenant (as it were riding in his chariot)
are preserved from the wrath of God, and their sins hid,
and so covered by that blood, that they are never called to
a reckoning for them, Psalm xxxii. 1, 2, Jer. l. 20. 8.
"The midst thereof is paved with love :" what can this be ?
gold is much but love is more ; what workman but Christ
can make this pavement : and what piece of work of his,
but the covenant of redemption, is so lined and stuffed
with love ? "the midst thereof" is the inward of it, as
great men in their chariots and coaches, have their pillows
and cushions of velvet, &c. to repose them ; but here
there is a far other thing, to repose and rest upon, love
lines all this chariot, so that there is none in the covenant,
but love is still next them, the word speaks good to them,

and all the promises run like pipes, with streams of love
to them : God's dispensations toward them breathe out
love, they walk on love, sit on love, rest on love ; it must
be good to be here ; and love is reserved for the midst of
it, to shew, that though its excellency and beauty may
someway shine, and glitter to those that are without ; yet,
none knows or can know the heart and bowels of the covenant, (to say so) and the love that is there, but those that
are within.   Love is put over the bottom of gold, and
made the pavement, 1. Because love in this covenant
condescends lowest to us, and there can be no lower stooping imaginable, than that to which the love of Christ hath
made him bow.   2. It is love that makes the riches of
Christ applicable to us, we could not walk on that gold,
if love paved it not, the freedom of his grace and love
makes all refreshful ; the believer, even though a sinner,
may ride and rest here.   3. It is to hearten a sinner to
come in and close with this covenant, and it shews what
fits it to be chariot for him to ride in, it is the pavement
of love ; a sinner may leap here, there is no hazard to fall,
or if he fall, he falls soft, for it is upon love : there will
be no rejecting of sinners that would enter and sit down
in it, why? they are to sit, stand, and lie on love, which
will cover their infirmities and not contend, otherwise
there would be no access to it, nor abiding in it, it would
cast them out.   Thus doth grace shine in the covenant,
as the lining and inside of all the promises, when they are
seen, therefore is it peculiarly called the covenant of grace.
9. It is "for the daughters of Jerusalem :" all the work
is for them, but especially the "pavement of love ;" it is
for them, who while they are in the way are subject to
infirmities, it is fitted for them to roll on, and rest in, even
when sense of sin would otherways sting and disquiet
them ; this suits well with that word, 2 Sam. xxiii. 5.
" although my house be not so with God," but there are
many things sinful to be found in it ; yet, " he hath made
with me an everlasting covenant well ordered in all things
and sure," this, saith he, (when he was to die) " is all my
salvation, and all my desire :" there needs no more for
carrying believing sinners through, and giving them ease
under their challenges and perplexities but this, it is so
well suited for believers' conditions. From all this she proceeds, verse 11, to point out Christ as precious, this covenant putting as it were the crown of grace, and loveliness
on him.

Observ. 1. The work of redemption, bringing sinners out of a state of wrath, and carrying them through to glory, is a noble design, a wonderful excellent work, and hath been deeply contrived. 2. O, the excellent wisdom, and wonderful grace that shines in his covenant! 3. They who would rest in Christ's bed, must ride in his chariot; they who would share his peace and be admitted to sweet fellowship with him, must accept of his offers, and enter into covenant with him. 4. The weight of all contained in the covenant lies on Christ, therefore it is his workmanship alone, as being the surety thereof to the Father, the messenger of the covenant to us, and in effect the sum and substance of it himself, therefore is he called " the covenant, Isa. xlii. 6. 5. Christ hath spared no invention nor cost, to make this covenent large and full for the believer's consolation and happiness. 6. Love is a main ingredient in this work of redemption, and the predominant qualification of this covenent, love being the thing which he chiefly intended to make conspicuous and glorious therein. 7. Every particular of the contrivance of grace will be found more precious than another, every step thereof proceeds to a greater excellency, and therefore there is mention made here, 1. Of " wood." 2. Of " silver." 3. Of " gold," &c. The further in we come in the covenant, we will find it the more rich. 8. Love is here mentioned in the last place, to shew the great excellency of Christ's love unto redeemed sinners; there is something beyond gold, but nothing beyond love, especially that of the mediator : it is left last also in the description, to leave the daughters of Jerusalem to consider the more of it, as being the great attractive commendation of this work, which should make it amiable and desirable unto them : love hath the last word, and there is nothing beyond it, but himself, whose glory and loveliness is spoken to in the following verse. Lastly, her scope is, 1. To commend Christ, for they will never esteem him that are not acquainted with his covenant. 2. To engage both herself and the daughters to fall more throughly in love with him; the right uptaking of the covenant is a most forcible argument for drawing souls to Christ; for, 1. It hath all fulness in it, for the matter. 2. All wisdom, for the manner. 3. All gracious condescending, in the terms. 4. It is most engaging in respect of its end, being made for this same very purpose, and designed for this very end, that it may bring about the peace and salvation of sinners; which considerations exceedingly commend it, and may much strengthen a sinner in applying himself to it. 5. It is most necessary in regard of the salvation of sinners, there is no riding or journeying to heaven, but in this chariot. " No other name by which men can be saved, but the name of Christ," that is manifested by this covenant.

Verse 11. Go forth, O ye daughters of Zion, and behold King Solomon with the crown wherewith his mother crowned him in the day of his espousals, and in the day of the gladness of his heart.

SHE proceeds in this verse, to hold forth the worker of this great work, and although all the pieces of the work be admirable, yet hath he much more glory, in as far as the builder is more glorious, and hath more honour than the house; and because his commendation is her scope, therefore she propounds him in his beauty and glory, with an exhortation filled with admiration; if (saith he) ye would wonder, " O daughters," &c. here is a wonderful object, Christ himself, on whom all eyes should be fixed; up therefore, come forth and behold him. There are four things in the verse, 1. The parties spoken unto. 2. A glorious object propounded to them. 3. This glorious object being Christ, is qualified and set out in his most lovely and wonderful posture, by three qualifications. 4. A duty in reference to him so qualified, is called for, and pressed upon the daughters.

1. The parties excited and spoken to here, are the " daughters of Zion :" by Zion oftentimes in scripture is understood the church: wherein Christ is set as king, Psalm ii. 6, and elsewhere; and so by " daughters of Zion," we are to understand members of the church; they are the same with the daughters of Jerusalem mentioned verse 5, and her scope being to speak to them who spoke, verse 6, and they being the same to whom she spake, verse 5, doth confirm it; for, the words run in one context. They are called here " daughters of Zion." 1. Because it was for Zion's sake that the Lord so much prized Jerusalem, Psal. lxxxvii. 2, his temple and ordinances being especially there. 2. To put the daughters of Jerusalem in mind, what was the especial ground of the relation which God owned in them, namely their being

incorporated into his church, whereby they had access to his ordinances: and that so they might know whoever was deficient, yet this duty called for, did exceedingly become them, Christ being king of Zion ; for which cause elsewhere, Zech. ix. 9, the exhortation runs in these terms, " Tell the daughter of Zion, behold thy King cometh," &c. It is no little thing to get professors taking up the relation they stand under to Christ, and engaged to walk accordingly.

2. The object proposed to these daughters, is King Solomon, even the King of Zion, the King of peace, and King of saints, in a word, their King : this relation makes him lovely to them, yet, it is not Christ simply that is here proposed to their view, but Christ with a crown, in most stately magnificence, such as kings use to be adorned with, when they are in great state, or on their coronation day. While it is said he hath a crown, hereby is not signified any material crown, but majesty and glory, as Psalm, xxi. 3, " Thou settest a crown of pure gold on his head," &c. and so Christ conquering on the white horse, Rev. vi, 3, is said to have a crown : and Rev. xix. 12, it is said, he hath on his head many crowns, to shew his great and manifold glory, such as becomes the Prince of the king's of the earth : every look of Christ is not enough, many think not much of him ; this shews how Christ's glory is to be seen, and how for that end he is to be considered by on-lookers ; he is to be looked upon as he doth discover and hold forth himself, otherwise his glory will never rightly be taken up : and therefore to help us in this, and to prevent an objection which carnal sense might make against her scope, she qualifies this crown and glory of his three ways. 1. It is the " crown wherewith his mother crowned him :" where we are to enquire, 1. What different crowns Christ may be said to have, and what this is. 2. Who this " mother" is. 3. How she is said to crown him.

Christ may be said to have a fourfold glory, or crown. 1. As God co-essential with the Father ; this crown is not put on him, being natural to him, who is " the brightness of the Father's glory and the express image of his person," Heb. i. 2, 3. 2. He hath a crown and glory as mediator, in respect of the power, authority and glory wherewith he is invested, as God's great deputy, and anointed upon the holy hill of Zion, having power and a rod of iron, even in reference to enemies : and seeing this is not of his mother's putting on, it is not that which is here understood.   3. He hath a crown and glory in respect of the manifestation of his glory in the executing of his offices, when he makes his mediatory power and glory apparent in particular steps : thus sometimes he is said to take his power to him, Rev. xi. 17, and is said to be crowned, when the white horse of the gospel rides in triumph, Rev. vi. 2.   The last step of this glory will be in the day of judgment : in short, this consists in his exercising his former power, committed to him as mediator. 4. There is a crown and glory which is in a manner put on him by particular believers, when he is glorified by them, not by adding any thing to his infinite glory, but by their acknowledging of him to be so, especially their acknowledging his rich and free grace, and by believing, putting their seal thereunto, John iii. 33, and giving him glory, as Abraham did, Rom. iv. 20, in which respect he is crowned, as on the contrary, when he meets not with this, he is despised, and it is a saying upon the matter, this man shall not reign over us : now this last is to be here understood.   Again, by "mother" here, is not understood his natural mother, but it must be taken in a spiritual sense for one of two, either, 1. For the church catholic, which being mother to Christ mystical, may be said to be mother to him, as Rev. xii. 5, the church is said to "bring forth a man-child," who is taken to heaven, and hath ascribed to him the properties due to Christ, and yet Christ mystical is there understood ; or, 2. For a particular, believer, who may be said to be Christ's mother in these respects, 1. For the near relation that is betwixt Christ and particular believers, and the account he hath of them : for which reason they are called " his sister, and spouse," chap. iv. 10, and Matt. xii. ult. He calls them "his brother, his sister ;" yea, "mother." 2. Because Christ is formed and brought forth in them, being as it were conceived in every one of them, Gal. iv. 19, Christ (as it were) getting a new being in them, which he had not before.   We conceive both may be understood here, and the last especially, as serving most to the scope of commending Christ to them : and if the first be included, to wit, the church universal, then particular believers (being homogeneous parts of the whole) cannot be excluded ; for, the church crowns Christ, when she brings forth children to him, which is, when by the ordinances Christ is begotten in them. Now they are said to crown Christ and glorify him, not by adding any new degrees of glory to him, considered in himself, but this his being crowned by them, doth especially appear in these three. 1. Their high estimation of them, beyond what others have, and what themselves were wont to have ; now he is highly esteemed who before was despised by them, and whereas to them he wanted a crown and dominion, now he hath it. 2. Their acceptation of him as their king, when by their consent, they ratify (as it were) God's donation of the crown to him, and in acknowledging thereof, they submit to his sceptre and government : thus he is crowned by them, when he is expressly with full consent of the soul acknowledged as king and Lord : even as David formerly crowned, anointed and made king over Israel by the Lord, is said to be made king of Judah, when they accept of him to reign at Hebron ; and afterward by the ten tribes in their submission to him, and consenting to the former appointment : even so believers' submission to Christ, is a crowning of him, as to themselves : and so there are particular coronations (to say so) of Christ, even as there are particular espousals betwixt him and believers. 3. This is in respect of the glory, that results to Christ from their submission and acknowledgment ; even as sinners despising him, put (as it were) a blot on him, put him to open shame, and say, we will not have him to reign over us ; so believers, yielding up themselves to Christ, do in a manner put honour and glory upon him, Isa. lxii. 2, 3. The married church or people are said to be "a crown of glory in the hand of the Lord," when the grace of Christ hath its native effect amongst them, as the conversion of souls proves to faithful ministers their "crown and joy," 1 Thess. ii. 14, so doth it to the great bishop and shepherd of souls : and, as Prov. xii. 4, "a virtuous woman is a crown," or ornament "to her husband," whereas if she be not so, she maketh him ashamed : so are believers some way a crown to Christ, because all the glory and beauty which is to be found on them, is his, and from him. This then is the meaning,—consider Christ in the beauty wherein he appears to believers, and with the esteem they have of him, as full of grace and truth, when they acknowledge him, and become subject to him, and he will be seen to be exceedingly stately and lovely.

The second qualification confirms this : this crown is put on him "in the day of his espousals ;" now Christ's general espousals are not yet come, and so the crown in that respect is not yet put on him ; it must be therefore the day of his espousals with particular believers (which is here understood, there being no other before his second coming) who are, 2 Cor. xi. 2, "espoused to him," by their consenting to accept him for their husband, as he is king to them, by their submitting to his dominion. His being crowned here, is mentioned with respect to this day of his espousals, because as bridegrooms used to be most glorious in their marriage-day, so Christ hath at the time of espousals, a special loveliness to the new married believer, what by the more kindly and tender manifestations of his love, and what by the fresh relish it hath then to them, when their spirits are broken with the sense of their sin, and warm with a deal of holy joy and fainness which useth then to abound in their heart, in reference to so good a bargain ; so Christ is then to believers wonderfully lovely : and although the effects of his kindness may be enlarged afterward, and their esteem of him may also grow, yet readily then as it is most sensible, so their admiration is most in exercise, and their thoughts of Christ's excellent worth, are most affectingly, and overcomingly ravishing ; and when in their after-thoughts they are taken up with him, the remembering of that day of espousals, when he took them by the hand, puts still a loveliness on him to them, that in his love he so wonderfully condescended unto them.

The third qualification confirms the same (for, it is in effect one qualification in three expressions) and it is in these words, "and in the day of the gladness of his heart ;" what is it (saith she) that cheers Christ, and makes him heartily glad ? it is even this, when poor sinners accept of him, that is Christ's marriage-day ; and as the bridegroom rejoiceth over the bride that day, so doth he rejoice : and as " the good shepherd" rejoiceth when he recovers his "lost sheep," or the father his prodigal son, Luke xv. 32, so doth Christ when sinners are brought in to him by the gospel : and this joy is called " the gladness of his heart," to shew the reality of it. Christ (in a manner) can enjoy no such satisfying thing as a marriage with a poor sinner ; then " he sees the travail

of his soul, and is satisfied," Isa. lviii. 11, that cheers him
and makes him smile (if I may say so) and this looks to
that glory which shines in Christ, and is expressed by
him when he is well satisfied with poor sinners, and that
is mainly when he gets welcome by them.   This signifies
not joy in Christ, as it is in us: but, 1. It shews how
acceptable a sinner's believing in him, is to him.   2.
What confident welcome they may expect from him,
when they come unto him. 3. How kindly he useth
them, by manifesting himself to be well pleased, as one
that is cheerful doth on his marriage-day to his bride.

3. The duty pressed upon the daughters is in two words,
holding forth two duties, the one whereof is the middle or
mean to the other, and the other the end of this.   The
first is, "behold," which points at the great scope and
thing called for ; and it imports, 1. A wonderful object,
and indeed Christ is so, being considered in his most royal
posture, as a crowned king upon his coronation-day ; and
in his most loving posture, as a beautiful bridegroom on
his marriage-day.   2. It imports a dulness in the daughters, needing upstirring to take up Christ in this lovely
and glorious posture.   3. A difficulty rightly to take him
up under this consideration, yet a necessity of it, and that
it be done with attention. 4. It implies an intenseness
or bensil of spirit in the act of beholding ; so rare an object calls for greatest intention of heart, and gravest consideration of mind in the beholder ; it is not every look
or glance of the eyes that will discern it ; but, 1. There
must be attentiveness and steadiness, a stayed looking,
and as it were dwelling on the object with their eyes.   2.
The exercise of faith must go along with this their looking, reading his worth by faith exercised on him, as Isa.
xlv. 19, " Look unto me and be ye saved ;" beholding of
him, as the stung Israelites did the brazen serpent. 3.
Also the exercise of love ; an affectionate look is here
necessary, delighting in him, and being taken up with
him, as one with that wherein they take pleasure, the eye
of the seer here, cannot but affect and inflame the heart.
4. This looking is attended with wondering at this glorious object, as one beholding a wonder, and ravishing with
the admirableness of it: all these are comprehended under this expression, " behold him."   The second word
(which hath in it another piece of their duty) is, " go
forth," and this is a help to the other : and (besides what

hath been hinted at in the former expression) it shews it is not in every posture that they will take up Christ thus, but there is a necessity they must come out from under the natural condition they were into : we take it to be the same with that precept, Psalm xlv. 10, 11, " Forget thine own people and thy father's house, so" (and no otherwise) "shall the King greatly desire thy beauty." Christ manifests not himself, as reconciled and pleased, till former lovers be given up with; and this beholding of his smiling and glorious countenance, cannot be obtained till then, even as one sitting in the house cannot discern a stately sight going by, except they go forth : thus the similitude is borrowed; to shew the necessity of rousing of affections within ; but not to signify any local mutation. This then is the sense and scope ; O professors (saith the Bride) would you see a stately sight ? then get up, and set yourselves to take up Christ, more glorious than Solomon, either on his coronation or marriage-day (to which there is an allusion here) and because few see great comeliness and beauty in Christ, why he should be desired; therefore she adds what a sight it is she understands. Endeavour (saith she) to behold, him as he is discernable to believers, when they close with him, and accept of him ; if so ye will exercise faith in him, so as ye may perfect espousals with him, and satisfy him by resting on him, ye will then have a stately and ravishing object to look upon, otherwise Christ is not alway and to every one, pleasant and cheerful company.

Observ. 1. Christ, when rightly conceived and taken up, is a most ravishing satisfying sight, and a most glorious stately person to look upon. 2. Though Christ Jesus be so stately a person, yet he condescends to espouse and marry himself to the believer : thus Christ by faith becomes theirs. 3. This marrying hath its day, and men are not born espoused to Christ, but their accepting of him, their espousals with him are consummated. 4. Christ is never taken up aright but by the believer, nor doth his glory ever appear as it is, but to the believer : others that are not spiritual cannot discern it. 5. Christ's condescending to marry sinners, and accept of them, is as the crown and diadem of his glory ; and that which makes him most singularly admirable, is that he is " full of grace and truth," John i. 18. 6. Christ accounts believing on him by a poor sinner, a singular piece of honour done unto him; it is as the putting of a crown on his head, when they make use of his grace; as he accounts it the greatest dishonour can be done to him, to refuse and slight him and therefore, misbelief (when Christ calls) is a most heinous sin, it is as it were the taking of Christ's crown from him. 7. There is no such pleasure that a sinner can do to Christ, as to believe on him; and Christ is ever cheerful then, when sinners are thronging on him by faith, and he is never discontented with that; for, that is the day of the gladness of his heart, as other days in the church are sad, when this design of his, is (as it were) obstructed and disappointed. 8. Usually the sight and sense of Christ's grace are most fresh and sensible to the soul, about the time of their closing with Christ, or of their being clear that they have closed with him. 9. Every lazy looking on Christ, or wishing for him, will not be acceptable to him, nor solidly comfort a sinner; but there must be a going forth, and a beholding of him. 10. This being spoken to the daughters of Zion, saith, many may have much of a profession and a name, yea, they may have a kind of high esteem of gracious people (as the daughters had verse 6,) and yet be such as have not rightly taken up Christ, but are exceeding ignorant of him, as these are, chap. v. 9. 11. Considering these words as spoken by the Bride, who was so much commended, verse 6, we may observe, that no particular esteem or commendation will satisfy a sincere believer, so long as Christ gets not his due: his honour will still be nearer them than their own.

CHAPTER. IV.

CHRIST.

Verse 1.   Behold thou art fair, my love; behold, thou art fair; thou hast doves' eyes within thy locks: thy hair is as a flock of goats that appear from mount Gilead.

THAT these are Christ's words spoken to the Bride, is at the first clear; he continues speaking from the beginning unto verse 16, and then verse 16, the Bride speaks by prayer to him, for the influences and breathings of the Spirit.

In Christ's speech there are two parts; the first to the eighth verse, wherein he gives both a general and particular commendation of the Bride. The second, from that forward to the last verse, wherein he begins with a sweet invitation, and then shews how he was affected towards her, and so breaks out in another commendation of her. The matter in both is sweet and comfortable; wonderful to be spoken by such a one as Christ, of such a one as a believer; but there is nothing in his love, but what is wonderful and like himself. The scope of the first part of Christ's speech is twofold. 1. More general, to intimate his love to his Bride, on the back of so much darkness; chap. iii. 1, 2, (in the midst of which, notwithstanding, her love did appear in her commending him;) and it is subjoined to the commendation that she gives of him to others, in the preceding chapter, to shew, 1. That when believers slight their own esteem, to have it accruing to Christ's commendation, it is never loss but gain to them; for, here Christ comes in to commend her himself, whereas it was but the daughters of Jerusalem who commended her, chap. iii. 6. 2. It shews, that time taken, and pains bestowed for the edification of others, and their instruction in the excellency of Christ, is acceptable to him, and proves often useful for attaining sensible fellowship with him; yea, it proves often to be some way as useful in reference to this as their own particular praying for themselves, the Lord doth so return their pains taken this way into their bosom. That to commend the Bride is the scope in general, is clear from verse 7.

More particularly we take the scope to be, his giving her an answer to her prayer, chap. ii. 17, where she prayed for his fellowship "until the day break," &c. Here he doth not only materially answer, but verse 6, formally repeats her words, that she may know what he speaks is a direct answer to her prayer: until that day come (saith he) it shall be so as thou desirest (as the words will make it clear) shewing, 1. That a believer's prayers may for a time lie beside Christ, (as it were) and yet he not forget a word of them, but mind well the answer and performance of them. 2. That sometimes he will not only give what is sought by his people, but make them know that he respects their prayer, in the giving of it; and so he not only hears their prayers, but lets them know he hath heard them.

This commendation, whereby he intimates his respect to her, hath four steps. 1. It is done in general, verse 1. Then, 2. He insists on particulars, from verse 1, to verse 6. 3. He shews how his respect to her affected him, verse 6. 4. He sums all particulars up in an universal commendation, verse 7, lest any thing should be missed, or being left out might vex her; whereby he shews, what was his scope in that which preceded.

The general commendation in the beginning of verse 1, is the same that was given her, chap. i. 15, yet here it is repeated with the two beholds: the reasons why he repeats it, are, 1. That Christ might evidence to her the reality of his love, and that he varies not, nor changes in it, even though fits of security on her side had intervened, chap. iii. 1. Christ's love and thoughts to his people, are still the same, whatever changes be upon their frame and way, which may occasion sad changes in his dispensations towards them. 2. That she might the more be persuaded of his love to her and esteem of her; Christ would have his own thoroughly persuaded that he loves them, 1 John iv. 16, and would have others to know, that he respects them, more than the most mighty in the world. 3. It is because often believers from all other hands, whether the men of the world, or from themselves, have but little comfort, therefore Christ renews his intimations to support and comfort them: believers' consolation hangs most on his kindness to them, and they who depend most on it are no losers. And further, we may here observe, that even a believer, especially after sad challenges, will need renewed intimations of Christ's love.

The more particular explication and commendation of her parts follows; where we would advert, 1. That bodily members or parts, are not to be here looked unto, but believers have an inner-man, as well as an outward, a new man as well as an old; and so that inner-man hath, as it were, distinct parts and members as the natural body hath, which act in reference thereto, with some analogy to these members in the natural body. 2. As the new or inner-man sets forth the new nature and habitual grace in the believer; so the particular parts, eyes, lips, &c. signify distinct graces of faith, love, &c. which are parts of that new nature. 3. These parts may be looked on as useful in the new man, as the external members are in the body, or as they are evidences of some thing in the renewed disposition.   4. They set forth the disposition, as they are qualified in the commendation, and not simply.   5. Although we cannot satisfy our own, or others' curiosity, in the particular application of these parts, yet there is a particular meaning of every several part here attributed to her, as well as of every part attributed to him, chap. v. 11, 12, &c. and he giveth no idle words nor useth any vain repetitions: we should therefore beware of thinking all this needless, seeing he knoweth best what is needful.   6. Being clear of the scope, that it is to commend graces, and to evidence the beauty of her several graces, we must regulate all the application by that scope, and what is subservient thereto, cannot be impertinent.   Yet. 7, There is much need of sobriety here; therefore we shall be short and peremptory in particular applications.   8. There being a connexion amongst all the graces of the Spirit, it must not be thought absurd that some of these graces may be signified twice in different respects, and that one part respect more graces (which are nearly linked) especially when the commendation gives ground to infer it.   9. We take this commendation to set forth especially the invisible church, or true believers, which are the members thereof, as the scope and application do clear.

If it be asked why he insists on particulars in this commendation? I answer, for these reasons; 1. That he may shew, that whoever hath the new nature, and a lively work of grace, hath also particular graces in exercise.   2. That it may be known that the new nature is not a dead body, but a living: and exerciseth itself by putting forth these particular graces in exercise.   3. That he may shew, that wherever one grace is, all are there, and as it is ordinarily with one grace, so it is with all; where believers are in a good and commendable case, it will not be one grace or two that will be in exercise, or one duty or two in which these graces are exercised, but it will be universally, all graces, and in all known duties.   4. To shew, who may expect Christ's commendation: those who have a respect to all his commands, and make conscience to exercise all graces.   5. To shew what particular notice he takes of believers' graces, he can tell how it is with every one of them; and takes this exact notice of them, because it is very acceptable to him, when he finds them in good case.

There are seven parts particularly mentioned, every

one having its own distinct commendation. The first two of them are in the rest of verse 1. The first thing commended is her " eyes," which here have a twofold commendation. 1. That they are as " doves' eyes." 2. That they are " within her locks." Eyes are the organs of seeing in the natural body, whereby we discern objects that are visible; and so our understandings are thereby set forth in scripture; " that the eyes of our understanding may be enlightened," saith the apostle, Eph. i. 18, By eyes also the affections are set forth, because the affection sets the eye on work to look here or there, (Hence is the phrase of a single and evil eye, Matt. vi. 21, 23,) and because it is some way the seat of these, and somewhat of love or hatred will be, and may be gathered from the eye. Here we understand, 1. A spiritual, sanctified enlightened understanding in the things of God, taking up Christ and spiritual things spiritually, 1 Cor. ii. 15, that is by faith, it being "the evidence of things not seen," Heb. xi. 1. And therefore looking is frequently put for believing in scripture, which presupposeth understanding. 2. Kindliness, or a spiritual, kindly and affectionate carriage to Christ; in a word, it is the exercise of love upon this spiritual and wonderfully excellent object, Christ; a having respect to him, as it is Isa. xvii. 7, his eyes shall have respect to his Maker, it is such an uptaking of Christ and spiritual things, as works love and delight in them.

The commendation will confirm this, which is twofold, 1. They are " doves' eyes:" this was opened, chap. i. 15, and it signifieth, 1. What is the great object they behold, and are taken up with, it is Christ; and they are chaste to him, and seek to know no other at all but him, 1 Cor. ii. 2. 2. It imports that the act of faith whereby they behold him, is simple, single and sweet, their understanding is not subtile, nor politic, nor are they puffed up with it, but it is taken up with studying Christ and him crucified, opposite to the vain wisdom of the world, 1 Cor. ii. 1, 2, 2. These eyes are " within her locks: locks are that part of the hair that hang about the face, handsomely knit, and was then instead of a vail to women, 1 Cor. xi. 7, and so the word in the Hebrew will bear; and it is differenced from that word translated hair, in the words following, which is that part of the hair that covers the head: it implies here, that the believer's knowledge is not used for frothy ostentation (as the knowledge that puffs up) but is kept

within its right bounds, and that they are wise unto sobriety, and that their knowledge is not at the first obvious,
but seasonably vents itself and looks out, as eyes that are
within the locks.

These things are sure, and may be observed from the
words, 1. That a believer should be filled with spiritual
knowledge and understanding. 2. Knowledge is no less
necessary to a believer, that he may go right in the way
of God, and not err, than eyes are to guide a man in a
journey; and this necessity extends both to faith and
practice. 3. A believer without knowledge, or weak
in knowledge, is very far defective in spiritual beauty, he
is as a man without eyes; it is not decent that a believer
should be so : from this it is, that many are called weak
in faith. 4. That knowledge of spiritual things, should
ever have faith, love and singleness going along in the
exercise thereof; for, every knowledge will not be commendable to Christ, more than every eye will be useful in
a body; believers' eyes must be as " doves' eyes." 5. A
believer's eyes, or knowledge, is different from the knowledge of all others. 1. In respect of its object, which is
Christ and spiritual things. 2. In that it is joined with
love, it respects him. 3. In that it is chaste, keeping the
soul for him alone. 4. It works delight in him. 5. It
is denied to other things. *Observ.* 6. Often the most
subtile in worldly wisdom, knows least of Christ truly;
whereas the most simple that have " doves' eyes," take
up most of him. 7. Christ respects not how much a
man knows, but how he is affected with it; it is not the
eagle's, but the " dove's eyes," which he commends. 8.
It is good to know and to think little of our knowledge,
and not to be puffed up with it. 9. Christ loves it well,
when his people seasonably use, and improve their knowledge and parts; then the new man becomes lovely, as
the eyes are within the locks. 10. There are extremes
in the use-making of knowledge, which are to be shunned;
we should neither altogether obsure it that it be not seen,
nor by ostentation make shew of it; it is good when it
runs in the right mids, then it gets to commendation, and
is as " eyes within the locks."

The second thing commended is her " hair," having a
twofold commendation also. The hair is no integral, or
essential part of the body (to say so) yet in all ages a
great part of men's decoration, hath ever been placed in it :

it is the most conspicuous thing of the body, being highest and most discernible, especially in the way it used to be dressed ; and this conspicuousness of it, by the commendation, seems mainly to be aimed at. By hair we understand the ornament of a christain, godly, and sober walk, having the right principles of saving grace within, and the fruits thereof in a well ordered conversation, and suitable profession appearing without in the practice. We take it so, not only because it is a main piece of a christain's or believer's beauty, but also for these reasons, 1. Because as hair sets out and adorns the natural body, though it be no substantial part thereof ; so a well ordered conversation commends grace within, and makes it lovely. 2. Because as hair is upmost, and most conspicuous, and therefore seen when the natural body is hid (therefore it was to women a cover, 1 Cor. xi. 5.) so a suitable practical profession, is (as it were) the cover of holiness, through which it shines, and by which it is conspicuous, which otherwise would not be discernible. 3. And especially, because in scripture this adorning with good works, and with a meek and quiet spirit, is put in the place of decking of the hair, and other external decorations (1 Tim. ii. 9, 10.) as that wherein christians' beauty should " shine before men," (Matt. v. 17.) and which should be to a believer, as decking of the hair is to those who take pains to adorn the body. For sure these do make them beautiful before God and men, more than hair and its decorations can make any person in the world appear beautiful to the men thereof, 1 Tim. ii. 9, 10, whose " adorning" (saith the apostle, speaking of believing women) " let it not be in costly apparel, broidered hair," &c. " but" (what then should be in the place thereof :) " shamefacedness, sobriety, and good works ;" so, 1 Pet. iii. 3, 4, 5, " Whose adorning let it not be the platting of the hair," but in the place thereof, let it be " a meek and quiet spirit, which in the sight of God is of great price." And this is also mentioned by the apostle, as that which is exceedingly engaging to the husband, for which Sarah there is commended. Next, the commendation of her hair, in both its parts, will confirm this, 1. It is like " a flock of goats :" goats are stately and comely in going, and a flock of them must be very stately, as they were especially in these parts, Prov. xxx. 21 and 31. And so this ornament of a good conversation, is an amiable, gaining and alluring

thing ; by it, saith Peter, the husband's affection may be
won (and that both to Christ and to his wife in the Lord)
more than by any outward decorating, and this puts them
to glorify God, when it shines before them, Matt. v. 16.
2. It is commended from this, that it is like a flock " appearing from mount Gilead :" this was a fruitful place,
and it is like the goats that fed thereon, were more ex-
excellent than others in their beauty : and being seen
afar, and discernible ere men came near them were pleasant and stately to beholders, and so good works, showing forth themselves in a well ordered conversation, do
also as from a mountain appear to others, and set believers up as " lights shining in a dark place," Phil. i. 15,
and also make them lovely and desirable in the consciences of on-lookers and beholders.   Observe then, 1. That
practice should wait upon knowledge, for it is the end
thereof, and without it all men's knowledge is void and
vain. 2.   Grace and holiness appearing in a christian's
practice, will shine, and be in some measure very discernible.   3. This is a thing that makes the believer's conversation very beautiful and lovely.   4. It is not enough
that believers should be tender, and conscientious in secret
before God ; but there ought to be a shining, even in their
outward conversation before men.   5. This doth exceedingly adorn a believer's walk, and make it stately to beholders, when the fruits of holiness visibly appear in his
conversation.

Verse 2. Thy teeth are like a flock of sheep, that are even shorn,
which came up from the washing : whereof every one bear
twins, and none is barren among them.

The third particular commended, is in verse 2, and it is
her " teeth," which have a fourfold commendation given
them.   The teeth properly taken, are useful for furthering the nourishment of the body, they being the instruments that fit meat for digestion ; and what comeliness is
in them, is not every way obvious ; they are not seen or
discerned in their proportionableness or disproportion-
ableness, but by the motion of the lips, otherwise they are
hid by them.   2. Again in scripture they are used to
evidence and signify these three things, 1. They are used
to signify the nature and disposition of a person, as good
or evil ; hence evil men are said to have " lions' teeth,"

and that their " teeth are as spears," Psalm lvii. 4. And
that beast, Dan. vii. 5, 7, is said to have " three ribs in
his teeth," pointing out its cruel disposition. 2. They
evidence good or ill food, that the person feeds on. 3.
A healthful or unhealthful complexion, which depends
much on the former: hence Judah's good portion and
healthfulness is set out by this, Gen. xlix. 12, " His teeth
shall be white with milk." According to the first, by
teeth in the new man may be understood two things ; 1.
Faith ; believing being often compared to eating, because
it furthers the soul's nourishment, and is the means by
which the soul lives on its spiritual food. This saith, 1.
That the inner man must have food, as the natural body
hath, for its sustaining. 2. That the believer actually
eats and makes use of that food, he hath teeth for that
end, and should not only look on Christ, but feed on him.
Secondly ; Meditation also may be here understood ; that
serving much to the feeding and filling of the soul, as
Psalm lxiii. 6, 7, " My soul shall be filled as with marrow
and fatness," how ? " While I meditate on thee on my
bed, and think of thee in the night watches ;" meditation
is as it were the soul's ruminating and chewing its cud,
feeding upon, and digesting what is understood and eaten,
as the clean beast did : which may be one reason why
her teeth are in the first part of their commendation, compared to " a flock of sheep," which were among the number of clean beasts by reason of this property : meditation
is exceedingly useful for a believer's life, and they who
are strangers to it, are not like Christ's sheep.

Again, as the teeth evidence first the nature and inward
disposition, so we conceive they are also made use of here
(as the commendation also clears) to shew, 1. The zealous
nature which is, and ought to be in believers, they have
" teeth," and ought not always to be soft, wherein the
Lord's honour is concerned : zeal though it bite not, and
devour not, yet it is not senseless, but easily touched with
the feeling of that which reflects upon the glory of God.
2. The similitude here is to shew what a meek and quiet
spirit believers have, they have not such teeth as lions or
tigers, but such as sheep have ; nor tusks like dogs and
ravenous beasts, but " even shorn," shewing a moderation,
and equitableness in their way, being " first pure, then
peaceable, gentle," &c. James iii. 17. This will agree
well to teeth, as they appear by opening the lips, for, the

new nature within is expressed, and doth appear in words, which afterward are spoken of under the similitude of lips. Now this christian moderation which keeps the right midst, is a notable piece of spiritual beauty (as is clear from the second piece of the commendation) for it is "as a flock of sheep even shorn," and not unequally, and unhandsomely clipped; so true zeal will not upon bye-respect or interest be high or low, up or down, but keeps a just equality in its way: and this speaks out a well constituted frame, that is, neither too soft, nor too sharp, in biting and devouring one another (as is said, Gal. v. 15.) which carnal zeal sets the teeth a-work to do.

2. This similitude doth evidence and signify a good subject they feed on, to wit, Christ and his promises; and a good subject they meditate on, the same Christ, and what is most precious in him: hence in the third part of the commendation, they are likened to sheep "coming up from the washing," white and clean: neither mixture of human inventions, nor of carnal passions or worldly delights, gets place and entertainment with them; their zeal is pure, their ends are single, their affections are chaste and clean, being "purged from all filthiness of flesh and spirit," and they appear so.

3. Not only their healthfulness is hereby evidenced, but further also their fruitfulness; whereupon their inward meekness and zeal moderated by pure and peaceable wisdom, have great influence, as is clear by the fourth part of their commendation, "every one" of these sheep "bear twins, and none is barren among them:" the scope whereof, is to shew their abundant fruitfulness, thus their sweet nature is a pleasant possession, like a flock of sheep that enriches their owner, they are so fruitful and profitable. *Observ.* 1. Feeding on Christ is ever fruitful to the soul that makes him its food; whereas other meats profit not them, that are occupied therein. Heb. xiii. 9. 2. Zeal moderated with meekness, hath also a deal of fruit waiting on it, James iii. 17, but bitter zeal (as it is there in the original) or strife, hath confusion, and every evil work following on it, *Ibid.* verses 14, 15, 16. It is much to be zealous alway in a good thing, and no little piece of spiritual commendation, to keep the right midst with our zeal.

Verse 3.   Thy lips are like a thread of scarlet, and thy speech is comely : thy temples are like a piece of a pomegranate within thy locks.

IN this 3d verse we have the fourth and fifth particulars that are commended in the Bride. The fourth thing commended is, her "lips ;" the commendation given them is, that they are like "a thread of scarlet," that is neat and lovely, and of an excellent colour, as scarlet, which (being of the richest dye) was made use of under the law to represent the blood of Christ, as Heb. ix. 19. Next, this is amplified, as we conceive, in the following expression ("and thy speech is comely") which is added for the explication of the former, and therefore is joined thereto with a copulative ("and") which is added to none of the other parts here commended ; and it may be here added, to shew 1. A way of opening the other expression; for speech is expressed by lips, because they are the organs (to say so) whereby it is formed and uttered. And, 2. To shew, that under lips, come in both our words to God in prayer and praise, and also our words to others, whatever is spoken or comes out of the lips, as often the phrase is used for both. Also it shews, that in a special way he takes notice of believers' speech (when it is savoury) as a main part of their spiritual beauty, which makes them lovely.

The commendation of her lips and speech is twofold. 1. More general; it is like "a thread of scarlet," 2. That is expounded by another expression more clear and particular, namely this, "thy speech is comely:" the meaning of both which may be comprehended under these four, 1. That her speech is profitable for its matter, as a scarlet thread is precious and useful : the subject of a believer's discourse is not common, but "good to the use of edifying," Eph. iv. 29. 2. It is pleasant and delightsome for its manner, like a sweet, comely, and pleasant voice, opposite to some kind of voices that are harsh and unpleasant ; it is by prudence and love sweetened, and made savoury, and therefore is said in scripture to be "seasoned with salt," Col. iv. 6, and to "minister grace to the hearers," and it is called a giving of thanks, Eph. v. 3. It is articulate and distinct, therefore called "speech" and not a sound ; having honest ingenuity in it, speaking as they think in their heart, Psalm xv. 2, and opposite to lying, dissembling, &c.

whereby one speaks to vail or hide his mind from another.
4. Hereby is also signified, that they hazard not even the
best of their prayers on their own bottom and worth, but
their work is to have them all dyed in the blood of the
Lamb, and to put them up in his name, Heb. xiii. 15. They
are all offered up by him.   Now these are special qualifications, commendations, and characters of a believer ; shewing, 1. That a believer, as a believer, is not dumb, but
hath renewed lips, whereby he can speak to God in praise
for his honour, in prayers for his own good, and also to
others for their edification : a believer that can speak
nothing to a good purpose, or if he can, doth it not, is not
like Christ's Bride ; much less those whose discourses
tend quite another way.   2. That words are in a special
way taken notice of by Christ, and are special evidences
of the frame of the heart, according to which we may
expect commendation or reproof from Christ, for by " our
words we shall be justified," or " condemned," Matt. xii.
37.   3. That there is nothing more commendable in itself,
beautiful in a believer, or acceptable to Christ, than the
well ordering of the words ; he who can " rule the tongue,"
is a " perfect man," James iii. 2.   4. That believers'
prayers are all dyed in Christ's blood, and put up in his
name : and we conceive prayer, or the believer's speech
to God, is especially understood ; partly, because prayer
gets this same commendation to be sweet and comely,
chap. ii. 14, and partly because mutual communication in
words among believers, is expressed afterwards more
clearly, verse 11, though it is not to be excluded here.

The fifth part of her commendation (or the fifth character or property of the Bride) is in these words, " thy
temples are like a piece of a pomegranate within thy locks."
The temples are that part of the face, that are betwixt
the ears and the eyes ; and sometimes the signification is
so large, as they take in the cheeks ; they are a special part
wherein the beauty of the face consists, and are the proper
seat of shamefacedness and modesty, wherein blushing
appears.   The commendation is twofold, 1. They are like
" a piece of a pomegranate :" they who write of it say, it
is a fruit, which when broken (as here the mentioning of
a piece thereof signifies) is pleasant with red and white
spots, not unlike blushing in a pleasant face.   The second commendation is, that these temples are " within her
locks," of the colour of a pomegranate, but not discernible

fully (as the eyes also were, verse 1.) yet something observable; as sometimes modesty will make blushing, and again will seek to cover it, when hardly will it be gotten done. Here we take tenderness, shamefacedness, modesty in spiritual things, and blushing before God to be understood; Christ's Bride hath a tenderness that is soon affected with wrongs done to him, she easily resents them; and this is opposite to impudence, and a whore's forehead, which cannot be ashamed, than which nothing is more displeasing to Christ, and unbecoming to his Bride; here the temples are not hard, (as the brow that is of brass) but like a piece of a pomegranate, opposite to it; here it is not stretched out impudently, but covered within the locks, and not shameless that cannot blush, but coloured (to say so) with shamefacedness and blushing, which though they seek to hide, yet it appears in them. And this application being safe in itself, and agreeable to the scope; (which shews what Christ is delighted with in her) and this being a main piece of her beauty, and also suitable to the commendation, there is no hazard to fix on it; for, without this she would not be so lovely. Now we may easily conceive, that this tenderness, modesty, or blushing, is not any natural endowment, which appears in the carriage of man to man; but it is a saving grace, which especially is to be found in believers' carriage before Christ as being their Lord and husband: and it evidenceth itself in believers in these, or the like steps. 1. In their being soon challenged, for any thing that looks like sin. 2. In their being affected easily with challenges, and with the infirmities that are in them. 3. In their thinking shame of them, as of things that are disgraceful. 4. In their not being tenacious of them, or of their own will, nor disputing with Christ in any thing, but passing easily from their compearance, as it were, and thinking shame to be taken in any sin, or to be found in mistakes with him. 5. In being sparing to speak of any thing that tends to commend themselves, or in seeking their own glory. These are commendable things in a believer, and make him look like the piece of a pomegranate, spotted with red and white: and it shews the result of a believer's looking on their own way, when they take it up, and see that wrong, and this right; and even that which is right, wrong in so many things, and so may ways; whereupon as there is ever some sincerity, so there is ever some shame, and holy blushing; and this is constant, and (as it were) native to them, still to blush when they look upon themselves.

2. This commendation, that her temples are " within her locks," imports, that Christ's Bride blushes when none sees, and for that which no other sees : and also that she seeks not to publish her exercises, but modestly covers them ; yet the evidences of all these in a tender walk, appear and are comely. *Observ.* 1. Shamefacedness or sobriety becomes a believer, or Christ's Bride exceeding well, 2. Tim. ii. 9. 2. Inward heart-blushing, when we look upon ourselves before God, is the best trial of true tenderness. 3. A believer will have many shameful representations of himself, and will think much shame of what he sees, which the world will never be acquainted with. 4. This grace of self-loathing and holy blushing, is much taken notice of by Christ, and most especially recorded by him, however it be much hid from others.

Verse 4.   Thy neck is like the tower of David builded for an armory, whereon there hang a thousand bucklers, all shields of mighty men.

THE sixth thing commended in the Bride, is her " neck :" the neck being comely and straight, adds much to the beauty of a person, and is placed by nature, as a more eminent and essential part of the body than the eyes, legs, lips, &c. or any other part here mentioned : for it is that whereby the head and body are joined together. The commendation thereof is, that it is " like the tower of David :" what particular place this hath reference unto, it is hard to say, possibly it is that mentioned, Neh. iii. 16, 19, 25, called the tower of the mighty, or the armory ; it is like, that some strong hold built by David, eminent for beauty and strength, is hereby signified ; which might have been employed for keeping of arms, for times of danger, as the words following seem to bear.

This tower is more particularly explicated. 1. From the end and use for which it was intended, it was built " for an armory," that men might be furnished with arms in time of need. 2. The store of arms there laid up, is here set down, " whereupon hang a thousand bucklers, all shields of mighty men," that is, it is furnished especially with defensive arms (the believer's war being most de-

fensive) as shields ; but with abundance of these, for number a "thousand ;" and for quality excellent, and such as
"mighty men" make use of. If we consider the neck
here, in respect of its use, it holds forth the vigorous exercise of the grace of faith ; for it is that by which a believer
is united to Christ the head : it is that which strengthens
them, and is their armory furnishing them with shields,
because it provides them out of Christ's fulness, which is
contained in the promises ; which promises, or rather
Christ in them, being made use of by faith, are for a believer's security, against challenges, temptations, discouragements, &c. as so many excellent shields : therefore, Eph.
vi. 16, it is called "the shield of faith," and for their safety, it is commended above all the rest of the spiritual
armour : and this being the believer's great defence, and
especially tending to their commendation when it is in
lively exercise, this similitude cannot be so well applied
to any other thing.

Observ. 1. Faith in exercise is a noble defence to a believer, against all assaults and temptations ; there is no
such shield as faith is ; every promise and every attribute
of God, is as a shield to those that exercise this grace of
faith thereupon   2. Faith exercised on these, is exceedingly well pleasing to Jesus Christ.   3. That all believers
have their arms out of one armory, there is but one store-
house for them all, to wit, faith acting on Christ's fulness.
4. Faith will never want a buckler, there is a thousand
laid up in a magazine for the believer's use.   5. He is
the most mighty and valiant man, who is most in the
exercise and use-making of faith.   6. Faith is the grace
that makes a man valiant and victorious, as all the "cloud
of witnesses," Heb. xi. proves.

Again, if we consider the neck, as it is commended
here, as being like a tower for uprightness and straightness, it signifies a quiet serene mind, and a confident
boldness in doing and suffering ; in which sense, it is opposite to hanging of the head, which speaks discourag-
ment : and as a stretched out neck, in a carnal sense, Isa.
iii. 16. signifies haughtiness and pride : so here in a holy
and spiritual sense, it implies cheerfulnesss of heart, and
confident holy boldness, which proceeds from the spirit of
adoption ; and this waits upon, and follows after the
exercise of faith, being fixed and stayed upon the Lord
and his word against all events, Psalm cxii. 6.   Bold in

duties, and valorous in sufferings, and in undergoing any difficulties. So then, this is no small commendation which Christ gives his Bride, and it is well consistent with that holy blushing, shamefacedness and sobriety, for, which she was commended in the former verse.

Verse 5. Thy two breasts are like two young roes that are twins, which feed among the lilies.

THE seventh and last part that is commended in the Bride, is her "two breasts," or paps. For clearing of this similitude, we are to consider, 1. That the breasts in nature are a part of the comeliness of the body, Ezek. xvi. 7. 2. They are useful to give suck and food to others. 3. They signify warmness of affection, and loveliness, as Prov. v. 19, " Let her breasts always satisfy thee ;" and chap. i. 13. the Bride expressing her affection to Christ, saith, " he shall lie all night between my breasts ;" and so the wife of the bosom is the chaste and beloved spouse ; and thus Christ is called the Son of God's love, or " of his bosom." For this cause, we conceive these things are here understood, 1. A believer's fitness to edify others, and that believers are in a condition suitable to a married wife, or mother, that brings forth children, and hath breasts to nurse them : and so to have " no breasts," chap. viii. 8. is opposed to this : a believer is, as it were, a nurse with breasts fitted to edify others. 2. That believers being in case to be useful to others for their edification, is a special ornament to their profession, and the third thing that is here understood, is believers' warmliness and kindliness to Christ, and those that are his, taking him and them (as it were) in their bosom ; the believer hath warm affections to receive them into. And two breasts are mentioned, to shew there is no defect as to the extent, but both her breasts are in good case, and always ready in love to communicate their furniture, for others' edification.

The commendation is in two steps, each whereof is qualified for the further enlarging of the commendation. The first is, they are like " two roes," that are lovely and kindly, Prov. v. 17, (often mentioned before) and like " young roes," because these are most lovely, and suit best to be a similitude to set forth the comeliness of that part of the body ; they are like young roes, not too big ; for, when breasts are too big, it is a deformity ; and so when private edification exceeds its true bounds, it is not approvable or lovely. And these roes to which her breasts are compared, are "twins :" which shews, an equality and proportionableness in their love to God and to others, giving each of these their own place, and keeping their love to creatures in the right subordination ; and also their communicating their love to others, in admonitions and rebukes, &c. equally, keeping a proportionableness in all.

The second part of the commendation, is, they "feed among the lilies :" as roes would not maintain their pleasantness long if they did not feed ; yea, if the pasture were not good : so, these must needs be pleasant and useful, because they feed, and that not in a wilderness, but amongst the lilies ; which shews, that believers in fitting and furnishing themselves that they may be forthcoming for others' edification, do not neglect their own advantage and edification, but feed on good pasture, whereby they are yet more fitted for being useful to others.

By feeding in this Song, is understood. 1. To be present in such a place, as chap. ii. 16. 2. To make use of that which is food for the entertaining of life. 3. To delight in a thing for satisfying of the affections. Next, by the Bride's "breasts" (being "like roes which feed amongst the lilies") three things may be understood. 1. As this expression respects Christ's feeding, (so to speak) for he is said to "feed amongst the lilies," chap. ii. 16, and so it says, that the believer loves to feed in Christ's company, and where he is. And, 2. That this makes believers' breasts run to others, when they are much with him, and in his company. 3. As it respects believers, who are called "lilies," chap. ii. 16, and vi. 2 ; and so it says, 1. That all believers have one pasture, they feed together as a flock doth. 2. That one believer loves and delights in the company of another, they are the excellent and the lilies of the earth, their delight is with them. And, 3. That this helps a believer's growth, and fits him to be useful for others' edification, and to improve well the spiritual fellowship of other believers. 4. As it respects Christ himself, who is called a "lily," chap. ii. 1. and his "lips" are said to be "like lilies dropping," &c. chap. v. 13. Whereby is holden out, his words, promises, ordinances, &c. And so it says, 1. That Christ and his word is the great and main food, upon which believers feed, that is their proper pasture ; to be much drinking-in the "sincere milk of the word" is their meat and drink. 2. That much acquaintance with Christ in the word, enables one for being very useful to others. In sum, it says, 1. That a believer is no bare novice, but hath breasts that yield milk and nourishment to others. 2. That a believer hath a good pasture to feed on. 3. That believers' breasts run to others, according as they feed themselves; if they hunger themselves, others will not be edified by them; if they feed on wind and empty notions themselves, it will be no healthful food that others will receive from them. 4. That it is a pleasant thing and acceptable to Christ, when a believer so communicates what he hath received to others, as he is still feeding on Christ himself, and not living on the stock he hath already received.

Verse 6. Until the day break, and the shadows flee away, I will get me to the mountain of myrrh, and to the hill of frankincense.

THE words in this sixth verse, express the second way, how Christ evidenceth his respect to his Bride, he is so affected with her beauty, that he tells her, he cannot but haunt her company and answer her prayers. For, comparing this verse with verse 17. chap, ii. we find it a clear answer of her petition she puts up there. The words contain, 1. A promise. 2. A term set to the performance of it, shewing the continuance of his performance. The promise is, " I will get me to the mountain of myrrh, and to the hill of frankincense :" by this in general is understood no withdrawing of Christ's, or shutting of himself up in heaven from her; for, that will not agree to the scope, which is to shew how he loves her, and comforts her; nor will that be an answer of her prayer, but the contrary: it must then hold forth some comfortable act of Christ's, evidencing his respect to her for her consolation; which we conceive to be a promise of his presence with her to the end of the world. By "mountain" is often understood the church (as Isa. ii. 1, and Mic. iv. 1.) called so for her endurance and stability; for typifying of which, the temple was built on mount Moriah. And it is called a " mountain of myrrh, and hill of frankincense," to difference this one mountain (which is in the singular) from the mountains, or excellencies in the world, after mentioned, verse 8, which are many: it is a sweet moun-

tain, not of leopards but of " myrrh" and " frankincense :"
these were spices much used in the ceremonial services,
Exod. xxx. 23 24, and signified the preciousness, and
savouriness of the graces of God's people, and of their
prayers, Psalm cxli. 2. " Let my prayer be set forth before
thee as incense," &c.   Here then is understood that place
of the world (namely the church) where the graces of
God's people flow, and their prayers (as acceptable sacrifices) are put up to him ; and so it answers the scope, and
is opposed to the mountains of the world, mentioned in
the eighth verse.   The church is called the " mountain of
myrrh," and " hill of frankincense."   1. Because it is the
place, where the graces signified by these are to be found ;
it is only in believers they do abound.   2. Because there
they abound in prayers and praises, which ascend before
him as incense from a high place.   3. Because he accepts
so kindly of their duties, that they are pleasant to him,
and he delights to rest amongst them beyond all other
places, as being a " mountain of myrrh :" in which respect,
the house of God is called the house of prayer, because of
the exercise of that duty frequently performed there.

The second thing is the term he sets to the performance
of this promise, in these words, " until the day break, and
the shadows flee away, I will get me" (saith he) " to the
mountain of myrrh," till that day ; the sense is, amongst
all the places of the world, the church is the place in
which I will choose to reside, and with believers abounding in the exercise of grace and prayer ; they shall not
want my presence, for there will I abide, until the everlasting day of immediate fellowship with them break up ;
and so this makes for the Bride's comfort ; thou mayest
my spouse (saith he) expect my company, and the acceptation of thy prayers (which are an incense to me) until
that day come, as thou desirest : where we may see, (besides what was spoken upon this expression, chap. ii. 17.)
1. That Christ conforms his answers to our suits, and
makes the one as extensive as the other ; the term she
proposed is that he accepts of.   2. His hearing of one
prayer, gives ground to his people to expect that he will
hear all their prayers, and so he is called the " hearer of
prayer" indefinitely, Psalm lxv. 2, and this is the reason
why he says not, he will turn to her : (which would look
to that one prayer, chap. ii. 17,) but he saith, he will " get
him to the hill of frankincense," which looks to all her

prayers, and so his answer is more extensive, than the particular sought; which shews, 3. That as Christ will not mince his answers to believers, and make them less than their prayers, so he will often enlarge them, and make them more extensive than their prayers.

Next, from this that he gives believers such a name, as the "hill of frankincense," which is a special way, with respect to their prayers. *Observe* 1. That believers ought to be very frequent in prayer, like a hill that abounds in incense. 2. That Christ's presence is ever to be found, where these spiritual sacrifices of prayers and praises abound; for, wherever he hath an altar built to himself, and records his name, there he will come and bless his people, Exod. xx. 24.

And that he sets down this by way of promise, it gives us ground to observe, 1. That even our sense of Christ's presence, is in, and by a promise; and it is the promise thereof that should comfort and satisfy the believer, even when sense is removed, and is not for the time enjoyed, John xiv. 21, 23. 2. Christ limits himself to no other term-day, for continuing of the fulfilling, and performing of his promises, than that very time when believers shall be entered into the possession of what is promised; for I will grant thy desire (saith he) "until the day break," &c. that is, until the great day come, I will keep this course with believers. 3. Christ's promise of coming, and his making that sure, is one of the greatest evidences of love which he can bestow on his people. 4. There is no society or place (to speak so) but the church, nor any person in the church, but such as abound in spiritual sacrifices, who hath a promise of Christ's presence. 5. Christ would have the thoughts of eternal life, and of immediate enjoying of himself, entertained in his Bride, and would have her confirmed in the faith of it; and therefore is there here a particular repetition of the term which had been mentioned, chap. ii. 17. 6. He would by this repetition also express, that (some way) he longs for that day of the consummation of the marriage, as well as she doth, and that he would gladly have all shadows gone betwixt him and her; which serves much to confirm her in the faith of it, and comfort her till it come.

Verse 7.   Thou art all fair, my love, there is no spot in thee.

THIS verse contains the last piece of the commendation which Christ gives to the Bride, and it is the scope of all; whereby, having spoken of some particular parts, he now sums up all in a general, 1. Positively expressed, "thou art all fair, my love," then, 2. Negatively, "there is no spot in thee." The reason why, thus in a general, he closes up her commendation, is to shew that his forbearing the enumeration of the rest of her parts, is not because of any defect that was in her, or that his touching of some particulars was to commend these parts only, but to shew this in general, that all of her parts, as well not named as named, were lovely. This universal commendation is not to be understood in a popish sense, as if she had had no sin; for, that will not agree with other express scriptures, nor with this Song, where she records her own faults, as chap. i. 6, and iii. 1, and v. 2, 3. And also this commendation agrees to all believers, who yet are acknowledged by themselves not to be perfect. Neither is it to be taken in an Antinomian sense, as if their sins and failings were not sins to them, and did not pollute them; for, 1. That is not consistent with the nature of sin. Nor, 2. With the Bride's regrets and confessions in this Song: nor, 3. With the present scope, which is to shew the Bride's beauty: and he doth thus highly commend her beauty, not because her sins were not sins in her, as they were in others, but because her graces were more lovely, which were not to be found in others: hence the particular parts of the new creature, or inherent holiness, are insisted on for the proof of this; further this commendation did agree to believers before Christ came in the flesh. And this love assertion, "thou art all fair," holds true of the Bride, in these four respects, 1. In respect of the justification and absolution; she is clean, though needing washing in other respects, John xiii. "Ye are clean by the word that I have spoken," yet they needed to have their feet washen. Thus a believer is in a justified state, and legally clean and fair, so as there is no sin imputed to him, or to be found in him to condemn him, because the Lord hath pardoned them, Jer. l. 20, 2, It is true in respect of sanctification and inherent holiness, they are all "fair," that is, they are wholly renewed, there is no part but it is beautiful in respect of God's grace (though in degree it be not

perfect.)   Thus where grace is true, it is extended through
the whole man ; aud makes an universal change.   3. It is
true in respect of Christ's acceptation ; and so where there
is sincerity in the manner, he over--looks and passeth by
many spots ; thus "thou art all fair," that is, in my account thou art so ; I reckon not thy spots, but esteem of
thee as if thou had no spot : Christ is no severe interpreter of his people's actions ; and where there is honesty,
and no spots inconsistent with the state of children, Deut.
xxxii 2, he will reckon of them, as if there were none at
all.   4. It is true of Christ's Bride that she is "all fair,"
in respect of Christ's design, he will make her at last
"without spot, or wrinkle, or any such thing," Eph. v.
25, &c.   And because of the certainty of it, it is applied
to her now, as being already entered in the possession
thereof in her head, in whom she is set in heavenly places.
Hence we may see, 1. The honest believer ere all be
done, will be made fully fair and without spot.   2. Christ
often expounds an honest believer, from his own heart-
purpose and design ; in which respect they get many
titles, otherwise unsuitable to their present condition ; and
believers themselves may someway reckon so also.   If all
were put together, it were a great matter for a believer
to conceive and apprehend these words as spoken to him
in particular from Christ's mouth, thou, even, "thou art
fair," and without this, they will want their lustre, for
certainly Christ speaks so upon the matter to some, and
he allows that they should believe that he speaks so unto
them.

Verse 8.   Come with me from Lebanon, my Spouse, with me
   from Lebanon : look from the top of Amana, from the top of
   Shenir, and Hermon, from the lions' dens, from the mountains of the leopards.

From this 8th verse to verse 16, follows a second way
how the Bridegoom manifests his love to his Bride in
other three steps, 1.   He gives her a kind invitation and
call, verse 8.   2. He sheweth her how he was taken with
her love, and in a manner could not want the enjoyment
thereof, verse 9, 10.   3. Upon this occasion, he proceeds
to a new commendation of her ; and all of these are wonderful, being considered as spoken by him.
   The invitation in this 8th verse, besides the title he

gives her, (which we may take in as a motive) hath three parts. 1. The state wherein the Bride was, is set down; and this is contained in the term from which she is called. 2. The duty laid on, included in the term to which she is called. 3. The motives pressing and persuading her to give obedience thereto.

I. The term from which she is called, gets divers names, 1. Lebanon. 2. Amana. 3. Shenir, and Hermon. 4. The lions' dens, and mountains of leopards, which are added for explication of the former. Lebanon is a hill often mentioned in scripture, excellent for beauty, and therefore Christ's countenance is compared (chap. v. 5,) to it: Moses desired to see the goodly Lebanon, Deut. iii. 25. It was profitable for cedar-wood, and sweet in smell by the flowers that grew on it, verse 11, and Hos. xiv. 6, it was on the north side of Canaan, a stately place, Isa. xxxv. 1. Therefore Solomon built his dwelling for pleasure there, in the forest of Lebanon, as some conceive, though others think it was built at Jerusalem, and gets the name of the forest of Lebanon, for the pleasantness thereof. As for Amana, we read not of it, except it be that which is mentioned, 2 Kings v. 12, called Abana, but on the margin, Amana. It is like that river there spoken of, flowed from it, which being pleasant and stately, is preferred by Naaman to Jordan, in which the prophet appointed him to wash. Next, Shenir and Hermon, were two hills (or two tops of one hill) mentioned, Deut. iii. 9, beyond Jordan, pleasant and fertile, and from which they might see the land of Canaan before they crossed Jordan : and which were conquered from Og, king of Bashan. The tops also of these are mentioned, to shew their height, and she is here supposed to be on the top of them. Lastly, it is added " from the lions' dens, from the mountains of leopards," not designing any new place; but shewing that lions and leopards often rove upon hills, and it is like upon these, notwithstanding all their beauty : therefore mountains are called " mountains of prey," Psalm lxxvi. 4, because wild beasts that used to make prey, often lurked in them. There is somewhat, Hab. ii. 17, that confirms this, where the " violence of Lebanon," and the "spoil of beasts," is mentioned, supposing that there, beasts used violently to spoil.

2. By these mountains here, we conceive are understood the most excellent, eminent and choice satisfactions that

are to be found amongst the creatures, wherein the men
of the world delight, who are often compared to ravenous
beasts : and the reason is, it is something that is conceived to be excellent, that is here implied by the description,
yet such as hath no true excellency in it ; therefore the
Bride is called from it, and commanded to look over it,
even at its height, and to leave it to the men of the world,
whose portion properly these heights and excellencies are,
for they have not another to enjoy or look after. By
lions and leopards, we understand covetous, worldly men,
who pursue the world to the destruction of themselves
and others ; so they are often called in scripture, as Psalm
lvii. 4, &c. 1. For their devouring insatiable nature,
that can never have enough, but use always to prey on
others. 2. For their unreasonable, brutish nature, being
in their way like brute-beasts, rather than men, Psalm
xlix. *ult.* 3. For their malicious nature, that are always
hurting the godly that are amongst them. Again, these
heights and excellencies of the world are called the dens
and mountains of these beasts, 1. Because often ungodly
men have the greatest share of those, and have no more
to claim unto ; " their portion is in this life," Psalm xvii.
penult. 2. Because they rest in them, and seek after no
more, as lions do in their dens. These mountains then
are the excellencies of the creatures ; for the enjoyment
of which, men often use great violence, therefore they are
called, Psalm lxxvi. 5, mountains of prey, as having such
beasts, as cruel men lurking in them, above which God
(who is the portion of his people) is there said to be far
more excellent ; and thus these mountains here are opposed to the mountain of myrrh, verse 6, where Christ
hath his residence. Next, the church (whose state and case
is supposed to be the same naturally with the men of the
world) is called from this her natural state, and from the
remainders of such a frame, in two words, 1. Come, quit
it, saith he, and come with me, which is the same with that
command chap. ii. 10, " Rise up and come away," implying
the exercise of faith in him, and the delighting of herself
in communion with him, (as the spouse should do with her
husband) and a withdrawing from those created concern-
ments, wherein men of the world sought their happiness.
The second word is, look from the top of these, which
word sets out faith also, so Isa. xlv. 19, " Look unto
me," &c. and looking from these, signifieth her elevating

and lifting of her affections higher than the highest excellencies of the earth, even towards heaven and the enjoyment of Christ, Col. iii. 1, 2. And so it saith, she is not to look to what is present, but to what is not seen, and coming, which is by faith only to be discerned and apprehended : and this is to be done, by looking over the tops of the highest of created excellencies. Now this word being added to the former, doth shew, that when they cannot " come," they are to " look," and that their looks are not to be fixed on created things, as their objects, but must ascend higher, as the Israelites from these mountains, Hermon and Shenir, beheld Canaan, with desire to be there.

Observ. 1. The world hath its own taking excellencies, its heights and mountains, whereby it looks very pleasant to many. 2. The most beautiful created excellency hath a palpable defect in it, the most pleasant hill hath a wild lion lodging in it, that mars all the satisfaction that can be found there to a believer : God hath wisely so ordered, that every gourd to them hath a worm at its root. 3. Often the men of the world are much taken with these created excellencies ; they love to live in them, and dwell in them, as beasts in their dens, and know no higher design to drive, than their satisfaction in created excellencies : yea, 4. Believers are in hazard to fall into this sin, when things go well with them in the world, they are ready to sit down there ; therefore are they here called upon, that this hazard may be prevented. 5. Addictedness to the world, when men excessively pursue either after its gain, honour, applause, or pleasure, transforms men into beasts, and makes them irrational, brutish, and violent, forgetting what should be their main work and end. 6. Often violence towards others, and oppression with much cruelty, is the fruit of addictedness to the things of the world : if he profit himself, such a man cares not whom he undo. 7. There is nothing more unreasonable, bitter and cruel, than a worldly Athiest, whose designs are only after things that are within time ; they are lions and leopards. 8. Carnal men are often by their neighbourhood to the saints exceeding troublesome, even as lions in a mountain. 9. Addictedness to the world, and a surfeit with its contentments, can hardly stand with fellowship with Christ, and is most unbecoming his Bride ; therefore he calls her from it. 10. Believers have, and ought to have a more

high, noble, and excellent design, than the greatest con-
queror that ever was in the world; the believer in this is
beyond Alexander the great, who desired more created
worlds; but he looks over from the highest top of all these,
as undervaluing them, and longing to be at something
else. 11. Believers should have their looks directed towards heaven, and their thoughts and affections (even
before hand) should be fixed there, Col. iii. 1 ; Phil. iii.
20, 21, their face should be set that way. 12. It is faith
that looks toward Christ, as coming, when he is for the
time absent; and when believers cannot win to walk and
move towards him, they may look to him; and sure,
Christ who calls for this, will accept of it, till the other
be attained. 13. Often in the most excellent parts of this
world, such as " Lebanon, Hermon," &c. men are most
cruel and carnal; and the Bride of Christ hath most
enemies, and fewest friends. 14. The most excellent of
created contentments, for profit, honour, and pleasure,
should be denied and forsaken when Christ calls. 15.
There is nothing a believer should watch more against,
(as that which mars fellowship with Christ) than taking
excessive contentment in created things. 16. Often a
condition which abounds in worldly contentments and delights, is very scarce of Christ's company; therefore when
he allows her his presence, he calls her to leave them, in
her affection at least.

3. Because he knows the world is most bewitching and
the affections of his Bride are not so soon weaned from it
(though this be most necessary) therefore three ways he
presseth her to deny herself in these, and follow him
(which is the sum of the call,) 1. Saith he, thou art " my
Spouse," that is, my Bride : it is the same word which
(Jer. ii. 32.) is translated Bride, " can a Bride forget her
attire ?" This title is frequently given her in this chapter,
and verse 1, chap. v. Importing, 1. A marriage-tie and
relation betwixt him and her. 2. Love in him, owning
that relation, and claiming thereby an interest in her. 3.
A duty in her to own him as her husband, and to forsake
all her lovers, that she go not a whoring after any other,
as a wife should cleave to her husband : it is the same
with what is pressed, Psal. lxv. 10, &c. My Spouse
(saith he) thou hast not thy portion in the world therefore
come away from it. 2. He presseth it from the advantage of his own company, which she should enjoy upon

her obeying his call: "come with me" (saith he) my
Spouse, and this is repeated, "come with me," that is,
thou art mine, and I am thy husband, wilt thou not then
come with me, "with me?" This is a weighty argument,
and none will prevail, if this do not; Christ's company
should have more weight and be of more force to engage
a believer to Christ, than all the pleasantness of the world
can have to divert them: he is more excellent by far than
the "mountains of prey." Psalm lxxvi. 4, therefore is his
company to be preferred to them all. 3. He presseth it,
from the heartless condition which she could not but have
in the most excellent things in the world without Christ,
they were but "dens of lions," not for her to stay with,
nor yet any way agreeing with her state and case. Hence
observe, 1. When Christ and the most excellent things
in the world are opposed, there will be great odds, and a
vast difference seen betwixt them. 2. All the defects
that abound in created excellencies, should necessitate the
believer to take himself to Christ, there is no satisfaction
for him till he come there. 3. Men have no great loss
that loose their affections from the world, and set them
on Christ; it is but leaving the dens of lions, &c. and
coming to him, who is more "excellent than all the mountains of prey."

We may also read these words, by way of promise,
"thou shalt come with me;" and the scope will not be
against this, it being no less an evidence of Christ's love,
and no less comfortable to the church, to have his promise,
than to have his call; and all his calls having promises
implied in them, both will well agree. And so that which
is set down by way of precept, Rom. vi. 12, "Let not sin
reign in your mortal body," is set down by way of promise, verse 14, of that chapter, "sin shall not have dominion over you."

Verse 9.   Thou hast ravished my heart, my sister, my Spouse;
thou hast ravished my heart with one of thine eyes, with one
chain of thy neck.

10.   How fair is thy love, my sister, my Spouse! how much
better is thy love than wine! and the smell of thine ointments,
than all spices!

ALTHOUGH what Christ hath spoken in the former
verse be wonderful, yet these expressions, verse 9, 10,
being spoken by Jesus Christ to a poor sinful creature,

passeth admiration : they may be looked on as the reason of his former call and promise, he thus seriously invites her to come to him, because he cannot want her company ; for, his heart is ravished with her. The scope in both verses is the same, but is more clearly expressed, verse 10. Not so much setting forth the church's loveliness (though that is not to be excluded) as his lovingkindness, who is admirably affected towards her, as every word in matter and manner of both shews. In them consider, 1. The titles given her, which are the same in both verses. 2. What is asserted, and that is, that his heart is ravished. 3. The manner how this is expressed, in a sort of holy passion, doubling the expression. 4. Wherewith it is his heart is so ravished, it is (saith he) " with one of thine eyes," &c. in the end of the 9th verse, and more fully amplified, verse 10.

The titles are two ; one of them, namely that she is his " Spouse," hath been spoken of; but his repeating of it, shews a kind of glorying in it, as being very much delighted therewith. The other title, " my sister," is added, and it doth import these five things, 1. A condescending upon Christ's part to be thus joined in kindred to the believer, and so it takes in his incarnation, whereby he was made " in all things like to his brethren," Heb. ii. 17. Our blessed Lord Jesus is man, believers are his brethren and sisters, they are bone of his bone, and flesh of his flesh ; and for his Bride's consolation this is asserted. 2. A privilege whereto she is advanced upon her part, and that is, that by adoption believers are become sons and daughters to the Lord God Almighty, not only friends but children, and so " heirs," and " joint heirs" with Jesus Christ, Rom. viii. So as now they are as brethren and sisters, which is an unspeakable advancement. 3. It imports a change of nature, as well as of state in believers, so that they partake of the divine nature and Spirit with Christ Jesus, as it is, Heb. ii. 11, " He that sanctifieth, and they that are sanctified, are of one ;" which is a special ground of his sibness and kindred to believers, not common to others, but special to them, and founded on their sanctification. 4. It implies sympathy, friendliness, and a kindly esteem in him that takes her up and speaks of her, and to her, in all the most sweet relations of " mother sister, Spouse," &c. Matt. xii. ult. 5. It shews his owning of all these relations ; he is not ashamed to call believers, "sisters" and "brethren," Heb. ii. 11. *Observ.* 1. There are many wonderful, near, and sweet relations betwixt Christ and the believer. 2. Christ is the most faithful owner of them, and is in a most friendly way forth-coming to them, according to them all.

2. The thing asserted here, is, " Thou hast ravished my heart:" The word in the first language is one, and it signifieth, " Thou hast hearted me," or so to speak, "Thou hast unhearted me;" it is no where in scripture, but here; Christ's unspeakable love, as it were, coins new words to discover itself by, it is so unexpressible: The word is borrowed from the passionateness of love, when it seizes deeply on a man, it leaves him not master of his own heart, but the object loved hath it, and (as it were) possesseth it, and commands it more than the man himself; so the gospel saith, " where a man's treasure is" (that is, the thing a man esteems most of) " there" (as it were) " his heart is," and not in the party that loves. Matt. viii. 21. So the common phrase is, such a man hath my heart, when he is dearly beloved; and thus in a subtile way, Absalom is said to have " stolen away the hearts of the people from his Father." It is in sum, " my Spouse thou hast my heart," thou hast won it, and as it were by violence taken it away, I am not master of it, I cannot but love thee.

It is hard to draw observations, that may suitably express the thing here spoken of; only we may hint at these things. 1. Love in Christ to a believer, hath strong and wonderful effects on him, in reference to them. 2. The believer hath Christ's heart, he hath a seat in his affection, he possesseth his love (for no other thing hath his heart) and he may promise himself from Christ, whatever he can desire for his good, even as if he had his heart under his command; for (so to speak) he can refuse believers nothing, which they seek, and which he knows to be for their good. 3. Love in Christ to a believer, it is at a height, or, it is a love of the highest degree: there is no greater intenseness thereof imaginable; for to have the " heart ravished," is the expression of the greatest love.

3. The manner how he expresseth this, is by doubling the expression, " Thou hast ravished my heart—thou hast ravished my heart:" and this is to shew, that this word fell not rashly from him, but was drawn out by the vehemency of affection in him. 2. That he allows be-

lievers to believe this great love and affection he hath to
them, and would have them dwelling on the believing
thoughts of it ; and therefore, he doubles the expression
while he intimates his love unto them : only remember
there are no disorderly passions in Christ, as in us ; yet,
that there is sympathy and love in him, and passionate
effects of love from him, cannot be denied.

The fourth thing is, wherewith it is his heart is so ravished : it may be thought it is some great thing that
thus prevails over Christ : now what it is, is set down in
two expressions, which are joined to the former, to make
this love of his the more wonderful ; that which was conquered or ravished, was his heart ; that which doth it, is
her eye, the eye or the look of a poor sinful creature, even
of such a person as as may be despised in the world, and
Lazarus full of sores, and not admitted to men's company.
It is not with "both her eyes," but (saith he) with "one
of thine eyes," that is (as it were) with a squint-look ; a
side-look of the Bride prevailed thus with him. One eye
is not there mentioned, as preferring the beauty of one of
her eyes to the other ; but to shew what excellent beauty
is in her, and much more what infinite love is in him, that
he could not (because he would not) resist a look of one
of her eyes cast toward him. We shew what is understood by eyes, verse 1, and it is explained in the following
verse, to hold forth love especially here, (lovers using to
signify affection by their eyes) yet it takes in knowledge,
as being presupposed ; and faith as going along with it.
The second expression is, " with one chain of thy neck :"
these chains are spoken of, chap. i. 10. Whereby we shew,
was signified her inherent holiness, with imputed righteousness, which by faith she possessed ; and so here also
it signifies her graces, especially her exercising faith on
him, for so the neck was expounded, verse 9, to be understood of faith, which joined the believer to Christ as
his head : and it is said to have chains, because it never
wants excellent fruits, wherewith it is adorned, when it
is exercised. One chain is spoken of, not as if she had
not had more, or as if he did not respect them all, but to
hold forth this, that one of her chains (as it were) did
overcome him ; and so it may be gathered, what will both
eyes do, and more chains, when one so prevails. The
scope then here doth shew, 1. That Christ is easily prevailed with by his people, O how easily is he overcome

by them, who have love to him, and faith in him ! 2. That
Christ stands not on the degree of his people's graces, nor
doth he suspend his love and acceptation of a person,
upon such or such a degree; but wherever reality and
sincerity are, if it were in the meanest degree, and but
one look, or one chain, he will yield to it, and accept of it.
3. It is to provoke and encourage believers to cast a look
to Christ, when they find their faith to be so weak that they
can do no more ; and to confirm them in the expectation
of good from him freely, without any rigid reckoning ; it
is not only the strong believer, and the strong acts of faith
and love, that prevail with Christ, but he condescends to be
overcome, even by the weakest, with whom the sincerity
of these graces is to be found.

This is further followed and explicated, verse 10, and
that two ways, 1. By an indefinite question, " how fair is
thy love !"   2. By two comparative questions, whereby in
two similitudes, her love is preferred to the most excellent
things, " how much better," &c.   The thing commended,
is, " her love," that is, the love wherewith she loves him,
wherewith her heart breathes after him, delights in him,
esteems him, and is zealous to please him, &c.   The commendation he gives her love, is, that it is " fair."   And
by the way we may observe, that this clearly shews,
that by all the former parts of her beauty, are understood
spiritual graces : now (saith he) " thy love is fair," that is,
it is lovely and acceptable to me : as beauty and fairness
are much esteemed among men : so this grace of love is a
beautiful thing in Christ's Bride.   The manner of the expression is by way of question, and admiration, " how
fair !"   I can get nothing (saith he) to compare it with :
a wonder, that Christ should be so taken with the love of
sinners, as to admire it, or think that their love exceeds
all expression ; for, so men use to express what they cannot express : but this doth indeed shew, that the height and
depth, and length and breadth of that love, which Christ
hath to believing sinners, passeth all knowledge, and is beyond all words.   *Observ.* 1.   That a believer is one that
loves Christ, and true faith hath always this grace of love
joined to it.   2. That love where it is sincere and true,
is a property of Christ's Bride and Spouse, there are no
other in the world who love him, but those who are espoused to him.   3. Where love to Christ is, there Christ
loves ; he cannot but love them, that love him, and there

is nothing more acceptable to him, than the faith that is working by love.   4. Our Lord Jesus takes special notice of the frame of the heart, and what seat he hath in the affections of his people, he lays more weight on their love, than on their work, though true love can never be without works.

The second way how he explains and illustrates this, is more particular, by two comparisons, yet keeping still the former manner of expression, by way of question and admiration : the first is, "how much better is thy love than wine!" wine may be looked on in two respects, 1. As it is useful in man's life, and refreshful, Psalm civ. 15, " It maketh glad the heart of man, and Eccles. v. 19, " It maketh the heart merry :" wine is one of the most comfortable creatures, therefore she calls " his love better than wine," chap. i. 2.   Thus observe, 1. Christ will not be behind with his people, neither in kindness, nor in the expressions of it ; for, this is beyond hers, chap. 1. 2.   Not that he hath a better object to love, but because the love wherewith he loves her, is like himself, and more excellent than hers.   3. There is no such refreshful thing in all the work of creation to Christ, no such feast, as the warming of a sinner's heart with love to him is : this (Luke vii. 47.) is thought more of by Christ in a poor woman, than all the great feast he was invited unto by the rich Pharisee.

Again, we may look on wine as used in the ceremonial services and drink-offerings, Levit. xxiii. 13, &c.   Thus the meaning is, thy love is preferable to all outward performances and sacrifices, as Hos. vi. 7.   Love being the principle within, from which all our performances should flow, it is not opposed to sacrifice simply or to obedience ; but, 1. Supposing these to be separate, he prefers love ; if it were to cast in but a mite of duty out of love, it will be more acceptable than the greatest bulk of duties without love, as is clear in the case of the widow, Luke xxi. Yea, if men would " give their bodies to be burnt," without this, 1 Cor. xiii. 3. it will avail nothing.   2. It saith, that where both the inward principles, and the outward fruit or work are, the Lord respects that more than this, and he respects this in a manner but for that.

The second comparison is to the same purpose in these words, " and the smell of thine ointments than all spices !" ointments typified the graces of the Spirit," the pouring out whereof, is called, " the unction," John ii. 20, and " the

oil of joy," Psalm xlv. 7. The "smell" thereof signifieth
the acceptableness of these graces, when in exercise : our
Lord Jesus finds a sweet savour in them, as ointments
cast a smell that is refreshful to men (as we said upon
chap. iii. 6.) the grace of love mentioned before is here
included ; but under "ointments" there is more comprehended, to shew, 1. That where one grace is, there are
all the rest of the graces of the Spirit to found. 2. That
love to Christ, and zeal for him, holds believers stirring,
and makes them send forth a sweet and savoury smell.
This smell is preferred " to all spices," not to one or two,
but to all : spices were either used as gifts, because they
were precious and costly ; so the queen of Sheba propined
Solomon with them, 2 Kings x. 2, and the wise men
offered such to Christ, Matt. ii. 11. And so it saith, there
is no such propine can be offered to Christ, as love, and
the graces of the Spirit, when they are in exercise. Again,
spices were used in the Levitical services, and holy oil,
Exod. xxx. 23, 24, and so they are to be considered as
wine was in the last sense formerly spoken of, and it
shews how preferable the inward exercise of grace, is to
all external duties. *Lastly*, They are not only preferred
while he saith, "thy love is better," &c. but as passing
comparison, they are extolled far above all these things
with which they are compared, How fair, or how much
better is thy love than wine ! &c. O my Spouse (saith
he) it is not to be wondered that thy love ravishes
my heart; for, there no is created thing so precious, nor
any external service so acceptable to me, as it is. Hence
observe, 1. That inward love, or the inward exercise of
grace, and outward performances are separable. 2. That
when outward performances are separate from the inward
exercise of love and other graces, the Lord respects them
not. 3. That love is a good and necessary principle of all
duties and especially of the duties of worship. 4. Those
who have any thing of the lively exercise of love to Christ,
want never a propine that will be acceptable to him ; if
it were but a mite, or a cup of cold water, or a look to
Christ, if love be the principle from which these flow, they
will be very acceptable with him.

Verse 11.   Thy lips, O my spouse, drop as the honey-comb:
honey and milk are under thy tongue, and the smell of thy
garments is like the smell of Lebanon.

HAVING thus expressed his affection to his Bride, he
breaks forth in a positive commendation of her) which
may be looked upon as the ground of the comparative
commendation in the former verse) and he describes and
commends her at once, these two ways, 1. Touching, as
it were, at some particulars (which are indeed generals)
wherein her loveliness appears in actual fruits, verse 11.
2. In seven comparisons he holds forth her fruitfulness
from the 12 to to 16 verse, wherein he not only commends
her by the fruits which she brings forth, but from her fitness or aptitude to bring forth these fruits, so that she
cannot but be fruitful; as if one commending an orchard
from the fruit, apples, pomegranates, &c. or whatever
other fruits are in orchards, should then fall upon the
commendation of the orchard itself, in its situation, fences,
waters, or kinds of the plants, &c. so is it here.   And this
last commendation, is to be looked upon as the cause of
the former.

In this 11th verse there are three particulars commended: under which we conceive much of the series of a believer's walk is understood.   The 1. is her " lips:" which
are commended from this, that they " drop as the honey-
comb."   By lips, as verse 3, and frequently in the Song
(and so in the Proverbs, a man of lips is taken for a man
of talk) is understood her speech, words or discourse,
especially to others.   These her words (or her speech)
are compared for the matter, to " honey" or " the honey-
comb," that is sweet, nourishing, healthful and pleasant;
as Prov. xvi. 24, " Pleasant words are as the honey-comb,
sweet to the soul, and health to the bones :" and by honey
in scripture, is often understood that which is excellent,
and useful for the life of man: and therefore it was a
property of Canaan, that it flowed with milk and honey,
which are put together in the following piece of her commendation.   2. Her speech or words, are commended from
the manner, or qualification of them, " they drop as the
honey-comb," &c.   Dropping words signify, 1. Seasonable
words, which are like dew, dropping for the edification of
others, as dew by its dropping makes the fields fruitful.
2. Prudence and moderation in discourse, and so dropping

is opposed to floods, that with violence overflow.   3. This phrase signifieth a continuance in seasonable, prudent, and edifying discourse, as Job xxvii. 22, " My words dropped on them," and Deut. xxxi. 2, " My doctrine shall drop as the rain :" Thus " the lips of the wise feed many," Prov. x. 21.   *Observ.* 1. A believer's words tend to edification, and are for the true benefit and advantage of others.   2. Every subject is not the matter of their discourse ; but, as the " honey," it is excellent and choice, and that which ministereth grace to the hearers.   3. Mens' words give a great proof of what is in them ; and when rightly ordered, they are a good evidence of their love and respect to Christ.   4. A well ordered tongue is a most commendable thing before Christ, and every word that proceeds from the mouth, is observed by him.   5. Christ's Spouse should be observably different, as to her words and discourse, from all others, " Thy lips, O my Spouse" (saith he) " drop as the honey-comb :" implying, that whatever be the way of others, it becomes the Spouse of Christ, to have her words seasonable, savoury, and edifying.

The second thing here commended, reacheth more inwardly, and it is in these words, " honey and milk are under thy tongue :" there will be sometimes smooth words as butter, when their is much venom within ; it is not so with Christ's Bride.   By " under the tongue," which is the part commended, we understand the heart or inward man, as it is distinguished from the bare expression of the tongue or words, which are only spoken (as we say) from the teeth forward : so, Psalm lxvi. 17, He was exalted under my tongue, (as it is in the original) is expounded in the following verse, by heart-regarding : there was an agreement betwixt his words and his heart, without which God would not have accepted his words.   And seeing, when it is said of the wicked, that mischief and vanity are under their tongue, Psalm x. 7 ; Rom. iii. 13, whereby their deceitful rotten heart, and the venom that is within is signified ; so here must be understood inward sincerity, and a good frame of heart within, as well as good words without.   The commendation is, that there are " milk and honey under her tongue :" it is almost the same with the former ; as her words were edifying, so there was much edifying matter in her heart, or under her tongue ; the honey-comb (as it were) was there, and it by words dropped to others.   " Milk" is added, because it is also sweet and nourishing. In a word, that which he here points at, is, that her inward constitution and frame is like a Canaan, flowing with milk and honey; so fertile and fruitful is Christ's Bride, Here, observe, 1. That Christ takes not only notice of words, but of what is under the words; the disposition and frame of the heart, and the thoughts thereof are observed by him. 2. There is a suitableness often betwixt the heart within, and the words without; when there is honey under the tongue, then the tongue cannot but drop, for, out of the abundance of the heart the mouth speaks. 3. It is a most commendable thing in the believer, when the inner-man is right, in a lively and edifying frame, and when the heart is watched over, so that no thought enters in, or word goes forth, but what is edifying. 4. The heart should be furnished with edifying, profitable purpose and thoughts, as well as the mouth with pertinent and useful words; and that is as the fountain, from which this must run and flow. 5. They will feed and edify others best by their words, who feed best upon the most healthful subjects, and savoury thoughts themselves.

The third thing commended, is, " the smell of her garments:" garments are that which cover our nakedness, and are for decoration externally put upon the body; sometimes by them is understood Christ's righteousness, which we are said to put on, Gal. iii. 27, sometimes our own inherent holiness, which makes our way comely before others, and hides our nakedness from them; so, Job xxix. 19, saith, " I put on righteousness, and it clothed me." Now, here it is to be taken especially in the last sense (though not only) as setting forth the outward adorning of her walk with holiness; and this is the third part of her commendation, distinguished from the other two, which pointed at her words and thoughts. And so it is the practice of holiness that is here commended, which is compared to " garments," because good works are called the clothing of such as profess godliness, 1 Tim. ii. 9, and 1 Pet. iii. 3, 4. The " smell" of them, is the savour and relish of these good works to others, and also to him; even as it is said, that Jacob's garments did smell to his father (to which this may allude) so our holiness, being washed in the blood of the Lamb, is very savoury to him, and is also savoury to others; yea, the smell thereof is as " the smell of Lebanon," which was a hill that abounded

with trees and flowers, exceeding savoury and delightsome: whereas a corrupt conversation, is exceeding unsavoury, as rottenness and dead mens' bones. In sum,
this completes believers' commendation, when their words
are edifying, their heart answerable to their words in true
sincerity, and their outward walk adorning to the gospel,
so as their natural nakedness and pollution appears not in
it. *Observ.* 1. Where there is true honesty within, it
will appear in the fruits of holiness without. 2. There is
no garment or clothing that can adorn or beautify men,
as holiness doth a believer. 3. Though outward profession alone be not all, yet is it necessary for the completing the commendation of a believer. 4. Although good
works be not the ground of our relation to Christ, but
follows on it, and though it be not on the account of our
works, that the Lord is pleased with us to justify us ; yet
are the good works of a believer and of a justified person,
when done in faith, acceptable to God, and an odour and
sweet savour to him. Phil. iv. 18.

Verse 12.   A garden inclosed is my Sister, my Spouse: a
spring shut up, a fountain sealed.

HAVING thus summed up her carriage in the former
threefold commendation, now he proceeds both to describe
and commend her, by a sevenfold comparison, wherein (to
say so) the rhetoric of our Lord's love abounds: each of
them may point out these three things, 1. They describe
somewhat the nature of a believer, or Christ's Bride. 2.
They evidence Christ's love and care, which he hath toward her. 3. They hold forth her duty in reference to
herself. We shall shortly explain them, as they relate to
this scope.
  In this 12th verse, we have three of these comparisons,
whereby she is described and commended. 1. She is
compared to a " garden enclosed:" a garden is a plot of
ground, separate from other places, for delight and recreation of the owner, having many flowers in it, and much
pains taken on it: so believers are, 1. Set apart by God
beside all others in the world, and much pains is taken on
them ; the trees in Christ's garden are digged about and
dunged, Luke xiii. 8. 2. They are his delight, being separate from others for his own use, with whom he dwells,
in whom he takes pleasure, and amongst whom he feeds,

chap. vi. 2. 3. They are furnished with many excellent graces, fruits of the Spirit, which are planted in them as flowers in a garden, Gal. v. 21. Next, this garden is "inclosed:" it is a special property of gardens to be so. To be inclosed, is by a wall or hedge to be fenced from the trampling and eating up of beasts, and also from the hazard of winds; so, Isa. v. 2, the "vineyard of the Lord of hosts," (which is his church) is said to be fenced, a wall is built about it, to defend it from the danger of beasts, and storms. And this sheweth, 1. His care of her, in watching over her, Isa. xxvii. 23. And, 2. Her watchfulness over herself, whereby she is not common or accessible to every one; but as she is defended by his care, so also she hath a watch herself at the door of her lips, of her eyes, of her ears, &c. she is not like a city without walls, obnoxious to every assault and temptation, but hath a hedge of divine protection, which is as a wall of fire about her to defend her; and also a guard of watchfulness and holy fear, in the exercise of which the believer hath rule over his own spirit, which (Prov. xxv. 28,) is implied to be as strong walls about a city.

The second similitude wherewith she is compared, is "a spring shut up:" springs were of great price in those hot countries, and served much for making gardens fruitful, as is implied, Isa. lviii. 11, where it is promised to the church, "thou shalt be as a watered garden:" hence the righteous is called, "like a tree planted by the rivers of waters," Psalm i. 3, and on the contrary, the barren condition of his people is described, Isa. i. 30, by the similitude of "a garden, that hath no water." In a word, she is not only a garden, but a spring, that is furnished with moisture and water, for making her fruitful. More particularly, by this may be set out the graces of the Spirit, compared to waters, John vii. 38, 39, and said to become "a well of water" in those that believe in Christ, John iv. 14, for, these graces of the Spirit, and his influence on them, doth keep all things in the believer's soul's case fresh and lively, as a spring doth make a garden green and fruitful. Next, this spring is "shut up," for so were springs in these countries, where they were rare, as we see by Jacob's rolling the stone away, Gen. xxix. 8. And this kept the waters from being corrupted by the sun, and also from being bemudded by beasts: this signifieth the preciousness of the graces and influences of the Spirit, wherewith believers are furnished. 2. Pureness and clearness in them, as in waters that are not bemudded. 3. A care she hath to keep them pure from carnal passions, or fruits of her own spirit, that would bemud all.

The third comparison is on the matter the same, but adds a further degree to the former ; she is (saith he) " a fountain sealed :" a fountain may signify waters springing in greater abundance ; and sealing doth signify not only shutting up, but securing it by a seal, after it is shut up : so the den of lions was sealed, after Daniel was cast into it, Dan. vi. 17. And the stone was sealed, that was put on Christ's grave, that so it might not be opened by any, but by those that sealed it. And though there be other uses of sealing, yet we conceive that which is aimed at here, is, 1. To shew that the church is not common, but well kept and sealed, so that none can trouble believers' peace without Christ's leave, who hath " sealed them by his Spirit to the day of redemption," Eph. iv. 30, &c. 2. To shew Christ's particular right to the church and her graces, and his owning of her and them, she bears his seal (as the one hundred and forty four thousand, Rev. vii. are sealed) there is none but himself, that hath access to these waters ; her graces and fruits are all reserved for him, chap. vii. 13. 3. It shews (to say so) her closeness, and resolute watchfulness, so that there is no gaining upon her to bemud her condition without advertency and observation, more than waters can be drawn from a sealed fountain, the seal not being broken : like that phrase, Prov. v. 15, " Drink out of thine own cistern, let them be thine own," &c. She hath her own distinct fountain, from which she draws influences, and that she preserves and secures to herself. 4. It shews a kind of sacredness in this fountain, so that nothing may meddle with it, more than that which is marked and separated by a seal. In sum, the first comparison shews that Christ's Bride or the believer is to be fruitful. The second, what makes her fruitful, the spring of the Spirit. The third shews her care to keep it clear, and to have it running and flowing, that she may be fruitful.

Verse 13. Thy plants are an orchard of pomegranates, with pleasant fruits ; camphire, with spikenard ;

14. Spikenard and saffron ; calamus and cinnamon, with all trees of frankincense ; myrrh, and aloes, with all the chief spices :

THE fourth comparison follows, verses 13, 14, wherein she is compared to an orchard (as before to a garden) planted with divers and excellent plants. Now this includes these three things, which he adds to the former commendation, 1. That the believer hath many graces, he is an orchard that is planted with many trees and plants. 2. That the believer's graces, as they are many, so they are various ; and therefore trees and spices of divers sorts are reckoned here. 3. That the believer's graces are excellent for kind, as well as many for number and variety, they are as "spikenard, saffron," &c. "with all the chief spices." And as it commends an orchard, to have many plants, and great variety, and to want none ; so to have them of the best kinds, adds much to the commendation, when it is fruitful of these. Thus the believer is furnished with many various graces of the Spirit, as plants planted in his soul, and these of the best kind, rising from the most excellent seed that can be, the Spirit of Christ. And so the graces of believers are rare and precious, in respect of any thing that natural men have, which are but like shrubs in a dry wilderness.

Besides these, we may further observe, 1. That to have fruit, and abundance of fruit, will not prove one to be a believer, except it be choice fruit which he brings forth. 2. Believers' fruits, and the graces that are in them, differ from the most excellent parts and gifts that can be in natural men, or most refined hypocrites. 3. It is excellent and commendable, when all the graces of the Spirit flow and increase together in the believer.

It is like, the Holy Ghost may here signify the effects and properties of divers graces, by these several spices and fruits ; and, it may be, Solomon understood the particular signification of every one of them ; for, having so great an insight in natural and spiritual things, it is like he did not conjecturally, but on knowledge, mention such spices and no others ; but we must hold on the general : they are precious, medicinal, savoury and delectable fruits, and so are the graces of the Spirit to one that hath them, to others they converse with, and to Christ in respect of his acceptation ; they are like an orchard, or garden, that abounds with these: this is the scope, wherein we rest.

Verse 15.   A fountain of gardens, a well of living waters, and streams from Lebanon.

THE fifth, sixth, and seventh similitudes, are contained in this verse, wherein the Lord, following the same scope, further insists and explains what manner of fountain this is, which makes the believer so fruitful. 1. She is " a fountain of gardens." A fountain was spoken of, verse 12, whereby is signified an inward principle (to say so) or spring, which from within sendeth forth and furnisheth waters : here she is called " a fountain of gardens," she was called a garden, verse 12, here " a fountain of gardens" in the plural number. By this is holden forth, 1. The end of grace in a believer, it is given him, not only for himself, but also for the use of others, as the gifts of the Spirit are given to every one " to profit withal," 1 Cor. xi. 7.   2. It shews that believers act and exercise their graces for others' edification, as a fountain that someway is common for the use of more gardens, and so it points out what public spirits they should have, intending the edification of all to whom they can conveniently communicate their gifts and graces. 3. It shews the abundance of spirit and life (to say so) wherewith Christ's Bride is furnished, so as she may communicate for the admonishing, strengthening, and edifying of others with herself, as it is, Rom. xv. 14, where believers are said to be full of goodness, filled with all knowledge, and able to admonish one another.

The sixth similitude is, " A well of living waters :" this is not only to difference her from a cistern that hath water, but hath no spring in it, but also to shew the nature of the Spirit of grace in believers, it proves quickening and healing to those that have it : both these are held forth, John iv. 14.   He that drinks of this " water shall never thirst," for it shall be in him " a well of living water, springing up to eternal life."   So is it also, John vii. 38, 39, where the Spirit of grace is, it will be springing ; and grace will never dry up, where it is true.

The last similitude is, " And streams from Lebanon :" which saith, that Christ's Bride is not only a fountain, but

also she is a stream : and it holdeth forth, 1. That grace
in her hath its rise from another, though it beget a spring
in her, as if Lebanon sent a stream to a garden, which did
become a spring by its constant flowing there. 2. By a
stream also is set forth the abundance of grace in believers, it is in them not as a brook, but as a stream. Next,
Lebanon was a hill much commended, it is like sweet
streams issued from it : it is written that Jordan which
watered much of the land, had its rise and spring there.
In the v. chapter, verse 15, Christ's countenance is compared to Lebanon, and so here, while the flowing of grace
in her is called a stream from Lebanon, the derivation of
grace, and of the Spirit from Christ Jesus is holden forth;
which though it have a seat, and becomes a fountain in
the believer, yet it hath its rise from him, and is kept
flowing and springing by him ; it is as a fountain derived
by a stream from Lebanon, and otherwise any spring of
grace, that is in a believer would soon run dry. All
these being put together, and compared with what is before, shew, 1. That the believer is fitted by Christ not
only with spiritual life, and a stock of habitual graces,
but also with every thing that may make him lively and
fruitful in the exercise of these. 2. This contrivance of
spiritual influence that makes believers fruitful, is a most
lovely and excellent thing. 3. The great commendation of
believers is grounded upon the graces of the Spirit that
is in them, and upon the influences of the same Spirit
that comes from Christ to them. 4. Where grace is, it
will have fruits, and be savoury in the conversation, in the
exercise thereof. 5. It is the best evidence of grace, and
of Christ's influence and Spirit, when it appeareth in the
fruits, these prove the believer to be an orchard and a
fountain. 6. Those graces that make a believer fruitful,
have not their rise in, or from a believer, but from Christ,
and the fountain that is in them, is but a stream that
comes from him.

BRIDE.

Verse 16. Awake, O north wind ; and come, thou south ; blow
upon my garden, that the spices thereof may flow out. Let
my beloved come into his garden, and eat his pleasant fruits.

CHRIST having now been large in commending the
Bride, she steps to in this verse (as it were, taking the

opportunity of his nearness) and puts up her desires to to him, briefly in two suits, which are grounded on the commendation that he gives her, and shews what is the great design that she aims at now when she hath Christ's ear ; and she follows these suits so, as she acknowledgeth all her fruitfulness (for which she is commended) to flow from him, and to depend on him, who is therefore so much the more to be commended and extolled himself.   In sum, the sense is this, though I be a garden (saith she) and have good plants, habitually in me, yet will they not bud nor flow, nor can they be fruitful except the Spirit (which is as the stream from Lebanon) blow to make them so ; therefore, O Spirit come, and let me partake of thy influences and breathings, that my beloved may have an invitation thereby, to come ; and when come, may be entertained upon his own fruits.

The first petition is, for liveliness and fruitfulness : the second is, for the beloved's presence, which is the end of the former.   And these two, life and sense, are (as it were) the air that kindly-believers love to breathe into. That both these are the Bride's words, may thus be collected.   1. Because they look prayer-like, and it is more suitable to her to say, " come," than for him : yea the Spirit being invited, " to come," to the garden, it is clear the party that speaks hath need of his presence : and that it is not said go, but " come," with reference to the necessity of the party that speaks, doth make it evident, that it cannot be spoken by the Bridegroom, but by the Bride ; for, so the phrase every where, and in the next, words, " let my beloved come," imports.   2. That the last part of the verse is her suit, none can deny ; and there is no reason to conceive two different parties, seeing both the matter of the suits, and the manner of speaking, will agree to the same party.

In the first petition, we may consider these two, 1. The thing sought.   2. The end wherefore that which she seeks and prays for, is held forth, as it were, in three steps or degrees, in three expressions, " awake, O north wind, come thou south, blow upon my garden."   For understanding whereof, we are to look, 1. What these " winds" signify.   2. What this " garden" is.   And, 3. What these acts, of " awaking, coming" and " blowing" are.   By winds often in scripture is understood the Spirit of God in his mighty operations, as Ezek. xxxvii. 3, and 14.   And the special work and operation of the Spirit is compared to wind, 1. For its purifying nature. 2. For its cooling, comforting, refreshing power and efficacy. 3. For its fructifying virtue, winds being especially in those hot countries, both exceeding refreshful, and also useful to make trees and gardens fruitful. *Lastly*, for its undiscernible manner of working, as John ii. 6, " the wind blows where it listeth," &c. yet hath this operation real effects with it. And it is clear that the Spirit is here intended, because it is the Spirit's blowing that only can make the spices or graces of a believer to flow, as the wind doth the seeds and flowers in a garden. Next, by " north and south wind," are understood the same Spirit, being conceived and taken up in respect of his divers operations (as it is, 1. Cor. xii. 6, 7, 8, &c. and therefore called " the seven Spirits of God," Rev. i. 4,) sometimes cooling, and in a sharper manner nipping, as the north-wind, sometimes working in his people more softly and warmly, and in a still and quiet manner like the south-wind ; yet, as both winds are useful, for the purging and making fruitful of a garden ; so are the divers operations of the Spirit, to the souls of believers. In a word, hereby is understood, the different operations of the Spirit, whether convincing and mortifying, or quickening and comforting, &c. both which contribute to make her lively and fruitful, which is the scope of her petition.

2. By " garden," is understood the believer, called a garden, verse 12, and an orchard, verse. 13, because the believer doth abound in divers graces, as a garden doth in many flowers. And she calls it " my garden," as he calleth the plants her plants, that were planted there, verse 13, and as she called the vineyard hers, chap. i. 6. and viii. 12, which also is his, verse 11, as also this garden is called his in the following words, chap. vi. 1. It is his by propriety, as the heritor and purchaser : as also, all these graces in her are hers as being the servant that hath the oversight of them, and who hath gotten them as talents to trade with for the Master's use. All that we have, viz. a soul, gifts, graces, &c. are given to us as talents, which we are to dress for bringing forth fruit to the owner, as the following words do clear.

3. The actings and workings of the Spirit, are held forth in three words, which are so many branches of her petition. The first is, " awake." This word is often used by God's

people in dealing with him, "awake, put on thy strength, O arm of the Lord," &c. Isa. li. 9. It is not as if the Spirit were at any time a-sleeping, but she desires that by some effects, sensible to her, he would let it be known he is stirring. The second word, "come," is to the same purpose: the Spirit considered in himself, cannot be said to come or go, being every where present; but this is to be understood, in respect of the effects of his presence, and so he is said to come and go: thus, while she saith, "come," the meaning is, let me find some sign of thy presence, quickening and stirring my graces. The last word is, "blow upon my garden:" blowing holds forth the operation, whereby the Spirit produceth his effects in believers; It is not the Spirit himself, nor the fruits of the Spirit that are in believers, that are here understood, but the operation of the Spirit, whereby, he influenceth, or (if we may so speak) infuseth them (as God breathed into Adam the breath of life) and whereby he stirs, excites, and quickens them for acting. The prayer then, is directed to the Spirit (as Rev. i. 14.) considering the Spirit essentially as the same God with the Father and Son, (in which respect, to pray by name to one person of the Godhead, is to pray to all the three, who in our worship are not to be divided) that he would by his operations (which are divers and various for believers' good) so stir and quicken his own graces in her, that, seeing she is a garden wherein the Beloved takes pleasure, her graces for his satisfaction may be exercised, and made to savour, to the end that he may the more manifest himself in sweet communion with her.

Next, The end wherefore she presseth this suit so much, is, that her spices may flow out: in a word it is, that she might be fruitful; for, though there were many graces in her, yet, without the Spirit's breathing and influences, they should be as unbeaten spices, that did not send forth their smell.

Observ. 1. Although a believer have grace, yet it is not always in exercise; yea, it may be, and often is interrupted in its exercise, 2. That the believer's great desire is to be fruitful, and to have grace in exercise, that he may be delighted in by Christ: it is not only his desire to have grace habitually, but actually to have it in exercise. 3. There is nothing can make a believer lively and fruitful, but the influences of the Spirit: and that same Spirit, that works grace, must quicken it and keep it in exercise. 4. There may be an interruption of the influences of the Spirit, so as his blowing may in a great measure cease. 5. The same Spirit hath divers operations, and divers ways of working and manifesting himself: sometimes as the south wind, more smoothly; sometimes as the north wind, more sharply. 6. All his operations, how rough soever some of them may appear, are always useful to believers, and tend to make them fruitful: and to this end the most sharp influences contribute, as well as the more comfortable. 7. Believers should walk under the conviction of their own inability to act their graces, and of the necessity of the Spirit's influences, for drawing them forth to acting and exercise. 8. They, who are thus sensible, may seek after the Spirit for that end: and it is a good frame in order to the obtaining of life and quickening by the Spirit of Christ, when the sense of their own inability, their love of fruitfulness, and the faith of attaining it by his Spirit, puts them to seek after it. 9. Prayer is a necessary and excellent means for stirring up one in a secure frame, and for attaining the Spirit to revive and quicken the work of his grace. 10. Believers may beg the Spirit to quicken them, when they find themselves lifeless; as well as they may ask pardon, when they find themselves under guilt. 11. Believers will be, and should be as desirous of liveliness and fruitfulness, as of sense: yea, this is the order by which they must come, and should seek to come to the obtaining of sensible presence. 12. No commendation of any attainment in believers, nor any clearness of interest, should make them sit down on their attainments, or become negligent; but, on the contrary, should stir them up to aim at the more liveliness and spiritualness, that they may be answerable to that interest they have in him, and to the commendation he allows upon them: for which cause, this petition follows immediately upon the former commendation.

The second petition, which goes along with the former, is for the Beloved's presence, "Let my beloved," (saith she) "come into his garden, and eat his pleasant fruits:" her desire here, is twofold, 1. That Christ would "come:" this doth respect a greater degree of nearness, notwithstanding of any thing she enjoyed. 2. That he would "eat his pleasant fruits," that is, familiarly, and friendly delight in his own graces; and therefore it was she prayed for the influences of the Spirit, that there might be abundance of fruits for his satisfaction. The way she presseth this petition is very kindly, though the words be short. 1. She presseth it from the relation she had to him, " Let my Beloved" (saith she) "come :" this makes her request and invitation warm and kindly. 2. From the kind of the fruits ; they are "pleasant fruits," that is, delectable in themselves, and acceptable to him. But, 3. Lest this should derogate from him, and arrogate to herself, she adds " his pleasant fruits;" they are " his," and that makes them pleasant, so that he cannot but accept them: they are " his" being purchased by him, wrought by him, kept in life by him ; though he hath made me the garden (saith she) wherein they grow (and the garden, as it hath weeds, is hers) yet all the good fruits, in so far as any of them are to be found in me, are his : in sum, all my desire is this, 1. To be fruitful, then 2. To have Christ's company, shewing himself pleased and present with me. *Observ.* 1. Whatever believers have, they neither will, nor can rest upon it ; nay, not in the most eminent measures of holiness attainable here-away, without Christ's presence and company. 2. Fruit-fulness and liveliness help and contribute much to the enjoyment of Christ's manifestations, John xiv. 21, 23. 3. Believers, that aim seriously at the exercise of grace in themselves, may confidently invite Christ to come, and may expect his presence. 4. All believers' fruits, even when quickened by the Spirit, are Christ's. 5. This should be acknowledged, and when we are most fruitful, we should look on our fruits, not as our own, but as his still. 6. Christ will feed or delight in nothing, but what is his own, and is acknowledged by his people to be so : and there can be nothing, which he will accept of set before him, but such. 7. Believers' end and design, in pursuing liveliness and fruitfulness, is not, and ought not so much to be their own satisfaction, and the feeding of themselves, as the satisfaction of Christ, and the pleasing of him ; for, that is his eating his pleasant fruits ; which is the Bride's great desire and design, when she calls for the north and south wind to blow upon her garden.

CHAPTER V.

Verse 1.   I am come into my garden, my Sister my Spouse : I
have gathered my myrrh, with my spice ; I have eaten my
honey-comb with my honey ; I have drunk my wine with my
milk : eat, O friends, drink, yea, drink abundantly, O beloved.

THIS chapter hath four parts, according to the parties
that sucessively speak.   In the first part, verse 1. Christ
speaks, and that it is he who speaks, doth at the first reading appear; they are kindly words, well becoming him, and
are the answer of her suit in the former words : and so depend on them (for the division of this Song, as also of
other scriptures into chapters, not being done by the penmen of the Holy Ghost, but by the translators, is not to
be stuck on where there is no question in the matter) she
desired him, verse last of the former chapter, to come, and
now in this verse, behold I am come, saith he, &c.   In it
we have 1. His yielding to come.   2 His carriage when
he is come, as to himself : and also his intimation of both.
3. His invitation to others, which may be also a part of
carriage when come, taken up in three.   1. He makes
himself welcome ; and, 2. Others.   3. He intimates it.

The title being spoken of formerly, the first thing is," I
am come into my garden" (as thou desired) "my sister," &c.
Hence observe, 1. Christ hath particular and peculiar ways
of coming to his people, and of nearness to them, even as
he hath of withdrawing from them.   2. There are some
peculiar times wherein he is more near than at other
times.   3. Sometimes he will not only draw near to his
people, but let them know that he is near, and put them
out of doubt that he is come.

Again, if we look to this as the answer of the former
prayer, we will see, 1. Christ is easily invited and prevailed with to come to his people ; and sometimes there will
not be long betwixt their prayer and his answer, it is the
very next word.   2. Few words may be an effectual
prayer to Christ (as the former suit was) a breathing or
sigh will not be rejected by him, where sincerity is.   3.
Christ will sometimes not only answer prayer in the thing
sought, but he will intimate, and let his people know that
he hath answered it.

More particularly, we may consider the answer, 1. As it agrees with her prayer. 2. As it seems defective. 3. As it is beyond it.

1. It agrees fully to her last suit, she prayed he would come and eat, he comes and eats. *Observ.* Christ will carve and shape out sometimes his answer, even according to his people's desires, as if they had the power of prescribing their own answers. For, when our prayers make for our good, Christ will alter nothing in them ; but will grant them in the very terms in which they are put up.

Again, I say there seems to be somewhat defective, there is no return recorded of the first suit of liveliness ; and her drowsy, lazy case, verse 2, 3, gives ground to think, that that petition was not as yet answered. *Observ.* 1. Christ may be particular in answering one petition of the same prayer, when yet he may for a time suspend an answer to another, in itself as acceptable to him. Yea, 2. He may answer the last prayer, and seem to pass over somewhat formerly sought for.

Finally, compare this answer with their last suit, he doth more than she required ; for she desired him only to come and eat, but he comes, eats, gathers, &c. Christ will often stuff in more in the answer, than was in the desire of his people ; and will do above what they asked or thought, Eph. iii. 20.

Next, his carriage (as to his own satisfaction) is in three steps, 1. " I have gathered my myrrh with my spice :" myrrh and spice signify (as hath been often said) the graces that grow in believers, who are his garden ; His gathering of them is his pulling (to say so) and dressing of them, as gardeners do their herbs and fruits, for making them useful ; here, ere he eat he gathers, signifying, that as the spices are his, so he must prepare them for himself ; she cannot prepare what provision Christ gives her, till he do it : she cannot put forth to exercise the grace she had received, till he breathe on it.

2. " I have eaten my honey-comb with my honey :" when he hath prepared, he eats : by honey-comb and honey, is signified the same thing (as chap. iv. verse 11.) because as that was savoury and wholesome food in these days and places, so are believers' graces a feast to Christ.

3. " I have drunk my wine with my milk :" milk was for nourishing, wine for refreshing ; Christ mentions drinking of both, to shew, how abundantly he was satisfied, and

fully feasted, both for meat and drink: and how heartsomely he entertained himself on it, as a friend that
thinks himself very welcome. Consider here, 1. Meat
and drink are mentioned : Christ will not want entertainment where he is, he will invite and treat himself, where
he gets welcome: where Christ gets welcome, he will
never complain of the want of fare, he hath there a feast.
2. He accepts all heartsomely ; as Christ is easily invited,
so is he cheerful and pleasant company: where he comes,
he takes what there is to give him, he is not sour and
ill to please. 3. There is myrrh and spice, milk and
honey and wine; which is not only to shew that there
are diversities of graces, but that Christ casts out nothing
of grace that is found in his people, he takes the milk as
well as the wine; he makes much of the weaker grace,
as well as of the most lively. 4. He gathers, and eats;
as Christ provides food for himself, (so to speak with reverence) he is his own cook, none can dress dishes for
Christ, but himself. 5. Where he gets the most serious
invitation to come, there may be much unpreparedness for
him when he comes, until he right it, and prepare his own
entertainment himself. 6. Though things be not prepared for him, yet sometimes he will not suspend his coming
on that, nor will it mar his cheerfulness in his carriage,
when he comes and is made welcome, he dresseth and
eateth. 7. He intimates all this : sometimes Christ may
be well pleased with believers, and be feasting himself on
their graces, and yet they not discern it, nor believe it,
until he intimate it and make it known to them: and
therefore that their joy may be full, he graciously condescends now and then to put them upon the knowledge
of it, and persuades their hearts of it.

The last thing, is his invitation to his friends to eat
with him, which is pressed, 1. By kindly compellations,
" Friends" and "beloved." 2. By three words, "eat,
drink," and that "abundantly," By "friends" and "beloved," are understood believers, there are none other
capable of these titles, and it was she that prayed, that is
here understood by friends and beloved, and so he answers
her. Hence we see, the believer is Christ's friend, as
Abraham, James ii. 23, and Lazarus, John xi. 11, were
called. It imports, 1. A privilege on the believer's part,
to be admitted to a special league of friendship with him,
when others are slaves or enemies. 2. A special friend-

liness in Christ's carriage to them; familiarly, freely, telling them all his mind, so far as is needful for them to know, John xv. 15, and lovingly manifesting himself to them, as one doth to his friend. 3. It holds out a duty lying on the believer, to carry friendly to Christ and them that are his, John xv. 14. " A man that hath friends must shew himself friendly" (Prov. xviii. 24,) to them: and seeing he trusts them, and expects no ill from them, they should be like Christ's friends, answerable to their trust. They are also beloved, the title that the husband gives the wife, for evidencing special love: all Christ's friends are beloved, and believers are (whatever they be as to their desert, or in the eyes of men) both friends and beloved: no friend hath such bowels for his friends, as Christ hath for his friends. " Friends" and " beloved" are in the plural, 1. To shew he excludes no believer, but includes all, and that with the same seriousness he invites and makes them all welcome to feast with him, whether they be strong or weak. 2. Because his mercy to one may be cheering to many, and he allows and would have others of his people to be cheerful, because of his kindness and mercy manifested to one.

His entertaining of them is held out in three words. 1. " Eat," that declares his desire to have believers partaking with him in the soul-refreshing blessings of his purchase, by their reflecting act of faith comforting themselves in the privileges, promises, and mercies allowed on them. *Observ.* 1. The same feast, is a feast to Christ and believers both. 2. Where he is cheerful, they should be so also. The second word is, " drink:" he drinks, that is, satisfies himself as fully feasted, to wit, with the graces of his people (such is the complacency he hath in them, when he stirs them up to any liveliness of exercise) and he allows them in this case to be refreshed, satisfied, and feasted also; it becomes them to drink when he drinks, and bids them drink. The third word is, "drink abundantly:" that shews the largeness of his allowance, and the heartiness of his welcome: as a gladsome host, so cherishes he his guests; and all this is to be understood spiritually, of the joy and comfort which he allows on his people, even to be " filled with the Spirit," in opposition to wine, Eph. v. 18, which is more satisfying, cheering, and refreshing to the inner man, than wine is to the body. The scope and dependance points out these things, 1.

There is much notable soul-refreshing to be had in Christ's company; wherever he is, there is a feast, Rev. iii. 20. 2. He allows his people largely to share of it; yea, it is his will that all should liberally improve this allowance, he willeth it. 3. If our joy run in a spiritual channel, there cannot be excess in it, if it were to be drunken with it, so as to forget our poverty, and to remember our misery no more. 4. Christ is never fully satisfied at his own feast, till he get his friends feasted and cheered also : he eats not his morsels alone, but is desirous to communicate his good things, according as they are communicable. 5. Christ's preparing and dressing is rather for the welcoming of his friends, than for himself. I have gathered, eat ye, saith he. 6. Christ is a most heartsome distributer to others, and entertainer of his friends : there needs be no sparing to eat where he invites. 7. Believers, even Christ's friends, need invitation, by reason of unbelief, sense of unworthiness (which makes them sinfully modest) and the dulness of their spiritual appetite ; and therefore they will need (to say so) bidding and entreaty oftentimes to eat their meat, and to cheer themselves in him, and he will not let them want that. 8. Wherever Christ is present, there is a feast with him for them that are in his company; he sups with them, and makes them sup with him ; and all is his own, and of his own dressing. 9. It is a gift of Christ's mercy, not only to have grounds of consolation, but to be enabled to comfort ourselves in these grounds ; (as in outward things, it is one gift to have, and another to have the cheerful use of that which we have) for the believer may have the one when he wants the other ; and when he hath the one, to have the other added is a double mercy, as the exhortation, " eat, drink," &c. imports. 10. It is not every one who is Christ's friend, nor every one that hath that honour to comfort and feast themselves with him ; it is a privilege that is peculiar to them who are his friends indeed.

BRIDE.

Verse 2. I sleep, but my heart waketh: it is the voice of my
Beloved that knocketh, saying, Open to me, my sister, my
love, my dove, my undefiled : for my head is filled with dew,
and my locks with the drops of the night.

FROM verse 2, unto the ninth, (which is the second part
of the chapter) the Bride speaks, and sets down a very
complex piece of her condition, which we take up in these
three. 1. Her condition is shortly set down. 2. The
mutual carriage of the Bridegroom and Bride are recorded ; wherein (as it were) grace and loving-kindness in
him, and unkindness in her, are wrestling together for a
time. 3. The out-gate, and the way how she attained it,
by several steps on his side, and hers, are particularly insisted on from verse 4, with what followed thereupon.
Her case is in short, " I sleep, but my heart waketh,"
or (as it is in the original) " I sleeping, my heart waking." It is made up of contraries, and seeming para-
doxes ; she is distinguished from her heart, and the sleeping of the one is opposed to the waking of the other :
both this sleeping and waking are spiritually to be understood ; the first signifies a ceasing from spiritual duties,
or a suspension of the acting of spiritual life, by a rising
of some inward corruption, that dulls and binds up the
spiritual senses, as in natural sleep the external senses
are dulled and bound up : so 1 Thes. v. 6, and Rom. xiii.
11, " Let us not sleep, but watch and be sober." This is
a further degree of spiritual distemper, beyond what was,
chap. iii. 1, 2, where she was on bed, and yet seeking, but
here she sleeps and lies still, as we see, verse 3. It imports, 1. An interruption of liveliness and actual exercising of grace. 2. An indisposition and laziness in the
frame of the spirit, added to that. 3. A sort of acquies-
cing and resting securely in that indisposition, with a
loathness to stir and be interrupted, such as useth to be
in the bodily sleep, and such as appears to be here from
the following verse : it is sleepiness, or to be given to
sleep, such as the sluggard is subject unto, who sleepeth
excessively and out of due time. This " I" that sleepeth,
is the believer, but considered in so far as unregenerate ;
as, Rom. vii. 18, " I know, that in me (that is in my flesh)
there dwelleth no good thing :" For, as the believer hath

two different natures, which have opposite actings; so are
they considered as two different persons. Hence is that,
Rom. vii. " I, yet not I," &c. by which Paul as renewed,
is distinguished from himself as unrenewed. By waking,
is understood, some liveliness and sensibleness, or at least
life, in opposition to the former deadness and dulness, as,
Rom. xiii. 11, " It is high time to awake :" and 1 Thess.
v. 6, " Let us watch, and be sober ;" which is opposite to
that spiritual drowsiness, wherein we are scarce at ourselves. " My heart," looks to the renewed part, which is
often called " the spirit that lusteth against the flesh," as
Gal. v. 17, and the " law in my mind," Rom vii. " Circum-
cision in the heart," Rom. ii. 25 ; the " new heart" in the
covenant Ezek, xxxvi. In sum, it is this, things are not
right with me, and indisposition to duty or lifelessness in it,
is great (as it is with one that is in a sleep) yet even then
there is some inward stirring of life, appearing in conviction of judgment, challenges purposes, prostestations of
the inward-man, against this dead and lazy frame, as not
delighting in it, but displeased with it, &c. wherein the
new nature wrestles and yields not, nor gives itself leave
to consent to it, although it can act nothing, at least in a
lively way, under this condition : thus she is sleeping because she acts nothing ; yet, the heart is waking, because
it is kept from being involved in that security though it be
bound up, and overpowered with corruption, that it cannot win to act according to the light and inclination that it
hath within. Hence observe, 1. That the believer hath
two different and opposite natures and principles within
him, leading him divers ways ; the carnal and sleeping
" I," and the renewed and waking " heart." 2. They
may be both at one time acting oppositely, " the one lust-
ing against the other," Gal. v. 17. 3. Sometimes corruption may prevail far over believers that have grace,
and lay them (though not quite dead, yet) fast asleep for
a time, and mar in a great measure the exercise of their
grace. 4. Believers at their lowest, have life in them,
and (by reason of their new nature) are not totally and
fully involved in their security and backsliding conditions.
5. There may be some inward apprehending of our
hazard, and dangerous condition, when it is very sad
and low ; so as believers may know it is not right with
them, and yet (as it is here with the Bride) may continue
under it and lie still. 6. Spiritual laziness and security

are incident to the strongest believers: the wise virgins may slumber and sleep, Matt. xxv. 7. Yea, after the greatest manifestations, and often on the back of the fullest intimations of Christ's love, and the most sweet invitations they have from him, and most joyful feastings with him, they may be thus overtaken, as the words preceding bear out: the disciples fell into this distemper, that same night after the Lord's supper. 8. Believers may fall over and over again into the same condition of sinful security, even after they have been roused and raised out of it; as this being compared with chap iii. will clear. 9. The more frequently believers (or any other) relapse into the same sin, they will go the greater length readily in it, and by falling more dangerously be more hardly recovered than formerly: now she sleeps, and when put at, will not rise, but shifts, which is a further step than was chap iii. 10. Lazy fits of indisposition and omissions of duty, do more frequently steal in upon believers than positive outbreakings and commissions, and they are more ready to please themselves in them, and to lie still under them. 11. Believers should be so acquainted with their own condition, as to be able to tell how it is with them, whether as to their unrenewed or renewed part; so here, " I sleep, but my heart waketh." 12. Believers in taking up their condition, should advert both to their corruptions and graces; and in their reckoning, should put a distinction betwixt these two, otherwise they will misreckon on the one side or the other: they should not reckon themselves wholly by the actings of nature, lest they disclaim their graces; nor yet by their renewed part, lest they forget their unrenewed nature; but they should attribute every effect in them to its own cause and principle, wherefrom it proceeds. 13. It is good for believers when overcome with corruption, and captivate by it, to disallow and disown it from the heart, as not allowing what they do, and to present this to God, as a protestation entered against their prevailing lusts. In some sense a believer may both condemn himself as sinful, and absolve himself as delighting in the law of God, at one and the same time; and where he allows not his corruption, but positively dissents from it, he may disclaim it as not being his deed.

This being her case, follows the Bridegroom's carriage, which is expressed in the rest of verse 2, and her carriage (implied only in this verse) is more fully expressed, verse

3. His carriage holds out the great design he drives, and that is to have access to her, and to have her roused up : for attaining of which, 1. He doth something, and that is, knocks at the door. 2. He endures and suffers "dew" and "drops" in the cold night, and yet doth not give over. 3. He speaks, and useth many persuasive arguments for that end ; all which she observes, and yet lies still. It is in sum, as if a loving husband, that is shut out by a lazy, yet a beloved wife, would knock, call, and waiting on still, use many arguments to persuade her to open ; so doth our spiritual Bridegroom, wait upon believers whom he loves, to have them brought again to the lively exercise of faith in him, and to a frame of spirit meet for communion with him. To take the words as they lie, there is, 1. The Bride's observation (as it were in her sleep) of the Beloved's calling at the door. 2. There is set down his call. 3. The arguments he useth for prevailing with her. By knocking is understood the inward touches of the word upon the conscience, when the efficacy of the Spirit goes along with it, which raps at the Bride's heart, as knocking doth at a door, and is the means of awaking her from spiritual sleep, as knocking at a door is a means of awaking from bodily sleep : So it is, Rev. iii. 20, "Behold I stand at the door and knock ;" in which sense the word is compared to a hammer, Jer. xxiii. 29. It takes in these three, 1. A seriousness in him that so knocks. 2. A power and efficacy in the word, that someway affects the heart, and moves it. 3. It implies some effect it hath upon the heart, as being somewhat affected with that touch ; therefore it is his voice or word, that not only calleth, but knocketh, implying some force it had upon her. By "voice" is understood the word, as chap. ii. 8, 10, yet, as backed with the Spirit and power, and as commended thereby to the conscience, 1 Cor. ii. 4, and convincingly demonstrated to be the very voice of Christ ; yet, so as rods, inward and outward, and other means, may have their own place, being made use of by him, yet still according to the word. His great end, for which he knocks, is in that word, "open ;" which, as it implies her case, that her heart was in a great measure shut upon him, and that by some carnal indisposition he was kept out of it, and was not made welcome ; so it requires the removing of all that stopt his way, and the casting open of the heart by faith to receive his word, and by love to receive him-

self: and in these two especially, this opening doth consist,
1. In the exercise of faith, Acts xvi. 14, the Lord opened
the heart of Lydia, and that is expounded, she gave heed
unto those things which Paul spoke. 2. An enlarging and
warming of the affections towards him (which ever comprehends the former) as, Psalm lxxxi 10, " Open thy
mouth wide, and I will fill it :" what that is, the refusal
following declares, " my people would not hear," (that is,
believe) " Israel would none of me," or loved not me, (as
the words in the original import) they cared not for me,
they desired me not, and would not quit their idols, as in
the foregoing words, verse 9, is mentioned. 3. There
resulteth from these two a mutual familiarity, as Rev. iii.
20, " If any man will open, I will come in and sup with
him, and he with me." This opening then, imports the
removing of every thing that marred fellowship with
Christ, and the doing of every thing that might dispose
for enjoying of it, as awaking, rising, &c. all which follows
in the 4th verse ; and while he commands to open, he calls
for the entertaining of fellowship with him, which now is
by her drowsiness interrupted : which two parts of the
verse put together, hold forth, 1. That Christ's own Bride
may shut the door on him, and so make a sad separation
betwixt him and her. 2. Christ's word is the great and
ordinary external means, whereby he knocks at mens'
hearts, and which he makes use of for begetting faith in
them. 3. That in a believer's secure condition there will
be sometimes more than ordinary convictions, stirrings,
and motions by the word. 4. That the word of God,
backed with power, will reach the securest heart and affect
it. 5. That believers will discern Christ's voice and call,
when their condition is very low. 6. It will be refreshful
to them to have him knocking ; she looks on it as a kindly
thing, even to have his knock bearing in convictions, challenges, or somewhat else on her ; though it please not her
flesh, yet in as far as she is renewed, it will be " the voice
of her Beloved" to her. 7. Christ hath a way of following his own, even when they are become secure ; and
sometimes then, will make his call, challenges, or convictions pursue more hotly and pressingly than at other
times. 8. When Christ knocketh and presseth hardest,
it is for our own good, and it is a token of love in him to
do so ; for there is nothing more deplorable, than when
he saith to one under indisposition, and in an evil case,

let him alone.   9. When Christ calls by his word, it is
then our duty to open to him, and to receive him; and
this can no more be slighted without sin, than prayer,
mortification, and other commanded duties, can be neglected or slighted without sin,   10. Christ may call very
pressingly, and his word may have some work on the
conscience and affections of hearers, and they be someway
affected with it, and yet the word be rejected, and the
heart not made open to Christ; as here she sleeps still
notwithstanding; and the following verse confirms it.
11. There are some operations of the Spirit, which though
they be more than a common work on the generality of
hearers, yet are not saving, and may be, and often are,
even by believers frustrated for a time, and by others for
ever; for, this knocking gets a refusal, verse 3.   So de-
ceiving, beguiling and dangerous are common motions to
rest on, when the finger of gracious omnipotency is not
applied, as verse 4.   12. Christ's design, when he knocks
fastest, is friendly, and yet it sometimes saith, things are
not right: this is the end of all his knocking and speaking
to a people, and then it is plainest when he speaks most
powerfully.

  2. The way how Christ presseth this, is, 1. By showing
who he is, it is " me," "open to me :" there can be no greater commendation given to Christ, nor weightier argument
used for him, than to make it known that it is he, the
Husband, Lord, &c, whose the house is, and to whom
entry by right from the wife ought to be given.   2. By
giving her loving titles, and claiming her as his in many
relations, as "my sister, love, dove;" and (which was not
mentioned before) "undefiled" is added, that is, my perfect one, or upright, sincere one, as it is often rendered.
These titles given now, and so many at once, shew, 1.
That believers, when secure, have very much need of the
Spirit to rouse and stir them up: souls are not easily
persuaded to receive Christ.   2. There is wonderful love
in Christ, that condescends so to entreat his people, when
in such a secure case: even then he changes not her name,
no more than if all things were in a good case; for our
relation to him, depends not on our case.   3. Christ will
sometimes very lovingly deal, even with secure souls in
his way, for obtaining entry, and persuading them to open
to him, and sometimes will apply the most refreshful gos-
pel-offers and invitations, and use the most kindly compel-

lations for that end. 4. Christ sometimes will overlook the lazy distempers of his people, and not always chide with them for these, but give them their wonted styles notwithstanding. 5. The kind dealing of Christ to his people will ever prove love to be on his side, but will not always prove that the persons so dealt with are presently in a good condition; for, he may accept their persons, and speak comfortably as to their state, although he approve not their present condition, as here. 6. We may see that Christ's love is not founded on our merit, nor is up and down according to our variable disposition, but he prevents both in his dealing with his people. These titles being made use of as a motive to answer his call, and to open to him, shew, 1. That the persuasion of Christ's love in souls, is a main thing to make way for their entertaining of him. 2. That it is a shame for a believer so beloved of Christ, to hold him without at the door, when he knocketh to be in. Grace would make a heart to blush, and in a manner look it out of countenance, that would refuse his kindness.

The third and great argument, is, "for my head is filled with dew, and my locks with the drops of the night:" very shame might prevail with the wife, when the husband useth such an argument as this : it is even as if a husband, standing long without doors in a tempestuous night, should use this motive with his wife to persuade her to let him in,—it will be very prejudicial and hurtful to my health, if thou open not unto me; for, I have stood long without: this may no doubt be presumed to be a very strong and prevalent argument with a loving wife; yet, it gets but a poor and very unsuitable answer from the Bride. By "dew, drops" and "night-time," are understood, afflictions, external crosses and lowness: so, Dan. iv. that king is said to be "wet with the dew of heaven" in his low condition, as having no house to shelter himself in, but being obnoxious to all changes and injuries of weather : and Jacob mentions it as a part of the toilsome labour, that he had with Laban, " I did endure the heat of the sun in the day, and the cold in the night," that is, he was ever watchful, and spared not himself for the hurt of either day or night: here Christ's spiritual sufferings also may come in, whereby he made himself obnoxious to the Father's wrath and curse, that he might have access to communion with his people ; and the ac-

count that he hath of being kept out by his people, as a
new piece of his sufferings, or as a painful reviving of the
remembrance of his old sufferings. The scope is to shew,
that as a kindly husband will so deal with a beloved wife,
and expect to prevail, being put to this strait; so doth
Christ with his people, being no less desirous of a room
in their hearts, and being as much troubled by their unbelief, as any man is, when put to stand in the cold night,
under dew and rain at his own door. This way of arguing saith, 1. That the believer, as such, loves and respects
Christ, and would not have him suffering, as a kind wife
would be loth to hazard her husband's health. 2. That
Christ expounds her so, even when she is lazy and keeps
him out, otherwise this argument would be of no force,
nor would he have used it: he will see much evil (to
speak so) ere he notice it in a believer; and is not suspicious, even when occasions are given. 3. Believers are
often exceeding unanswerable to the relation that is betwixt Christ and them, and may suffer Christ to stand
long waiting without. 4. It affects Christ much (and is a
suffering to him, and a kind of putting him to open shame,
and a crucifying again the Son of God) to be kept out of
hearts by unbelief, and there can be no pardonable sin
that hath more and greater aggravations than this; for,
it is cruelty to kind Jesus Christ. 5. Believers, even
when Christ is in good terms with them, may fall into this
fault. 6. Christ is a most affectionate suitor, and patient
Husband, that thus waits on even when he is affronted,
and gives not over his kind suit: who would bear with
this that he bears with, and passeth by, and continues
kindly notwithstanding? Many strange and uncouth
things are comported with, and overlooked betwixt him
and believers without hearing, that the world could not
digest. 7. Our Lord Jesus hath not spared himself, nor
shunned sufferings, for doing of his people good: Jacob's
care of, and suffering for Laban's flocks, and Nebuchadnezzar his humiliation was nothing to this. 8. The love
of Christ is manifested in nothing more for his people
than in his sufferings for them, and in his patient on-
waiting to have the benefits thereof applied to them. 9.
Christ's sufferings, and his affectionate way of pleading
from them, should melt hearts in love to him, and in desire
of union with him, and will make the refusal exceeding
sinful and shameful, where it is given; O so strong argu-

ments as Christ hath, to be on the hearts of his people! and how many things are there, to plead for that?

Verse 3.　I have put off my coat; how shall I put it on? I have washed my feet; how shall I defile them?

THE Bride's answer is here set down, but O! how unsuitable to that which was his carriage? He stands, she lies : he without, she within; he calls friendly ; she ungratefully shifts it, at best : as if a wife should answer her husband so calling, I am now in bed, and have put off my clothes, and washen my feet, and so have composed myself to rest, I cannot rise, it would hurt me to rise ; so doth the Bride thus unreasonably, and absurdly put back this fair call, upon a twofold shift, both which are spiritually to be understood, as the sleep and opening, formerly mentioned, were. In it consider, 1. The answer. 2. The manner of it. 3. The particular grounds which she layeth down to build it on. And, 4. The faults of this reasoning of hers, which at first may be concluded to be unsound. The answer in general is a denial, as the event clears ; and it is like that, Luke xi. 7, " I am in bed, and my children with me, trouble me not," &c. Yea, " how can I put it on?" these words (being the interrogation, not of one doubting but of one shifting) imply a vehement denial, as as if it were a most unreasonable and impossible thing for her to give obedience to what was called for : which shews, that Christ may get most indiscreet refusals to his fairest calls : which refusal is thus aggravated, 1. It was against most powerful and plain means : the most powerful external ordinances may be frustrated. Even Christ himself in his word, when he preached in the days of his flesh, had not always success. 2. It was against her light, she knew it was Christ's call : even believers may sit challenges against their light, and sin wittingly through the violence of tentations, though not wholly willingly. 3. She had invited him by prayer, chap. iv. 16, yet now lies still : which lets us see, 1. That believers, in their carriage, are often unsuitable to their prayers : there may be, and is often a great discrepancy betwixt these. And, 2. Often believers may be more desirous of an opportunity of meeting with Christ, or any other mercy, when they want it ; than watchful to make the right use of it, when they have gotten it.

Her way is to give some reasons for her refusal, as if she could do no otherwise, and were not to be blamed so much for her shifting off Christ, as the words, "how can I," &c. import. Observe, 1. The flesh will be broody and quick in inventing shifts for maintaining of itself, even against the clearest convictions and duties. 2. It is ill to debate or reason a clear duty, often Satan and the flesh get advantage by it. 3. Folks are oft-times very partial in examining their own reasons, and are hardly put from their own grounds once laid, although they be not solid ; and the most foolish reasons will be convincing to a spiritual sluggard, who, in fostering his ease, seems wiser to himself, than one who can render the most conclusive arguments, and strongest reasons to the contrary, Prov. xxvi. 16. The opening of the particular reasons will clear this ; the first is, " I have put off my coat," and the conclusion is, " how can I put it on ?" putting off the clothes is an evidence of men's betaking themselves to rest, as keeping them on, is a sign of watching, as in Neh. iv. 23. " None of us put off our clothes, save to washing ;" hence keeping on of the clothes is borrowed, to set out spiritual watchfulness, and hiding of spiritual nakedness, as Rev. xvi. 15. " Blessed is he that watcheth and keepeth his garments, lest he walk naked :" and on the contrary putting off of clothes, signifieth not only a spiritual drowsiness, but a high degree of it ; as having put off, and fallen from that tenderness and watchfulness in her walk, wherewith she was clothed, chap. iv. 11. and is now somewhat settled in her carnal ease and security. From this she argueth, " how shall I put it on ?" the force of the reason may be three ways considered, 1. As it imports a difficulty in the thing, how shall I do it ? O it is difficult ! 2. As it imports an averseness to it, in herself : it stands against her heart, as a seeming unreasonable thing, as Gen. xxxix. 9, " How shall I do this great wickedness," &c. 3. A sort of shame may be in it. I am now out of posture, and I think shame to rise, and to be seen : which shews, 1. That it is hard to raise one that hath fallen into security. 2. To lazy souls every thing looks like an insuperable difficulty, their way to duty is as an " hedge of thorns," Prov. xv. 19. and " there is a lion in their streets," and sometimes, as it were, even in the house-floor, when any duty is pressed upon them that would rob them of their carnal ease, Prov. xxvi. 13, and xxii. 13. 3. It is much for one in a secure frame to wrestle with his own indisposition, it is a weariness then to take the hand out of the bosom, Prov. xxvi. 15. 4, It is not a commendable shamefacedness, but must needs be a very sinful modesty, that keeps one from duty: it was indeed more shameful to lie still, than to rise.

Her second ground is of the same nature, " I have washed my feet:" washing the feet, fitted and prepared for rest ; men's feet in these countries, being, by walking bare-footed, some way stiffened, beaten and bruised, which by washing were eased and refreshed, as we may see, Gen. xviii. 19, in Abraham and Lot's carriage to the angels, supposing them to be men : so here, it is, I have fitted and composed myself for rest, as being wearied with the painfulness of holy duties and now she cannot endure to stir herself toward these, as if that would again defile her; in which reasoning, there are these faults, 1. That she doth at all offer to debate a clear duty, this makes way for the snare. 2. That she interprets the study of holiness, and communion with Christ to be a trouble, and carnal security to be an ease: there will be strange misrepresentations sometimes, both of our faults and failings, and of Christ's worth and excellency, which have much influence on our deadness and sinful distempers. 3. She makes one sinful action the cause of her continuance in another, there is often a connexion amongst sins, and one draws on another ; the premises, that the flesh lays down as principles, will still bear conclusions like themselves : it is unsound and unsafe reasoning from these. 4. That which should stir and persuade her to rise, to wit, that she was not right, she makes a motive of it to strengthen herself, in her lazy inclination to lie still: carnal sense draws conclusions most unreasonable in every thing, and tends still to foster itself; whereas faith and tenderness would reason the quite contrary. 5. She puts too honest a name upon her security, and calleth it the washing of her feet, which was indeed the polluting of them : fairding and plaistering over our own evils, is a great fostering of security, yet too common; as to call unbelief humility ; presumption, faith ; security, peace, &c. We give to sin the name of virtue, and then without a challenge maintain it ; which is a degree of putting darkness for light, and bitter for sweet, and a sort of calling evil good, which brings under the hazard of the pronounced wo, Isa. v. 20. 6. She fails here, that she expects more ease in lying still, than in opening to Christ, whereas it is but the flesh that is troubled at Christ's presence ; but, solid satisfaction is only to be had in his company : flesh hath ever secret fears of Christ's company, as if it were intolerable, irksome, and troublesome to be a Christian in earnest ; and these whisperings, and wicked suggestions of the flesh, may have sometimes too much weight with a believer. 7. She mistakes Christ's word, which pressed that he might be admitted, who was a most loving husband, and had suffered so much in waiting for entry ; but, she states the matter otherwise, if she that was at ease should trouble herself, that so the shift might seem reasonable ; though Christ be not directly and down-right refused, and the heart dare not under convictions adventure on that, yet by opposing respect to ourselves to him, and by shifting to open to him when he knocks, many are guilty upon the matter of refusing and slighting Christ himself, when they think they slight not him, but would only shun something that is troublesome to themselves ; these words are not so to be looked on, as if explicitly believers would so argue but that in their lazy and drowsy spiritual distempers there is such arguing on the matter, and such or such like shifts prevail often to make them keep out Christ, when directly they dare not refuse him ; which doth evidence the power and subtilty of corruption, even in a believer, and the greatness of the love of Christ that passeth it by.

If it should be asked, why is this sinful distemper of hers registrated, and put on record ? We say, 1. For her own good ; it is profitable for believers to mind and record their miscarriages to Christ, as well as his kind dealings with them. 2. It is for the honour of the Bridegroom, whose love appears and shines most brightly, when it is set forth against her miscarriage ; believers should acknowledge their infirmities and failings, as well as their mercies and graces, when it may make to the Bridegroom's commendation. 3. It is for the edification of others ; often one believer's infirmities, through God's blessing, may prove edifying to others, for making them watchful, and bidding them stand, and sustaining of them when fallen : the infirmities of Job, under his sore trials, have strengthened many, as his patience hath convinced them.

In sum, this reasoning is indirect and frivolous, shewing in the general, 1. That men incline to cover their secret misregard of Christ, as if it were rather tenderness to themselves, than indiscreet disrespect to him, yet he expounds it so: as, Matt. xxii. 5, when they alleged it as a necessary excuse, that they behoved to wait on their farm and merchandise, he interprets it, they made light of the invitation to the marriage of the king's son. 2. It shews, that the shifts, whereby men put back Christ, are exceeding frivolous, there can be no strong nor relevant reason alleged for our slighting Christ, and for our ruining ourselves in slighting of him in the offers of his grace in the gospel; although corrupt nature exercise and rack its invention, to find out reasons to plead our excuse, yet when such reasonings are examined, they will not abide the trial. 3. That when men's hearts are in a declining frame, very trivial and weightless arguments will prevail to make them keep out Christ; and, for as trivial as they are, they would prevail even with believers, did not grace refute them, and make way for his entry into the soul.

Verse 4. My Beloved put in his hand by the hole of the door, and my bowels were moved for him.

THERE follows in this fourth verse, a second step of Christ's carriage, with the effects of it: he gives not over, but puts in his finger, and powerfully makes application to her, by a saving work of the Spirit upon her heart, which hath the desired and designed effect following upon it: she riseth and openeth.

In this we have, 1. The means applied and made use of. 2. The manner of application, (for that the worker is the Beloved himself, is clear; the means is his hand, which in scripture signifieth three things, when attributed to God. 1. His omnipotency, whereby he doth what he pleaseth. Exod. xv. 6, " Thy right hand, O Lord, is become glorious in power:" Exod. viii. 19, it is said " This is the finger of God," that is, his power. 2. It is taken for the Spirit, or the common operations of the Spirit, whereby miracles, beyond the power of man are wrought; as by comparing Matt. xii. 28, with Luke xi. 20, will be clear. 3. It is taken for the saving work of the Spirit, applied for the working of faith in the elect at the first, or renewing and confirming of it afterward in believers; as, Acts xi. 21, " The hand of the Lord was with them, and a great number believed." This is it which is pointed at, Isa. liii.

1. where, " who hath believed?" and " to whom is the
arm of the Lord revealed ?" are made of equal extent :
and so especially it is to be taken here, as the scope clears,
to wit, for the immediate powerful work of the Spirit,
made use of in the working of faith, as a key is made use
of for the opening of a door.

The way of applying this means, is, he "put in his hand
by the hole of the door :" where (following the similitude
of a husband's standing at a shut door, and not getting
entry) he shews what he did, when knocking prevailed
not ; to wit, he took an effectual way of opening it himself, which is ordinary by putting in the key or somewhat else at the hole of the door : so Christ by his Spirit
made open the heart, in a kindly native way, not by
breaking open, but by opening ; he indeed having the
key by which hearts are opened, even " the key of David,
that opens and no man shuts, and shuts and no man
opens," Rev. iii. 7. Which words do shew, 1. That
besides the call of the word, and any common conviction
that is thereby wrought in the heart, there is in the conversion of sinners, an immediate, real, powerful, and peculiar work of the Spirit that accompanies the word. 2.
That the application of this is necessary, and that men
being now asleep, and dead in sin, cannot without that be
stirred and quickened by the most powerful external ordinances, or common operations ; nay, even to the believer's reviving, from his backslidden and drowsy case,
this work of omnipotency is needful. 3. This work of
the Spirit is effectual, and when peculiarly applied by
Christ, cannot be frustrated ; for, he " puts in his hand,"
and the effect follows. 4. Although it be a most powerful work, yet it works kindly, and brings about the effect
without wronging of the natural faculties of the soul, but
makes use of them formally for bringing forth the effect,
as one that openeth the door by the lock, makes use of a
key, but doth not hurt nor destroy the lock : there is
therefore no inconsistency betwixt Christ's opening and
ours ; for, he co-acts not, nor forceth the will, but sweetly determines it, so that it cannot but be willing ; he
takes away unwillingness from it, and makes it willing,
Psalm cx. 3. Christ hath the keys of hearts, and can
open and shut at his pleasure, without wronging of them.
5. Grace being the work of a high hand, it cannot be easy
to procure welcome to Jesus Christ even amongst believ-

ers, and much less with others, who have no principle of grace within to co-operate with Christ. 6. Christ Jesus as he is a most powerful worker, so is the work of his power most free, sovereign, and wonderful; which clearly appeareth in that it is applied on the back of such a slighting answer, and not before: yea, 7. Oftentimes the work of grace surpriseth his own, when they are in a most unsuitable case, and when in respect of their deserving they might have expected the quite contrary; certainly, we are not obliged to our free-will for our conversion, but to his Spirit; nor to our predispositions for his applying of it, but to his own grace, who in his gracious way of dealing with his people, comes over many obstructions, and packs up (to say so) many affronts and injuries.

If any should ask, why Christ did not apply this work, and put in his hand at first, but suspends it till he had gotten a refusal, and be now at the very withdrawing? *Answ.* 1. He doth this to shew the sovereignty of grace, that works as well when it will, as on whom it will: grace must not be limited by us in the manner or time of its working, more than in its work, or subject-matter upon which it worketh. 2. By this he discovereth, what believers would be without his grace (and so would teach them to walk humbly) which otherwise had not so well appeared. 3. His wisdom and tenderness appear herein, that he will not withdraw from her, and leave her lifeless too, but ere he awake challenges in her, he will make her lively in the exercise of her graces: otherwise she might have lien still in her deadness: Christ times his operations, his appearings and withdrawings with much tenderness, wisdom, and discretion.

This work of the Spirit puts a stir in the Bride, which vents itself it four steps. 1. Her bowels are moved 2. She ariseth. 3. Her fingers drop with myrrh. 4. She opens. All which may be considered, either, 1. As effects following the work of the Spirit, whereby she is recovered from such a condition: or, 2. As duties lying on a believer: or, 3. As they hold out the order of the effects wrought by the Spirit. In general, it holds forth, 1. That the work of the Spirit, when it is effectually applied, makes a very great, palpable, and universal change upon the persons in whom it works: there is a great difference betwixt the Bride's carriage here,

and what it was, verse 3. 2. Although it be not absolutely necessary, nor ordinary for a believer, to know the
instant of his conversion : yet when the change is sudden,
and from an extremity of a sinful condition, it will be
discernable, and the fruits following the change will be
the more palpable. 3. A believer should endeavour to be
clear in the change of his condition ; and when this clearness is attained by the distinct uptaking of the several
fruits of the change, it is very useful and profitable for
establishing the believer in the confidence of his interest
in Christ, and that there is a saving change wrought in
him ; so here, the Bride both asserts him to be her Beloved, and likewise the reality of the change he had
wrought in her.

The first effect is, " my bowels were moved for him ;"
Which, in short, holds forth the kindly exercise of serious repentance, affecting and stinging (as it were) the
very inward bowels, for slighting Christ so long : which
will be cleared by considering, 1. What is meant by
bowels. 2. What by moving of the bowels. 3. What
that is, "for him." By bowels, are understood either sorrow, and that in an intense degree, as, Job xxx. 27, "my
bowels boiled," Lam. i. 20. " My bowels are troubled."
And Jer. iv. 19, " My bowels, my bowels, I am pained
at the very heart :" Or, bowels are taken for affection
and tender love in the highest degree, such as mothers
have to the children of their womb, Philip. ii. 1, 2, " If
there be any bowels." And Philemon, 12, " Receive
him that is my own bowels." Thus they are taken, Isa.
lxiii. 15, " Where are thy bowels ?" and frequently elsewhere, both in the Old and New Testament. By " moving of the bowels" (or sounding or making a noise, as the
word is elsewhere translated, Isa. xvi. 11, and lxiii. 15,)
is understood a sensible stirring of the affections, when
they begin to stound, and that kindly, and in a most affectionate manner, either severally, or jointly, such as is
" the turning of the bowels," Hos. xi, and the " troubling
of the bowels," Jer. xxxi. 18, 19, 20. It is even such as
is kindly sympathy with persons that are dearly beloved,
when any sad change befals them : it is called the yearning of the bowels, spoken of that mother, 1 Kings iii. 26,
who was so affected towards her child, out of love to him,
that she had rather quit him to the other woman, that was
not his mother, than see him divided, her bowels were

so hot towards him; (another thing than was in any on-
looker) it is the same word here, which shews, that this
motion of the Bride's bowels proceeded from love to
Christ, and from sorrow for wronging of him, which two
jumbled her within, and pierced and stounded her to the
heart, as a kindly parent useth to be for the death or distress of his only child, which is the character of true repentance, Zech. xii. 10, 11. 3. " For him," holds out, 1.
The procuring cause of this trouble, that it was for
wronging of Christ, and the slighting of so kind an husband and friend, that stounded her at the heart above all,
as, Zech. xii. 10. " They shall look on him whom they
have pierced, and mourn for him." 2. It holds forth the
final cause wherefore she was so stirred and moved ; it
it was " for him," that is, that she might enjoy him, as
the word is, Hos, vii. 14, " They assemble themselves for
corn and wine," that is, to obtain them : so her bowels
were moved for or after him, to obtain and enjoy him :
and thus, sense of the wrong done to him, in her bye-past
unkindly carriage to him, and desire to recover him again,
so affects her, as if it were the pangs of a travailing
woman, till Christ be again formed in her heart. *Observ.*
1. The first work of the Spirit, is, by powerful convictions
to beget evangelic repentance in the heart, and to make
the soul sensible of bye-past failings, Acts ii. 37. This
although it be not in time before faith, nor in nature (for,
seeing it proceeds from love, it supposeth faith) yet it is
the first sensible effect, that sinners (surprised in a sinful
condition) are touched with, and it is never separate from,
but always joined with, the exercise of faith, Zech. xii. 10.
2. This work of repentance is necessary to be renewed,
even in believers after their failings, and it is the way by
which they recover ; Christ's Bride is thus affected, and
it becomes them well who have sin, to be deeply moved
and afflicted with the sense of it. Where most love to
Christ is, and where most sincerity hath been, when awakening comes, it will be the more sensible, and affect the
heart the more throughly. Particularly, we may gather
hence these properties of true repentance or godly sorrow.
I. Godly sorrow is no fruit of nature, but is a work and
effect of the Spirit of Christ, and a peculiar saving grace,
beyond common conviction, and a believer is not the
worker of it in himself. 2. This sorrow consists most in
the inward pangs and stings of the heart, wherein love to

Christ, and indignation against ourselves for wronging of him, struggle, and put all within in a stir. 3. True repentance is different from, and beyond convictions, and challenges (which the Bride had before when this was wanting in her) and makes another kind of impression, and a more sensible touch upon the heart and inward bowels: I say not that it is always terrible; for, that is accidental to it, but sensible it is. 4. Though this godly sorrow affect the heart deeply, yet doth it work kindly, sweetly and affectionately, as a mother's affection warms to her child, or, as a man is troubled for his first-born: love hath a main influence upon, and goeth along in this godly sorrow; both in the rise of it, love kindles this heart-indignation, and also in the exercise of it, love to Christ keeps it lively; and in the manner how it vents itself, it makes it a kindly and no torturing or terrible exercise. 5. Nothing more affects a kindly repenting heart, truly touched with godly sorrow, than that it should have sinned against Christ; its own hazard is not the predominant cause of this sorrow (she is clear of her interest still (nor is it any sad event that might follow, which so affects her (though she was not senseless as to these) but it is "for him," and his cause and not her own, that she is thus moved: the Spirit's conviction, John xvi. 8, is, "because they believe not on me." 6. Considering the words with what follows, "I rose," &c. and comparing them with what went before, *Observe*, that true repentance brings forth always a change in a believer's carriage to the better, in those things by which Christ their Beloved was formerly provoked; and it doth stir up to universal activeness, in the study of holiness: this makes her arise from the laziness in which she formerly was. 7. Consider, that she rests not till first she open to Christ, and thereafter obtain his presence; which sheweth, that where true repentance is, the soul will never sit down on challenges, convictions, or making amends in the conversation, or any thing in itself; but it will be restless until by faith it close with Christ; yea, it will be pressing after the intimation of his favour, on the back of any peace attained in closing with him, as David doth, Psalm li.

Verse 5. I rose up to open to my Beloved ; and my hands dropped with myrrh, and my fingers with sweet smelling myrrh, upon the handles of the lock.

THERE are two steps of her carriage, or effects of the Spirit's work, verse 5. The first is, her bowels being thus stirred and moved, she ariseth to open, as being sorry she had lien still and shifted him so long ; " I rose up :" this is opposite to her former lying still, and refusing to give him entry ; now she yields, and begins to bestir herself, to draw her clothes to her, &c. Which imports not only more diligence as to the matter of duty, but much seriousness as to the manner : it seems to differ from opening (which is the actual receiving of Christ into the heart when all things are ready and prepared) not as if it were simply contradistinguished from faith (for, this being a fruit of her repentance, and he acknowledged to be her Beloved, there behoved to be faith in it) but only, as one degree or act of faith is distinguished from another, as, Luke xv. in the prodigal's case, it is said, after he came to himself, before he act, he deliberates and stirs himself ; so this holds forth, her rousing and quickening herself, for receiving Christ, which is not separate in time, either from her repentance in the former words, or her faith in those that follow : she " rose to open," that shows her design, that she resolved now not to stand at, but to go over her former reasonings ; and purposed by this stirring, to have the way rid for Christ's entry, and to make him welcome ; which shews, it was no confused exercise that her repentance put her unto, but distinct and digested, like the prodigal's " I will arise, and go to my Father, and say," &c.

Observ. 1. Repentance will put the securest sinners to their feet, when it is real. 2. There is no settling of an exercised mind, but in receiving of Christ, and in making of him welcome. 3. When the heart is affected with the sense of sin, and desire to have Christ, it is not time to delay or dispute what to do, but to rise and open, and by faith to receive Christ. 4. Where a soul hath been plunged in security, or (like the prodigal, Luke xv.) in profanity, there will be need of gathering, composing and rousing of itself, for exercising of faith in Christ ; this is not from any difficulty that is on grace's side to receive a sinner, but from the difficulty that is on the sinner's side, in acting of grace, who being at a low ebb, must by several steps of grace ascend out of it, with a kind of violence to corruption, discouragement and unbelief, from under the power of which the penitent must arise, when they combine to entangle and detain him, as she doth here. 5. Believers should be distinct in their exercises, especially in reference to their end and design, that in their activity and stirrings it may be discerned by themselves what they would be at: some exercises are confused, neither having a distinct cause, nor a distinct end; kindly exercise hath both, though much confusion may be with it. 6. Faith in Christ, and making way for him into the heart, should be, and is the native end of all inward exercises, diligence in duties, &c. This must be the great scope of all pains whatsoever; those stings of exercise that put not the soul to open to him, though they put the person through other, are not to be fostered, nor laid much weight upon. 7. Though faith and duty differ, and the most active frame is not to be rested on without faith, yet activity in duty, and liveliness in the exercise of faith go together: as her rising and opening do, even as before, her lying still, and the keeping of him out, went together. Yea, 8. This activeness runs especially to perform what he called to: he called to open, and she accordingly riseth to open; which shews, that the penitent's activity doth principally bend itself towards those duties that Christ in a more especial manner calls for.

She proceeds to set down her experience which she found when she had risen, which is the third effect of the work of grace on her by Christ's putting in his hand: when she arose to open, her hands and fingers dropped " sweet smelling myrrh upon the handles of the lock :" she continues the comparison of opening a shut door, he, as it were, put in the key without, and she came to draw the handle or slot within (as is usual in some locks.) The door is the heart, as Psalm xxiv 7, called " the everlasting doors :" The lock that closeth, is unbelief and security, indisposition and declining in the exercise of grace; whereby, as by a fast lock, Christ in his access to the heart is kept out: now she puts to her hands and fingers to the lock within, which imports her stirring herself again in the exercise of faith and diligence, being now arisen to open. Therefore by faith we are said to grip and take hold of Christ, and to work righteousness, and by it the heart is opened to him, as follows. This "sweet smelling myrrh" that drops, is the flowing of habitual grace, which formerly was not vigorous and active, but now it flows and vents, and is to the heart as oil applied to moisten and make easy a rusted lock, to make it open without difficulty: this grace is ordinarily compared to myrrh, and the anointing typical oil was made of it and of other spices, Exod. xxx. 23. It is said here, to drop, from her "fingers," implying the active stirring of her faith; because when faith becomes lively, it puts all other graces to exercise, and thereby (as it were by oil) her former hardness and indisposition was softened and removed, and her heart made meet to act lively. In sum, it is this, that when she, in the exercise of faith and holiness, set herself seriously and effectually to make way for Christ, and to remove what formerly had kept him out, through her indisposition, unexpectedly she found, that by his putting in of his hand, it went much more easily and sweetly than she expected, all had been so anointed and quickened; and thus conduced to the opening of her heart, as dropping of oil doth to the easy opening of a lock: which shews, 1. That the work of grace upon the heart, being applied by Christ from without, doth leave an inward fitness on the heart within for the opening of itself to him: grace infused and quickened by Christ's Spirit, will make the most indisposed and secure heart to open to him heartsomely. 2. That though Christ apply grace from without to open the heart, yet will he have the heart formally opening itself to him; and though the heart open itself formally to him, yet it is by the virtue of his application from without; for, this putting to of her hand, and its dropping myrrh, is the effect of his putting in his hand first. 3. Often when the most spiritual and difficult duties (if it were even faith itself) are essayed, they will be found more easy than was expected, and none can tell how they will go with them, till they undertake and set about them. She, while lying in her security, thought it impossible to get this done, yet now it goes easily and sweetly with her. O! but when grace goes along and flows, the exercise of a duty is a sweet and easy work. 4. Although the exercise of grace make duties easy, and a supply of help be given thereby for doing of spiritual duties, yet the Lord will have the person essaying duty ere he find it so; nor can he find or expect that supply that will facilitate duties to him, till he first set himself about them, as she first rises to open before her fingers drop with myrrh. 5. Those that set themselves to open to Christ, and mind that singly from the sense of their need of him, and being affected for wronging of him, will not find grace wanting and deficient to help them; and by this all the mouths of unbelievers will be stopped, that are ready to say, and usually say, they had not grace to open. 6. Faith in exercise hath a great influence on the keeping of all other graces in a believer fresh and green; because it acts by Christ's strength, and therefore when it is in exercise, it makes all the rest to "drop" as it were, "with sweet smelling myrrh."

Verse 6.   I opened to my beloved; but my beloved had withdrawn himself, and was gone: my soul failed when he spake: I sought him, but I could not find him; I called him, but he gave me no answer.

THIS 6th verse contains five particulars of the Bride's experience in this case: the first of them, " I opened," &c. is the last effect following upon his putting in his hand, verse 4.   This work of grace left her not in an indifferency, whether to open or not, but having given her to will in the former verse, now he gives also to do, and actually determines the will, or makes it determine itself to receive him: but now Christ is found to be absent, whereupon follows the other steps of her carriage, and the disappointments that she met with in seeking of him. This opening is the very thing called for by him, verse 2, which (considering the words following) is especially to be understood of her exercising of faith in him, whereby the heart is dilated to receive him, hence believing is called a "receiving of Christ," John i. 12.   And it being a heart-receiving, it must be the very thing understood here by opening.   Now although faith, according to its several acts, may be several ways considered; yet that act of faith whereby the heart consents to receive Christ, and to rest on him, is that which is mainly here aimed at, 1. Because this opening, is opposed to refusing, Psalm lxxxi. 10, 11.   It must therefore be consenting.   2. It is not giving of consent, that mainly keeps Christ at a distance from souls, or keeps them without interest in him, as opening to him, or receiving of him, entitles them to him, John i. 11, 12, and Acts xvi. 14.   3. This opening is both different from conviction, resolutions, repentance, and what may be supposed to precede; these were in the words going before: and is also distinguished from sense and the fruits of believing, which follow after: it must therefore be the heart's yielding to Christ's call, and submitting thereunto, Rom. x. 3, as actually consenting to be his: yet all these acts should not be looked on as distinct in respect of time, as they proceed from grace (which puts all together) but in nature, and in respect of the distinct uptaking of the same grace, in its effects: in a word, saith the Bride, the Lord having applied the work of his Spirit to me, it effectuated one step after another, and left me not until I yielded myself to him to be his, as a mansion for him to dwell in. Which shews, 1. That grace doth not only work upon the understanding to enlighten it, but that it doth also immediately work on the will, and determines it; for, this opening of the heart is an effect of that work of grace, verse 4, as the former steps were. 2. The act of believing and opening to Christ is both the effect of grace, and also the work formally of the believer: therefore the Lord is said to " open the heart," Acts xvi. 14, because the effect flows from his putting to his hand; and the Bride is said to open her own heart, because she formally brought forth, or elicited the act of faith, by the strength of grace. 3. This (being compared with his call, verse 3.) shews, that it is by faith that way is made for Christ into the heart, and it is that which especially entitles one to Christ, closes with his call, receives him, and enters covenant with him; for, if opening or believing be that which he calls for, as giving him access to the hearts of his people, then believing being the performance of that called for condition, must unite the soul to him, and enter him into the heart. 4. There is some peculiar efficacy in faith, in the uniting of one to Christ, in accepting of Christ's call, and making way for him to come into the heart, which is not in any other grace: or, it hath a peculiar way of concurring, in effectuating the person's union with Christ and (and so in justification) which no other grace hath: hence this opening is peculiarly to be attributed to it, and is distinct from repentance spoken of before, verse 4, and from other duties mentioned in the words following. 5. Whoever honestly, from the sense of sin and need of Christ, and desire to have him to supply their need, essays believing, and opening their heart to him, shall certainly come good speed, and without fail attain their design; " I rose to open" (saith she) " and I opened." 6. Although the distinct exercise of faith be not attained instantly, (but there must be first a rising, and an offering of violence to our corruptions in the pursuing thereof, before we win to the distinct opening of the heart) yet it should be prosecuted till it be perfected. 7. Sometimes the exercise of faith will be distinct and discernible, so that a believer can tell he hath believed; and it is no less comfortable to be clear from serious reflection on ourselves, that we have indeed by faith yielded to Christ, than to be clear of it by the fruits following thereupon: for she is clear and confident in this, that she had opened to him.

Having opened, now the beloved is gone: like as a husband, being offended at his wife's disrespect to him, should withdraw, when she at length with much ado were brought to rise; so our Lord Jesus takes that way of rebuking kindly the former unkindness of believers, by after-desertions and withdrawings. The word is doubled, " but my Beloved had withdrawn himself, and was gone," or " he was gone, he was gone;" which doth not only import in his carriage a sad withdrawing, and in hers an observation of it; but also a sorrowful regret and weightiness, as having met with a sad disappointment (as the following words clear) as if she had said, at last I opened, but alas he was gone and away! what this withdrawing of Christ is, we may know by considering what his being present is, which is not to be understood of the omnipresence of the Godhead, there being no coming or going that can be attributed to that infinite essence, which is every where, at all times present; but it is in respect of the out-letting of his especial love, and that in the peculiar way of manifesting it to his people, and not in regard of his love itself, or of their interest in him; for, here her interest stands in him, and faith in him is exercised, and the lifelessness that she was under is removed, so that now she is acting faith, and there is a presence of grace making her active and lively, even under this withdrawing: the thing then which is wanting, is a sensible manifestation of Christ's love to her, which now upon her yielding to open, she expected to have been filled with, as a wife opening to her husband should expect his embracements, and yet in place thereof, find that he were gone: this withdrawing is no real al-

teration on Christ's side, nor are we to look upon it as if
now she had less than before she believed and bestirred
herself; for, her union with him, and the influence of his
grace on her remained: but, 1. She missed that comfortable and sweet sense of love that she expected from him ;
that was kept up. 2. She was then more sensible that
he was provoked, and found that her peace was not so
well grounded, which formerly she pleased herself with,
as she conceived. 3. Upon this also followed some kindly
exercise, whereby Christ might make his dissatisfaction
known, as a husband doth his, by his withdrawing ; so
that although interest be not disputed, and the heart be
kept in the exercise of duties yet disquietness may grow
above what it was : and Christ wisely times this sense of
his absence now, with the presence of his grace, because
she might both better endure it, and it would also be more
profitable thus to chasten her now, than if he had done it
in her dead condition. Hence, *Observ*, 1. That believers,
in the lively exercise of faith and duty, may have many
more exercies, and sharper spiritual dispensations, than
they had formerly in their security. 2. Christ hath a peculiar way both of presence with, and absence from his
own. 3. Often believers when they are in the exercise of
faith and duty, expect satisfying manifestations of Christ
to their sense ; for, it is supposed here, that she looked
for him this way, when she opened. 4. Sometimes Christ
will keep up the sense of his love, and withdraw himself
from his own, even when in the exercise of faith and duty.
5. Christ's withdrawing is not always an evidence of the
worst frame, even as his presence doth not speak out his
satisfaction every way with his people's condition, but
these are often acts of sovereignty, timed according to
his good pleasure ; for, she is now in better case than
formerly, and yet he is withdrawn and gone. 6. Christ
by his withdrawing may be chastening for some former
sin or disrespect, done to him before the believer became
lively, who yet for good ends did suspend the taking notice of that sin, till he was in a frame to bear it, and profit by it. 7. Christ's withdrawings ought to be observed
by his people, as well as other pieces of their own experience : it is profitable to know what he doth, as well as
what they do themselves. 8. There is a great difference
betwixt faith and sense ; yea, betwixt clearness of interest, and sensible presence : the one may be in a great

measure, where the other is not, as in this case here. 9.
It is the exercise of faith in Christ, that makes his absence to be discerned : (for that is not known here, till
the door be opened) and the more lively a person be in
the exercise of grace, the more will Christ's absence be
marked and regretted ; whereas in a believer's secure
frame, or in a person still unacquainted with Christ, his
absence is not discerned nor laid to heart. 10. Although
sense be not satisfied, yet believers should not disclaim
their faith when it is real, but acknowledge that they do
believe, and open to Christ when they do it : so it is
here, " I opened," or yielded by faith to him, even when
he was gone, and I could not find him.

What effect this disappointment had upon her part,
follows, " my soul failed when he spake :" This effect is
sad and heavy, the sense of her sin, and the apprehension
of her grieving of him, kindled by love to him, pierceth
and stoundeth her so to the heart, that it becomes almost
lifeless : so the word is used, Gen. xlii. 28, of Jacob's sons,
when they found the money in their sacks' mouths, they
were sore afraid, and " their hearts failed them," or went
out of them ; it is a surprising unexpected heaviness, and
that in a high degree, holding forth, how deeply believers
will be affected when disappointed of the expected presence of Christ, and that by their own guilt : the cause or
occasion of this failing of heart, is in these words, " when
he spake," which look to the time past, though the effect
was present ; and they may be two ways understood. 1.
As being a remembering how it was with her while he
spake (for now he speaks not) she now observes, and calls
to mind, that when he called and she shifted, yet even
then her heart was affected with his word ; and this smites
her now, that she should have so long smothered so much
kindness, and have brought all this upon herself; it is
like that of the disciples, Luke xxiv. 32, who after Christ
was gone, say one to another, " Did not our hearts burn
within us, while he talked with us by the way, and opened
up to us the scriptures ; though before they little heeded
it, yet afterward they observe ; and when they recollect
themselves, it becomes more distinct than it was in the
time. 2. It may be looked on as being the present effect
of the words formerly spoken, which although they did not
so sensibly affect her when he spoke them, yet now being
brought to her remembrance (as, John xiv. 16,) they

pierce her, that she should have slighted and neglected them, as, Matt. xxvi. when Peter is admonished, the word for the time affects not, but afterward, verse 75, when he remembers it (as challenges bring back words formerly spoken) " he went out and wept bitterly ;" so her resentment of what she formerly slighted is now bitter. *Observ.* 1. The time of Christ's absence is a time when by-gone challenges, or challenges for by-past offences, use to recur. 2. Often believers, when brought through a secure fit, will find some stirrings and effects of the grace of Christ to have been in them, even then, which were not so discernible to them while they were under their distemper. 3. Christ's word may have effects long after it is spoken and heard ; yea, a word long since heard, may be an after-remembrance (being brought again to mind by the Spirit) John xiv. 26, and have operation more than at first : or, although for a time it have had none at all, but may be as seed under the ground, till the Spirit blow on it to bring it above, yet afterward by the Spirit's influence, it may have many blessed effects. 4. There is nothing that will affect a gracious soul more, than to miss Christ's presence, when the disappointment hath been procured by its own sin ; if it be but a withdrawing for a time, that will make the hearts of his own even to fail ; but O ! if it be eternal, by reason of sinners' constant slighting of him now in the offers of his grace, what desperate anguish will it produce !   And there are none that slight Christ's call now and put him away, but one time or other it will be heavy to them and cost them dear. 5. It is a kindly thing, when a believer misses Christ, and wants presence, to be affected with it ; and it is unkindly to discern absence, and not to be affected. 6. Repentance, where it is kindly, or right heart-sorrow will have its continuance and growth from one degree to another : this failing of heart is a continued, but a further step of the moving of her bowels, verse 4. 7. Although interest in Christ be clear, and matters otherwise not in an evil case, yet want of Christ's presence for the time, and the remembrance of by-gone guilt, will be a very sad exercise to the believer, and affect his heart very much.

This is a sad posture ; yet she gives not over, notwithstanding of this or any following disappointments, till she obtain the holy design she drives : where faith and love are exercised together, for attaining Christ, nothing will scare nor discourage the soul in its pursuit of him. Her carriage follows in four steps (whereby she endeavours to recover him) with the success that she found in each of them. 1. She gives private diligence. 2. She applies herself to public ordinances, verse 7. When that also fails, she, 3. Betakes herself to the exercise of mutual fellowship with the daughters of Jerusalem, and seeks their help, verse 8, and at last, rests on the exercise of faith in him, chap. vi. 3, Her secret painfulness, with the fruit thereof, is set down in two steps, in the rest of this verse. 1. " I sought him," that is, painfully used all means to meet with him, as one searcheth earnestly for what he wants ; so the word is taken, Prov. xv. 14. It shews her seriousness as to the end, and also her holy solicitude in the manner of pursuing it : " But" (saith she) " I found him not ;" he was now obtained, but she continueth still under the want of the sensible manifestations of his presence. Again, the second is, " I called him," that is, prayed to him ; "but" (saith she) " he gave me no answer :" that is, I had no sensible ease, and return of prayer ; though the prayer was not altogether unheard : for, her continuing to seek after him, shews, that she was answered with strength in her soul, Psalm cxxxviii. 3. There was sustaining grace even then, though there were not the soul-satisfying and comforting enlargements, or sensible embracements of Christ, and his warm speaking of peace to her heart, which she aimed at ; and the greatness of her ardour after these makes her think that she had received no answer at all. It is in sum, as if a wife, by searching and running to and fro, did seek her husband ; and when that succeeds not, she calls him by his name ; so did she leave no means unessayed, but did not obtain what she sought. Which shews, 1. That God often blesseth want of sense to a believer, to be a spur to much diligence. 2. When desertions are most sensible, then ought the believer to be most diligent in the use of all means, especially of prayer, for an outgate. 3. There may be much life in duty, even then when there is little sense and satisfaction as to the event ; there is here seeking and calling on him, though she found him not, and he gave her no answer. 4. It is a blessed heart-sorrow, that vents in diligence and prayer to God for his presence. 5. The remembrance and resentment of our by-gone wrongs to Christ should not so affect as to scare us from

him, but should press us to seek to be again in his company ; otherwise, if we scare at him, or bide away from
him, because of the sense of guilt, it will be the mending
of one fault with another : it is ever best reckoning our
own guilt, when he is present. 6. Christ's presence is the
only cordial that can satisfy a soul, fainting under a sense
of the wrongs it hath done to Christ : therefore when her
heart fails, she sits not down under it for ease, but seeks
and calls for himself and his own presence. 7. There
may be much seeking and prayer, which may be so indeed,
and accepted of by God, and yet his comfortable presence
be kept up, and the particular sought for suspended. 8.
Often the having our eye in prayer upon one particular
(suppose upon one comfort) may make us construct our
prayers to have less of an answer than they have, while
as indeed they are not fruitless, but may be answered in
other things, which we do not observe. 9. The Lord may
deny comfort when it is sought, and yet shew his grace
in sustaining his people, and quickening them to follow
him in their duty, when they in the mean time may take
it for a sort of refusal, 2 Cor. xii. 9, 10.   It is ever good
for believers to reflect on their duty, and on the success
of it, whatever it be ; and that not in one step only, but
in the whole tract of their way.   10. If we compare this
with her former carnally easy and secure condition, verse
2, 3, we see, that sensible desertion, when a believer is
holily active under it, is no ill condition ; comparatively
it is better with her now when she is swooning and fainting without Christ, than when she did lie still carelessly
without him ; grace is working more actively now (as
from verse 4, is clear) and she is nearer unto him, and
hath much more solid ground of peace than she had at
that time.

Verse 7.   The watchmen that went about the city found me,
they smote me, they wounded me ; the keepers of the walls
took away my vail from me.

WHEN private means do not the business, the Bride
betakes her to public ordinances, and frequents them ;
and this 7th verse shews that she found, in the use of
that means, a sad disappointment also, which is several
ways aggravated ; Christ's presence is easily lost, but it is
not easily recovered ; this will cost much pains, and the

enduring of many perplexing disappointments : it is much
more difficult to win to enjoy Christ, than it is to lose him :
lying on the bed in ease may bring on that, which much
labour and watching will not remove.

That this verse points at her going about the public
ordinances, the scope makes clear, that being the next
ordinary means used for enquiring after an absent Christ,
when private diligence hath had little success. The matter of the words as was cleared in chap. iii. 3, doth also
evidence this ; the church is the " city" which hath " walls"
(that is, the ordinances) for preventing her hurt, and promoting of her edification : the " watchmen" are her ministers, appointed and designed to keep the walls, and to
go about the city ; they are said to go about the city, in
respect of their care and solicitude to prevent inward
difficulties and hazards, and are called " keepers of the
walls," as they stand to repel what from without may disturb the church's edification, and ecclesiastic peace ; in a
word, they are the same by office, that these were, chap.
iii. 3, but their carriage to her is more unlike the relation
they stood in : which is set forth in four steps, all which
are to be looked on as a special piece of untenderness in
them, and of suffering in her ; which now the Lord in his
wisdom permits her to meet with, that so she may find
how unwisely she had done to neglect Christ's kind call,
verse 2, when as now other hands deal more roughly with
her : the reasons hinted, chap. iii. 3, do confirm this ;
besides, there being so much spoken of their wounding of
her, either she or they must be wrong ; now she is (for
the main) in her duty, and under a fainting condition,
seeking after Christ, and there is no warrant to wound a
poor seeker of Christ in such a condition, even where
there have been former failings, (2 Cor. ii. 7, the apostle
will have the incestuous person in such a case tenderly
dealt with, lest he "should be swallowed up") but it is
duty rather to bind up their wounds, and to pour oil into
them, by speaking a word in season to such weary souls.
This was, no doubt, their duty, and the Lord himself doth
so. Isa. l. 4. Neither could her former security be a
ground to reach her such blows now, especially her offence
being betwixt Christ and her alone, and so no object
of ·public reproof ; and she being a burden to herself, ought
not to have been made more heavy by them : besides,
chap. iii. iv. the watchmen dealt more tenderly with her,

when yet she had been in security also. This dealing of theirs cannot be to speak a word in season to the weary soul of a tender person, whose carriage is so convincing even to others, that verse 9, they give her a high commendation, which is a clear testimony against the malignity of these watchmen; they must therefore be looked on as untender, or unskilful, or both, who do thus misapply the word contrary to the end for which it is appointed, and as miserable comforters talk to the grief of such as he hath wounded. 1. The first step, is, " they found me:" it is not the finding of a friend, as chap. iii. 3, but (as the effects clear) the finding of an enemy, and is, as if a minister should digress of purpose, to take in the case of some poor tender soul, that he might reach it a blow, though beside his text: thus, Ezek. xxxiv. 21. The idle shepherds (who it may be, had a true external call) are said to thrust with the side and shoulder, and push at the diseased with the horns: and, verse 4, to rule with force and cruelty: and in Ezek. xiii. 20, they are said to hunt the souls of God's people: a part of which cruelty and oppression, is verse 22, in making the righteous sad: this is their finding, a seeking occasion to load them with bitter invectives and reproaches. It is observable also, that here at the very first finding they hurt her, without so much as suffering her to tell her own case, as she did to the watchmen, chap. iii. 3, so that, without taking notice of her condition, they presently fall upon her ; which saith, that in their smiting her, they did not respect her case. 2. They smote her ; that is, more gently at first ; however, they suffer no occasion to slip, whereby they have any access to give a wipe to such heart-exercised souls, but it is laid hold upon ; and what infirmity is in any of them, or inconsiderateness in their zeal, that is casten up, and often somewhat of less moment is much magnified. The word takes in also wronging with the tongue, Jer. xviii. 18, " Come let us smite Jeremiah with the tongue:" and it is like, by the words following in that verse, the profane priests had no little accession to it. 3. They wound her : this is a further step, and imports such a smiting as continues till the person be wounded, denoting a higher degree of cruelty, such as is the persecuting of those whom God hath smitten, and talking to their grief, Psalm lxix. 26, which will exceedingly wound a tender exercised soul who is soon affected; and the Psalm

especially points at Judas, who, John xii. 4, 5, 6, was
ready to condemn the holy zeal of an honest soul, which
our Lord vindicates and leaves on record to her eternal
commendation. 4. The last step is, " they took away my
vail from me ;" the word that is rendered " vail," comes
from a root that signifieth to subdue, it is that same word
which we have, Psalm cxliv. 2, " who subdues the people,"
&c. It hath a threefold use, 1. For decoration, as Isa.
iii. 23. 2. For a sign of modesty, pleaded for by the
apostle, 1 Cor. xi. 6. 3. And mainly, for a sign of
women's subjection to their own husbands; for which
cause Rebekah puts on her vail, when she meets Isaac,
Gen. xxiv. 65. And therefore it is called power, as being
the sign of the wife's being under the power of her husband, 1 Cor. xi. 10. Here her vail is the tenderness of
her profession, whereby, in a decent, modest and humble
way, she professed herself to be a believer, seeking after
Christ Jesus, as one bearing the badge of subjection to
him as her Husband. The taking away of the vail, is
their wronging of that honest profession she had, and the
giving of her out, not to be that which she professed herself
to be, and so not worthy of a vail; but that her profession
was hypocrisy, her painfulness and tenderness, conceited-
ness, even as Judas, John xii. 5, nicknames that good
work wrought upon Christ by the honest woman, calling
it wastry : and by these, and such other means, often
tender souls are affronted, and proposed as a reproach to
the multitude ; even as if a wife that is chaste, were de-
nuded of her vail, and reputed as a gadding harlot, while
she is seeking her own husband : so when the Lord
threatens his people, that their lewdness should be made
to appear, he useth this expression, Ezek. xxiii. 26, 27,
They shall " strip thee out of thy clothes," &c. that being
a manifest shame to a woman, that should be covered, 1
Cor. xi. 6. This is added, to shew that they pretend they
have reason for their smiting : they disgrace her, and take
away her vail, that they may not be thought to smite
holiness or tenderness, but a hypocrite under such a vail,
or a whore more decently adorned than became her to be.

  This is the sum ; when I prevailed not in the private
diligence, I frequented the public ordinances; but those
who were watchmen and healers by office, being untender
(as if they had intended it) did by malice, or want of affection, or through unskilfulness and want of experience,

so apply the word, that they sewed pillows under the arm-holes of the profane, and made the righteous sad : whereby I was not only nothing profited, but returned, more weight-ed and ashamed, and had no encouragement to seek any more of their help, as I had done, chap. iii. 3, but was ne-cessitated to turn to others : which shews, that she ac-counts them untender, and therefore, sets it down here as a piece of her sad trial ; whereas, had it been the wound-ing of a friend, it had been a " kindness to her," Psalm cxli. 5, and would have engaged her to follow on for heal-ing from that same hand, so far it would have been from being the matter of her complaint, neither would it have been complained of by her.

These words afford many such doctrines, as, chap. iii. 3. As 1. That the visible church is a distinct incorporation by itself, and all its members have right to its privileges, to wit, such whereof they are capable : it is the city, and they are the citizens, Eph. ii. 19.   2. It is a city that is not without fear and hazard, though it have walls ; but it had need to be watched both within and without : or, the visible church hath many enemies, she is in constant war : hence therefore, she is called the militant church ; and for this cause, she hath walls and watchmen.   3. The Lord hath provided her with sufficient means against all assaults. 4. A lawfully called ministry, or watchmen peculiarly de-signed for that end, are the great means Christ hath ap-pointed for preventing the hurt, and promoting the good and edification of his church, Eph. ii. 12, 13.   They are as the sentinels, which he hath set on the walls, for giving advertisement and warning ; and this well becomes their office, Isa. lxii. 6. Ezek. iii. and xxxiii. chapters, and else-where.   5. Tender believers will put a great price upon public ordinances, even when they seem to themselves to come little speed in their private duties ; private diligence furthers public, and public furthers private : these two ought not to be, neither will they be separated in a tender person, but go together.   6. Tender believers may have weights added to their exercise, and a load put above a burden, even by those whose stations and relations call for much more sympathy and healing.   7. Public ordinances may be sometimes unfruitful to believers, even when they have great need, and are under great sense of need.   8. When one that is tender gets no good nor ease by public ordinances, often there is an addition made to his burden

thereby.   9. Untender, unskilful, and unfaithful men may
creep in, and be admitted to the ministry, and to watching
over the church, as Judas was.   10. When such are gifted
and (as to order) lawfully called, they are truly ministers,
though not true ministers, and have authority for discharging of all duties ; and duties discharged, or ordinances
dispensed by them, according to Christ's warrant, are valid,
and the word from their mouth, is to be received as from
him : therefore they are called watchmen, which imports
them to be really in office, which could not be, if the former assertions were not true.   11. Very often, tender believers, in their exercises, suffer much from such ministers :
or, an untender minister is often a great affliction to tender
exercised believers ; yea, of all men, these prove most
sadly afflicting to them ; no man wounds godliness more,
or wounds and affronts the profession thereof more in them
that are the most real and tender professors, than a gifted
untender minister may do, and often doth ; though sometimes the Lord will make use of him for their good, to
humble them and yet more to provoke them to the study of
more seriousness in secret duties, and to more close and
constant waiting on the Lord himself.   12. Where enmity
against godliness once ariseth, and vents itself against the
godly, it often grows from one degree to another as here,
men, especially ministers once engaged in it, are not
easily recovered and brought out of that evil, but are
carried, yea, often hurried from one step to another : yet,
she accounts them watchmen, as holding out the respect
she bare to their office, even then.   Whence observe, 13.
That it is a piece of spiritual wisdom and tenderness, to
distinguish carefully betwixt the office of the ministry, or
the ordinance itself, and the faults and untenderness of
persons, who may miscarry in the exercise of that office ;
and not to fall from the esteem of the ordinances because
of them, or of what faults may be in them, but even then
to respect the ordinance out of respect to Christ, and his
institution and appointment.   14. Believers should observe
the fruit of public ordinances, as well as of secret diligence,
as the Bride here doth.

Verse 8.   I charge you, O daughters of Jerusalem, if ye find
    my beloved, that ye tell him, that I am sick of love.

When this means fails her, she gives not over, but betakes herself to the use of mutual fellowship with the

saints (which is the third step of her carriage) verse 8, that she may have their help for recovering of Christ's presence : she propounds her case to them, and presseth for their bearing burden with her ; her case is in the last words, " I am sick of love :" a strange disease, yet kindly to a believer : this sickness implies pain as of a woman in travail, whose showers are sharp, and pangs vehement till she bring forth : the same word is used to this purpose, Isa. xxvi. 17. " Like as a woman that draweth near her delivery, is in pain," &c. And it imports in this place, these two, 1. Vehement desire after Christ, from ardent love to him, so that she could not endure to want him. 2. Much heart-affectedness following upon that ardent desire, which (under her former disappointments) did beget such pain and fainting, that it was as a sore sickness, though not dangerous : this sickness differs from that spoken of, chap. ii. 5, as the scope shews ; that is like the pain procured by an overset of the stomach ; so the sense of his love being let out in a very great measure, was like to master her ; not, that sense of his love is simply or in itself burdensome, but she is weak like an old bottle, or a queasy and weak stomach that cannot bear much : but this is like the pain that proceeds from hunger, and a strong appetite, when that which is longed for is not obtained, which augments the desire, and at last breeds fainting and sickness. This shews, 1. That love to Christ, where it is sincere, is a most sensitive thing. 2. That the more disappointments it meets with, in seeking after sensible manifestations of Christ, it grows the more vehement. 3. That continued absence to a tender soul, will be exceeding heavy and painful ; hope deferred maketh the heart sick, especially when the sweetness of Christ's presence hath been felt, and his absence distinctly discerned. 4. That Christ's presence is the soul's health, and his absence its sickness, have else what it will. 5. That love to Christ will sometimes, especially after challenges and disappointments, so overpower the soul, that it cannot to its own sense (at least) act under it, or sustain it (it seems so heavy a burden) as sickness will do to the body, if it get not an outgate.

The way she takes to obtain Christ, after all other means fail her, is by making her application to the daughters of Jerusalem : indeed it is Christ, and not they that can cure her, he is the only medicine for a sick soul ; therefore, her design is not to rest in their company, but

to make use of it for obtaining his company : for, the company, although it were even of angels, will not be satisfying to a soul that seeks Christ; the best fellowship is empty
without him, John xx. 12, 13, " Why weepest thou?"
(say the angels) " Why?" (saith she) "they have taken
away my Lord." In this consider, 1. The parties she betakes herself to, " the daughters of Jerusalem," spoken of,
chap. i. 5, professors not of the worst stamp ; yet (as after
appears) under much ignorance of Christ, and of spiritual
exercise : this is the means she goes now unto. Where
observe, 1. Spiritual communion, amongst professors or
believers, is not only a duty, but a special means, being
rightly made use of, to further our fellowship with Christ.
2. Believers, in their sad cases, may, and ought freely to
make use of this means, by desiring other's help ; and for
their own ease and furtherance in meeting with Christ, by
communicating their case to them, as she doth here. 3.
Even the strongest believers (whom the Bride represents)
may be helped by those that are much weaker than themselves in gifts, grace, and experience ; as the daughters of
Jerusalem are here : and so Paul often requires of others,
inferior to, and much short of him, the help of their
prayers. Consider, 2. Her desire to them, " Tell him"
(saith she) "that I am sick of love ;" make my case known
to him, and hold it up by prayer : she had been doing so
herself, and had not come speed, and therefore she puts
them upon it, that they might help her to obtain an answer.
Observ. 1. That prayer for one another, is a duty of
mutual fellowship, especially for those that are exercised :
others should be in that exercise with them, James v. 17.
2. Believers sometimes will not trust themselves with the
opening of their own case to Christ, and will not be satisfied with their own way, but will think others can do it
much better. 3. Praying for ourselves, and desiring of
help from others, should go together ; or, it will give most
clearness and peace to believers, to desire the help of
others, when they have been serious in the use of all means
by themselves, as she had been. 4. It says, That believers
holding up the case of another, will be very acceptable to
Christ. And, 5. That there is nothing, we can tell Christ,
of our own or other folk's case, that will be more pleasant
to, and taking with him, than this, that we are they who
are "sick of love" to him : this is propounded, as that
which may and will be most acceptable to him : what shall

ye tell him ? (so the words run) these are the best and
most acceptable news to him. 6. Such a case as love-
sickness is a good motive, upon which to press for the help
of others' prayers, and that which may also give confidence
to any, to bear such a message to Christ. 7. Believers,
in their communion with others, should more insist upon
their own cases, than on the faults of ministers, or miscarriages of others: although she was formerly smitten
by the watchmen, yet this is the great thing she propounds
to them. Consider, 3. A qualification, put in her suit to
the daughters of Jerusalem, " If ye find him :" that is, if
ye get access, which now she thinks herself excluded from.
And it imports, 1. That there is a peculiar finding of, and
and access unto Christ at one time beyond another. 2.
That a weak believer may sometimes have much more
access to Christ, and sensible communion with him, than
others of greater parts and experience : she supposes that
they might find, while she did not. 3. That when any
get access for themselves, then especially they should remember others, and improve their court with Christ. for
their good who may be in bonds, and under sad exercise :
then (saith she) when ye get access, remember my case :
she would share of the fruit of their most warm enjoyments. 4. She doth not resent nor envy this, or become
jealous of it, but humbly submits to be helped by them :
Christ will have every one useful to another, and the
strongest should not disdain to be in the common of the
weakest.

The last thing is the manner of her proposing of it " I
charge, or adjure you" (saith she) which hath the force of
an oath proposed to others as if she had sworn them that
they should do it ; the same charge or adjuration is set
down, chap. ii. 7, and iii. 4. She puts them to it, as they
will be answerable. Which shews 1. Great seriousness
in her ; the matter of Christian fellowship, and our desiring of the help of others' prayers, is no matter of compli-
ment, but should in earnest be sought for. 2. She desires
seriousness in them, in their discharge of this duty : in our
praying for others, conscience should be made of it, as
seriously as for ourselves, and we should beware of super-
ficialness and overliness in it. 3. Our expressions in our
fellowship, especially concerning the most serious purposes,
should be suitably serious. A light manner of speaking
in serious things often spills the beauty of them, mars

edification, and diminisheth from the weight of the matters themselves.

Verse 9.   What is thy beloved more than another beloved, O thou fairest among women? what is thy beloved more than another beloved, that thou dost so charge us.

IN this 9th verse, is the third part of the chapter, where the daughters of Jerusalem are brought in speaking; where we may see what effect the Bride's serious charge had upon them : it someway surpriseth and astonisheth them, to see a person convincingly approvable in her carriage, so taken up with that which the most part of the world slights; this makes them think that he whom she asketh for, must be a person beyond ordinary, and in this they conclude right : there is much infirmity in this question (as often many professors are upon the matter really ignorant of Christ's worth) yet some honest-like things (at least) are in it.   There is, 1. Respect to her as a beautiful and goodly person, even when she was thought little of by the watchmen.   2. Docileness, and a desire to know.   3. Some suspicion of their own knowledge of Christ: and, 4. Ingenuity in seeking help.   All which, are good symptoms in beginners; and we will see that the question ended well with them, chap. vi. 1, and it is like was awakened in them by her serious carriage.   The return they make to her charge hath in it, 1. The title they gave her.   2. The question they propose to her.   3. The rise of it, or that which gives them occasion to ask, and which puts them to it.   The title is excellent, " O thou fairest among women :" it was given to the Bride by Christ himself, chap. i. 8.   It implies, 1. A spiritual beauty in her who now was thought little of by the watchmen, and had her own crosses in the world, yet even in this case lovely in herself, and lovely to those daughters, *Observ.* 1. That believers should be eminently convincing, and commendable in their carriage even before others ; they should be fairest among them, and for spiritual beauty conspicuous, as lights shining in a dark place.   2. Grace, when seriously in exercise, is that which makes any person (though outwardly mean and contemptible) truly beautiful and lovely : it makes them so really, and also in the eyes of all spiritual beholders. 3. Sometimes God will make honest seekers of him the more lovely to others, when corrupt ministers seek most to defame them: the watchmen's wounding her, mars not the daughters' estimation of her; and this shews that they did smite her without reason. Again, 2. It implies respectfulness on their part, and also honesty; for there is now no external thing to commend her to them: which saith, 1. That to the spiritual eye of honest souls, none will be so beautiful as the person that is holy; yea, sometimes holiness will have a commendation in the consciences even of them that are strangers to it. 2. Often holiness may be more esteemed of, and holy persons more respectfully dealt with, by men of little either knowledge or profession, than by those who may be much more knowing, and whose station and place calls them to be much more tender; the Bride here is like the wounded person, Luke x. 31, &c. whom the Samaritan succoured, when both the Priest and the Levite had passed by him. 3. Where grace shines, it should be highly esteemed of and respected; and such as are but babes in Christ, ought much to reverence those that are of older standing. 4. Tender souls when under exercise, if we can do no more to ease them, should be respectfully spoken unto at least: these daughters do not wound the Bride, as the watchmen did, but speak discreetly and respectfully unto her, although they can further her little. 5. The right use of freedom, and seriousness with humility in mutual fellowship, is a great help to entertain mutual respect among professors; when the weak see the strong ones not puffed up, but condescending to take their help, it will conciliate love and respect: thus the daughters meet the Bride here with respectful carriage. 6. Respectful expressions of one professor to another, with gravity and seriousness, becomes Christian fellowship well; and is a great furtherance of edification and mutual confidence; so we see here, and chap. vi. 1, as also in the Bride's expressions preceding.

2. The question propounded by them is, "What is thy Beloved?" as scarce knowing him, or acquainted with him themselves: it is not spoken out of disdain, but out of desire to know, being convinced that there behoved to be some excellency in him, beyond others, as the following effects clear. The question is proposed by way of comparison, and doubted, "What is thy Beloved more

than another beloved ?" or "the beloved of another ?" By beloved, all along is understood that which the soul loves and cleaves unto ; therefore Christ is sometimes designed by the one name, the soul's love ; and sometimes by the other, the Beloved, as we may see by comparing chap. iii. 1, 2, 3, with chap. ii. 16, 17, because he eminently and above competition had the Bride's heart. By other beloveds are understood these things that men of the world set their love and affections upon, and which bear most sway with them, as that which in a singular manner their souls love ; the same that ordinarily are called idols, because they are put in God's room ; there is the same reason here, why they are called other beloveds, and strange lovers elsewhere : such are the belly, Phil. iii. 19, " the world," 1 John ii. 15, 16, " Love not the world, nor the things of it," &c. " the lust of the eye, the lust of the flesh, the pride of life :" so it is as they had said, there are many things which the men of the world seek after, it is none of all these that this Bride is enquiring for, she rests not satisfied with these, nor valueth them ; he must then be some excellent person, a singular and non-such Beloved, that she is so serious in the enquiry after, and therefore they desire to know from herself what he is. The question is doubled as being the result of a serious desire to know, and of high admiration, what he might be, who was thus enquired for.

3. The words added, shew what is the rise of their question and wondering, to wit, these, 1. " That thou doest so charge us :" every word hath weight, it is " thou," the " fairest among women," who certainly can make the best choice. 2. Thou art not only in earnest thyself, but chargest us also. And, 3. Not only thou chargest us, but so vehemently, pressing, and weightily ; this sure must be some excellent Beloved. This question carrieth in it not so much an enquiry who is the believer's choice, as their desire to know what Christ was indeed, in respect of his real worth, whose name only (or little more) they knew before ; therefore they say not, who is, but what is thy Beloved ? as knowing his name, but being much ignorant of his worth. Again, it supposeth such a question to be moved by these professors, upon occasion of her exemplary carriage ; and indeed it cannot be told, what thoughts, serious challenges, and exercising questions the convincing carriage of believers will have

amongst those with whom they christianly converse; and so it shews, that this seriousness in one may put others to it, to question what the matter may be, and through God's blessing may commend Christ to them in the end, which is the scope.

Observ. 1. There may be some respect to godly persons, where there is much ignorance of Christ himself. 2. Where there is esteem of godliness and of those who study it, there is some begun enquiry for Christ himself, and it leads on to further, although the beginnings be weak. 3. True tenderness in beginners, appears in nothing sooner than in respect to those who were in Christ before them; they are now but beginning, yet this shews itself in the respect they carry to the Bride. 4. It is no shame for those that are unacquainted with Christ, to enquire for him at such as know him. 5. What Christ is, and the necessity of praying for others, is a suitable subject of discourse in Christian fellowship. What is Christ? say they to her; and pray for me, saith she to them. 6. Christ's name may be known to many to whom his worth is unknown, or but little known, and who are not acquainted with what he is. 7. All men naturally have some lust, idol, or beloved, that their affection is set upon besides Christ; it is some other thing, from which he is distinguished, and to which he is opposed. 8. Men lay out their affections liberally upon their idols, and upon those things their hearts cleave unto besides Christ; they are beloveds, and opposed to Christ, as being that to the men of the world, that Christ is to his own; they are as Gods and Christs to them, they run so mad upon their idols and are so joined to them, Hos. iv. 17, men naturally have an high esteem of their idols, as placing some worth in them which is not, and they have a low esteem of Christ, and prefer their idols to him. 9. This mistake is a great cause of Christ's being slighted in the world, that they think other beloveds as good as he, and other lives as good as the life of holiness; therefore they go to the farm, plough, market, and make light of Christ, Matt. xxii. 4. 10. The questioning of this grand principle of corrupt nature, that Christ is no better than other beloveds, or the enquiring whether he be indeed better than these, is one of the first rises of a soul's making forward to enquire for him. 11. The growing of the esteem of Christ in a soul, and the decay of the esteem of all idols (formerly beloveds) go together; as the one stands, the other falls, as the one grows, the other decays. 12. The right up-taking of Christ's worth, is the great thing that commends Christ to a soul (therefore the Bride describes him afterward) and the thorough conviction of the vanity of all other things looseth the grips of our affections from them, and makes way for setting Christ more high. 13. The convincing carriage of a believer may stir and raise an exercise in those that formerly were secure : and God can make the words of a private humble Christian, the rise of a serious enquiry after Christ in another ; thus her serious charging of them doth so stick to them, as if that word, " I charge you," had pierced them. 14. Nothing more adorns the gospel, and commends Christ, and makes him lovely to others, than the convincing, serious carriage of believers.   15. Those who are not acquaint with Christ's worth, or the exercises of believers, are ready to wonder what moves them and puts them to make such a stir about Christ, more than others, that live satisfied and contented without him.

BRIDE.

Verse 10.   My beloved is white and ruddy, the chiefest among ten thousand.

FROM verse 10, to the end (which contains the fourth part of the chapter) the Bride speaks : and in answer to the daughters of Jerusalem their question) in a sweet, pithy, taking manner, commends her Beloved. She is not long in returning answer to their question, as being fully clear and ready to demonstrate Christ, her Beloved, his worth above all : and as impatient that any other should be put in competition with him, (especially by the daughters of Jerusalem, whose edification she studies by this to promote) instantly she steps in with a large commendation of Christ, (though in few words) whereby she doth so demonstrate him to be an object infinitely worthy to be her soul's Beloved beyond all others, that chap. vi. 1, they as convinced yield, acknowledging that her Beloved was preferable to all other beloveds, and that therefore they are engaged to love and seek him with her.

In this commendation, she, 1. Asserts Christ's preferableness in the general, verse 10.   2. She confirms and illustrates it in particulars, to verse 16. And then, 3. verse 16, sums it up in an universal expression, as being in its particulars inexpressible. Lastly, Having fully proved her assertion, she resumes the conclusion as un-answerable : " This" (saith she) " is my Beloved," a sin-gular beloved indeed, and therefore it is no wonder that I am so serious in pursuing after him, and so sick of love to him, and so much pained at the very heart for the want of him.

The first general in this 10th verse sets out Christ positively, and comparatively : do you ask (saith she) what my Beloved is ? he is a non-such, an incomparable Beloved, " he is white and ruddy," O so lovely as he is in himself ! and being compared with all others, he hath the pre-eminence by far, as being " the chiefest among ten thousand." By " white and ruddy" we are to conceive Christ's qualifications, according to the strain of the alle-gory, there being no bodily qualification set out here, Christ at that time not being incarnate, yet even then was he white and ruddy ; the due and just mixture of these colours maketh a man lovely, and evidenceth a good com-plexion of body : so by them in Christ is understood a concurrence of all fit qualifications and excellencies, that may make him lovely to the soul, when by faith looked upon, and taken up, there is sweet beauty and comeliness, or a comely beautiful sweetness that lustres and shines in him, through the excellent qualifications wherewith he is furnished, as the husband of his church, that ravisheth spiritual affections far beyond the greatest beauty that can be in the fairest face ; for, indeed he is fairer than the sons of men : there is nothing that may make a Mediator lovely but it is here. Again, as if that did not fully set out his amiableness, she adds, " He is the chiefest among ten thousand :" this is a definite great number for an in-definite ; in sum it is this,—there are many beloveds indeed in the world, but compare them all with Christ, they are nothing to him : without all controversy he is the chiefest, 1 Cor. viii. 5, 6, For " though there be gods many, and lords many" (to the world) " yet to us there is but one God, and one Lord Jesus ;" in all the world there is but one Christ. The word used here is, he is the standard-bearer, or it may be rendered passively, he is standarded above ten thousand ; all tending to the same scope ; love kythes its rhetoric in seeking words to prefer Christ, as

having indignation that his precedency and pre-eminence
(who is "above all things," Col. i. 17,) should so much as
once be questioned : it is like, that in these times the most
comely persons were chosen to carry the standard, a piece
of dignity being thereby put upon them; so then, if all
the most choice, comely, and excellent persons in the
world were mustered together, Christ would be preferred
eminently and deservedly above them all.   Whence, *Observe*, 1. That Christ is the most lovely and excellent object that men can set their eyes on, that they can cast
their love and affection upon: there is not such an one as
Christ, either for the spiritual soul-ravishing beauty that
is in him, or the excellent desirable effects that flow from
him.   O what a singular description is it which follows,
if it were understood! 2. Christ is the most singularly
excellent Husband that ever was closed with : under that
relation he is commended here, as singularly lovely, and
loving ; it is a most honourable, comfortable, happy, and
every way satisfying match to have him for a Husband.
3. Christ's worth in itself is not expressible, and whatever
he can be compared with, he doth exceedingly surpass it.
4. Where right thoughts of Christ are, there is nothing
admitted to compete with him, other excellencies and beloveds are in their greatest beauty darkened beside him ;
he is set up as chief, and they are not to be taken notice
of beside him, but to be accounted loss and dung. 5. Christ's
absence, when believers are right, will never lessen their
esteem of him, but even then believers will be warm and
fresh in their love to him, and high in their esteem of
him.   6. Neither will the great mistakes of others shake
believers that have a thorough esteem of Christ's worth,
but will rather with holy zeal awake them to commend
him the more.   7. As where there is true love to Christ,
there Christ will be lovely ; so when he is looked on as
lovely, that makes the heart to flow and abound with holy
rhetoric in commendations of him.   8. True love to
Christ, and to others for his sake, will not suffer one to
despise the weakness of another, but make them rather
take occasion from it, to honour him and edify them so
much the more, as the Bride doth here in answering the
question proposed.   9. The more nearly and fully any
thing be compared with Christ, though it be otherwise
lovely, yet then it will be seen to be nothing, he so infinitely excels all things he can be compared with ; and it is

ignorance of him that makes other things get such a place in men's affections : but, when once they are set for against him, he is found preferable, as incomparably chief, for dignity, riches, and satisfaction, or whatsoever is delightsome, desirable, and truly excellent, verse 11, 12, 13, &c.

She passeth from the general, to demonstrate it in particulars, and therein she insists in the following verses. If it should be asked, why she descends into particulars, especially now, considering her deserted case ? I answer, for these good reasons, 1. That she might the more fully demonstrate, and the more satisfyingly unfold Christ's worth ; for, his worth cannot be soon nor easily told, nor conceived, nor soon believed by others, it needs to be demonstrated, amplified, and insisted upon ; yet, his worth can bide the trial : there is no truth may more fully and demonstratively be made out than this, that Christ is a most excellent object of love, and infinitely preferable to all others. 2. This is for the edifying of the daughters of Jerusalem, and in reference to their question, that they might be the more convinced and satisfied anent the incomparable worth and matchless excellency of her Beloved, she brancheth it forth and insists upon it, that so a deeper impression of it might be left upon their hearts, *Observ.* 1. There is nothing more useful for the gaining and edifying of others, than to help them to the right uptaking of Christ's worth. 2. That is a great part of the work that should take up Christians in their fellowship together, to be spending their mutual conferences on that subject for one another's instruction. 3. To edify another, is no diverson from pursuing after him, to souls that love Christ, and would be helped by others to meet with him ; this is well consistent with her pursuing after sensible presence for herself, to stay a while instructing them. A third reason of her insisting is, that it is suitable unto, and agrees well with her own sad condition, when he is away, she loves to think and speak of him, and of his loveliness, and that gives her some ease. *Observ.* 1. Where love to Christ is, there will be a delight in speaking of him, and setting out his commendation, even when he is absent ; it is a kind of ease to tell over his qualifications when he is absent. 2. It is a good diversion under a deserted condition, and a suitable way to an outgate, to be dwelling rather upon the excellency of Christ, than on the comfortless aggravations of our own sad condition ; this is more honourable to

Christ, more edifying to others, and more pleasant to our-selves: O, it is sweet to think of him! it is more useful also for confirming of our faith in him, for warming our affections to him, and for keeping the mind stayed in de-pendance on him for the outgate; every attribute or property of his is a cordial to the soul fainting under a deserted case. 4. Her insisting on this subject, shews the nature of true love to Christ, that a soul affected with it, being once entered to speak of this theme or sub-ject (namely the excellency of Christ) it expatiates on it, and is not soon withdrawn from it; this (to say so) is the very native element of it: and it doth the heart good to enumerate, and tell over distinctly the commendable quali-fications and excellencies of Christ: all which (being his own) are unspeakably delightsome and refreshing to reck-on: if there were any good measure of love to Christ in men's hearts, they would not be easily withdrawn from meditating on him, nor from speaking of him; and the great haunt that other things have in our hearts, and the rarity of any expression that tends to Christ's commenda-tion, shews plainly that there are (alas!) other beloveds abounding with us besides him.

In the opening of the following particulars, we would consider, 1. The scope, which is to demonstrate, that Christ Jesus is altogether lovely and desirable beyond all other things that the hearts of men are set upon; the question proposed, ver. 9, and the closing answer to it, ver. 16 makes this clear. This then being the scope, these particulars must be so taken up, as they best contribute to clear this scope, and so must necessarily imply the excellen-cies that are in Jesus Christ; the Mediator himself being as the body, and the several qualifications, properties, and excellencies wherewith he is furnished, being as the several members, and parts of that body. Now, seeing Jesus Christ is so excellent himself, and these being instanced as the choice excellencies that are in him, they must needs be exceeding and passing excellent, as the aggreging and heightning of every commendation doth shew: there will be need therefore of much sobriety, holy admiration and reverence, in the opening of them, lest we spill so ex-cellent a subject as is the transcendent excellency of our Lord Jesus. 2. That the Spirit intends by these parts, distinct considerations of Christ's loveliness in so many distinct particulars, seems also to be without all question;

for the particular enumeration is brought in to demonstrate this general, that he is the chiefest among ten thousand, which is done (as it were) by an induction of so many commendable things that are in him; besides in other scriptures, and especially, Rev. i. 13, 14, where our Lord is thus considered, and also in the second and third chapters of that book of the Revelation, particular respect is had to the foresaid description; and these parts are there (being equivalent to them that are here mentioned) expounded of divers attributes and properties of his, and not unlike in many things to the description following, as the particulars will clear. Consider, 3. That it is both difficult and dangerous to be peremptory in the application of these particulars to the object described, it being so exceeding glorious, and the Spirit's expressions so very comprehensive, we dare not so limit the words to one thing, as if they were exclusive of another, nor say this is meant and no other thing; although such and such things as have a necessary connexion with the scope to confirm it, may warrantably be included, and for instances pitched upon, especially when from the analogy that is in the expressions which are borrowed, and from other scriptures, we have some ground to fix upon : but to be sure, the words should be so taken up as they best afford the most solid general doctrines, which are sometimes (because of our darkness, and to prevent our curiosity) to be rested in ; for, whatever be meant, it is Christ, and he by these commendations is set forth as most excellent: that all these are to describe a divine person, and no human body, we conceive so clear that it needs no advertisement. 4. All these parts hold him forth, not only as excellent in himself, but as lovely to his people, and as making up their privilege and happiness in having an interest in him to be theirs ; and therefore as this is the scope, so it is to be applied as setting out his excellency, and the blessedness of all that have him for theirs ; as on the contrary to cry down all other beloveds of the world, of whom these things cannot be said, for they are singularly peculiar to him.

Verse 11.   His head is as the most fine gold ; his locks are bushy, and black as a raven.

THERE are ten parts mentioned, that are brought in as proofs of Christ's singular excellency, each of them almost

having a double commendation ; two of them are in the
11th verse. The first is, "his head," the most eminent
part of the body ; that furnisheth influence and direction
to all the rest : it may signify (if we dare adventure) these
three in Christ, 1. His Godhead, which is the most eminent nature of Christ's person, sustaining the other, and
furnishing it for its office ; thus, 1 Cor. xi. 3, as " the
head of the woman is the man," in respect of his dignity ;
so "the head of Christ is God," as the Godhead " dwells
in him bodily," Col. ii. 9, by a wonderful and unspeakable
personal union, the like whereof is not to be found in any
other. 2. It may hold out Christ's headship, or sovereignty which he hath as Mediator, being made head of
" the body, the church," and " over all things for the
church," Eph. i. 12, and his instalment into this office is
the rise of all the other commendations that follow, which
are as parts thereof : thus Nebuchadnezzar's sovereignty,
as being a king of kings, is set out by a head of gold,
Dan. ii. 32, 38. 3. It may signify the qualifications,
wherewith he, as head to the body, is furnished for its behoof and good : so he is an excellent head, for contriving
of what is good for the body, and for furnishing life and
motion to all his members ; thus Eph. iv. 16, he is the
head, from whom the whole body, being fitly compacted
together, doth make increase of itself in love : and to
this purpose, a man of a great reach and profound wit,
useth to be called a great head. All these agree with the
scope, being instances of Christ's excellencies, and also
with the commendation following ; yet, the first seems
most agreeable to the analogy of head and members, and
it is not unlike that Christ's Godhead is begun at in his
commendation : surely it cannot be excluded, seeing, in
Rev. i. 14, by his head (as there described) is set forth
his eternity, the same nature may well be here understood, though Christ be otherways represented in the
colour of his locks, because here he is described as a lovely
Bridegroom, there as coming to judge, as also in Dan. vii.
But it must be some excellent thing that is meant, as the
commendation annexed clears. " His head is as the most
fine gold :" in the original, there are two words indifferently
made use of, to signify gold, the first because of its shining brightness and beauty ; the second is applied to it, because of its solidity and firmness ; so it runs, his head is
gold of gold, or gold and gold, or fine shining and solid

gold, as if gold were not enough to set out the excellency of this head : gold is rich in the quality, solid and strong as to the efficacy, (as in chap. iii. 10.) sovereign as to usefulness and profitableness ; it is above other metals, and so in the heavenly Jerusalem, the streets are said to be of pure gold, Rev. xxi, 21. Therefore that dominion of Nebuchadnezzar's, spoken of Dan. ii. 32, is compared to a head of gold, for its excellency above the rest that followed, and especially for the shelter that the church of God had under it : and this being gold of gold, must hold forth such sovereignty, riches of grace, solidity and happiness, as is unsearchable ; gold cannot reach it, no not gold raised to the highest worth conceiveable.

This first particular may put us to a stand, when (as it were) the Bride is at a stand in the commendation, and must double the word, as gold, gold ; and it is hard to draw observations from it, yet warrantably this may be said, 1. Christ hath a head (however we take it) that is exceedingly excellent, he is God, and in that respect is unsearchable, " being the brightness of the Father's glory, and the express image of his person," Heb i. 3. He, as Mediator, is furnished with sovereignty and eminent graces for the good of the body ; and these, as they are for their nature most solid and excellent, so as to their virtue they are most efficacious and quickening. 2. If we take it in general, *Observ.* That the excellencies wherewith Christ is furnished, are in the highest degree of excellency ; therefore it is gold of gold, whatever it be, and this general will necessarily infer the former, that he is God and Mediator, and in such and such offices furnished for the good of his people, and the former doctrine is the proof of this : all Christ's properties, wisdom, love, counsel, &c. are of more than an ordinary depth, being in him to the very uttermost, Heb. vii. 25, and without measure, John iii. 34. 3. Christ's excellency is not only lovely in itself, but useful to others ; he is not only rich in himself, but enriching those that possess him, as gold doth enrich the owners of it : Christ is a golden possession where there is a well grounded claim to him. 4. Gold and all external riches, are empty things to a spiritual discerner of Christ's worth ; as it were, a new sort of gold must be invented, or imagined, to shadow forth the excellencies of Christ, gold itself is but an insufficient and dark shadow to represent him ; whoever loves gold, may have (and

that freely) the most fine and choice gold in him. Yea,
5. This is peculiar to him, in opposition to all other beloveds : men's idols and other beloveds may be gilded,
like the whore's cup, spoken of, Rev. xvii. 4, but Christ
only is the golden Beloved ; for, this is so attributed to
him, as it is denied to them, which are but clay, or "thick
clay" beloveds, Hab. ii. 6.

The second thing commended is " his locks," which are
no essential part of the body, yet are (when lovely) a
special decorement, and ever have been so esteemed : the
signification of locks (being joined to the head) will be so
much the more clear, if we consider the commendation
given them, which is threefold, 1. " They are bushy," or
curled : not such as old men have, hairs here and there,
but his are bushy, thick, and handsome, such as young men
in the flower and vigour of their youth use to have. 2.
They are black ; and that, 3. As a raven : black hair in
those times and places was comely in men, and betokens
strength of youth, and vigour of age. Therefore the
same word, which is here blackness, signifieth youth also
in the Hebrew, as Eccles. xi. 10, " childhood and youth,"
&c. So black hair here, is opposed to white hairs, whereby decay is signified (as Hos. vii. 9, by " gray hairs" on
Ephraim, is understood) and thus all other idols get a
dash, as if they were gray haired, decaying beloveds ; but
Christ is always in youth and vigour, he continues always
vigorous, as his love is always green. They are compared
to the blackness of a raven, because that is native black,
and lovely beyond other things that are black. As by
Christ's head then was signified that which is in Christ
(to speak so) most intrinsically excellent ; so here, by locks
we understand the most extrinsic thing that is in him (if
we may say any thing of Christ is so) that is, if any thing
seem less necessary than another, yet is it in itself excellent, and serves to commend Christ to others. And
again, by bushiness and blackness, we understand the
vigour and perfection of Christ's lovely and desirable excellencies, that as loveliness and desirableness are in a
man, when in his youth, at their height and perfection, so
are they in Christ, with all commendable aggravations, as
in their prime and vigour. Gold did set forth the intrinsic
worth of Christ's qualifications, this aggravates it so, that
it lifts up that worth to the highest pitch that is con-
ceivable : as a lovely man is yet loveliest in the flower of

his age and youth, so it is with Christ, his perfections are
ever in their flower, and never decay, nor does he ever fail
in the exercising of them for his people's good, Isa. xlii. 4,
" He shall not fail nor be discouraged ;" and, as Rev. i.
12, Christ's eternity is holden forth by white hairs, so by
black hairs is signified his continuing young, vigorous and
flourishing (to say so) through all eternity ; which serves
much to the scope of commending Christ ; for, whatever
is attributed to him, is in an implied way denied to all
other beloveds : otherwise he were not the chiefest among
them, and preferable to them all, which is the scope.
Observ. 1. There is nothing for completing Christ's beauty
but it is in him ; yea, even these things in him, that are
least taken notice of by us (though nothing in him be little
in itself) they are in themselves, and in their use when
discerned, exceeding lovely ; his locks, yea, all his garments are so, Psalm xlv. 8.   There is nothing superfluous,
and useless in our blessed Bridegroom. 2. What perfections are in Christ (as there are none wanting) they
are in him in their perfection ; what unspeakable commendation is here ? 1. He hath infinite numbers of perfections.
2. All these are rich, like the " most fine gold." 3. If
there be a season (to speak so) wherein these perfections
may be conceived more lovely and shining than another
(for in themselves they are ever the same) they are so in
our Lord Jesus Christ ; it is ever harvest, summer and
youth with him ; he is that tree spoken of, Rev. xxii. 2,
which bears fruit always : this Sun is ever at the height,
and never goes down.   Christ's perfections are continuing
perfections ; he is a Beloved that never decays, that never
waxeth sick, weak, nor old ; but is ever in youth, with his
hair black, although he be eternal, and the Ancient of
days, for all his properties are unchangeably in him, and
ever agree to him, even now as well as in Solomon's time,
and will do so for ever : this is good and very comfortable
to his people ; Christ sets not up nor fails ; his Spouse
weeps not for the death, decay, or waxing old of her Beloved and Husband, which can be said of no other. 3.
All other beloveds, besides Christ, are decaying beloveds,
they evanish and are growing gray-headed ; even all this
clay world shall wax " old as doth a garment," and the
beauty of it shall be stained, and it will become weak,
like an old dying harlot, with whom many hath gone a
whoring : for, if this, to be black and bushy, be peculiar

to Christ, it cannot agree to them; for, " they shall wax old," but he is the same, Psalm cii. 27, which words are peculiarly applied to Christ, Heb. i. 10. 4. This continued flourishing of Christ's excellency in its perfection, doth put Christ supereminently above all compare, as having no match amongst all beloveds; they decay, but he is the same; they are broken cisterns, and can hold no water of comfort, and appear with no beauty at death and judgment, and through eternity they will be as clothes worn out and failed ; but Christ is fresh and vigorous at death to the believer, and will be so for ever : how blessed are they, when they come to eat of the tree of life, that never wants fruit, to possess him, who is " yesterday, to-day, and for ever" the same, " God over all, blessed for evermore !" O the happiness ! the eternal happiness, that there is in being espoused to Christ, when the breath of all clay idols and beloveds will be out, and Christ still fresh in the communicating of his fulness to his people! O what a sad heart will many have, who have forsaken this fountain of living waters, aud chosen such broken cisterns to themselves as the creatures are, that have set their heart on " that which is not," Prov. xxiii. 5, and "laboured for the wind," Eccles. v. 16, loading themselves " with thick clay," Hab. ii. 6, and have neglected him who gave, and who continues the being of all things, and who then will be, when they will not be found, or have a being! In sum (saith she) my Beloved is the golden Beloved, others are but of clay and earth; my Beloved is in his flower and youth, other beloveds are decaying, waxing old, and drawing to their grave, therefore is he incomparable beyond them all.

Verse 12.   His eyes are as the eyes of doves by the rivers of water, washed with milk, and fitly set.

THE third thing commended in him, is in verse 12, and it is " his eyes," which are several ways described.   Eyes in the natural body are the organs, whereby we discern external objects : the Lord, as he is a Spirit, hath no body, nor bodily members ; but eyes are attributed to him, to hold forth his omniscience, who, having formed the eye, cannot but see, Psalm xciv. 9, and therefore eminently is said to see, in opposition to the idols, " who have eyes and see not," Psalm cxv. 5.   This, then, sets out our Lord's omniscience, before whom " all things are naked and open," Heb. iv. 3, even the most secret things are

open to his view, as if by the most sharp-sighted bodily
eye he did behold them, and much more; so, Prov. xv. 3,
" The eyes of the Lord are in every place, beholding the
evil and the good :" and, Prov. v. 21, " The ways of man
are before the eyes of the Lord," he knows them, as if he
were looking on them with his eyes, all things are so
naked and discernible to him : this agrees also with that,
Rev. ii. 18, where Christ is said to have " eyes as a flame
of fire :" which title, verse 23, is expounded, (as all the
titles throughout those epistles are) and said to be given
him, that men may know that he " searcheth the heart, and
trieth the reins ;" even the most inward things are fully
reached by his all-seeing eye.

The excellency of his eyes (or omnisciency thereby
pointed out) is held forth under several similitudes, 1.
They are " as doves' eyes," such as were attributed to
the Bride, chap. iv. 1, that is, eyes that are quick, lovely
and loving, having much affection in them to his own. 2.
They are as doves' eyes " by the rivers of water," where
doves are most lovely after washing, or bathing and beek-
ing themselves at river sides. 3. They are washen " with
milk," that is, most clean, white and pure. 4. They are
" fitly set," or (as the word is) set in fulness, like the
stones in Aaron's breast-plate, Exod. xxxix. 10, (where the
same word is) signifying that there is no deformity in them,
but like curious jewels, they are most equally and beautifully set, being neither too hollow, nor sticking too far out,
which are the two extreme deformities in eyes. In sum,
it saith, 1. That Christ's knowledge is sharp and piercing.
2. Pure and clean. 3. Pleasant to his people to look on.
And, 4. That it is kindly vented, and well qualified for
the good of his people, whereby he is made exceeding
lovely to them. These notes are sure here, 1. That our
Lord Jesus is omniscient, knowing all the designs of
enemies, knowing all the straits and necessities of his
people, he actually takes notice of all these. 2. Christ's
omniscience is one of his chiefest excellencies, that qualifies
him for the good and comfort of his people, and doth exceedingly commend him to them above all others : it is a
very pleasant comfort to his people, especially in the time
of trouble, that their Beloved knows all, what we are,
what we have need of, and what is good for us, and what
is designed to our prejudice by any of our adversaries,
and cannot mistake. 3. Christ's omniscience, though it

be terrible to his enemies (so his eyes are as a flame of fire) yet it is very amiable to his people, his eyes to them are as "doves' eyes," his all-seeing knowledge is kindly and comfortable, and exercised for their good (as all his other attributes are) and is still at work for their good and advantage, 2 Chron. xvi. 9, "His eyes run to and fro throughout the earth, to shew himself strong in the behalf of them, whose heart is perfect towards him:" He takes notice of the case of his own, that he may succour them in their wants, as he takes notice of his enemies, that he may disappoint and bring them down. 4. When the tie of the covenant with Christ is once fastened, those attributes in him which are most terrible to flesh and to men in nature, are exceedingly lovely, and make Christ beautiful to his people, as his omniscience, justice, faithfulness, &c. 5. As it is our duty, so it is our advantage to walk under the conviction of Christ's omniscience, and to converse before him with the faith of his beholding what we are doing. 6. It is a good evidence of sincerity, when his omniscience becomes delightsome to us, and when the heart is made glad with this, that Christ knows the secrets thereof, as Peter speaks, John xxi. 17, "Thou that knowest all things, knowest that I love thee:" it is much to abide Christ's search, as omniscient, contentedly. 7. All other idols and beloveds are blind, they have no eyes, or though they seem to have, "they see not," Psalm cxv. 5, that is, they can take no notice of, nor give any succour to, their worshippers. Our Lord's eyes, that are upon his people, make him singularly preferable to all that come in competition with him, 8. It is a singular commendation of Christ's knowledge, that it is pure and holy, that it cannot approve of sin, nor take any complacency in it; for, his eyes are as "doves' eyes, by the rivers of water, washen with milk:" "He is of purer eyes than that he can behold iniquity," O how doth he delight in purity; and what a strong motive may and ought this to be with his people, to make a covenant with their eyes, that they get not leave to wander and gad on sinful objects!

Verse 13.   His cheeks are as a bed of spices, as sweet flowers; his lips like lilies, dropping sweet-smelling myrrh.

THE fourth and fifth instances of Christ's loveliness are in this verse. The fourth is, that "his cheeks are as a bed of spices, as sweet flowers :" the cheeks, being comely, are a special part of the loveliness of the face : his cheeks are here commended from two things, first, they are " as a bed of spices," that is, like garden-beds furnished with excellent smelling and refreshful spices : it sets out, 1. A proportionable height of them, as cheeks are in the face, and as beds are higher than the rest of the ground. 2. A preciousness and sweetness of Spirit-refreshing savour, as such beds use to yield to those who walk in a garden. The second commendation is, " as sweet flowers," or as the words may be read, as flowers of perfume : it tends to the same purpose, but holds forth an abundance of delight, to the spiritual sense of smelling in the believer, when Christ is made the object of it ; O the sweet savour he finds in him ! it is fit to be sober here, these excellencies being mysteries : it is not unlike that lesser glimpses of Christ's manifestations, whereby he makes himself known, may be understood here ; as if she said, he is so lovely, that the least glimpse or waffe of him, when it is seen, if it were but of his cheek, is very delightsome: and this sense may be gathered, 1. From this, that the cheek is a part of the face and countenance, yet not the full countenance ; now by seeing his face and beholding his countenance, often in scripture (and it is like also, verse 15,) is understood his most sensible manifestations of himself to his people ; by proportion then the cheeks would hold forth the same, though in a lesser measure and lower degree. 2. It makes well for the scope of commending Christ above all, whose incomparable worth by his manifestations, is much evidenced and confirmed to his people, and when a little glimpse of him doth this, how much more would a full view of him demonstrate it ? and indeed such a view doth effectually demonstrate it to those who have experimentally known the excellency that is in him, although others who are unaquaint with his face, do therefore undervalue him, which may be hinted at as a cause of their so doing. 3. This agrees with the commendation, which sets him forth in this as pleasant to the spiritual sense of smelling, and so would imply, that it must be somewhat whereby Christ becomes sensibly sweet and refreshful, as his sensible manifestations make him more delightsome and refreshing to the soul's senses, than flowers of perfume are to the bodily senses ; therefore is his love compared to " ointment," chap. i. 3, and elsewhere : however, these things are certain, 1. That the least glimpse of Christ's countenance is exceeding refreshful and savoury to the spiritual senses. 2. That Christ's excellencies are delightsome to all the spiritual senses, to the smell as well as to the eye, ear, &c. The whole soul, and all its faculties have abundant matter in him, for delighting and refreshing them all. 3. The more senses be exercised on Christ, and the more sensible (to speak so) he become unto us, he will be the more lovely and pleasant: beds of spices, and flowers of perfume in a garden, to them that lie amongst them, are not so savoury as Christ is, when the senses of the soul are exercised to discern him.

The fifth thing instanced is "his lips;" the bride's lips were spoken of, chap. iv. 3, 11. and cleared to signify her speech: by proportion they hold forth in him the loveliness of his word, wherein he is especially lovely, in that he magnifies it above all his name, Psalm cxxxviii. 2, and makes it often sweet as the honey and the honeycomb to his people. This may be looked on, 1. As it respects the matter spoken by him, out of whose mouth many gracious words proceeded (while in the flesh) even to the admiration of his hearers, Luke iv. 22, so that upon conviction they say, never man spoke as this man speaks, John vii. 46. Or, 2. It may look to Christ's manner of speaking, and his fitness to communicate his mind to his people (as lips are the organs of speaking) so he hath "grace poured into his lips" Psalm xlv. 2, that makes all his words gracious, as being formed or anointed by it. Thus it takes in that holy art, skill, and dexterity, wherewith Christ is furnished, to speak for the consolation of a believer, especially under sad exercises; as it is, Isa. l. 4. "He hath the tongue of the learned, to speak a word in season to him that is weary:" both these in the result come to one; and this being a special piece of Christ's loveliness to his people, conducing exceedingly to the bride's scope here, and the analogy being clear, and lips being frequently made use of in scripture to signify speech or words, we conceive that they may well be taken so here, especially considering, that all the parts of the commendation will agree well to his words. 1. They are "like lilies," that is, pleasant and savoury; so words spoken in season are often called pleasant and sweet like honey, Prov. xvi. 24, yea, they are said to be "like apples of gold in pictures of silver," Prov. xxv. 11. His words then may well be compared to lilies. 2. They are not common words, therefore it must not be ordinary lilies that will set them forth; but they are like "lilies dropping sweet-smelling myrrh:" such lilies we are not acquaint with; and nature though excellent in its effects, yet comes short in furnishing fit resemblances to represent Christ, and what is in him, to the full. These "lilies dropping myrrh" signify, 1. A savouriness and cordial efficacy in the matter, like myrrh proving comfortable to those it falls or drops upon. 2. "Dropping" shews abundance, seasonableness, and continuedness therein, so as he still furnisheth such strengthening efficacy and influence, as if it were ever dropping, and never dried up; as the phrase was, chap. iv. 11. All these agree well, either to Christ the speaker, who never wants a seasonable word; or to the word spoken, which, in respect of its effects, endures for ever.

This must be an excellent Beloved (saith she) who speaks much, and never a word falls from his lips, but it is precious and savoury, like any cordial to the souls of his people, especially in their fainting fits; and there is ever some good word to be gotten from him, far from the rough speeches that many use, but O, so pleasant and kindly as all his words are! *Observ.* 1. There is a special loveliness in our Lord Jesus' words to to his people; how much of this appears throughout the 4th chapter of this Song? and what love appears in all his promises! yea, in the titles that he gives to his people, every one is (as it were) big with child of strong consolation to them. 2. Christ's words have a special refreshing efficacy in them, and can comfort, refresh and sustain drooping sick souls; he sends out his word and it healeth them. 3. Those who love Christ himself truly, have also an high esteem of his word, and are much delighted with that; and where there is little esteem of his word, there is but little esteem of himself: they who have tasted the sweetness of the word, do highly esteem of Christ himself. 4. The word of Christ is as Christ's own lips, and doth sweetly set out his thoughts of love to sinners; it is good reading of Christ's loveliness out of his own word, and from his own mouth. 5. Where there hath been a sweetness felt in the word, it should be turned over to the commendation of Christ that spoke it, as a proof of the reality of his excellent worth. 6. The word is never rightly made use of, though it should fill the head with knowledge, till it be savoury to the inward man and spiritual senses; and it is that which makes it lovely, when the virtue and consolation that flows from it is felt.   7. All the consolations of the word, they come not out at once, neither can we so receive them, but it drops by little and little in continuance; and therefore daily should men draw from these wells of salvation.   8. Observe from the scope, that Christ's word, known by experience, will lift and set Christ up in the heart beyond all beloveds; and that the unacquaintedness of many with Christ's lips, and the consolations that abound in his word, makes them so ready to slight him, and set up their idols above him. The scope saith further, that she was acquaint with his words, and the refreshfulness of them, and in this she is differenced from others.   Whence, *Observe*, 9. That believers are acquaint with the sweetness of Christ's words, otherwise than any in the world are; Christ is another thing to them, and his word is so also, than to all the world beside: it is a good sign, where Christ's lips are so lovely.

Verse 14. His hands are as gold rings set with the beryl; his belly is as bright ivory overlaid with sapphires.

THE sixth and seventh particulars instanced to commend Christ, are in verse 14.   The sixth is, "his hands:" the hands are the instruments of action, as the lips are of speaking: they are commended that they are as "gold rings," that is, as men or women's hands are adorned with gold rings, so his hands have a native loveliness beyond these: yet, this commendation (as all the former) answers not fully, therefore it is added, they are "set with beryl:" this was a precious stone put in Aaron's breast-plate, Exod. xxxix. 13.   To be "set" with it, signifies, as preciousness, so rare artifice; and such is seen in the right setting of precious stones.

By our Lord's hands, may be understood that powerful activity whereby he is fitted to bring about what he pleaseth, and that power which he exerciseth especially in the works of grace, as on verse 4, was cleared: or, we may understand the effects produced by that his power, or his works which are exceeding glorious; as, Psalm cix. 27, "That they may know, O Lord, that this is thy hand," that is, "that thou, Lord, hast done it."   So his hands

signify such works especially, wherein his divine power,
art and skill do manifest themselves for the good of his
people : both agree well together ; for, excellent power
and skill produce excellent effects, and excellent effects
demonstrate the excellent qualifications of the worker.
This being a main piece of Christ's commendation, and
which doth hold him forth to be exceeding lovely above
all to the believer, (which is the scope) may well be taken
here as the meaning, especially being subjoined to the
commendation of his words : for, our Lord Jesus doth
not only say well, but also doth well ; he is a "prophet,
mighty both in word and deed," Luke xxiv. 19.

The commendation suits with his works, as if there were
none of them but what are adorned (as it were) with excellent gold rings, there being much glory, grace, wisdom,
and skill shining in them all ; they are " honourable and
glorious," Psalm cxi. 3, yea, " great and marvellous are the
works of the Lord God almighty," Rev. xv. 4.   These
are the deserved epithets of his actions : in sum, it is, as
if she had said, Ask ye what my Beloved is, more than
others ?   If ye saw but a glimpse of the white and red
that is in his cheeks, and if ye heard the sweet words that
proceed from his mouth, and if ye knew the excellent
works which he hath performed, even to admiration, for
the good of his people, and how much loveliness appears
in all these, ye would (no doubt) say with me, He is the
chiefest among ten thousand.

Observ. 1. Christ is an active husband, having hands,
and working with them for the good of his Bride : a piece
of his work we heard of chap. iii. 9, in that noble chariot :
he is no idle spectator ; he " worketh hitherto," John v.
17.   2. All our Lord Jesus his works, are exceeding excellent and beautiful, and when rightly discerned, they
will appear wonderful, honourable, and glorious, as proceeding from him " who is wonderful in counsel, and
excellent in working," Isa. xxviii. 29.   What a curious
and excellent piece of work is that chariot, or the covenant of redemption signified thereby, chap. iii. 9.   There
are many shining well set jewels, and rings upon every
finger of his hands : there is nothing that can be done
better than what he hath done.   The works of Christ, in
our redemption, do hold forth infinite skill, and glorious-
ness to be in the worker, all of them are so wisely contrived and exquisitely executed.   3. Christ's works do ex-

ceedingly endear him, and that deservedly to his people, and do infallibly demonstrate his worth above all beloveds in the world; who is like unto him? and who can do great works, such as he hath done? This makes heaven to resound with the praises of what this beloved hath done for his people. 4. Believers should be acquaint both with Christ's words and works, and should be well versed in the knowledge of the excellencies that are in them both, that so they may be the more affected with him themselves, and be more able to commend him to others. 5. Where Christ is lovely, all his works will be delightsome: and it is by acquaintance with, and observation of, his excellent works, that the hearts of his people come to take him up, and to be rightly affected with him. 6. As ignorance of the excellency of Christ's works (especially of the work of redemption) makes many slight Christ, and prefer others to him (for, she would discover the daughters of Jerusalem their mistake of him, by instancing this among other things) so it is a kindly-like thing to have an honourable esteem of Christ's works in the heart. 7. Although the devil and mens' idols seem to promise much to their lovers, when they suit and entice them: yet never one indeed can equal Christ, or compare with him in respect of what he hath done for his Bride; and this sets him up incomparably above them all: his hands, in respect of his magnificent works, are adorned, as it were, with gold rings; whereas they have hands, but work not for the help and relief of their lovers. Psalm cxv. vii.

The seventh part of this demonstration of Christ's worth is from his "belly:" the word in the original is the same word, which verse 4, is rendered bowels, and we rather use it so here as it signifieth bowels, in the native signification of it, as not knowing why it should be altered in this verse; especially considering, that whatever it is attributed to God, it is translated bowels, as, Isa lxiii. 15, "where is the sounding of thy bowels?" and, Jer. xxxi. 20, "my bowels are moved for him:" reading it then thus, "his bowels are as bright ivory," &c. The words at the very first, would seem to signify the intense love and tender affection, wherewith our Lord Jesus (who is full of grace) is filled and stuffed (to say so) for the behoof and good of his people; so that no mother is so compassionately affected towards the fruit of her womb, as he is towards his own. This exposition is confirmed, 1. From the ordi-

nary signification of the word bowels, when it is applied
to God, as, Isa. lxiii. 15, and Jer. xxxi. 20, and it is
borrowed from the affection that mothers have to their
children, whose bowels yearn on them, as, 1 Kings iii. 26.
and so Joseph was affected toward his brethren, Gen.
xliii. 30 Hence the word, both in the Hebrew and
Greek, in the Old and New Testament, which is made
use of to set forth the Lord's tender compassion, flows
from a root that signifieth bowels. 2. The scope will
confirm this : for, is there any thing that makes Christ
more lovely and admirable than his love? which makes
the prophet cry out, Mic. vii. 18, " who is a God like unto
thee, that pardoneth iniquity ?" &c. " because thou delight-
est in mercy ;" or, is there any other thing that more commends him as a Beloved preferable to all, than his love ?
love in a husband is a special property. Now " Christ
loved his church and gave himself for it," Eph. v. 25, it
is not like therefore, that this is omitted : and, 3. It follows well on the commendation of his works for, and
about his people, as shewing the fountain from whence
they proceed : the commendation of this is excellent. 1.
It is as " bright ivory :" ivory is rarely and singularly
pure, and pleasant, being made of elephants' teeth: "bright,"
is added, to shew, that it is of the best sort, as all that is
in Christ is. 2. It is " overlaid with sapphires ;" that was
a stone in Aaron's breast-plate, and also is reckoned one
of the foundation stones of the " New Jerusalem," Rev.
xxi. 19, which shews, that it is very precious, though we
know not the particular properties of it : the word " overlaid," may be from the original rendered curiously set,
or, enameled : in sum, here, his love is described as most
lovely, clean and pleasant, like ivory ; rich and precious
like sapphires ; and well ordered and wisely vented for
the good of his people, as bright ivory curiously enameled
with sapphires : his love is a most excellent, curious, and
pleasant object, the like whereof is not to be found amongst
all the beloveds in the world. This verse commends
Christ's heart and inside, which is unsearchable as to its
height, depth, breadth, and length : it may therefore be
hard, and someway hazardous to offer doctrines on, or to
form expressions concerning, that " which passeth knowledge," Eph iii. 18, 19, the comprehending experimental
knowledge of it will be the best commentary on it ; yet
these things are clear and safe.

1. There is singular love, affection, and bowels in our
Lord Jesus to his people; so singular, that there is none
can compare with him in this, no husband, nay nor wife,
it passeth the love of women; no tender hearted mother,
and much less any idol can compete with him in this; it
is inconceivable in itself, and it is wonderful in its effects.
2. There is nothing that will contribute to make believers
see Jesus Christ as admirable in himself, and lovely to
them, than right apprehension of his love: this is the
constraining, ravishing, engaging, and soul-inebriating
consideration of Christ, the conceiving of him rightly in
his admirable love; and they will never esteem of Christ
rightly, who discern not that; it is (as it were) his
crown: and the believing of it, is in a sort the putting the
crown on his head. Amongst all his excellencies, none
takes the believer more up than his love: and nothing is
more remarkable in him than that; and right thoughts of
Christ's love is no ill token. 3. Our Lord Jesus his love
and bowels are a rich jewel when seen, a precious stately
sight; "bright ivory overlaid with sapphires" is but a
small and dark shadow of it; Christ's love is a possession
beyond jewels, a very beautiful object to look on, beyond
the most excellent creature: it is both a wonder and a
heart-break that it is so little thought of, and that men are
not more delighted in it. 4. Although there be much in
many mouths of Christ's love, yet there are few that really
know and believe the love that he hath to his people,
1 John iii. 1. As this is the cause that so few love him,
and why so many set up other beloveds beside him; so
the solid faith of this, and the expectation of good from
him, hath a great engaging virtue to draw sinners to him,
Heb. xi. 6, and for that end it is made use of here. 5.
Whatever seeming smiles idols may give to their lovers,
yet will they not prove lovers in the end to them; for,
that is proper to Christ, he only hath strong love and
bowels of affection to his own to the end, but other lovers
in the end will fail men, only our Lord Jesus continueth
a loving husband to the end: for, whom he loves he loves
to the end. 6. It is, beyond all peradventure, good and
desirable to be matched with Jesus Christ, where so much
honour, riches, power, wisdom, loveliness, and love, meet
all together; for, the scope of this, and of all the rest of
the commendations, is to engage sinners to match with
him. 7. There is no cause to be jealous of Christ's love,

his people have a most loving husband, and never a spot
or ground of jealousy hath defiled his bowels since the
world began, but they to this day are, and will be for
ever "as bright ivory." 8. Christ's love is excellent in
itself, and is also excellent in the way of communicating
itself to his people; therefore it is not as sapphires that
are confusedly casten together, but that are artificially
set; or, our Lord Jesus vents not his love fondly (to
speak with reverence) or imprudently, but most wisely,
skilfully, and seasonably, so as it may be for the good of
his people; not as a fond and too indulgent mother, that
gives that which is even hurtful because the child desires
it, but as a wise father who gives that which is useful,
though it be unpleasant: he guides his love by discretion,
and according to expediency, as John xvi. 7, " It is
expedient for you that I go," and therefore he will go,
though they were even made sad with it. 9. Although
some pieces of Christ's love, being considered in themselves, seem not so pleasant and lovely, like precious stones
not rightly set, yet when all are seen together, and every
thing taken up as in its own place, and proportionably
corresponding with one another, and especially in respect
of the fountain of love from which they come, they will
then (being all looked on together) be seen to be very
beautiful and pleasant and well ordered, like " bright
ivory," that is regularly and curiously enameled, or in-
dented with sapphires: the time comes, when Christ's
love will be thought to be exquisitely and wisely let out
and conveyed, even in these things wherein it is most
suspected now by his own.

Verse 15.   His legs are as pillars of marble set upon sockets of
   fine gold; his countenance is as Lebanon, excellent as the
   cedars:

THE eighth and ninth particulars of Christ's commendation are in verse 15. The first of them here commended is " his legs:" the word " legs," comes from a
root in the original, that signifieth to walk; and so takes
in thighs and feet, which are also useful in motion. In
scripture, and by analogy, they are made use of to signify
these two, 1. A man's way in the series of his carriage
and deportment, as ordinarily his life is called a walk:
so, Eccl. v. 1. " Take heed unto thy feet," that is, to thy

carriage ; hence the "iniquities of the heels" are spoken of, Psalm. xlix. 5, to set out men's defects, that cleave to them in their conversation, as their feet leave prints and footsteps behind them in their walking. 2. This metaphor signifieth strength and activity, Psalm cxlvii. 10, " The Lord delights not in the strength of an horse, nor in the legs of a man ;" wherefore (very probably) Eccl. xii. 3, they are called " the strong men," because they sustain or bear up the body : here being applied to Christ, we conceive they signify his way, or administration of providence, which he useth with his people, it being by his dispensations that he walks amongst them. Hence the series of common providence is so often in scripture called the way of the Lord, as Ezek. xviii. 26, " The Lord's way is equal," his carriage in his dispensations is still just, opposite to their way or walk, which is there called unequal : and the dispensation of grace is called a way, Rom. xi. 33, " How unsearchable are his judgments and his ways past finding out ?" which take in the contrivance, and administration of his grace, as the scope there doth clear. His way is more general and comprehensive than his works, and takes in these three (for which it is called, a way.) 1. His design and end, that he proposeth to himself. 2. His wise and powerful plot in contriving and applying means suitable thereunto, for bringing it about, especially the principle (to say so) by which he walks and works, to wit, his wisdom, power and love. 3. His convoy of, and the progress which he makes in these by which he is ever proceeding towards his end, as a man doth in his way by walking with his legs : in all these respects, the Lord's way of carrying on his design is said to be unsearchable : this we take as intended here, to set forth and commend the gracious and glorious steps of the Lord, in the administration of his grace, both in its contrivance and application amongst his people, whereby his wisdom, power, and goodness are in these paths of his (that are all mercy and truth to his own, Psalm xxv. 10,) made exceeding lovely and stately, as the commendation following imports. This is confirmed, 1. By the analogy that is betwixt the legs and walking, and the frequent use that the scripture makes of this similitude for that end, and no other thing can suit so well. 2. In Rev. ii. 18, where Christ's legs and feet are spoken of, with a commendation not unlike what follows here, namely, that

they are "like fine brass," as his eyes are expounded,
verse 23, by this, that " he searcheth the heart, and trieth
the reins ;" so his feet are set out by this, " that he renders
to every one according to his works," that is, he keeps an
equal and just way in his administration towards every
one. 3. The scope likewise confirms this, Christ being
by his way to his people commendable above all, and this
being a special commendation of his, that " all his works
are perfect, and all his ways are judgment," Deut. xxxii.
4. As also the property attributed to his legs, and from
which they are commended, will clear this, which is, that
they " are like pillars of marble :" marble is a stone that
is firm, good and pleasant, therefore was it prepared by
David, for the temple, 1 Chron. xxix. 2 ; " pillars" signify strength, orderliness and beauty, as was cleared on
chap. iii. 10, which may be applied here : so pillars of
marble say, that his ways are curiously, skilfully, and
sickerly contrived ; and wisely, dexterously and infallibly
executed, and firmly settled like pillars, and that of marble, for unmoveableness : the amplification of the commendation confirms this also; they are not only like pillars
of marble, but also like pillars " set on sockets of fine
gold." Pillars are durable, according to the basis or
foundation upon which they are set and founded, now
gold (as often hath been said) signifieth preciousness and
solidity, so all of them are settled and fixed on a good and
precious ground, which cannot fail, therefore they cannot
shake, slide, nor slip, but prosper he must in his ways, and
nothing can mar his design, " for he is of one mind, and
who can turn him? and what his soul desireth, that he
doth," Job xxiii. 13. Yet not only are his feet or legs of
brass, (which shews severity against enemies, in his treading
on them, Dan x. 6) but the sockets are of gold, as his head
was, verse 11. all is of gold that is in him, he is a golden
Mediator and Beloved from head to foot, whereas others
are clay beloveds : the sockets are of gold, to shew his
graciousness to his people, as Psalm xxv. 10, all his ways
are settled on mercy and truth, all his decrees anent them
are made lovely and sure by grace, and so cannot be but
precious and excellent as to them.

Observ. 1. Our Lord Jesus hath a design, a gracious
design, that he is carrying on amongst his people, and he
is ever promoving therein for the end which he hath proposed ; he is not like the idols of the Gentiles, Psalm cxv.

7, "which have feet and walk not," but as he sees with his eyes, and works with his hands, so doth he walk and make progress with his legs. 2. Christ's way with his people is a most excellent and stately way; or, in all his convoy of grace towards his people, there is a special excellency shining ; "all his ways and works are holy and righteous," Psalm cxlv. 17; "just and true," Rev. xv. 3. Gracious and loving, even "all mercy and truth," Psalm xxv. 10. This King of saints is marvellous in his way of grace, as he is in all his works. 3. Christ's purpose cannot fail, neither can his design be altered, the contrivance thereof is so wise, and the execution so powerful, he cannot but attain his point. 4. However men may quarrel with Christ's way, and say it is "not equal," as Ezek. xviii. 25. And although his way may be sometimes "in the deep waters," and not discernible, Psalm lxxvii. 19, yet it is ever ordered in deep wisdom, that there can be nothing more just, holy and glorious, so that there is no reason to complain thereof; and this holds, not only in one step or two, but in the whole series of his way. 5. A right sight of Christ's wise, glorious, and omnipotent way of grace, will make him singular in the estimation of his people, and put him above all other beloveds, whose ways are neither for wisdom, nor stability, any way comparable to his; for, all the counsels and designs of the world beside his, will come to nought, and be made, nill they will they, subservient to his; clay idols have their breath in their nostrils, and in that same very day " when it goeth out, their thoughts perish," Psalm cxlvi. 4, but it is not so with his, they are more solidly founded, and these strong legs, that are of marble, can neither be bowed nor broken: it must then be most sure and safe for the Lord's people to drive this as their design, to side and share with Christ in his designs; and it must be a most desperate thing to drive contrary designs to him, whose "legs are as pillars of marble," and before whom none can stand. 6. Where there is respect to Christ, there will be an high estimation of his way ; and it is a good sign of an especial esteem of Christ, when his ways are admired and loved.

The ninth particular instance, brought to prove that he is the chiefest among ten thousand, is, that "his countenance is like Lebanon:" the word "countenance," as it is in the original, comes from a root that signifieth to see,

therefore countenance is used in scripture, not only to
signify the face, but the whole stature and presentation
of a person, or that which gives a full sight of one in all
his parts together; and so it is here, and differs from the
cheeks mentioned, verse 13, as being more extensive and
comprehensive: therefore that phrase, which, 2 Sam. xxii.
12, is rendered a goodly man, or man of countenance
(as it is in the original) is, 1 Chron. xi. 23, (where that
same story is recorded) expressed by this, that the Egyptian was a man of stature, as if it were said, a brave per-
sonage of a man, and so it takes in face, legs, body and
altogether, when all these are so proportioned, as they
make one a person goodly to be seen and looked on: now
this being applied to Christ, as subjoined to the particulars formerly mentioned, we conceive it takes in his matchless stateliness, as it results from all his properties together: so that not only this or that part of Christ is
lovely, but whole Christ, when seen, is exceedingly stately
and lovely to the view and faith of a discerning believer,
whatever, others think of him; so then, the meaning is,
—Ask ye what my Beloved is? (saith she) as all his parts
are beautiful, severally considered, so all being put together, he is a most stately and lovely object to behold,
when he gives a full view of his countenance.   It sets
out then, a more full view of Christ, or Christ in a more
full view, as if not only a man's head or legs were seen,
but his whole stature, whereby he is more fully discernible: thus Christ's countenance in scripture, is put to signify his manifestations to his people; and here, being
subjoined to the cheeks, as more extensive, it signifieth
more full manifestations, whereby a view (as it were) of
whole Christ is attained at once, by the believer's faith;
as, by faith, Heb. xi. 27, Moses is said to have seen him
that is invisible: and this will agree well with the scope,
and the commendation following, which is in two things,
1. It is "as Lebanon," a most pleasant, stately hill; and
therefore, that which is excellent, is often compared to it,
as was said on chap. iv. 8, 11, 15.   2. It is amplified, that
it is "excellent, as the cedars:" they were useful, stately,
and tall trees, especially those that grew in Lebanon;
the word is, elect, or choice as the cedars, which agrees
well with a goodly presentation, to be tall, straight and
stately, as they were: therefore the Bride's stature, is
compared to a palm-tree, chap. vii. 7.   In a word, my

Beloved (when seen) looks excellently and passing well (saith she) so as there is no other beloved in the world, that hath such an aspect as he; who can look on him and not love him?

Observ. 1. Although there is no fully comprehensive view of Christ to be gotten here, even by the faith of a believer (while we are upon the earth we cannot see him as he is, that being reserved for heaven) yet there are more full uptakings of him attainable, even here-away, than ordinarily believers meet with; yea, such full views of him are to be had, which in respect of our other ordinary attainments, may be called, a beholding of his countenance, whereas these are but a beholding of his cheeks; for, he hath a countenance which is discernible: neither doth the Bride speak of that she never saw, but of what she hath seen; and it imports a more full, near, thorough and distinct sight of him than is usual. 2. There is no such lovely, delightsome, spiritually gallant, stately and glorious object, as our Lord Jesus, complexly considered as in himself; and there will be no sight more satisfying to a believer than this, when admitted to behold it. 3. All other beloveds, whatever they be in themselves, are yet exceedingly, nay, infinitely short of him, when he is seen; this differenceth him from them all, the more and the better other beloveds be seen, they are found to be the more feckless, insignificant and little worth; but the more full view be gotten of Christ, he is found to be the more excellent. 4. Slight and passing views of Christ, make men think the less of him, whereas more full, distinct and near beholding of him doth heighten the esteem of him, and lessen the esteem of all others beside him. 5. Faith in Christ will make a real impression of him, and of his excellency upon the heart of a believer, even as if he had been seen by sense: therefore she speaks so of his countenance; and it is a good sign, to be distinct and confident in our apprehensions of Christ's excellencies.

Verse 16. His mouth is most sweet; yea, he is altogether lovely. This is my Beloved, and this is my Friend, O daughters of Jerusalem.

THE tenth and last particular, commended in him, is in the beginning of the 16th verse, and it is " his mouth," which is compared to " sweetness" or sweetnesses in the plural number. By "mouth" sometimes is understood the words of the mouth, but it is not so used in this Song. The Bride's words, and his also, are set out by their lips, and it is not like, that that being spoken of, verse 13, is repeated here. Again, the "mouth," and its "sweetness" especially, may be mentioned to signify friendliness and love, or ra- rather the sensible manifestations of these, as the husband doth by kissing his wife ; and in this sense is taken, chap. i. 2, and we take that to be aimed at here, to wit, the sweet- ness of Christ's more immediate manifestations of himself unto the spiritual sense of his people, by "shedding the love of God abroad in their hearts, by the Holy Ghost," Rom. v. 5. For, this sensible manifestation of his love is a thing that much commends him to his people, and is their satisfaction, in opposition to all the creature satisfactions that others have, Psalm iv. 6, 7, therefore it agrees well with the scope. Again, it is a different commendation from any that is mentioned, 1. It differs from his "lips," or the comfort that one hath from the word, as from the word (though it is not to be separated from that, but to carry that along with it) yet this is more immediate and sensible, and that is mediate, though real and sure unto faith. 2. It differs from seeing "his cheeks," in that this is more full, near and immediate also, she being, as it were, admitted to enjoy Christ's sweet embracements. 3. It differs from "beholding his countenance," because that may be, and only can be taken up by faith, beholding him in his excellent qualifications and offices ; but this is dis- cernible to the believer's spiritual sense, when Christ ap- plieth his love, as chap. i. 2. In which (to say so) we are more passive, as being fed by him, and having it infused and shed abroad in our hearts by the Spirit. If we may in a holy way follow the similitude in a spiritual sense (which is necessary for understanding of the thing) "kisses of his mouth" are his applying and venting of his love, as one doth by kissing another ; this also will agree with the commendation, it is "most sweet," it is but one word in the original, in the abstract, and that in the plural number, "sweetnesses," to shew the exceeding sweetness and loveliness, the soul-ravishing delight that is in that, to which no similitude or comparison can come up, clearly and perfectly to resemble it, it is very sweetness itself. If we might allude to what Philosophers say of fire in its element, or water in its element, that being there, they are more properly and eminently fire and water; so sweetness is in its element here; or, Christ's mouth is the very element thereof, in respect of its sensible refreshfulness to the spiritual senses of his people, to whom he manifests it. Ask ye then what my Beloved is? (saith she) he is indeed stately to look on; but his mouth, when it is felt in his kissing of his own Bride, by manifesting his love to her sense, there, there, O there, exceeding, unexpressible and unconceivable, delight and satisfaction is to be found!

Observ. 1. Christ hath more near and sensible ways of manifesting himself to the spiritual sense of his people, as if he had a mouth to kiss them. 2. There is nothing comparable to the refreshing sweetness, that these manifestations have with them; it is " a peace that passeth understanding, Phil. iv. 7, and a "joy that is unspeakable and full of glory," 1 Pet. i. 8. 3. This sensible feeling of the sweetness of Christ's mouth, should be aimed at, and sought after by believers; although the manner, measure, time, and other circumstances thereof, should be submitted to him; yet this is not only commendable in itself, but also, as such, is proposed and commended to the daughters of Jerusalem, to be sought after by them. 4. The experimental feeling of this, doth notably demonstrate Christ's worth to the soul that enjoys it, and makes him incomparably sweet and lovely above all things whatsoever, Psalm iv. 7. 5. There is no other thing can have any such sweetness or relish to a believer as Christ hath; and to a spiritual taste, the excellency of all created beloveds will be as the white of an egg in comparison of this. Only Christ's mouth is sweetness; and so he differs from all others: and it is a good sign, when our affections, or spiritual senses, can relish nothing but Christ.

Next, it is added, " yea, he is altogether lovely." Although she hath spent many sweet words (and indeed there hath been no straitening in her) in commending Christ, and although all her words be sweet, and especially when she draws near the close, her expressions be the more massy and significant, yet as being necessitated to succumb under the great task of describing the excellency of her Beloved, she must give over particulars, and conclude with a general, as if she would say, Would ye know him? O, I, even I cannot tell you all his excellent properties: for, he is most justly called " Wonderful," Isa. ix. 6, but in sum, I may say, " he is altogether lovely :" the word is, " he is all desires," or, " all he desires :" the word that is rendered " lovely," comes from a root that signifieth to covet, as in Josh. vii 21. it is said of Achan, when he saw the "wedge of gold," that he coveted it, so it is such a desire as ardently covets the thing desired : and thus Christ is not simply lovely, but of such an attractive excellency, as makes him the proper object of the most ardent and holy-coveting desires, or after which all desires should go forth, as towards the best and most desirable object ; the words are meant to express somewhat that is not expressible, or rather the unexpressibleness of that Beloved she had been commending, lest they should think she were satisfied, as if she had fully described him.   We may consider the words several ways, 1.   Negatively, as they shew there is nothing in him, but what is desirable : as if she said, " all he is desires," there is nothing of any other nature in him, but such as I have mentioned, he is a " God of truth, and without iniquity, just and right is he."   2. Take them positively, and so they shew whatever is in him is exceedingly desirable ; go through all his parts, qualifications, attributes and works, whereof I have given you but a hint (saith she) and ye will see them all exceedingly desirable.   3.   Take them conclusively or comprehensively, and so while she saith, " he is all desires," the meaning is, there is nothing truly desirable, but it is to be found in him, the soul cannot rationally imagine that satisfaction that is not to be found in Christ, otherwise all desires were not in him : this is sweet, even very sweet ; what idol is perfect ? there are many defects in all other beloveds, but (saith she) my Beloved is perfect : all the beauties and perfections that are scattered among all creatures, are in an eminent and transcendent way gathered together, contracted and to be found in him at once, so that whatever can be desired, whether it be for this life, or that which is to come, whether for sanctification justification, or consolation, it is eminently to be found in our Lord Jesus, " in whom all fulness dwells," Col. i. 19, and who alone is " all and in all" to his own, as being " full of grace and truth," John i. 14.   4.   We may take them exclusively, or privately, as they deny any thing desirable to to be in any beloved, but in Christ ; he is all, and so consequently they must be nothing, he is altogether lovely, and so they must be altogether loathsome : Christ is never rightly conceived of, nor commended, but where other things come down, evanish and disappear, when compared with him; " Whom have I in heaven but thee? and I desire none on earth beside thee," saith the Psalmist, Psalm lxx. 25, as having full satisfaction, and all that can be wished for in him. It is hard to observe what may be suitable to Christ's loveliness, when the Bride gives it over: but we may say, 1. The more that believers insist on Christ's loveliness, their hearts will warm the more with it, and it will be found to be the greater depth; for, now her expressions grow, till at last they be swallowed up. 2. Where there is true respect to Christ, no commendation of Christ that believers can invent (whatever it be) will be satisfying to them : for, there have been, 1. Many excellent commendations given of Christ, as being like gold, myrrh, spices, &c. Yea, 2. Like such gold, lilies and ivory, as are not in the world; and finally she hath left and given over comparisons, and betaken herself to the abstract, sweetness itself; yet all comes short, and she must quit the thing as unexpressible : it is the very height of soul's love-rhetoric, to close with a kind of holy amazement and admiration, which ends in silence, because they cannot say enough, when they have said all they can say. O what a lovely object then must Christ Jesus be! They never knew him rightly, who were satisfied with their own apprehensions of him, or expressions concerning him. 3. There is an universal loveliness in Christ, whole Christ is lovely, neither is he to be divided in our apprehension and esteem, but as every thing in him is wonderful and lovely, so is it to be admired and loved; even his lowest sufferings, and seeming infirmities, his frowns and seeming greater. austerity, are lovely and profitable ; he is altogether lovely. 4. There is a wonderful desirableness in our Lord Jesus, and incomparable satisfaction to be gotten in him ; there can be nothing more to draw a soul to love it, than what is here ; whatever may be attractive, is here ; and there is nothing wanting to satisfy the soul that enjoys him, and hath yielded to his call; to such he is all desires. 5. Christ is never rightly taken up, so long as any thing desirable is supposed to be gotten elsewhere, he must be all desires : and therefore, where any thing hath the least share of the affections beside him, he hath not his own place. 6. Empty and undesirable are all beloveds in the world beside Christ, and broken cisterns will they all prove; and it is no marvel; for, all desires are in him, and therefore, not one desirable thing is or can be found in them. 7. They have a good bargain who have Christ; it is the short cut (to say so) and compendious way to happiness, and to the inheriting of all things, to unite with Christ by faith, and to possess him; for, all desires are in him; and miserable will the persons be who shall miss Christ, although they were gainers of the whole world.

Having somewhat answered the daughters of Jerusalem their question, by insisting in this excellent description of Christ, now by way of application and holy boasting, in the close of the verse, she reasons thus: ye asked what my Beloved was more than other beloveds? and for your satisfaction, I have described him as I can, many several ways, though all fall very short of full expressing of his matchless worth: now (saith she) this excellent person is "my Beloved, and this is my friend, O daughters of Jerusalem;" bring all other beloveds, and compare them with him, and see if he be not the chiefest and standard-bearer amongst them all; and in this confident boasting of the excellency of her Beloved, she closes: which sweet discourse wants not its fruit on them, as we will see in the chapter following.

Consider the words four ways, 1. In the matter, they hold forth two sweet relations betwixt Christ and the believer, and this sweetens all, not only that this Beloved is an excellent person, but that he was hers, she saith, he "is my Beloved," and also "my friend;" he is her friend (as she is his friend, verse 1,) that is, one that is friendly to her, and will do for her, beyond what a brother, or mother, or the nearest of all relations will or can do; he is one that is born for the day of her adversity, and one whom she trusts as her own soul, he is so dear to her, and she to him; for, this tie of friendship is mutual betwixt them. In a word (saith she) he is much in himself, and much to me, unspeakably excellent in himself, and very dear and precious to me, my husband, and my friend: in sum, my friendly husband, and my loving friend.

Observ. 1. There are many sweet relations that Christ stands in to the believer, as husband, friend, brother, &c. even as there are many relations that she stands in to him, as spouse, sister, dove, &c. 2. Christ fills all the relations that he stands in to his people, and that exceedingly well; he is a singularly loving, faithful, kind and tender husband;

and a singularly kind, faithful and unchangeable friend, the best friend that ever a believer had ; for, the expression, "this is," &c. saith, that what Christ is, he is indeed, and singularly so, as having no equal, he is a matchless husband and friend : this is the scope. 3. Christ and the believer are upon one side, they are friends, there is a league of friendship betwixt them, and they have common friends, and common adversaries. 4. Those who are Christ's friends, (as verse 1. "eat, O friends") Christ may be claimed by them as their friend, and what that can infer, they may expect from him ; for, he hath no bare title, neither sustains he any empty relation. 5. Believers should lean much to Christ, trust him, and expect good from him, as their friend. 6. It is a notable and singular consolation for folks to have Christ their friend, it is comfortable in life, death, and judgment, in prosperity and adversity, it implies these things in which he is forthcoming to his friends, 1. Constant kindness and faithfulness at all times, " he loves at all times," Prov. xvii. 17, and, chap. xviii. last : he never fails, nor can he at any time be charged with that which Absalom casts up to Hushai, 2 Sam. xvi. 17, " Is this thy kindness to thy friend ?" 2. Sympathy, and condescending to supply their wants, he cleaves "closer than a brother," Prov. xviii. 24 ; it is such a love, as one hath who aimeth at his friend's good, as well as his own. 3. Familiarity in mutual communion, as useth to be betwixt friends, and freedom in conversing, as, Exod. iii. 11, " The Lord spoke with Moses as a man doth with his friend." 4. It takes in a mutual confidence that one may have in another, as in his very own self, and more than in any other ; all which are eminently in Christ, as "ointment and perfume rejoice the heart, so doth the sweetness of a man's friend," and eminently of this friend, " by hearty counsel," Prov. xxvii. 9. No other friends are comparable to this friend : happy, happy for evermore are they, whose friend Christ Jesus is. 7. Where Christ is a friend, there is he also the soul's Beloved, or, believers' choosing of Christ for their Beloved, and his being kindly to them as a friend, go together ; these two relations, " my Beloved ;" and " my friend" are never separate. Now to be the soul's Beloved, implies these things, 1. That comparatively, Christ is eminently and only loved by his people, and nothing is admitted to share in their affection with him, Phil. iii. 8. 2. That there is in the soul

an high esteem of him, which begets this love. 3. That
there is such an ardent affection to him, as makes them
long for union with him, as love naturally desires union
with that which it loves, it desires to be with Christ here,
and hereafter, as that which is far the best of all, Phil. i.
23. 4. It supposes a delight and satisfaction, that their
souls take in Christ, and expect from union with him;
their happiness lies in it, and they are disquieted, and
someway holily discontented and weighted, when they
miss it, and under desertion and absence, easily fear, lest
their heart beguile and delude them in that concerning
matter, as the scope of this place, and her present exercise
shew. 5. It supposes a kindliness in their love, and
well groundedness, such as a wife hath to her husband,
and not such as is betwixt the adulteress and the adulterer,
which is all the love that the men of the world have to
their idols, but the love that the Bride hath to Christ, is
a native and avowed love, of which she hath no reason to
be ashamed (as men will one day be of all their idols) but
to boast and glory in him; and Christ is to the believer,
not what idols are to the men of the world, but what a
most loving husband is to his wife, being the object of her
heart-contenting and satisfying love; wherever these properties of true love to Christ are, there may the soul lay
claim to him as its friend, and be confident to find him its
true and kindly friend; for, where he is the soul's Beloved, he is the soul's friend. 8. This is implied, that whatever other beloveds men set their love upon besides Christ,
they will prove unsound, and unfaithful friends in the
time of need; or, confidence in any thing but Christ will
fail a man at last; for, he is their friend, and no other
beloved deserves that name. All other things will be like
"a broken tooth, or a foot out of joint," Prov. xxv. 19,
or like pools in the wilderness, that run dry in the heart,
and make the wayfaring men ashamed, such as Job's
friends did prove to him, Job vi. 15, miserable comforters
will they be to men, in the day of their greatest need;
but then especially will Christ Jesus be found to be a
friend indeed; for, there is an excellency in Christ in
every relation which he stands under to his people, and
an infinite disproportion betwixt him and all creatures, in
respect of this.

A second way that we may consider the words is, as
they relate to the daughters of Jerusalem their question,

verse 9.   Ye ask what he is more than other beloveds?
now (saith she) this is he, who is singular and matchless
in all his properties; and so, it looks not only to her
choice of him, to be her Beloved and her friend, but saith
also, that he is singularly and matchlessly such, even a
non-such Beloved and friend, and one who will be found,
after trial, only worthy to be chosen and closed with as
such.   *Observ.* 1. Believers in their answers to others,
should, as particularly as may be, bring home what they
say to some edifying use (for, this best clears any question
proposed) and should not insist on generals, much less
evanish in empty speculations, but should level at edification, and frame what they say, so, as it may best reach
that end, and therefore she applies her answer to their
question.   2. When Christ in his excellency and worth
is a little insisted and dwelt on, he will be found to be incomparable; and the more souls search into him, the
more confidently may they assert his incomparable excellency: this she here doth, and saith, as it were, is he not,
and see ye him not now to be the chiefest among ten
thousand, and more excellent than all others? as having
made her assertion demonstrative, and undeniable.   3.
Christ's worth can bide the trial, and there are, and may
be gotten, good grounds to prove that he is well worthy
of all the respect, that can be put upon him; and in reason, his worth and excellency may be made convincing
unto others, and it may be demonstrated to consciences,
that Christ is of more worth than all the world; and her
resuming of it thus, supposeth it now to be so clear, that
they could say nothing against it, as appears more fully
from the words following.   4. No other beloved, nor
friend that men choose beside Christ, can abide the trial;
the more they are inquired into, and searched out, they
will be found to be of the less worth: therefore she appeals
(as it were) to all men to bring their beloveds before Christ,
if they durst compare with him, as being confident none
durst enter the lists, purposely and professedly to compete
with him.

   3. We may consider these words, as her application
made to the daughters of Jerusalem, holding forth her
scope, to edify them by this description of Christ, and
pressingly (for their good) to bear it in upon them, that
they might be made to fall in love with this Christ, that
had so high a room in her heart; for, so the very strain

of the words seem to run. Hence, *Observ.* 1. Those who love Christ themselves, will be desirous to have others knowing and loving him also: and this may be a mark of love to Christ, an earnest desire to have him esteemed of, and loved by others. 2. Those who love Christ and others truly, will endeavour nothing more, than to have Christ made known to them, and to have them divorced from their idols, and engaged to him; thus love to them, as well as to him, manifests itself. 3. It is a piece of the duty of mutual communion, to which the Lord's people are obliged, to instruct others in the knowledge of the excellencies of Christ, that they may be brought in love with him; and where that end is proposed, according to mens' several places and stations, no opportunity should be missed, nor pains spared, which may attain it. 4. That this duty of commending Christ to others, so as it may be profitable, should be exceeding warily and circumspectly gone about, as all the Bride's strain clears; for, she goes about it, 1. Tenderly, not upbraiding their ignorance. 2. Lovingly, speaking still to them as friends. 3. Wisely and seasonably, taking the fit opportunity of their question. 4. Fully, solidly, and judiciously, bearing forth the main things of Christ to them. 5. Affectionately and gravely, as being affected with the thing, and in love with Christ herself. 6. Exemplarily and convincingly, as going before them in the practice of that herself, which she endeavours to press upon them; that is, by loving and seeking Christ above all herself, she studies to commend that to others the more effectually. 5. *Observ.* That the right uptaking of Christ in his excellency, and the pressing of him upon the heart, is the most solid way of wearing all other beloveds out of request with the soul: if he once get room, the esteem of other things will quickly blow up; and there is no way to have the heart weaned from them, but to have Christ great in the affections of his people; therefore, when they ask, what he is more than other beloveds? she answers, not by crying them down, or by discovering their worthlessness, but by the describing of his worth, and thereby giving them a solid proof of his excellency to be a ground of their faith, which doth necessarily infer the other; for, " Who is he that overcomes the world, but he that believes that Jesus is the Son of God? 1 John v. 5.

4. We may consider this close, as it holds forth the

holy exulting, and boasting of her soul in Christ, who is
so far in excellency beyond all others: this is clear from
her claiming of interest in him, and her repeating of the
phrase, "this," this, singular "this, is my Beloved;" and
again, "this is my friend," especially compared with the
scope, whereby now she holds him out, not only as a
matchless beloved and friend, but to be hers, and she
thinks no shame of him; her heart with holy gladness and
joy doth exult in this excellent choice of hers above all
others: as if she said, ask ye what he is? this, now so
described, is he that is mine; he is not like the worthless,
empty, and stinking beloveds, which others have, I avow
him, and count myself happy, and well come to in him;
the contentment I have in him is incomparably beyond
the counterfeit contentment, that all other beloveds can
give.   This the manner of expression, and the frame of
her heart in the uttering of it, and the scope (which is to
shew her confidence in this his commendation, as most
worthy to be commended) do imply. *Observ.* 1. That
there is matter of boasting and holy bragging in Christ
Jesus, whether we consider the excellency that is in himself, or the confidence that his people may have in him,
as one who will make all that is in him forthcoming to
the utmost, for the good of his own. 2. That there is
nothing besides him, that one can confidently boast of;
for, this her boasting is so appropriate to him, as it is implied, to be utterly unsuitable that men should boast of
any other thing. " Let him that glorieth, glory in the
Lord," that is, in him, and in no other thing beside. 3.
That believers who have interest in him, and have taken
him to be their Beloved and their friend, may make their
boast in him, Psalm xxxiv. 2; may glory in him, Isa.
xlv. 25; and may bless themselves, as happy eternally in
him, Isa. lxv. 16. This holy boasting implieth, 1. An
high estimation of him. 2. Confidence in him, without
fear. 3. Satisfaction with him, and having full contentment in him. 4. An eminent joy resulting from these,
which cannot be shaken, all the former being in an eminent degree. 4. *Observ.* That it is incumbent on the
believer who hath chosen Christ, sometimes to boast in
him, and in a lovely and holy way to vaunt and boast (if
we may so speak) of him above all, so are we commanded,
to " glory in his holy name," Psal cv. 3, and this is one of
the ways we are to commend him, and Christ will take it as a

piece of notable respect put upon him, when it is seriously done. 5. When a believer is in a right frame, and clear anent his interest, he will boast himself in Christ, as having " the lines fallen to him in pleasant places," Psalm xvi. 6, whatever else be his lot in the world: Christ is a bargain, that one day will be found worth the boasting of.

CHAPTER VI.

DAUGHTERS OF JERUSALEM.

Verse 1.   Whither is thy beloved gone, O thou fairest among women? whither is thy beloved turned aside? that we may seek him with thee.

THE sweet conference begun in verse 8, of the former chapter, and continued to the end thereof, betwixt the Bride and the daughters of Jerusalem, is further drawn out in this chapter; and first they return a new serious question, verse 1.   In the second place she replies, verses 2. and 3.   After which, in the third place, the Bridegroom himself comes in, with a notable expression of his love to his Bride, and an affectionate commendation of her graces: and so, according to the number of the parties that speak, we have three parts of the chapter.

The question proposed by the daughters of Jerusalem, is, verse 1. and it supposeth them to be convinced of Christ's worth, by the former discourse; and that they now are provoked, as being deeply in love with him, to desire and thirst after him, and communion with him. Now, as it depends upon the former discourse, and this is the continuance thereof, it gives ground to observe, I. That serious and faithful endeavours to gain those that are weak, are often followed with a blessing on those upon whom such pains are taken; for, now the daughters are engaged to seek him with the Bride: and this should notably encourage to the discharge of this duty. 2. As it is the duty of one to admonish and instruct another, so it is all men's duty to accept of admonition and instruction from others, and in the Lord to yield themselves thereunto, as these daughters do. 3. It makes Christian fellowship sweet and pleasant, where there is faithful tenderness upon the one side, and submissive yielding on the other : " A wise reprover upon an obedient ear is an

excellent jewel, even as an ear-ring of gold, and an ornament of fine gold." Prov. xxv. 11.   4. Yielding to instruction, and acknowledging of a conviction after a mistake
(especially concerning Christ) is one of the first things,
whereby desire of obtaining Christ doth appear ; whereas
such grumblings, as, " Who made thee a reprover, or
instructor ?" &c. evidence an unhumbled frame, out of case
for any true desire after Christ.   5. This may give some
directions for Christians' profitable conversing one with
another : as, 1. A necessary and profitable subject should
be proposed to be spoken of ; for, so much the matter of
the daughters' question imports.   2. It should be entertained by both sides when once tabled, and all diversions
barred out, and the subject proposed, closely followed
with answers suitable to it.   3. The end designed should
be practice and edification (for, so it is here, to seek him
with them) and not a mere notional contemplation.   4.
The manner should be grave and serious, suitable to the
matter.   5. Compellations, and expressions that are used,
should be respectful of each one to another.   6. Those who
are weak should not shun to speak, and move questions,
in those things that may edify them, as we may see in the
daughters' carriage here.   7. They who have knowledge
should not despise those who are weak, but condescend
unto them.   8. It is sometimes useful to suspend explicit
following of our own case, (especially when those who are
present seem strangers to it) and to condescend to insist
upon the case of others for their edification : thus doth the
Bride with the daughters.

More particularly in the words of verse 1. consider 1.
The title which the daughters give the Bride, " O thou
fairest among women :" It is the same which was, chap. v.
9, but here it shews their continuing in respect to her,
which they vent by suitable grave expressions ; it is not
much at the beginning to carry respectfully to the lovers
of Christ, but it is much after some familiar acquaintance
to continue so doing, which is the lesson that may be
learned here.   2. Consider the question, " whither is thy
Beloved gone ?" and it is repeated, to shew how serious
they were in it, and how desirous of an answer.   3. There
is the end, or motive, that draws this question from them,
and that is, " That we may seek him with thee."

She had told them that her Beloved was withdrawn ;
now they when convinced of his worth) ask, "whither ?" &c.

which is a farther step of their desire of being acquaint
with Christ and his way, than what was holden out in
their question, chap. v. 9, yet having infirmity also : and
it shews, 1. That where there is any conviction of what
Christ is, then the great design and main enquiry should
be to know where he is, and how he may be attained. 2.
There may be some acknowledgment of Christ's worth,
and affection to him, where yet there is much ignorance of
the way how to come by him. 3. It is no less necessary
for a person to know rightly where and how to seek Christ,
than to know what he is. 4. There may be some honesty
of desire after, and love to Christ, where faith dare not
claim his as the believer's own ; for, say they, where is
thy Beloved? they say not, where is our Beloved? beginners are often very anxious and afraid to make this
application, although it may be, before their conviction
and conversion, they did never question it.

Next, we would consider, that the daughters here leave
the Bride's case, and enquire for instructing of themselves,
whence observe, 1. Whosover have any affection to
Christ, and any opportunity to be instructed anent him,
should thriftily improve it ; if they had but the fellowship
of an intelligent private Christian, it should be made good
use of to that purpose. 2. Young beginners often forget all
others cases but their own, and the more experienced should
bear with that, and for others' good pass over their own case,
and be content it be laid aside and forgotten for a time. 3.
They ask this, that they may be the more enabled to sym-
pathize, and concur with her, in what she required of them :
which teacheth, that they can be most useful to others, that
have some distinctness in their own condition : for, confusion in our own condition doth much obstruct the sympathy,
faithful burden-bearing that we owe to others in theirs.

The end they propose, is " That we may seek him with
thee :" which may be considerd, first, as their end in enquiring ; Tell us (as if they had said) for, we ask not for
curiosity, but to be helped in practice. Whence observe, 1.
The great end and design of all endeavours for knowledge,
should not be to rest in speculation, but to be furthered
in practice. 2. It saith, no sooner should folk be clear
in a duty but instantly should they set about the practice
of it. 3. Men's practice should be according to their
knowledge ; their seeking, and knowing where to seek,
should go together. 4. The finding of Christ is the great

end of all religious duties, wherein we are to seek him, as
these duties are the end of knowledge. 5. Often good
desires after Christ, are much impeded by ignorance and
confusion, even in the judgments of those that affectionately love him.

Again, we may consider the words as a motive proposed
to the Bride, to make her to answer; which is, shew us
we pray thee where we may find him; for we are in earnest, and would gladly seek him with thee. And from
the words so considered, *Observe*, 1. Nothing will nor
should more prevail with a tender believer, to move him
to be helpful to others, than this, that they are serious and
yet weak: yea, 2. Singleness of desire to profit by the
means, is a piece of that frame that is necessary in order
to our edification by them ; for, thus they strengthen themselves in the expectation of an edifying answer, which
otherwise they could not have expected ; they who are serious and single, though feckless, may look for God's
guiding of them.

3. These words may be considered, as holding forth the
daughters' purpose, and (as it were) an obligation that
they come under ; tell us (say they) " and we will seek
him with thee :" And this teacheth, that humble, single
purposes, are neither unsuitable, nor unprofitable to beginners : yea, it is very necessary, that they seriously devote,
and engage themselves in that blessed work of seeking
after Jesus Christ.

Further, the words, " we will seek him with thee," considered in themselves, import not only a seeking, but a
joint seeking with her, as coming in to share in the same
exercise that she was taken up with. Which shews 1.
That they acquiesced in the same way of religion, which
they that were in Christ before them did follow. 2. That
there is an union to be kept amongst the worshippers of
Christ, and a joint cordial concurrence in going about of
duties. 3. That this united, or joint-way is profitable to
all, both to beginners, and to those that are more experienced ; otherwise it would not be such a motive, as it is
here held forth to be. 4. Although believers, and all professors, have an union and communion amongst themselves
(as the Bride had formerly kept with the daughters of
Jerusalem) yet when sincerity is begun to be more fresh
and lively, or when it is begotten where it was not before,
there follows a more near union and communion than that

which was before : now they mind another joint-way of
seeking him, than formerly they had done. 5. Often the
persons, by whom souls have gotten good, are very dear
to them, and in much respect with them, so that their way
hath a testimony from them, as approvable ; for (saith the
daughters) we will seek him with thee, who instructed us.
It is true, that this may sometimes degenerate (so that
folks may drink in the dregs from such persons with their
wine) yet it seems, in the main principle of practical godliness, not to be unsafe : as, Heb. xiii. 7, 8. 6. The great,
main and native use of what is spoken of Christ's excellency, is to have souls brought in love with him ; and engaged to seek him ; and if this be not gained, any other
effect of what is spoken, is little worth, as to what mainly
concerns themselves. As this was the scope of all the
Bride spoke concerning Christ, so it is attained on these
daughters to whom she spoke ; and it is the great thing
we should aim at, when either we speak of Christ's worth,
or hear it spoken of.

BRIDE.

Verse 2. My Beloved is gone down into his garden, to the beds
of spices, to feed in the gardens, and to gather lilies.

THE Bride is not long in returning her answer, but
being glad to have the opportunity to further their edification, instantly she replies, verse 2, " My Beloved is
gone down," &c. as being well acquaint with the place,
where he useth and haunts : if ye would find him (saith
she) his withdrawings are not far off, but as a man re-
tires sometimes to his garden, and is not in his chamber,
so Christ when withdrawn from sense (which is the chamber, chap. i. 4,) he is to be found in the assemblies of his
people, in his church and ordinances, which are (as it
were) his garden, there ye should seek him : this is the
sum of verse 2 ; and then, verse 3, having instructed
them by this notable digression, she returns to quiet herself (when all outward means fail) in the faith of her
interest in him.
  If it were asked, how the daughters could ask the
Bride, where Christ was, or how she now can tell them,
when she herself is seeking, and knoweth not (as she
seemed to profess chap. v. 6, 7, 8,) where to find him ?

Answ. 1.   Believers will often give more distinct advice to others, in their difficulties, than they can take to themselves in their own exercises ; because light and reason guides them unbiassedly, in reference to others, and sense, inclination, and affection sway too much in their own cases.   2.   Believers may complain they know not how to find him, not so much from defect of light as of life, when either in their own practice, or in their success in duties, they are not answerable to what they aim at ; exercised souls are ready to aggravate their own infirmities ; and what is indeed in them, is to their own account as not in them, till the Lord shine upon it and quicken it, and so bring it out and make it appear.

In the first part of her answer, verse 2, she speaks to these two, 1. Where Christ is. 2. What he is doing. The first gives them direction where to seek him ; the second encourages them to fall about it, as a thing acceptable to him ; the place where he is, is set forth by two expressions, 1. He is "gone down to his garden," which implieth the similitude, formerly expressed, of a man's retiring from his chamber or closet to his garden : this "garden" signifies the church, as chap. iv. 12, 15, and here, as opposed to gardens, in the words following, it holdeth forth the catholic visible church, as gardens signify particular societies, or congregations : the church is like a garden that is within one precinct, yet divided into divers quarters and inclosures : this being the church that hath the promise of Christ's presence, and where he is ever to be found, must be understood of no particular church, of which that cannot be asserted, that Christ shall be always there : it must therefore be the catholic church, distinguished from particular churches, or gardens. **2.** He is gone "to the beds of spices :" as gardens have distinct plots of flowers, and beds of spices, and some particular parts are allotted for these, where especially they grow ; so in the church Christ hath his plants, whereof some are sanctified with grace (therefore compared to spices) and these, in some parts of the visible church, are more abounding than in other parts, (as spices in beds together, that may be elsewhere but in particular stalks, and not so frequent) and as men love and frequent that plot of their garden most ; so doth Christ most manifest himself in his ordinances ordinarily, where he hath his spices and lilies in greatest abundance : and thus this last part qualifies the former, he is in his church, but especially where his spices are most abounding: and therefore would you have him? seek him in his church and amongst his people, and especially in such societies of his people, where true and lively believers are most to be found. Here observe (besides what was observed on chap. iv. 12,) Christ's church, though it have many subdivisions, yet is it one church, one whole catholic church, whereof particular churches are parts, 1 Cor. xii. 28. 2. It is in that church and no where else, that Christ's presence is to be found, and where believers, the spices and lilies are planted. 3. There may be, in that one visible church, many more real converts in one part thereof, than in another; spices in beds are not in every place of the garden. 4. Though Christ hath a singular care of, and respect for, his whole church, and hath a peculiar presence there wherever there is any part thereof, yet where he hath much people, beyond what he hath in other places (as in Antioch, Acts xi. 21, in Corinth, Acts xviii. 10, and Ephesus, Acts xix. 20,) there especially is he present, and there ordinarily continues he the power and life of his ordinances. 5. Those who desire Christ, should not run out of the church to seek him, or expect any way of finding him, which others have not found out before them? but should seek after him by the ordinary means, in his church; for, this answers their question, where is he? proposed for that end, that they might seek him and find him.

He hath a twofold exercise in his gardens, for he is not idle, he is gone there, 1. " To feed in the gardens." By " gardens," in the plural number, are understood the subdivisions, and particular plots of that one garden, formerly mentioned; the Jews had their synagogues, where the people did meet, and the law was read (as we have our distinct congregations) as Psalm lxxiv. 8, and Acts xv. 21, do evidence. To " feed" taken actively (as chap. i. 7, " where thou feedest," &c.) signifieth his taking care, to provide for his own in the church; if taken passively, he is gone down " to feed," that is, that himself may eat, and it is the same with what was, chap. v. 1, " I have come to my garden, I have eaten," &c. and the scope in both, looks to the same, and so the meaning of the similitude is, that as men have their gardens, wherein they solace themselves, and feed upon the pleasant fruits that are in them, so doth Christ delight himself in his church, and take pleasure therein, as Psalm cxlvii. 11, he " taketh pleasure in them that fear him ;" and " he delighteth in the habitable parts of the earth," Prov. viii. 31, that is, where saints dwell, and where the place of his rest and haunt is : other places being but as uninhabited wildernesses to Christ, the church is the garden, wherein he delights and finds fruit. He is said to feed in " the gardens," and not in the garden, 1. To shew, that the way of his manifesting himself to his church, is by erecting his ordinances in particular societies, and thus they derive his blessing. 2. To shew, that though there be divers societies, or particular churches, yet his presence is not excluded from, or tied to, any one of them : He walks amongst the candlesticks," as observing every one of them, and manifesting himself among them, as he seeth good.

The second part of his exercise is, " to gather lilies :" By " lilies," in this garden (as often hath been said) are understood believers, chap. ii. 2, 16. To " gather" is a borrowed expression from men that use to gather some flowers they delight in, to bring to their chamber with them, or some fruits, that they may dress and prepare them, as we heard, chap. v. 1. Christ's gathering of his lilies, points, 1. At his calling of them effectually who belong to him ; the elect may be called lilies to be gathered, as they are called sons of God to be gathered, John xi. 51, 52. Thus also, Matt. xxiii. 37, Christ's expression, " I would have gathered you," &c. whereby their bringing in to him is signified. 2. It points at his glorifying of them, which is in part, when particular believers are gathered to their fathers, as the phrase is, Gen. xxv. 8, and xxxv. 29. This is, as his pulling of some lilies for his own satisfaction : and this gathering will be perfected, when all the elect shall be " gathered from the four winds," Matt. xxiv. 31, and the " angels shall gather the good fishes into vessels, but cast the bad away," Matt. xiii. 48. In a word then, the sense and scope of the whole is this,—would ye (saith she) have my beloved, or know where he is, that ye may seek him ? he is in his church, seek him in the way of his ordinances ; for he is there, purposely to delight himself in doing good to his people, it is his errand to welcome and gather them " as a hen doth her chickens under her wings ;" therefore (saith she) seek him there ; for, ye can find no better opportunity. *Observ.* 1. Our Lord Jesus takes pleasure to be amongst his people, and to do them good ; he feeds on this with delight, as a hungry man doth on his meat. 2. The more Christ gains (to say so) he feeds the better, and is the more cheerful: he feeds and gathers at once, and this gathering of souls, is as sweetly refreshing and delight-some to our blessed Lord Jesus, as the plucking of the sweetest flowers is to a man walking in a garden; and there is nothing more acceptable and welcome to him, than a seeking sinner. 3. Wherever Christ's ordinances are, there may his presence be expected, in one particular church, as well as in another; for, he " feeds in the gar-dens." 4. The great scope of ordinances, is to gather in believers, and build them up: and there is nothing more acceptable to Christ, than to have some to gather, some whom he may save. That is a refreshing feast to him, John iv. 34. 5. Our Lord Jesus hath delight in all his people, and in every one of them, where sincerity is, though it be not in the greatest measure: therefore it is said he gathers lilies indefinitely, that is, one of them as well as another. 6. So long as our Lord Jesus hath a church and ordinances in it, as long doth he continue to gather, and he is not idle, but is still gathering, though at sometimes, and in some places, this may be more sensible and abundant than ordinary. 7. It is a great encourage-ment to poor sinners to seek for Christ, to know, that this is his very errand in his ordinances, to gather them, and that he is waiting on, like the prodigal's father, ready to run with delight to welcome them; this is proposed as a motive to the daughters, to seek him. 8. Although be-lievers may seem for a time to be neglected, and, as it were, forgotten, yet will the Lord gather them all in at last, as his choice of all the world, they being the flowers of his gardens; there is a good day coming to believers, when not one of them shall be left to grow in this fighting church, but he shall take them in to the king's palace, there to be for ever with him. 9. The readiness of Christ to welcome sinners, and the delight that he hath in doing them good, should exceedingly provoke and hearten sin-ners to seek him, while he may be found: this is the great scope of this verse.

Verse 3. I am my Beloved's, and my beloved is mine; he feedeth among the lilies.

THE second part of her answer to the daughters' ques-tion, is, verse 3, and it contains the great ground whereon

she quiets herself, and wherein she rests, as being that
which makes Christ lovely to her, even though absent;
" I am my Beloved's, and my Beloved is mine :" this now
is the anchor which she casts, when all other means seemed to disappoint her.   We had the same words for substance, and to the same scope, chap. ii. 16, wherein she
first asserted her interest, and secondly maintained it
against an objection, even as she doth here.   Besides what
was said there, we may consider the words here, first, as
in them her interest is repeated, though it was once formerly asserted : which shews, 1. That believers, though
once clear anent their interest, may have their difficulties
and doubts recurring upon them.   2. That when new
difficulties recur, there is no new way to be taken for
discussing of them, but the same way of believing, which
is again to be renewed and kept in exercise.   3. It shews
that miscarriages do not break off that union, which is betwixt Christ and his people ; for, although there had been
many failings in her former carriage, yet her interest is
still the same.   4. Believers, even over, and notwithstanding of, many challenges, may lay claim to an interest
in Christ, when they are in the exercise of repentance,
faith and, other graces.   4. Her thus repeating and again
owning of her interest, shews, that she was exceeding
clear and persuaded thereof : whence observe, believers
may attain a great degree of assurance, and may and
should not only aim to have it, but to preserve and keep
it clear ; for, that is of great concernment as to their
peace ; and the weight of their consolation, in their confident application of all the promises, depends on it.

2. Consider, although the words be the same, yet the
order is changed ; it was, chap. ii. 16, " my Beloved is
mine," &c.   So there she begins at asserting her interest
in him, but here she begins at asserting his interest in her,
or her betaking of herself to him, for clearing of her interest in him.   " I am" (saith she) " my Beloved's" or,
I am to my Beloved ; and from her betaking herself to
him, and adhering to the bargain, she concludes he also
is hers : which shews, 1. That they, who are clear of
their adhering to Christ, and of their fleeing to him, as
their choice, may warrantably conclude, that Christ is
theirs, even though sense should say the contrary.   2.
When there is nothing in Christ's dispensation to us, that
looks convincing-like of his love to us, it is good to reflect

on our acting on him, and if it be found that we have fled
to him, and closed with him, then there is ground to con-
conclude our union with him, and interest in him: and
there cannot be a sounder way of reasoning than that.
For, if we on our part be answerable to the call, we are
not to question his part (namely his bestowing of himself
on us, according to the tenor of his offers) but to believe
it according to his word: believers may sometimes be put
to this way of arguing, and it is sure.

If we consider the words, as following on her former
desertion and exercise, and as being now intended by the
Bride (as her scope) to fix herself; they give ground to
observe, 1. That faith is still a refuge; when all God's
dispensations, and every thing in the believer's case, seems
to leave the heart in disquietness, faith is then the last
and great refuge. 2. Faith is then most satisfying when
repentance is exercised, and all other means diligently
gone about; therefore may she now cast this anchor, after
she hath been in the exercise of repentance, and in the
use of other means (as we have seen in the former chapter) which had been presumption to have been done at
first, these being slighted; faith will sustain souls in duty,
but presumption puffs up (as in verse 3,) even when they
are out of it; faith preserves from fainting under discouragements in the way of God, presumption strengthens
against just challenges, when folks are out of his way.

The second part of the verse, " He feeds among the
lilies," was also spoken to, chap. ii. 16.   It is brought in
here to remove that objection, if he be thine, where is he?
Is he not away? and if he be away, why claimest thou
interest in him?   She answers them, though he be not
present to sense, yet is he ever kind to his people, and
therefore cannot but be kind to me, which makes me
conclude, that though he be not present to sense, yet he
is mine, and I am his. Believers are called lilies often,
1. For their native beauty, Matt. vi. 29. 2. For their
savouriness, chap. v. 13. 3. For their growing, and
making increase, as the lily, Hos. xiv. 5. And so the
similitude points at these three excellencies of the believer, 1. The native beauty and loveliness of Christ's
grace in them. 2. The sweet relish and savouriness of
their graces. And, 3. Their spiritual growth in grace,
from one degree of it to another. Christ's feeding among
his lilies, shews, the great delight he takes in them, and

the pleasure he hath to do them good, as was cleared, chap. ii. 16. *Observ.* 1. Christ is exceeding loving to, and tender of, all his people, of one as well as of another, and hath been so from the beginning, that none had ever any reason to complain. 2. Christ's way in general to his people, when well taken up, may notably quiet, content, and comfort any of them, when a difficulty comes on, or when under any darkness or desertion, as the Spouse here was; he never did any of his own wrong. 3. A believer, that hath clearness anent his fleeing to Christ, by faith, may draw comfortable conclusions from, and comfortably apply, the way of Christ with others of his people to themselves, and expect that same kindness from him, that they have met with; for, the covenant is one and the same with them all. 4. Believers may sometimes be put to gather their comfort, and to sustain their faith, more from the experience of others, in what they have found, and how Christ hath carried to them, than from any thing that is in their own present condition. 5. She propounded Christ's kindness to his people (the lilies) to encourage the daughters of Jesusalem to seek him, verse 2, now here, she makes use of the same ground, for quieting of herself. Hence learn two things, 1. That same which warrants believers at first to approach to Christ, may encourage them to renew, and continue the exercise of their faith, in making application of him and his comforts. 2. It is good in our own practice, to make use of the same grounds, and to walk by the same rules, that we would propose to others.

BRIDEGROOM.

Verse 4.   Thou art beautiful, O my love, as Tirzah, comely as Jerusalem, terrible as an army with banners.

In verse 4. (which begins the third part of the chapter) Christ, the Bridegroom, comes in and speaks: our Lord Jesus (as it were) hath been long silent, and here he breaks in, without any preface, and makes up all his former absence and silence, by his singular kindness, when he manifests himself to his Bride; which kindness appears in the warmness and sweetness of his many and various expressions. He continues speaking unto verse 10, of chap. vii. after he had knocked at her door, chap. v. 2, he had been longing, as it were, to be in, and now when he wins in, he insists the more, and several ways prosecutes, and amplifies the commendation of his Bride. This is, 1. generally propounded in three similitudes, verse 4. 2. It is aggreged in one instance thereof, verse 5. 3. He descends to particulars, verses 5, 6, 7. 4. He takes her up in divers considerations, that speak her to be lovely and beautiful, verse 8, 9. 5. This is confirmed by two instances and proofs, 1. What the daughters did esteem of her, and their praise is marked, verses 9, 10. 2. It is instanced in the influence that her loveliness had on him, verses 11, 12, 13. And, 6. He proceeds in a different method from what he had, chap. iv. to set out the particulars of her loveliness, chap. vii.

Generally she is set out, verse 4. by three comparisons, 1. She " is beautiful as Tirzah :" this was a city of the tribe of Manasseh, the word in the original comes from a root that sigifieth acceptable ; whereby it seems, that this city had been exceeding pleasant ; it was the seat of one of the kings of Canaan, Josh. xii. 24, and of the kings of Israel, after the rent of the ten tribes from the house of David, until Zimri burnt it ; after which Omri built Samaria, as is to be seen at large, 1 Kings xvi.. Thus the spiritual beauty of holiness in believers (Psalm cx. 3.) is set out as having in it so much loveliness as may commend it, and make it desirable and acceptable to others. 2. She is " comely as Jerusalem :" this was the head city of Judah, " beautiful for situation, and the joy of the whole earth, Psalm xlviii. 2, but most beautiful for the ordinances and worship of God, which were there ; therefore glorious things are spoken of it, more than any thing that was to be seen by carnal eyes, and it was loved on that account, " more than all the dwellings of Jacob," Psalm lxxxvii. 2, 3. It is ordinarily taken for a type of the church, which is set out by it, as, Psalm cxxii. It seems here the Lord doth respect the believer's spiritual beauty, with reference to that comeliness and orderliness, which is to be seen among them, and is maintained by them in the exercise of his ordinances ; and also in respect of his estimation, every believer is a Jerusalem to him, where he dwells, where he is worshipped, and to whom he hath given the promise of his presence : believers are to him as Tirzah and Jerusalem, the most beautiful cities of that land, for the time. Or, the first similitude, taken from Tirzah, may look to outward beauty; for, Tirza was a beautiful city: and the other similitude, taken from Jerusalem, may look to church beauty, as the ordinances were there; and so the sense runs, My love thou art to me as the most excellent thing in the world; yea, as the most excellent thing in the visible church, which is more precious to him than any thing in the world. 3. She is "terrible as an army with banners:" an army is strong and fearful; a bannered army is stately and orderly, under command and in readiness for service; an army with banners, is an army in its most stately posture; the church is terrible as such an army, either, 1. Considered complexly or collectively, her ordinances have power, authority and efficacy, like a bannered army: so the church's spiritual weapons are said to be "mighty and powerful through God," 2 Cor. x. 5. 6. This being compared with the 6th and 10th verses, may have its own place. But, 2. The scope here, and the words following, look especially at the stateliness, majesty, and spiritual valour that is in particular believers, who are more truly generous, valorous and powerful, than an army with banners; when their faith is exercised, and kept lively, they prevail wheresoever they turn; they carry the "victory over the world," 1 John v. 4. over devils, which are enemies whom no worldly army can reach; but by the power of faith they prevail, even to quench the "violence of fire," as it is in Heb. xi. 34, and by faith they "waxed valiant in fight:" but mainly this holds in respect of Christ himself, they prevail over him in a manner, by their princely carriage, as Jacob did, Gen. xxxii, 28. "As a prince hast thou had power with God and men, and hast prevailed:" see Hos. xii. 4, " He had power over the angel, and prevailed:" and indeed, no army hath such influence upon him, as believers have, which is such, that he cannot (as it were) stand before them, or refuse them any thing, that they with weeping and supplications wrestle with him for, according to his will: now, that it is in this respect mainly, that the believer is called terrible as an army with banners, is clear, 1. From the scope, which is to comfort a particular believer, who hath been wrestling with him already under desertions. 2. The next words confirm it, " Turn away thine eyes from me" (saith he) " for they have overcome me:" what stateliness (might one say) is in a poor believer? It is easily answered, that this is not any awful or dreadful terribleness that is here intended, but the efficacy of faith, and the powerful victory which through the same by Christ's own condescending, the believer hath over him ; and so in his account, as to prevailing with him, Christ's Bride is more mighty than many armies, in their most stately posture ; therefore (saith he) "thine eyes" (that is her faith) "have overcome me" (that is her terribleness) turn them away, I cannot (to say so) abide them : and these three together, make the believer (or rather Christ's love, who useth these expressions) wonderful, 1. The believer is beyond all the world for beauty. 2. The visible church, and believers in her, in respect of ordinances and her ecclesiastic estate, is very comely and lovely ; and yet the believer's inward beauty is beyond that also, "the King's daughter is all glorious within. 3. Believers, in regard of the power of their faith, are more terrible than armies, or all military power among men : thou art (saith he) so to me, and hast such influence on me, and may expect thus to prevail with, and in a manner to overcome me : and so Christ is so far from quarrelling with her, for her by-gone carriage now, that he effectually comforts and commends her. Hence, *Observe*, 1. Our Lord Jesus is a most friendly welcomer of a sinner, and the sweetest passer-by of transgressions that can be ; there is no upbraiding here for any thing, but every word speaks how well he takes with her. 2. Our Lord Jesus, his manifestations are seasonable and wise: seasonable, that now he comes when the Bride hath left no means unessayed, and was at a stand ; wise, that he comes not until she had found the bitterness of her own way, and was brought to a more lively exercise of faith, repentance, holiness, and profitable experiences therein ; of which we have spoken in what goeth before. 3. The Lord is not displeased with humble believing, and with the claiming of interest in him by his own, even when his dispensations to sense are dark, but takes very well with it, and hath a special complacency in it, and therefore comes in with this intimation of his love here, importing his hearty accepting of her. 4. The Lord's commendations of his people, and the intimations of his love to them are such, as it may be seen he conforms and proportions them to their conditions and exercise ; and when they have been under any long and sharp exercise, (as the Bride was in the former chapter) he makes, when he comes, his manifestations the more sweet and full, as here. 5. Believers, when grace is exercised, must needs be beautiful creatures, and much esteemed of by Christ, who thus commends them. 6. Grace and holiness in a believer's walk are much more beautiful and acceptable to Christ than the external ordinances (though excellent in themselves) as separable from it ; for, Jerusalem, that was very beautiful as to ordinances, is but an emblem of this. 7. There is an awfulness and terribleness in believers, as well as loveliness, which makes them terrible to the profane, even whether they will or not, a godly carriage puts a restraint on them. 8. Loveliness, terribleness, and authority in holiness, are knit together ; when a particular believer, or church, is lively in holiness, then have they weight and authority, and when that fails, they become despicable. 9. The believer hath great weight with Christ, he is the only army that prevails over him, as faith is the only weapon, being humbly exercised, by which they overcome : this is more fully expressed in the next verse.

Verse 5. Turn away thine eyes from me, for they have overcome me :

THE first part of the fifth verse contains the amplification and heightening of the Bride's lovely terribleness, and the great instance, and proof thereof, is held forth in a most wonderful expression, " Turn away thine eyes from me," and as wonderful a reason, " for they have overcome me," saith the Beloved : wherein consider, 1. That, wherein this might and irresistible terribleness of hers consisted ; it is her " eyes," which are supposed to be looking on him, even when she knew not, to her sense, where he was. By eyes, we shew, chap. iv. 9, were understood her love to him, and faith in him, whereby she was still cleaving to him under desertion, and in the present dark condition she was in, seeking to find him out. 2. This phrase, " Turn away thine eyes," is not so to be taken, as if Christ approved not her looking to him, or her faith in him ; but, to shew the exceeding great delight he had in her, placing her faith and love on him ; which was such, that her loving and believing looks ravished him (as it is chap. iv. 9,) and (as it were) his heart could not stand out against these looks, more than one man could stand out against a whole army, as the following expression clears : it is like these expressions, Gen. xxxii. 28, " I pray thee let me go," and Exod. xxxii. 10, " Let

me alone, Moses;" which shews, that it is the believers
strength of faith, and importunity of love, exercised in
humble dependence on him, and cleaving to him, which is
here commended; "for" (saith he) "they have overcome
me," this shews, that it is no violent, or unwilling victory
over him. But (in respect of the effect that followed her
looks) it holds forth the intenseness of his love, and the
certainty of faith's prevailing, that (to speak so with reverence and admiration) he is captivated, ravished and
held with it, as one that is overcome, because he will be
so : yea, according to the principles of his love, and the
faithfulness of his promises, whereby he walks, he cannot
but yield unto the believing importunity of his people, as
one overcome. In sum, it is borrowed from the most
passionate love that useth to be in men, when they are so
taken with some lovely object, that a look thereof pierceth
them : this, though in every thing (especially as implying
defects) it cannot be applied to Christ, yet in a holy spiritual manner, the effects, for the believer's comfort, are
as really and certainly, but much more wonderfully in
Christ. These expressions are much of the same nature
with those spoken of, upon chap. iii. 4, and chap. iv. 9,
and therefore the doctrines there, will follow here. But
further from the scope and repetition. *Observe.* 1. That
believers' eyes may look, that is, their love and faith
may be exercised on Christ, even in their dark and deserted conditions ; and it is their property to look always
to him, even when their eyes are, as it were, blind through
desertion, he is still the object they are set upon. 2.
That when these graces of faith and love are exercised on
Christ, they are never fruitless, but always prevail and
obtain, though it be not always sensible to the believer.
3. The love and faith of believers have weight with
Christ and affect him, even when he keeps up himself;
he may be overcome even then ; for, the expression in the
text looks to what was past. 4. Faith working by love,
is a most gallant, and holy daring thing, bold in its en-
terprises to pursue after, to grip, and stick to Christ over
all difficulties (as may be seen in her former carriage)
and most successful as to the event. 5. The more staidly and stoutly, with love, humility and diligence, that
faith is set on Christ, it is the more acceptable to him,
and hath the greater commendation, as the eleventh of
the Hebrews, and his commendation of that woman's

faith, Matt. xv. 25, do confirm: tenaciousness, and importunity in holding of, hanging on, and cleaving to Christ by faith, may well be marvelled at, and commended by Christ, but will never be reproved nor rejected. They greatly mistake Christ, who think that wrestling by faith, will displease him; for even though he seem to keep up himself, it is but to occasion, and to provoke to more of the exercise of the graces, in which he takes so much delight.

Verse 5.—Thy hair is as a flock of goats, that appear from Gilead:
6.   Thy teeth are as a flock of sheep which go up from the washing, whereof every one beareth twins, and there is not one barren among them.
7.   As a piece of a pomegranate, are thy temples within thy locks.

The following particulars of her commendation, in the end of the 5th and in the 6th and 7th verses, are set down in the same words, chap. iv. 1, 2, 3, and therefore we need say no more for their explication, only we would consider the reason for repeating them in the same words, which is the scope here, and it is this; although he commended her formerly in these expressions, yet considering her foul slip, chap. v. 2, 3, and his withdrawing on the back of it, she might think that he had other thoughts of her now, and that these privileges and promises which she had ground to lay claim to before, did not belong to her now, and therefore she could not comfortably plead an interest in them now as before: to remove this mistake or doubt, he will not only commend her, but in the same very words, to shew that she was the same to him, and that his respect was not diminished, to her, therefore he will not alter her name, nor her commendation, but will again repeat it for her confirmation, intimating his love thereby; and also for her instruction, teaching the Bride her duty by these particulars of her commendation and shewing her what she should be: and this commendation had not met so well with her case, nor expressed so well his unchangeable love, if it had been given in other terms. From this we may *Observe*, 1. as believers are ready to slip and fail in their duty, so are they ready to suspect Christ to be changing towards them because of their failings; they are very apt from their own fickleness and changes, to apprehend him to be changeable also, and to refuse comfort from all by-gone evidences and intimations of his love, and from all words that have comforted them, till they be restored and set aright again. 2. Our Bridegroom is most constant in his affection to his Bride, continuing still the same, and as he is the most free forgiver of wrongs to his own, so he is the most full forgetter of them, when they return; and therefore he continues speaking to her in the same terms as formerly, without any alteration, as if no such wrong on her side had been committed. 3. Renewing of repentance and faith by believers after failings, puts them in that same condition and capacity with Christ, for laying claim to his love, and their wonted privileges and comforts, wherein they were before, even as if such failings and miscarriages had never been. 4. Our Lord Jesus would have his people confirmed, and strengthened in the faith of the constancy of his love, the unchangeableness of their interest, and the privileges following thereon : and seeing he thus loves his people, he allows them to believe it. 5. It is not easy to fix and imprint Christ's words on believers' hearts, and to get them affected with them : therefore often, both promises and duties must be repeated; and what was once spoken must be again repeated for their good, especially after a slip and fit of security, the same word hath need to be made lively again, and fresh to their relish, which the Lord doth here. 6. Unless Christ speak and make the word lively, the sweetest word, even that which once possibly hath been made lively to a believer, will not savour, but will want its relish and lustre, if he repeat it not.

Verse 8.   There are threescore queens, and fourscore concubines, and virgins without number.
9.   My dove, my undefiled is but one; she is the only one of her mother, she is the choice one of her that bare her : the daughters saw her, and blessed her; yea, the queens and the concubines, and they praised her.

THIS kind Bridegroom proceeds in the commendation of his Bride, verses 8, 9, and shews the rich excellency that is in her, by considering her several ways, whereby she is preferable to what is most excellent : and then in the following verses, he confirms this by a twofold proof;

and lastly, verse 13, closeth the chapter with a kind invitation, whereby, as it were, by a new proof of his love, he puts the commendation given her, out of doubt.

For understanding the 8th and 9th verses, we are to conceive, that by "daughters, virgins, queens, concubines," by this "dove" that is "one," and the "mother" that bears, are not understood any party distinct from the church or Bride, but the same Bride diversely, considered, taking in first the church as visible, which is beautiful in her ordinances, external profession and order ; for, she is the mother that bears the daughters (who are the daughters of Jerusalem) and that is said to be seen : both which expressions hold forth this, and accordingly mother and daughters have hitherto been understood in this Song, chap. iii. 4, 5. Secondly, and especially, the church as invisible, and the real believers who are members of the church invisible ; for, the scope here is to commend her graces ; and if we consider the commendation preceding, and the proofs given, it will appear that they especially belong to her, and by analogy agree to the visible church, wherein she is comprehended.

This diverse consideration of the church as one and more, is not, 1. disagreeable to other scriptures, in which Christ useth to commend her, as we see, Psalm xlv. 9, 13, 14, where there is the queen, called the king's daughter, and the virgins or daughters, her companions, who are with her, yet by all is understood the same invisible church, considered collectively as one body, or distributively in her several members. Nor, 2. Is it unsuitable to the strain of this song, nor is it absurd, as was shewn in the preface, and needs not now be repeated. And, 3. It agrees well with Christ's scope here (where he is, to say so, seeking how to express fully the commendation of his Bride, as singular and eminent,) thus to consider her ; for, the more ways she be considered, her excellency appears the more, she being excellent, whatever way she be looked on : and if as visible, she be glorious, and someway one in him, much more as invisible she is so, which is the scope, as is clear, verse 9. By queens, concubines, and virgins then, we understand believers of different growths and degrees : I say, believers, 1. Because these titles agree best to them, according to the strain of this Song, and of Psalm xlv. 2. They are supposed to be of one mother. 3. They praise the Bride, which is an evi-

dence of honesty and sincerity, and a greater argument
of her excellency, that she is praised and commended by
such as had discerning : I say, we are here to understand
believers of different growths and degrees, so that some
believers are queens, that is, more glorious, and admitted
to the highest privileges; some are as concubines, who
were accounted lawful wives as to conjugal fellowship,
but differed in this, that they had not such government over the family, and their children had not right to
inherit, therefore they are as half wives, as the word in
the original will bear : some are virgins, that are not so
far admitted, yet are of a chaste carriage, and so differenced from others, as was said on chap. i. 3.   Next, the
commendation is, that though there be " many queens,
more concubines," and " virgins without number," (that is,
though there be many believers of different sizes and degrees,) yet there is but one Bride : which is a singular
excellency in her, and an unheard-of thing, that so many
make up but one Bride? the like whereof is not to be
found in any marriage that ever was in the world : or,
we may conceive thus, though men, for their satisfaction,
sought out many queens, concubines, and virgins, because
there was not to be found in any one what was satisfying,
yet, saith he, my one Bride is to me many virtually, as if
the worth of so many queens, concubines, and virgins
were combined in one : and thus as she set him out chief
of all husbands, so doth he set her out as chief of all
Brides, and as comprehending in her alone all that was
desirable, as the next part of the 9th verse clears.   By the
number, " threescore," " fourscore," and " without number," we conceive an indefinite number is to be understood,
that is, they are many, only they of the inferior ranks are
maniest, that is, there are more concubines than queens,
far advanced in christianity, and again, more virgins than
concubines, because experienced believers of an high degree are most rare, and those who are not grown up to
have their senses exercised, are most numerous : in a
word, there are more weak than strong believers.   Which
saith, 1. That there are degrees amongst true believers,
all have not the same degree of grace, though all have the
same grace for kind, and though all be in the same covenant; there are old men, or fathers, young men, and
little children or babes, 1 John ii. 12, 13.   2. Among
believers, there are many more weak than strong.   3. He

accounts of them all as honourable, and reckons even the
virgins as commendable, though come not up to be queens.
Yet, 4. Where grace is most lively, and faith most strong,
there he dignifies believers with a most special and ample
commendation, verse 9th.

The 9th verse makes up the scope with the former.
By "dove" and "undefiled," we said, is understood the
church, especially the invisible church of believers, who all
partake of the same nature and property, and so of the same
privileges : the titles are spoken of before : the commendation is threefold, 1. She is one, which sets her out not only
with unity in her affections, but (to say so) with a kind of
oneness in herself : thus the visible catholic church is one
garden, verse 2, comprehending many beds of spices ; one
church, made up here of many particular churches : and
thus, oneness or unity is a great commendation to her, or
a special part of her excellency. But, 2, The invisible
church is but one, all believers make up one body ; though
there be many of different growths, yet there is but one
Bride : this is a singular thing, and this makes for the
scope of commending the Bride ; and points out two
things, 1. That all the excellencies in believers combine in one, and that must be excellent ; every one of
them partakes of another's excellency, by virtue of the
mutual union and communion they have with Christ, the
head and husband, and one with another ; as the beauty
of the face adorns the leg, and the straightness of the legs
commends the face, because both hold forth one glorious
body. 2. It illustrates her commendation thus, there are
many queens stately, many concubines and virgins lovely
amongst men, yet one cannot be all ; but (saith he) although there be many of these in the church, yet is she
one, and although she be one, yet is she all, collectively
summing up all.

2. "She is the only one of her mother :" this sets her
out singularly and exclusively, there is not another but
she : by mother here is understood the catholic church,
wherein children are conceived and brought forth, she is
the mother of all that believe, Gal. iv. 25, "Jerusalem
that is above, is free, which is the mother of us all :" this
church considered, as from the beginning of the world to
the end, is one ; and is the mother, in respect of the church
considered as being in this or that place for the time present,
which is understood by us all, wherever we live, we be-

long to that mother, Gal. iv. 26.   There is no church but
that one, and who are begotten to God, are brought forth
by her, and belong to her.

3. " She is the choice one of her that bare her :" this
sets her out comparatively, 1. She is the choice one in respect of the world, this one church is more excellent than
the multitude of all the societies that are there.   2. She is
the choice one in respect of all visible professors as such,
she is beyond the daughters : amongst all her mother's
children, or professing members of the church, the believer
doth excel.   3. The church considered complexly doth
excel particular believers as having all their excellencies
combined together ; or the scope of these two verses, being
to prefer the Bride as singular, and eminently beyond all
other beloveds, whether queens, concubines, such as are
joined unto men, or virgins, such as are yet suited and
sought for, we may conceive it thus,—my love, (saith he)
my dove hath not a match, but is chief ; and as she called
him the chief of all beloveds, chap. v. 10, so here he commends her as the most lovely of all Brides, that can be
wedded or wooed : although there be many of these ; yet,
1. My dove is but one, that is, in respect of her singular
excellency, she comprehends all.   2. " She is the only one
of her mother," there are no more of that family, that are
born of that mother, besides herself, that I can set my heart
on, or can match with : and thus all the world besides the
believer is cried down.   3. Comparatively " she is the
choice one of her that bare her ;" that is, not only by comparing her with the world, but by comparing her with all
mere external professors, she is still the choice of all.

That this is the scope, is clear ; and the enumerating of
so many queens, concubines, and virgins, doth illustrate it,
either by shewing her singularity and perfection, as having
all in her alone, which is to be had in many ; or, by prefer-
ing her to all, although they be many : and thus, in his
commending of her, he is even and equal with her in the
commendation she gave him, which was both comparative,
that he was " chief of ten thousand ;" and also absolute and
comprehensive, that he was " all desires," that nothing was
wanting, but that all things desirable were comprehended
in him : so now he commends and extols her above all
other, as having more in her alone than was to be found
in all others ; to shew that his love to her, and his estimation of her was nothing inferior to hers of him ; and that

he was satisfied with her alone, without seeking to multiply queens or concubines, as many men of the world did.

This commendation out of Christ's mouth, of a Bride so undutiful, may seem strange; therefore, to make it unquestionable; he brings in a double confirmation, both which respect what goeth before, to make it the more convincing. The first is in the end of the 9th verse, and it is taken from that esteem that others had of her " The daughters saw her, and they blessed her," &c. This beauty (saith he) is real and singular, even such that it makes onlookers, the most glorious and discerning (not only the daughters but even the queens and concubines) to be much affected ; the beauty of my Bride is such as takes them all up. The daughters, that is, professors, saw her ; they beheld this beauty of hers (as chap. iii. 6.) and "they blessed her," that is, 1. They were convinced of her excellency, and accounted her blessed and happy, as Mary saith of herself, Luke i. 48. And 2. they wished well to her, desiring God to bless her, as, Psalm cxxix. 8, " We bless you in the name of the Lord;" for, these two are comprehended in one man's blessing of another. Next, "the queens and concubines," that is, those who either in the world, or in the church, are thought most of, "they praised her ;" by which is understood some external expression of their esteem of her, and their endeavour to paint out her excellency and beauty to the view of others, so as they might fall in love with her : as the first then looks to the high thoughts, and inward esteem they had of her ; so this looks to the outward expression of that esteem, by which they study to set her out in the eyes of all others : so they yielded the Bride to be excellent, and called her "fairest among women," chap. v. 9, which is an evidence of her loveliness, and of the loveliness of grace in an exercised believer ; and whatever others thought of her, yet that such praised her, it shews, there was reality in the ground thereof. This is also spoken to their commendation, who did thus commend her ; and it holds out. 1. The notice which he takes of the thoughts and words which men have of his Bride; our Lord knows what men say or think of his people, and records it. 2. How pleasing it is to him, to have them speaking respectfully of her, especially when she is exercised with any dark or afflicting dispensation.

Verse 10.   Who is she that looketh forth as the morning, fair as the moon, clear as the sun, and terrible as an army with banners?

THE tenth verse may be taken as the expression of his own esteem of her, and so it begins the second proof of her excellency, that not only they, but he esteems of her. Or, the words may be looked on as the continuance of their praise, and be read thus, " They praised her," saying (as often that word is to be supplied) " who is she ?" &c. If they be thus taken, the scope is the same, holding forth their esteem of her ; and his repeating of it, shews his approbation thereof : and we incline to take the words in this sense, because it continues the series better, and shews their concurring in their thoughts of her, with what were his thoughts, verse 4, which is his scope.   This is peculiarly taken notice of by him as well grounded praise, upon this account, that their thoughts were conformed and agreeable to his.   It will also difference the two confirmations better to begin the second, verse 11, than to take the words simply as the Bridegroom's words, wherein the same thing for substance with what was said, verse 4, is repeated.   However, in these words, her loveliness is set out, 1. In the manner of expression here used, " who is she ?"   Like that chap. iii. 6, which was spoken by the daughters, and so this looks the liker to be spoken by them also, as wondering at her, What is she ? this she must be some singular person, and so it proves his scope, laid down, verse 9.   2. The matter of the words sets out her loveliness in four expressions or similitudes, tending to one thing, namely, to shew the lightsomeness (to say so) of the church, and her ravishing beauty.   The first similitude is, that she " looketh forth as the morning :"   The morning is lightsome, compared with the night, and refreshful; so the Bride is like the morning, compared with the world that is darkness, and she is lovely, cheering and heartsome to look on beyond all others, so the morning is often opposed to affliction and heartlessness, Isa. lviii. 8, for, then birds and fields look cheerful, that before were dark and drooping.   2. She is " fair as the moon :" the moon is the lesser of the two great lights, and was made to guide the night, and is a glorious creature, shining above all stars ; so is the Bride like the moon in a dark night, very conspicuous and beautiful, and useful withal, to them that are acquaint with her. 3. She is " clear as the sun :" This speaks yet more of her splendour, her taking excellent beauty, and usefulness, for the direction and comfort of the daughters that behold her : the sun being the most bright, lightsome and glorious creature of the world, and the greater light that is singularly useful to the world. 4. She is " terrible as an army with banners," which was spoken to, on verse 4, and is here repeated, to shew that it is no common, effeminate beauty, but a stately majesty, wherewith she is adorned, that hath an awfulnesss in it towards men, and a prevailing efficacy towards God. In sum, it describes the spiritual beauty of the Bride in these properties. 1. That it is light-some and shining, there is no true glory but this, which is like the light, all other beauty is but dark ; grace maketh one shine " like a light in a dark place," Phil. ii. 15. 2. It is a growing beauty, every step of these similitudes ascends higher and higher till the sun be rested in, " The way of the just is as the shining light, that shines more and more until the perfect day," Prov. iv. 24. 3. It is comprehensive, therefore it is compared to lights of all sorts ; there is somewhat in grace that resembles every thing that is lovely, God's image being therein eminently. 4. It is stately and awful, being convincing and captivat-ing to onlookers. 5. It is a beauty attended with a military and fighting condition, and therefore compared to armies : the highest commendation of believers doth insinuate them to be in a fighting posture, and the more staidly they maintain their fight, and keep their posture, they will be the more beautiful. 6. A believer that prevails with Christ (as she did, verses 4, 5,) will also be awful to others, as here she is, and will prevail over them, as the Lord saith to Jacob, Gen. xxxii. 28, " Thou hast prevailed with God," and then follows, "thou shalt also prevail with men."

Verse 11. I went down into the garden of nuts to see the fruits of the valley, and to see whether the vine flourished, and the pomegranates budded.

12. Or ever I was aware, my soul made me like the chariots of Ammi-nadib.

FOLLOWS now in the 11th and 12th verses, the second proof of the reality of the beauty and stateliness of the Bride, which puts all out of controversy ; and this proof

he takes from his own experience, respecting what was
said, verses 4, 5, and it may be summed thus.   That must
be stately beauty, that ravisheth me ; (that is understood)
but hers is such ; this is proved from experience, " I went
down" (saith he) " to the garden of nuts" (having withdrawn from that sensible communion which was entertained with the Spouse, as a man doth out of his chamber
to his garden) and was looking to the case of my plants,
according as the Bride had informed the daughters of
Jerusalem, verse 2, but (saith he) " ere I was aware,"
she did cast an eye after me, that so suddenly and effectually ravished me, that I could not but return, and that
speedily, as if I had been mounted upon the swiftest
chariots, and therefore this cannot but be stately loveliness : which agrees with, and relates to what is said,
verse 5, " Thou hast overcome me :" and so we may look
on the words, as if he therein, for her consolation, were
giving her an account of his absence, and what he was
doing ; and he shews her that even while he was absent,
her cries (which chap. v. 6, she thought had not been
heard) and her looks to him, were not forgotten, nor
slighted, even when to her sense she saw him not, yet
even then (saith he) they pierced me, and made my affections warm, that I could not but be affected, and return,
as now thou seest.

The 11th verse shews where he was, and what he was
doing, when he was absent : the 12th verse how he returned.   The place whither he went, was to the " garden
of nuts," that same which was called the garden and beds
of spices, verse 2.   His going down, is his withdrawing
from her sense, and as in that same place, so here his end
is set out in two expressions (which expounds how he
feeds in his gardens.) 1. It is to " see the fruits of the
valley."   The church, called the garden formerly, is here
called the valley, because she is planted, as it were, in a
good valley-soil, where fruits use to thrive best.   His
going to see them, holds forth his accurate observing in
general how it is with them, and his taking delight (as it
were) to recreate himself by beholding of them, as men
do who visit their gardens.   Next, and more particularly, it is " to see whether the vine flourished, and the
pomegranates budded :" by vine and pomegranates, are
understood particular believers, who are as several trees
of his garden, as was cleared on chap. iv. 13.   Their

flourishing or budding, looks to the beginnings of grace, scarce come to ripe fruit, but (as in the bud, chap. ii. 15,) being exceeding tender ; and these are mentioned distinctly, besides the former general, of seeing the fruits ; to shew, 1. His taking particular notice of every particular believer, as a man that goes from tree to tree in his garden. 2. His special notice taking of beginners, and of the beginnings of his work in them, as being especially delighted with the first buddings of grace, and careful that nothing wrong them : this is his feeding in his gardens, and his gathering lilies, to be delighted with fruitfulness in his people, even with their weak and tender beginnings, and to be solicitously careful of their good, as men use to be of the thriving of their fruit-trees.

Observ. 1. Where our Lord Jesus hath a garden, which he hath planted, and on which he takes pains, he looks for fruits ; his garden should never want fruit. 2. There are diverse growths, degrees, or measures of grace amongst his people ; for, some of his trees have fruits, and some but blossoms. 3. Our Lord Jesus takes special notice of his people's fruitfulness, and that as particularly of every one of them, as if he went from one to another (as the gardener doth from tree to tree) to discover it. 4. Our Lord Jesus is especially delighted with the kindly blossomings of beginners, and he takes especial notice of the young and tender buddings of their grace, and will be so far from crushing them, because they are not ripe fruits, that he will more tenderly care for them. 5. Our Lord Jesus accurately takes notice of his Bride's carriage, and fruitfulness, when he seems to her sense to be absent, and is especially much delighted with it then ; for, when he is gone down to his garden, this is the errand, to " see the fruits of the valley, whether :" &c. when he withdraws he hath a friendly design, yet, saith he, although this was intended, I was made, (as it were) to alter my purpose, and not to stay.

And so we come to the 12th verse, in which is set down, how suddenly he is transported with affection to his Bride ; while he is viewing her graces in his absence from her, he is so taken with love to her, that he can stay no longer from her, we may consider in the verse, these three things, 1. An effect, as it were, wrought on him, He " is made like the chariots of Ammi-nadib," or " set as in the chariots of Ammi-nadib :" Chariots were used to travel with, and that for the greater speed; or, they were used in war, for driving furiously (like Jehu) and mightily, over difficulties and obstructions in the way; the word "Ammi-nabid" may be read in one word, and it is to be taken for a proper name of a prince, and thus the expression sets out excellent chariots, such as belonged possibly to some such valiant men of that name; or it may be read in two words, "Ammi nadib," which in the original, signifies "my willing people;" so, "Ammi," signifieth, "my people," as, Hos. ii. 1. Say to your brethren, "Ammi," that is, "my people;" and "Nadib" is the same word that is rendered, Psalm cx, 3, "willing," "thy people shall be willing;" it is a princely beautifulness and willingness, the word, chap. vii. 1. O Prince's daughter, is from the same root, and we rather take it so here, as being more suitable to the scope, which shews what effect his Bride's affection had on him, and the word is often so elsewhere translated; and so it may be rendered, the chariots of my princely willing people: they get this name for their princely behaviour, in wrestling with him under difficulties. Again, the word, "I was made," may be rendered, "was set," (according to the more usual interpretation of the word) thus the effect may be taken two ways to one scope. 1. I was made like the most swift chariots for speedy return, that nothing could detain me from returning to my Bride. Or, 2. If we may call the prayers, faith, and love of his people, their chariots, he is set on them, as taking pleasure to ride and triumph in them, and to be brought back by them, as if by chariots sent from them he had been overcome: and this suits with what is spoken, verse 5, for, while he accounts her as an army; these must needs be her weapons and chariots, to wit, a longing willingness to be at him, and soul-sickness, casting her eyes after him, and in a manner, even fainting for him.

2. There is the manner how this effect is brought about. He is suddenly, as it were, surprised, "or ever I was aware," &c. I knew not (as if he had said) till I was transported with an irresistible power of love toward my Bride, who in the exercise of faith, repentance, and prayer, was seeking after me, while I had withdrawn myself. The expression is borrowed from men (for, properly it agrees not to him) who by sudden effects that fall out beyond their expectation, use to aggravate the wonderful-

ness of the cause that brings them about : thus I know not how it was, it was or I was aware, or, while I was not thinking on it, so forcibly and, as it were, insensibly the thing prevailed over me: Chriст expresseth it thus, to shew the wonderfulness of the thing that came on him, that he could not but do it, and could not shun it, more than if he had had no time to deliberate about it. This narration of Christ's, is not to resent that effect, but to shew how natively it was brought forth, so that when they (to say so) sent their chariots to him, and did cast a look after him, he could not but yield, because he would yield, as the third thing in the verse shews, and that is, what it was that so easily prevailed with him ; the cause is within himself that set him on these chariots of his willing people, and made him to be overcome: it was even, his soul, "my soul made me," or, set me, that is, my inward soul, my affections, my bowels were so kindled, (as it is Jer. xxxi. 20,) and my soul cleaved so to my loving and longing Bride, and was so stirred with her exercise, that I could not but hastily and speedily yield, because I could not resist my own affections. Hence, *Observe*, 1. willingness is much prized by Jesus Christ, when the soul yields to open to him, and longs for him, verse 5, and cannot want him, there Christ (as chap. v. 6.) will not, and cannot continue at a distance. 2. Although Christ's affection doth not properly surprise him, nor do the effects thereof fall from him inadvertently, but most deliberately, yet both his affection and the effects thereof, are most wonderful and astonishing in themselves, and ought, as such, in a singular manner to affect us. 3. The first rise and cause of all believers' good, and that which makes their faith, prayer, love, &c. bear weight with Christ, is in himself; it is his own soul, and good will that overcomes and prevails with him in all these: it is not any worth or power in their graces, as considered in themselves, that hath this influence upon him, but his intimate love to believers themselves, that makes their graces have such weight with him : all that ever came speed with him, were prevented by his love. 4. The believer hath a notable friend in Christ's own bosom, his soul is friendly to them, and is in a kindly way affected with their conditions, even though in his dispensations no such thing appear : and while he is man, and hath a soul, they want not a friend. 5. Considering this as the exercise of his soul, when he was withdrawn to her sense, and she was complaining. *Observe,* That Christ's bowels and soul are never more affected toward his people, than when he seems most offended with them, and when they are most offended with the wrongs done to him, Jer. xxxi. 19, 20, Judges x. 16. There be many inconceiveable turnings in his bowels, even when he seems to speak against them to the sense, then he earnestly remembers them still, and their friend love steps to, and takes part for them, and so prevails, that by his own bowels he is restrained from executing the fierceness of his anger (Hos. xi. 8, compared with 9,) and constrained even when he is provoked to take some other course to express marvellous loving kindness to them.

Verse 13.   Return, return, O Shulamite ; return, return, that we may look upon thee.   What will ye see in the Shulamite? As it were the company of two armies.

The thirteenth verse continueth the same scope, and is a confirmation of the interpretation given of the former verse, and a new expression of his love, whereby as a kind husband having forgotten by-past failing in his wife, he invites her to return to her former familiarity, with a motive signifying the love which he had to her, and that upon so good ground (in his gracious estimation) as that by her yielding to return, he puts no question, but what he had spoken of her stately terribleness, would be found to be a truth.   The verse contains these three, 1. A most affectionate invitation. 2. A most loving motive proposed, persuading to embrace it, which is his end. 3. An objection removed, whereby the motive is confirmed and illustrated.   In the exhortation or invitation, Consider, 1. The party invited, or called. 2. The duty called for. 3. Its repetition.   The party called, is a Shulamite: this word comes either from Solomon as the husband's name is named over the wife, Isa. iv. 1, and it is from the same root that signifies peace, from which Solomon had his name ; and it is in the femenine gender, because it is applied to the Bride: thus it holdeth forth, 1. The strict union betwixt him and her, that she with him partakes of the same name: see Jer. xxiii. 6, compared with Jer. xxxiii. 16, where ye will find the like communication of his name to her. 2. It shews the privilege she was admitted unto, through her tie to him and union with him, by which she is made his, and is admitted to share with him in all that is his ; for, it is not an empty style she gets, while called by his name, it being to signify that she was his, and that whatever he had (whereof she was capable, and might be for her good) was hers. 3. It shews his affection that he so names her now, wishing her a part of his own peace, and entitling her to it. Or, 2. This word may be derived from Salem, which properly taken, is Jerusalem, Psalm lxxvi. 1. and Heb. viii. 1. Melchisedec was king of Salem, which signifieth peace, and so, as Shunemitish comes from Shunem, so Shulamite comes from Salem, and so taking the derivation thus, it comes to the same thing with the former, both being derived from the same root; and this holds forth his respect to her, as acknowledging her new-birth and original from the new Jerusalem. 2. The exhortation is, "return:" this implies, 1. A distance whether in respect of sin, Jer. iii. 1. for, sin breeds distance betwixt Christ and his people, Isa. lix. 2, or, in respect of sensible manifestations of his love ; for, howsoever, the distance brought on by sin, was in some measure taken away, and she returned to her former obedience and wonted tenderness, yet she wants the sense of his love, and is seeking after it: "return," here then, supposeth somewhat of these. 2. A duty laid on her, to quit this distance and to return ; this the very expression bears. 3. A kind offer of welcome, which is implied in his offers and exhortations, whenever he calls : so Jer. iii. 14 ; Jer. iv. 1, and thus the sense is, as if he had said, there hath been a distance betwixt us, and thou art suspicious of my love : but return and come hither, and neither thy former faults, nor present jealousy shall be remembered ; and this shews, that the words are his, both because the scope is continued, and also because none can call the Bride properly or effectually to return but he, neither would the voice of another be so confirming to her of his affection, and his scope is to confirm her, as to that.

3. This exhortation is twice doubled, "Return, return," and again, "return, return :" 1. To shew the hazard she was in. 2. Her duty to prevent it. 3. The necessity of speedy putting the exhortation in practice. 4. The difficulty that there was to bring her over her discouragements. 5. His great and earnest desire to have them all

removed, and to have the duty performed. These words
shew, 1. That there may be a distance betwixt Christ
and his Bride; even the beautiful believer may fall into
a distance of sin. 2. Of indisposition. 3. Of comfort-
lessness. And, 4. Of discouragement and heartlessness, which follows on the former. 2. There is often a
loathness to come home, when there hath been a straying; discouragement and shame may prevail so far, as to
scare fainting believers (who fain would have him) from
hearty applying of his allowances to themselves. 3.
Souls that are at a distance from Christ, whatever kind of
distance it be, should not sit down under it, or give way
to it, but wrestle from under it, over all difficulties that
are in their way. 4. This should be done speedily, and
without all delay, dispute, or dallying; therefore doth the
Lord so double his call; there will sure be no advantage
by delaying or putting off this great business of returning
from our distance to him. 5. The return of believers
after a slip, to confident walking with Christ, and comforting of themselves in him, is allowed by him and well
pleasing to him, as well as the conversion and coming
home of a sinner at first. 6. Believers after their slips,
are not easily persuaded of Christ's kindness, in the measure that he hath it to them; nor are they easily brought
to that confidence of it, that formerly they had. 7. Our
Lord Jesus allows his people to be fully confident of his
love, and of obtaining welcome from him; for which reasons this return, as a sure evidence and testimony of his
kind and hearty welcome, is four times repeated to shew
that he is entreating and waiting for it, and cannot abide
to have it delayed.

2. The end proposed, that makes him so serious, is in
these words, "that we may look upon thee:" it doth him
good (to speak so) to get a sight of her: this looking of
his, is not for curiosity, but for delightsome satisfaction to
his affection, as one desires to look upon what he loves,
so, chap. ii. 14, speaking to his Bride, "Let me see" (saith
he) "thy face, for thy countenance is comely." This is
to take away all jealousy from the Bride, and to shew
how he was taken with her, so that her returning would be
a singular pleasure to him, which is indeed wonderful.

Observ. 1. Our Lord Jesus allows the Bride, when
returning to him after her departings from him, to be confident in him, and familiar with him. 2. The more that

nearness to him be sought after and entertained, he is the
more satisfied.   3. When believers hide themselves from
Christ, even though it be through discouragement, and
upon just ground and reason, as they think ; yet doth it
someway mar Christ's delightsome complacency, and he
is not satisfied till they shake off their discouragement,
and shew themselves to him with confidence.

Again, we should consider, that it is not said, that I
may look on thee ; but that " we," &c.   Which is to shew,
that she is delightsome to many, her beauty may be seen
by any that will look upon her : this word, " we," 1.
May import the blessed Trinity, the Father, Son, and
Spirit, as chap. i. 11, " we will make," &c.   A returning
sinner will be welcome to all the persons of the Godhead.
2. " We," that is, " I," with the angels, who (Luke xv.
10,) " Rejoice at the conversion of a sinner."   And, 3.
" we," may import, " I," and all the daughters that admire thee.   The thriving of one believer, or, the returning of a sinner may make many cheerful, and is to be accounted a lovely thing by all the professors of religion.

3. The third thing in the verse, comes in by way of
question, either to heighten the loveliness that is in Christ's
Bride; what is it that is to be seen in her ? as, Luke vii.
24, &c. " what went ye out for to see ?"   No common
sight : or, it is to meet with an objection that strangers
may have, what delightsome thing is to be seen in her,
that seems so despicable ?   Or, she herself might object,
what is in me worth the seeing ?   It may be, when it is
well seen, that it be less thought of.   The Lord to prevent such doubts, especially in her, moves the question,
that he himself may give the answer ; " what" (saith he)
" will ye see in the Shulamite ? (that is) which may be
pleasant and delightful : and he answers, " as it were the
company of two armies ;" which in general holds out, 1.
We will see much majesty and stateliness in her; even
so much as I have asserted, in comparing her to an army
with banners. 2. Two armies may be mentioned, to
shew, that when she is rightly, and with a believing eye
looked upon, her beauty will appear to be double to what
it was said to be ; and so, "two armies" signify an excellent army, as, Gen. xxxii. 1, 2, God's hosts of angels
get the same name in the original, it is Mahanaim, that
same which Jacob imposeth as the name upon the place,
where these hosts of angels met him ; and there may be

an allusion to this, these two ways, 1. Ask ye what is
to be seen in her? even as it were Mahanaim, that is, for
excellency she is like an host of angels, such as appeared
to Jacob; she is an angelic sight, more than an ordinary
army: this is a notable commendation, and serves his
purpose well, which is to confirm her: and therefore,
that his poor Bride may be encouraged to press in on him,
and return to him, he tells her, she may be as homely
with him as angels, that are holy and sinless creatures;
which is a wonderful privilege, yet such as is allowed on his
people, by him who hath not taken on the nature of
angels, but of men, that he might purchase them a room
amongst angels "that stand by," Zech. iii. 6, 7. 2. It
may allude thus, what is to be seen in her? whatever it
be to the world, it is to me (saith he) excellent and refreshful, as these hosts of angels were to Jacob at Mahanaim, when he had been rescued from Laban, and was to
meet with Esau: either of these suits well the scope, and
saith, it will be, and is a sweet and refreshful meeting,
that is betwixt Christ and a returning sinner, a little view
whereof is in that parable, Luke xv. 20, of the prodigal
his father's hearty receiving of his lost son, and making
himself and all his servants merry with him.

Observ. 1. Our Lord Jesus is very tender of believers'
doubts and perplexities, and therefore prevents their objections which they may make, by giving answers to them,
before the objections be well formed or stated in their
hearts. 2. Believers may and usually do, wonder what
ground there is in them, for such kindness as Christ shews
to them, when he magnifieth them and their graces so
much, that are so defective and full of blemishes: and
indeed it is such that are readiest to wonder most at his
love, and esteem least of themselves, whom he makes
most of, and of whom he hath the greatest esteem. 3. It
is a wonderful welcome that Christ gives to repenting
sinners, he receives them as angels, and admits them to
such freedom with him, and hath such esteem of them, as
if they were angels; for, to be received " as an angel,"
signifies honourable and loving entertainment, Gal. iv. 14.
4. The returning of sinners to Christ, and Christ's loving
welcome which he gives them upon their return, makes a
heartsome and refreshing meeting betwixt him and them:
and O what satisfaction and joy shall there be, when they
being all gathered together, shall meet with him at the
last day!

CHAPTER VII.

BRIDEGROOM.

Verse 1. How beautiful are thy feet with shoes, O prince's
daughter ! the joints of thy thighs are like jewels, the work
of the hands of a cunning workman :

2. Thy navel is like a round goblet, which wanteth not liquor :
thy belly is like an heap of wheat set about with lilies :

3. Thy two breasts are like two young roes that are twins.

This chapter hath two parts ; in the first, reaching to the
tenth verse, Christ continueth in the commendation of his
Bride : in the second, thence to the close, the Bride expresseth her complacency in him and in his love, her enlarged desires after communion with him, and that she
might be found fruitful to his praise.

That it is Christ, the Bridegroom, who was speaking
in the end of the former chapter, that continues his speech
throughout the first part of this, there is no just ground
to question, the scope, style and expressions being so like
unto, and co-incident with what went before ; and what
is spoken in the first person, verse 8, can be applied to
none other, neither would it become any to speak thus but
himself, his love is enlarged and loosed (as it were) in
its expressions, and this love of his is indeed a depth, that
is not easily reached.   In this commendation, he doth first
enumerate ten particulars (as she had done when she
commended him, chap. v.)   Then, 2. He shews his ac-
quiescing in her, as being ravished with her beauty, verse
6, &c.   We had occasion to say something in the general
of such commendations, chap. iv. 1, which is now to be
remembered, but not repeated ; we take this to be understood after the same manner as that was, and although
the visible church be in some respect Christ's Bride, and
therefore, we will not condemn the application of some of
the parts of this commendation to her as so considered ;
yet, since the scope is mainly to comfort true believers,
as differenced from others, and that it is she to whom he
speaks, who had ravished him with her eyes in the former
chapter (which can agree properly to the true believer only)
and considering also, that some parts of the commendation
do respect inherent grace in his people (and indeed it is

this, which is the great ground of the Bride's commendation) we therefore incline still to take these commendations, as holding forth the continuance of the expressions of Christ's love to those, who are his own by saving faith; and so much the rather, as the words being taken so, are of special and particular use for believers.

There are four differences in this commendation, from that mentioned, chap. iv. and that which was spoken to, on chap. vi. 6, 7, which by answering four questions, we shall clear.

Quest. 1. Wherefore is this subjoined now, after so large a commendation in the words immediately preceding. *Answ.* The former commendation shews Christ's love to his Bride (to say so) immediately after the marriage, or on the back of some agreement, after an outcast; but, this is added, to shew what is Christ's ordinary way of carriage to his people, and what are his usual thoughts (to say so) of them; he is not kind only at fits (as men sometimes use to be, and do no not continue) or, when he was surprised (as it were) with a sudden gale of affection, chap. vi. 12; no, he is constantly kind; and therefore, these expressions are now renewed, to show that such are his ordinary kind ways of dealing towards them, even when there is no connexion betwixt his dealing and their present condition, nor any thing in them that can be looked on as the immediate rise thereof: our blessed Lord is a most fair, loving and friendly speaker unto, and converser with his Bride.

Quest. 2. Why is this commendation enlarged beyond the former, having more particulars in it? *Answ.* Thereby the Lord shews, 1. The sovereignty of his love, in making the intimations thereof, less or more as he pleaseth. 2. The last commendation is most full, in expressing the riches of his love, to shew that Christ never speaks so kindly to one of his own, but there is more behind in his heart than hath yet vented itself, and that there is more which they may expect from him, than they have yet met with, however that may be very much. 3. It is to make it the fresher unto them, when by this it is evidenced to be a new intimation of his kindness, although it proceed on the same grounds, on which former intimations did; and this may be a reason also of the third difference, and question following, which is,

Quest. 3. Why are the same parts named, as "eyes,

hair," &c. and yet the commendation is different from what it was, for the most part? *Answ.* 1. This is to shew the beauty of grace, which is such, that one commendation cannot reach it. 2. The account that he in his love hath of her, which is so great, that one expression doth not fully answer it. The various and abundant ways, that love hath to speak comfortably to a believer, there is strange eloquence and rhetoric in the love of Christ, when he thinks good to vent it.

Quest. 4. Why is the way he followed before changed? He began formerly at the head, now at the feet? *Answ.* This is also a piece of his sovereignty, and shews how he delights to vary the expressions of his love to his people; and that it may be seen, that whatever way we will follow in looking upon grace in a believer, it is still beautiful in itself, and acceptable to him.

The first verse contains two pieces of the Bride's commendation: the first part that is commended is the feet, "How beautiful are thy feet!" &c. In this consider the title she gets. 2. The part commended. 3. The commendation itself. 4. The manner of expressing of it. First, The title is, " O prince's daughter!" This was not given her before, it is now prefixed to this commendation in general, to usher in all that follows, and to make it the more gaining on her affection: the word in the first language is, Nadib, which signifies a bounteous prince, or, one of a princely disposition, Isa. xxxii. 5. It is given to the visible church, Psalm xlv. 13, " The King's daughter is all glorious within." For more full taking up of the meaning, consider, that it doth here include these three, 1. A nobleness and greatness in respect of birth, that the Bride is honourably descended; from which we may learn, That believers (whatever they be in respect of the flesh) are of a royal descent and kindred, "a royal priesthood," 1 Pet. ii. 9, " Sons and daughters to the Lord God Almighty," 2 Cor. vi. 18. 2. It respects her qualifications, as being princely in her carriage, suitable to such a birth, Eccles. x. 17. Hence observe, the believer should be of a princely disposition and carriage, and when he is right, he will be so; for, he is endued with princely qualifications, with noble and excellent principles beyond the most generous, noble, gallant and stately dispositions of men in the world: a believer when right, or in good case, is a princely person indeed. 3. It respects her provision and expectation; that she is provided for, waited upon, and to be dealt with, and even caressed not as children of mean persons, but of princes, to whom it is her "Father's good pleasure to give a kingdom," and such a one as is "undefiled, and fadeth not away," Luke xii. 32 ; 1 Pet. i. 4. Hence observe, That the believer is royally dealt with by Jesus Christ, and hath a royal princely allowance bestowed on him ; the charter of adoption takes in very much, even to "inherit with him all things :" no less than this may be expected, and is the claim of a daughter to the King of kings, Rev. xxi. 7.

2. The part commended is, "the feet," by which a believer's walk and conversation, as grace shines in it, is understood, as we may see frequently, Psalm cxix. verses 59, 101, 105. So likewise shedding of blood, or other defiling sins, such as leave foul prints upon a man's conversation behind them are called the "iniquities of the heels," Psalm xlix. 5, by which the nakedness and offensiveness of one's conversation is set forth : and on the contrary, the Bride's feet thus commended, sets out her good conversation.

3. Her feet are commended from this, that they are not bare, but, "beautiful with shoes." To be bare-footed, imports three things in scripture, 1. A shameful condition, Isa. xx. 4. 2. A present sad affliction, the sense whereof makes men careless of what is adorning ; so David, 2 Sam. xv. 30, under heavy affliction, walks bare-footed. 3. An unfitness for travel ; therefore, when the people were to be in readiness for their journey, Exod. xii. 11, their feet were to be shod : so then, to have on shoes, doth on the contrary import three things, 1. The honourable estate and dignity to which believers are advanced ; and more especially, it holds out a singular beautifulness in their walk, whereby their shame is covered. 2. A thriving in their spiritual condition. 3. A readiness and promptness of obedience, to what they are called unto : all which are beautiful in themselves, and adorning to the believer. We take it, in a word, to hold out a conversation, such "as becomes the gospel," Philip. i. 27, which is, to have "the feet shod with the preparation of the gospel of peace," Eph. vi. 15, because, that as by shoes, men are enabled to walk without hurt in rough ground, and are in the company of others not ashamed of their nakedness ; so, a gospel conversation quiets the mind, keeping it in peace against difficulties, and doth exceed-

ingly strengthen the confidence of believers in their conversing with others, and becomes exceeding lovely, that
they care not (as it were) who see them ; as, Ezek xvi. 10.
" I shod thee," &c. Whereas a disorderly conversation is
shameful, even like one that is bare-footed.

4. The manner of the expression is, to heighten the
loveliness of a well ordered walk. " How beautiful are
thy feet with shoes !" It cannot be told how beautiful a
tender and well ordered conversation is ; it is exceeding
lovely, and acceptable to me (saith he) to see thy holy walk.

Observ. 1. Our Lord Jesus takes notice of every step
of a believer's carriage, and can tell whether their feet be
shod or bare, whether their conversation be such as adorn-
eth or shameth the gospel. 2. The believer hath, or at
least ought to have, and, if he be like himself, will have
a well ordered walk, and will be in his carriage stately
and princely. 3. A conversation, that is well ordered,
is a beautiful and pleasant thing : grace, exercised in a
Christian's practice, is more commendable to Christ, than
either greatness, riches, wisdom, or what the world esteems
most of ; none of these hath such a commendation from
Christ, as the believer, who, it may be, is not much in the
world's esteem : practical holiness is a main part of
spiritual beauty, and is valuable above speculative knowledge and many gifts. 4. Believers should be walking
creatures, therefore hath the new nature feet ; that is,
they should be much in the practice of holy duties, according to the commands he hath given in his word : and in
their way they should be making progress towards perfection ; for, that is their mark, Phil. iii. 13. Sitting still,
or negligence, much more going backward, is unlike a
believer. 5. The conversation of all others, though never
so fairded with much civility, and great profession, and
many parts, is yet naked and abominable before God, and
subject to bruisings, stumblings, and such inconveniences
as feet that are bare are liable to. 6. A well ordered
walk is sure and safe : " He that walks uprightly walks
surely," Prov. x. 9. And, saith the Psalmist, " Great
peace have they who love thy law, and nothing shall offend
them," Psalm cxix. 165. Their feet are shod against an
evil time, and there is nothing safer when offences abound
than that.

The second part of the commendation is to the same
scope, " The joints of thy thighs," &c. It is the coupling

and turnings of them, as the word bears; they are also useful in motion, and help the feet to stir, the same thing is intended as in chap. v. 15, by his thighs or legs; only it seems to look to the principles of their walk, as the feet do respect their way more immediately: these are compared to jewels, which are precious and comely, serving much for adorning; and it is not to ordinary jewels, to which they are compared, but such as are the "work of the hands of a cunning skilful artificer, or workman," that is, such as are set orderly and dexterously, by skill and art; the work, not of a novice, but of one that is expert; by which, not only the matter of their practice is holden forth to be solid, but also, in respect of the principles from which their way and duties have their spring and rise and the manner of their performing them, they are rightly gone about, with an holy kind of art and dexterity: which saith, 1. That there are many things necessarily concurring in a well ordered conversation; there must be skill to do rightly, what is in itself right, to make it commendable: it is needful that holy duties, and what is on the matter called for, be done in the right manner, and according to art, and not put by thus, and so.　2. Believers are singularly expert, in doing of the same duties of religion which other men do, they do them in another manner.　3. The several pieces of a holy walk, are in a manner but split, when not rightly ordered, and every one put in its own place, like jewels undexterously set by one that is unskilful.　4. There is an holy art required to those that would walk commendably, and men naturally are unskilful in such practices, until they be taught them.　5. Being right in the manner, is no less necessary to make a man's way commendable, than to be right in the matter, as much of the commendation lies in this, as in the other; when these two go together in a believer's conversation, it is excellent and beautiful; there is no jewel, most finely set, comparable to a well ordered walk.　6. Believers that use to walk in the way of godliness, may attain to this spiritual dexterity and skilfulness in a great measure: and there is no other way of attaining it, but by accustoming ourselves to it; when her feet are once shod, this commendation follows, that "the joints of her thighs are like jewels."

In the second verse, the Lord proceeds from the "thighs," to the "navel" and "belly:" which parts, were not touched in her commendation, chap. iv. These parts in men's bodies have not much beauty in them ; and therefore, it seems, that by them the Lord points rather at what is inward and useful, in the spiritual complexion and constitution of believers, than what is outward and visible in their walk, that serving no less to their commendation than this.

The navel hath much influence on the intestines ; and when it is sound, it furthers much the health of the whole body; so, Prov. iii. 8, it is said, the fear of the Lord " shall be health to thy navel, and marrow to thy bones ;" that is, it will be exceeding useful and profitable for thy well-being, as it is useful for the body to have that part in good case : and, on the contrary, a wretched miserable condition (such as is our condition by nature) is described by this, " thy navel was not cut," &c. Ezek. xvi. 4. It is known also, that in nature, the navel hath much influence on the child in the womb, which may be especially taken notice of here, as appears by the following commendation, namely, that it " is like a round goblet," that is, well formed and proportioned (opposite to a " navel not cut," Ezek. xvi. 4.) " which wanteth not liquor," that is, furnished with moisture for the health of the body, or entertainment and nourishment of the child in the womb.

Before we further clear the words, or observe any thing from them, we shall join to this the fourth part here commended, and that is, the " belly :" the word differs in the original, from that which is translated belly : being spoken of him, chap. v. 14, and it is taken for the inward parts, Jer. xv. 35 ; Prov. xviii. 8. It hath a special influence on the health of the body, and on the bringing forth of children : it is here compared to " an heap of wheat ;" to " an heap," to shew her bigness, as being with child, and still fruitful, and that in abundance : to " an heap of" the grain of " wheat," to shew, it was not big with wind, but with good grain, even the best, whereby she feeds him herself, and others : and so, as in the former similitude, she is represented to be furnished with liquor, so here she is set forth to be furnished with bread, whereby her spiritual liveliness and healthfulness may be understood. Again, this heap of wheat is said to be " set about with lilies," not only thereby to express its beautifulness, with its usefulness, but also the fruitfulness thereof, in having particular graces as lilies growing about it, which are moistened and nourished by these two parts, the navel and the belly. Now we conceive, that most likely (though it be hard to be peremptory) the graces of the Spirit may be understood here, which being infused in their habits, and drawn forth in their actings by the influences of the Spirit, are compared to waters and liquor, and are said to be in the belly of the believer, John vii. 38, (" He that believes on me, out of his belly shall flow rivers of waters") because they have such influence on the new man, and (to speak so) are the health of the navel thereof. In sum, the sense of the words comes to this, O prince's daughter, thou hast a lively spiritual constitution, by the inward flowings of the Spirit, whereby thy navel is formed and beautified (which was by nature otherwise) and therefore thou art not barren, but fruitful, and that of the most precious fruits. Hence observe, 1. That believers' inward constitution and frame, is no less beautiful than their outward conversation and walk : this " King's daughter is all glorious within," Psalm xlv. 13. 2. Soundness within, or heart-soundness is no less needful than outward fruits, for completing a believer's commendation ; to have the navel well formed, is as necessary and requisite, as to have the feet beautiful with shoes. 3. Inward liveliness, or a well furnished inside, hath most influence on a believer's liveliness in all external duties : this keeps all fresh, being like precious liquor which makes Christ's Spouse fruitful and big, and that not with wind, but wheat.

The two breasts (which is the fifth part here commended) are spoken to in this third verse : they were spoken of, chap. iv. 5, with the same commendation, and we conceive the same thing hinted there, is aimed at here, namely to shew, that as she was healthful in herself, and prosperous (like that which is said, Job xxi. 24, " his breasts are full of milk") so was she both fitted to communicate, and loving in communcating the graces that was in her, as nurses their milk to their children : which clears, that the scope in short is to shew, that the believer is not only a beautiful bride, but a fruitful mother for bringing forth, verse 2, and nourishing and bringing up, verse 3, which was (especially in those times) a great commendation of a wife, and a thing that engaged husbands to them, Psalm cxxviii. 3 ; Gen. xxix. 34, as on the contrary, barrenness was a reproach to themselves, and a burden to their husbands : now, Christ's Bride hath breasts, and

is furnished as becomes a mother and a wife, contrary to
that of the "little sister," chap. viii. 8, whose desolate
condition is set out by this, that "she had no breasts;"
and this is repeated particularly, to shew the Lord's particular taking notice thereof, and his respect thereunto.

Verse 4. Thy neck is as a tower of ivory ; thine eyes like the
  fish-pools in Heshbon, by the gate of Bath-rabbim; thy nose
  is as the tower of Lebanon, which looketh toward Damascus.

In the fourth verse, three more of the Bride's parts
(which make the sixth, seventh, and eighth) are commended.   The sixth is the neck : it was spoken of, chap.
iv. 4, neither doth the commendation differ much : there,
it was said to be like "the tower of David," here it is
" as a tower of ivory," that is, both comely and precious,
being made of the elephant's teeth, a tower whereof, must
be very precious : and by this we conceive, the great defensive efficacy of faith is set forth, which is still a tower,
yet comparable to many, it is so excellent and sure ; they
dwell safely who are believers, because they dwell in
God, and in his Son, Jesus Christ.   And so we may here
observe, 1.   Faith is a precious defence ; for, Christ is a
precious hiding-place, and faith must be precious, because
Christ is precious: hence it is not only precious as ivory,
but "much more precious than gold," 1 Pet. i. 7.   2.
Faith is a sure defence, and is the believer's tower, whereto he betakes himself when he hath to do.   3. It is lovely
and pleasant to Christ, when believers by faith betake
themselves to him ; he will never quarrel with them for
it, seeing he so commends it.   4. There is no safe tower
to any of the world, but what the believer hath ; for, he,
and he only, hath a tower of ivory to make use of : Christ
is the only rock and sure foundation, and it is only believers that build their house upon him.

The seventh part instanced, is "her eyes," which were
several times mentioned before ; they point at her spiritual discerning, and understanding of spiritual things, and
the believing uptaking of them ; in which respect, all natural men are blind, because of their ignorance and unbelief; she only hath eyes.   They are compared to "fish-
pools in Heshbon, at the gate of Bath-rabbim:" this city
Heshbon is mentioned, Num. xxi. 25, 26.   It was a royal
city, where Sihon king of the Amorites dwelt ; and it is

like, there hath been some place there called Beth-rabbim, for the great resort that was made thereunto : and the fish-pools that were there, it seems, were excellent and clear, and fit to give a shadow to those who looked into them. Now it would seem, that believers' eyes are compared to these pools, because of the clear, distinct, and believing knowledge they have of themselves, of Christ, and of other spiritual objects. And from this we may observe, 1. That solid and distinct knowledge in spiritual things, is very commendable. 2. That a believer hath another kind of insight in spiritual things, than the most understanding natural man : he hath eyes in respect of him ; the natural man (who hath no experimental nor believing knowledge of spiritual things) is but blind. 3. He is sharpest sighted that discerns himself, and can rightly take up his own condition ; " the wisdom of the prudent is to understand his way :" so believers' eyes, or knowledge, is compared to a fish pond, that gives representations of a man's face to him.

The eighth particular is, the nose, (it was not mentioned in her commendation, chap. iv.) It is not to be taken here for the whole countenance, but for a part thereof : therefore it is distinguished from the eyes, and is described as being eminent (like a tower) beyond the rest of the face, and so it is to be applied to the nose properly, which ariseth with a height on the face, like a tower, and is the seat of smelling to discover what is hurtful, or savoury ; also anger or zeal appear in it, therefore is it in the Hebrew language in the Old Testament, sometimes put for these, because it shews a real indignation, when a man's anger smokes forth at his nose, Psalm xviii. 8. It is said, 1. To be like " the tower of Lebanon :" there is no particular mention of such a tower, but, that Solomon built there a stately house, 2 Chron. viii. 3, called the " house of the forest of Lebanon," wherein, 2 Chron. ix. 15, 16. he put many " targets" and " shields ;" and Lebanon being on the north side of Judah, near to Syria (where enemies soon brake out against Solomon) it is not unlike, but either this house was made use of as a frontier-tower, or that some other was there builded, for preventing of hurt from that hand, to which this alludes. Next, this tower is said to look " towards Damascus :" Damascus was the head city of Syria ; so, Isa. vii. 8, it is said, " the head of Syria is Damascus :" those that dwelt in it, were at that

time amongst the most malicious enemies that Israel had ;
they were so in David's time, 2 Sam. viii. 5, he slew two
and twenty thousand of them ; they were so in Solomon's
time, 1 King xi. 34. Rezon (whom God raised up to be
an enemy to him) did reign in Damascus ; and generally
they continued to be so. They lay on the north of Judah
(therefore it is called evil from the north, which came
from Syria) and Lebanon was on the north border of
Israel next to it : and it is like, that for this cause, either
Solomon did change that place into a tower, or built some
other of new, to be a watch especially against that enemy,
which was his chief enemy, to prevent the hurt that might
come from that hand ; therefore, it is said to look toward
(or to the face of) Damascus, as having a special respect
to that enemy. Now we conceive, that by this, the Bride's
watchfulness and zeal, in prosecuting and maintaining her
spiritual war against her enemies, is understood ; as also,
her sagacity, in smelling and discovering the stirrings and
motions of her spiritual enemies, as the nose doth easily
smell and discover what is pleasant or hurtful to sense.
Christ's Bride hath many enemies, and some more terrible
than others ; therefore, she hath her watches, and (as it
were) sentinels at the post, to observe their motions,
especially she hath an eye upon her most inveterate and
malicious enemy, the enemy nearest her doors, that is
naturally most predominant, and her great care is to be
kept from " her iniquity," Psalm xviii. 21. This we conceive, agrees both with the scope, and also with the dis-
cription and comparison here made use of.

Observ. 1. The most beautiful Bride of our Lord Jesus
hath enemies, and such enemies, as are strongly seated and
fortified (as the Syrians at Damascus were) to watch
against. 2. There are some particular quarters, or enemies,
from which, and by which, believers often suffer most ;
and although they have enemies on all hands, yet is there
ordinarily some one particular enemy, more terrible, malicious and predominant than others, from which they are
most in danger. 3. Believers should ever be on their
watch against those enemies, and must neither make peace
with them, nor be negligent to provide against them. 4.
Although the believer should not be secure or careless,
in reference to any ill, but every evil is to be carefully
watched against ; yet, where one ill doth more often
assault him than others, and is more strong, by the con-

currence of tentations from without, or from his own inclinations within, there the believer hath need of a special watch. 5. This watchfulness impartially extended, and constantly maintained, is a main piece of spiritual beauty, and hath much influence on the adorning of a believer, and is a good evidence of a person that is commendable before Jesus Christ.

Verse 5. Thine head upon thee is like Carmel, and the hair of thine head like purple : the king is held in the galleries.

THE first part of verse 5, contains the ninth and tenth particulars, that are commended in the Bride : the ninth is her head ; it looks here to be taken for the uppermost part of the head (from which sense and motion do flow) as being distinct from eyes and nose ; therefore it is said, " Thy head upon thee," to wit, upon and above those parts before mentioned : next, it is said to be " like Carmel ;" which may be understood, 1. As it relates to a fruitful place, mentioned with Sharon, Isa. xxxv. 2, " The excellency of Carmel and Sharon." 2. It may be translated scarlet or crimson, as the same word is, 2 Chron. iii. 14, thus it is a rich colour, wherewith princes and great men used to be decorated ; and the hair being in the next words compared to purple, it is not unlike that it is taken for a colour here also.

By " head," we must understand either Christ himself, who stands in that relation to the believer, and in respect of dignity is called " a head to all men," 1 Cor. xi. 3.   Or, 2. (which is not inconsistent with the former) some grace in the believer, acting on Christ, and quickening the new life ; and seeing the scope is to commend the believer from inherent grace, and the new nature being compared to an inner-man, which is described from its several parts, and so must have an head, we think that it is some particular grace that is here especially aimed at.   By " head" then, we conceive the grace of hope may be understood, it being the grace whereby the soul sticks to Christ, expecting the enjoyment of him ; for, not only is hope a grace necessary and commendable (and so it cannot be unsuitable to the scope, to take it in upon one branch or other) but it may be called the head, 1. Because it is above, having Christ himself for its object ; and though the word may be said to be the object of hope, yet it is not so much the word, as Christ held forth in the word ; and therefore, hope is said to be " within the vail," Heb. vi. 19, for, properly we hope for him, because of his word, and so he is "our hope," 1. Tim. i. 1.　2. Hope is a grace, which hath its rise from faith, and is supported by it, as the head is by the neck ; though hope be someway above faith, yet doth faith sustain it, and give it a being ; the believer hopes, because he believes.　3. It hath much influence on all spiritual duties, and especially on our consolation, and is useful in the spiritual war, as being an essential piece of the believer's spiritual armour, and is therefore called the " helmet" or head-piece " of salvation," 1 Thess. v. 8, and the head-piece may be someway called the head ; so hope, which keepeth (to say so) grace's head, may not unfitly be called the head, seeing without it the head will be at least without its helmet ; and taking it so, for this special piece of the believer's armour, it follows well on watchfulness : however, it is certain, that hope bears up the believer under difficulties, Rom. vii. 24, and that it rests on Christ, who therefore is called our hope : and so, co-relatively being considered, as acting on him, it may get the name of head, as faith is upon the like account called our righteousness, and thus our head is Christ hoped upon : and the commendation, that is, like crimson, will suit well this interpretation, the red or crimson colour having a special reference to Christ's death and sufferings, which puts the right colour on our hope, and makes it of this dye, that it is never ashamed or stained, Rom. v. 3. *Observ.* 1. The exercising of hope is a necessary piece of a believer's beauty, and as to have the heart sustained and comforted in the hope of what is not seen, is both necessary and profitable ; so, when by the power of hope, a believer's head is helped up, and kept above in all waters, that he sink not, it is his singular ornament.　2. Hardly will a believer be in good case, without this grace of hope, and when other graces are lively, hope will be so also : these pieces of armour, and spiritual decorating go together. 3. There is no other in the world that hath a well-grounded hope but the believer ; it is only the believer, whose head is like crimson : all others, their hope makes ashamed, and their confidence shall be rooted out ; whereas, his will be always fresh and green.

The tenth and last particular here commended in the Bride, is her " hair :" this was spoken of, chap. iv. 1.

But here, both the word in the original, and the commendation that is given of it, do differ from that which is
there recorded: the word here translated, "hair," is not
elsewhere to be found, it comes from a root that gives
ground to expound its smallness, or tenderness: therefore, it is taken by some, to signify a pin, or some of the
small decorations of the head: and it is compared to
"purple," for its preciousness, loveliness, and other reasons formerly mentioned in speaking of that colour.

We take the scope here to be, to shew the universal
loveliness and preciousness of grace in a believer, even in
the least things; what shall I say (saith he) that thy
"feet, navel, eyes" and "head" are beautiful? even thy
"hair," or the pins that dress it, are lovely and excellent:
so glorious, princely, and stately a creature is this Bride,
that there is not a wrong pin or hair to be found upon
her: and thus, all the commendation is well closed with
this. By the "hair" then, we conceive is understood,
even the meanest gestures and circumstances of a believer's
walk, which being ordered by grace, are beautiful, and
serve much to the adorning of the gospel.

Observ. 1. That grace makes an observable change
upon the whole man, it regulates even the least things, it
orders looks, gestures, and circumstances, wherein often
men take too much liberty. 2. Grace vented in the
meanest piece of a christian carriage, is very beautiful;
it puts a special beauty and lustre upon the meanest circumstances of the christian's actions: or, when a believer
squares all his walk, even in the least things, by the right
rule, it makes his way exceeding lovely; whereas, often
a little folly, or unwatchfulness in such, proves like a
dead fly, that makes a whole box of ointment to stink,
Eccl. x. 1. 3. Our Lord takes notice of the smallest
things in a believer, even of the hair, yea, of the smallest
thereof; there is nothing in his people so mean, but he
takes notice of it, and there is nothing so little, but grace
should be exercised therein; in a word all things in a
believer should be suitable, "eyes, hair, head," &c.

The particulars of the Bride's commendation, of which
we have spoken (if they were understood) certainly they
contain much; but, as if these were little, he proceeds in
expressing this beauty of, or rather his love to, his Bride,
in three wonderful expressions, as proofs of what he hath
said concerning her loveliness and beauty, or (if we may

improperly so call them) aggravations thereof, whereby that commendation is raised and heightened to an exceeding great height. The first is in the end of the fifth verse, and it is this, "the King is held" (or bound) "in the galleries:" the sense in a word is, what ravishing loveliness is this that is to be found in this Bride, that the king is thereby (as it were) held and bound, and must stand to look upon it, he is so delighted with it? 1. This "King" is our Lord Jesus, the prince of the kings of the earth ; he is not only here, but elsewhere often styled "the King," because he is eminently so, and it is much to the believer's consolation that he is so ; if the faith of it were fixed in them. Our Lord is a most royal kingly person. 2. The "galleries" here, are the same that were, chap. i. 17, called there "rafters," the word there, is our galleries : galleries are places where great men use to walk, and here (Christ and the believer having one house, wherein they dwell together) the galleries signify the means or ordinances, wherein, in a more special way they come to walk together. 3. To be "held" (or bound as the word is) signifies a holy constraint that was on him, that he could do no otherwise, because he would do no otherwise, it was so delightsome to him, as, chap. iii. 4, and, iv. 9, and chap. vi. 5, 12, where, on the matter, the same thing is to be found. The word here used, is borrowed from the nature of affection amongst men, that detains them to look on what they love : in sum this in an abrupt manner comes in on the close of the particulars of the Bride's commendation ; as if it were said, so lovely art thou, that Christ as captivated, or overcome, cannot withdraw, but is held (as, chap. iii. 4.) to look upon thy beauty; which is the more wonderful, that he is so royal a person, whom enemies, death, and devils could not detain, yet he is so prevailed over by a believer. And it is observable, that there is not one thing oftener mentioned in this Song, than the wonderful expressions of Christ's yielding himself to be prevailed over by them, as if his might were to be employed for them, rather than for himself, and as if he gloried in this, that he is overcome by them, which is indeed the glory of his grace. *Observ.* 1. There are some more than ordinary admissions to nearness with Christ, that believers may meet with ; which are more than ordinary for clearness, so as they may be said to have him in the "galleries," and also for continuance, so as they may

be said to have him "held" there.   2. Christ Jesus by the
holy violence of his peoples' graces (so to speak) may be
held and captivated to stay and make his abode with
them; it is good then to wrestle with Christ, that he may
be held and prevailed with.   3. Holiness in a believer's
walk, hath much influence on the attaining and entertaining of the most sensible manifestations of Christ: thus he
is "held in the galleries."   4. Our Lord Jesus thinks no
shame to be out of love prevailed over by his people; yea,
he esteems it his honour, therefore is this so often recorded
for the commendation of his love, and the comfort of believers.

Verse 6.   How fair and how pleasant art thou, O love, for
delights!

THIS verse contains the second expression, whereby
the Bride's commendation is heightened, in three things,
1. By the title he gives her, " O love, for delights;" he
calls her in the abstract, love itself, there can be no more
said, she is not only lovely, but love itself; " for delights"
is added as the reason of it, because of the various and
abounding delights that are to be found in her; she is (to
say so) a person so excellently beautiful, and hath so many
lovely things in her.   The second thing is the commendation he joins with this title, and it is in two words, 1.
She is " fair:" this looks to the external loveliness of her
person.   2. She is " pleasant:" this respects the sweetness, and amiableness of her inward disposition: these
two may be separate in others, but they meet in the believer, as they do in Christ; therefore she had given him
these two epithets, chap. i. 16.   The third thing is the
manner of expression, which heightens all this: it is expressed with an " how!" " how fair!" &c? (as chap. iv.
10,) shewing an incomparableness, and an inexpressible-
ness to be in her beauty: whereby in sum, the love of
this blessed Bridegroom shews his satisfaction in his Bride,
by multiplying such wonderful expressions, as holds forth
the high esteem that he hath of her.   Observ. 1. There
is nothing so lovely in all the world, as grace in a believer; the most delightsome pleasant thing in the world is
nothing to this.   2. The love that Christ hath to his
people, is inexpressible; although he useth many significant ways to express it, yet must it close with an indefi-

nite expression and question, to which an answer cannot be made, "how fair!" it cannot be told how fair, and men cannot take it up otherwise than by wondering at it. 3. This loveliness of the Bride, and the king's being kept in the galleries, or the sense of the enjoyment of his presence go together; and therefore it is subjoined here, as the cause of the former, like one that is ravished with the admiration of some excellent sight, he stays and beholds it, and O (saith he) how pleasant it is! the believer is the uptaking object of the love of Christ, wherein he delights. 4. There is no lovely nor delightsome thing in all the world, that Christ cares for, or esteems of, as he doth of the believer: grace makes a person Christ's "love for delights:" riches, honour, favour, parts, will be of no value without this: whereas one without these, may with this, have Christ's affection engaged to them.

Verse 7. This thy stature is like to a palm-tree, and thy breasts to clusters of grapes.
8. I said, I will go up to the palm-tree, I will take hold of the boughs thereof: now also thy breasts shall be as clusters of the vine, and the smell of thy nose like apples;
9. And the roof of thy mouth like the best wine for my beloved, that goeth down sweetly, causing the lips of those that are asleep to speak.

The former two expressions, verses 5, 6, have fallen from him (to speak so) in a ravished abrupt manner, by way of exclamation: the third way how he amplifies the commendation of the Bride, follows, verses 7, 8, 9, (as subjoined to the preceding particular description) and this amplification is expressed these three ways: 1. By commending her stature, as the result of all her parts (formerly described) put together with a repetition of one of these parts mainly taken notice of, verse 7. 2. By shewing his resolution to haunt her company, by which his respect to her appears, verse 8. 3. By promising gracious effects to follow on his performing the former promise, of his keeping company with her, verses 8, 9.

The seventh verse then speaks to two things, her stature and her breasts: her stature respects all the by-gone parts being now put together, for so they represent the whole stature: and by stature is understood the proportionableness and comeliness that is in the whole, being considered as jointly united in one body, as well as severally (as was said of him, chap. v. 16,) and the relative "this," clears it, "this," that is, "this" which is made up of all the several parts I have been enumerating, they being put together, make thy stature, and thy stature thus made up of these members and parts, is "like the palm-tree:" and so from this similitude, her stature is commended: the palm-tree is recommended in scripture to have divers commendable properties, 1. It is straight: therefore it is said of the idols that they are "upright like the palm-tree;" Jer. x. 5, straightness is comely in a stature, he was "like to a cedar" chap. v. 15, she is like to a "palm-tree" here. 2. A palm-tree hath good fruits, the dates are the fruit thereof. 3. It is a tree of long continuance, and keeps long green; hence, Psalm xcii. 12, 14. It is said of the righteous, "they shall flourish like the palm-tree:" therefore, Joel i. 12. It is an evidence of great drought, when "the palm-tree withereth." 4. They were looked on as most fit to be used in times when men were about to express their joy in the most solemn manner, and so when Christ is coming triumphantly to Jerusalem, John xii. they cut down "branches of palm-trees," to carry before him, and, Rev. vii. 4, these victors have "palms in their hands," and in Levi. xxiii. 40, we find branches of these trees commanded to be made use of in the joyful feast of tabernacles, and the "seventy palm-trees" that were found by the Israelites at Elim, are mentioned, Num. xxxiii. 9, as refreshful, so is the city of palm-trees also mentioned as a most pleasant place, Deut. xxxiv. 3. All these may be applied to believers, who, both by the change that is wrought upon them by the grace of Christ, and also, as they are in him by faith, are such; they are straight not crooked, but beautiful and flourishing, and to him refreshful, as the next verse shews, being the living signs and monuments of his victory over death and the devil. *Observ.* 1. There ought not only to be in a believer, a thriving of graces distinctly, but a right joining, ordering, and compacting of them together, that they may keep a proportionableness, and make up complexly a lovely stature: that is, not only should all graces be kept in exercise together, but as members of one new man, each ought to be subservient to another, for making up of a sweet harmony in the result; love should not wrong zeal, nor zeal prudence; but every grace, as being a distinct member of the new man, should be settled in its own

place, to make the stature lovely. 2. When this proportion is kept, and every grace hath its own place, it is exceeding lovely, like a beautiful stature ; whereas grace,
when acting unorderly (if then it may be called grace) is
like an eye, beautiful in itself ; but not being in the right
place of the face, doth make the stature unlovely and dis-
proportionable : it is not the least part of spiritual beauty,
when not only one hath all graces, but hath every one of
them acting according to their several natures, even when
they are acting jointly together. 3. This furthers much
believers' usefulness, and continues them fresh and green,
when the whole stature of grace is right, and kept in a
due proportionableness.

The particular that is again repeated, is her "breasts,"
which are compared to a " cluster of grapes," or " wine,"
as it is in the eighth verse. We conceive, by " breasts"
here, is signified her love and affection, whereby he is entertained ; so, chap. i. 13. " He shall lie all night between my breasts ;" and so it agreeth well with that expression, Prov. v. 19, " Let her breasts satisfy thee at all
times, and be thou always ravished with her love :" this
is confirmed from the similitude unto which it is compared, and that is, "grapes," or "wine;" shewing that her
love is refreshful, and cordial (to speak so) to him : thy
breasts (saith he) that is, to lie between thy breasts, and
to be kindly entertained by thee, is more than wine to
me : and this is the same thing which was said, chap. iv.
10, " How much better is thy love than wine ?" And
the similitude being the same, we think the thing is the
same that is thereby set forth and commended ; and it is
singularly taken notice of by Christ through all the Song,
and marked in chap. iv. and here, as that which makes all
her stature so lovely in itself : love makes every grace
act (therefore is it " the fulfilling of the law") and makes
grace in its actings beautiful and lovely to him. These
words then, may either express, 1. The loveliness of
her love : or, 2. The delight which he took in it, as
esteeming highly of it ; she was so very lovely, that nothing refreshed him so much as her breasts : which expression (as all the rest) holds out intense spiritual love, under the expressions that are usual amongst men. And it
says, 1. That the beauty of grace is a ravishing beauty ;
or Christ's love delights in the love of his people ; a room
in their hearts is much prized by him. 2. Christ hath a

complacency and acquiescence in his people, which he hath in none other, and where more grace is, there his complacency (though one in itself) doth the more manifest itself. 3. When a believer is right and in good case, then his love to Christ is warm : and particularly, a right frame is by nothing sooner evidenced, than by the affections ; and it is ordinarily ill or well with us, as our love to Christ is vigorous or cold.

The second way how our Lord expresseth his love to his Bride, is in the beginning of verse 8, and it is by expressing of his resolution to accompany with her, beyond any in the world : she was compared to a palm-tree in the former verse, now (saith he) " I will go up to the palm-tree" (that is, to the palm-tree before mentioned) it is on the matter the same with that promise, chap. iv. 6, " I will get me to the mountain of myrrh," &c. Consider here, 1. The thing promised or proposed, and that is, his going " up to the palm-tree," and taking " hold of the boughs thereof :" that the scope is to hold forth his purpose of manifesting himself to her, is clear, 1. By the dependence of this on the former, he had said, Thou art a palm-tree, and now (saith he) " I will go up to the palm-tree," which speaks his prizing that tree above all others. 2. The effects also of his going up, in the following words, do clear it ; it is such a going up as hath refreshful and comfortable influence upon her : the importance of the similitude is, as men love the trees they converse much about (and it is like, palm-trees were much used for that end) or as climbing up upon trees, and taking hold of their boughs, do shew the delight and pleasure men have in such or such a tree, and how refreshing it is to them to be near it ; so having compared her to a palm-tree, he expresseth his delight in her, and his purpose of manifesting himself to her, under the same similitude, as is ordinary in the strain of this Song. 2. Consider, that this resolution is laid down as no passing thought, but is a deliberate and determined resolution, " I said I will go," &c. " I will take hold," &c. which doth shew, 1. Christ's inward thoughts and conclusions with himself, this is his heart language. 2. The expression of these, and so the words come to be a promise, which the believer may make use of, as of a thing which Christ hath said. 3. It shews a deliberateness in both, that they were not sudden, but the advised result of a former deliberation, and that of

old, I said it: in a word (saith he) my Bride is my choice
in all the world, the tree that I have resolved, for my
delight, to climb up upon, beside all others. *Observe,* 1.
The scope and result of all Christ's commendations of
his Bride, is, that she may be brought to look for, and
expect to be made happy with his own company, and to
be unspeakably made up in the enjoyment of his presence.
2. It is not every one that hath the promise of Christ's
company and fellowship, or that may expect it; it is the
believer only who may look for it, he hath Christ's word
for it, and none but he.   3. Christ's most passionate expressions of love are not from any surprise of affection
in him, but are deliberately resolved, and that of old, so
that now they cannot be altered; his delight was in the
habitable parts of the earth, and his resolution was laid
down to "go up to the palm-tree" before it was.   4.
Christ's thoughts to his people (if known) would be found
to be precious, thoughts of peace and not of evil; many
a good purpose hath been in his heart of old, and there is
no greater evidence of love, neither can be, than to intimate and accomplish these, as he doth here; I laid down
this resolution (saith he) long ere now, and I will follow
it out.   5. A holy tender walk in believers (which is
indeed to have the stature lovely as the palm-tree) will
obtain the manifestation of Christ's heart to them; and
there is no greater evidence of Christ's respect, than that,
John xiv. 21, and 23.

The third way how he expresseth his love, is by the
effects, which he promiseth shall follow on his presence
with her, as his presence is subjoined to her lovely stature
(which connexion is observable) the effects that follow, are
three, the first two are in the second part of the eighth
verse, and the first of them in these words, "Now also
thy breasts shall be as the clusters of the vine;" this is
the first fruit of his going up to the palm tree, which (as
also the rest of them) may be taken as comprehensive
of these two.   1. Of some gracious effect that shall be
wrought in the Bride, and so these words bring him in
speaking to this purpose, when I come to thee, then by my
presence thy grace shall flow, and thou shalt be in a capacity
to edify others, and to satisfy me, as if thy breasts were
clusters of the vine, to furnish what might be refreshful: thus he comforts her, from what should be wrought
in her, by his presence with her: and the scope and con-

nexion shews, that this cannot be excluded, it being a native consequence of his presence, and comfortable in itself to her, 2. They are to be looked upon as comprehensive of his gracious acceptation of her and her fruits, as being well satisfied with her; and thus the meaning of these words, " Thy breasts shall be as clusters of the vine," is this, when I shall come to thee, thy love and company, thy bosom (to say so) shall be to me more refreshful than clusters of the vine, I will feed upon it, and delight in it, as, chap. iv. 10, this completes her consolation, and the evidence of his love, that he undertakes it shall be well with her inward condition, and that he shall accept of her also, and be well satisfied with her : these are not only consistent together, but do necessarily concur for making up the scope, which is to evidence his love, and to comfort her ; and the one of these follows on the other, therefore, we comprehend both in all these effects. *Observ.* 1. Christ's presence hath much influence on believers' liveliness ; their breasts run when he is present. 2. Liveliness is a singular and comfortable mercy in a believer's estimation ; therefore it is promised as a thing that is in a special way comfortable to her. 3. Christ's presence, or nearness with him, and fruitfulness, go together : and where thy breasts are not as clusters, no condition the believer can be in, is to be accounted presence.

The second effect is in these words, " And the smell of thy nose like apples :" apples are savoury fruit, the smell of the nose is the savour of the breath, that comes from it, which in unwholesome bodies is unsavoury ; saith he to the Bride, thine shall not be so, but thy constitution shall be lively, and all that comes from thee shall be savoury, and so shall be accepted of me ; it shall be savoury in itself, as apples are to the smell, and it shall be delighted in by me, as having a sweet air and breath with it: this imports a conspicuous inward change, by the growth of mortification, whereby believers being purified within from all filthiness of the flesh and spirit, there proceeds nothing from them but what is savoury, whereas a loose and ragged conversation, as corrupt breath (Job xvii. 1.) evidenceth much inward rottenness. *Observe*, 1. Christ's presence, is of an healing, cleansing virtue, and makes an observable inward change. 2. An inward change evidenceth itself in the outward fruits and effects, the very smell and savour of the conversation, and of all external duties, is changed.

3. This inward purity is very desirable to the believer; for so it is here a piece of his comfort, to have a promise that the smell of his nose shall be as apples, and it is a special evidence of Christ's respect, to have that performed.

It may also take in the savouriness of the believers' breathing, in respect of themselves; when Christ is present, they shall draw in a wholesome, pleasant and refreshful air; whereas now ordinarily we breathe in a corrupt air: it shall not be so then, saith he, the smell of thy nose shall be as if thou didst savour of apples: Christ's company makes all both fruitful within, and refreshful to the believer, and also makes all duties and all dispensations he is exercised with, savoury and acceptable to himself; all which follow on Christ's presence, and suits with the scope, that saith, both taste and smell are satisfied.

The third lovely effect of Christ's presence, is in the 9th verse: and, 1st, The effect itself is set down, then its commendation is amplified. The effect, or advantage of Christ's presence, is in these words, "The roof of thy mouth" (or thy palate) "shall be as the best wine;" the palate, or roof of the mouth, is the instrument of taste, and so is sometimes taken for the taste itself, and is so translated, chap. ii. 3, " His fruit was sweet to my taste :" so Job xxxiv. 3, or by palate may be understood the mouth, as, chap. v. 16. Next, it is compared to wine, yea, the best wine (the reasons of the comparison have been often spoken to) the best wine is that which is most refreshing and exhilarating: now this wine is three ways set out in its excellency (for, that the following expressions are to this purpose, is clear) 1. It is " for my beloved," that is, such wine as he allows his friends, whom he styles beloved, chap. v. 1. (and this shows what kind of wine is understood) and so it must be excellent wine, being that which is allowed on Christ's special friends. Or, it is an abrupt expression, whereby he speaks in name of the Bride; it is such wine as I (as if she were speaking) allow on thee, my beloved, and which I reserve only for thee; for which reason, she is called a fountain sealed, and garden inclosed, as being set apart for him, and not common to others; and thus is he expressing in her name, what she expresseth herself in the last words of this chapter, it is all " for thee my beloved ;" and it implieth both a commendation of its sweetness, and her devoting of it to him. However, the words hold forth something that

proves it to be excellent and not common, but such as is
found among those who stand in this spiritual relation.
2. It is commended from this, that "it goeth down
sweetly," that is, it is pleasant to the taste, and is not
harsh, but delightsomely may be drunk off; or, it may
respect that property of good wine, mentioned, Prov. xxiii.
31. (that it "moves itself rightly") if the words be translated as the margin imports. 3. It is commended from
the effects, it drinks sweetly, and when it is drunk, "It
causeth the lips of those that are asleep to speak :" wine
is cordial and refreshful, but this wine must be in a singular
way refreshful, that makes men that are infirm, or old (as
the word may be rendered) and almost dead, to revive
and speak, or those that were secure (as the Bride was,
chap. v. 2.) and in a spiritual drowsiness, it can quicken
them, and make them cheerfully speak ; thus the wine
is commended. Now we conceive, by this comfortable
effect, that is promised to her upon Christ's coming to her,
these two things are here holden forth. 1. How refreshing it shall be to herself, all her senses shall be taken with
it, both the smell and the taste ; it shall be singularly
sweet to her spiritual taste, as it is, chap. ii. 3. And thus
the wine of the Spirit is commended, which accompanies
his manifestations, and is reserved for his beloved, chap.
v. i. And it is a joy that no stranger is made partaker of :
this wine is indeed peculiar for his beloved, (and is suitable
to himself) and is the wine that goeth sweetly down ; and
is most refreshful, and makes secure sinners to speak,
and those that are faint it revives them, as Eph. v. 18,
" Be not filled with wine," &c. but " be filled with the
Spirit, speaking to yourselves in psalms, singing and making melody in your hearts to the Lord :" this effect agrees
well to the Spirit, yea, only to this wine of the Spirit : and
it suits well the scope, which is to shew what comfortable
influence Christ's presence should have on her, so that when
he comes to his palm tree, her taste shall relish as with the
best wine ; his presence shall thus revive and quicken her,
and be a special evidence of his singular respect to her.
    2. It holds out (which follows on the former) that not
only her breath shall savour well to him and others, and
her inward senses abound with refreshings to herself, but
also the expressions of her mouth, to others shall be
savoury, and to him refreshful, as a delightsome fruit
flowing from her : thus (saith he) when I betake me to

fellowship with thee, and come near by sensible embracements, to take hold of thy boughs (as a man embracing
one whom he loves ; for thus the allegory is spiritually to
be understood) thou shalt be to me, and in my esteem,
exceedingly lovely ; thy breasts, smell, and mouth, will
be cheering and savoury, like grapes, apples, and the best
wine : and here spiritual affections and holy reason
should be made use of, to gather the life of Christ's love
from the effects of it, with some resemblance of what useth
to be betwixt man and wife, in their mutual loving carriage (for so runs the strain of this song) although our
carnalness makes it hazardous, and unsafe to descend in
the explication of these similitudes : and thus, as chap. v.
16, by his mouth or palate, was understood the kisses
thereof, or the most sensible manifestations of his love to
her : so here, by her palate or mouth, is understood her
most affectionate soul-longings of love to him, which being
warmed and melted by his presence, doth manifest itself
in a kindly way, in spiritual embraces and kisses (as from
verse 11 and 12 will be clear) which are exceedingly delightsome to him : and so the sense of this promise is,
when I come to thee, then, yea even now, thy love with
the sense of mine shall be warmed and refreshed, so that
it shall in an affectionate way vent itself on me, and that
shall be as the most exhilarating cordial unto me, as the
manifestations of my love will be cheering and refreshing
unto thee; both which are notably comfortable to her,
and special evidences of his respect, which is the scope.
Observ. 1. There are some secret flowings of love, and
soul-experiences between Christ and believers, that are
not easily understood ; and that makes the expressions
of his love so seemingly intricate. 2. These flowings of
love that are betwixt Christ and his people (how strange
soever they be) are most delightsome to the soul that
partakes of them, they are as "wine that goeth down
sweetly." 3. Christ's presence hath many benefits and
advantages waiting on it, which contribute exceedingly
both to the quickening and comforting of the believer ;
many things hang on this one, "his going up to the palm
tree." 4. The joy of the Spirit hath notable effects, and
can put words in the mouth of those that never spoke
much before, yea, can make the dumb to sing, with a sensible warming of the heart and inward affections, stirring
up melody in their souls, which yet will be distinct in the

impressions and effects of it. 5. Our Lord Jesus hath designed the comfort of the believer, which he holdeth out in comfortable promises, and alloweth them to make use of it, and it is pleasant and delightsome to him to have them so doing.

BRIDE.

Verse 10. I am my Beloved's, and his desire is toward me.

THE Bride hath been long silent, delightsomely drinking in what she hath been hearing from the Bridegroom's sweet mouth, and so suffering him to say on : now in this tenth verse, and those that follow, she comes in speaking, and having well observed what he said, the result and effect thereof upon her heart doth appear in what she saith. And, 1. She comforts herself in her union with him, as now being clear in it from his owning of her ; and she lays down, and begins with this conclusion, verse 10. Now (saith she) I may say, " I am my beloved's," &c. Then, 2. Looking to his promise, verse 8, she puts up her great desire after communion with him, that according to her interest in him, she might be admitted to enjoy him ; which suit is put up, qualified or enlarged, and by several arguments pressed on him, verses 11, 12, 13.

The conclusion which she gathers, verse 10, from his discourse, comes not in altogether abruptly, but is the expression of a heart comforted with the intimations of Christ's love, and wakened with the wine that makes them that are asleep to speak ; and so breathing out the great ground of her consolation : now (saith she) seeing he loves me, and out of the infinite freedom of his grace is pleased to commend unworthy me so much, certainly, I may conclude, " I am my Beloved's, and his desire is towards me." The first part of this verse, wherein she asserts her interest in him, was spoken to chap. ii. 16, and vi. 3, and it is now repeated on this occasion, for these reasons, 1. Because it is the great compend of all her consolation, and that wherein it consists, that she is Christ's, and Christ is hers : this is indeed matter of solid consolation, and whatever is comfortable doth flow from it. 2. To shew that she kept the clearness of her interest in him, in some measure constantly, and carried it along with her in the several parts of her exercise, she

can assert it this day, and the next day, and the third day.
3. It is now a full tide with her, as to Christ's manifestations, and the flowings of his Spirit; he hath been liberal
and large in the intimations of his love, and she makes
this use of it, to put her interest in him out of question,
while the evidences of it are so legible. *Observ.* 1.
Believers may at sometimes, more clearly and distinctly
gather and conclude their interest in Christ, than at other
times. 2. When believers are admitted to nearness with
Christ, and clouds that would darken their faith are scattered, then they should endeavour to fix their confidence,
and put their interest out of question; that when their
sun comes under a cloud, and they see not to read their
evidences so distinctly, they be not put to question their
interest, and all by-past experiences, as delusions. 3.
When the Lord owns his people, and speaks comfortably
to them (as he hath been doing to the Bride) then they
should own him, and acquiesce in that consolation allowed
upon them by him.

The last part of the verse, in these words, "and his
desire is towards me," shews not only that the interest
was mutual, and that he loved her, as she did him; but
that he loved her affectionately, so that in a manner he
could not be without her, his desire was to her. 2. That
he condescended to love her with such a kind of love and respect as a woman hath to her husband; for, so this is spoken
of the first woman, Gen. iii. "Thy desire shall be towards
him," that is, subordinate to his, or seeking to conform to
his, that she may please him: and so here it shews Christ's
great condescending, to have the believer carving (as it
were) to him, so ready is he to please and satisfy his people
for their good. 3. It shews a deal of satisfaction that she
had in this; it was the matter of her humble spiritual
boasting, that Christ so loved her, hate or condemn her
who would. 4. She thinks still much of this privilege of
an interest in Christ, and esteems nothing the less of it that
she had attained clearness in it before now : clearness is
ever of much worth, and those who are clearest anent this,
will esteem most of it : that holy fainness (to say so) that
this word, "My Beloved is mine," brings in to the soul,
easeth and comforteth the more that it is often renewed.

Verse 11. Come, my beloved, let us go forth into the field ; let us lodge in the villages.

12. Let us get up early to the vineyards ; let us see if the vine flourish, whether the tender grape appear, and the pomegranates bud forth : there will I give thee my loves.

13. The mandrakes give a smell, and at our gates are all manner of pleasant fruits, new and old, which I have laid up for thee, O my beloved.

When she hath laid down this ground of her interest in him, she proceeds to improve it, verse 11, by giving him a kindly and familiar invitation, which she, first, qualifies in the end of the eleventh verse, and beginning of the twelfth, and then in what followeth, adds some motives to press it. The similitude of a loving wife's carriage to a kind husband is continued, as if such a loving wife, desirous of her husband's company, did invite him to the fields, thereby in a retired way to be solaced with his company, especially by going abroad with him in a pleasant spring time, and staying some nights in villages for that end, and that they might the more seriously and comfortably view the state of their orchards and gardens, which is both pleasant, profitable, and delightsome to be done in the husband's company ; even so doth the Bride follow the similitude, to shew what she desired from Christ in desiring of his company, and for what end, to wit, both for the profit and comfort she expected to reap thereby.

The invitation she gives him, is, " Come, my Beloved ;" Come, is a word much used betwixt Christ and the believer, and is a kindly word. He saith, " Come," chap. ii. 10, and now she useth the same word ; her putting up this desire, expresseth a desire of communion and nearness with him, and also much affection, and is the language both of the Spirit and the Bride, who saith " Come," Rev. xxii. 17, here it imports a petition, pressing for a greater degree of communion, which, by comparing this with the former words, may be gathered ; for, she possessed it in a good measure for the time, and yet here she saith, " Come." First, considering this invitation in itself, we may observe, That communion with Christ is the one, principal, and common suit of the believer, wherein he is never satisfied till it be perfected. Next, comparing these words with the preceding, Observ. 1. The more that

Christ be manifested to his people, the more near they be admitted to him, and the better that their frame be, and the more clear they be anent their interest in him, the greater will their desire be of more near communion with him. 2. Clearness of interest in him, when it is solid, is a good ground to press for his fellowship, and still it presseth the person who hath it to pursue after more full manifestations of Christ. Again, considering these words as they respect his promise, verse 8, " I said" (saith he) " I will go up to the palm tree," &c. Now she having heard it, layeth hold on this promise, and is not long in saying, " Come." *Observ.* 1. That believers should improve the promises they have, for attaining what is promised in them, and should not suffer promises to lie by them not made use of. 2. What is promised to a believer may, and should be prayed for by him. 3. Believers in their prayers and suits to Christ, should have a special respect to the promises, not only to conform their desires to them, but to ground them upon them. 4. The more tender believers be in their frame, they will the more carefully gather up all Christ's words and promises, and strengthen their faith thereby in their dealing with him.

Next, she contents not herself to put up this suit, but she further qualifies it, in several repeated petitions (whereby the ardency of her desire, and the strength of her faith doth appear) all which are recorded, both as a pattern to teach believers how they should carry in prayer, and also as evidences what will be their way and manner in that duty, when their spirit is in a good condition. The first qualification of the former petition is, " Let us go forth into the field." Going forth into the field, holds forth these two, 1. The extent of her desire, she would have him at home and abroad also, she desires not to go out of doors without him. 2. A desire of retiredness with him, that she might be alone in his company, as a wife going abroad to the fields alone with her husband, as Gen. xxiv. 63, it is said, that " Isaac went out to the fields to pray." that is, that he might be the more retired in that duty. *Observ.* 1. That where desire of fellowship with Christ is right, it breathes after a walk with him every where, at home and abroad, they cannot endure to go out at doors, or to the fields without him. 2. Delight in Christ's company seeks to be retired with him, to be alone with him, to be freed from all other companies, and abstracted from all distraction, the more freely to be solaced with him.

Again, the pronoun, "us," "let us go," is not without good purpose added: it is not, go thou, nor, I will go ; but, " Let us go," as bearing in it a double motive, and evidence of her affection. 1. That she offers herself to bear him company. *Observ.* When Christ's company is loved and respected, the soul will be content to leave all others, and go with him, for the entertaining of it. 2. It implies, that though she had an errand, and desire to be abroad ; yet, she could not endure to go about it without him ; therefore (saith she) " Let us go." *Observ.* 1. The fields, and most pleasant recreations, are heartless and wearisome without Christ's company in the believer's esteem. 2. His company is the believer's great encouragement to undertake any thing, and that which makes his out-going and in-coming pleasant : she is content to go with him, and cannot abide to go without him. Lastly, It shews her respecting that which was her part in the exercise, as well as his, and her resolution to conform her practice to her prayers ; for, as she desires him to go, so she is willing to go herself : if we would expect the answer of prayer, our practices should be like our prayers.

The second qualification is, " Let us lodge in the villages." Villages are rural, or land-ward places, by that name distinguished from towns or cities ; in these, men travelling, or continuing a time in the fields for their recreation or business, do lodge, as retired from their ordinary vocations in cities. Her desire, " let us lodge" in these (or, as the word is, let us night or dwell there) shews that she desired him abroad with her, nor for a piece of a day, to return at night, but for a greater length and continuance of time, as loving rather to lodge with him in the villages, and to take what might be had in his company, for lengthening their retirement, than to return hastily to the city, or business whereby she might be distracted, and in hazard of an interruption of her communion with him. *Observ.* 1. True desire of communion with Christ in the enjoyment of his presence, as it presseth for retiredness with him, so is it desirous to have that lengthened, and cannot endure to think of parting with him, when it gets him in a corner. 2. A back-side, or a corner alone with Christ's company, is good lodging to a lover of Christ : solitariness with his presence, is more frequented and delighted in by such, than more public fellowship and societies.

In the twelfth verse we have some more qualifications
of her petition, and some of the motives, that press her to
seek after Christ's company.   The third qualification is in
these words, " Let us go up early to the vineyards :" the
similitude is continued, but this word " early," is added,
and it implies (as it is used in scripture,) 1. Timeousness,
so the women came to Christ's grave " early," Luke xxiv.
1, " while it was dark."   2. Seasonableness, so it is taken
in that expression, " the Lord will help, and that right
early," Psalm xlvi. 5.   3. Seriousness, so Hos. v. 15.
" They shall seek me early," that is, seriously.   Here it
implieth, that she, as one impatient of delays, desires to
go with expedition, and for that end offers him her company. *Observ.* 1. Sincere desire of fellowship with Christ
cannot endure delays, but would presently be at enjoyment.   2. There is a season of earliness, a fit opportunity
of keeping company with Christ, and that should not be
neglected.   3. As privacy is a great friend to communion
with Christ, so is earliness and timeousness in setting to
it : the more early one begin, they may expect to speed
the better.   4. As no duty should be put off, or delayed,
so especially this great and concerning duty of endeavouring for fellowship with Christ, should by no means be
delayed or shifted, but early and timeously should be gone
about.

The fourth qualification follows in the motives, that she
might see how the several fruits budded : and it shews,
that she desired not his company only for her satisfaction,
but for her profit also, that thereby she might he helped
to thrive in her spiritual condition, and might be enabled
the better to do her duty.   *Observ.* A sincere and right
desire of communion with Christ, studieth to improve it
for spiritual advantage, when it is attained.   So then, all
these put together, shew, that she desires Christ's presence retiredly, constantly, timeously, and in order to her
spiritual advantage and profit : this last will appear more
in the motives, especially the first.   This is indeed a main
desire, and therefore, in what follows she presseth it with
motives, which put her to it, and also (as being well
pleasing to him) give her ground to expect it from him :
and though she useth these motives, as if they were arguments to induce him to grant her desire, yet they are
mainly for strengthening her own faith in pressing her
suit.   The using of motives, and her thus qualifying of

her desire, saith, that believers in their petitions, should
insist and press them : for, although Christ be not informed by words, nor persuaded by our arguments, yet this
both helps to warm the affections, and strengthen the
faith of the believer himself, and is becoming believers in
their prayers to him, who calls for, and admits of reasonable service.   The motives in particular are four, the first
is taken from the end of her petition, which is to see how
her graces prosper: the similitude continues, as a wife
intending to visit her husbandry (to say so) is helped and
encouraged therein by her husband's presence, and therefore desires his company; so, the believer hath a husbandry, "vineyards, grapes, pomegranates," and divers
plants to oversee, which are the graces of the Spirit, and
divers duties committed to him (as was said upon chap.
iv. 12, 13, and vi. 11,) and his visiting of these, is the
taking of a reflect view of himself, in an abstracted retired
condition, that thereby he may be distinctly acquainted
how it is with him, and with his graces: in following of
which duty, Christ's presence in some secret corner is exceeding helpful ; therefore, for that end doth the Bride
seek it, and makes use of this motive to press it, because
it is a duty of concernment to her to search herself; it is
pleasing to him, and a thing that she would be at, yet,
cannot win to it in a common ordinary frame, it is so
difficult ; therefore doth she propose this (which is her
end) as that which would be respected and well taken off
her hand by him.   *Observ.* 1. Believers have a task, and
husbandry committed to them to manage, that is, several
duties and graces, holden forth under the similitude of
" vines, pomegranates," &c. which they are carefully to
notice.   2. It is necessary, in the managing of this task,
for a believer to be well acquainted with the condition of
his graces, and it is his duty to be reflecting on himself
for that end ; and if men ought to look to the state of
their flocks and herds, Prov. xxvii. 23, how much more
ought they carefully to look to this.   3. This duty should
be purposely, retiredly, and deliberately intended, undertaken, and gone about, with a resolute design for attaining
to the discovery of her own case, as she doth here.   4.
This duty hath difficulties in it, and ordinarily the heart
is not prevailed with to be kept serious about it, except
the frame thereof be more tender than ordinary.   5. To
a tender believer it will be a great favour to get this duty

of self-examination profitably and unbiassedly discharged :
it is a mercy worth the seeking from God, and the more
tender believers be, they will be the more in this. 6.
Although believers be clear as to their interest (as the
Bride was, verse 10,) yet may they be indistinct as to
the knowledge of their own condition, and therefore
ought not to neglect this duty of self-examination : but
where clearness is solid, they will be the more careful in
the searching of themselves. 7. Christ's presence, as it
is a notable help to all duties, so particularly it is in a
special way helpful to believers in searching themselves,
by making the heart willing and pliable, to follow it
sweetly, by discovering things as they are, and by making
the eye single, rightly to judge of every thing, and impartially to take with that which is discovered : much
presence should encourage the Lord's people to follow
this duty, which otherwise is gone about in a heartless
way. 8. It is a good use of Christ's presence and company, when it is improved for attaining of more thorough
and distinct knowledge of our own condition ; and then
especially believers should take the opportunity of putting
themselves to trial. 9. A believer, when tender, will be
particular in his search, he will search even to the least,
he will not disapprove any thing of God's grace that is
real, although it be weak and tender, therefore she looks
to buds, as well as more mature fruit, and acknowledgeth
them, because Christ doth so, chap. vi. 11. 10. Believers
promise not much in themselves, or, they expect not great
things anent their own fruitfulness ; therefore, it is to see
what is budding or appearing, rather than what is ripe,
which she proposeth here to herself, as her design. 11. A
tender believer will esteem much of little grace where it
is real, a bud is much to him, if it look fruit-like, as it is
the evidence of Christ's Spirit in him, and the work of his
grace : he that is humble will have a high esteem of it,
though he expect no great thing, nor yet think much of
it, as it is inherent in him, yet he will not cast what is
least, if solid. 12. The more tender one is, he will be
the more desirous to search his own condition, as being
unsatisfied with what he hath attained. Again, if we
compare this with chap. vi. 11, where it is said " He went
down to his garden" for this very end, for which she desires his presence ; we may see, 1. A co-incidence betwixt
Christ's work and the believer's (to say so) they have one

task. 2. A going alongst both of their ends and ways to attain them ; he takes pains on his people by the means of his grace to make them fruitful, and they diligently haunt and improve the means for that same end,   And, 3. Christ's words are near the same with hers, the more to strengthen their faith in obtaining what she sought, when it so concurred with his design : a believer that aims at fruitfulness and tenderness by Christ's company in the means and ordinances, may expect to obtain his desire ; for, that same is his work, which he drives by the means of grace amongst his people.

The second motive which makes her press for Christ's company in this retired way, is in these words, " There will I give thee my loves ;" that is (in short) as in retirements the Bridegroom and the Bride rejoice together, in the expressions of their mutual love, with more than ordinary familiarity : so (saith she) let me have thy company continued with me, that thereby my heart being warmed, I may get opportunity to let out my love in a lively manner on thee.   By " loves" here, love simply is not meant, but love in the highest degree of it, manifesting itself in the most sensible manner, when the heart is melted, as it were, and made free to pour out itself in love to him : it is therefore called " loves" in the plural number, to shew the many ways it will vent itself, as, in thoughts delightsomely making the heart glad, in cheerful exulting in him, and affectionate embracing him in its arms, feeding and delighting on him, and such like ways ; there is nothing kept up from him, and all doors, whereby love useth to vent, are opened.   While she saith, " I will give thee my loves," it is not to be understood, as if then she would begin to love him, (for, the thing that made her put up this suit was her love to him) but that then she would with more freedom do it, and with ease and delight get it done, which now would not do for her, (till his presence warned her) at least in the manner she would be at. The word, "there," that in the latter relates to the "fields, villages," &c. is to be understood of that retirement in fellowship, which she desired with him ; in the scope it looks to his secret manifesting of himself to her, in admitting of her to his bosom ; O ! saith she, come, my heart longs to be near thee ; and this advantage I expect from it, I would then get my heart drawn from idols, and my affections engaged unto thee, which in thy absence I cannot get done so as I would : as a person cannot vent love so in company, as when he is alone in solitariness with his bosom friend : thus Joseph, being to manifest his love to his brethren, Gen. xlv. 1, commanded all to go out, that so he might with the greater freedom let forth his affections on them : and as Jonathan sent away his boy, when he was to embrace David in the fields, 1. Sam. xx. 40, &c. so here, the secret manifestations of Christ, by his Spirit to his people, being that which gives them liberty to let forth their hearts on him, especially in their unknown access to him, to which no man is witness, are by this word " there," signified. *Observ.* 1. There are many more good things than one which accompanies Christ's presence : and where love is in a believer's heart, there will be no scarcity of arguments to hold forth the advantage thereof. 2. As there are some more than ordinary manifestations of love from Christ to his people, which are not constant; so, there are some more than ordinary flowings of the love of believers towards him; there are some times, and cases, wherein especially the heart will melt in affection to him, and wherein it will be made to pour out itself with ease and delight upon him. 3. It is no less the desire of believers to love Christ, and to have their affections flowing on him, than to have the manifestations of his love to them ; therefore speaks she of this as of a benefit she exceedingly desired, to get leave to pour her heart out in love upon him. 4. Believers that love Christ, will not be satisfied with the degree of their own love, but will be desirous to have it more withdrawn from other things, and more fully venting on him. 5. Although sometimes, yea, oftentimes, the believer's heart comes not up that length in love to Christ that he would have it, yet he designs to set it on Christ alone, and there is none that willingly he gives it unto with consent but Christ, it is on him only he allows it. 6. There is no greater gift can be given to Christ, than his people's love ; this is therefore the motive that is proposed by the Bride in her dealing with him, as holding forth the propine or entertainment which he should receive. 7. Christ's presence, and the manifestations of his love conduceth notably unto, and hath great influence upon, the gaining of our affections to him ; it doth not only, as it were, give us the opportunity of his company, but it gains the heart, softens it, ravisheth it, and heightens the esteem

of Christ in it, (which no report of him can do so effectually as his own presence) and also it oileth all the affections, that they have a freedom to flow out (like the
ice before the sun) which otherwise are key-cold. 8.
Love to Christ, loves solitariness and retirements with
him; it is neither so stirred itself as when it is alone with
him, nor are the men of the world able to bear, or understand the intimate familiarity, that will be in the flowings of the love of Christ to a believer, or of a believer's
liberty and holy boldness with Christ; nor were it meet,
that they should be witnesses of the love-secrets that are
betwixt him and them. 9. It is an evidence of single
love to Christ, when his presence is longed for, that we
may the more ardently and affectionately love him, and
when all opportunities are sought for that may increase
this; this is singleness and spiritualness in a great length,
when this makes us glory in Christ's love to us, and desire
the manifestations thereof, that we may have access thereby to love him: a believer will love heaven, because there
he will have access fully to love Christ, as well as to be
loved of him; and will abhor hell, not only because there
are no intimations of Christ's love there, but also because
there is no access to love him there: to get the heart
loving Christ is indeed the believer's great delight, and
in a manner his heaven. 10. Love in a believer to Christ,
is the result or reflex of Christ's love to him, it is the sun
which begets this heat in the soul that loves him: and the
more brightly he shines on believers, the more is their
love hot toward him: for " here is love, not that we loved
him, but that he loved us" first. 11. It is an evidence of
true love to Christ, and esteem of him, when the heart is
longing, praying and using means that it may love him,
and get its love to him heightened till it be all bestowed
on him allenarly.

In the 13th verse, we have the third and fourth motives, whereby the Bride presseth her suit: the third is,
" The mandrakes give a smell," &c. It is like that motive
which he useth in pressing her to hearken to his call,
chap. ii. 12, " The flowers appear on the earth," &c. The
graces of the Spirit, growing up (as in a garden) in the
believer's walk with Christ, are like flowers in the spring,
which by their pleasantness and savour, invite men to the
fields: thus the sense of this motive comes to this, all
things (saith the Bride) are in a good condition, and there

is a thriving amongst my graces, which are for pleasantness as flowers; therefore come. This avowing of the
flourishing of her graces, is not from any vain boasting,
but in humble sincerity, acknowledging what she found
in herself to his praise, and what she knew to be acceptable to him, as a confirmation to her faith in the expectation
of what she prayed for; for (which is a lesson we should
learn) although the goodness of our condition can merit
nothing which we pray for, yet, it may give us confidence
and boldness in prayer, when we have a good conscience
and testimony within us, 1 John iii. 20, this fruitfulness
of hers is four ways set forth, 1. That these her fruits
are ripe, and in their flower, "the mandrakes give a
smell:" mandrakes were much longed for by Rachel,
Gen. xxx. 14, and by their savouriness of taste there, and
of smell here, it appears that they were some lovely fruit,
and now in their prime most pleasant, because they give
their smell. 2. Her fruitfulness is set forth in its comprehensiveness and variety, she is adorned "with all manner of pleasant fruits;" whereby is holden forth, that as
believers have many divers graces, like variety of spices,
chap. iv. 13, 14, which they should entertain, so all of
them were in good case with her. 3. These fruits were
"new and old," whereby the plenty of the same kind is
set forth, both (to say so) of this and the former year's
growth; whereby is signified, a thriving or increase of
the believer's grace, there being a new degree of faith and
love, &c. of this year, added to the former degree she
attained before: she preserves the old, and she brings
forth new, as Matt. xiii. 52, the scribe, taught in the
kingdom of God, "brings out things new and old;" he
hath the old stock, and the new increase, the talents that
were given him, and five more gained by them. 4. These
fruits are said to be "at our gates;" this looks most simply
to signify this, that it is pleasant to have such fruits at the
doors, and it betokens a frequency or plenty, and great
abundance of them, when not only in the garden, but at
the gates they so abound; so this abounding of grace in a
believer, makes (to say so) Christ's entry savoury and
pleasant, and shews, that all things are in a good readiness
for him, as the last motive (that they are laid up for him,
even while they are at the gates) doth shew: in sum, all
things (saith she) are in readiness, and for thee only my
beloved; although not in perfection, yet in sincerity, pro-

vision is made for thy entertainment. *Observ.* 1. There are many various kinds of graces in a believer ; and when it is right with one, or when one of them is thriving, it is ordinarily so with all. 2. Grace hath its growth, and should be increased by new additions, where it is begun ; and when it goes well with the believer, there will be of these spiritual fruits, " both new and old." 3. There is no keeping in good case of the old stock of grace, but by continuing and growing in fruitfulness ; where the old is preserved, there will be found new also, otherwise, what seemed once to blossom, becomes almost withered. 4. Those who are seriously desirous of Christ's company, should be making ready for him, by liveliness of all manner of graces, new and old ; and they who aim at such a condition, may with some confidence expect his presence and company. 5. Believers who seriously, tenderly, and humbly follow holiness, may attain a great length in it, as this expression of her case signifies : and therefore, the blame is only our own, that our attainments in grace are so small.

The last motive is in the last words, these are the fruits (saith she) " which I have laid up for thee, O my Beloved ;" these fruits are many, and at the doors, yet they are laid up for him ; they are then such fruits, as are reserved for Christ. And this motive completes the former, whereby having asserted her fruitfulness, lest she should seem to boast of it, that her graces did so abound, whatever increase they have made, O my Beloved (saith she) I have devoted them to thee ; they shall not be for my own satisfaction or boast, but for thy glory ; therefore (saith she) come : as one would say, I have such good fruits of purpose kept for thee, which no other shall share of, and therefore I invite thee to come and enjoy them : which is a kind invitation, turning over the acknowledgment of what she had on Christ, as indeed belonging to him, and as only to be made use of for his honour : so then, to lay up, signifies, 1. A carefulness and solicitousness, carefully to gather together as covetous worldly men use to lay up riches, and to gather them together. 2. It signifies the success which she had in her endeavour, that there was much gathered, a store of fruits, as in a treasure ; so we find laying up, to have this sense, Psalm xxxi. 19, " How great is thy goodness which thou hast laid up," as it were in store, &c. 3. It signifies a setting apart of that store from common uses, as men do what they lay up, and a reserving of it for some peculiar use. And the peculiar uses for which she laid them up, follows in these words, " for thee, O my beloved !" which implies, 1. That in her gathering and storing up, respect was had to Christ; and that her provision was not to rest herself upon it, but to honour him with it. 2. That even when it was attained, she was denied to it, and did not look upon it as if it could be any stock to herself to live upon, but that she had prepared it as an offering to present or entertain him with : even as a kind wife would provide what might be for the husband's refreshment and honour, and would be still laying up for his return, aiming singly to satisfy and entertain him with it ; (so saith the Bride) this store is for satisfying and honouring of thee, and for thee only, O my Beloved ! it is for thy cause, because thou commandest it, lovest it, and art honoured by it. " O my Beloved," is added, to shew how affectionately she insisted in this discourse ; and in particular, how well bestowed she thought all that she had laid up was, when it was bestowed upon him ; " O my Beloved !" it is for thee, and I have willingly and affectionately laid it up, for that use, therefore come and lodge, and dwell with me, which is the scope. *Observ.* 1. Increasing in fruitfulness, or growing in holiness, is a work that will not be done in one day ; but it will take time, and both carefulness and diligence to gather together and lay up these spiritual fruits. 2. When Christ is absent to sense, it is a suitable and seasonable duty to be laying up provision by fruitfulness in holiness, for his coming and return : or, when Christ seems not presently to come and accept of a believer's prayers, duties, or graces, yet are they not to be rejected, and cast at, as null and useless ; nor is the believer to desist from performing of them, but to continue and persevere in stirring himself up in the exercise of graces and duties, until he come. 3. Although Christ come not at the first, but suffer many of the believer's duties, and the exercise of his graces (if we may say so) to lie long on his hand, yet they are not lost, but laid up (and grace is no ill treasure) and Christ will one time or other come and make good use of them. 4. It is no less practick (to say so) or it is no less difficult in believers' walk, to reserve what store they have gathered for Christ's use alone, and to be denied to it themselves, than

to get duties performed, and spiritual provision laid up.
5. It is not enough to do duties, and to lay up fruits, unless
they be laid up for Christ; and this is no less a duty than
the former. 6. It is no small attainment in a believer,
and a strong motive for attaining of Christ's company
(without which all will be nothing) when not only he hath
store of fruits, and is painful in holiness, but also is denied
to these, as to any use-making of them for his own ends,
more than if he had never been taken up in attaining
them, and when he reserves the praise of them to Christ
Jesus alone, that they may be subservient to his honour;
this laying up of fruits for him, is opposite to the laying
up for ourselves, as living, eating, fasting, &c. to him, 2
Cor. v. 15; Zech. vii. 5, 6, are opposite to living, eating,
fasting to ourselves, which in God's account is to be as
an empty vine, Hos. x. 1. 7. Grace is of a durable nature, it can keep, or it will endure laying up; all other
treasures are fading; if men lay them up, they will rust
and canker; but, the laying up of this spiritual treasure,
which makes men rich in good works is profitable, commendable; and the riches thereby treasured up, are most
durable.

CHAPTER VIII.

BRIDE.

Verse 1. Oh that thou wert as my brother, that sucked the
breasts of my mother! when I should find thee without, I
would kiss thee; yea, I should not be despised.
2. I would lead thee, and bring thee into my mother's house,
who would instruct me: I would cause thee to drink of spiced
wine of the juice of my pomegranate.

THIS chapter carries on the copy of that spiritual communion, which is betwixt Christ and the believer; the
Bride speaks most here, and the nearer she comes to a
close, her expressions become the more massy. It may
be divided into these parts, 1. The Bride continueth, and
heightens her one great request, of more intimate familiarity with Christ: which is propounded, amplified and
pressed, with the insinuation of her success, and after-
carriage in the first four verses. 2. The daughters of
Jerusalem being charged by her, verse 4, break out with
a commendation of her, verse 5. 3. She forbears to own

them, but proceeds, verse 5, to speak to him (as loath to be interrupted or diverted) with two further petitions: the first whereof, is for fixedness in her fellowship with him, that it be not liable to the frequent interruptions of a declining heart, verses 6, 7. The second, is for those not yet brought in, verse 8. 4. The Bridegroom replies to this last suit, in good words and comfortable, verse 9. From which, in the fifth place, she gathers a comfortable conclusion to herself, verse 10, which she confirms, verses 11, and 12. 6. The Bridegroom gives his farewell-request unto her, verse 13. Which, seventhly and lastly, she meets with the ardent expression and putting up of her first, last, and great suit to him, to wit, that he would make haste, that is, haste his coming for completing her happiness, beyond which she hath nothing to say, and until which, she is never silent, Rev. xxii. 17, so then, this chapter doth consist of seven parts, according to the several intercourses of the speakers.

In the first part, the Bride first propounds, and amplifies, or qualifies her suit, verse 1. 2. It is pressed with motives, verses 1, 2. 3. Her attainment and success in her suit is mentioned, verses 3, 4. And 4. her care of entertaining Christ, is recorded, verse 4.

The suit is in the first words, " O that thou wert as my brother :" this I conceive looks not mainly to Christ's incarnation, but to something that might have been by believers obtained even then before his incarnation, and may yet be desired by those who now love him : but, that which is chiefly intended in these words, is the following forth of the love strain of a heart longing for Christ's company, in the terms and expressions that are in use amongst men : it hath been ever thought unseemly for virgins, too familiarly to converse with men that are strangers, even though they were suited for by them, this hath been cause of reproach to many : but, for brethren and sisters to be familiar, hath not been subject to mistakes ; they who are in that relation may use more freedom, than without offence can be used by others ; therefore, Abraham fearing to call Sarah his wife, gave her out to be his sister, that their conversing together might be the less suspected ; thus, the scope here is to press, that Christ would condescend to be so homely with her, as she with boldness and without fear might converse with him : O ! (saith she) that thou wert so familiar with me, that I

might confidently converse with thee, as a woman may do
with her brother : and because, there is great odds betwixt brethren that are of the same father, yet born of
divers mothers (as Joseph, Simeon, and Judah were) and
brethren that are also of the same mother (as Joseph and
Benjamin were, who therefore more dearly loved one another) she doth therefore add that qualification, "that
sucked the breasts of my mother," that is, such a brother
as hath been conceived in the same womb, and nourished
by the same breasts (mothers being then both mothers
and nurses to their own children) whereby, a brother in
the most near and warm relation is signified : in sum, the
sense is this, O ! if thou wert to me so condescending, as
a brother is to one born of the same womb with him, that
I might with the more freedom, boldness, and confidence,
and sensible out-letting of my affections, converse with
thee : such sensible breaking forth of affections, we find
to have been betwixt Joseph and Benjamin, Gen. xliii 34.
She looks upon all the familiarity that she had attained,
but as that which might be amongst strangers, in respect
of that which she longed for and expected : and that this
is the scope of this part of the allegory, the words after
do clear, " then I would kiss thee, and not be despised,"
or reproached for it ; whereas now in her present condition, which had much of estrangement in it, any claim
she made to Christ, was by tentation cast in her teeth,
and she upbraided, as if it were unsuitable for her to carry
so to him : but (saith she) if thou wilt condescend to me,
and be familiar with me as a brother, I would not be
ashamed for any challenge of that kind.

This suit, and its qualification, import, 1. That there
should be much loving tenderness betwixt those that are
in so near a relation as this, to be born of one mother, &c.
2. That mothers who bear children, and are fitted to give
suck, should not decline that duty to their children ; the
giving of suck being a duty no less natural, than bringing
forth, where the Lord hath put no impediment to the contrary in the way. 3. It imports, that there are steps of
access to Christ, and degrees of fellowship with him, beyond any thing that the most grown believers have
attained : there is somewhat of this, even by the Bride to
be wished for, that she hath not yet attained. 4. There
ought to be no halting or sitting down in any attainment
of nearness with Christ, till it be brought to that measure

that no more can be enjoyed, and till it be at the utmost
height that is possible to be attained.   5. To have sensible
warmliness, and condescending familiarity from Christ,
and confident freedom with him, is the believer's great
design ; that is, to have him as a brother : and these two,
to wit, confident freedom with Christ, and his warm condescending to them, go together; which the reasons following will clear.   They are set down in seven motives,
or advantages, which his being as a brother would bring
along with it to her ; and hereby it will be further cleared,
what it is that is here intended.   The first is hinted at in
these words, " When I should find thee without :" when,
is supplied, and the words read in the original, " I would
find thee without:" now (saith she) I have sought thee
often without, and have for a long time not found thee
(chap. iii. 2, 3, and 5, 6, 7.) but if thou wert thus familiar
with me, I would have thy company every where, and
think no shame of it.   This supposes, 1. That Christ may
be without, or at a distance, even with his own sister and
spouse : the most sensible manifestations have interruptions.   2. When Christ is without, or at a distance, then
the believer's work is to seek him till he find him ; he
loves not to be separated from Christ, and therefore he
pants after his manifestations : an absent Christ, and a
seeking, painful, diligent believer, should go together.
3. That where Christ is familiar, all interruptions of presence are easily superable, yea, more easily superable
than to others, with whom he is not so familiar and intimate : he may be found by them even without, that is,
in cases that have in them some obstructions unto intimate
fellowship, as without is a place that is not convenient
for familiar communion.   4. It is a great benefit to a believer, to have Christ's presence easily recoverable, or recovered; it is no small mercy to find him when he is
sought.   Other things rising from this expression may be
gathered from chap. iii. 2, 3, and 5, 6, 7.   In general,
from all these arguments we may observe, that they all
include advantages to the believer, yet she makes use of
them as motives to press her suit ; which says, that whatever may be any real advantage to a believer, doth sway
much with Christ.

  The second reason why she desires this, is, that she
may embrace and kiss him, and it follows on the former
(as each of them depends upon another) I would find thee

without (saith she) and " I would kiss thee," having found
him, she would with delight let out her affections on him.
Kisses amongst men, are the most kindly evidences of
their love, as was cleared, chap. i. verse 1, upon these
words, " Let him kiss me :" his kisses are kindly intimations of his love to her ; and therefore her kissing of him
must be a most sensible flowing and abounding out-letting
of her affections on him, as affectionate relations do when
they kiss one another. It is much to the same purpose,
with what she said, chap. vii. 12, " There will I give thee
my loves :" in sum, if thou wert familiar with me (saith
she) when I find thee, I would sensibly, confidently, and
with freedom solace myself in thee, which now I dare
scarce do when I find thee, being possessed with fear of
thy removal. The difference between this expression,
and that in chap. vii. 12, seems to be this ; there, she desired communion with him, that her heart might be by
his presence disposed (to say so) for letting out her love
on him, and that she might have the opportunity to do it:
here, she desires that he would manifest himself more
familiarly, that with the greater holy boldness and confidence, she might satisfy herself in pouring forth her love,
by spiritual soul-embracings, and kissings of him whom
she loved. This imports, 1. That there are degrees in
the way of believers' letting out their love on Christ, as
there is in his manifesting of himself to them ; there are
some times they " give him their love," when they have
no access to kiss him ; and other times they are admitted
to kissing of him, as at some times he doth them. 2. The
more familiarly his love lets out itself on them, the more
doth their love flow out on him. 3. It is a mercy to the
believer, and highly prized by him, to have access to kiss
Christ, and to let out his heart and love on him. 4. It
says, that at all times believers will not get themselves solaced in Christ ; this is an exercise to which their hearts
doth not frame, till he familiarly manifest himself ; they
cannot kiss and embrace him, until his embracements come
first. More particularly, if we consider the scope of
these words, " I would kiss thee," and that, " without :"
they imply, 1. A more present sensible object, such as
may be kissed : whence, observe Christ's familiar out-
letting of himself, that makes him exceedingly obvious
unto the believer ; it makes him so sensibly present, as
he may be in a spiritual way embraced and kissed. 2. It

holds out the out-letting of the believer's love on him : from which, *Observe* 1. The great duty of one that finds Christ, is to love him, and to let the heart flow out on him. 2. This should be done whenever, or wherever, Christ is found ; and so soon as opportunity is offered, the heart should close with it without delay. 3. Familiarity with Christ will not be displeasing to him, but exceedingly acceptable ; otherwise, this could be no motive to press her suit.

3. Kissing him, imports, both a holy confidence, and satisfaction or delight, in her letting out her heart upon him : which shews, that it is sweet not only to have Christ loving us, but to get him loved ; and so this is both satisfying to her, and acceptable to him.

The third motive or reason (which depends on the former two) is, " yet, I should not be despised," or, they should not despise me : that is, although I found thee without, and were seen kissing thee, and by confident boldness delighting in thee ; yet, if thou wert familiar with me as " my brother," and according to the nearness of that relation would familiarly own me, neither men, devils, temptations, nor any thing else, would have access to despise, upbraid, or reproach me for it, I would be confident against all ; as a virgin that is shewing her respect to her own born brother, needs fear no reproach from that. *Observ.* 1. Believers are subject to be despised, even the beloved Bride of Jesus Christ is not freed from this trial, to be little esteemed of, even as the off-scourings of all things, to be reproached and shamed by men (as she was, chap. v. 7.) to be baffled (to say so) as an hypocrite, by the devil and temptation, as Job was, Job, chap. i. and ii. 2. Believers are not senseless or stupid ; when reproached or despised, they may be affected with it, and may endeavour rightly to have it prevented or removed. 3. Often the more tenderly that believers let out their affection on Christ, or their zeal for him, they are the more subject to be despised ; for, when she kisses Christ, she looks upon despising then as waiting on her, if he prevent it not. 4. Christ's familiar presence, or, his being as a brother owning his Bride, is the great thing that guards off, and prevents despising, and procures freedom from reproach, or at least is a bulwark to the soul against reproaches : it is no little advantage that familiarity with Christ brings along with it ; for, by his owning of believers, either their carriage is made so convincing, that malicious mouths are stopped, as having nothing to say against them; or they are so sustained, under all these outward or inward despisings, that they trouble them not, and so they are to them as if they were not. 5. Christ's keeping up of himself, is the dispensation under which the believer is most obnoxious to be despised: the devil, temptations, and men, usually cast up to them then, " Where is their God ?" Psalm xlii. 9, 10, and that pierces them: so our Lord was dealt with on the cross; Job calls this the Lord's renewing of his witnesses against him, whereby (as it were) temptation is confirmed in what is asserted.

There follows in the second verse, four more arguments, she makes use of to press her suit: we heard of three in the first verse; the fourth is in these words, " I would lead thee :" the word in the original signifies such a leading as useth to be in triumph, a leading that is joined with respect and honour to the person who is led. Christ leads his people as a shepherd doth his flock, or a nurse her child; and this signifies tenderness in him, and weakness in them: the believer again, leads Christ, as a servant or usher doth the master, or as men do kings and victorious conquerors whom they honour; and this supposes stateliness in him, and respect and attendance in the Bride, she looks upon him as a glorious, magnificent person, in whom, and with whom, she desires only to triumph. In sum, the meaning is this, If (saith she) thou wert as my brother, when I found thee myself, I would not soon quit thee, but wait with all honourable attendance upon thee. *Observ.* 1. Honourable attendance on Christ, and respectful service, is a duty that well becomes believers. 2. To give him this honour, is a thing which they mainly aim at. 3. It is a great mercy to them (and they will so look upon it) when they are helped, in a way suitable to his majesty and stateliness, to wait upon him, and do him service. 4. Christ's familiar presence, both gives believers the occasion, and also the fitness and disposition, for giving him this honourable attendance; she speaks here, as if one would say to another whom they respected, if thou wert in our quarters, I would wait on thee, and think it a favour to have the opportunity to do so: this, or the like, is alluded unto here.

The fifth argument follows on this, and it is, " I would

bring thee into my mother's house :" this is a resolution, to perform what she had practised, chap. iii. 4, and was spoken to there: the sense is, if thou wert familiar with me (saith she) I would usher thee into the church, whereof I am a member, for the good of all the family; as if a virgin, living in her mother's house, should press one whom she loved, and with whom she might be familiar as with a brother, when she had found him without, to go in and abide with her in her mother's house, as the greatest evidence of her respect, and that they of the family might have the benefit of his company, as well as she : so it is here. And it shews, 1. That she would leave no respect, that was possible to her, unexercised towards Christ; she would not only honour him herself, but she would endeavour to have him made known to others, that they might have a high esteem of him also; believers whom Christ is familiar with, they will not be satisfied with any respect they can put upon him, but are careful to have him known and honoured by all others that live in the church with them. 2. That in her seeking for him, she minded the public good of the church, as well as her own : which teacheth us, to purpose to ourselves the public good, as well as our own particular advantage, whenever we haunt the means, wherein we are called to seek him. 3. That she thought it a great mercy, to be any ways useful for the good of her mother's house : and so believers will look upon it, not only as their duty, but also as their mercy, to be useful to others. 4. That Christ's presence familiarly manifested to particular believers, doth exceedingly capacitate them, for being usefully instrumental in the church wherein they live.

The sixth argument amplifies this, from the benefit that she would have by his being brought into her mother's house, in these words, " who would instruct me ;" that is, then she would instruct me, if thou wert there: the ordinances in the church, whereby believers are edified and instructed, would then be lively and profitable, in a greater measure than formerly: whereby it appears, that by " mother," is understood the visible church; for, there only are the ordinances which do instruct; and by the Bride, is understood particular believers, because it is to them that these ordinances become " the power of God unto salvation :" or, the words may be read, thou wouldst instruct me ; that is, if thou wert brought to the church, thou by thy ordinances wouldst teach me. The scope in both these readings is one, to shew, that by Christ's presence in the church, she expected to be taught, which she looked for no otherwise, nor by any immediate way; therefore, she would have him there. *Observ.* 1. The most grown believer needs instruction, and is still a scholar while he is in the church upon earth. 2. The ordinances in the visible church, are the means, whereby Christ ordinarily teacheth his people; otherwise, there were no force in this reasoning, to desire him to her mother's house, that she might be instructed. 3. The most eminent believer, even the Bride of Jesus Christ, is not above the reach of ordinances, but is to be instructed by them in the visible church. 4. Believers should endeavour the enjoyment of Christ's company in the same church that was their mother, and seek to be instructed there, and should not endeavour to carry Christ away from their mother-church. 5. Christ hath a more full way of manifesting his presence in his church at one time than at another; even as also at different times, there are different measures of his manifestations to particular believers. 6. Christ's presence in his church and with his people, singularly furthers their edification and instruction, and gives a blessing to the ordinances. 7. Believers, when in a right frame, will account it no little mercy to be instructed by Christ in his ordinances, and to have the word blessed unto them. 8. The most sensible and full manifestations of Christ, should not, yea will not, lessen the esteem of the ordinances; but both should, and will put the Lord's people in a capacity to be edified by them, and will incline and fit them to profit under them.

The last motive is taken from the entertainment she would give him; if (saith she) thou wouldst familiarly manifest thyself, and if once I had found thee, and gotten thee brought to my mother's house, then " I would cause thee to drink of spiced wine, of the juice of my pomegranate :" in a word, I would entertain thee as well as I might, and thou shouldst be very welcome, and kindly taken with, as guests who are respected, use to be. By "spiced wine," and "the juice of the pomegranate," is understood the most excellent entertainment; as in these countries, it is like (as we may see from Prov. ix. 2, and Song, chap. v. i.) they used to mix the wine they gave their friends, that it might be the more savoury. Now through this

Song, by such similitudes are understood the graces that are in believers; as, chap. iv. 10, 13, &c. chap. v. 1, and in sum, the sense comes to this, if thou wert familiar with me, and by thy presence in my mother's house, were making the ordinances lively, then I would feast thee on my graces, and my love, faith, hope, &c. (which are to thee, more savoury than wine, with which men use to entertain their most special friends) should flow out abundantly on thee. Hence, *Observ.* 1. That believers' design and aim at the feasting and entertaining of Christ, when they have his company, as well as to be entertained thereby themselves. 2. It is no little mercy to get respect to Christ discharged; and a believing soul will think it no small privilege to get him to entertain, if he have wherewith to entertain him. 3. Christ's coming to a soul brings sufficient provision for his own entertainment: the Bride makes no question, but there shall be a feast, if he will come; and if he come not, there will he nothing but emptiness there: she doubts not, but if once he would come to her mother's house, his presence would make enough of good provision. 4. The Lord respects, even the offer of welcome from his people, when he is not actually entertained as they would: or though they be not in case for the time to entertain him, yet their serious desire to do it, is very acceptable to him; otherwise, this would be no argument for our Lord Jesus, to grant her suit.

Verse 3.   His left hand should be under my head, and his right hand should embrace me.

THE third verse is the same, and to the same scope with verse 6, of chap. ii. and the words being the same in the original, we conceive they will read better here as they are there, " his left hand is under my head;" here it is, " should be under my head," but " should" is supplied: and so the words hold out here (as in chap. ii. 6,) a return, which the Bride had to her suit; our Lord Jesus coming, and putting in his left hand under her head, and as a kind brother taking her in his arms, answereth her suit, and satisfieth her desire: this agrees best with the words, as they were formerly used, chap. ii. 6, and with the scope here. The verse following confirms it also, where she chargeth the daughters not to stir him up, which supposes him to be present: so we find the same charge following

the same words, chap. ii. 7, as also, her finding him, and
bringing him to her mother's house, is followed with the
same charge, chap. iii. 5, and she is said to be leaning on
him here, verse 5, and yet is by the daughters commended,
and not despised, which is a proof that he was present;
for, this is it that made her not to be despised. The
meaning then is, now (saith she) I have obtained what I
desired, and he is become very friendly and familiar with
me, like a brother, which was my desire. And this shews,
1. That Christ easily condescends to his longing Bride,
to give her such a degree of his presence as she called
for; and that he doth this so suddenly, is great kindness
and confidence: Christ will in this sometimes condescend
very quickly to the desires of his longing people. 2.
That she observes and acknowledgeth it; it is no less
duty to observe and acknowledge a return, than to put up
a prayer. 3. Christ hath a singularly tender way of
communicating his love, and of embracing his people, he
can take them in his arms, and make much of them, when
he sees it fit. 4. There is a sweet satisfaction, and
unspeakable heart-quieting refreshment to be found in
Christ's arms; she thinks it so good to be here, that she
speaks of it with much complacency, and carefully sets
herself not to have it interrupted in the verse following.

Verse 4.　I charge you, O daughters of Jerusalem, that ye stir
not up, nor awake my love, until he please.

HAVING now access to much familiarity with Christ, as
she desired, and being in his arms, she expresseth her care
in this verse, to prevent any new interruption of his blessed
presence; as if a woman having her friend or husband
sleeping in her arms, should command all in the house to
be quiet lest he should be awaked: so the Bride sets herself to watch so tenderly over every thing that is in her,
that nothing give him just ground to withdraw: and
though she speak to the daughters of Jerusalem, yet the
scope shews, she looks to herself; but it is thus expressed,
partly, to keep the form used in this Song, and so having spoken of bringing him to her mother's house, she
makes use of the similitude of keeping the house quiet;
partly, to shew her seriousness and reality in this her
care, and the great need that there is of being watchful, even as David provokes all the creatures to praise, and

lays that charge on them, thereby to show his own seriousness in the thing, and the greatness of the work of
praise which he was taken up with : so to the same purpose is this resemblance here.   The same words were
found, chap. ii. 7, and chap. iii. 5, where they were opened :
there are two little differences in the original, which yet
alter not the scope.   1. That expression, "by the roes
and hinds" (which was formerly used) is here left out,
not because this charge is less weighty, but it shews
a haste and abruptness in her speaking, which makes her
omit that, the more speedily to express her charge.   2. It
was before, " If ye stir or awake :" here it is (as the margin reads from the original) "why will ye stir or awake ?"
which doth more plainly import, 1. A readiness, or bensil
in them to stir him up.   2. A certainty of the effect of
his withdrawing, if they should stir him up, or awake him.
3. An unreasonableness and absurdity in the doing of it,
Why will ye do it? saith she.   4. A pressing seriousness,
in her proposing of this question, and urging it so vehemently.   From this, and the frequent repetition of this
charge,   Observe, 1. That it is a difficult piece of work,
to keep the heart tender and watchful for entertaining of
Christ, even when he is present.   2. The strongest believer will take one charge after another, and all will have
enough to do, to make him watchfully tender in keeping
Christ : there is so much laziness in the hearts of the best,
and there is so great need to stir them up to renew their
watchfulness.   3. When the heart hath had frequent
proofs of its own declining, there is the more need to be
very serious in the preventing of it again.   4. There is
nothing that a kindly loving believer will have more indignation at, whether in himself or others, than at this,
that Christ should be provoked, and thereby put to withdraw ; this he cannot abide, why (saith she) will ye stir
him up? 5. They who have Christ's presence, will not be
peremptory with him, for the constant continuing of the
sense thereof, although they love it ; but will be peremptory with themselves, that by their sin they provoke him
not to withdraw before he please.   6. Communion with
Christ is an uptaking exercise to the believer, it takes him
so up that he is never idle : if he be waiting for Christ,
he is breathing, " O that thou wert," &c. and seeking to
find him ; if he enjoy him, he is endeavouring to keep and
entertain him, and these two take him up : believers are

either seeking while they obtain, or watching that they
may entertain what they have attained.

Verse 5. Who is this that cometh up from the wilderness leaning upon her beloved?—

THE daughters of Jerusalem come in speaking to the
Bride's commendation, in the first part of the fifth verse,
" Who is this" they say, (or who is she?) " that cometh
up from the wilderness, leaning upon her beloved?" This
part of the verse stops the Bride from following the purpose she was upon, with a kind of an abrupt exclamation
to her commendation. The daughters now beholding her
resting in her Beloved's arms, as it is, verse 3, to shew
the commendableness of that posture of leaning on him,
they are brought in admiring it : and therefore, both the
Bride and the Bridegroom are spoken of in the third
person, and that by way of question, which supposeth no
doubt in the thing, who it was of whom they speak, but implieth an exceeding high estimation of the party spoken
of, as being (especially in that posture) exceedingly lovely.
The words hold out a believer's walk, 1. In the nature of
it : it is a coming up, or ascending.   2. In the term from
which, it is from the wilderness : by which too (as was
cleared, chap. iii. 6.) is understood the believer's spiritual
progress heaven-ward, with their backs on the contentments of the world, as being unsuitable for them to rest
in : these two are spoken of chap. iii.   3. There is added
here a more express description of her posture, in this
ascending, she is " leaning on her Beloved:" that is, as
they who are weak, make use of a staff, in climbing of a
straight and steep ground, or ease themselves by leaning
on one that is strong, and especially one whom they love,
for helping them on their way ; so the believer is said to
come up from the wilderness, " leaning on her Beloved,"
because she being weak in herself, and unfit for such a difficult voyage, by faith rests on Christ, for helping her in
the way, whereby she is sustained, and carried through
in the duties of a holy walk, and the difficulties in her
way, till she come through the wilderness unto the land
of rest.   So then this leaning imports, 1. Felt weakness
in herself, for encountering with the difficulties of this

walk or journey. 2. Strength in Christ, sufficient for enabling her. 3. Her use-making of this strength by faith ; for, that is to lean or rest on him, or to be joined or associated to him, as the word is rendered by some ; and it is ordinary for faith to be expressed by leaning, resting, taking hold ; and so leaning to Christ, is opposed to "leaning to our own understanding," Prov. iii. 5. 4. Her quieting of herself delightsomely in her leaning or resting on Christ, which gave her security against all fears and difficulties in her way, as John when he leaned on Christ's bosom, John xiii. 23, so the believer thinks himself sure and safe, when admitted to lean his soul there. 5. A progress that she made by this in her way and journey, and that this leaning had much influence on her advancement therein, and upon this account is her leaning mainly commended. *Observ.* 1. That even believers are insufficient of themselves, as of themselves, for the duties of a holy walk. 2 That believers should walk under the sense of this their insufficiency and weakness, and when they come the greatest length in a holy walk, they should not lean unto themselves, or any inherent stock of gifts or grace ; which two supposes, that a believer's conversation, when right, is a heavenly and tender walk. 3. Christ Jesus hath a sufficiency and efficacy in him, not only for the justification of believers that rest on him, but for the furthering of their sanctification also, and helping of them to a victory over the world ; 1. Cor. i. 30, " He is our sanctification," as well as our justification. 4 Believers in their way, should not only by faith rest on Christ, for attaining pardon of sin by his righteousness ; but, should also depend on him, for furthering of their mortification and sanctification : and thus in the exercise of faith and holy dependance, we are to " acknowledge him in all our ways," which is opposed to " leaning to our own understanding," Prov. iii. 5. This was practised in an exemplary way, by the worthies, recorded, Heb. xi. 5. The exercising of faith on Christ for sanctification and life, and for performing of the duties of holiness, hath much influence on the believer's success in all these ; for, " this is our victory," whereby the world is overcome, " even our faith," 1 John v. 4, 5. And therefore, those that are most in the use-making of Christ, for the helping them forward in their way, cannot but come best speed ; for, " leaning on him," and " going up," are here joined together : and so they can never make progress in holiness, that make not use of Christ in their endeavours after it ; God hath so coupled use-making with Christ, and progress in holiness together, that Christ may bear all the glory of the believer's success in the way of holiness, and that he that glories may glory in him. 6. The believer's walk toward heaven is both a stately, and also an easy and successful walk ; for, he is to go about all duties in the strength of Christ, and so Christ bears the burden, and his yoke becomes easy : it is the neglecting of him, that makes all duties wearisome. 7 It is no little piece of the dexterity of a holy walk, and is the great commendation of it, to do all we do by faith, to walk and go on in the faith of his strength, as leaning on him ; this makes the Bride's posture wonderful, for its rarity and commendableness. 8. Although doing of duties will not prove an interest to Christ, and although believers come not to perfection, or any exact suitableness in them, yet the doing of them in the strength of Christ, and walking, as leaning on him, will make out an interest in him : none can actually employ him, for bearing them through in duty, who have not first closed with him, as their beloved, for obtaining of pardon ; this is the Bride's property, Christ is first her beloved, and then she leans upon him to be helped in her walk. 9 That this solid faith, which doth empty the believer of himself in the performance of all duties, as well as of righteousness in the point of his justification : the native work of faith, is to make the soul rest on Christ, yea, and actually it makes the soul rest on Christ alone ; for, all true faith lays the burden of all duties and difficulties upon him, and so it is compared to leaning.

BRIDE.

Verse 5.—I raised thee up under the apple-tree : there thy mother brought thee forth ; there she brought thee forth that bare thee.

THE second part of this verse, in these words, " I raised thee up," &c. are not without obscurity : we take the words to be a new argument of the Bride's, whereby (after this exclamation of the daughters of Jerusalem) she comes in to press her former suit upon the Bridegroom,

and proceeds in it, as being loath to be interrupted or
diverted from her direct application to him; wherefore
she seems to take no notice of what the daughters spoke,
and makes no reply, but instantly goes on in her wrestling
with him, as if nothing had been spoken by them. That
they are words spoken to him, the affixes in the original
make it clear; for, although there be no such difference
in our language, whereby we may discern whether the
word "thee," be masculine or femenine, as spoken to man
or woman, yet in the Hebrew there is a clear difference:
and so, the word "thee, I raised thee," being in the
original of the masculine gender, it is "thee" man, or
"thee" my beloved, or husband: and therefore, they cannot be understood as his words to her, but as hers to him,
seeing it may be clearly discerned in the original that
they belong to a man and it is a different word from that
which is ordinarily spoken of a woman; and there being
no convincing example to the contrary, we must so understand the words here, and to understand them otherwise,
would bring in needless confusion in that language. Next,
that her scope is to press for nearness with him, both what
went before, and what follows, do demonstrate: which
also the opening of the words will confirm. In them
there are two experiences asserted, which tend both to
this scope: the first is her own experience, " I raised thee
up under the apple-tree." The second is, the experience
of all other believers, "there thy mother brought thee
forth, there she brought forth" (for "thee" in this repeated
expression, is not in the original) "that bare thee."

By the "apple-tree," we understand Christ himself,
who is so called, chap. ii. 3, because of his fruit and shadow, under which she sat down. To be "under the apple-
tree," supposes her to be near him, and actually delighting
herself on him, as being abundantly refreshed under his
shadow, as was cleared, chap. ii. 3. Her raising up of
Christ, imports these three things. 1. A duty on her part
(to say so) putting him to shew himself someway for her,
more than formerly he had done; so to raise, or awake,
when it is applied to God, signifies, as, Psalm vii, 6;
Psalm xliv. 23, " Awake, why sleepest thou? arise, cast
us not off?" So then, the meaning of this expression,
" I raised thee," is, I dealt with, and importuned thee in
this. 2. It implies importunity in dealing with Christ,
incessantly she stirred him, and with petitions pressed

him; so, when it is said, Isa. lxiv. 7, "No man stirs up himself," &c. The word, "stirs up," is the same word, and imports more than to pray : it signifies liveliness and wrestling in it, as fowls use to stir their young ones when they would have them flying, from which the word is borrowed. 2. It implies success, I not only made application to thee, and was helped to be serious; but I prevailed, and thou wast awaked and raised, and did make thyself in more than an ordinary way manifest to me, and for me, when I being admitted under thy shadow, took that opportunity to deal with thee. This then is the scope and strength of this first assertion, it is no marvel (saith she) that I long for thy company; for, by former experience I have found the good of it, not only for present ease under sad difficulties, but also I have been thereby helped to more liberty in prayer, and have had success for attaining new experience of thy love; therefore, I desire thy company still, and cannot but desire it.

The second assertion is more broad and extensive, not only I (saith she) have found it so; but all thy people have found access to thee, or thy blessed company and presence singularly useful, to make them fruitful, as having much influence thereon, so, by Christ's mother, here we conceive is understood the believer, in whom he is formed and brought forth, as we cleared on chap. iii. 11, and they bring forth Christ. 1. By giving him a being in their hearts, where he had it not before; his image is in some respect herself, and when his image is brought forth in the soul, Christ is said to formed and brought forth there. 2. By bringing forth of the fruits of Christ's Spirit before others, when being, as it were, in travail in the pursuit of holiness, they are helped to manifest his image (after which they are created) in their conversations. 3. By attaining to the knowledge of this, that Christ is in them; believers being, as it were, in travail, till they know their delivery; but when that is clearly made out, and intimated to them, then (as the woman that brings forth a man-child, John xvi. 21,) they are at quietness, as being delivered. The force of the argument lies in the word "there," which relates to the "apple-tree;" under the apple-tree (saith she) where I raised thee up, being admitted to thy fellowship; there also they were made fruitful, and delivered from their former pangs and travail, even as I was; and when it is found in the experience of all thy people, as well as by me (saith she) that thy presence and company is so useful, it can therefore be no delusion, nor is it any wonder that I so press after it· and by this it seems, that bringing forth of Christ in this second part, is the same in substance with raising him up in the former, to wit, the obtaining of some sensible manifestation of Christ's respect, by which, those who were formerly in pain to have Christ formed in them, are now delivered and eased from the flames of jealous love, that are as pangs to such as travail in birth (as it were) to have their interest in Christ made clear, as the words in the following verse express. *Observ.* 1. That which in a believer's experience hath proven useful, is in a special manner lovely and commendable to him: experience is a most convincing demonstration of the worth of any thing, and leaves the deepest impression thereof behind it. 2. The more any by experience have learned Christ's worth, and the more they have "tasted that he is gracious," their affections do the more vehemently stir after him. 3. Christ's presence hath many great and excellent advantages waiting on it; it brings ease and quietness to the soul, and gives refreshment under his shadow, it gives access to pray with freedom, and duties then have usually a sensible success. 4. The believer looks upon it as a great mercy to have freedom in prayer, and to be heard when he prays; that by prayer she raised Christ up is remembered as a mercy not to be forgotten, and this yet commends unto her the good of sitting under his shadow. 5. Access to Christ is no time for security, but for prayer; and when the believer is admitted to solace himself in Christ's presence, then should he be diligent in wrestling with him, and improving that opportunity for pressing after a farther manifestation of him. 6. There are some experiences that are unquestionable to all believers, though they be mysteries to all others in the world. 7. It is not a little strengthening, yea, exceedingly confirming to believers, when their experience and the experiences of other believers co-incide, and jump in the proof of the same thing. 8. Although believers may in some things differ, yet there are some things commonly found good in experience by them all: this is the advantage of Christ's company, there was never a believer that attained it, but he found much good of it; and those who still travail for it, apprehend groundedly that there is an unspeakable good in it.

Verse 6. Set me as a seal upon thine heart, as a seal upon thine arm: for love is strong as death; jealousy is cruel as the grave : the coals thereof are coals of fire, which hath a most vehement flame.

7. Many waters cannot quench love, neither can the floods drown it : if a man would give all the substance of his house for love, it would utterly be contemned.

In the sixth verse, she proceeds to her second petition, wherein she is strengthened from her former experience : the suit is in two expressions, to one purpose ; and it is pressed with several reasons, in the end of the sixth and seventh verses ; whereby she shews, that less could not be satisfying to her, and this much she behoved to have granted her. The first expression, holding forth her suit, is, " Set me as a seal upon thine heart :" the second is to the same purpose, in the words that follow, and " as a seal upon thine arm." By Christ's " heart" is signified his most inward affections ; for, it is frequent in scripture by the " heart" to signify the most inward affections; so, Matt. vi. 12, " where the treasure is, there the heart will be." And chap. iv. 9, " Thou hast ravished my heart," &c. a " seal" is used for confirming evidences, or closing of letters ; they have some peculiar engraving on them, serving to distinguish the deed of one man from the deed of another ; wherefore men use to have a special care of their signet or seal (for both are one upon the matter and in the original) thus Ahasuerus kept his seal upon his own finger, Esth. iii. 10, 12. So then from this we may see, that a seal, or signet, signifieth, 1. What one hath a precious esteem of ; and therefore, Jer. xxii. 24. the Lord said of " Coniah, though thou wert the signet on my right hand," &c. Hag. ii. 23, the Lord expresseth his love to Jerusalem in this, that he would take Zerubabel and make him as a signet. 2. By a " seal" is signified something that makes an impression, and leaves a stamp thereof behind it, that doth not wear out again, as a seal doth on the wax. Next, by Christ's " arm," may be understood, his care of his people, outwardly expressed in the effects, wrought by his power for their good : so, Isa. xl, 11, it is said, he " will gather the lambs with his arms," &c. thus then, to be set as a seal on his heart, doth imply, 1. Exceeding great nearness to Christ, even to have a special room and seat in his heart. 2. It imports, a settledness in that condition, that she may be set there, as the Lord

T

saith of Jerusalem, 2 Kings xxi. 4, there I have put or
set my name, and as it is, Psalm cxxxii. 14, there will
I dwell. 3. To be set as a seal on his arm, takes in
further, that, as she would be always minded by Christ,
and have him loving her; so would she have him in all
his dispensations making that manifest, and that (as it
were) they may bear it engraven upon them, that he
minds her; like that expression, Isa. xlix. 14, "I have
graven thee upon the palms of my hands," whereby he
expresseth his mindfulness of her, that he could look to
nothing in all his works, but he saw (as it were) her name
engraven thereupon; for, all his works express love to
her. In sum, we conceive the words look to one, or both
of these similitudes, or allusions: 1. In general, to men
who have such respect to their seals or rings, that they
wore them on their fingers, and carried them still about
with them; now, she would be carried about on his heart,
and have him sympathizing with her in every thing that
she meets with. 2. And more especially, it may allude
to Aaron's breastplate, whereby he did carry the names
of the children of Israel on his heart, Exod. xxviii. 12,
29, which engraving is said to be like the engraving of a
signet, in which the high-priest was certainly a type of
Christ: however, this is certain, that she would be established in her union with Christ, so that neither desertions on his part, nor backslidings on hers, might mar
that; but that she might be fixed as to her union with
him, and made to abide in him, as the impression of a
seal is fixed upon the wax, and made to abide in it.
Observ. 1. True love to Christ, will be bold, pressing and
importunate, in its suits to him; it will not stand to seek
any thing that may endear him to the soul, to have him
as a brother, and to be worn upon his heart, &c. 2.
Christ's heart and inside, are most heartsome to the believer, who hath had any discovery thereof made unto his
soul; and true love can settle no where, till it get a lodging in his very heart, that is the proper resting place of a
believer, and that is the refreshing, which can make the
weary to rest. 3. Love to Christ would not only be near
him, but would be fixed and established in nearness with
him. 4. A stayed, immoveable condition, or frame of
heart, in the enjoying of communion with Christ, is most
desirable and profitable; and therefore, it is no marvel it
be longed for. There is no staying or settling of a be-

liever, till he be admitted to dwell (as it were in Christ's heart) that is, to dwell near him in the believing and enjoying of his love; all other grounds are wavering, but this is stable; and dwelling here, if it were pressed after, would bring more establishment.

This seems to be a peremptory suit, she doth therefore give two reasons to press it, both which shew that it will not be unpleasant to Christ, nor can it be condemned in her, for (saith she) the love that presseth me to it is of such a vehement nature, I cannot resist it, more than death, the grave, or fire can be resisted. This reason is contained in the rest of the sixth verse. The second reason in the following, wherein she shews, that the love that pressed her, was of such a peremptory nature, and so untractable (if we may so speak) as to this, that there was no dealing with it, if it did not obtain its desire, no other thing could quench or satisfy it. The strength of her love is amplifyed in the sixth verse, by three steps, in several similitudes. By love here is understood that vehement, ardent desire, after Christ's presence, which is kindled in the heart of the believer. And first, it is called strong, in respect of its constraining power, whereby the person that loves, is led captive, and brought down as weak under it, so that he cannot withstand it : saith she, love masters, and will undo me, if it be not satisfied ; love-sickness so weakens the soul, when it once seizeth on the heart, till it be cured with Christ's presence. Next, it is called "strong as death," which is so strong, that it prevails over the most powerful, wise, mighty and learned in the world. Eccles. viii. 8, " there is no discharge in that war ;" neither can the most mighty monarch encounter death, and stand before it : so (saith she) I can no more stand against the strength of this love, it overpowers me, and is like to kill me, if it be not satisfied. The second step or degree of this love, and the similitude illustrating it is in these words, " jealousy is cruel as the grave :" it is the prosecution of the same purpose, only, what she called love before, is here termed jealousy : jealousy may be taken in a good sense, or an evil : in a good sense, jealously is the highest degree of love, or love at its height, and is the same with zeal : thus the Lord is said to be " jealous for his glory :" and it imports, 1. Ardent affection. 2. Desire of enjoying. 3. Impatiency of delay. 4. A deep measure of grief, mixed with love, for any

seeming appearance of a disappointment in the enjoying
the person they love, or, when they do not meet with love
again from the person whom they dearly love ; so jealousy in this sense is applied to both God and men, but
properly it agreeth only to men ; for, there are no such
passions in God, though he, condescending to our capacity,
speaks thus of himself, after the manner of men. Now
this jealousy is said to be cruel, or hard : it is called,
Prov. vi. the "rage of a man ;" and this was the jealousy,
or zeal that did eat up David, Psalm lxix. and so it is
compared to the grave, which Prov. xxx. is the first of
those four things that are never satisfied, but wastes all
the bodies that are laid in it : so (saith she) this love of
mine, being at a height, torments me restlessly, as if it
were cruelly persecuting me, till it be satisfied, with a
good answer from thee, O, my Beloved ! In an evil sense
jealousy signifies not a simple fear of missing the thing
men desire, or a suspicion of their own short-coming in
attaining of it, but a groundless suspicion of them whom
they love, as if they did not entertain their love as they
ought ; and thus, jealousy is called " the rage of a man,"
Prov. vi. 34, and so here this cannot be altogether excluded ; jealousy thus taken, having in it some unbelief,
which torments believers horribly, when the suspicion of
Christ's not taking notice of them grows ; and this is
frequently to be found in the saints' cases, in times of desertion ; they are then very apt to suspect God's love,
and this exceedingly disquiets them, the want of the faith
and sense of his love being a death unto them, Psalm
lxxvii. 8, 9, 10. And so the reason runs thus, let me be
admitted to thy heart, for my love will be satisfied with
no less ; and if this be not obtained, jealousy and suspicion
of thy love may steal in, and that will be torturing and
tormenting : and therefore, she puts up this suit, that she
may be set as a seal upon his heart, to have that prevented ;
for she cannot abide to think of it. 3. She compares this
jealousy to coals of fire (the coals thereof are coals of fire)
for their vehement heat, tormenting nature, and consum-
ing power ; all which are to be found in this strong and
jealous love ; it is vehement for heat, and painful and de-
structive as fire is : yea further, it is compared to coals
that have "a most vehement flame," or as it is in the
original, the " flame of God ;" for so the Hebrews do
name any thing that is superlative in its kind, and this is

added, to shew the horrible torture that Christ's absence, and love-sickness hath with it, to a tender loving soul, especially when carnal unbelieving jealousy enters and prevails, they cannot abide it, but would choose any rod before that, if it were at their election. *Observ.* 1. Love to Christ, where it is strong and vigorous, will make strange and mighty impressions on the heart, which others are not acquainted with, and will break out in such expressions, as men of the world may wonder what they mean, none of them having any such feeling or sensibleness of Christ's absence or presence. 2. Where true love to Christ is, it is a most constraining thing, the soul, that hath it, cannot but pursue for Christ, and go about all means which may any way further its communion with him. 3. Where love begins to pursue after Chrsst, the longer it be in meeting with him, it increaseth the more, where it is real ; and the more disappointments it meet with, it grows the more vehement, till it break out in jealousy and zeal. 4. Believers that have true love, are ready to fall in jealousies of Christ, and to be suspicious of his love, especially in his absence ; this is supposed here, that where true love to Christ is, there may be jealousy of him. 5. Where jealousy enters, is cherished and prevails, it is not only dishonourable to Christ, but exceedingly torturing to the believer : there is not a more vexing guest can be entertained, than jealousy of Christ. 6. Jealousy of Christ's love may be where there is little cause , and often where there is least cause, it is most ready to enter : the reason whereof may be taken from the ardency of the soul's love to him, joined with the mistakes they have of his way ; so, Isa. xlix. 13, 14, for considering what is gone before, it might be thought, that, whatever any other might seem to have, the Bride had no cause of jealousy. 7. Believers should endeavour to prevent all jealousy of Christ and his love, and by all means seek to be established and confirmed in the faith of his love to them, as that which can only keep and guard the heart against these sinful suspicions and jealousies. 8. Though this jealousy be vexing, yet sometimes the believer cannot rid himself of it, it will so prevail, and is so cruel against him. In the similitude of death and the grave, that is here made use of, it is implied that no man shall escape death and the grave, they are as strong and mighty conquerors, that prevail over all that come in their way : it is clearly hinted here, that the believer carrieth this conviction in his heart, that some time he will be prevailed over by death and the grave, this is no ill impression, "the graves are ready for me, and, I have said to corruption, thou art my father : and to the worm thou art my mother, and my sister," Job xvii. 1. 14.

Her second reason is contained, verse 7, and it is taken from the peremptoriness of her love ; for, her love is such as it will have love from Christ again, or no other thing will satisfy it. This is two ways illustrated, 1. From its invincibleness, which appears in this, no opposition can extinguish it, "many waters cannot quench love, neither can the floods drown it :" waters will quench fire, but nothing will quench this love. By waters in scripture, often (as Psalm xlii. 7, and xciii. 4, and frequently) are understood afflictions, crosses, and even spiritual desertions, Psalm xl. 7, "all thy waves and billows have gone over me," Psalm cix. 1, 2, and so here it saith, love to Christ is of that nature, and is so strongly fixed on him, that no cross or rod, nay not the blackest dispensations and desertions can make it alter ; but it will stick to him through and over all, as, Rom. viii. 35, "neither famine, sword, pestilence," &c. can do it, but it triumphs over all, though floods of trial and opposition were let out upon it. The second way how the peremptoriness of love is illustrated and proven, is, that it rejects all offers, that may be made to it by any other that would have Christ's room : there are two sorts of trials, that ordinarily carry souls away from Christ, the first is on the left hand, from crosses ; and when these will not do it, but the thorny ground will abide the heat of the sun ; yet, the second sort of trials, to wit, the cares of the world, and the deceitfulness of riches, which are tentations on the right hand, may choke the word, and carry the soul away : but (saith she) true love to Christ, will be prevailed over by neither, it will tryst and capitulate with other lovers upon no terms ; nay, though a man would give it "all the substance of his house ;" that is, all that can be given, though he would leave nothing behind, but give it all to one that loves Christ, for love, that is to purchase and buy away the soul's love from Christ, that it may be given to some other thing that comes in competition with him, so to bud and bribe the soul's love from Christ, that it may settle on some other thing that is offered in his place : what entertainment would be given to such offers and treaties ? true love (saith she) in so far as it is true, and lively in exercise (otherwise where something of true love is the soul may often be ensnared) " would utterly contemn it," or as it is in the first language, " contemning it should be contemned" that is, not only would all such alluring offers be rejected, but with a holy disdain and indignation, they would be despised, abhorred and abominated, as unsuitable once to be mentioned : so that true love to Christ, will not once enter to capitulate, what to have in Christ's room ; but all possible overtures, which may be made by the flesh and the world to divert it, will be loathed, abhorred utterly, and " accounted as loss and dung," Phil. iii. 8. And there-fore, the reason concludes, at thy heart I must be, for my love will neither be boasted from thee, nor bribed or allured to be satisfied with any other thing in thy room ; but thee I must have upon any terms, and must not be refused of this my suit, of being set as a seal upon thy heart : and this sort of peremptoriness from love, will not be accounted presumption by Christ, nor is any ways dis-pleasing, but most acceptable to him. *Observ.* 1. Where true love to Christ is, there will be many essays to cool it, or to divert it, and draw it away from him : it is no easy thing to get love to Christ kept warm ; for, the devil and the world, will especially aim at the throwing down of this hold and bulwark, that maintains Christ's interest in the soul. 2. The devil hath several kinds of tentations, which do all drive especially at this, to cool the believer's affections in the love of Christ : and these tentations may be contrary, some of them mustering the difficulties that follow those that love him, and such as the tempted seekers of Christ may be oftentimes exercised with ; for, they often meet with reproaches, or other afflictions in the world : others of them again, alluring the heart to embrace some other thing in Christ's room, and making fair offers of advantages, to those that will take the way of the world in following of them. 3. The lovers of Christ may be assaulted by both these extremes successively ; and when tentations from the one hand fail, then tentations from the other begin, so that the believer should con-stantly be on his guard. 4. The tentations that come from the right hand, and entice the soul with the offers of worldly pleasure, honour, riches, &c. are more strong and subtile than the other, and more frequently do prevail, yea, sometimes when the other may be rejected ; there-

fore, this is mentioned after the other, as being that wherewith the soul is assaulted, when the first cannot prevail,
and so the devil leaves this till the last; when he was
permitted to tempt Christ, having tried him with several
tentations, at last he makes offer of the world to him, Matt.
iv. 9. 5. Tentation will sometimes make great offers, as
if nothing more could be offered, " even all the substance
of the house," and still it offers more than it can perform,
when it is in its offers most specious : the devil at once
offered all the world to Christ, Matt. iv. 9, though he had
not power of himself to dispose of one of the Gadarene's
swine. 6. The great scope of the world's courting a man
with its offers, is to gain his love from Christ; this they
had need to look well to, on whom the world smiles most,
for then the tentation to this ill is strongest. 7. It is a
proof of true love to Christ, when it can endure and hold
out against tentations upon all hands, and that when they
are most speciously adorned. 8. Where love is true,
although it may be sometimes (as it were) violated, or
the soul in which it is, circumvented and beguiled by tentations (as the experiences of saints do clear) yet when it
is at itself, or in good case, it will not deliberately capitulate to admit any thing in Christ's room, but will reserve
itself wholly for him : where love cedes, and yields finally,
it is a sign that it was never true. 9. Tentations though
most pleasant, yet tending to divert the love of the soul
from Christ, should be with indignation, at their first
moving and appearing, rejected. 10. Love will not only
refuse a consent to some tentations, but will have a great
abhorrency at the moving of them ; whereas others, though
they may, as to the external actings, resist these tentations, yet their wanting of this indignation, bewrays their
want of love. 11. As it is good to be actuated in doing
duty, from a principle and motive of love ; so it is good and
commendable, to reject tentations upon that same account.

Verse 8.   We have a little sister, and she hath no breasts ; what
    shall we do for our sister in the day when she shall be spoken
    for ?

THE Bride's third petition, for those that are not yet
brought in to Christ, followeth in this eighth verse : her
love is strong in pressing for the enjoyment of Christ ;
and seeing it hath two arms, as it reacheth out the one to

embrace Christ, so it reacheth out the other to bring others
in to him; love is very desirous to have others enjoying
him with itself; and by this arm of love, the Bride is
pulling in those that are yet strangers, that they may be
engaged to love Christ; and she forgets them not, even
when she is most serious for herself: this being an un-
doubted truth, that, whenever our love is most fervent
after Christ for ourselves, it will also be most sensible and
sympathizing, in respect of the condition of others; when
love is hot and fervent the one way, so will it be the other
way also, and when it cools to the one, it also decays in
respect of the other. We may take up this verse in these
three, 1. She remembers and propounds her little sister's
case to Christ. 2. There is her suit, in reference thereunto. 3. This suit is qualified, in the last part of the verse.

   1. Her little sister's case is proposed in these words,
" We have a little sister, that hath no breasts:" here
much love and sympathy appears in these three things,
1. That she is called a "sister," 2. " Our sister," 3. " A
little sister," and without breasts, which do express much
tenderness of affection and sympathy. By "sister," is
sometimes understood, more strictly, such as are renewed
converts to the faith, whether in profession only, or really,
1 Cor. vii. 15, but that is not the meaning here; for, the
sister here mentioned "hath no breasts," and is not yet
spoken for. Again, "sister" may be more largely taken,
for one, or all of these three. 1. For all men, as partaking
of one common nature. 2. For men of one stock and
nation; so Samaria was sister to Jerusalem, &c. Ezek.
xvi. 46. 3. For the elect who are yet unconverted, who
are sisters in respect of God's purpose, as they are Christ's
sheep, John x. 16, and sons of God, John xi. 52, even
before their conversion; for which cause, the "sister" here
spoken of, is said "to have no breasts," as not being yet
changed from her natural condition; and so we take this
especially to look to the unrenewed elect, not excluding
the former two. The sense then is, there are yet many
who have interest in, and many that belong to, thy election, yet uncalled. Now, it is their in-bringing, and the
making of them ready to be Christ's Spouse and Bride,
that she breathes after, and prayeth for. Next, it is
said, " We" have a sister, and so she is called "our"
sister, that is, thine and mine; Christ's sister, because of
his purposed respect to her; the believer's sister, not only

because of their native and kindly sympathy, but also because of the common adoption, to which they are designed. She is called "a little sister," and that "hath no breasts,"
1. To shew the sad condition that the unconverted elect are in, like little young children that are unfit to do any thing for themselves, and altogether unmeet for the duties of marriage, as those at age, who have breasts, are: thus, Ezek. xvi. 7, the wretched condition of that people, before they were taken into God's covenant, is set out by this, that their breasts were not formed; and the good condition that followed their being in covenant is expressed thus, that their breasts were fashioned. This then is the scope here, to shew that this little sister was yet in nature, unmarried to Christ, yea, (as to many of the unconverted elect) not spoken for, or called. 2. She is called "little," to express the Bride's pity and sympathy, as one would say of a young one, that cannot do any thing for herself, what will become of her? she is a little one.

2. The suit is, "what shall we do for our sister?" This is a petition, that seems to have more affection than distinctness in it: it is proposed by way of question, the better to express her sympathy; where she disputes not, but again asserts his relation to her, and puts no question but he will be tender of her; and withal acknowledgeth that there is a duty lying on herself, in order to the case of her little sister, but would be informed and taught by him in the right discharge of it: and so this question supposeth necessity and wretchedness in this sister, affection and duty in herself, but unclearness how to discharge it. Now, the way she takes to be helped in it, is the putting up this petition to Christ, "what shall we do?" saith she; not as if Christ knew not what he would do, but it shews her affection to this sister, and her familiarity with him; and also, that she will not separate his doing from hers, but looks upon it as her duty to co-operate with him, in bringing about the conversion of their little sister.

The qualification of her suit is, "what shall we do for her, in the day that she shall be spoken for?" This phrase, to speak for her, is in allusion to the communing that is used for the attaining women in marriage: we find the same phrase in the original, 1 Sam. xxv, 39, "David sent messengers to commune with Abigail, that he might take her to wife:" now (saith she) our little sister is not ready, nor spoken for, but when she shall be suited or communed with, what shall we do then? This communing, is the Lord's dealing by his ministers in the gospel, with people, to marry and espouse his Son Christ Jesus, so it is often called, Matt. xxii. 3, " He sent forth his servants, to call them that were bidden to the wedding :" the ministers of the gospel are his ambassadors, to tryst this match, and to close it, 2 Cor. v. 19, and xi. 2 " The day" when they shall be spoken for, is either whilst the means are amongst people, and so that is the acceptable time, 2 Cor. vi. 2, or more especially, when the means have any force on them, and God seems in a more than ordinary way to treat with them, then it is the day of their visitation, as it was in the days of Christ's ministry, though that people were treated with before. In sum, the meaning of the verse is this, there are many who in thy purpose are designed to be heirs of life, who yet are strangers, and not suited or engaged ; now when the gospel comes amongst such, or, by stirring them now and then, puts them in some capacity to be dealt with, what shall be done for them, to help on the bargain, that the marriage be not given up, when it hath come to a treaty, and thou hast by the gospel bespoken them, and propounded it? it may look to sister-churches, and no question the believing Jews, who understood the prophecies of the Gentiles' conversion, did then long for their in-gathering, and inchurching of them (for we were then to them a little sister without breasts) yet we cannot astrict it to that, but now, and to the world's end, it speaks out the believer's desire of the perfecting of the saints, and the building up of Christ's body, as well as it spoke out their desire after this then: and by the same sympathy, the converted Gentiles long, and should long for the in-bringing of the elder sister, the Jews, who now have no breasts, and also of the fulness of the Gentiles, who are as yet unconverted ; and according to the strain of the song, it takes in the believer's respect to the conversion of other church-members, who being indeed not converted, and not effectually called, they are without breasts, and so to be helped forward in the time when God is bespeaking them and trysting with them.

Observ. 1. There may be relations betwixt one in grace, and those who are yet in nature, which grace doth not dissolve, but sanctify ; the little sister is " a sister," though unrenewed, and the Bride's desire is to have her

gained. 2. There is a jointness, and community of relations betwixt Christ and the believer, they have common
friends and interests, and as it is betwixt husband and
wife, the sister of the one is the sister of the other. 3.
Before men be by faith married to Christ, even the elect
in that estate are lying in a most miserable, wretched
condition, as we may see, Ezek. xvi. 3, they are loathsome
before God, and indisposed and unfit for being fruitful to
Christ in any duty, as a little damsel without breasts is
unfit for marriage. 4. The converted elect should be
tenderly affected with the sad condition of the unconverted
especially of those that are in any relation to them, and
to whom God hath respect in his secret purpose, though
definitely they be not known unto them : and this tender
affection ought to appear, in sympathizing with them,
pitying of them, holding up of their condition to God, and
praying for them, as the Bride doth for the little sister :
and when the case of believers is right, they will be making conscience of longing, and praying for the gathering
in of all the elect, that Christ's work may be thoroughed
and perfected, and that his kingdom may come in the
earth. 5. It is a most difficult business, how to get the
conversion of sinners promoted, and Christ's kingdom
advanced ; believers will be non-plussed in it, as being
put to say "what shall we do ?" 6. The Lord hath a
way of espousing, and marrying to Christ Jesus, even
such as are by nature most sinful and loathsome ; it is
such that he suits, wooes, and speaks for, that they may
be married to him. 7. Christ's great design in the gospel,
by sending ministers from the beginning, was, and is to
espouse a Bride to himself, and to make up a spiritual
marriage betwixt him and such as by nature were lying
in their blood. 8. He hath a special time of carrying on
this treaty of marriage, a day before which he treats not,
and after which, there is no opportunity of a treaty of
grace ; it is the day of sinners' merciful visitation, and an
acceptable time for a people. 9. In this treaty, by the
ministry of his ordinances, the Lord will sometimes more
effectually drive the design of the gospel, namely the
matching of sinners to Christ, than at other times, and
will bespeak them more plainly and convincingly, as he
doth, chap. v. 2. 10. When the Lord presseth closing
and matching with Christ home upon sinners, there is
great hazard lest it miscarry, and be given over uncon-

cluded, through their own default. 11. It is a main and
special season for believers to step in, to further the engaging of others to Christ, when the Lord is putting
home upon them the suit and offers of the gospel, and
when they are put to some stir, and made something
serious and peremptory about it. 12. It is a great happiness to be spoken for to Christ, every one is not admitted to that privilege : and it is our great concernment,
to see how we make use of that our day, when he treats
with us. 13. There is nothing wherein a believer's love
to his friends, or to any others, will appear more, than in
endeavouring their conversion, and in longing to have
them engaged to Christ. 14. As God's call in the gospel,
is a wooing, or bespeaking for marriage betwixt Christ
and sinners, so believers' believing, is their consenting to
accept of Christ for their husband, according to the terms
of the contract proposed ; and this closeth the bargain,
and makes the marriage ; for, then the proposed offer of
matching with Christ is accepted of.

BRIDEGROOM.

Verse 9. If she be a wall, we will build upon her a palace of
silver ; and if she be a door, we will inclose her with boards
of cedar.

THIS verse contains the Bridegroom's answer unto the
Bride's last petition : our Lord loves to have his people
praying for others, as for themselves, and therefore, he so
accepts this petition for the little sister, that instantly he
returns an answer thereunto, by a gracious promise ; in
which we are to consider these four things, 1. The
party to whom the promise is made. 2. The promiser.
3. The promise itself. 4. The condition that it is made
upon. First, the party to whom this promise is made, is
implied in the words, " she," and " her," that is, the little
sister yet unconverted, who is mentioned in the former
verse. 2. The promiser is, " we," that is, the Bridegroom and the Bride, to whom this sister stands in relation, verse 8, or rather, " we," the Father, Son, and
Spirit (as we took the like expression, chap. i. 11,) for,
this work which is undertaken and engaged for in the
promise, doth belong especially to them. 3. The promise
is in two expressions (as is also the condition.) 1. " We

will build upon her a palace of silver:" a palace (if the word be so rendered) is a place for dwelling in ; and here it signifieth the adorning of her to be a mansion for his Spirit, and wherein himself will dwell, which is a privilege that the believer in him is admitted unto, 1 Cor. iii. 16, 17. and vi. 19. and this is more than to be a "wall," which is an house, but not so completed and adorned. He is no common guest that is to dwell there, therefore it is no common palace, but " of silver," both precious, and also durable, and stately for its matter, which we must have to dwell in : we will make her such, saith he. The condition proposed in this part of the promise, is, "if she be a wall:" a wall is different from stones, considered in themselves, and supposeth them to be built on a foundation: now Jesus Christ being the only "foundation," 1 Cor. iii. 10. upon which the believer, who is the spiritual temple, is built. This to be a " wall" supposes her to be by faith united to him, whereby she becomes fixed and settled as a wall, who before was unstable : and so the sense runs thus, if she, the little sister when she shall be spoken for by the gospel, shall receive the word, and by faith close with Christ, then (saith he) we we will throughly adorn her, as a mansion fit to be dwelt in, and we will "make our abode" with her, John. xiv. 23. If we render the word, towers, we will build on her towers of silver, it comes to the same scope ; walls are for defence, and they are defective till towers be built on them : and so the promise is to strengthen and adorn her more, if Christ be received by her. The second part of the promise, is, " we will enclose her with boards of cedar :" cedar was a precious wood, and durable (as hath been often said) and to be enclosed with it, signifies the adorning of her, and strengthening of her more. The condition annexed to this part of the promise, is, if " she be a door :" doors make way for entry, and are the weakest part of the wall : the opening of the heart to receive Christ, is compared to the opening of a door, Psalm xxiv. 7, and chap. v. 4, here he saith, although she be weak (possibly like a door of fir) yet if she be a door, and give entrance to Christ (for, all, without faith, are as houses without doors to Christ, that cannot receive him) we will not only adorn her, but also fix and strengthen her more. From all which it appears, that these two things are clearly to be found in the scope, 1. That there is an access,

and addition of beauty and strength promised to the little
sister, even so much as may fully perfect her beginnings,
and carry them on unto perfection; as a "palace," or
towers "of silver," are beyond a wall; and "boards of
cedar," beyond an ordinary door. 2. That these things
promised, are here made to hang upon the condition of
her receiving Christ, and being by faith united to him,
and built on him. That this is the meaning of the supposed condition, is clear, 1. From the promise that is
annexed to it, faith in Christ is the condition, upon which
all the promises of increase of grace, and establishment,
do hang; and the thing promised her can be no other
thing: therefore, the condition must be her union with
him by faith. 2. It agrees with scripture, to expound her
being a "wall," to signify her union with Christ; for,
Christ being the foundation, and believers being the wall,
there must be supposed an union betwixt them, otherwise
these names could not denote that relation which is betwixt Christ and the believers, even such as is betwixt
the wall and the foundation: now this union, by which
believers are built on him, is made up by coming to him,
which is believing, 1 Pet. ii. 4, 5, "To whom coming as
unto a living stone" (or foundation) "ye also as lively
stones, are built up a spiritual house:" their coming to
him builds them upon him, as the foundation: and, Eph.
ii. those that are by nature "aliens to the common-wealth
of Israel" (as the little sister is here, while she hath no
breasts) are by their believing on Christ, said to be of "the
household of faith, and to be built on the foundation of
the prophets and apostles" doctrine, whereof Christ is
"the chief corner-stone," verses 19, 20, &c. 3. It is clear
by the opposition implied; for, to be a wall supposeth
her to be that which she is not now, when she hath no
breasts; and what that is, is clear from the next verse,
where the Bride saith, "I am a wall, and my breasts like
towers," and so I have found favour in his eyes: therefore, to be a wall, is to be a believer, whatever it includes
more: for, none is a wall but the Bride, and who find
favour in his eyes, as her argument will conclude; and
therefore, to be a wall, must include faith. So then, the
meaning of the words comes to this, I tell thee (saith he)
what we will do with our little sister, when she shall be
spoken for; if she by faith come to Christ, and be built
on him, we will perfect that work, for her eternal com-

munion with him; yea, though she be weak and unstable, yet if she yield to Christ, we shall make her grace grow, till she be stable and firm, even as thou, by becoming a wall, hast thy breasts made as towers, and hast found favour to be friendly dealt with, so shall she, and upon the same terms.

Observ. 1. That receiving of Christ by faith, puts them that have been strangers to him in that same capacity, for acceptation and communion with Christ, that his Bride hath, or that those who were formerly believers have by their union with him, 2. All that are bespoken by the gospel, have not interest in the things promised, nor can they apply them, till by faith they be united to Christ, and fulfil the condition to which the promise is annexed, and that is faith. 3. One may really close with Christ, and so be "a wall," and yet have many things to be perfected: grace is not perfect at the beginning, but that "wall" hath a "palace" or tower to be built upon it. 4. The believer's growing in grace, even after his union with Christ, is a great mercy, and is as such promised here. 5. Growth and increase in grace, after conversion is no less a work of Christ's, and a gift of God's, than conversion itself. 6. Christ hath given a promise to the believer, for furthering and perfecting of his sanctification, as well as of his justification. 7. Where there is any honest beginning or foundation laid by real union with Christ, although it be weak, yet it will be perfected, and that may be expected; for, Christ's word, is here engaged for it. 8. There are none of the promised blessings that can be expected from Christ, without performing of the condition of believing in him; and they, who rest on him by faith, may expect all.

BRIDE.

Verse 10.   I am a wall, and my breasts like towers: then was I in his eyes as one that found favour.

IN this tenth verse, and the two verses that follow, the Bride comes in speaking and accepting the Bridegroom's gracious answer and promise: and first, she doth confirm, the truth of it from her own experience, verse 10, and then she doth more fully clear and strengthen her experience, by laying down the grounds from which she draweth that comfortable conclusion (of finding favour in his eyes) in reference unto herself, verses 11, 12.

First, then, in the tenth verse, the Bride brings forth her experience, for confirmation of the truth of what the Bridegroom had spoken: that they are the Bride's words, we conceive is clear; for, this " I," is she that put up the suit for the little sister, and by her description is opposed to her, as being " a wall," and having breasts like towers, which " she" the, little sister had not; and there is none other that hath found favour in Christ's eyes but she. What the scope is, shall be cleared when we have opened the words; which have three things in them. 1. A short description of her own good condition. 2. An excellent advantage that followed thereupon. 3. The connexion of these two. First, Her condition is set forth in two expressions. 1. " I am a wall:" that is, what the little sister was not, and what the condition, proposed by the Bridegroom in the former verse, required: in a word, that condition is fulfilled in me (saith she) by faith I am built on Christ, and like a wall stand stable on the foundation. The second expression, setting forth her condition, is, " and my breasts like towers:" this supposeth a growth, and further degree of her faith and other graces, as having not only breasts, which the little sister had not, verse 8, but " breasts like towers," i. e. " well fashioned," Ezek. xvi. 7, and come to some perfection; and so she is a wall with towers.

Next, the privilege, or advantage which accompanies this her good condition. is held out in these words, " I was in his eyes as one that found favour," or peace; to find favour in his eyes, is to be kindly and affectionately dealt with, and to have that manifested by some suitable evidence: so it is said, Esther found favour in the eyes of the King, and he held out the golden sceptre to her, Est. v. 2. The thing that Moses pitched on, as the evidence that he and the people found favour in God's eyes (Exod. xxxiii. 16, 17,) is, that his presence might go with them, " whereby" (saith he) " should it be known that we have found grace in thy sight, is it not in that thou goest with us?" So then, to find favour in his eyes, is to have his presence in a gracious manner manifested to his people, as John xiv. 23. And in sum, this expression implies these three, 1. Love in Christ's bosom to her. 2. His manifesting of this by his complacency in her, or his making the delight which he had in her, manifest in the effects of it on her. 3. Her being comforted and delighted in the favour that she found from him.

3. The connexion of this comfortable attainment, with her gracious state, is implied in the word then: "then, was I," &c. that is, when I was a wall, and by faith rested on him, I found this favour, and not before: it holds out no casuality betwixt the one and the other, but a peremptory connexion of order and time; for though God's love of benevolence, whereby he purposeth good to us (such as was his love to Jacob, "before he had done good or evil," Rom. ix. 13,) and also his love of beneficence, whereby he actively confers, and brings about our conversion and regeneration, go before our believing in him, and our love to him, and is the cause of our loving of him (who love him because he first loved us) yet his love of complacency, whereby he shews himself delighted with the graces, which by his love he hath bestowed on us, doth follow, in order of nature, upon our faith in him, and love to him; so, John xiv. 21, 23, " He that loveth me, shall be loved of my Father, and I will love him;" and what is meant by this love, the words following clear " I will manifest myself to him ;" and so, verse 23, having said, " my Father will love him," it is added, " we will come and make our abode with him." This then is the sum of this verse, I am by faith founded on him, and united to him, and so am a wall, and have breasts, who by nature once was not a wall, and had no breasts; by which union my breasts becoming as towers, I did find favour from him, and had his presence friendly manifested to me. The scope, as appears from the coherence of this verse with the former, is to make good, from her experience, the truth and certainty of the promises, which he had made for the encouragement of the little sister and for comforting of herself, who had been seriously pleading with him on her behalf: thus, these promises are faithful, saith she ; for, in my comfortable experience, I have found it so : I was once without the evidence of his love, as now others are ; but being by faith engaged to him, I have found favour of him, so as others may be assured of obtaining the like, and on the same terms, if when he is bespeaking them by the gospel, they will close with Christ, and by faith unite with him.

Observ. 1. There are great, real, and discriminating

differences betwixt one in nature, and one that is in
Christ; the one is not a wall, and hath no breasts; the
other is a wall, and hath breasts, which shows a great
odds. 2. Believers may come to know that marches are
cleared betwixt their estate and condition, now while
they are in Christ, and their estate and condition as it was
before; or, believers should set themselves to know,
whether marches be cleared or not, or if they may say
that of themselves, which cannot be said of others that are
not in Christ. 3. It is no little advancement, to be able
upon good grounds to assert our union with Christ, to
to say that " I am a wall," &c. each one cannot do it. 4.
Although none ought to be proud of their attainments,
yet may believers humbly (where there is good ground)
acknowledge the reality of grace in them. 5. Although
the Lord loves the elect, and the believer always, yet
there are special times or occasions upon which, or ways
by which, he manifests his love to them. 6. The believer
hath Christ's favour otherwise let forth and manifested to
him, than it was before his conversion, although this love, as
it is in God himself, be ever the same. 7. It is a singularly
refreshful thing to find favour in Christ's eyes, and to
have that love of his sensibly manifested, and clearly
made out unto us. 8. There is an inseparable and peremptory connexion betwixt holiness in a believer's walk, and
Christ's manifesting of his favour thus unto them. 9.
Those that have felt by experience, the fulfilling of Christ's
promises, are both more clear in the meaning of them, and
more thorough in the faith of them : experience is both a
good commentary upon, and proof of, the promises of
Christ, which the Bride makes use of here. 10. The experience of one believer in the way of grace, which is
founded upon the essentials of the covenant, and is agreeable to it, may be an encouragement to strengthen others,
in expectation of the accomplishment of the same thing,
when the same way is taken in suing for it. 11. Believers
that are more versed in, and acquainted with experiences
than others, should fitly and conveniently bring them out,
and communicate them for the benefit of others, who yet
have not attained that length. 12. It is the duty of
hearers, when they hear gospel truths and offers (such as
were held forth in the ninth verse) to reflect on themselves, and try if their experience suit with them, if they
have such conditions in themselves, and have felt the ful-

filling of such promises in their own particular experience: and it is comfortable, when their experiences and the promises agree so together, that when he saith, " If she be a wall, we will build on her": or, "who loveth me, I will manifest myself to him," they may groundedly answer, and say, " I am a wall," and so have "found favour" in his eyes; I love him, and so he hath manifested himself to me.

Verse 11. Solomon had a vineyard at Baal-hamon ; he let out the vineyard unto keepers: every one for the fruit thereof was to bring a thousand pieces of silver.
12. My vineyard, which is mine, is before me : thou, O Solomon, must have a thousand, and those that keep the fruit thereof two hundred.

IT is a great assertion which the Bride laid down, verse 10, that she was a wall, and had found favour in his eyes : and it being of high concernment, if well grounded, therefore, to make out the warrantableness thereof she proceeds to demonstrate it, verses 11, 12, thereby to give believers advertisement, that they should be well seen in the grounds of their own peace, and to shew the solid way how the well groundedness thereof may be found out : and because, the conclusions, asserting our union with Christ and interest in him, follow on premises, whose major proposition is in the word, and whose assumption is to be searched, and confirmed from the conscience, speaking from inward experience and feeling, she doth formally proceed : first, by laying down a sum of the gospel, in a complex general doctrine, verse 11, to this purpose, Christ had a church, which he took pains on, for this end, that it might be fruitful, and that in such a measure.   Then in the twelfth verse she compares her practice with that rule, and finds it suitable, therefore the conclusion follows. We may take it up thus in form, They who improve the trust well that is put upon them, to bring forth such fruits as Christ calls for in his covenant, may conclude, that " they are a wall, and have found favour in his sight :" this truth is confirmed in the eleventh verse, because it is for that very end, and on these very terms, that Christ hath appointed the ordinances in his house, and made the promises to his people, that they should " bring forth a thousand for the fruit thereof to him," and he will not reject a consequence drawn from that which he himself hath appointed in his covenant; for, such grounds, as the word and covenant confirm, are only sure to reason from. Then she assumes, verse, 12. But I have been sincere in that trust which was committed unto me, conform to the terms of the covenant, and have a thousand (according thereto) to give to Christ, Therefore, &c. And because this hath need to be well grounded also, she proves it, partly, by instancing the fruits that belonged to him and to the keepers, which she had brought forth, to shew that his ordinances were not in vain to her; and partly, by attesting himself immediately, in these words, " Thou, O Solomon," speaking to him in the second person, thereby to evidence her sincerity before him, who alone could bear witness thereof, and that it was not mere external performances (which, as such, are manifest to others) upon which she grounds what she asserts in the assumption. This is the native series and scope of the words, whereby they depend on the former, and by which, now before death, leaving this way of communion with Christ, which she enjoyed here-away mediately in ordinances, and before that eternal and immediate way beyond death (which is prayed for, verse 14.) she doth collect her interest, and confirm her assurance: the particular exposition of the words will clear it more. From the scope, *Observ.* 1. That thorough persuasion of interest in Christ had need to be solidly grounded, and believers should be distinct in the grounds thereof, and not go by guess with their confidence. 2. The nearer that people come to dying, they should be the more accurate in this search, and have the evidences of their interest in Christ the more clear. 3. We may gather from her example that the solid and only way to be thoroughly cleared of our title to Christ, is when the grounds thereof are comprehended in the Lord's covenant; as he that believes, repents, hath the fruits of the Spirit, &c. he is justified, sanctified, &c. And when the assumption, bearing the application of these grounds to ourselves, will abide the trial in Christ's sight, and may be instanced before him in the effects thereof, thus, but it is so with me, therefore, &c. this is her way of concluding.

We come now to expound the words more particularly: and first, we conceive it is out of doubt, that they are mystically and spiritually to be understood, that is, by Solomon, Christ is meant, and by the vineyard, the church, &c. for, so the strain and nature of the allegory throughout this Song and the manner of speaking all along doth require; and there being but one Solomon that is spoken of in this Song, his having of a vineyard must be understood as his making of a chariot, chap. iii. 9, 10, which being paved with love, could not be a piece of work framed by David's Son: we are not therefore, curiously to enquire here, what place this is, called Baal-hamon: or, whether Solomon had such vineyards or not, let out at such a rent? these things make not to the scope.

Again, that they are the Bride's words, is clear not only from the scope and matter thereof, but also from these things, 1. She not only speaks of Christ (by the name of Solomon) in the third person, verse 11, but to him, " Thou, O Solomon," &c. in the second person, verse 12. It cannot therefore be the Bridegroom that here speaks, but the Bride, as personating a believer. 2. She is differenced from strangers and hypocrites, in this, that she hath fruit to give him, and hath that proposed to herself for her end: and she is differenced from the keepers of the vineyard, the ministers, verse 12, they get from her two hundred; it must therefore be the Bride, as personating a believer, who was speaking in the former verse, and continueth here in speaking. 3. The expressions, verse 12, where she applieth to herself what she had in the general asserted, verse 11, agree well to her, as the opening of them will clear.

The words do contain the proof of a believer's sincerity and reality in the covenant of God, made out by two things put together, 1. By laying down distinctly the nature and terms of the covenant, verse 11. 2. By comparing herself exactly and impartially therewith, verse 12. The general doctrine of the covenant, verse 11, runs on three heads; the first looks to the sum and end of all, that Christ had a church or vineyard, committed or given him. The second looks to Christ's administration in his church, by external ordinances, " he let out to keepers." The third holds forth the ends of his letting out this vineyard, or the terms upon which it is leased, " every one was to bring for the fruit thereof, a thousand pieces of silver."

For explaining of the first, we are first to remember, that by Solomon, we are to understand Christ; for, as ever hitherto, so here, the allegory is continued, to express and set forth Christ in his way with his church, under that name. Next, the vineyard here is his church,

Isa. v. 7, &c. the visible church in some respect is his vineyard, as she is separate from others, and appointed to bring forth fruits to him ; but especially the church invisible and elect, who in a peculiar respect are Christ's as given to him and purchased by him, and so frequently in this Song, the believer is called a garden or vineyard. 3. The place where this vineyard is planted, is called Baal-hamon : which is the name of no proper place any where mentioned in scripture, but is borrowed for its signification, and it signifieth " father of a multitude," and so it points out that Christ's vineyard is planted in a soil that is fruitful, and bringing forth much ; and it is on the matter the same with that, Isa. v. 1, " my beloved had a vineyard in a fruitful hill," or, horn of oil, as the word there in the Hebrew signifieth, to shew that it was well situate in a good soil, and did lie well, and was by his industry well fitted for bringing forth of fruit.   Now, Christ is said, and that in the peterite time, to have " had" this vineyard, which shews his interest and propriety therein, and title thereto, and that by an eternal right, and a far other kind of title than he hath to the rest of the world beside : now this right of Christ's (in respect of which it is he had this vineyard) is not to be understood with relation to his essential dominion and sovereignty, whereby with the Father and Holy Ghost he created all things, and so as Creator, hath a conjunct interest in them ; but this looks to that peculiar title, which Christ hath to the church of the elect, especially as mediator, by the Lord's giving of such and such particular persons to him to be saved, John vi. 38, 39, &c. for, he hath this vineyard as distinct from the world, and claims title to the given ones, when he disclaims the world, John xvii. 6, 8, " they are mine" (saith he) " because thou gavest them to me :" yet, in so far as the visible church is separated to him by external ordinances (and so all Israel are said to be elected, Deut. vi.) they may be said to be Christ's ; but it is those who are by God's election separated from others, given to Christ, and undertaken for by him, in the covenant of redemption, that especially are intended here, and it is necessary to advert, that there are four divers parties, to which the church in divers respects is said to belong.   1. She is the Lord's the Father, Son, and Spirit, his by eternal election ; this is the first right, John xvii. 6, " thine they were," to wit, by thy eternal purpose : and from this flows the second, to wit, the mediator's right, "and thou gavest them me;" the Father is the owner and proprietor of the vineyard, Matt. xxi. 40, called, John. xv. 1, "the husbandman;" for, the church is first his, and next Christ's who as Mediator is the great deputy, and universal administrator of grace, to whom the elect are given as to the great bishop and shepherd, and to whom all the ordering of what concerns their good is committed: this right is by donation, and differs from the former. 3. The vineyard is said to be the Bride's, verse 12, and chap. i. 6, in respect of the believer's particular trust, with oversight of, and interest in, those things that Christ hath purchased for them, and bestowed on them, which they are to improve and trade with: in which respect, Matt. xxv. and Luke xix. the talent is said to be not only the master's, but also the servants because the right improving of it, brings advantage unto the servant more properly than to the master: and each believer in some kind hath a vineyard, because each of them shares of all the graces, privileges, benefits, &c. that are saving. 4. The vineyard is also the minister's; they have a title as under-keepers, overseers and dressers, therefore it is said to be let out to them by Christ; they are as farmers; Hence when Christ, Rev. ii. 5, writes to the angel of the church of Ephesus, speaking to the angel, he calls the church, "thy candlestick," and chap. ii. 15, while the vines are called "our vines," the minister's interest is asserted as well as Christ's: so all these interests mentioned in these two verses are well consistent. *Observ.* 1. That our Lord Jesus hath some who beyond all others are his, by peculiar right and title; and he had this title to them before ever actually there was a church, this vineyard did belong to him otherwise than others, in the world, even before it was, which could not be but the Father's giving the elect to him. 2. Christ hath a notable right to, and propriety in, these elect who are given him, so that the vineyard is his, and it cannot be that one of these perish, without the impairing and prejudice of the property of our Lord Jesus. 3. There is an old transaction, concerning the salvation of the elect betwixt the Father and the Son, which can be no other thing but the covenant of redemption; for, the Son's having an interest in some and not in others, supposeth that some were given to him and accepted by him, as that word, John xvii. 6, bears out, "thine they were, and thou gavest them to me," and so they are mine.   4. Christ's church or vineyard, hath the only choice soil in all the world to live into, it is Baal-hamon where they are planted, though often their outward lot be not desirable, yet their "lines have fallen in pleasant places."

The second part concerns Christ's managing of his church when he hath gotten it; he doth not immediately dress it by himself, but "he lets it out to keepers," as a man having purchased a field, or planted a vineyard, doth set it, or farm it for such a rent; so hath Christ thought good to commit his church to keepers, that is, to watchmen and farmers, that by their ministry, he might in a mediate way promove their edification and salvation, which he accounts his rent: the very same parable, almost in the same words, pressing this scope, is recorded, Matt. xxi. 33, " A certain householder planted a vineyard, and let it out to husbandmen, and sent servants to gather the fruit ; the husbandmen are the ordinary office-bearers in the church (the scribes and pharisees did fill that room for the time) the servants are extraordinary prophets raised up of God, to put them to their duty; so here the keepers are the ministers, who are intrusted with the church's edification under Christ, as stewards are with distributing provision to the family, or shepherds with feeding their flocks, or a farmer with the labouring of his farm that he possesseth : and this name, of keepers given here to ministers, agreeth well with the names that ministers have in scripture, watchmen, overseers, stewards, builders, husbandmen, &c. and also with the nature of that office, which, 1 Cor. iii. is to plant and water this vineyard : and lastly, with the scope of this and the like parables, whereby Christ's mediate way of building up of his church, by the intervention of ordinances and ministers, is expressed.   Particular professors are as vines, the ordinances like the press that presseth the grapes, the ministers like the dressers that dig, dung, prune, and water the trees, and put the grapes in the press, and gather the fruits, by applying of these ordinances convincingly to the consciences of hearers. Next, his setting of this vineyard, or church to the keepers, is borrowed from a proprietor, his farming of his heritage, and giving of a lease, or tack under him, to some other, both for the better labouring of his land, and for furthering of his rent; and this is opposed to his immediate labouring of it himself: so here, as Christ is the proprietor (whose own the vineyard is) ministers are the farmers: which implieth, 1. That the minister hath a title and interest in the church of Christ, which no other hath, he is a farmer and keeper of it. 2. It supposeth, that it is but a subordinate title the minister hath; he is not as a lord of Christ's vineyard, or master of the faith of God's people, but as a farmer or subordinate overseer, he is to be a helper of their joy. In sum, the sense comes to this, that this trust that was put on Christ of governing his church, he thought meet not to discharge it all immediately, but hath appointed some others as instruments under him, to promote their edification, whom singularly he hath entrusted for that end. *Observ.* 1. Since our Lord Jesus had a church militant, he hath thought good to guide it mediately, by a standing ministry and ordinances; and that is to set out his vineyard to keepers. 2. There ought none without Christ's tack or lease, enter upon the ministry, and become keepers of his vineyard; for, they are but tacksmen, and what right they have, it is from him: thus that which is here called his setting a lease, is, Mal. ii. 4, 5, called the "covenant of Levi." 3. Although Christ employ ministers, yet he makes them not masters, but he reserves the propriety of his church to himself, and they are such as must give an account. 4. Though ministers be not masters, yet are they keepers, and have a special trust in the church; they are intrusted with the affairs of Christ's house, for carrying on of his peoples' edification; which is a trust that no others have committed to them.

The third thing in this verse, is the end for which he lets it out, or the terms upon which; and these are, "that every one may bring a thousand pieces of silver for the fruit thereof:" and so the condition, upon which it is set out, is, that he might have a competent revenue and fruit, as is clear from Isa. v. and Matt. xxi. and the rent is agreed on by himself, and it is "a thousand silverings," which is mentioned, Isa. vii. 23, as a great rent. The number is a definite for an indefinite, saying, in sum, that Christ's scope, in letting out his church, is thereby to make her fruitful, that by his servants' ministry he might have rent from her, as he saith, John xv. 16. "I have chosen and ordained you, to go and bring forth fruit." &c. Which is especially to be understood in respect of their ministerial fruit (to say so) or the fruit of their ministry.

The sum required is alike to all, that every man may bring, &c, not implying, that all ministers will have alike fruit in effect, or *de facto*, but to shew, that all of them have one commission, and *de jure*, or of right, ought to aim at having much fruit to the landlord, and should by no means seek to feed themselves, but seek the master's profit. The words aim at these four things, 1. That Christ's great design in planting of a church, and sending of a ministry, is to have souls saved, that is the fruit which he aims at, for the travail of his soul : and so to have his people brought on towards heaven, by every step of knowledge, conversion, faith, repentance, holiness, till they be brought completely through. 2. It supposeth the people's duty, that they who are planted in the church, should be fruitful : this vineyard bears well, else the keepers could not pay so much. 3. The minister's duty is implied here also, and it is to crave in Christ's rent, that is his office, as a factor, or chamberlain to gather it in ; so, Matt. xxi. 31, " He sent his servants to gather in the fruits of the vineyard." Ministers are to labour amongst the people, and either to bring fruit, or a report of ill success unto Christ. 4. Whatever fruits the minister have to render to Christ, he must return a reckoning ; so the word, bring, imports a returning of an account to the owner that sent him. The last thing is the peremptoriness of this lease, in respect of the fruits or rent, which is held forth in two things, 1. It is determined it must be " a thousand :" which saith, 1. It is not free to ministers to call for or to accept of what they will, or what men will, as enough for Christ's due ; he must determine himself what he will have, and none other, and he hath determined it. 2. There can be no alteration of the terms which Christ hath set down and imposed, it is definite in itself what every one must bring. Again, 2. Its peremptoriness appears in this, that " every one," none excepted, are put at for this rent : this is the great article in all their leases, fruit, fruit. *Observ.* 1. Every minister of the gospel hath a weighty trust put on him, in reference to the church's edification. 2. Ministers' right discharging of their trust, may have much influence on a people's thriving, and Christ's getting of his rent from amongst them. 3. All Christ's ministers have every one of them the same commission, for the same end, and every one of them should endeavour fruits proportionable thereto. 4. The Lord hath every minister's fruit, as to the event, determined, as well as their duty is appointed them. 5. Though all ministers have not alike success, in respect of the number of souls brought in by their ministry; yet, where there is honesty and diligence, the Lord will account it a thousand, as well as where the fruit is more : therefore are they alike in his reckoning, though not in the event. O! but an unfruitful minister, and unfaithful also, who, besides what fruit a common Christian should render, ought to render a thousand for his ministry, will be much in Christ's debt, when he shall reckon with him! Let ministers consider well this double reckoning.

Having laid down the general doctrine, verse 11, she doth now in the twelfth verse make application thereof to herself: and this she doth. 1. By asserting of her own sincerity. 2. By proving it in two instances. Her assertion is, " My vineyard, which is mine, is before me :" the Bride's vineyard is the particular trust which is committed to her, in reference to her soul's estate ; called a vineyard, 1. Because every particular believer, intrusted with his own soul's concernment, is a part of, and of the same nature with the church of Christ, which is called a vineyard in scripture, 2. Because of the variety of graces bestowed on her, and the ordinances and privileges, whereof she is a partaker with the whole, as is said. It is called hers, because she must make a special account for her own soul, and the talent that is given to her, according to the trust that is put on her. We have almost the same phrase, chap. i. 6, where the Bride calls it, " mine own vineyard :" this vineyard is said to be before her, which is like the expression, Psalm xviii. 22, " all thy judgments were before me ;" which the scope, by the words foregoing and following, shews to be, not a pleading of innocency, but of sincerity and watchfulness in keeping himself from his iniquity; and it is to be understood in opposition to departing wickedly from God, mentioned verse 21. And thus, to have her vineyard before her, signifieth watchfulness and tenderness, as those who have their eye always on their orchard, or vineyard ; and it doth import, 1. Watchfulness, as has been said. 2. Diligence and carefulness; so it is opposed to the hiding of the talent, Luke xiv. She did not so, but had the talent she was intrusted with, still before her, and among her hands, that she might trade with it. 3. It imports ten-

derness and conscientiousness, and so is opposed to mens'
casting of God's law behind their backs, Psalm l. 16.
This she did not, but the work God had appointed to her,
and the trust which was committed to her, was always in
her eye. 4. It implies sincerity and honesty in aiming at
her duty, and that by a constant minding of it, as suffering
it never to be out of her sight : all which, being put together, holds forth the sense of the words, Christ hath
given every one in his church a trust (which is, as it were,
the vineyard that every believer ought to have before him)
and that (saith she) which was committed to me, I have
been singly and conscientiously careful to do my duty in
reference thereunto, so as I have a testimony in my conscience of it.   And thus her case is far different from
what it was, chap. i. 6, where she acknowledgeth that her
own vineyard she had not kept.   *Observ.* 1. It is no matter how well one be acquaint with the general truths of
the gospel, if there be not a conformity of practice ; whatever knowledge christians have, it will never further their
peace, except their practice be suitable.   2. Every member of the church, and every believer, hath a particular
trust committed to him ; and he must be accountable for his
carriage in reference thereto.   3. The right discharging
of this trust calls for watchfulness and diligence, and it
will require daily oversight and attendance, that so the
believer's vineyard may be always before him.   4. They
who assiduously wait upon the work committed to them,
may through grace make good progress in it, and attain
to a good testimony from their own consciences thereanent.
5. It is exceeding comfortable to believers, when they
have a testimony within them, that they have been diligent and careful in the duty committed to them.   6. Believers should reflect on their carriage in the trust committed to them, that they may be able to make some
distinct report concerning the same.   7. They who are
most tender in their duty, are also most diligent to search
how it is with them, that they may know the condition of
their vineyard, whether it thrive or not.   If it be moved
here, how she could assert so much of her condition, seeing, chap. i. 6, she acknowledgeth the contrary, that her
own vineyard, or, the vineyard which was hers, she had
not kept ; and it is evident, chap. v. 3, that she was under
a great measure of security, in which case she fell into
many escapes?   I answer, both may be true, in diverse

considerations, 1. As David in one place acknowledged sin, yet, Psalm xviii. 21, 22, &c. pleadeth sincerity; so doth she here. *Observ.* 1. There may be a just ground of a plea for sincerity, where there is much guilt to be acknowledged: these are not inconsistant, otherwise she could not assert her sincerity so confidently here. 2. Believers' plea for peace in the discharge of their duty, and the testimony of their conscience thereanent, is not founded on perfection of degrees, but on sincerity. 2. *Answ.* Chap. i. 6, contains the Bride's case at one time; this speaks of her case afterward, when by repentance she was recovered and restored to his friendship. *Observ.* 1. There may be a great difference in the way of one and the same believer, in respect of different times: at one time (possibly in youth) most unwatchful, at other times tender and serious. 2. Those that sometimes have been under many challenges for unwatchfulness, may through God's blessing afterward obtain a good outgate, both from their sins and challenges. 3. Bygone failings, will not, nor should not, mar a present favourable testimony from the conscience, when God hath given to one the exercise of faith, repentance and true tenderness. 3. *Answ.* Since these failings, Christ hath spoken peace to her, and therefore now she remembers them not, for marring of her peace, though otherwise she hath regretted them for her humbling. *Observ.* When Christ speaks peace, believers should not obstruct it, by continuing the resentment of former provocations and quarrels to the prejudice thereof, though they should still mind them for furthering of their own humiliation.

She comes, in the next place, to make out this assertion: which is done, 1. By the matter of her words, while she instanceth the fruits, that belonged both to the owner and to the keepers. 2. By the manner of her words, while she turneth her speech over to Christ himself, " Thou, O Solomon, shalt have a thousand;" (for so it will read as well as, must have, &c. seeing either of the words, shall, or must, may be supplied) and this shews both what he should have, and with what cheerfulness she bestowed it on him. And, 1. She instanceth the fruits that Christ should have, and these are " a thousand:" by the thousand that Christ is to get, is understood that which was appointed and conditioned in his lease of the vineyard, and is mentioned, verse 11. It is, in a word, thou shalt have

what thou hast appointed, the terms shall not be altered
by me.   Hence it appears, that the "thousand" which the
minister was to bring in as the revenue of the vineyard,
is the engaging of souls to Christ, and the making of them
fruitful; for, then gets Christ his rent from his people,
when this is effectuated by the ordinances.   *Observ.* 1.
That fruits are the best evidence of sincerity.   2. That
there can be nothing offered to Christ as fruit, or which
can be an evidence or proof of sincerity, but that same,
for the matter and manner, which is prescribed by him in
his covenant; our fruits must be suitable to what is called
for, and accepted by him, or they will be no ground of
peace.   3. True sincerity will never alter the terms that
Christ hath set down in his covenant, nor lessen his rent,
which he hath prescribed as his due, but will think that
most suitable which he hath prescribed, and will think it
a mercy to have that to render to him.

The second instance, proving her fruitfulness, holdeth
forth what the keepers should receive; the keepers shall
have "two hundred:" two hundred is a definite number
for an indefinite.   The scope is to shew, that she acknowledged Christ's care, in providing watchmen and ordinances to her, and as they were not useless to her, but were
blessed for her good so he should have honour, and their
pains taken on her, by her fruitfulness, should redound to
their commendation and glory, yet (as it becomes) in a
lesser degree than to the Master, and without wronging
of the rent due to him; this "two hundred," (saith she)
ought not, and shall not diminish his thousand.   Now, this
may relate either to the reward that faithful ministers
shall have from Christ, spoken of, Dan. xii. 3.   O what
joy and glory will result to them, from the people's fruitfulness (amongst whom they have laboured) in the day
of the Lord! that they have not run in vain, but with
much success, will bring them much joy in that day; so,
1 Thess. ii. 19, 20, " What is our hope" (saith the apostle)
" or crown of rejoicing, are not even ye in the presence of
our Lord Jesus Christ, at his coming? for ye are our
glory and our joy."   It is a piece of their life and satisfaction, to see the work of the gospel thrive amongst the
people: " We live" (saith Paul, 1 Thess. iii. 8) "if ye
stand fast in the Lord."   Or, 2. It may look to that
which is called for from a people to their ministers, even
here, they are to acknowledge them that are over them

for their work's sake, to obey and submit to them, yea, to give themselves to them by the will of God, having given themselves first to Christ, 2 Cor. viii. 5, and this being a testimony of believers' sincerity, it looks like the scope ; and so the sense is, thou shalt have (saith she) that which is called for, as thy due, and the keepers shall have what respect and encouragement is due to them, for thy sake.

This "two hundred" belonging to the keepers, is added here, and was not mentioned in the former verse : because there the terms that were required of the keepers themselves were set down, here the duty of every particular believer is expressed, which is to give Christ his due, and in doing that, to give to his ordinances and ministers as commissionate from him what is their due ; and this is to be given them, not as men, nor as believers, but as keepers ; which though immediately it be given to them, as to the ambassadors of Christ, yet that obedience, submission, &c. being to his ordinance, and given them only for their work's sake, 1 Thess. v. 3, it is rent also due to him, and called for by him.

If it be asked, why her giving of "two hundred" to the keepers, is subjoined to the giving of him "a thousand ?" The answers to this are so many observations from the words ; and the first is, that those who are trusted by Christ to be keepers of the vineyard, and his ministers, ought also to be respected by the people over whom they are set ; and Christ allows this on them. 2. Where Christ is respected and gets his due, there the keepers will be respected and get their due : if Christ be made welcome, the feet of them that bring good tidings will be beautiful, Isa. lii. 7. 3. It is a good sign of honesty and sincerity before Christ, when ministers and ordinances are respected in their own place, with subordination to the respect that is due Christ ; therefore it is mentioned here. 4. It is no burden to an honest believer to acknowledge Christ's ministers, to obey their doctrine, and submit to their censures ; for sincere believers both willingly do this, and engage to do it, as the Bride doth here. 5. The respect that is given to ministers, should be given to them as to his ministers, without derogating from, or encroaching upon, that which is the Master's due ; therefore, his thousand is reserved whole for him, and this two hundred is no part thereof. 6. Where Christ gets his due among a people, and where his ordinances be received, there, and there only do ministers get their due ; for, it is (as Paul saith) not yours but you, that we seek : and less will not be accepted by faithful ministers: they will never think they get their due, if the gospel be not taken well off their hand.

The last thing in the verse, is the way she takes to prove her uprightness, by attesting Christ to bear witness to the sincerity of her fruits ;   and this is held forth in the change of the person, from the third to the second, " Thou, O Solomon" (saith she) " shalt have a thousand :" which, in short, is done for evidencing of her sincerity, that it was such as might abide his trial ; and so she doth pass sentence upon herself, as in his sight, who knew what was truth : and this doth not proceed from boasting, but from humble confidence, being desirous that he would accept of it, and approve her in it.   *Observ.* 1. Sincerity gives one boldness in approaching to Christ. 2. It is a good evidence of sincerity, when believers are not very anxious, and careful what is the judgment of men concerning them, if they may have Christ's approbation ; and therefore they consider their case and practice as speaking to Christ, and before him. 3. It is delectable, in the most spiritual passages of our inward walk, to turn them over into addresses to Christ, and to speak them over betwixt him and us. 4. It is best gathering conclusions concerning our condition, and best learning how to esteem of it, when we are set as in Christ's presence, and are speaking to him : every thing will then be best discerned, and the soul will be in the best posture for discerning itself.

BRIDEGROOM.

Verse 13. Thou that dwellest in the gardens, the companions hearken to thy voice : cause me to hear it.

THE thirteenth and fourteenth verses contain the last part of this kindly conference, that hath been betwixt these two loving parties, and express their farewell and last suits, which each of them hath to the other.   He speaks in this verse, and being to close, as a kind husband, leaving his beloved wife for a time, he desires to hear frequently from her till he return ; this is his suit : and she, like a loving wife, entreats him to hasten his return, in the next verse, and this is the scope of both these verses.   That the words in this thirteenth verse are spoken by him, appears by the title he gives the Bride, " Thou that dwellest in the gardens," which in the original, is in the feminine gender, as if one would say, " thou woman," or, " thou Bride," or, " thou my wife :" or, take it in one word, as it is in the original, it may be rendered, " O inhabitress of the gardens ;" which can be applied to none other, but to her ; and therefore, these words must be spoken by him to her, and thus the scope laid down is clear.

There are three parts in the verse, 1. The title he gives her. 2. A commendation, that is insinuated. 3. A request made to her, or duty laid on her. The title is, " Thou that dwellest in the gardens :" by gardens, in the plural number, we understand (as chap. vi. 2.) particular congregations, where the ordinances are administered, called gardens in the plural number, as contradistinguished from the catholic church, and from a particular believer, who are also called a garden in the singular number. To " dwell in," or inhabit these gardens, imports three things, 1. A frequenting of these meetings. 2. A continuance in them ordinarily, as if there were her residence. 3. A delight in them, and in the exercises of his worship and service there. And in sum, the meaning is, "thou, my Bride, who frequentest and lovest the assemblies of my people, and my public ordinances," &c. *Observ.* 1. That Christ Jesus loveth to leave his people comforted, and therefore, is distinct in this his farewell, that there be no mistakes of him in his absence : and this way he used also with his apostles, John xiv. 13, 14, 15, &c. before his ascension. 2. Christ hath ordinarily ever preserved the public ordinances, by particular assemblies, in his church. See, chap. vi. 2. 3. Where God's people are in good case, there the public ordinances are most frequented and esteemed of; and still the better in case they be, the ordinances are the more prized, and haunted by them ; for, this is a special character and property of such, that they love to dwell among the ordinances, Psal. xxvii. 4. Also, this is pleasant and acceptable to Jesus Christ, and the title he gives the Bride here, shews his approbation thereof.

The second part of the verse, namely the commendation he gives her, is insinuated in these words, " The companions hearken to thy voice." By companions here, are understood particular believers, members of the church, called also " brethren" and " companions," Psal. cxxii. 8.

and the "brotherhood," 1 Pet. ii. 17, so also, Psal. xlv.
14, and cxix. 63. " I am a companion of all that fear
thee," &c. and this title is given them for these two reasons, 1. Because there is a jointness and communion
amongst them, in all their interests, both of duties and
privileges, and also in sufferings, &c. and so John, Rev.
xix. calls himself their brother and companion in tribula-
tion : they are all fellow-citizens of one city, Eph. ii. And,
2. Because they have a familiar way of living together,
according to that joint interest, by sympathizing with
each other, freedom to each other, and kindness of affection to one another, opposite to that strangeness and par-
ticularness that is amongst the men of the world : and
this is the right improving of the former, and results from
it. Next, by the Bride's " voice," is here understood her
instructions, admonitions, and such parts of Christian
fellowship, which tend to edification, wherein that companionry (so to speak) doth most appear : an example
whereof we find in the instructions she gave to the
daughters, chap. v. The companions, their hearkening to
her voice, is more than simple hearing (for hearkening
and hearing are much different, and have different words
in the original) and it implieth, their laying weight on
what she said, by pondering of it, and yielding to it, as
the daughters did, chap. vi. 1, to which this may relate.
And so the meaning is, thy fellow-worshippers (saith he)
with reverence and respect, receive thy words, thou
speakest so weightily unto them. And this doth import
not only the practice and duty of the Bride and her companions, but also a commendation of them, both which we
may take up in the doctrines. *Observ.* 1. That there is
a most friendly union and familiar relation amongst all
believers ; they are companions in this respect, though
there may be many differences in externals, which this
takes not away. 2. Believers ought to walk friendly together, according to that relation ; and it is pleasant when
they converse together as such, Psal. cxxxiii. 3. Believers ought not to be useless in their fellowship and mutual
conversing one with another, but should be speaking, by
instructions, admonitions, and exhortations, that others with
whom they converse may hear their voice. 4. Believers
should not only hearken to public ordinances, and the
word spoken by the office-bearers in the church, but also
to that which is spoken by a companion when it is edify-

ing. 5. It is a thing pleasant to Jesus Christ (who takes notice how companions walk together) when there is conscience made of mutual fellowship, with fruit and freedom amongst his people: this were good companionry. 6. God's making the stamp of his Spirit on a particular believer to have weight on others, so as their fellowship with them hath success, should provoke the believer to pursue more after fellowship with Christ himself; which is the scope of this part of the verse, compared with that which follows.

The last part of the verse, containing his desire to her, or the duty he layeth on her, is in these words, " Cause me to hear it." The words, as they are in the original, are, " Cause to hear me :" which occasioneth a twofold reading. 1. " Cause me to be heard," and let me be the subject of thy discourse to others, seeing they give ear unto thee, improve that credit which thou hast with them for that end : thus this same phrase is rendered, Psal. lxvi. 8, " Make the voice of his praise to be heard," or, as it is in the original, " Cause to be heard the voice," &c. 2. They may be read as they here stand, " Cause me to hear it ;" and thus Christ desires, he may be the object spoken unto, as by the former reading he is to be the subject spoken of; so this same phrase is rendered, Psal. cxliii. " Cause me to hear thy lovingkindness :" and this translation agrees well with the scope here, where before he brake off communing with the Bride, as in the first part of the verse he had commended her for her frequenting of public ordinances, and in the second, for her keeping fellowship with others, in both which her duty is insinuated ; so here he calls for her keeping of fellowship with himself, by her sending frequent messages to him in prayer ; which he not only requires as a duty, but now requests as a favour (to speak so) that he may hear often from her, which he will account as much of, as any man will do of hearing from his wife in his absence. And, thus, to make him hear her voice, is by frequent prayer to make addresses to him, as, Psal. v. 3. " In the morning shalt thou hear my voice :" and, chap. ii. 14, of this song, speaking to the Bride, " Let me hear thy voice," saith he. *Observ.* 1. That though Jesus be a great Prince, and sometimes be absent to the sense of his people, yet hath he laid down a way how his Bride may keep correspondence with him, and let him hear from her when she will, in his greatest distance : he hath, as it were, provided posts for that end, prayers, ejaculations, thoughts, looks, if wakened by his Spirit, which will carry their message very speedily and faithfully.   2. The Bride ought to be frequent in sending posts and messages to her blessed Bridegroom, that he may hear from her ; and both duty and affection call for this.   3. Messages from the believer are most welcome and acceptable to Jesus Christ, they are as messages from a loving wife to an husband at a distance, and believers may expect that such messages shall be well entertained ; they cannot be too frequent in suits and prayers to him, when these duties are rightly discharged ; and there will be no letter sent to him so short, or ill written, but he will read it : and sure, the neglecting of this, is a sin doth exceedingly displease and wound our kind Bridegroom.   4. In this verse, frequenting public ordinances, fellowship with believers, and much corresponding with Christ in secret prayer, are all put together, to shew, that they who rightly discharge the duties of public worship, and the duties of mutual fellowship, and the duties of communion and corresponding with Christ in prayer, must necessarily join all together ; and when it goes well with a believer in one of these, they will all be made conscience of ; and this last is subjoined, as the life of both the former, without which they will never be accepted by him.

BRIDE.

Verse 14. Make haste, my beloved, and be thou like to a roe or to a young hart upon the mountains of spices.

THE last verse hath in it the Bride's last and great suit to her Bridegroom, that he would haste his return : as in the former verse the Bridegroom compended all his will, as it were, in one suit to the Bride ; let me often hear from thee that I may know how it is with thee, said he : so here, she sums up all her desire in one suit, which to her is both first and last, I beseech thee (saith she) my Beloved, " make haste" and do not tarry.   In the words there are, 1. Her suit. 2. The title she gives him. 3. Her repeating and qualifying of her suit.   Her request is, " make haste :" the word, in the original signifieth " flee away," importing the greatest haste and speed that may be, so would she have Christ hasting his coming in the most

x

swift manner; whereby the holy impatience of her affection, that cannot endure delays, doth appear; therefore
abruptly she breaks out with this as her last suit, and that
which especially her heart desires of him. That it is for
a speedy return, the scope, her love that expresseth it,
and the manner which she useth through the Song, doth
clear; and there being two comings of Christ spoken of in
scripture, 1. His coming in grace, which already she had
prayed for, and it is promised, John xiv. 21, 23. 2. His
coming in glory at the last day to judge the world; we
conceive that it will agree with her scope here, to take in
both, but principally the last, that is, her desire, that
Christ Jesus would hasten his second coming: not that
she would have him to precipitate, or leave any thing undone that is to do before the end: but her desire is, that
in due time and manner it may be brought about, and
that what is to go before it, may be hastened, for making
way for it; for, the phrase, "haste, my Beloved," is indefinite, and therefore it may look both to his second
coming, and to all that must necessarily precede it; and
therefore, so long as there is yet any thing to be performed, as previous to his coming, she bids him hasten it. 2.
We take this desire to look mainly to his second coming,
because that only can perfect believers' consolation, and
put an end to their prayers: till he come, their consolation
cannot be full, and all shadows are not away, chap. ii. 17.
There is ever something to be done, and therefore they
have ever something to pray for (to wit, that his kingdom
may come) till that time. 3. This is the great, joint, and
main suit of all believers; they all concur in this, Rev.
xxii. 17. "The Spirit and the Bride say, come." &c. It
is essential to all who have the Spirit, to join in this suit;
and the Bride cannot but be supposed to love the last appearing of our Lord Jesus, which will perfect all her
desires: and this coming of his, was prophesied of by
Enoch, the seventh from Adam, Jude, verse 14, and was
delighted in by believers (Psalm xcvi. 12, &c. Psalm
xcviii. 6, 7,) before Solomon wrote this.

2. The title which she gives him, is, "my Beloved,"
that which ordinarily she gave him, and is here inserted, 1.
To be a motive to press her suit, and it is the most kindly
motive which she could use to him, that there was such
a relation betwixt him and her, and therefore she prayeth,
that he would not leave her comfortless, but return again.

2. It is made use of as a stay to her faith, for sustaining of her against discouragement: and that there is such a tie standing betwixt him and believers, is a notable consolation, seeing he is faithful and kind in all his relations; and by this she sweetens this her farewell-wish. 3. It is an expression of her affection, she cannot speak to him, but her heart is kindled, and must speak kindly: and it shews that their parting is in very good terms, like friends. 4. It shews, her clearness of her interest in him, on which she grounds this suit, so as heartily she hereby makes ready, and prepares for his coming, knowing that he is hers.

3. The qualification of her suit is in these words, " Be thou like to a roe, or a young hart, upon the mountains of spices:" roes and harts frequent mountains, and do run swiftly, speedily and pleasantly on them, as hath been often said: see upon chap. ii. 8, 17, the allusion and scope here is, as roes and harts run swiftly over mountains, so, my Beloved (saith she) make haste to return with all diligence: or, because " the mountains, of spices" signify some excellent mountains, such as it may be, were not ordinary for roes and harts to run upon (though in these countries it might be so in part) therefore we may read the words, thus, my Beloved, be thou upon the mountains of spices, like a roe, &c. and so heaven may be compared to such savoury and refreshful mountains. The scope is one, and speaks thus, "now my Beloved, seeing there is a time coming, when there will be a refreshful meeting betwixt thee and me, never to be interrupted, therefore I entreat thee, so to expede thy affairs which are to precede, which in reason I cannot obstruct, that that blessed and longed-for meeting may be hastened, and thou may come to receive thy Bride at the last day." From all these. *Observ.* 1. which is supposed, that there is a final and glorious coming of our Lord Jesus to judgment, which will be when all that he hath to do in the earth is perfected otherwise this could not be prayed for by the Bride. 2. It is implied, that this coming of Jesus Christ, is a most comfortable and desirable thing to believers; there is nothing that they more aim at and pant for, than his company; and that being so desirable here, it must be much more so hereafter, when all his people shall be gathered to him, and the queen shall be brought to the King in raiment of needle-work, and shall enter into the

palace with him, there to abide for ever : that cannot but
be desirable, and therefore it is pressed as her farewell
suit. 3. This suit of the Bride's implies, that this glorious
coming of our Lord Jesus is much in the thoughts of his
people, and useth to be meditated on by them ; for, this
prayer of hers, is the expression of what useth to be in
her heart. 4. It implies, that believers ought to be established in the faith of Christ's second coming, so as it may
be a ground of prayer to them. 5. Even the thoughts of
this second coming, which flow from the faith thereof,
long ere it come, will be refreshful to the believer. 6.
It is peculiar to the believer to be delighted with, and to
be longing for Christ's second coming ; for, it agrees with
this relation the Bride hath to him as her Beloved : and
whatever others may say, yet this coming of Christ Jesus,
really is, and will be dreadful to them : and therefore are
believers differenced from all others by this name, that
they are such who love his appearing, 2 Tim. iv. 8.

That we may further consider this prayer of the
Bride's we may look upon it, first, more generally, and
so gather these. *Observ.* 1. Faith and love will compend
much in few words, and will thrust together many suits
in a short expression ; there is much in this same word,
flee, or haste ; it is not the longest prayer that is made
up of maniest words. 2. Faith in Christ, and love to
him, where they are in exercise, will make the believer
to meddle in his prayers with things of the greatest concernment : so doth this prayer of the Bride's, it looks not
only to his second coming, but also takes in the overturning Satan's kingdom, the calling of Jews and Gentiles,
the dissolution of heaven and earth, &c. which go alongst
with, and before, Christ's coming : these are great things,
and yet that they may be accomplished, is that which she
here prayeth for. 3. Faith will look far off in prayer, it
will be minding things that are to be performed long after
the person's removal out of this life.

Again, we may consider this suit as it followeth on the
former long conference, and goes before the off-breaking
thereof : and so, *Observ.* 1. That the most lively and
longest continued enjoyments of Christ, that believers
have here upon earth, may, and will have their interruptions and off-breakings for a time : uninterrupted communion is reserved for heaven. 2. Believers that have
been admitted to familiar access unto, and fellowship with

Christ Jesus, should endeavour to have it distinctly breaking off: so that although they cannot entertain it always,
yet they should be careful that it slip not away, and they
not knowing how, nor understanding in what terms their
souls stand with Christ; neglects here ocaasion many
challenges. 3. Those who are best acquainted with fellowship with Christ here-away, and are clearest of their interest in him, will be most desirous of, and most pressing
after his second coming : and the little acquaintance that
many have with him here-away, is the reason that so few
are taken up with this suit. 4. When believers have been
admitted to much sweet fellowship with Christ, before
their sun decline, or before his sensible presence be withdrawn, they ought to have a new design and desire tabled
for his returning ; and this is a good way to close such
sweet and comfortable conferences with Christ, by refer-
ing distinctly to a new meeting, especially to this last,
which will never admit of a parting again. 5. When temporal enjoyments of Christ break off, believers should endeavour the clearing of their hope of that eternal enjoyment which is coming, and should comfort themselves
in the expectation of that, which no time will put an end
unto.

3. We may consider the words in themselves, as this
particular prayer holds forth a pattern and copy of prayer
to believers, and as the Bride evidenceth the nature of
true love by this suit.   And so we may *Observe*, 1. That
it is the duty of a believer to long and pray for Christ's
second coming, and when they are in a right frame and
case, they will do so : love to Christ himself, who at his
appearing is to be glorified ; love to the church in general,
which that day is to be adorned as a bride for her husband,
and fully to be freed from all outward crosses and inward
defects; and love to a believer's own happiness, which
that day is fully to be perfected, do all call for this. 2.
This second coming of our Lord doth fully satisfy the
believer in all respects ; they have no suit nor prayer after
this, when that day is once come, there will be no more
complaints, all sorrow and sighing flies then away   there
will be then no more prayer, for there will be no more
necessities and wants, but all they can desire will be then
enjoyed, and praise will be the work of that blessed world,
amongst all the saints to all eternity: there will be no
such use of the promises and of faith, as we have of them

now, but all will be in possession ; our warfare will be
ended, and our victory completed, when we shall see him
as he is, and be like him : it is no marvel then that the
" Spirit and the Bride say, come," and cry constantly,
" haste, my beloved," until this desire be fulfilled. " Even
so, come, Lord Jesus."

FINIS.

1981-82 TITLES

TITLES CURRENTLY AVAILABLE

0101	Delitzsch, Franz	A New Commentary on Genesis (2 vol.)	27.75
0201	Murphy, James G.	Commentary on the Book of Exodus	12.75
0301	Kellogg, Samuel H.	The Book of Leviticus	19.00
0901	Blaikie, William G.	The First Book of Samuel	13.50
1001	Blaikie, William G.	The Second Book of Samuel	13.50
1101	Farrar, F. W.	The First Book of Kings	16.75
1201	Farrar, F. W.	The Second Book of Kings	16.75
1701	Raleigh, Alexander	The Book of Esther	9.00
1801	Gibson, Edgar	The Book of Job	9.75
1802	Green, William H.	The Argument of the Book of Job Unfolded	10.75
1901	Dickson, David	A Commentary on the Psalms (2 vol.)	29.25
1902	MacLaren, Alexander	The Psalms (3 vol.)	43.50
2001	Wardlaw, Ralph	Book of Proverbs (2 vol.)	29.95
2301	Kelly, William	An Exposition of the Book of Isaiah	13.25
2401	Orelli, Hans C. von	The Prophecies of Jeremiah	13.50
2601	Fairbairn, Patrick	An Exposition of Ezekiel	16.50
2701	Pusey, Edward B.	Daniel the Prophet	19.50
2702	Tatford, Frederick	Daniel and His Prophecy	8.25
3801	Wright, Charles H. H.	Zechariah and His Prophecies	21.95
4101	Alexander, Joseph	Commentary on the Gospel of Mark	15.25
4201	Kelly, William	The Gospel of Luke	16.95
4301	Brown, John	The Intercessory Prayer of Our Lord Jesus Christ	10.50
4302	Hengstenberg, E. W.	Commentary on the Gospel of John (2 vol.)	34.95
4401	Alexander, Joseph	Commentary on the Acts of the Apostles (2 vol. in 1)	27.50
4402	Gloag, Paton J.	A Critical and Exegetical Commentary on Acts (2 vol.)	27.50
4501	Shedd, W. G. T.	Critical and Doctrinal Commentary on Romans	15.75
4601	Brown, John	The Resurrection of Life	13.25
4602	Edwards, Thomas C.	A Commentary on the First Epistle to the Corinthians	16.25
4801	Ramsay, William	Historical Commentary on the Epistle to the Galatians	15.75
4901	Westcott, Brooke, F.	St. Paul's Epistle to the Ephesians	9.75
5001	Johnstone, Robert	Lectures on the Book of Philippians	16.50
5401	Liddon, H. P.	The First Epistle to Timothy	6.00
5601	Taylor, Thomas	An Exposition of Titus	17.50
5801	Delitzsch, Franz	Commentary on the Epistle to the Hebrews (2 vol.)	29.95
5802	Bruce, A. B.	The Epistle to the Hebrews	15.00
5901	Johnstone, Robert	Lectures on the Epistle of James	14.00
5902	Mayor, Joseph B.	The Epistle of St. James	19.25
6501	Manton, Thomas	An Exposition of the Epistle of Jude	12.00
6601	Trench, Richard C.	Commentary on the Epistles to the Seven Churches	8.50
7001	Orelli, Hans C. von	The Twelve Minor Prophets	13.50
7002	Alford, Dean Henry	The Book of Genesis and Part of the Book of Exodus	11.50
7003	Marbury, Edward	Obadiah and Habakkuk	21.50
7004	Adeney, Walter	The Books of Ezra and Nehemiah	11.50
7101	Mayor, Joseph B.	The Epistle of St. Jude & The Second Epistle of Peter	15.25
7102	Lillie, John	Lectures on the First and Second Epistle of Peter	18.25
7103	Hort, F. J. A. & A. F.	Expository and Exegetical Studies	29.50
7104	Milligan, George	St. Paul's Epistles to the Thessalonians	10.50
7105	Stanley, Arthur P.	Epistles of Paul to the Corinthians	20.95
7106	Moule, H. C. G.	Colossian and Philemon Studies	10.50
7107	Fairbairn, Patrick	The Pastoral Epistles	14.95
8001	Fairweather, William	Background of the Gospels	15.00
8002	Fairweather, William	Background of the Epistles	14.50
8003	Zahn, Theodor	Introduction to the New Testament (3 vol.)	48.00
8004	Bernard, Thomas	The Progress of Doctrine in the New Testament	9.00
8401	Blaikie, William G.	David, King of Israel	14.50
8402	Farrar, F. W.	The Life and Work of St. Paul (2 vol.)	43.95
8601	Shedd, W. G. T.	Dogmatic Theology (4 vol.)	49.50
8701	Shedd, W. G. T.	History of Christian Doctrine (2 vol.)	30.25
8702	Oehler, Gustav	Theology of the Old Testament	20.00
8703	Kurtz, John Henry	Sacrificial Worship of the Old Testament	15.00
8901	Fawcett, John	Christ Precious to those that Believe	9.25
9401	Neal, Daniel	History of the Puritans (3 vol.)	54.95
9402	Warns, Johannes	Baptism	11.50
9501	Schilder, Klass	The Trilogy (3 vol.)	48.00
9502	Liddon, H. P. & Orr, J.	The Birth of Christ	13.95
9503	Bruce, A. B.	The Parables of Christ	12.50
9504	Bruce, A. B.	The Miracles of Christ	17.25
9505	Milligan, William	The Ascension of Christ	12.50
9506	Moule, H. C. & Orr, J.	The Resurrection of Christ	16.95
9801	Liddon, H. P.	The Divinity of our Lord	20.25
9802	Pink, Arthur W.	The Antichrist	10.50
9803	Shedd, W. G. T.	The Doctrine of Endless Punishment	8.25